SALT OF THE DESERT SUN

AFRICAN STUDIES SERIES   46

Editorial board

John Dunn, Reader in Politics and Fellow of King's College, Cambridge
J. M. Lonsdale, Lecturer in History and Fellow of Trinity College,
   Cambridge
A. F. Robertson, Fellow of Darwin College, Cambridge

The African Studies Series is a collection of monographs and general studies
which reflect the interdisciplinary interests of the African Studies Centre at
Cambridge. Volumes to date have combined historical, anthropological,
economic, political and other perspectives. Each contribution has assumed
that such broad approaches can contribute much to our understanding of
Africa, and that this may in turn be of advantage to specific disciplines.

OTHER BOOKS IN THE SERIES

(SALT OF THE DESERT SUN)

A History of Salt Production and Trade in the Central Sudan

PAUL E. LOVEJOY
Professor of History, York University, Toronto

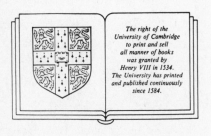

The right of the
University of Cambridge
to print and sell
all manner of books
was granted by
Henry VIII in 1534.
The University has printed
and published continuously
since 1584.

CAMBRIDGE UNIVERSITY PRESS

CAMBRIDGE
LONDON NEW YORK NEW ROCHELLE
MELBOURNE SYDNEY

Published by the Press Syndicate of the University of Cambridge
The Pitt Building, Trumpington Street, Cambridge CB2 1RP
32 East 57th Street, New York, NY 10022, USA
10 Stamford Road, Oakleigh, Melbourne 3166, Australia

First published 1986

Printed in Great Britain at the University Press, Cambridge

British Library cataloguing in publication data

Lovejoy, Paul E.
Salt of the Desert Sun: a history of salt
production and trade in the Central Sudan.–
(African studies: 46)
1. Salt industry and trade – Sudan – Central Sudan
– History
I. Title   II. Series
338.4'766142'09626   HD9213.S8/

Library of Congress cataloging in publication data
Lovejoy, Paul E.
Salt of the Desert Sun.
(African studies series; 46)
Bibliography; p.
Includes index.
1. Salt industry and trade – Africa, West – History.
I. Title.   II. Series.
HD9213.A56L68 1986   338.2'763'0966   85-12837

ISBN 0 521 30182 3

TM

To Hugo, whose Dad's job is salt

*This book has been published
with the help of a grant from
the Social Science Federation of Canada,
using funds provided by the
Social Sciences and Humanities
Research Council of Canada.*

Contents

Contents

Tables

Maps

All maps were drafted by the Cartographic Service, Department of
Geography, York University, Ontario, Canada

Figures

Illustrations

Preface

When I first became interested in African history, it was apparent that the growth of the African economy was little understood. At the time only Raymond Mauny's monumental *Tableau géographique* dealt adequately with aspects of economic history, filled as it is with countless numbers of research projects that needed more detailed attention. I initially chose one of these, the kola trade between the Hausa cities of the central Sudan and the forests of Asante. My decision to concentrate on this sector of long-distance trade led to several important discoveries, all of which logically turned my attention to salt. First, the kola traders exported natron to the middle Volta basin, and it became necessary to learn more about the source of these supplies. Secondly, most of the kola traders were associated by origin with other merchants who dealt specifically in salt. Finally, the kola traders often acted as brokers for itinerant salt traders, or else they lived adjacent to other broker-merchants who catered to the salt trade. It became abundantly clear that the salt trade required as much attention as the kola trade if the regional economy of the central Sudan was to be analysed historically. This book is the result of the logical development of my research on the kola trade.

The project began, therefore, in 1969, although at that time my concern was specifically with kola nuts. None the less, from March 1969 to June 1970 my research in Nigeria, Ghana, Senegal and England resulted in my acquisition of considerable data that pertained to salt. Subsequently, I returned to Nigeria in the summer of 1973 to explore the possibility of concentrating on the salt trade and learned much at that time that has since proved invaluable. I also became acquainted with Aliyu Bala Umar, who was to be my research assistant until 1975. Because I observed a close connexion between the salt trade and the regional economy of the central Sudan, I realised that the salt trade could only be analysed within a larger context. Both my earlier work on kola and the concentration on long-distance trade influenced my research in this broader direction. Therefore, I planned a broadly conceived research strategy that was intended to explore salt, agricultural production, slavery, and other aspects of the economy. Thanks to an invitation from R. J. Gavin, then chairman of the history department at Ahmadu Bello University, I returned to Nigeria to inaugurate a course on the economic history of West Africa and to initiate a large research project to recover oral data relevant to economic history. Salt was an integral part of that project, which lasted from 1974 to 1976 and resulted in the taping of hundreds of interviews over scattered parts of northern Nigeria. Among the many people who assisted me in this project, J. S. Hogendorn was perhaps most crucial to its success. Together we mapped out a strategy to supervise what turned out to be an unduly large programme of research.

Subsequent to the economic history project of 1974–76, I turned my attention specifically to salt, now that a substantial body of oral data had been collected that included information on the salt trade and production at some locations and after I had completed archival research on salt in the Nigerian archive at Kaduna. Now I needed to concentrate on the production sites in Niger and Chad. Consequently, I travelled to Niger in the summer of 1977, where I found an unexpectedly rich collection of colonial documents in the Niamey archives. The years from 1977 through 1979 were generally spent collecting published material on the salt industry, and I finished the research for this book with a trip to Paris and Aix-en-Provence in the summer of 1979, where once more considerable documentation was obtained, most especially copies of documents from the Bilma archives, made available to me by Marguerite Le Coeur. Unfortunately, a trip to Chad was not possible because of its civil war.

The progression in both my thinking and in my research is best reflected in my earlier publications, which can be considered as interim reports for this study. The kola trade, for example, resulted not only in a Ph.D. thesis but also a book, *Caravans of Kola: The Hausa Kola Trade, 1700–1900*, which contains some discussion of salt and an analysis of the origins of the kola traders mentioned above. The social and economic aspects of the desert-side sector are discussed more fully in two essays undertaken with Stephen Baier. Both Baier and I have separately explored other dimensions of the desert-side sector, which is central to the study of the salt industry. In Nigeria, I wrote a first essay on the salt industry, which was presented at the Seminar on the Economic History of the Central Savanna, held at Kano in January 1976. This preliminary survey was designed to explore two problems. The first was to establish the wide range of uses and types of salt in the economy, and the second was to arrive at a rough estimate of the scale of production. The Nigerian experience also enabled discussions with J. S. Hogendorn on the economic history project, its organisation and results. A second interim report, following on the Kano Seminar paper, was presented at the Canadian Association of African Studies annual meeting in 1978 and subsequently published. This essay examined the salt of Borno alone in order to show that salt was of fundamental importance to the Borno economy. Finally, another paper, 'The Trans-Saharan Trade and the Salt Trade of the Central Sudan: A Comparison of Nineteenth Century Patterns', was presented at a conference on the history of the trans-Saharan trade routes in Libya, which attempted to place the salt trade in the context of other desert-side commercial patterns. There are other relevant essays that contain information on aspects of the salt trade, and information from them is incorporated in this book. The focus of the present book is on reconstructing a picture of a premodern salt industry – one of the few recoverable pictures – rather than the transformation of that industry under colonialism.

The study of the central Sudan salt industry is now well advanced, as the appearance of this book hopefully demonstrates. In large part this is the result of the research of a number of scholars, whose work is incorporated here. Many of these scholars have been particularly helpful in my research: most especially, Stephen Baier, who has written on the economy of Damagaram, through which much of the desert salt passed, Suzanne and Edmond Bernus, who have studied the salt industry of Teguidda n'tesemt, P. L. Gouletquer, whose work on Manga salt production and Teguidda n'tesemt has been done in the context of his considerable knowledge of the salt industry of Europe, and Madame M. Le Coeur, whose years spent at Bilma resulted in a first-hand knowledge of that important site. There are, of course, numerous other scholars who have worked on the salt industry, and references to their studies are contained in the notes and bibliography. Knut Vikør's study of Bilma, Peter Fuchs' research at Fachi, and A. Chukwudi Unomah's work on Awe should be mentioned.

The interdisciplinary nature of research on the topic of salt has been significant. Baier is an historian; Suzanne Bernus is an anthropologist; Edmond Bernus is a geographer, and Gouletquer is an archaeologist. Léon Soula, who studied the Manga salt industry in the 1940s, was a pharmacist, while H. Faure, who completed a detailed study of salt sources in the 1960s, is a geologist. Besides these, there are many other geologists, chemists, botanists, and other specialists who have been involved in research, including a number of scientists sent to the Lake Chad basin in the last years of the nineteenth century and the first decade of the twentieth century. The scientific training of members of such missions as those under Foureau and Lamy, Tilho, Chevalier, and others makes their reports particularly valuable from a technical perspective.

Despite this considerable body of research, there are still some sizeable gaps in the documentation available for this study, and it may well be that additional research, particularly in Niger and Chad, will modify the findings analysed in this book. The most serious gap is the lack of adequate field work in the many salt-camps of the sahel, including Dallol Bosso, Dallol Fogha, Muniyo, Mangari, Kadzell, and the eastern shores of Lake Chad. Fortunately, archival materials are very good on some of these locations, but the number of actual sites is so great that there is probably much additional history to be recovered. Clearly, detailed field work, involving interviews with local people, would add considerable material on some aspects of the history of the industry, particularly the nature of access to salt sites, the social origins of salt workers, and the relationship between salt production and other aspects of the local economy. Archival data for these sites are particularly valuable on production techniques, output and trade. Data are far less complete on the social relations of production. Furthermore, it has not been possible to collect archival material in Chad or at some local offices in Niger, including Goure, Nguigmi, Maine-Soroa, Myrria and Zinder. Undoubtedly, additional material of value is to be found in these places.

It should be amply clear that I am indebted to many people for the successful completion of my research, including: M. Le Coeur for Bilma documents and her hospitality in Paris; S. Bernus and E. Bernus for access to unpublished material; S. Baier for working out a model of desert-side trade; D. Lange for discussions in Niamey and by letter; J. Lavers and N. Alkali for encouragement at early stages of research; J. S. Hogendorn for support of my project and his co-operation in Nigeria; D. Tambo for information on trade in the Jos Plateau area and for tracking down materials; M. B. Duffill for help in conducting research in the Benue Valley and for assistance with German sources; Peter Knights for his help with German translation; A. S. Kanya-Forstner for French translation; and M. Klein for his continuous comments on and support of my work.

I have had several research assistants: in Toronto, Murray Hoffbauer, Stephen Giles, Jeff Da Silva, Elaine McCready and Heather Esser, and in Nigeria, Aliyu Bala Umar, and members of the economic history project, particularly Ahmadu Maccido. Ann McDougall, Martin Klein, M. B. Duffill, Richard Roberts, J. S. Hogendorn, James Webb, Jr, and Allison Jones read the manuscript in draft form, and their comments have been largely incorporated here.

Financial support has come from the Ford Foundation through the Program in African Economic History at the University of Wisconsin for research in the summer of 1973; the Social Science Research Council of New York for research support, 1975–76; Ahmadu Bello University Research Board and Department of History, Ahmadu Bello University for funds, 1975; Social Sciences and Humanities Research Council of Canada, 1977–79, 1981–82, and the York University Faculty of Arts, Research Grant for funds to cover maps and diagrams. Typing was done by Secretarial Services, under the direction of Ms Dorris Rippington, at York University.

Algonquin Park, Canada
August 1984

xvi

1

Salt in the history of the central Sudan

THE NEED FOR SALT: AN HISTORICAL OVERVIEW

Salt satisfies a physiological need, and it may well be that salt is also man's earliest addiction.[1] The body requires salt because of its role in regulating osmotic pressure and its part in hormonal and enzymatic processes, but recent studies suggest that the addition of salt to food is usually not necessary. Most foods contain enough salt naturally to meet body requirements, and the body can adapt to salt-free diets. People who consume relatively high proportions of animal products need the smallest amount of salt, since meat and milk are naturally saltier than cereals and vegetables. Diets that are dependent upon grain as a staple food are more apt to be supplemented with additional salt than diets based on animal products. Consequently, nomads have usually consumed less salt than sedentary farming populations. Although the amount of salt needed as a dietary supplement is open to dispute, salt does reduce the danger of dehydration because salt intake encourages people to drink more fluids. In a particularly hot climate, the usual physiological requirements that are largely satisfied through the salt contained naturally in animal and vegetable products have usually been supplemented in order to counteract the effects of the tropical sun. The normal level of salt consumption in temperate zones – 4.5 kg per year – can be satisfied largely through the salt contained in food sources, but in the tropics this level can easily double; at least people have wanted to consume more salt when and where it is available.[2]

Whether or not salt is a necessary additive, people have valued it as a necessity. Salt was always a major item of trade; it could be given as a gift and was a treat on special occasions. The poor usually had to make do with impure substitutes made from local plant ash, while the wealthy compared different salts as a gourmet savours different foods. In addition, salt has been fed to livestock in considerable quantities, and one salt or another has had important medicinal and industrial uses. These other uses, combined with the culinary demand for salt, increased the value of salt as a commodity. Only in recent times, as the result of advances in science and technology, has salt become less important in trade, partly because salt has become cheaper and more plentiful and partly because salt is more often recognised by its chemical constituents than by its generic term.

Robert Multhauf, a leading historian of common salt (sodium chloride), explains contemporary ignorance of the historical role of salt in terms of the

1

major technological and scientific advances that have occurred over the past several centuries. Common salt is a principal source of sodium and chlorine for use in industry; today its culinary usage is far less important than in the past. Moreover, it used to be that salts were impure mixtures, often containing carbonates, sulphates and chlorides of potassium, magnesium and soda. Scientific works and encyclopedias once listed salt as a major item for discussion, but now it is more common to find the chemical ingredients instead. This practice has reflected the increasingly esoteric nature of scientific knowledge and the greater isolation of the general public from their immediate surroundings.[3]

The search for salt to fill culinary requirements and medicinal needs involved considerable technological and scientific experimentation, which were important factors in the development of chemistry and geology as distinct sciences. This process affected large parts of the world; such has been the universal interest in salt. Before the seventeenth century the most advanced production was in China, but thereafter European centres underwent a transformation that led to the major scientific discoveries that have turned salt from a scarce commodity into an extremely common one.[4] A brief review of the advances in salt technology and scientific knowledge demonstrates how variations in geological conditions and the knowledge of salt chemistry have shaped the development of the salt industry in different settings.

Salt is found almost everywhere, although this has been known only as a result of scientific advances in the past two hundred years. The Chinese were the first to discover that salt could be found deep under the earth's surface, at depths of several hundred metres or more.[5] As long ago as 500 AD, the Chinese began to drill for brine, a technique that was only discovered in Europe in the eighteenth century and was not known in Africa until the twentieth century. Drilling led to the discovery that large and easily recoverable deposits were located in many places and could be either mined or turned into brine and pumped to the surface.

Perhaps no other aspect of salt production experienced more experimentation than techniques to concentrate brine.[6] Most devices were elaborations of the arrangement for promoting atmospheric evaporation and included elongated pieces of porous clay in long wooden troughs (Schwabisch Hall), graduation houses in which brine was manually circulated over bundles of straw (Langensalz, Naisheim, Sulz, Sulza, Lombardy), thorns (Wilhelmsgluckbrunn), or ropes. Graduation houses were increased in size; at Sulz manual pumps and siphons were employed to circulate brine in houses that were as long as a kilometre, with two or three walls for greater surface area. These techniques reduced the need for fuel to boil brine dry, but the introduction of furnaces and improvements in furnace design also increased production. Chimneys made it possible to achieve greater temperatures and conserved fuel. Pans were adopted as a replacement for pottery; the pans could be used again; they conveyed heat better and could be pre-heated.

2

Chemical discoveries also improved production techniques. In the course of the eighteenth century, the various salts in the different European salines were isolated, which allowed the production of purer salt and the development of subsidiary chemical, principally medical, compounds.[7] At Luneburg, blood and beer were introduced to the brine to remove impurities as early as the fourteenth century, but the discovery of Epsom salt (magnesium sulphate), Glauber's salt (sodium sulphate) and soda (sodium carbonate) helped salt-makers isolate sodium chloride in ever purer amounts. These discoveries depended upon experiments with the mother liquor, the residue in the salt pans after total evaporation, and the recognition that salts precipitate out of solution at different concentrations and temperatures.

Salt was once that rare commodity sought after by man in much the same way that petroleum is today. The two are linked historically, in fact. Early petroleum discoveries were frequently associated with the extraction of salt, and petroleum soon became a source of chemicals used in combination with the elements contained in salt. Today, however, the association between salt and petroleum has been reversed. New sources of salt are located as a result of the search for petroleum, and now salt is so common that no one looks specifically for it. Indeed, the availability of salt has changed its attractiveness to man. Where it was once the rare commodity that required intensive labour to secure it, today, thanks to technological breakthroughs in chemistry, physics, engineering, and other fields, the salt industry is no longer labour intensive. Where once it took thousands of man-hours to produce a small quantity of salt, now it requires only a few man-hours to produce vast quantities.

Throughout the sixteenth, seventeenth and eighteenth centuries, salt was an important component of European economic and political history.[8] The European industry was the concern of governments interested in tax-ing output – salt was an easy target because the sources of salt production were fixed. Salzburg and other places were sometimes associated with small principalities; at other times salines were associated with political struggles on a larger scale. In France and many other countries the salt tax was a political issue.

The virtual unimportance of salt in the politics of contemporary North America and Europe is in sharp contrast to its role in the past. Salt is still dis-cussed; salt-free diets and other popular, quasi-scientific interest in salt or the lack of salt has periodically been a topic of conversation at social gatherings, sometimes having relatively passionate advocates whose political stance – in the great scale of things – only serves to emphasise the relative unimportance of salt. Only when it comes to the use of salt on icy highways – with the destructive impact on automobiles and leather boots – does a passion concerning salt reach epidemic proportions. As is the case with anti-salt faddists, moreover, the use of salt to melt ice raises cries of frustration, not desire. The contemporary age is anti-salt, in part because of a negative public image and in part because salt is so cheap that it cannot be taken seriously in

3

an economic sense. The present attitudes are so remarkably in opposition to the once lofty position of salt in society as to be an accurate testimony of the advances of technology. Once a luxury, now salt is truly common.

The salt trade in Africa has an importance historically that is parallel to its history elsewhere, but unlike its European and Asian counterparts few technological innovations took place that led to other breakthroughs in modern science and industry. Indeed the African industry has remained technologically backward, despite some modest advances developed locally and introduced from outside. The African industry can be said to be dying a slow death, as its counterparts elsewhere in the world have long since experienced. Whether or not modern technology can exploit the geological conditions that account for salt remains to be seen, but the relatively recent decline of salt production in Africa enables scholars to examine this primitive industry in some detail, both to throw light on the industry in its own right and also for comparative purposes in understanding the history of salt production at other times and places.[9] Technological innovation may revolutionise production at some salt deposits – so that various chemicals other than salt are produced. Most sources of salt will probably fall into disuse, as some already have. The most vulnerable are brine springs whose brine content is too low to make them economically attractive when so much salt is available elsewhere. Explorations have failed to reveal large underground salt deposits at most brine sites. The surface deposits of the Sahara and sahel are another matter, however, and some of these are attracting attention and possibly can be developed. Trona deposits near the shores of Lake Chad, for example, are very large, with a possible annual output of 120,000 tonnes, should the need for sodium or carbon ever warrant the development of a modern industry there.[10] It may be that valuable deposits of other minerals are located close to these and similar salt sources. Commercial quantities of uranium are now being mined near Teguidda n'tesemt in Niger, long a source of salt and once a source of copper, too. Perhaps future discoveries of other modern treasures await the salt districts.

Salt deposits in Africa have drawn the attention of outsiders – Arab geographers and European adventurers – for a long time, not because these observers were particularly interested in salt as such but because salt was sometimes associated with the gold trade. Indeed gold and salt were reputedly exchanged measure for measure, which can only be a myth but one that does serve to highlight the importance of salt.[11] The salt of these myths came from rock salt deposits – in Ethiopia and in the western Sahara. At Taoudeni, Teghaza, and Ijil, the salt is relatively pure sodium chloride in tremendous deposits which date back thousands of years into the geological past. In fact salt was not as scarce as these myths would lead us to suppose, but relatively pure sodium chloride was. Deposits of impure salt – mixed with other compounds and dirt – and methods of making salt from ocean water, the ashes of plants and other means have satisfied the demand for sodium chloride when rock salt deposits were lacking or insufficient.

4

THE SALT INDUSTRY OF THE CENTRAL SUDAN

This book analyses the production and distribution of mineral salts in the central Sudan, a region that encompasses the Lake Chad basin, the south-central Sahara Desert, the Benue River basin, and the Niger Valley from the confluence with the Benue northward to the sahel (the southern border zone of the Sahara). In the nineteenth century, the central Sudan included a loose federation of Tuareg nomads centred on Agades and two major savanna states, the Sokoto Caliphate and Borno. Together they dominated the whole region. Before the middle of the eighteenth century, Borno included most of the Chad basin and parts of the central Sahara northward along the axis of the Kawar oases. In the nineteenth century Borno was reduced to half its former extent but still controlled much of the Chad basin. The Sokoto Caliphate emerged after 1804 through the amalgamation of over thirty emirates that had come into being through the Islamic holy war (*jihad*) of Shehu Usuman dan Fodio (d. 1817). Previously a series of smaller states had dotted much of the territory that was subsequently united under the caliphate. The most important of these were the Hausa states of Katsina, Kano, Zamfara, Zazzau (Zaria), and Gobir – an area which became the heart of the caliphate. Military expansion also extended southward to incorporate Nupe and large parts of Oyo (the major state in the interior of the Bight of Benin during the height of the Atlantic slave trade), south-eastward into the Benue basin and the Cameroon highlands, and westward across the Niger River. The Tuareg federation was centred on the Air Massif and neighbouring parts of the sahel, including Adar, Damergu and Azawaq. The tribes that led a nomadic existence in this area recognised the Sultan of Agades as their titular ruler, but in fact each fraction ran its own affairs, as had been the case for several centuries.

Most of the salt sources under consideration were located in Borno; a few were found in the Sokoto Caliphate, while the Tuareg controlled several important desert salines. The Borno industry can be subdivided according to province; Muniyo, Mangari, Kadzell and Foli. Furthest west was the hilly region of Muniyo, where 23–40 deposits were found; immediately to the east were the depressions of Mangari, with an additional 100 or more deposits; and between Mangari and Lake Chad was the province of Kadzell, located north of the modern boundary between Nigeria and the République du Niger. Kadzell was a source of wells infested with salt. The final salt district in Borno was Foli, a part of Kanem, located on the eastern shores of Lake Chad, which was the location of a number of trona depressions. The major sources in the Sokoto Caliphate included two valleys, Dallol Fogha and Dallol Bosso, that run south into the Niger River immediately to the west of the present boundary between Nigeria and Niger, and a dozen or more brine springs in the Benue River basin. The most important springs were found at Awe, Keana, Azara, Akwana, and Bomanda. The Tuareg-controlled salines included the Kawar oases (especially Bilma), Fachi (located 170 km west of the

5

Kawar oases), and Teguidda n'tesemt (located west of the Air Massif).

A regional perspective is adopted here for analytical purposes because the major sources of salt supplied much of the same area; the salt market can be thought of as constituting a series of overlapping distributional systems that radiated outward from each source. Many of the more important salines competed throughout the region, but the smaller ones had more localised networks. The markets for the different salts also depended upon chemical composition and purity, as well as proximity to competing sources, because the use of the salts varied with their chemistry. By focussing on the central Sudan as a region, it is possible to examine the competition between the various salts and thereby assess the relative importance of each. This market-centred approach also allows a study of different methods of salt production, since salt technology depended upon various geological, climatic and demographic settings. As a consequence of a regional perspective, therefore, it is possible to compare differences in production techniques and marketing strategies and how these have changed over the years.

Three major benchmarks can be identified in the history of the central Sudan that had important consequences for the development of the salt trade. The first was the Great Drought of the middle of the eighteenth century (1738–53); the second was the *jihad* (1804–12); and the third was the imposition of British and French colonialism (1897–1903). This study of the salt trade reconstructs the industry in the late nineteenth century, and from this baseline attempts to uncover changes that resulted from the Great Drought and the *jihad*. The colonial conquest destroyed the political structure within which the salt industry had operated, and because much of the documentation for this study is derived from early colonial reports and recently-collected oral data, a major methodological problem has been deciphering the impact of the conquest.

The Great Drought of the eighteenth century upset a balance of power in the central Sudan that had existed since the fifteenth century, when Borno had achieved its ascendancy in the region and the Tuareg confederation at Agades had come into being.[12] Until the Great Drought, Borno virtually dominated the salt market of the central Sudan, since most salt districts, including Kawar and Fachi as well as those in the Borno sahel, were within its political frontiers. The other salines were subdivided into three districts, each independent of the others. The Tuareg of the Agades Confederation controlled Teguidda n'tesemt; Dallol Fogha (and probably Dallol Bosso) were part of the Hausa state of Kebbi; and the Benue salines were in the Jukun confederacy of Kwararafa.[13] After the Great Drought, Kawar and Fachi were brought into the orbit of the Tuareg, thereby reflecting a shift in the balance of power between Borno and the Agades Confederation. This change in commercial patterns destroyed the dominant position of the Borno state in the salt trade, an adjustment that presaged the far more serious economic decline after its losses in the *jihad* of 1804–12, when the consolidation of the Sokoto Caliphate to the west resulted in the emergence of a far larger and more prosperous state in the region. The caliphate not only came to dominate the salt trade, in part through a commercial alliance with the Tuareg and in part through the incorporation of a substantial market within its domains, but the caliphate also seized the Benue salines, Dallol Fogha and Dallol Bosso. With the rise of the caliphate, a new division of the salt industry was achieved. Borno continued to control the provinces of Muniyo, Mangari, Kadzell and Foli; the Tuareg dominated the marketing of the desert salts, and the caliphate held the Dallols and the Benue salines. The distributional networks for all the salt sources became centred on the caliphate because of its market. This basic division between Borno, the caliphate and the Tuareg lasted until the European conquest.

THE LIMITS OF THE CENTRAL SUDAN SALT MARKET

A regional perspective that concentrates on the central Sudan depends upon a rough correspondence between the market for the various salts and the major salt sources of Borno, the Sokoto Caliphate and the desert immediately to the north of these two states. Such a correspondence is invariably rough because some of the salts produced at the central Sudan locations were exported further afield than Borno and the caliphate, while salt from outside the central Sudan was imported into parts of the region. In order to place the following study in perspective, it is necessary to identify the limits of the market for central Sudan salts.

Broadly speaking, the central Sudan included that territory that was self-sufficient in salts and hence can be distinguished from the northern Sahara and North Africa, the western Sudan, the area east of the Chad basin, and the forest region along the Guinea Coast to the south. While the boundaries separating these different regional markets were never clearly delineated, a number of generalisations are useful in establishing the relative autonomy of the central Sudan from other sources of salt. First, the many salt sources of the northern Sahara supplied North Africa and local Saharan markets, so that very little – if any – salt flowed across the desert in either direction. The only exception to this generalisation was the transport of some salt – perhaps a few hundred tons – from Amadror in southern Algeria to the central Sudan. Secondly, the frontier between salt from the Guinea Coast and the savanna to the north was never clearly defined because some types of salt from the central Sudan were needed in the forest zone for medicine, livestock and tobacco, while other types of salt could not compete with sea salt or imported European salt. Locally-made sea salt penetrated the interior all along the coast, from the Niger Delta and the Cross River estuary in the east to the mouth of the Volta River in the west (and indeed continuing along the coast to Mauritania to the north-west and Angola to the south). European salt became a major import by the late eighteenth century and accounted for at least 8,000 tonnes for the Bight of Biafra alone by 1845.[14] European imports gradually undermined local salt production and appear to have penetrated further and further into

7

the interior, reaching the central Sudan in appreciable quantities by the last decades of the nineteenth century.

The eastern and western limits of the central Sudan salt market can be established as follows: the eastern boundary passed south through Kanem, east of Lake Chad, to the Chari River valley, while the western boundary was roughly parallel to the Niger River valley, downstream from Timbuktu to the confluence with the Benue. The regions to the east and to the west were similar to the central Sudan in that they straddled the ecological divide between desert and savanna, and consequently similar patterns of desert-side trade prevailed in all three regions.[15] The location of salt sources was an important factor in distinguishing separate desert-side regions; the central Sudan stands out because the various sources (Kawar, Fachi, and Teguidda n'tesemt) satisfied the same geographical area. The western Sudan and the region east of Lake Chad constituted similar regions in which several sources of salt supplied overlapping markets within each region. Invariably there was some overlap between adjacent regions.

To the east of the central Sudan, salt came from a number of deposits in the Borkou–Tibesti–Ennedi region. Demi in Ennedi and Bedo in Borkou were the most important sites, and their output supplied much of the area east of Lake Chad and southward to the upper Ubangi River basin. The Donza, who lived at Bedo and Tigui, worked the Bedo deposits. The salt was formed into moulds that weighed 2–2.5 kg. In 1955, 3,000 camels were used to transport about 400 tonnes of Bedo salt to markets in Kanem and Batha; some salt was sent as far as Marrua in Cameroon. The salines at Demi supplied 80 per cent of the salt for the region east of Kanem. A subgroup of the Bideyat – the Taoua – worked the salines, although at one time the Gaeda also were involved in production. Many different nomadic groups – Teda, Gaeda, Bideyat, Zagawa and others – carried the salt south to Wadai and Batha. The volume of the trade appears to have been of the order of 1,150–2,000 tonnes annually.[16] Soda (sodium carbonate) was available at Ouadi Doum, Ouni-anga, Mogoro, Teguedei, Mardingai, Sa, Dourab and Toro, which is one reason why trona – a substitute for soda – produced on the east shores of Lake Chad tended to flow west and south. As much as 1,500 tonnes were produced at the Borkou sites (Mardingai, Sa, Dourab and Toro) alone.[17] Salt was also found further east still. The Ethiopian region represented another distinct area of salt production and trade. Salt was found in the Dunahil depression in Eritrea, in the immediate interior of the Red Sea, and was extracted in bars for use as a currency and for consumption. This salt was distributed widely in the interior of Ethiopia as far west as the borderlands with the modern Republic of Sudan.[18]

The principal inland sources of salt for the western Sudan were Ijil, Taoudeni and Tichitt, and there were also important salines along the Atlantic coast as well. The history of these sites is relatively well known, thanks to the research of E. A. McDougall on Ijil and Tichitt and to a variety of scholars who have studied Taoudeni and its predecessor, Teghaza.[19] Ijil rock salt came

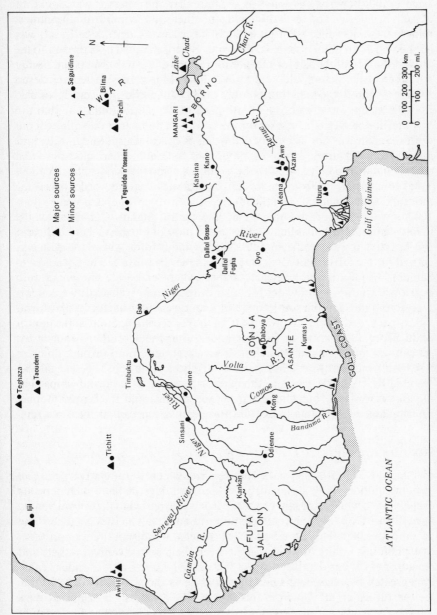

Map 1.1 Sources of salt and natron in the western and central Sudan

9

from the basin of what appears to have once been a vast Saharan lake, while Taoudeni rock salt was mined in shafts from the remains of a similar lake. Tichitt salt, known as *amersal*, was less pure than the others; it was a mixture of sodium chloride and probably soda and other salts. Water from the annual rains in the sahel collected in a number of basins near Tichitt, and the salt was left behind as an efflorescence as the water evaporated.[20] These three sources produced much of the salt for the interior regions of the western Sudan; one or the other of the desert salts was found along trade routes to Asante in the south-east and to the kola forests south of Wagadugu further west. Rock salt from Taoudeni was even brought into parts of the central Sudan, so that the dividing line between the market for this salt and a number of the salines of the central Sudan was not as clearly defined as between central Sudan salts and other external sources. Natron (mixtures of soda and other salts) from the central Sudan also flowed west to the Volta basin and the middle Niger Valley. Total volume of trade from the western Sahara sites was of the order of several thousand tonnes annually; in the nineteenth century probably no more than 100 tonnes of Taoudeni salt entered the central Sudan. Camel caravans, involving thousands of animals, transported most of the salt to Timbuktu and the Maraka towns of the middle Niger Valley, from where the salt was carried further afield. Salt also came from the sea coast. In Sierra Leone, Sine-Saluum, the mouth of the Senegal, and elsewhere, elaborate salt works were developed to trap ocean water for solar evaporation.[21] This salt was of two types; from the Gambia south to Sierra Leone, sea salt was in granular form, tightly packaged in mats to preserve it. In the region of Gandiole, at the mouth of the Senegal River, and in the depressions along the Aftouth in Mauritania, sea salt was mined in bars. Finally, salt was imported from Europe – much of it sea salt from near Marseilles – at a relatively early date.[22] The Senegal and Gambia Rivers made access to the interior possible for European ships, and the many overland routes inland from Senegambia and the Upper Guinea Coast enabled merchants to deal in European salt as well as local sea salt.

THE CHARACTERISTICS OF THE CENTRAL SUDAN SALT MARKET

The central Sudan lacked rock salt deposits which were relatively pure in sodium chloride. Only at Amadror, in southern Algeria, were such deposits available, and while some salt from Amadror was exported to the central Sudan, at least since the early nineteenth century, Amadror salt has never satisfied the demand for salt in the central Sudan.[23] Problems in transport and supply seem to explain this failure; the distance between the major savanna markets and Amadror was considerable – over 1,000 km. The salt from Taoudeni came even greater distances, and again there was never the possibility of satisfying the central Sudan market from this source. The deficiency in relatively pure salt was overcome in other ways. Most important, people settled for less pure substitutes – mixtures of sodium chloride and other compounds which were used in the place of pure sodium chloride.

This market situation explains an important characteristic of the central Sudan industry: the competition between various impure salts and mixtures of different salts. Very little pure sodium chloride entered the market. Because of its absence, people developed a taste for different mixtures; the kind of salt that was available influenced cultural values in a remarkable way. In contrast to modern advertising, which can have a strong influence on demand, here was a market situation in which demand was enshrined in culture. People had no choice but to use impure salts; in time they came to prefer such salts so that when pure sodium chloride became available in the late nineteenth century and then became plentiful and cheap in the early twentieth century, most people still chose to buy local salts because they had their preferences for different salts for use in cooking and as medicines. Virtually all these salts had substitutes so that people used what was available, but they voiced a preference that influenced the market. The preoccupation with salt, as reflected in proverbs, folk medicine, culinary recipes and tobacco use, ultimately demonstrates that salt was a subject of considerable debate among consumers.

The lack of rock salt and other salts relatively pure in sodium chloride explains the unique nature of the central Sudan salt industry. There were many competing salts; some came from the desert and some came from the sahel and savanna. Production techniques varied from saline to saline. The great complexity of the industry can be explained by the quest for acceptable substitutes for pure sodium chloride; unlike neighbouring regions to the east, west, north and south, the people of the central Sudan had to develop numerous small salines that were widely scattered. Many of these sites were located in the sahel and had no counterparts in the western Sudan (except for the single example of Tichitt) or the region east of Kanem. Furthermore, the Benue basin brine springs were also unique. Except for the relatively small brine spring at Daboya in the Volta basin, there were no major brine springs in the western Sudan nor in the eastern Sudan. The salt of the Benue brine springs – Awe, Keana, Azara, Akwana and neighbouring sites – filled the vacuum in salt supply between the desert and the sea coast. It was not possible to produce enough salt to satisfy the region incorporating the Benue, lower Niger and Cross River basins, but there were many other brine springs further south, the most important of which were at Uburu and Ogoja.

It is estimated here that the central Sudan required an annual output of 4,500 tonnes of salt per year per million inhabitants, based on a figure of 4.5 kg per person per year. The salt content in various foods accounted for much of the normal bodily needs, but if allowance is made for higher salt consumption in the tropics, a figure of 4.5 kg per person per year still seems a reasonable estimate for the amount of salt added to food or otherwise consumed by humans, at least for sedentary populations that depended upon cereal and vegetable products. Some of this additional salt intake was consumed as medicine and as an additive to tobacco. Consumption was on such a large scale that one professional observer – Dr W. E. McCulloch – reported in 1929

11

that 'Native salt is used in amounts which astonish the European'.[24] Dr McCulloch, describing the dietary habits of the Hausa in the *West African Medical Journal*, was critical of local consumption patterns; he felt that a number of dietary disorders could be traced to the use of impure salts. He was probably correct in his diagnosis, but his observations also demonstrate the cultural bias of someone from Britain, where salt had been plentiful, cheap and pure for well over a century and where medical advances had reduced the need for the use of salts in the treatment of illnesses. None the less, Dr McCulloch's observations confirm the hypothesis presented here – average salt consumption by the human population of the central Sudan was high.

While the total population of the central Sudan or the wider region of West Africa served by the central Sudan salt industry can be estimated only approximately, there were at least several million people in Borno and the Sokoto Caliphate in the nineteenth century, and there were several million more in neighbouring countries and areas that were partially satisfied by the central Sudan salt industry. It is unlikely that 20,000 tonnes of salt would have been sufficient to meet the average minimum requirements for salt consumption.

Hill's estimate that the caliphate had a population of 10,000,000 at the end of the nineteenth century is probably too high,[25] but if such a figure were adopted, then the potential salt market, based on an average consumption of 4.5 kg per person, would have been 45,000 tonnes per year for the caliphate alone. Neighbouring Borno probably had another one or two million people, which would have raised the upper level for salt consumption to 50,000–55,000 tonnes. Since salt was used for purposes other than cooking, the market was correspondingly greater. Livestock consumption alone certainly required thousands of tonnes; it is estimated here that 500 kg of natron was required for every thousand head of cattle, donkeys, and horses and half as much for sheep and goats.[26] It may be that farmers and herders were not able to supply these amounts, but it is still clear that the quantity of natron or salt that was needed was very large. Some cattle, horses, camels and other livestock received their requirements from salt-licks and wells that were naturally laced with natron, but many animals in the savanna had no such access. They only obtained salt through the food they ate; animal diseases were often treated with salt or natron supplements. Besides this quantity of natron, culinary and medicinal uses of salt outside of Borno and the caliphate required additional supplies – probably another thousand tonnes or more. Market demand for all types of salt in the central Sudan may well have totalled 60,000–65,000 tonnes per year or more.

Although it is impossible to establish a baseline for salt demand with any accuracy, a range from 20,000 to 65,000 tonnes of salt seems reasonable in the light of probable consumption patterns and the scale of population in the area of salt distribution. That portion of this potential market which filled human biological needs, and probably livestock needs as well, was probably characterised by a relatively inelastic price structure, but that portion of the market which supplied industrial, medicinal and tobacco uses was more price elastic. If the price was too high, consumers did without or substituted other raw materials for salt. Even biological needs could be satisfied with impure vegetable salt, so that a correlation between mineral salt supply and price was less direct than neo-classical theory might suggest. People could do without salt because they could make their own. It is impossible to estimate the scale of vegetable salt production and the extent to which people consumed less than the average 4.5 kg that has been projected here. A range of 20,000–65,000 tonnes of mineral salts represents a potential market situation that was not necessarily satisfied.

As is argued below in Chapter 5, total production of salt from the major production sites probably did not exceed 15,700 tonnes, and this output had to satisfy all requirements – culinary, veterinary, medicinal and other uses. It is clear, therefore, that production lagged behind potential demand, despite Dr McCulloch's observation that local salts were used in 'astonishing' amounts. This excessive demand accounts for the situation in which salt assumed such a prominent place in trade. Salt was an essential item of trade, but people could do without salt if they had to; the use of vegetable salts, impure and vile-tasting as they often were, filled the gap between industrial production and market demand, but people preferred the better salts found in the market. Many poor people simply could not afford the better salts, no matter what the price. Hence poverty served as a brake on the expansion of salt production, particularly on relatively pure salt.

This market situation in which potential demand exceeded supply could have resulted in the creation of a monopoly or oligopoly, in which a state or group of merchants came to establish its ascendancy in production or trade and thereby could reap monopoly profits. If a state could dominate most of the production sites or a group of merchants could control the marketing of most of the salt, then either the state or the merchants could have benefited from a monopoly–oligopoly situation. These conditions existed at certain periods in the past. Before the middle of the eighteenth century – probably for 150 years or more – a single state (Borno) dominated most of the production sites of the central Sudan; after that time a single group of nomads (Tuareg) controlled the salt trade from the desert salines. Despite these important exceptions, however, several factors militated against the development of a monopoly or oligopoly situation. First, there were too many sources of supply, and it was difficult for a single state to control enough of the sources to influence the market. Secondly, the organisation of production and the problems of transport varied considerably, so that it was impossible to co-ordinate all the factors of production and trade. Thirdly, the availability of transport animals limited the amount of salt that could be marketed. Fourthly, political and climatic crises periodically upset the economy to such an extent that the production of salt and the flow of trade were altered significantly. Finally, the poverty of large sections of the population hampered those who would have

13

created a monopoly or oligopoly; there was a price threshold beyond which people could not afford to buy salt.

The study of salt production and trade is an important subject in understanding the influence of ecology on history. As an examination of the geology, chemistry and technology of salt production reveals, the constraints of the natural environment on human activity helped shape the course of history. Where people lived and worked was partially determined by available salt resources and the ability to exploit them and partially by political and other factors, but the ecological setting was important. Fluctuations in rainfall not only affected agriculture but also salt production. Although man altered his ecological conditions through the kinds of agricultural, pastoral and other activities he pursued, more often than not ecological factors beyond human control had a more profound influence on history. Certainly this observation is true for the central Sudan salt industry.

A variety of ecological settings characterised salt production in the central Sudan. Most salt and natron came from desert sites or the sahel, places where the scarcity or absence of rainfall made human occupation difficult. Agriculture was practised wherever possible – in oases, relatively fertile valleys in the sahel, and on the dunes when rain came. Hunting and gathering were also important occupations, because animals that had value not only as food but also for export lived in the sahel and southern desert. Ostriches and civet cats were the most prized, ostriches for their feathers and cats for their perfume. Pastoralism was the dominant human activity, and nomads controlled settlement patterns, production along the desert-edge, and exchange in the sahel and desert, unless a strong savanna state could restrict nomadic movements. Invariably the tug of war over scarce resources – water and arable land – along the desert-edge, not only between desert and savanna but among nomads themselves, resulted in considerable raiding and pillage. Theft offered another way of life that could either supplement agriculture, trade, hunting and pastoralism or replace these pursuits altogether.

The production of salt in the Benue Valley represented a different pattern in the organisation of economy and society from the desert-side region. While rainfall could fail, usually water was not a problem for agriculture. It could be for salt-making, if there was too much rain or the brine stopped flowing because there had been too little rain over a series of years. None the less, the differences are striking. The movements of nomads and the political impact that nomads had along the desert-edge were not factors in the politics or the economy of the Benue Valley. A study of the brine springs, therefore, offers a useful contrast to the study of the desert-side salines. The inclusion of the Benue salines here has been determined primarily because of an overlap in markets for its salts with those from further north. Salt and natron from the sahel and desert served an extensive region that encompassed the same territory supplied by the Benue salines. The reason that this overlap should have occurred relates to the differences in the various salts that came onto the market.

14

2

Consumption of the central Sudan salts

The salts of the central Sudan were used for a variety of culinary, medicinal, industrial, and other purposes, but broadly speaking two important distinctions can be made (Table 2.1). First, some salts (*beza, gallo, foga, awai, keana, kige*) were predominantly sodium chloride in content, and their use was most often purely culinary, although the presence of other salts, particularly sodium carbonate, sodium sulphate, and other chemicals, meant some salts with a high sodium chloride content (*balma, fachi, mangul*) had medicinal uses as well. Those salts with higher concentrations of sulphates and carbonates were also used in cooking and as medicine, but their composition meant that they could be used for industrial purposes too. This second category of salt mixtures is often referred to as natron, and sometimes, erroneously, as potash.[1] Technically, almost all the salts were mixtures, but it will be useful here to distinguish between 'salt' and 'natron', following the distinction recognised in the central Sudan. In Hausa and Kanuri, for example, the salts with a significant sodium chloride content are called *gishiri* and *manda*, respectively, while the other salt mixtures are called *kanwa* (Hausa) and *kalvu* (Kanuri). Unless otherwise noted, *gishiri* and *manda* are translated as 'salt', and the mixtures with a predominant sodium carbonate content as 'natron'.

CULINARY USES

In the central Sudan and other parts of Africa, salt was an ingredient added to food, but an analogy to European consumption of salt is misleading. Certainly the Fulani proverb, *manda resatake nden takai lamma*, 'if the salt is stored, the soup will not be good',[2] accurately reflects a universal appreciation of that property in salt which brings out the flavour of food. For North American and European taste, the desire for salt is satisfied simply by adding a pinch of sodium chloride – common table salt – in the preparation of food or after the food has been cooked. In this way the physiological need for salt is satisfied too; only rarely is salt used for other human needs – occasionally as a medicine to treat eye disorders or minor skin irritations. The very purity of European and North American salt is responsible for this relatively simple correlation between salt and its use. In recent times, the consumption of sea salt instead of salt mined commercially has gained favour among some food purists; the additional minerals other than sodium chloride which are

15

Table 2.1 *Uses and known distribution of central Sudan salts* (Hausa terms)

	Type	Source	Uses	Extent of distribution
I.	*Farin Kanwa* (*kwaras kwaras*) (white or grey natron)	Muniyo, Mangari, Kawar, Asben, Zaberma	1. Culinary 2. Medicinal 3. Soap-making 4. Snuff-making 5. Dyeing textiles	Central Sudan, Benue–Cross River areas, Yoruba states Dahomey, Borgu, Timbuktu
II.	*Gari* (powdered *farin kanwa*)	Same	1. Fed to livestock 2. Medicinal	Sokoto Caliphate, Borno, Southern Sahara
III.	*Jar kanwa* (red natron)	Muniyo, Mangari, Kawar	1. Medicinal 2. Culinary	Sokoto Caliphate, Borno
IV.	*Ungurnu* (trona)	Foli (Kanem)	1. Medicinal; general health 2. Snuff-making and chewing tobacco (*garin-taba*) 3. Culinary	Sokoto Caliphate, Asante, Borno, Chari basin, etc.
V.	*Gwangwarasa* (sodium sulphate)	Mangari	1. Tanning 2. Animal medicine	Borno, Sokoto Caliphate
VI.	*Gallo* (sodium chloride predominant)	Taoudeni	1. Medicinal 2. Culinary	Kano, Zaria, probably elsewhere
VII.	*Kige* (sodium chloride predominant)	Chad shores, Mangari	1. Culinary	Borno, perhaps Mandara

	Salt (description)	Source	Uses	Regions
VIII.	*Mangul* (high in sodium chloride content)	Mangari	1. Culinary 2. Medicinal	Borno, Mandara, Sokoto Caliphate
IX.	*Beza* (best sodium chloride salt)	Kawar, Fachi, Asben, Taoudeni, Teguidda n'tesemt, Amadror	1. Medicinal 2. Culinary	Sahara, Sokoto Caliphate, Borno, elsewhere
X.	*Balma, kantu* (most common Kawar salt, inferior to *beza*)	Kawar	Same	Same
XI.	*Fachi* (like *kantu*)	Fachi	Same	Same
XII.	*Gishirin foga* (sodium chloride predominant)	Dallol Fogha	1. Culinary	Western Sokoto Caliphate, Borgu, Songhay
XIII.	*Dan awai, dan wase* (sodium chloride and impurities)	Awe	1. Culinary	Bauchi, Kano, Zaria, Benue basin, Jos Plateau
XIV.	*Dan keana* (sodium chloride and impurities)	Keana, adjacent sites	1. Culinary 2. Medicinal	Jos Plateau, Benue basin
XV.	*Kakanda* (adulterated sodium chloride)	Niger–Benue confluence	1. Culinary	Benue–Niger Valleys, Kano, Zaria
XVI.	*Beji* (sodium chloride)	Teguidda n'tesemt	1. Culinary	Hausa territory, Adar

contained in sea salt are considered to be healthier and more 'natural' than commercial salt. This distinction between sea salt and pure sodium chloride is the closest analogy to the far more elaborate distinctions which were and still are recognised by the consumers of the central Sudan salts.

The tastes of the central Sudan salts differ, and this property was probably the basis of the most important distinctions made between the various salts which were used in food. Unlike the distinction between sea salt and commercial salt in western cuisine – where taste is not usually considered the most significant difference, being subordinate to considerations of health and 'nature' – West African recipes required specific salts, as if each type were a different spice. A Hausa proverb demonstrates the sophistication of the taste factor: *hanci bai san dadin gishiri ba*, 'the nose does not know the flavour of the salt'.[3] The analogy with smell suggests that the distinctions in taste of the various salts were subtle and important. Because the various kinds of salt were not always available, consumers could not always choose one salt over another. None the less, the distinctions were clear, as reflected in recipes for different dishes.

The purer salts – higher in sodium chloride content as well as cleaner – most closely correspond to western table salt, and were usually the highest in price. Because of their expense, these salts were used on special occasions, and of course aristocrats, merchants and others who could afford to purchase these better salts were the principal consumers. Except for certain special recipes, these salts could be used in the preparation of any food, including the staple Hausa grain dishes, *tuwo* and *kunu*, but cheaper salt or natron was more often used. *Tuwo* has the consistency of a thick porridge or hasty pudding and is prepared from the winnowed flour of guinea corn or other grains. The flour is added to boiling water and stirred continuously, until a thick paste forms and it becomes nearly solid. A little salt or much more natron is then stirred into it. It is then taken off the fire and left to stand for about ten minutes. *Kunu*, a thin porridge which is drunk, is prepared in the same manner as *tuwo*, except that less flour is used, and bulrush millet rather than guinea corn is the more common grain.[4] *Miya*, the soup or light stew which is served with the staple grains, also uses different salts, particularly natron, which is thought to soften leaves, which are often an important ingredient. Pepper, locust-bean cakes, beans, tomatoes, onions, pumpkin, meat, ground-nut oil, and many condiments are frequently used in *miya*; their proportions and combination depend upon the recipe, the wealth of the consumer and the availability of the ingredients. Salt was also sprinkled on roasted peanuts or added to rice, with some butter. These and other uses are similar to the use of salt in western cuisine, even if the dishes are often different.[5]

The wealthy used *beza*, which was a generic term for high quality salt. Originally, *beza* referred to the pure white salt from Bilma, which was marketed in small leather bags.[6] There is a place in the Kawar oases known as Beza, but the salt came from the same salines as the far more common – and less pure – *kantu* or *balma*. Subsequently *beza* was applied to salt from other sources and the term came to signify quality rather than place. Merchants even tried to pass off *kantu* as *beza*.[7] The salt of Teguidda n'tesemt (*tigadda*) was considered a type of *beza*, as was the salt from Amadror and Taoudeni (*gallo*). The variety of terms which identify the different origins of *beza* is an indicator of the fine distinctions which were made by consumers. *Aza* or *gikau* (*jik'au*) came from Aïr, perhaps from Teguidda or Amadror, while *zumba* (*sumba*), and *cingiraba* referred to other distinctions which are no longer clear.[8] Although *kige*, a relatively pure salt from the Kadzell region of Borno, appears not to have been considered a type of *beza, kige* was in fact as pure as the various types of *beza* and had a similar price. The salts from the brine springs of the Benue basin – Awe, Keana, Bomanda and elsewhere – were high quality salts which competed for the same market. European salt, which began to command a small market by the middle of the nineteenth century, was actually adulterated to bring its taste more in line with those of the local, high quality salts.[9] In its adulterated state, European salt was referred to as *kakanda*, named after the Nupe trading communities along the Niger River that were responsible for its introduction to the central Sudan.[10] Each of these sodium chloride salts tended to satisfy a relatively small market because quantity was often limited, and locally produced salt of similar purity was found beyond the Sokoto Caliphate and Borno. These other sources of sodium chloride salts included those from Uburu and other brine sources south of the Benue basin, the salt from Daboya in western Gonja in the middle Volta basin,[11] and the sea salt from the numerous salt works found along the Guinea Coast from the Bight of Biafra westward to the Gold Coast.[12]

The less wealthy used salts which were lower in sodium chloride content but which were still classified as *gishiri* or *manda*. The most important of these were Kawar and Fachi salt (*kantu* or *fachi* and *balma*), the salt of Mangari in Borno (Hausa: *mangul*) and the salt of Dallol Fogha (*gishirin foga*). Usually, *kunu* and *tuwo*, the two Hausa staple foods, were made with *mangul* or *kantu*; *foga* was common in western Hausaland, while *mangul* was common in the populous Kano, Katsina and Zaria areas and of course in Borno. The Kawar and Fachi salt (*kantu*) was slightly more expensive but was also widely consumed. *Mangul*, slightly cheaper, was used more in the countryside, while *kantu* was in greater demand in the towns and cities, at least as far as the Kano area was concerned.[13]

Poorer people, and indeed many people for everyday fare, used natron in preparing *kunu* and *tuwo*, and there were many special dishes as well which required natron (*kanwa*) rather than salt (*gishiri*).[14] The best quality white natron from Borno (*farin kanwa or kwaras kwaras*) was used in making *d'an wake*, ground bean cakes, thickened with water and mixed with pepper. A slightly poorer quality *kwaras kwaras* could be used in making *kunu* (*kunun kanwa*), usually made of millet or sorghum. *Kunun kanwa* was thought to be healthy for nursing mothers. Natron could be added to *zogale* or *rama* leaves and ground-nut cakes (*kuli kuli*). *Kunu, d'an wake* and other dishes could also be made with red natron (*jar kanwa*). Bean dishes in particular were made with natron, rather than salt, because, it is said, 'natron takes the fart out of the beans'. The best quality natron, actually trona, which came from the eastern shores of Lake Chad, was used in making *birabisko* – millet, wheat, rice, or sweet potatoes, boiled in water. *Kayan yaji*, another meal, was prepared from pepper, *citta* (ginger), *mai koko, kimba* pepper, and red natron, which were ground up. *Fankaso* (Katsina: *algaragi*) was a wheat cake boiled in oil and seasoned with tamarind and natron. Sesame was also made into cakes fried with *kantu* salt from Bilma and pepper as a food that could be taken on journeys. The young leaves of *Stylochiton ancifolius* (Hausa: *gwandai*) were used as a herb after long boiling with *beza* salt, while the marrow of the bulrush (*Typha australis*) was eaten in Borno with *manda*.[15]

One particularly tasty snack consisted of deleb-palm shoots (*muruci*) which were roasted or boiled. Young girls sold these in the streets of Kano and other places for 15 cowries at the end of the nineteenth century, although in Zamfara and Kebbi, where deleb palms were common, the shoots (known there as *gazari*) sold for only 5 cowries.[16] *Muruci* was considered to be an aphrodisiac when prepared in the following manner: the shoots were dried and pounded into a powder, then mixed with salt, red pepper (*barkono*), ginger, and *kimba* pepper. The mixture was sprinkled onto fatty meat which was then roasted but left rare. Whether or not this snack actually 'makes the penis strong', the salt was an important ingredient. Other preparations which also used salt or natron were considered essential to male virility as well.[17]

As I have already suggested, the use of salt and natron in food can provide some indication of the scale of the salt trade, if some estimate of total population can be made. The demand for salt in food is particularly inelastic; since a population as a whole consumes an average of 4.5 kg per person per year, only an increase in population alters salt consumption significantly. In the central Sudan, however, a direct correlation between population and salt consumption did not exist. As Imam Imoru observed, poverty was a severe problem in society, to the point that many people could not afford even to buy salt:

> The common people, *talakawa*, make their soup [*miya*] without meat, and the destitute, *matsiyata*, are forced to make it without salt and it is called 'tasteless', *lami*. Some people, due to poverty, cook beans and eat them with salt at night. Some even cook beans to eat at night without salt, and again, this is because of poverty.[18]

Perhaps there is no better measure of poverty than the inability of people to afford salt, particularly in a society in which the salts were impure mixtures that varied greatly in price.

MEDICAL USES

Hausa medical practice was a well-established tradition in the nineteenth century. The specialist practitioners included traditional doctors (*boka*),

20

medical dispensers (*mai magani*), barbers (*wanzami*), bone-setters (*madora*), midwives (*ungozoma*) and Muslim clerics (*malam*).[19] Each of these specialists used one or another salt, depending upon the medical treatment being administered. Of course many prescriptions did not require salt or natron, and there was a division between Islamic medical theory, which relied on religious texts, incantations, amulets, and prayers, and *materia medica* that included a knowledge of herbs, minerals and other raw materials. *Boka*, for example, tended to treat common colds, headaches, digestive disorders, and general complaints; *mai magani* provided the medicines for treatment and hence served more as pharmacists than as doctors. In both cases, however, a knowledge of the properties of salt and natron was essential. Bone-setters had to treat swelling and infections, and they too had to know about salt and natron. Only *malam*, who relied on Islamic theory, used less salt and natron, although they too had considerable knowledge of *materia medica*.

This medical tradition of *materia medica* and Islamic science was the subject of numerous medical treatises written in the early nineteenth century that were widely disseminated among the literate *malam* class of the caliphate and beyond. Foremost among these medical writers was Muhammad Bello, son of Usuman dan Fodio and first caliph of the empire. Bello wrote treatises on senna as a purgative, eye diseases, piles, 'the medicine of the Prophet', 'how to treat women', and religion and medicine. Other important writers included Muhammad Tukur and Abdullahi ibn Fudi (the brother of Usuman dan Fodio). Bello in particular was fascinated with *materia medica* and attempted to codify local remedies by recording Arabic, Hausa and Fulfulde terms for various herbs and minerals.[20] Precisely because of this tradition, Dalziel was able to complete a far more detailed survey of botanical plants and their medicinal (and other) uses. Dalziel brought together an indigenous tradition with the developed science of botany. His survey, *The Useful Plants of West Tropical Africa*, is the successful culmination of a long tradition of local observation and recording.[21]

The central Sudan salts must have been used for medicinal purposes over a vast area for a very long time, although it may be impossible to learn exactly how old such practices are or how knowledge of their properties spread. Abdallah, a Borno pilgrim who was in Cairo in the first decade of the nineteenth century, reported that both red and white natron were used as a stomach medicine, as indeed both still are.[22] In 1817, Bowdich found that natron was a common treatment in Asante; the natron was dissolved in water and drunk 'for pains in the bowels'.[23] At virtually the same time, Hausa traders took 'congwa' to Timbuktu, from where it may well have been re-exported as far as Segu.[24] Again, one of its uses was as medicine. Natron was found on the Guinea Coast – at Ardrah at least – in the 1790s, and Clapperton observed its medicinal importance when he was in Oyo in 1826; his information confirms its use as medicine on 'all parts of the coast'.[25]

These accounts demonstrate the wide geographical extent of natron use by the late eighteenth and the early nineteenth centuries. There is every reason to

21

believe that these practices were well established before this time, at least for areas to the west and south-west of the central Sudan. Although reports for the area south of the Benue River and Lake Chad only begin after the middle of the nineteenth century, it seems likely that the importance of natron as a medicine was as well established there as in the areas to the west.[26]

Perhaps the most important use of medicinal salt and natron was to counteract digestive disorders. Dr McCulloch reported in the *West African Medical Journal* that digestive disorders were common throughout Nigeria – representing 22 per cent of all hospital cases in 1926–29, but in the Hausa north the percentage was more than double that figure – 46.5 per cent in Katsina province.[27] Although medical reporting, the availability of treatment, and the presence of trained doctors were all inadequate, to say the least, Dr McCulloch's observations are interesting because they demonstrate the importance of salt and natron in local medical practice. Of the cases reported in Katsina, 16.8 per cent related to constipation, which suggested to McCulloch that dietary problems were serious in northern Nigeria. The prevalence of constipation explained why 'purgatives are extremely popular with the Hausa and are probably taken largely on principle because of the fear of constipation, rather than because the condition exists'.[28] It might have been difficult for Dr McCulloch to convince his patients that the condition did not exist; folk knowledge anticipated the effects of particular foods, so that the addition of natron to food was a good example of preventive medicine in a situation in which a balanced diet did not safeguard people from constipation. P. Noel, M D, who observed the medicinal practices of people in Bilma, attributed the relief from constipation to the presence of sodium sulphate in the natron of Kawar.[29]

The purest red natron (*wariza*) was used to 'wash the stomach' – it induces diarrhoea. The natron, dissolved in water and drunk, was considered particularly effective in the relief of cramps. A less pure form of *jar kanwa* was used for the same purpose by older people.[30] *Ungurnu* – trona from Kanem – was also used for constipation. It cost more but was stronger than other varieties of natron. Pregnant women in particular tended to use *ungurnu*, especially to counteract excessive sweetness. During the month of Ramadan, when people rose early in order to eat before the sun came up, *ungurnu* was used to prevent indigestion. The early meal was the only food all day so people mixed *ungurnu* in some water and drank it after they finished eating. Then most people went back to sleep. Although other kinds of natron were used, *ungurnu* was preferred because it was purer and hence stronger. Among men, regular users of *ungurnu* were credited with increased virility and better sight.[31] Nursing mothers and sick people were given extra doses of white natron, often in their food. The salt from Bilma (*kantu*) was cooked with senna leaves (*filasko*) in boiling water and drunk as a medicine to 'wash out the stomach'. Inducing diarrhoea in this fashion was done if a person had little appetite. The 'dirty stomach' was cleaned out on one day, and the next day the patient ate a huge meal. Mild doses of *kantu* were also given to newborn babies with stomach aches; the *kantu* was mixed in water.[32] If a woman was pregnant, the whitest part of a *mangul* cone could be substituted for *ungurnu*, mixed with water and drunk to counteract indigestion from too much sugar or honey. This part of the *mangul* cone (*d'an farifari*) was not sold separately, but it was broken off. *Mangul* was often given to women just after delivery to relieve stomach pains, and it was also cooked with cattle hooves (*k'afa*) to soften them. *K'afa* was served to new mothers, five or seven days after giving birth. This family feast (*k'auri*) was considered healthy for the new mother and also an important occasion, recognising the successful birth and the fact that the new baby had passed safely through the first days of life. The mother was also given *mangul* in water for indigestion.[33] Natron was mixed with cereal flour, shea butter or oil, and *Trichodesma africanum* (Hausa: *walkin tsofa, walkin wawa*) and boiled to make a paste that could be eaten to counteract diarrhoea. A cold infusion of the bark of *Sclerocarya birrea* (Hausa: *danya*) along with natron was also a remedy for dysentery, and *Maytenus senegalensis* (Hausa: *k'unk'ushewu*) and *Vernonia amygdalina* (Hausa: *shiwaka*) were boiled with natron for gastro-intestinal troubles. Senna (*Cassia italica*; Hausa: *filasko*), when mixed with natron and tamarind, was a common laxative. *Sumbu-sumbu*, another salt, was also mixed with pieces of mahogany (*mad'aci*), which were ground up for the oil content in the wood and used as a stomach medicine. As a medicine, ground *sumbu-sumbu* and mahogany were considered good for the blood and for one's virility. Red natron, by contrast, was thought to reduce sexual desire and was drunk in solution by single men.[34]

Local doctors had their own uses for natron and salt: *salala* could be made from powdered guinea corn, ground wood, and red natron. Or a doctor could prescribe other mixtures which contained natron, although he would not necessarily mix the ingredients himself.[35] Imam Imoru referred to a medicine for teeth, made of indigo root and natron. The loose tooth was darkened with the indigo, covered with natron and then rinsed with hot water to reduce swelling.[36] *Beza*, relatively pure sodium chloride, was also used for guinea-worm (*kurkunu*). But red natron mixed with the fresh fruit of *Crinum glaucum* (Hausa: *albasar kwad'i*) and plain natron, garlic and leaves of *Aristolochia albida* (Hausa: *gad'akuka*) were also used to counteract guinea-worm. *Mangul* in water was also administered to people who lost blood in an injury or beating; it was thought to assist in restoring blood to the body and in removing the dead blood from the bruises. Red natron was also used by barber-doctors who were treating bruises or infections. The barber-doctor made an incision into the infected part of the body and administered the red natron directly on the wound. *Salala*, medicine made with red natron and different fruits or wood, was applied to fractures, swelling, and dislocated bones. It consisted of a paste which was spread on the affected part of the body to reduce the swelling. *Salala* was also used for scalp diseases. Powdered natron. *gari*, was also used as a preparation for scalp diseases and other scaly skin problems. And natron could be chewed with the bark of *Commiphora africana* (Hausa:

dashi) and then administered to scorpion bites, or it was chewed with the bark of gum of *Acacia campylacantha* (Hausa: *farchen shaho*) to relieve sore throat.[37]

Other types of *salala* were used for internal disorders related to gonorrhoea, various forms of gastritis accompanied by tympanites (*kabba*), and complications related to pregnancy.[38] Depending upon the illness, various medicinal woods were also ground up in the mixture. *Kunun salala*, a powerful abortifacient, was administered in generous amounts; the patient drinking as much as possible. In the case of gonorrhoea, this mixture – to which white natron was also added in considerable quantities – produces severe diuresis, which even causes the passing of blood. Other remedies for venereal diseases included mixtures of natron with *Annona senegalensis* (Hausa: *gwandar daji*), *Polygala arenaria* (Hausa: *hankaki dako*), *Securidaca longipedunculata* (Hausa: *sanya*), *Alchornea cordifolia* (Hausa: *bambami*), *Cissus cornifolia* (Hausa: *rigar biri*), *Solanum incanum* (Hausa: *gauta*), *Merremia angustifolia* (Hausa: *yimb'ururu*), *Stereospermum kunthianum* (Hausa: *sansami*), *Leonotis africana* (Hausa: *jamb'arawo*). Often these mixtures were also powerful purgatives that could be used for intestinal disorders too. The immediate effect in pregnant women is violent diarrhoea with subsequent abortion. In complicated pregnancies where there was danger of death, a saline solution of *gallo, sumbu-sumbu,* or natron could also be used as a means of inducing delivery or the expulsion of the embryonic sac, a procedure that is extremely dangerous but which was administered in the absence of better medical treatment.[39]

After his survey of Hausa dietary practices and health problems, Dr McCulloch concluded that the use of salt and natron to the extent he observed was a major problem.

> It is obvious from the analyses...that the natrons are unfit for human consumption and that their use should be discouraged. Gallo and Bilma salts are impure sodium chlorides of which Gallo is easily the better, both because of the small silica content and the presence of iodine in sufficient amount to be estimated.[40]

McCulloch may well have been right in questioning the use of natron as medicine and as a culinary salt, but in conditions where modern medical facilities were lacking his recommendation to discourage the use of local medicines was premature, to say the least. He may well have been 'astonished' by the amount of 'native salt' used in northern Nigeria, but his observations are excellent proof of the importance of the salt industry.[41]

Some of the 'medicinal' uses of salt had even less basis in scientific theory than the uses criticised by McCulloch, as is often the case in folk medicine. Natron or salt – but usually *beza* – was mixed with ink, for example, which was then used to write Quranic verses and prayers on the slates of the Muslim clerics. The words were then washed off the slate and drunk as a potion to cure ills. The solution was considered magic (*tsubbu*). Often women sought this kind of cure, particularly to counteract false pregnancies. In a typical prescription, a person drank the *tsubbu* for seven days. *Gallo*, from Taoudeni, could also be used in *tsubbu*, although it was very expensive.⁴² The *malam* who performed these rites may well have provided psychological and religious support to people in time of emotional or physical stress. While the believers undoubtedly benefited from this attention, the use of natron was only an incidental factor in the rite. Dalziel found that *Jussiaea suffruticosa* (Hausa: *sha shatau*) was mixed with natron for similar purposes: 'The uses are superstitious, both in Hausa and Yoruba, e.g. to prevent forgetfulness, escape punishment, ensure favour, etc. The first Hausa name is apparently connected with *shashasha*, an idiot or weak-minded person with whom one cannot be angry. Thus a slave who does wrong rubs his body with the plant or sucks it with red natron to escape detection or to avoid pain if beaten for his fault.' Another remedy, including *Loranthus spp.* (Hausa: *kauchi*), *gallo* and shea butter – a thick white fat made from the nuts of the shea tree – was used by hunters. If the mixture were eaten in the morning, so it was believed, 'the hunted game will be drowsy and easy to kill'.⁴³ It may well be that these practices began because natron was known as a good medicine for other ailments. As with other concoctions in which natron was an ingredient, natron was readily available for use in quasi-medicinal situations. In pre-scientific society, patients could not easily distinguish between real and imaginary cures, but in either case they demanded one or another salt.

TOBACCO CONSUMPTION

When Hugh Clapperton visited Borno and the Sokoto Caliphate in the 1820s, he found that 'snuff mixed with trona is a favourite habit'.⁴⁴ Both chewing tobacco (Hausa: *taba gari*) and snuff (Hausa: *tabar hanci*) were mixed with natron. Although smoking was also common in the 1820s, the reform government of the Sokoto Caliphate indirectly encouraged the spread of snuff and tobacco chewing, since it actively discouraged people from smoking by invoking Islamic prohibition.⁴⁵ When Clapperton returned to the central Sudan in 1826, travelling from the coast through Oyo into the interior, he found that the practice of mixing natron with tobacco was equally widespread; indeed by the time he was once again in the caliphate, he referred to 'the universal custom of chewing snuff mixed with tobacco'. In much of the caliphate, he observed, men and women alike used snuff, while in Borno, 'where the indulgence is not permitted to women', only men had succumbed to the habit.⁴⁶

The practice had spread over much of West Africa by the early nineteenth century and, as has already been noted with respect to the use of natron as medicine, the mixing of natron with tobacco was probably much older than our sources allow us to conclude safely. Again, the earliest reference in the central Sudan is the account of Abdallah, the pilgrim from Borno who was in Cairo around 1808. But its use is reported in Tunis in the 1830s, and it was common among the Tuareg, Teda and other nomads of the central Sahara.[47] The natron which Adams saw in the market at Ardrah in the 1790s, for example, was probably used with tobacco, as well as being a medicine, if the evidence of Clapperton in the 1820s can be used to indicate the probable extent of snuff use three decades earlier. A major import on the Slave Coast was tobacco from Brazil,[48] and tobacco and natron went together, even though tobacco was also smoked. The Asante, for example, as Bowdich found, ground up natron with tobacco 'as it gives it a pungency agreeable to them'.[49] Bowdich reported that chunks of natron the size of ducks' eggs could be purchased in the Kumasi market for the equivalent of 2 shillings. In Asante, people not only mixed ground natron with their chewing tobacco, but they often ate a small piece of *trona* after finishing the tobacco. Some people even chewed powdered *trona* without tobacco.[50]

The practice of mixing natron with tobacco was also common in Timbuktu, another centre of the tobacco trade, in the early nineteenth century. The Kunta were actively involved in the tobacco trade through Timbuktu, while Hausa traders brought the natron from the east.[51] The Igbo also mixed natron with tobacco, although it is unclear how old their use of natron for this purpose is. It is likely, moreover, that natron was probably chewed with tobacco much further east, in the regions south and east of Lake Chad.[52]

Consumers in those places at considerable distance from Lake Chad wanted trona from the eastern shore of Lake Chad. It was relatively pure and came in chunks, as Bowdich observed.[53] But trona was not the only type of natron, and sometimes – knowingly or not – consumers in the distant places purchased other varieties of natron, which were also mixed with tobacco. Closer to the sources of production, however, consumers consciously distinguished between types. Many were popular, not just trona, and the different taste provided by the various kinds of natron was an important factor in determining the volume and direction of trade. Trona was often considered an expensive additive; its expense was higher in part because of its relative purity and in part because the demand of distant markets kept its price up. Consequently, other varieties were more common in the Hausa cities and along the desert-edge.

A Tuareg nomad would have made the following kinds of distinctions in picking his natron supply.[54] Tobacco would taste good with natron from Kawar, where there were two major varieties available in the desert-edge markets. But salt from Teguidda was also prized; many consumers further south would not have thought about using Teguidda salt because of its expense, but for the Tuareg, who had easy access, such a consideration was not as important. Other natron was also found; a journey to Zinder would enable a Tuareg band to buy the natron of Muniyo, while trona was always to be found in the Hausa cities. Whether it was the red natron of Dirku, the grey *manda* of Borno, the white salt of Teguidda, or the natron from Dallol Bosso, chewing tobacco was a luxury to be enjoyed.

The Hausa connoisseur kept his supply in a small leather or metal container, strung around his waist or buried deep in the pocket of his gown. Both tobacco and natron were subjects of debate. Quality, price, taste and availability were the concerns of the old men studying Arabic texts under the trees outside their compounds. Tobacco chewing was as much a part of local culture as it was in Asante, only for the Muslims of the savanna tobacco chewing had the sanction of religion. Drinking alcohol and smoking tobacco were forbidden, but chewing tobacco and kola nuts was not. Supported by Islamic prohibition, local taste promoted a market for natron which was based on these cultural values, not on biological necessity. Kola nuts came from Asante and were used to finance the import of natron. This market situation brought about the exchange of commodities which had far-reaching consequences for the economic history of West Africa. Consumption patterns were equally crucial in the central Sudan, where tobacco smoking would not have encouraged the consumption of natron as an additive. Chewing tobacco and snuff did, and as a result the market for salt expanded with the spread of these habits.

INDUSTRIAL USES OF SALT

Leather goods, textiles, and livestock production were three of the most important sectors in the economy of the central Sudan, and each had a need for salt. Tanning – more properly tawing – used salt, especially sodium sulphate, to change the raw hide into an imputrescible substance not capable of being restored to its original form by outside influence; textile dyeing used natron in solution to reduce indigo to a soluble state; and livestock needed natron for medicinal purposes similar to those common to man. Soap too needed natron; soap was made from fats and soda. The salts needed for these purposes – with the exception of the salt for tanning – were the same as those used in cooking, as medicine, or with tobacco. The tanning salt – *gwangwarasa* – was highly concentrated sodium sulphate and was poisonous, but *gwangwarasa* came from the same places in Mangari as natron, often from the very same locations. Consequently, the trade in industrial salts was identical to the trade in salt for other purposes. For these purposes, moreover, the commerce in salt was not a luxury trade but essential to the central Sudan economy.

Tanning dates back at least to the early sixteenth century, probably to many centuries before then. Leo Africanus, who visited sub-Saharan West Africa in 1516, observed that shoes and other leather products were made in the Hausa cities.[55] These goods were exported to Songhay and elsewhere. It may well have been that the tanners used sodium sulphate from Mangari at that date, although direct evidence is, of course, lacking. Curing of hides can be done with vegetable substances, salts or oils, but it is likely that in the central Sudan salts were always used for this purpose. In the Middle East and other places where tawing was also the common method of tanning hides, alum was used as the active agent. Supplies of alum were limited in the central Sudan; some

27

alum was found in Kawar and was an item exported to North Africa in the medieval period.[56] Various other salts could be used, and perhaps were, but sodium sulphate was the most important tawing agent by the nineteenth century, and probably earlier still. Whether it was sometimes mixed with alum is not known. The sodium sulphate was pounded in a mortar, mixed with water, and put on the skin. Hausa tanners made leather aprons and loincloths, cushions, bags, sandals, saddles and other horse gear, containers, and sword sheaths.[57] From Leo Africanus' day to the nineteenth century, these leather goods were the subject of an important export trade.

Natron was also used in dyeing leather. Tawed leather is most easily stained with vegetable dyes, which is a major reason why the leather industry of the central Sudan became so famous. So-called Moroccan leather was in fact often leather imported from the central Sudan or other parts of West Africa. Natron was used in red and yellow dyes.[58] In Kano, Clapperton learned that in order to dye leather red, the tanners 'daub it over with a composition, made of trona and the outer leaves of red Indian corn, first beaten into a powder and mixed up with water'.[59] As Clapperton observed, red dyes were made from a red variety of sorghum (*Sorghum guineense*; Hausa: *karan dafi*). A watery extract of wood ashes or natron was allowed to sit for 3–4 hours; the dyestuff was pulverised in a wooden mortar and mixed with the extract; the tanned hide, dressed with ground-nut oil or shea butter, was immersed in the mixture for a minute or two and then wrung out and shaken; and finally the hide was rinsed in cold water which had been acidulated with lime juice or tamarind pulp. Yellow dye was made from turmeric (Hausa: *zabibi*) or *Cryptolepis sanguinolenta* (Hausa: *gangamau*) and occasionally several other vegetable sources. The method of dyeing was similar to that used for the red, except that tamarind paste was added to the mixture for a second coating of the dye. The effect of the tamarind pulp was probably to purify the colour; it removed the red tint left by the alkali. Green dyes combined copper or brass filings with a white salt, *sunadri* (ammonium chloride). Sheep skins were more often used, and the skin was not tanned. Sometimes *kantu* was added to the dye.

The most common dye used in textile production – blue – was made from indigo, which strictly speaking is not a self-fixing dye. The active ingredients in the plant are insoluble in water but can be made soluble through fermentation and direct chemical treatment. Hausa techniques employed a combination of both methods, and natron was one of the chemicals that made the dye soluble. In solution the dye remains unfixed but exposure to oxygen fixes it; hence dyers raised the material from the vat and exposed it to the air before reimmersion. Hausa dyers practised a method that involved over-dyeing; which means that they tried to build up a surplus deposit of dye on the impregnated, and now stable, dyed cloth. This deposit is unstable in the physical sense; it comes off through abrasion and in washing. While the natron – containing sodium sulphate and sodium carbonate – facilitates the conversion of the insoluble indigo into a soluble form, it is not a true mordant; that is, it does not fix the dye but rather allows its reduction to a form that can be fixed. Natron from Mangari was used for this process in Kano and northern Zaria, where the textile industry was most heavily concentrated. By the nineteenth century, however, dyers also used the residue (*kasko*) from the dyepits to reduce the indigo.[60] *Striga hermontheca* (Hausa: *k'uduji, k'ujiji, makasha, makasar dawa*) was also used as a red dye; it was pounded, mixed with red natron and the ashes of guinea corn stalks. *Sorghum caudatum* (Hausa: *karan dafi*) was another red dye; when mixed with natron and black dyestuffs it was used for cloth and also mat fibres, calabashes and as a body pigment.[61]

Soap was made from shea butter (*Butyrospermum parkii*), extracted from the kernel of the shea butter tree, which was mixed with animal fat and natron. The soap was soft and Denham found it to have a pleasant smell when he observed its manufacture in 1824. The soap was put in small wooden boxes.[62]

By far the greatest industrial use was as a salt and medicine for livestock. Livestock breeders could obtain salt locally or move their herds to the sites of salt deposits, as indeed they still do, but even in the case of livestock production, the keeping of livestock by sedentary farmers presupposes the availability of salt, just as the presence of a human population is indirect evidence for the consumption of salt. White natron in powdered form (*gari*) was bought for this purpose throughout the central Sudan and beyond. *Gari* was given to all livestock; donkeys, cattle and camels were fed the natron in their drinking water, while horses, sheep and goats were fed it with their food. *Gari* could be spread on the pastures for cattle. For horses, the *gari* was added to leaves, which were ground up together, or it was mixed with millet chaff and administered daily. Sometimes ash was added. The *gari* was mixed with millet or guinea corn chaff as a food for sheep and goats.[63] Lander reported in the 1820s that natron was given to horses, sheep and other animals in Borgu; livestock ate 'large lumps of it with the greatest avidity'.[64] Bowdich found that natron was dissolved in water and fed to cattle and mixed in the guinea grass fed to horses in Asante.[65] Similar practices were found in the central Sudan, where natron was dissolved in water or mixed with fodder and sometimes spread on the fields, and it was used as a medicine for livestock if diarrhoea was evident. Estimates from east of Lake Chad indicate that camels consume 10–15 kg of natron per year, although the amount probably varied considerably in the past.[66]

There were a number of special preparations for livestock that used one or another variety of salt and natron. Baobab leaves, coarsely pounded, mixed with natron and bran and then boiled, were the most usual ingredients in a horse food called in Hausa *cusar doki*. Mahogany bark (*Khaya senegalensis*) was mixed 'with native natron (*kanwa*) or with a sort of salt from Adar called *boi-boi*; it is given to horses as a tonic and to improve their appetite'. *Lactuca taraxacifolia* (Hausa: *nonan b'arya*), a wild lettuce, was mixed with natron and given to sheep and goats 'to produce multiple births'. Red pepper, mixed with natron and soot, was rubbed into the lips of cattle and horses if they were suffering from a disease (Hausa: *cizal*) – probably 'woody tongue' – that was characterised by a hard, black tongue. Woody tongue is caused by bacteria, which are in fact a secondary invader of wounds on the tongue that are derived from grazing on prickly plants. Finally, *Vernonia amygdalina* (Hausa: *shiwaka*), a bitter leaf, was crushed in water, and mixed with bran and natron as a tonic to fatten and to strengthen horses.[67]

While *gari* and purer forms of natron were transported over great distances, livestock herders also moved animals to places where natron could be obtained, particularly to the sites of wells impregnated with natron. Such wells were common in much of the sahel – north of Borno, in Kanem, in Adar, and on the Air Massif, among other places. Herds were also taken to the sites of natron deposits in Mangari, Muniyo, Air, and Azelik–Guelele (near Teguidda n'tesemt). This part of the transhumant cycle was known by the French as the *cure salée*.

The salty water of the Azelik–Teguidda region is still particularly important to livestock herders. Today some 10,000 herders visit the region during August and September for the *cure salée*. The different groups of herders frequent the same sources each year, and they move the herds carefully, because of the difference in salinity of the various waters, in order to accustom the herds to the salt. Certain of the waters are considered to have therapeutic value, as much for humans as animals – notably those at In Gitane and one of the sources at Teguidda n'tesemt, situated in the Agaya quarter of the salines, which forms the pond called Bangu Beri. At In Gitane and Bangu Beri, people drink the water for several days or several weeks as a cure for skin ailments, digestive problems, and rheumatism.[68]

Less ritualised practices of livestock movement were pursued in the savanna wherever natural salt-licks were located. The ebullient springs found in the narrow mountain valleys of the Bamenda grasslands of Cameroon, for example, were used as salt-licks. Sodium salts predominate in the springs: sodium carbonate represents 821 parts per 100,000, sodium bicarbonate 117 parts per 100,000 and sodium chloride 31 parts per 100,000. Jeffreys, who observed these salt-licks in the 1930s, reported that 'at these springs the Fulani make wooden troughs out of hollowed tree trunks, and regularly bring their herds thither to give them a drink of 'salt water' as they call it'. The lick at the foot of Bamessing Hill has so many palaeolithic stone implements that it is possible that before the introduction of Fulani cattle to the area a local salt industry may have flourished.[69]

Jeffreys even found artificial salt-licks – to catch wild game – among the Igbo in Awka Division:

> I had at times found a foul-smelling cooking-pot, reeking of ammoniated urine, standing just inside the compound gate. It struck me that it wasn't there as a result of a Medical Officer of Health's protests against indiscriminate micturition. Inquiries revealed that the collected urine was evaporated down and the resulting 'brine' was spread about on a piece of cleared land in a disused farm. In this way a salt-lick was established and by the skilful setting of traps a steady supply of 'stewers' in the way of small 'beef' was ensured. The aim was to

maintain the salt-lick: hence the vessel at the gate-post and a gentle hint given to visitors that all contributions would be thankfully received. Visitors queued up before departing, and in the public eye contributed to the common object.[70]

Salt was once important in the smelting of copper at Azelik, near Teguidda n'tesemt, west of the Air Massif. The smelting process required the use of salt to free the copper from its ore. Copper was mined around Azelik, which was the capital of an important agricultural and industrial region in the sahel until it was destroyed in a war with Agades in the fifteenth century. As Gouletquer and Bernus have established, the town of Azelik was once in the midst of an irrigated district where the remains of numerous smelting furnaces, ore pits, and other debris have been found.[71] In 1353, Ibn Battuta passed through Azelik, which he called Takkeda ('Teguidda' means 'place', as in 'place of copper', to be compared with Teguidda n'tesemt, 'place of salt'). Ibn Battuta found the copper industry and agriculture flourishing, but he did not report the existence of salt processing.[72] None the less, it appears that salt was produced near Azelik, at Guelele, which was convenient to the smelting furnaces.

This wide variety of uses and the correspondingly large area of distribution demonstrate the importance of salt in the economic history of the central Sudan. Consumer demand covered culinary, medicinal and other uses which are not always easy to classify. As Dalziel observed, for example, 'in pagan districts in N. Nigeria the leaf [*Lonchocarpus laxiflorus*; Hausa: *shunin biri*] is chewed with natron, or with wood ashes, to darken the teeth'. The purpose appears to have been cosmetic, but since people sometimes chewed natron alone this particular practice may have combined cosmetic and culinary tastes. It is even less easy to categorise the use of natron in the Hausa gambling game of *caca*. The root of *Biophytum petersianum* (Hausa: *tsuku, tsuwuku*) was chewed with red natron and then rubbed on the cowrie shells before staking them in the game.[73] Such practices probably varied from place to place and over time, and hence it is not possible to determine what proportion of total demand was directed into these kinds of activities. It is safe to conclude, none the less, that culinary, medicinal and industrial uses were far more important.

Because of the absence of source material, it is not possible to correlate the expansion and contraction of the salt market with changes in population, but it can be supposed that such changes – both human and animal – affected the market. Such major climatic disasters as the Great Drought of the middle of the eighteenth century (1738–53) or the upheavals of the *jihad* (1804–12) must have had a severe impact on the salt trade, although efforts to assess this impact must be speculative and imprecise. Demand for many culinary and medicinal salts, which are usually highly inelastic and increase proportionally with population growth or the inclusion of greater territory in the distributional network, certainly varied with political and climatic factors. Disruption of production, political insecurity along trade routes, and reduced purchasing power among consumers certainly occurred at different times, but there is virtually no way to quantify the effects of these factors. The

31

production of the Benue basin salts, which were used for virtually no purposes other than culinary ones, must have been more directly affected by such disruptions. The other salts had more varied uses, and the scale of production varied with changes in industrial output as well as changes in human consumption. Textiles, leather and soap depended upon salt as a raw material, but wood ash and other substitutes could be used if necessary. Nevertheless, the expansion of the Hausa textile and leather industries in the nineteenth century is most certainly evidence for the expansion of the salt trade. The increase in the size of Fulani cattle herds also affected the demand for salt, as the amount of *gari* that was consumed almost certainly rose with the size and number of herds. The broad outlines of Fulani expansion are known; these herders first penetrated the central Sudan in the fourteenth century and perhaps increased dramatically in numbers in the eighteenth century. They pushed their herds further south and south-east in the nineteenth century under the aegis of the caliphate. Despite inadequate data, it is safe to conclude that this phenomenon also resulted in increased production of salt.

Other examples of the interaction between commercial expansion, population growth and political consolidation could also be cited, and an effort to establish the broad parameters of economic and political change that affected salt production is necessary in order to establish the historical development of the industry. Various attempts to provide an historical context are presented in the chapters that follow. Here it is only necessary to establish first, the correlation between the medicinal and culinary uses of salt, on the one hand, with the size of the human and animal population, on the other hand; secondly, the importance of climatic and political factors in the functioning of production and trade; and thirdly, the relationship between industrial uses for salt and the expansion of the economy. An understanding of the salt industry helps provide a perspective on the regional economy centred on the Sudan. The growth in population, the expansion of pastoralism, and the development of industry provide the parameters for studying the production and distribution of salt.

3

The chemistry and geology of the central Sudan salts

THE CHEMICAL COMPOSITION OF THE SALTS

The mixtures which constitute the salts of the central Sudan often contain relatively large percentages of impurities. Essentially, the distinctions between the types of salt relate to the proportion of sodium chloride and sodium carbonate in the mixtures. Unlike salts from other parts of West Africa, which contain very high proportions of sodium chloride, the amount of NaCl in the central Sudan salts often was less than 80 per cent, and some had as little as 20 per cent or none at all. Indeed some salt from Borno had such low concentrations of sodium chloride and far more significant proportions of sodium carbonate (soda), sodium sulphate (thenardite or Glauber's salt) and other salts, that they were referred to as natron (*kanwa*). The distinction in the central Sudan between salt and natron related to the relative amounts of sodium carbonate in the salt mixture, not to the relative amount of sodium chloride alone. When sodium chloride, potassium chloride or some combination of these salts predominated, it was called 'salt' (Hausa: *gishiri*; Kanuri: *manda*; Tamachek: *tesem*). When sodium carbonate was predominant, sometimes in combination with sodium sulphate (Na_2SO_4) or trona ($Na_3H(CO_3)_2 \cdot 2H_2O$), then it was referred to as natron (Hausa: *kanwa*; Kanuri: *kalvu*; Tamachek: *kanwa*) (Table 3.1). Hence the crucial factor in 'natron' was the relative concentration of sodium carbonate.[1]

This distinction has often been confusing to observers, although not to merchants and consumers. Indeed *kanwa* and *kalvu* have been translated as 'potash' rather than 'natron', but this is inaccurate, despite the occasional presence of small quantities of potash, that is potassium salts, in a few mixtures. References to potash, therefore, are here corrected.

Many distinctions relate to the geographical source of the salt and often correspond to a particular combination of chemicals and the degree of purity. *Beza* and *kantu* came from the same salines – those in the desert oasis of Bilma – but *beza* was also a generic term for a high quality salt which was found at other oases in Kawar besides Bilma and also in Fachi, a related saline west of the Kawar complex. *Kantu* was similar to *beza*, only less pure and far more plentiful. A similar quality salt was also obtained at Fachi (Table 3.2). The same can be said for the salt from the Benue Valley salines. Awe, Keana and Azara were the largest sites, but except for merchants in the immediate

Table 3.1 *Terms for the different salts of the central Sudan*

English	Hausa	Kanuri	Tuareg	Predominant chemical composition
salt (generic)	gishiri	manda	tesum	NaCl and other chemicals
natron (generic)	kanwa	kelvu	kanwa	Na_2CO_3 and other chemicals
white natron	farin kanwa	kelvu buktur	—	Na_2CO_3, Na_2SO_4, NaCl
red natron	jar kanwa	kelvu kime	—	Na_2CO_3, Na_2SO_4, NaCl
Chadic trona	ungurnu	—	—	$Na_3H(CO_3)_2 \cdot 2H_2O$
Manga salt	mangul	manda	—	NaCl, Na_2CO_3, Na_2SO_4
Bilma salt	kantu	manda kur	—	NaCl, Na_2SO_4, and other chemicals
Bilma salt	beza	yergal	beza	NaCl
Taoudeni salt	gallo	—	—	NaCl
Kige salt	—	kige		NaCl, KCl
Awe salt Dallol	d'an awai	—	—	NaCl
Fogha salt	foga	—	—	NaCl, Na_2CO_3
thenardite	gwangwarasa	gangorasa	—	Na_2SO_4

Table 3.2 *The desert salts: chemical mixtures of various samples*

Location	NaCl	Na_2CO_3	Na_2SO_4	KCl	Ca_2SO_4	$MgSO_4$
Bilma (beza)	65	—	20	—	—	—
Bilma (beza)	82.0	2.6	9.8	—	—	—
Bilma (kantu)	33.83	7.43	46.44	4.47	traces	—
Bilma (kantu)	12	—	79	—	traces	—
Fachi (kantu)	13	—	83	—	traces	4
Teguidda	70	—	22	—	—	—
Teguidda	87.70	—	6.65	0.20	0.72	—
Amadror	96.23	—	—	—	—	—
Arrigui (red natron)	20	50	—	—	—	—
Seguidine (salt)	80	—	—	—	—	—
Achenouma (natron)	—	40	—	—	—	—

Sources: Greigert and Pougnet (1967), 186; Faure (unpublished, 1965), 54, 63, 77, 118; Régnier (1961), 254; Lambert (1935), 371; Lacroix (1908), 42; Lhote (1933), 735; Lahache and Marre (1911), II, 558; Fuchs (1983), 69.

Table 3.3 *Composition of salts from the brine springs and other sources of the Benue trough*

Location	NaCl (Salt)	Na$_2$CO$_3$ (soda)	Na$_2$SO$_4$ (thenardite)	KCl	CaCl$_2$	CaCO$_3$	CaSO$_4$	MgCl$_2$	Al$_2$O$_3$	MgCO$_3$
Awe	85.37	—	trace	—	2.39	—	—	0.65	—	—
Awe	86.3	1.5	—	—	—	3.0	—	—	0.2	1.6
Awe	81.0	2.6	—	—	—	2.9	—	—	1.2	1.4
Awe	86.0	—	—	—	—	1.2	—	—	0.5	0.7
Awe	91.5	1.9	—	—	—	1.7	—	—	0.4	2.1
Awe	87.54	—	—	0.34	0.70	—	0.43	0.71	0.30	—
Azara	85.49	—	—	0.61	2.35	—	—	0.69	—	—
Jebjeb	91.43	1.45	1.01	0.22	—	3.24	—	—	—	—
Ameri	81									
Azara	90 +									
Okpoma	75									
Kanje	91									
Bomanda	93.3									
Muri natron	—	56.22					0.24			

Sources: Dunstan, Second Report on the Results of the Mineral Survey, 1904–05 [Cd. 3914], 8; Dunstan, Mineral Survey 1907–08, 1908–09 [Cd. 5899], 39, Public Record Office, London; and Beltaro and Bojarski (unpublished, 1971).

Table 3.4.   *Chadic salts: chemical composition*

Location	Sample	Na_2CO_3 (soda)	$Na_3H(CO_3)_2$ (trona)	Na_2SO_4 (thenardite)	NaCl (salt)
Kaya	trona	32.51	67.11	—	—
Keya	trona	23.15	53.14	—	1.81
Mao	salt earth	24.0	—	—	4.48
Hangara	natron	35.5	—	traces	12.95
Napal	thenardite	—	—	42.1	55.6

Sources: Pochard (1943), 180–181; Garde (1910), 263; Maglione (1970b), 82.

area it appears that little distinction was made between them, primarily because all were high in sodium chloride, despite the presence of varying amounts of impurities (Table 3.3).

Natron – that is some combination of sodium carbonate, sodium bicarbonate, sodium sulphate, and sodium chloride – was classified into different categories according to the degree of impurities and according to colour. Hence the natron that was scraped from the ground in Muniyo and Mangari was referred to according to its appearance: it came in powdered form, not in large pieces. The term was *gari*; it was poor in quality, with no refining to remove impurities. The better quality natron – which came in pieces of various sizes – was distinguished as red or white, but white was actually called 'black' if the impurities were so great that the colour was influenced. In fact 'red' is a pinkish colour, and 'white' is varying shades of grey. One type of *kanwa*, *ungurnu*, was of such high quality, that, like *beza*, it was recognised as a separate type. *Ungurnu* came in large, pure slabs from the east shores of Lake Chad. The *ungurnu* from the eastern shores of Lake Chad actually contains soda and trona and, as J. Y. Gac has noted, the dominant mineral is trona $(Na_3H(CO_3)_2 \cdot 2H_2O)$[2] (Table 3.4).

The greatest variations in the relative proportions of the different salts in a particular mixture are found in the salt and natron of Mangari (Table 3.5.). Each site in Mangari produced a different mixture because the salt was either obtained from the natural evaporation of surface water or the boiling of brine which had been concentrated as a result of solar evaporation. In both cases, there was no attempt to separate different salts out of solution, except for the collection of crystals which formed in the filtering of brine or which gathered on the edges of the depressions that were contracting because of natural evaporation. As a result Mangari salt and natron fell on a continuum: at the one extreme was *gwangwarasa* which was relatively pure sodium sulphate, and at the other extreme were salts which had different concentrations of sodium chloride and sodium carbonate and, correspondingly, a lower concentration of sodium sulphate.

Finally, the salts of the western Dallols varied in composition to the same extent as the salts of Mangari and Muniyo. The highest concentration of NaCl

Table 3.5 *The salts of Mangari, Muniyo and Kadzell*

Location	Type	NaCl (salt)	Na$_2$CO$_3$ (soda)	Na$_2$SO$_4$ (thenardite)	KCl	CaCO$_3$	Na$_2$HPO$_4$	K$_2$SO$_4$	CaSO$_4$	MgSO$_4$	MgCl$_2$
Gourselik	manda	24.24	12.50	25.98	—	—	—	—	—	—	—
Gouboria	natron	1.95	60.0	—	—	—	—	—	—	—	—
Adebour (Gamgawa)	manda	76.7	15.7	7.1	—	—	—	—	—	—	—
Adebour (Gamgawa)	manda	68.50	5.20	15.30	—	1.80	—	—	—	—	4.00
Adebour	manda	28.70	13.80	57.50	—	—	—	—	—	0.5	—
Zumba	manda	53.07	0.70	45.46	—	—	—	—	—	0.73	—
Zumba	manda	16.10	2.50	56.40	—	2.50	—	—	—	—	1.00
Adebour	gwangwarasa	2.64	4.40	80.96	—	—	—	—	—	—	traces
Kalakama	salt-earth	3.47	20.00	26.53	—	30.80	—	—	—	—	—
Zumba	gwangwarasa	3.03	traces	66.97	—	10.30	—	—	1.00	—	traces
Zumba	gwangwarasa	2.46	0.37	55.17	—	6.80	—	—	3.20	—	traces
Zumba	manda	14.16	9.60	66.80	—	—	—	—	—	—	—
Tatoukoutou	gwangwarasa	0.40	0.50	97.50	—	—	—	—	—	—	—
Tatoukoutou	gwangwarasa	traces	traces	95.50	—	—	—	—	—	—	—
Adebour	gwangwarasa	0.23	traces	98.27	—	—	—	—	—	—	—
Muniyo	stone natron	.35	75.06	trace	0.12	—	—	—	—	—	—
Muniyo	loose natron	1.04	69.66	8.45	0.18	—	—	—	—	—	—
Mangari	manda salt	24.27	5.23	30.17	4.76	—	—	2.14	—	—	—
Mangari	manda salt (ordinary)	15.71	26.53	36.21	—	—	—	—	—	—	—

(cont.)

Table 3.5 (cont.)

Location	Type	NaCl (salt)	Na$_2$CO$_3$ (soda)	Na$_2$SO$_4$ thenardite	KCl	CaCO$_3$	Na$_2$HPO$_4$	K$_2$SO$_4$	CaSO$_4$	MgSO$_4$	MgCl$_2$
Cheri	manda	12.60	—	40.05	0.77	—	—	—	—	—	—
Karia	manda	50.07	4.99	29.39	2.54	—	5.46	—	—	—	—
Shedanno	(1)	22.52	12.00	56.14	2.76	—	—	—	—	—	—
Shedanno	(1)	14.98	2.36	37.45	4.67	—	—	—	—	—	—
Diiru	(2)	36.58	11.56	28.16	1.84	—	—	—	—	—	—
Diiru	(2)	15.75	.18	42.42	2.47	—	—	—	—	—	—
Wongangawa	(3)	16.96	17.32	46.02	1.37	—	—	—	—	—	—
Wongangawa	(3)	16.20	31.42	41.86	0.62	—	—	—	—	—	—
Mangari	natron	3.47	20.00	26.53	—	30.80	—	—	—	—	—
Mangari	salt	68.50	5.20	15.30	—	—	—	—	2.00	—	—
Kadzell	kige	83.78	—	0.90	8.98	1.73	—	—	1.13	—	—
Kadzell	kige	19.17	—	—	66.36	2.43	—	1.91	—	—	—
Zumba	gwangwarasa	0.50	0.69.	87.81	—	—	—	—	—	—	—
Kadzell	kige	9.62	—	0.73	81.16	—	—	—	1.92	—	—
Kadzell	kige	26.83	0.22	0.67	57.88	—	—	—	—	—	—
Kadzell	kige	67.60	—	1.42	28.76	—	—	—	1.48	—	—

Sources: Dunstan, Second Report on the Results of the Mineral Survey, 1904–05 [Cd. 3914]; Dunstan, Mineral Survey, [Cd. 4719], Public Record Office, London: Lahache and Marre (1911), II, 555, 564, 569, 571–573, 583, 587; Gouletquer and Kleinmann (unpublished, 1973), I2; Garde (1910), 262, 263.

Table 3.6   *Salts of the Dallols and neighbouring areas*

Location	NaCl (salt)	Na_2CO_3 (soda)	Na_2SO_4 (thenardite)	KCl	$CaCl_2$	$CaSO_4$	$MgSO_4$
Dallol Fogha	53.0	—	35.0	—	—	—	—
Dallol Fogha	70.00	—	23.01	.82	—	.92	.50
Bunza	88.10	—	—	2.72	.53	1.51	—
Zaura	—	52.43	0.95	1.48	—	—	—
Bengu	31.60	—	48.70	1.19	—	—	10.73

Sources: Lambert (1938), 49–51; Lahache and Marre (1911), II, 555; Dunstan, Mineral Surveys 1907–08 and 1908–09 [Cd. 5899], 17–18; Dunstan, Second Report on the Results of the Mineral Survey, 1904–05 [Cd. 3914], 8, Public Record Office, London.

was found in the valley of Dallol Fogha and on the Kebbi River at Bunza, although only Dallol Fogha had considerable deposits (Table 3.6). Elsewhere, the salt mixtures included high proportions of sodium carbonate or sodium sulphate. At Dallol Bosso, for which there are no samples available, these were the dominant salts too.[3]

THE GEOLOGY OF THE SALT DEPOSITS

The presence of salt in the southern Sahara and sahel is the result of geological change over the past ten millennia. As the more humid conditions of the quaternary gave way to drier eras, the great lakes of the Sahara gradually receded, depositing salt in a few locations, most notably at Amadror, Kawar, and Fachi in the central Sahara. During the particularly dry times of the past millennium, a second phenomenon – efflorescence – resulted in the concentration of salt in parts of the sahel where rain water formed temporary ponds and lakes which retreated as the dry season progressed. The drainage of the countryside into these depressions leached the ground of its salt and, as evaporation occurred, the salt was left as an efflorescence on the edges of the larger ponds and lakes and in the dried bottoms of the more shallow ones. The deposit of trona and soda on the eastern shores of Lake Chad occurred as a result of a related phenomenon; the lake expanded after the rainy season but then evaporation removed its water. As part of the annual desiccation of the sahel, some efflorescence occurred in the valleys of Kanem and the Bahr el Ghazal, but the vast deposits on the eastern shore were left behind as water seeped out of the lake towards the north-east. The trona and soda were pushed out of the lake through capillary action which deposited these salts some distance from the edge of the lake.[4]

THE DESERT SITES

The depression of Kawar results from a gap originating in the quaternary age. There is a high cliff on the eastern side of Kawar, which is often greater than 150 m above the depression, while on the eastern side the water table is at a shallow depth, with surface water at Dirku, Seguidine, and Bilma. The cliff contains layers of sandstone, lime, and fossilised algae, which are very rich in salts. Some layers have as much as 50 per cent NaCl and Na_2SO_4. The impregnation of salt is found to heights which are more than 6 m from the bottom of the depression.[5]

The evidence establishes clearly that Kawar was once the basin of a great lake which probably stretched 120 km north of Bilma and 20 km westward from the cliff. The lake may have extended further south than Bilma, perhaps having an outlet in that direction. The great lake was at its fullest more than 10,000 years ago: the desiccation of the region gradually resulted in its contraction, a process which probably took several hundred years before the water was confined to the basins at Bilma and elsewhere in Kawar.[6] The contraction resulted in the concentration of salt through precipitation, which accounts for the salt layers in the cliff at Bilma and elsewhere in the Kawar region. Faure, who has conducted the most thorough geological survey of Kawar, estimates that the quantity of salt deposited as a result of the desiccation of the great lake was probably in excess of 1 million tonnes, perhaps as much as 6 million tonnes.[7] Subsequently, these deposits were largely scattered as a result of erosion.

The salt at the bottom of the depressions – the salt which has been actually exploited for commercial purposes for at least the past millennium – traces its origin to a later development. After the disappearance of the great lake, smaller lakes continued to occupy the depressions at Bilma, Dirku, Seguidine and elsewhere in Kawar. Evidence of hippopotami at Fachi, 120 km west of Kawar, indicates that wetter times still prevailed, despite the long term process of desiccation.[8] The lake at Bilma would have covered the 24 km² of the basin; its area was perhaps only 1 per cent the size of the great lake. The drainage of the surrounding countryside reconcentrated salt in these smaller lakes. The salt inflow included some of the eroded deposits from the great lake but other salt too. Faure estimates that these later deposits, occurring over many thousands of years, could have resulted in accumulation of 500 tonnes of salt per year. The total deposit was certainly of the order of another million tonnes and perhaps as much as 3 million tonnes.[9]

These reserves provide the basis of the salt industry. Later additions are infinitesimally small by comparison. The present conditions of evaporation and regeneration through the inflow of water account for an addition of about 44 tonnes per year, which demonstrates that the water table itself is remarkably free from salt.[10] The surface brine is almost entirely enriched from the ancient salt deposits, not from the inflow of new brine. The chemical composition of the brine also confirms the relationship between the brine and the original lake. The brine is a mixture of thenardite (Na_2SO_4) and NaCl, the same salts which are found in the cliff. Alum has also been found in Kawar in the past.[11]

Various factors influence the precipitation and crystallisation of the salts in the basin at Bilma: the relative concentration of the various salts, the temperature of the brine, the agitation of the brine, and the presence of bacteria and other microbes in the brine. Of these factors, the most important is the temperature, both seasonal variations and the differences between day and night.[12] NaCl has a solubility in water which is relatively constant from $10°$ to $70°$ C. By contrast, Na_2SO_4 has a solubility which varies directly with temperature. Below $32°$ C, the salt which precipitates is mirabilite ($Na_2SO_4 \cdot 10H_2O$); its solubility increases rapidly from $0°$ to $32°$. Between $30°$ and $40°$, the salt crystallises as thenardite (Na_2SO_4). From $40°$ to $80°$ C solubility gradually decreases. At low temperatures, therefore, hydrated sodium sulphate precipitates in great quantities, thereby increasing the percentage of NaCl in solution. Since the total amount of salt in the brine is decreased as a result of the crystallisation of the mirabilite, the sodium chloride does not become saturated and therefore remains in solution. In fact the altered brine is able to absorb more sodium chloride but is not able to absorb additional sodium sulphate. At night and in the cold months of the dry season, sodium sulphate accumulates around the basin. When the temperature rises, the mirabilite crystals form a paste in the bottom of the basin. Some mirabilite redissolves with the change in temperature and then recrystallises as thenardite. The effect is similar, however. Sodium sulphate separates out of solution, thereby allowing a higher concentration of NaCl.[13]

As will be clear in the discussion of the technology of production, these geological and chemical conditions were understood to a great extent, and the salt workers were able to take advantage of the natural conditions in producing salt. It was easy to remove the mirabilite and thenardite crystals and as a result increase the NaCl content of the salt. It was also possible to extract the paste-like substance as a means of promoting the concentration of NaCl. Other methods were also followed which affected the mixture of the brine, although in each instance the salt workers were only maximising the natural conditions of production. There were no technological innovations of a mechanical or scientific nature.

The geological conditions at Fachi, 170 km west-south-west of Bilma, were similar to those in Kawar. The Agram depression was also the deepest portion of an ancient lake which covered an area much more extensive than the oasis itself. The deep basin, located in the erg of Tenere (a vast region of dunes in the Sahara), is about 25 km long, in a north–south direction. It is dominated to the east by a cliff which rises 200 m above the bottom of the depression. As at Bilma, there is evidence in the cliff of fossil algae and layers of relatively concentrated salts, indicating that the formation corresponds to the remains of other lakes in the southern Sahara. The desiccation of the great lakes about 10,000 years ago and the fluctuations of the smaller lakes in the next several millennia are responsible for the deposits of salt which are the basis of the more recent salt industry.[14]

The geology of Fachi is significantly different from that of Bilma in two important respects. First, the artesian water supply is not as clearly defined as at Bilma. The water has a much higher salt content, which suggests that the desiccation of the ancient lake resulted in a water table closer to the surface than at Bilma. Consequently, the water has been contaminated with salt. In the depression itself, salt production has been pursued at several places, interspersed with areas of cultivation. At Bilma, the salt works and agricultural zone are separated. Secondly, Fachi is at a higher elevation than Bilma, so that the ancient lake may have drained quicker than the one in Kawar, with a correspondingly smaller deposit of salt. The effects of these differences are clear: the surface area exploited at Fachi is greater than the surface area at Bilma, but the quantity of salt produced is much smaller. While $NaCl$ and Na_2SO_4 are also the dominant salts at Fachi, the differentiation between the two is incomplete.[15]

The same natural process of precipitation occurs at Fachi as at Bilma. Na_2SO_4 crystallises out of solution and forms into distinct pieces either at the bottom of the brine pools or on the edges of the basin. This precipitation enriches the concentration of chlorine in solution, but because the brine is weaker as a result of the dilution in the water source, less salt is produced. In this case, the salt workers deliberately reintroduce thenardite back into the solution in order to increase the quantity of the salt produced. The result is a salt less pure in $NaCl$ than the salt of Bilma, although at Bilma too quality is sacrificed for quantity.[16]

Elsewhere in the desert, salt deposits were found at scattered places in the Air Massif and in the valleys to the west of Agades.[17] Most of these deposits are the result of efflorescence occurring after rain-water from the occasional shower has drained off. Usually, the salt-earth was scraped for livestock or used as a salt-lick. Only at Teguidda n'tesemt was the amount of this efflorescence sufficient to enable the development of a salt industry. The geological formations of the Teguidda area consist of calcareous sandstone in the middle of Irhazer clays; water seeps to the surface in little springs. During the rainy season the area is covered by more or less brackish water, which leaves a white salt deposit on the clay and the rocks when it evaporates in the dry season. The natural springs regenerate the water supply, although the water is very salty.[18]

THE SAHEL SITES

The Manga region – sometimes called Mandaram, the country of salt – extends 150 km between the hilly country of Muniyo and the valley of the Komodugu Yo River along an axis which is virtually identical with the modern boundary between Niger and Nigeria. The region extends about 40 km north of this axis in the west, but only 8 km north in the east. The most intensely exploited portion of this zone lies between Adebour in the east and Dabalia 100 km to the west. In a belt which is only 7–15 km wide, there are numerous depressions which produce an efflorescence of salt during the dry season. In the region as a whole, there are probably 1,000 depressions – many 20–30 m deep – where salt can be found on the surface, but the number exploited at any one time was much smaller.[19] In 1950, only 138 depressions were worked, while in 1963 production was centred at 184 sites.[20] Most of these sites fall along a NW–SE line which once was part of Lake Chad but later may have been an ancient affluent of the lake. Two or more rivers appear to have drained the higher ground of Muniyo, probably connecting with the Komodugu Yo near Adebour. The depressions appear to be the low points along these ancient valleys.

The amount of salt deposited in these depressions is a function of the level of the water table, which depends on the extent of rainfall each season. Rainfall can vary from about 200 mm to as much as 600 mm or more per year, although in years of drought, as in 1913–14, the amount of rain can be much less than 200 mm.[21] Since the water table depends as much on the run-off from the higher ground of Muniyo as it does on the rain in the immediate vicinity of the depressions, the annual level of salt production is not a direct function of rainfall. Water is also stored in the ground. None the less, over a period of years, the fluctuations in rainfall have a direct effect on the quantity of salt available for exploitation.

The salt is brought to the surface as the water table fluctuates between the rainy season and the dry months. During the rains, when water collects in the depressions, some salt is brought into the depressions with the drainage from the surrounding countryside. Additional salt is brought to the surface through capillary action, whereby the ground acts as a filter. As the water in the depressions evaporates during the dry months, the salt is increasingly concentrated. Either chunks of crystalline thenardite form in the water as a result of the concentration of brine through evaporation, or the evaporation of the damp ground produces an efflorescence which is directly controlled by the level of the water table.[22]

Where the water level is several metres below the surface, there is very little efflorescence; production is usually minimal or non-existent. Where the water table is about 2 m from the surface, the efflorescence begins to be significant; chlorines are slightly enriched but not much is retained. The capillary action which raises the water through the ground is too weak to produce much salt. When the water table is less than half a metre below ground, the efflorescence becomes extensive. Soda, trona, thenardite and common salt appear in mixture. The variation in the mixture depends upon the history of the depression – the extent to which it has been worked before and its geological evolution. When there is a lake or pond, evaporation is considerable, often more than 2 m per year. In this condition, the water is progressively enriched with the various salts. In some cases, bacteria transform the sulphates into ferrous sulphide, which increases the trona and soda content. This stage of evolution is most pronounced in the depressions in the south and west. When the water evaporates completely, the different salts precipitate out of solution in different concentrations. As thenardite, mixed with soda and trona, crystallises, the sodium chloride content of the brine increases. This stage requires a small inflow of relatively pure water, which is possible because the water table is very close to the surface. In the various tests conducted by F. Pirard, the salinity of the soil decreased in direct proportion to the depth below the surface. At the beginning of this phase, when the seasonal variation in the water level has resulted in the formation of a lake, the crystallisation of salt is most pronounced. The evaporation is so intense that the salt is able to precipitate in pieces of various sizes.

When the drop in the water table is particularly rapid, the formation of salt by efflorescence is prolonged as a result of the capillary action of subterranean water. This phase is often charged with more salt than the preceding stage and is the most favourable to those salt workers who exploit the efflorescent phenomenon. The quantity of salt is increased if there is some fresh water still coming into the depression. Salt is formed on the top soil; often there are crystals of thenardite.

Finally, the full cycle of the efflorescent phenomenon in Mangari is reached to the south of the salt-producing area, where the water table is again well below the surface of the ground. The formation of salt ceases completely, and instead an area of agriculture dependent upon rainfall cultivation replaces the relatively infertile areas of the Mangari depressions. Whereas agriculture is practised in Mangari on the edges of the lakes and in some valleys where the efflorescence is minimal, the salt zone is generally not suitable for intensive agriculture, which is characteristic of parts of Muniyo to the west or of the Komodugu Yo River valley to the east.

The full cycle of efflorescent conditions is best illustrated through an examination of the depressions along a north–south gradient. In the north, the water table is relatively deep; occasionally well water has a fair amount of salt – often in evidence as a strong natron taste. In these cases, the residue of diluted salts indicates the probable existence of salt efflorescence in some ancient cycle. Further south, the water table is less than 2 m deep; there efflorescence is common, although only in the extreme south and towards the west do the depressions actually contain natron lakes. The lakes which are furthest north are generally not deep; they yield slabs of thenardite when they dry up. Those lakes situated toward the frontier with Nigeria are generally deeper and more extensive. This area is the region of most intensive salt production.

The efflorescent cycle appears to shift, with short-term cycles lasting about fifteen to twenty years during the present century. As the production zone shifts to the north – as it did from 1950 to 1965 – a number of depressions in the south which have produced considerable quantities of salt are drowned under the enlarged lakes.[23] Conversely, in the north during such relatively wet times, some depressions appear to be replenished as the level of the water table rises and the possibility of efflorescence is correspondingly enhanced. While it is not clear if this cycle also occurred in the past, there is no reason to think it did not. The depressions at Guidimouni, for example, appear to have experienced a twenty-year cycle from c. 1901 to 1923. In this period, the main lake at Guidimouni evaporated progressively and regularly, and the production of natron was considerable. Between 1924 and 1926, however, there was virtually no output at the main lake because the lake did not evaporate completely. The elders of the village remembered that a similar phenomenon had taken place in the past; they considered such fluctuations as a necessary and natural part of a longer production cycle.[24] Heinrich Barth, who passed near the salt-producing region of Mangari three times – in 1851, 1852 and 1854 – took no notice of salt production, although he did observe the collection of natron at several places.[25] Although it may be that salt output was minimal or non-existent because of political instability – or Barth may simply not have heard about or seen the industry – it seems far more likely that very little, if any, salt was being made at that time. Barth was a particularly astute observer and reporter. If there had been a major industry, he would have seen it or heard about it. Furthermore, the level of the water table must have been different from later times; it was higher than in periods of intensive salt production (as opposed to scraping natron from the ground), which may indicate that salt could not always be manufactured. Barth reported extensive production of natron at Bune and Keleno, neither of which have been important in the twentieth century.

For several centuries at least, the activities of man have also affected the cycle.[26] Deforestation and the spread of agriculture are responsible for the general restoration of the water table, while irrigated agriculture in areas adjacent to the production areas has artificially segregated salt and fertile basins, with the result that in some places salt production has been greater than otherwise might have been the case. The biggest influence, however, is the removal of salt for export. Unlike the deposits at Kawar, Fachi and Amadror, the salt of Mangari is not replenished from ancient reserves. The salt has to be restored continuously for production to be maintained. The cycle is not a closed circuit; the intervention of man has prevented the accumulation of salt reserves in the depressions. Although it is not possible to estimate with any degree of accuracy when salt production began in this region, it may well not date back more than a few centuries.

On the basis of the scientific observations from the beginning of the century to the 1960s, Faure has reconstructed a tentative chronology of the efflorescent cycle of Mangari. Although this chronology is necessarily imprecise because of the lack of data, the evolution of the water table can be divided into periods as follows: around 1860 the water table was relatively high; between 1910 and 1930 the level was low; between 1932 and 1939 the level had been restored, but from 1941 to 1946 the level fell again. By 1950 the level had fallen about 2 m from previously recorded levels. By 1960–63 it had risen between 2 and 3 m.[27]

Faure's analysis of cycles in the geology of Mangari does not account for variations in climatic episodes between drier and wetter times. These are long term changes, within which the 15–20 year cycles must have operated. In wetter episodes, the water level probably varied more considerably than in these short cycles, and the focus of salt production may have shifted further north or south depending upon the overall pattern of rainfall. Or it may have declined considerably. Since the sixteenth and seventeenth centuries were generally wetter than the eighteenth and nineteenth centuries, salt production may once have been centred north of the present area of production. What cannot be determined at present is the extent to which longer climatic episodes affected production – specifically how many kilometres the production zone would have varied with each episode.[28]

The zone of efflorescence extends further east than Mangari; in fact a wide region which arches around the northern end of Lake Chad and extends as far as Kanem on the eastern side of the lake experiences a similar phenomenon, although under different conditions and on a much more limited scale than in Mangari. The water table is relatively deep throughout this great arc. Kadzell – the region north of the Komodugu Yo River valley between Mangari and Lake Chad – is a relatively infertile area where nomads graze their herds but where little agriculture is practised, except very near the lake. Salt still comes to the surface, or very near the surface, and is often in evidence in well-water.[29] Salt production is not based on efflorescence, however. Instead, plants (*Salvadora persica*, in particular) which have absorbed considerable quantities of salt are burned and their ashes filtered with well-water. The plants serve as agents which extend the capillary action of the earth. Efflorescence is minimal, but the roots of the plants raise salt out of the earth. The combination of the salt-laden plants and the weak brine of the wells enables the production of relatively pure chlorine salts to take place.[30]

Efflorescence also occurs far to the west of Mangari, but nowhere is the natural concentration of salts as extensive as in Mangari. In Dallol Bosso and Dallol Fogha – two valleys which run north from the Niger River into the sahel – efflorescence under conditions similar to those in Mangari has made possible a local salt industry for some unknown period into the past.

The salt zone of Dallol Fogha is divided into two parts. A southern section extends along the valley, 6 km from the confluence with the Niger River to Azemouraba, 60 km north. In this zone the centres of exploitation are numerous and dispersed, depending upon the extent of efflorescence. A branch of this section extends a few kilometres up the Dallol Maouri, and in the west efflorescence is common as far as Malgourou and Gari-Malam.[31] The lower basin extends to the confluence of the Dallol Fogha and Dallol Maouri. The banks of the valley, which is 400–600 m wide, are small cliffs which rise a dozen metres or so above the base of the valley. The basin is not really a river but a series of ponds and small lakes during the rainy season which then evaporate.[32]

The salt is rich in sodium sulphate and sodium chloride. Production has been extensive enough over the past three or four hundred years for there to be piles of debris at Sado, Kawara-Debe and other places.[33] The origins of the salt are related to the relatively shallow depth of the water table and the concentration of salt as a result of evaporation.

A northern zone is centred around a salt lake at Bara, near Sabongari. The upper and lower basins of the Dallol Fogha are separated by higher ground which extends for about 20 km.[34] The lake extends about 12 km from Kawara-Debe to the north of Tounga Gandou. The lake forms where the water table is above the basin of the Dallol and is maintained by a number of effluents which replenish the water supply. None the less, the lake contracts in the dry season, especially on the northern edge, where the water turns into brine. Efflorescence also occurs on the borders of the lake, as in the south. It appears that the exploitation of salt in this area is more recent than in the southern part of Dallol Fogha.[35] As is the case in other areas of efflorescence, the quantity of salt is relatively limited; there are no salt reserves, but instead the salt is brought to the surface each year as a result of fluctuations in the level of the water table.

A similar phenomenon occurs in neighbouring Dallol Bosso, which lies to the west of Dallol Fogha and also runs into the Niger River, two lakes near Dosey and Itesan, 12 km from Birnin Konni, and several places on the Sokoto River. The Dallol Bosso efflorescence and also the one at Bunza, on the Sokoto River, are much more restricted than in Dallol Fogha. The salt is primarily a mixture of carbonates and bicarbonates of soda (soda and trona). Only at the small salt lake of Koudye and at Bunza is there any significant evidence of NaCl.[36] The two lakes near Birnin Konni are permanent; a crust of magnesium sulphate and sodium sulphate, with some calcium sulphate, forms on the shores, particularly on the northern side, as the lake retreats during the dry season.[37] The Bunza and Zaura efflorescences are also relatively small. The Bunza deposit is mainly sodium chloride, while the salt at Zaura is soda. In addition to these sites, salt has also been found at Sengulu, Ginga, Bakoshi, Dendene and Sabe – all located in Dendi country.[38]

Elsewhere in the sahel, salt is deposited in a belt stretching 300 km along the north-eastern littoral of Lake Chad for a distance of 25–30 km inland. The salt forms in the depressions between the dunes. This region corresponds to an ancient erg, running NNW–SSE, whose depressions between the dunes fill with water each year, either from the overflow from the lake or from rainfall or both. Efflorescence occurs in 500 depressions, whose salinity and alkalinity vary. Sometimes there is a simple efflorescence on the surface; but the quantity of the deposit is particularly heavy in a region – Foli – between 13°40′ and 14° north and 14°10′ and 14°20′ east.[39] In the region as a whole, the depressions can be divided into two representative conditions. Either the water table is not very deep, averaging 1–180 cm, or water accumulates on the surface as a result of capillary action in the predominantly clay sediment. In the first case, the depressions are alkaline; the strong salinity is a result of the poor drainage system in the depressions, which is why the level of the water table remains

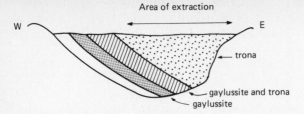

Figure 3.1 A trona depression

close to the surface. In the second case, the capillary action continues to feed water into the depression, even in the dry season, with the result that the water becomes increasingly saline and eventually salt precipitates out of solution. This condition allows the extensive exploitation of trona mixed with soda in the zone of highest concentration. On the surface, the soluble salts exude a sediment which forms a saline crust. Below this crust, the brine continues to evaporate and deposits salt as the limit of solubility is reached.[40]

The water table of Kanem is replenished from the west by an influx of water from Lake Chad. The water infiltrates the littoral zone through a 'seepage' phenomenon.[41] On the lake front, the water has a weak concentration of calcium bicarbonate, but as the water seeps into the interior, the alkalinity increases. Capillary action results in the concentration of sodium; the calcium is deposited in the ground. This process of seepage not only accounts for the deposit of trona and soda but also regulates the salinity of Lake Chad, maintaining the lake as a fresh water lake.

Maglione has analysed the salinity and the process of salt formation at four production sites (Liwa, Kaya, Anjia and Bedarra).[42] He has been able to determine that four salts are formed as a result of the mechanism of infiltration from the lake. Gaylussite ($CaCO_3 \cdot Na_2CO_3 \cdot 5H_2O$) is the first salt to crystallise. Where the water table is relatively deep (180–200 cm), as at Koulfa-Kama, gaylussite is the only salt that forms. Secondly, in the depressions where the water table is immediately below the surface, the gaylussite is found along the edge, but it coexists with other salts in the centre. The salt which is dominant is black trona ($Na_2HCO_3 \cdot Na_2CO_3 \cdot 2H_2O$), although some gaylussite is also present. Thirdly, in the depressions where the brine is concentrated on the surface, white soda ($Na_2CO_3 \cdot 10H_2O$) crystallises in slabs which are 30–40 cm thick. There is also some trona in the mixture. Finally, in parts of the same depressions and in those depressions where the level of the water table is deep, the surface collects a crust of salt in the course of the dry season, which can be 15–20 cm thick. This efflorescence also characterises the border of Lake Chad on the northern shores. The deposit is mixed with sand from the surrounding dunes and also contains some trona and quartz. Maglione's contribution in understanding the process of salt formation is this identification of gaylussite as the first salt to crystallise; on rare occasions when the temperature is high enough pirsonnite ($CaCO_3 \cdot Na_2CO_3 \cdot 2H_2O$) also precipitates at an early stage.[43] Normally trona is the second mineral to crystallise. In the depressions where the brine attains a temperature greater than 32° C, soda is the salt which is produced; otherwise trona predominates. According to Maglione, the equation of equilibrium between trona and soda is the following:

$$2(NaHCO_3 \cdot Na_2CO_3 \cdot 2H_2O) + 25H_2O \rightleftarrows 3(Na_2CO_3 \cdot 10H_2O) + CO_2$$

trona   soda

Trona or soda predominates, depending upon the temperature.[44] When the temperature is greater than 34° C, the balance is tipped towards the production of soda.

On at least one of the islands in the south-eastern part of Lake Chad – at Napal, south of Bol – a different phenomenon occurs. There the dominant salts are sulphates and chlorides, which are not present in the depressions of the north-eastern littoral. The deposits at Napal contain sodium chloride (55.6 per cent) and thenardite (42.1 per cent). There are other depressions which also have considerable deposits of sodium sulphates, especially mirabilite and thenardite. Of these, Ngarangou is one of the most important.[45]

Most of the salt brought into Lake Chad comes from the Chari River, which feeds the lake from the south. Other tributaries and the annual rains are relatively insignificant by comparison with the flow of the Chari. Hence an analysis of the mineral content of the Chari is an excellent gauge of the annual inflow of sodium, the chemical which is necessary for the deposit of the soda and trona on the north-eastern littoral. According to Roche, the amount of sodium passing Fort Lamy between 1932 and 1966 varied from a minimum of 47,100 tonnes to a maximum of 105,100 tonnes.[46] Since only a small portion of this inflow is actually extracted each year through the production and export of trona, it is clear that there are considerable reserves of trona on the north-eastern littoral. Although there are no estimates as to the size of the reserves, Mosrin has estimated that potential production could reach 120,000 tonnes per year.[47]

The level of Lake Chad does not appear to affect the amount of trona which can be exploited along the north-eastern littoral, primarily because the reserves are so enormous. The lake was exceptionally large in 1823, 1853–54, 1866–70, and 1892–98, probably exceeding 20,000 km². At these times, the trona pans must have had more water on them – with a corresponding delay in the production season – but once the water evaporated, production was probably as great as in other years.[48] From 1840 to 1850, in 1905, and 1908, and again from 1914 to 1916, the lake was very small, less than 12,000 km².[49] In dry years, less trona would have been deposited, but the reserves are so extensive that production would not have been affected. Indeed the season would have been lengthened.

Table 3.7 *Brine concentrations in the Benue basin*

Source	Per cent solids	Source	Per cent solids
Awe	0.80		
Awe	0.74	Arufu	2.04
Awe	0.76	Akwana	0.56
Awe	0.78	Akwana	1.95*
Azara	2.0	Akwana	5.97*
Kanje	0.94	Bomanda	weak concentration
Keana	very dilute	sea-water	3.50
Moi Igbo	0.4		

* It is likely that these samples were contaminated with brines which had already been concentrated as a result of evaporation.
Sources: Beltaro and Bojarski (unpublished, 1971); W. Thomson, 10 March 1949, Nigerian National Archives, Kaduna.

THE BRINE SPRINGS OF THE BENUE TROUGH

The Nigerian brines are located in four main areas: Gombe, Shendam, Abakaliki and Ikom–Calabar, an area which is referred to as the Benue trough. Brines are also found in the Mamfe region of Cameroon. The springs and ponds occur in a relatively narrow territory which extends in a NNE–SSW direction from Gombe to Afikpo, along generally low lying and gently undulating plains of the Benue and Cross River basins. The brines issue from clays, shales, silty sandstones and conglomerates of Upper Cretaceous age. Most are situated in valleys which flood during the rainy season and often retain the water for one or two months into the dry season. A series of folds and fractures related to several tertiary intrusions account for the occurrence of the brines and are also responsible for such mineralisations as silver and galena. The distribution of the brines appears to follow two parallel narrow belts which are discordant with the Benue trough. This pattern is particularly clear if the Ikom brines are considered in conjunction with the Mamfe brines of Cameroon.[50]

The brines are generally very weak, much weaker than sea-water. The most concentrated brines are those at Arufu and Azara – minor sites where the flow of brine is weak. The more important sources, notably Awe, whose brine supply is substantial, have very weak concentrations, less than one-quarter the concentration of sea-water (Table 3.7). Only the brines at Ameri and Okposi have a significant salt content, but these sources were discovered only in this century as a result of mining activities. Otherwise, the brines were able to produce relatively modest amounts of salt.[51]

The cluster of brine springs near Gombe totals fifteen sites, most if not all of which were centres of salt production in the past. Three of these were at or near Pindiga; two were at Tumu. The most important appear to have been Bomanda and Jebjeb. The only analysis available shows the Bomanda salt to have a concentration of 93.3 per cent NaCl.[52] The Gombe cluster lies in the Gongola River basin, to the north of the Benue River. The springs at Pindiga and nearby at Gujba and Takulma and the two springs near Tumu (Tumu and Zanga) – which are to the south-west of the bend in the Gongola River – originate in the Gombe sandstones; all the other springs in this cluster, including Ayabe, Bomanda, Gyakan, Jebero, Jebjeb, Jende, Langa, Mutum Daya, and Todi, emerge from the Bima sandstones. Over time the surface sands and clays at these locations have become impregnated with salt from the rocks below. This alluvium forms the only source of salt at Jebjeb, Jenoe, and Langa and accounts for most of the salt at Bomanda. At Jebjeb, only a few square metres were productive in 1905, while at Langa the salt was only sufficient to enable production every other year. The Bomanda salting was the largest of the group in 1905; approximately 260 ha of alluvium were worked. Jebero possessed a saline alluvium and four fairly good brine springs.[53]

The most important group of brine springs are those located between the Jos Plateau, on the north, and the Benue River, on the south. There are at least eleven sites in this region, including Abuni, Akiri, Akwana, Arufu, Awe, Azara, Kanje, Keana, Langrel River, Lankaku and Ribi. The Arufu and Akwana springs issue from shales; the rest emerge from marine sediments of the Lafia–Wukari facies. Awe, Azara and Keana were the most important, although all the sites appear to have been worked for at least the past century.[54] But there were numerous minor sites. At Barkar, between Jungeb and Muzu, a few square metres of alluvium were worked in small quantity; while Karkure, opposite Umaisha on the Benue River, was another small site. Lafin Gishiri, Doja, and Nassarawa all had alluvial workings too, but again the scale of output was very small, and these sites may have resulted from efflorescence rather than brine springs.[55]

There were at least another 44 brine springs, most of which were south of the Benue River. There were seven workable salt deposits in Tiv Division: one near Nyam in Mbaikuran area of Mbaduem, one in Mbatoho area of Mgabwem (near Makurdi), three in Mbakine and Mbayom areas of Ngohor, one between Mbakper and Mbamar in Njiriv, and one between Mbaiger and Mbagusu in Yonov. The Nyam deposit is about 260 ha in extent.[56] There is another site at Moi Igbo, near Oturkpo.[57] Further south, there are ten springs near Ogojo; another 11 sites are in the Abakaliki–Ameri area. Further south still, there are five sites near Afikpo, the most important of which is at Uburu Lake. Others are found in the Cross River basin from Ikom to Mamfe and including the Abakaliki area. There are at least ten sites in this last zone.[58]

CONCLUSION

The salt producers of the central Sudan understood and used the geological endowment of their region, even though they did not fully understand the chemistry of salt. Not only did they know where salt was to be found, but they also realised that different geological conditions required specific techniques of exploitation. The Benue brines derived from springs which had to be cleared of rain-water before the reduction of the brine could begin. The salt reserves of Bilma and Fachi could best be worked when temperatures were at a maximum, during the months after April. Only at this time was evaporation intensive enough to allow a concentration of sodium chloride. In short the salt workers of Bilma and Fachi understood that salts separate out of solution at different temperatures and in different concentrations, although they did not know how to control these conditions or how to measure them exactly. Similarly, it is clear that the salt workers of the sahel were fully aware that efflorescence occurred every year as the dry season progressed; there were no apparent reserves, but production could be undertaken each year. Output varied with rainfall – or at least appeared to – and while the scientific reasons for this fluctuation were not known, experience had taught the workers that there were always some depressions where salt was plentiful, even if particular depressions could not be depended on every year.

Despite an imperfect understanding of salt chemistry, it is perhaps amazing how much was actually known about the central Sudan salts. This knowledge is reflected in the distinctions that were made between the salts from the various sources. The Benue brines, for example, were clearly distinguished from other salts, and the Benue brines were relatively pure sodium chloride. Trona from the eastern shores of Lake Chad was a virtually pure carbonate of soda, and it was distinguished from natron found elsewhere. This distinction establishes that people knew that all types of *kanwa* contained the same chemical ingredient and that that ingredient was a carbonate of soda. The removal of mirabilite and thenardite crystals from the salines of Bilma and Fachi also demonstrates that sodium sulphate had been clearly identified. Indeed, thenardite was collected in Mangari and shipped west for use in the leather industry. Hence the three principal salts – sodium chloride, sodium carbonate and sodium sulphate – were all known and were processed in varying quantities in relatively pure forms.

An examinaton of the technology of production, which is undertaken in the following chapter, demonstrates that workers exploited their knowledge of the geology and chemistry of salt, but they did not bring this knowledge together into a coherent form that could have constituted the basis of a scientific understanding of salt production. Many of the details of scientific observation were present, without the institutional capacity to combine observation with practice. In short, applied technology benefited little from the knowledge of salt geology and chemistry that had been acquired over the centuries. People understood more than they could use to advantage and consequently could not exploit their knowledge in order to maximise production.

4

The technology of production

The technology of the salt industry has developed in the context of the natural advantages of the south central Sahara and neighbouring parts of the savanna: the heat of the sun and the low humidity during the dry season make evaporation rapid. The temperature at the desert sites of Bilma and Fachi, for example, can exceed 40° C during the height of the production season; the brine reaches 70° C. In Mangari temperatures rise from a mean of 22° in December and January to 24.8° in February to 27.9° in March, 31.8° in April and 33.4° in May, before dropping with the beginning of the rainy season.[1] Even at the savanna sites in the Benue Valley, temperatures can rise as high as 35° during the early weeks of the dry season, when the evaporation of rainwater is a necessary precondition to working the brine springs. There are cool months – January and February – when evaporation is not as rapid, but the generally cloudless skies and low humidity partially compensate for the lower temperatures.

Rates of evaporation vary with these natural conditions. At Bol, near the trona depressions of Foli, annual evaporation – measured in the dunes and on Bol Island over a period of seven and five years respectively – averaged 3,180 mm in the first case and 2,322 mm in the second.[2] Lake Chad loses water at a phenomenal rate, both through seepage into the north-eastern littoral, from where moisture is then taken off into the air, and through direct evaporation. This high rate of evaporation can be demonstrated through the variation in conductivity, which increases from 60 mMho in the Chari delta, in the south, to 400 mMho in the northern part of the lake.[3] Rates of evaporation elsewhere in the sahel and the desert are comparable to those for Lake Chad.

Four distinctions can be made among the methods of utilising these high rates of solar evaporation: first, salt-earth from depressions, valleys or the shores of receding lakes was taken from the ground; there were few technological developments which affected production. Secondly, brine taken from the basins of evaporating lakes and depressions was also processed through filtering and boiling. In this case, production took advantage of natural evaporation, but various techniques were employed to increase production. Thirdly, the ashes of plants which had come from salt-laden earth were manufactured into brine, which was then filtered and boiled. The manufacture of this brine relied indirectly on the deposit of salt in the earth as a result of solar evaporation. Finally, brine from natural springs was exposed

53

to the sun as a means of concentrating the weak salt content in the brine. Salt-earth, rock salt, salt formations on the edges or surfaces of lakes and ponds, and natural brine each required different processing; the technology developed to increase yields depending upon climate and geological conditions. Hoes, picks, and other iron tools have long been used to scrape and dig. Pottery, baskets and the trunks of palm trees have provided the moulds used to shape the salt into cakes and cones that could be transported more easily. Calabashes have also been used to carry brine, and pots have held the brine when boiling has been employed to increase concentration. Filters have been made from straw and mats, with branches in their natural shape constructed into frames. Mats and rope have been important in packaging and transport, and, for the highest quality salt, leather bags have been used. This survey demonstrates the relatively low technological state of the industry, which even today has remained largely unchanged in those places where salt is still produced in the traditional fashion.

KAWAR AND FACHI

The desert sites took advantage of the high rate of natural evaporation, and consequently techniques of production were very simple. There was no filtering or boiling. Instead salt was removed from the surface of pits, lakes or other depressions where water was deposited. These sites were surrounded by waste, often heaped many metres high, which transformed surface deposits into pits because of the accumulation of debris. Local conditions determined whether or not the water supply was sufficient to be transferred into man-made pans for greater evaporation.

In the Kawar oases, there were two large red natron pits near Dirku, salt pits and depressions at Kalala, near Bilma, and white natron pits at Djado and Seguidine. There were also salt basins at Fachi, to the west of Kawar. In the nineteenth century, the sites at Bilma and Fachi were by far the most important, but it is possible – indeed likely – that the other sources were once more productive than they were in the nineteenth century. Once the northern Kawar sites were important sources of salt, and if the tradition is true then more salt must have been produced there in the past than in the nineteenth or the twentieth century.[4] There was also some alum, although the production of alum was of minor significance by the eighteenth and nineteenth centuries.

At Seguidine, in northern Kawar, natural evaporation occurs so fast that a thin layer of salt forms on the surface of the water. This crust was broken several times each day in order to increase its thickness, and once a week or so it was removed. Crystals of salt, in the form of stalactites, also formed where water could drip, and this very pure salt was also exploited.[5] Because of the great distance to market and the availability of salt further south in Kawar and at Fachi, only the highest quality salt has been worked at Seguidine in recent times, although there is some indication that in the distant past the Tuareg travelled to Seguidine for salt, perhaps to obtain far greater quantities than in the past century or two.[6] Certainly, the salt-earth is sufficiently high in concentration to have been utilised if transportation facilities were available.

Djado, a series of six oases, slightly to the west of the main north–south axis of Kawar, was the source of relatively small amounts of natron, consisting of sodium and magnesium sulphates and chlorides. As at other desert sites, the main production season was from April to November. The natron was removed from the edges of the water that forms at the oases.[7]

Similarly, the natron lakes of Dirku – one at Achenouma and the other at Arrigui – have similar characteristics to those elsewhere in the desert.[8] The lake at Achenouma, for example, can fill a basin 2 km long and 200 metres wide. Of course the level of this lake varies from year to year, as do all bodies of water in the desert. Indeed, the lake itself can evaporate so that only several smaller ponds are left, but water is close to the surface, and the production of natron is therefore possible. In the past natron was removed from the borders of the water, where it formed as a result of solar evaporation. The natron lake of Arrigui can fill a basin 7 km by 4 km, and because of the rapid evaporation, chunks of natron often form around the edges of the water. Dirku was sometimes a permanent settlement, but in unstable conditions it had to be abandoned, except when salt was being worked. It lay in a wide valley, 1.6 km across, between the two *jar kanwa* lakes. In 1823 Denham described the soil in the neighbourhood of these lakes as

> very powerfully impregnated by saline substances; so much so, that incrustations of pure, or nearly pure, trona [natron] are found, sometimes extending several miles. The borders of these lakes have the same appearance: they are composed of a black mud, which almost as soon as exposed to the sun and air becomes crisp like fresh dug earth in a frosty morning. In the centre of each of these lakes is a solid body or island of trona, which the inhabitants say increases in size annually; the lake to the east is probably fourteen or fifteen feet in height, and one hundred in circumference; the edges quite close to the water are solid , . . . ; it breaks off in firm pieces, but is easily reduced to powder . . . .[9]

Denham's account contains some inaccuracies, but it demonstrates the importance of production at Dirku in the early nineteenth century. The 'island of trona' in the centre of the lake was in fact the pile of waste left by the salt workers, and besides the lakes that Denham observed there were two others to the north of the town.

The saline at Bilma consisted of an area fifteen hectares in size which was subdivided into a series of large holes, two to three metres deep, and five to six metres square, which were continually dredged in order to allow salt to form on the surface of the water.[10] When Rohlfs watched production in 1867, he found the water so saline and the evaporation so rapid that within a few days several centimetres or more of thick crust (*minto*) surfaced on the water. Workers broke this crust and removed it, allowing more salt to form,[11] as Vischer witnessed in 1906:

Illustration 4.1   Bilma salt works

> The mode of preparing the salt for commerce at Bilma is very simple. In places where the salt deposits are richest, large holes are dug in the ground, four to five feet deep, and of varying diameter. The water then fills the hollow and in doing so dissolves the salt; after a few days a crust of salt crystals covers the surface like a thin sheet of ice: this is broken up and the bits sink to the bottom; a new crust forms and is treated likewise, and thus the water-hole gradually fills up with the sun to dry [sic]. The salt is next beaten up and compressed into large cones called Kantu, each weighing about forty pounds, or into flat cakes, locally known as Kunkuru (tortoise), which are much smaller.[12]

The moulds for *kantu* were made from the trunks of palm trees, and the workers filled these with the salt that formed on the surface and edges of the water. It took several days before the salt was dry and could be removed from the moulds.[13]

The evaporating surface was actually divided into basins which were located in the middle of huge piles of debris which accumulated over the centuries. The basins varied in size from 3 m to 5 m by 15 m.[14] Many of these basins were irregular in shape; in the 1960s Faure found many basins abandoned and others used for only part of the salt season. The principal craters numbered about 250; another 1,000 smaller ones were also worked. Although the total surface area of these basins was about 6,400 m², it may well be, as Faure assumes, that only about 5,000 m² produced salt.[15]

At the beginning of the salt season in March, workers cleared the basins of refuse. In April, normal production began. A specialist (Bilma: *kalla baktuma*; Fachi: *kalla saroma*) broke the *minto* layer of salt which had formed on the surface of the basin twice each day. The *kalla baktuma* usually worked a large number of basins. The *minto* was forced to the bottom, although some of the salt returned to solution. The effect was to increase the concentration of the brine as evaporation took place. Gradually a layer of salt (*kali*) accumulated on the bottom; as this layer became thicker it formed *beza*, which was then removed by other workers and stored beside the basin. The workers had to trample the salt in the basin in order to loosen it for removal. The cycle was repeated about every eight days.[16]

The *beza* was a relatively white salt, with crystals ranging from the size of sugar granules to 1 cm in diameter. In the middle of the season, which lasted from April to October, the *beza* which was produced was slightly soft, and it was sometimes packaged in palm leaves in this form. Usually, however, the *beza* was put in moulds of different shapes, after it had been rinsed in the brine of the basin to remove impurities. The *beza* was made into columns (*dembul-dembul*) (often called cones) which were about 33 cm high, weighing 5–6 kg. The softer *beza* was also sold in rectangular cakes, 35 cm wide, called *tagama* or *asrom*, which weighed about 4 kg.[17]

The *beza* was also used to make *kantu*, which were larger columns of salt that contained more impurities and were therefore a commodity of poorer quality. Much of the *beza* was left alongside the basins for the production of *kantu*, which was made at the end of the salt season. The busiest time of the season was from May until November, during the hottest months of the Saharan summer. By this time, the water in the basins had decreased and eventually evaporated completely. Workers (*magema*) broke up the salt in the basins with the aid of several iron implements which were imported from the Hausa country to the south-west. This deposit was mixed with the *beza* previously set aside, and the mixture was put into moulds made from the trunks of palm trees (*kantu*) or smaller moulds (*foshi*). Lime (Ca_2SO_4) was added; it acted as a binder that held the *kantu* together. A salt-taster (*furti-duma*) determined if the mixture had the appropriate combination of *beza* and impurities. The *gektuma* were the workers who put the mixture in the moulds to dry. The *naktuma*, a child or old woman, smoothed the base of the salt.[18] The column of *kantu* took 4–6 days to dry, before it was removed from the mould and turned upside down so that the base – which was thicker than the rest of the *kantu* – could finish drying.

The major distinctions between *beza* and *kantu* have existed at least since the early nineteenth century, although it is likely that the process of *kantu* manufacture is much older still. Denham, who was at Bilma in 1823, learned that salt was extracted from the borders of the salt basins at the end of the dry season 'in large masses'. 'This transparent kind [*beza*] they put into bags, and send to Bornou and Soudan; a coarser sort is also formed into hard pillars [*kantu*], and for which a ready market is found.'[19] The bags were known as *sukulmi.* Denham also discovered that people collected the pure salt crystals (*yergal*) which formed on the edges of the basins, although the *yergal* – 'beautifully white, and of an excellent flavour' – was not a major export then, nor has it been in more recent times.[20]

According to Grandin, who studied the industry in 1946, work units consisted of four men and a woman or child; two *magema* working in the basins, two *gektuma* putting the mixture into the moulds, and a *naktuma* finishing the moulds.[21] In a single day, a team could make as much as 200–250 *kantu*. An average salt basin could produce about 30 goat-skins of *beza*, 400 columns of *kantu*, and lesser amounts of *foshi*, the smaller moulds which are similar to *kantu*. This amount is approximately 3–4 tonnes of salt, enough for 40–50 camels.[22] The actual ratio of *beza* to *kantu* depended upon demand, since *beza* could be made for its own sake or mixed with impurities to make *kantu*. Finally, the difference between *kantu* and *foshi*, and indeed between the different sizes of *beza*, was related to a sexual division of labour. Men made the large-sized varieties, including *kantu*, which accounted for the great bulk of the salt exported, while women used the smaller moulds, including *foshi*.

Based on these production figures, Vikør has concluded that a family of four could make approximately 40 tonnes of *kantu* in 3–4 weeks, assuming that each basin produced 200 *kantu* per day and that a family owned a dozen or so basins.[23] In fact his figures are based on annual output, not just the final stages of production. The output of an average basin could be achieved in about two days, although it is likely that work units normally moved between several basins during production. Vikør's analysis demonstrates that the output of a work unit was extremely high, at least by comparison with other salt sources in the central Sudan. Of course, the output of a dozen basins depended upon the preparatory work which preceded the period of *kantu* production. In fact the accumulation of *beza* in the months after the opening of the salt season also involved considerable amounts of labour. Grandin reported that the whole population of Bilma worked in the salines from May until November, sometimes spending long periods in the ruins of Kalala. In 1946, additional workers came from Aney and Arrigui during the peak of the season.[24]

Productive capacity was a function of surface evaporation, the salinity of the initial brine, and the rate of annual evaporation. Faure has calculated each of these factors. The initial brine varied in concentration, ranging from approximately 250 g per litre to as much as 400 g per litre. Evaporation resulted in the removal of about 3 m of water each year, assuming that the rate of water inflow was constant. The water at the bottom of the basins was about 50–75 cm deep. In these conditions, it was possible that a surface area of 5,000 m^2 produced 3,750 tonnes of salt each year, during which time 10,000 m^3 of water evaporated. This estimate includes debris, as well as salt. Faure believed that the actual amount of salt and debris produced has been of the order of 2,000 tonnes per year if variations in temperature and the amount of water are taken into consideration.[25]

The quantity of debris at Bilma attests to the antiquity of salt production at the site. The debris, made up of thenardite and other salts in different concentrations, dominates the landscape. There is so much debris that the salines themselves are scattered about, forming artificial craters. The actual area of the salines is small by comparison with the accumulated debris, which Faure estimated at one half to two million metres^3. This volume indicates that at least one million tonnes of debris are present at the site. This quantity suggests that 1,000 tonnes of salt could have been produced each year for the past millennium, assuming that the amounts of debris and salt were equal in volume. Of course, it may be that there are more than one million tonnes of debris present and the ratio of debris to salt is lower than Faure has allowed, in which case the amount of salt produced for export would have been correspondingly greater.

The earliest reference to salt production in Kawar is contained in the geographical writings of al-Idrīsī (548 AH, 1154 AD), although the term he used to describe the Kawar salts was *shabb*, which strictly speaking is alum, that is, a double aluminium sulphate $(Al_2(SO_4)_3)$.[26] Lange has discovered that there is some alum near Bilma, but Faure's detailed geological survey of the oases failed to uncover significant deposits. Alum was used widely in North Africa, the Middle East and Europe in the medieval period; it was used in tanning, medicine and amulets, but al-Idrīsī's account seems to refer to other salts, although he probably meant to refer to alum too. First, he distinguished between different qualities and noted that poorer qualities were mixed with better types for the market. Secondly, his description of how the salt was formed is remarkably similar to later observations of the rapid evaporation that left the salt deposits:

> This alun [alum] which is in the land of Kawwār is outstanding in quality. It is abundant and is extracted (and sent) each year to every land in such enormous quantities that its weight cannot be measured. Its mines are inexhaustible. The people of the region say that it grows like plants and is replenished within hours by the same quantity as is taken from it. If this were not the case, the land would have become quite exhausted because of the quantities which are extracted and sent out to every land.[27]

The allusion to salt 'growing like plants' probably refers to the formation of a salt crust on the lakes and ponds of Kawar, while the quantity of production, as reflected in trade, indicates a scale of production that could have been satisfied only from the known deposits of the various salts – not alum, which is found in small amounts. It is unlikely – indeed highly improbable – that geological conditions and the chemical composition of the various salines have changed significantly since the twelfth century.

Al-Idrīsī learned that 'alun' was found at many places in Kawar, including Qasr 'Umm 'Isa, whose chief wealth was the trade in this salt; Ankalas, which was the most important commercial centre and which had 'mines of pure alun, of outstanding quality'; and Abzar, with its 'mine of alun of first-rate quality, but which because of its softness tends to disintegrate'. The trade of all these centres was in alum, according to al-Idrīsī. The mine at Tamalama (which Lange identifies as Bilma) was of little use because of the 'many layers of earth' in the source, but it was still mined and the alum mixed with other alum from other places.[28] With the exception of Tamalama, the places in al-Idrīsī's account have not been identified with later settlements, but the number of places strongly suggests that the references are to Seguidine, Dirku and other oases.

As at Bilma, production at Fachi was divided into three stages. First, the salines were prepared for production by removing sand and debris that had blown or fallen in during the off-season. Walls were also repaired. Most of this maintenance was done in April. Secondly, the flow of brine had to be guaranteed so that the salt could 'ripen', that is saturation of the solution could be achieved. The layer of salt (*kali*) that formed on the bottom of each saline had to be broken. Thirdly, the *beza* was removed and allowed to dry before being stored in warehouses near the basins. Some production techniques were different than those at Bilma, however. The raw salt from the basins was pounded in order to break the crystals and produce a more even mixture. Brine was then sprinkled on the salt before the mixture was put in the palm-tree moulds. The columns of salt were dumped out on the ground to dry and the mould was used again to make more *kantu*.[29] Whereas at Bilma the salt pits were quite small, approximately five to six metres square, at Fachi there were several large basins scattered throughout the oasis. In the nineteenth century, the most important basin was Fosso, but Kalala, Birgam, Dafogorom and Kaudi were probably worked at different times, depending upon political conditions and the availability of labour. The Fachi basins were subdivided into several hundred smaller workings, which were individually operated and separated by dykes. Furthermore, at Fachi the surface water flows, while at Bilma it is stagnant. At Bilma individual salt pits had to be abandoned when the waste heaps became too high, for sand can fill in the pits. The relatively small size of each pit became a problem because the height from the bottom to the top of the waste piles could exceed 20 metres. At Fachi this problem did not exist. The basins were large enough to permit extensive output, when political and other factors were conducive to such a production level. Fuchs has demonstrated that work units of 2–5 men can produce 2.6 tonnes of salt per flat per year. In 1972 flats averaged 1.5 m^2, and work units operated as many as ten flats. Some flats could produce as much as 8 tonnes. Fuchs estimates that 50 per cent of the flats in 1972 produced the average of 2.6 tonnes; 30 per cent produced only 1.6 tonnes; and the remainder produced more than 2.6 tonnes.[30] When compared with Bilma, output appears to have been less – perhaps 25 per cent less – than at Bilma.

TEGUIDDA N'TESEMT AND THE AIR MASSIF

The production of salt at Teguidda n'tesemt was based on a system of decantation basins in which salt-earth and brine were mixed to increase the concentration of the brine. The basins were shallow, which facilitated solar evaporation. The concentrated brine was then removed to the village of Teguidda for final processing into blocks of salt. In the 1930s, the salt was shaped into squares, rectangles or triangles, measuring 10 cm by 15 cm to 40 cm by 90 cm, depending upon the mould. In 1963, there were two moulds, *taralalt*, 12–15 cm by 20–25 cm by 3–4 cm, weighing about 1 kg; and *afassas*, 80–90 cm by 50–60 cm by 5–6 cm, weighing about 50 kg.[31]

The decantation system included four types of basins, all of which were located on the natural sandstone bed, which acted as the bottom of the basins.[32] The *abatol*, the first type of basin, was a large, shallow basin which was higher than the other basins. Salt-earth and water were mixed in the *abatol* as a means of enriching the brine. A second set of large basins, *farandaw*, was located at a slightly lower elevation than the *abatol*. Through a tunnel at the base of the clay wall of the *abatol*, the weak brine was allowed to flow into the *farandaw*, where more salt-earth was added to increase the concentration of the brine. The waste material which remained in the *abatol* and *farandaw* was put in another basin, *fasendaw*, until it was dry. The waste was then thrown onto the piles of debris which surrounded the workings. The process of decantation in the *abatol* and *farandaw* lasted about five days, with more water and salt-earth added as evaporation proceeded. Eventually, the concentrated brine in the *farandaw* was placed in a series of small basins, *tarsiyo*, whose location and size depended upon the available surface on the sandstone floor. There could be from 10 to 90 *tarsiyo* around the larger basins. The diameter of the *tarsiyo* averaged about 20–60 cm, but some were as large as 3 m. A crust of salt, which was regularly broken by sprinkling water on it, formed on the *tarsiyo*. This operation (*mouss*) was continued for 5–10 days until the *tarsiyo* was filled with salt. The salt was then scraped from the sandstone bed and taken to the village.

When Faure studied the Teguidda industry in 1963, there were 700 units (*ibitelen*).[33] Each unit consisted of two large basins (*abatol* and *farandaw*) and a series of *tarsiyo*. He calculated the surface area of the *abatol* at 1,400 m², with a volume of 350 m³; the *farandaw* at 840 m², with a volume of 210 m³, and the *tarsiyo* at 4,000 m², with a volume of 400 m³. The area where the waste was dried (*fasendaw*) occupied an area of 1,100 m² and could contain 250 m³. The variation in size made accurate measurement impossible, but Faure's rough calculations indicate the extensive surface area for evaporation. The *tarsiyo*, where the final evaporation of the brine occurs, were much shallower than the two larger types of basin.

Nearby, at Guelele, salt-earth (*taferkast*) was also scraped off the ground and packaged in bags for shipment south to the markets of Barmou, Shadawanka and Kao. This salt was fed to livestock. It was gathered after the *cure salée* was over, when the ground had dried up completely. Salt-earth (*ganda-ganda*) was also gathered at Teguidda n'tesemt.[34] Natron was collected in the Air Massif, too. Barth saw people collecting natron a day's march north of Agades;[35] Chudeau witnessed a salt harvest between

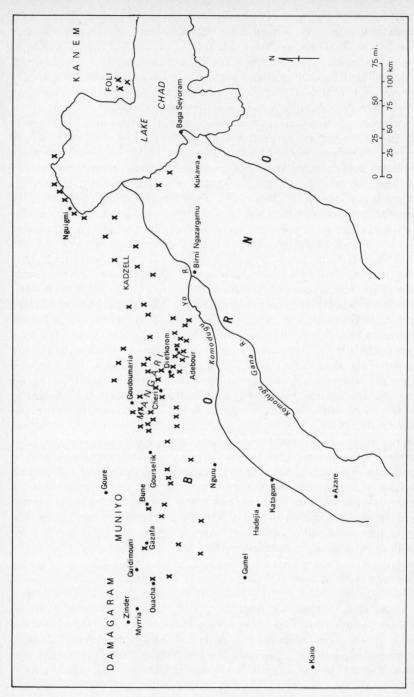

Map 4.1 Salt and natron sources in the Chad basin

Aoudereas and Bidei in Air in the first decade of the twentieth century.[36] The natron crust (*ara*) was about 50 cm thick. It was taken as far south as Damergu, where it was fed to camels.

THE BORNO SAHEL: MANDA AND KIGE

Salt production in Mangari and Muniyo was far more scattered than the desert industry. First, *manda* salt was made at perhaps one hundred sites from western Muniyo to an area which was only a few kilometres from the site of Birni Ngazargamu. This salt required filtering devices and furnaces, and hence production centres gained a degree of permanence. Some sites were quite large, but there were also many small ones.[37] Secondly, *baboul* or *kige* salt, which was also filtered and boiled, was even more dispersed; there were no large sites. Salt-camps consisted of only one or two furnaces. located at wells in Kadzell, although some were found in northern and eastern Mangari. There were also sites south of the Komodugu Yo and along the western shore of Lake Chad.[38]

Production techniques in Mangari, Muniyo and Kadzell were varied. More different kinds of salt came from those regions, and the volume of production was probably greater than at any other place, except perhaps the Kawar oases. The types of salt from these provinces included *manda, kige, kwaras kwaras* (*farin kanwa*), *gari, gwangwarasa*, and *jar kanwa*. The first two are largely sodium chloride salts, while the latter varieties are natron. *Manda* production was very extensive, and distinctions were made between numerous sub-varieties (Table 4.1). Since *manda* was a mixture of sodium chloride, soda, and thenardite, these distinctions relate to different proportions of salts, as well as purity. A sampling of the numerous reports on the production of *manda* reveals how extensive the industry was; furthermore it was closely associated with the collection of natron (Table 4.2).

In order to make *manda* (Hausa: *mangul*), workers gathered salt-earth which had been left on the ground as the water from the rainy season retreated. This salt-earth was placed in filters and washed with brine from the depression. The more concentrated brine was then placed in ovens, which contained from 40 to 170 moulds (Figure 4.1). The brine was boiled dry, and the moulds were then broken to remove the salt, which varied in weight from 3 to 6 kg.[39] The product, often referred to as cones of salt because one of the most common moulds was in the shape of a cone, varied in purity and chemical composition. The techniques of production, however, were relatively similar throughout the country of salt.

The technique took advantage of a natural system of graduation, based on the shallowness of the depressions and the rapid evaporation during the dry season. As the water receded, salt was deposited along the edges of the lakes and ponds. Water was trapped in shallow hollows, while efflorescence also occurred as a result of the proximity of the water table to the surface of the ground. By collecting the salty earth as well as the brine, workers were able to

63

Table 4.1 *Types of manda salt in northern Borno*

	Type	Characteristics	Sources	Distribution (19th century)
1.	*Mangul*	Most common form; shaped in round cones	Numerous depressions	Borno, Mandara, Kano, Zaria
2.	*Pieske*	Rectangular loaf, smaller than *mangul*, but same type, though often purer	Scattered depressions	Borno
3.	*Kariamu*	Like *mangul* but larger and better quality	Scattered depressions	Borno
4.	*Kubule*	Tube-shaped, very good quality; only from best workings		Only purchased at workings; never went to market
5.	*Alawusai* (*Allah wuse*)	Made like *mangul* and *pieske*, but from brine which involves no filtering; special for export; has reddish tinge		Kano and western market
6.	*Yergal*	Salt crystals, excellent quality but rare	*Gwangwarasa* beds	Largely consumed locally, when found
7.	*Bangul*	Pot-shaped, involves filtering and boiling	Koremaram, Garrua, Madda, Dabilia, Dara	Fika, southern Borno

10.	*Shedanno* or *Cheri*	Purer than *bangul*, but similar – no filtering, hence could be type of *alawusai*. First class *manda*	Chocknapchumni, Cheri, Shedanno
11.	*Diru*	Second grade *manda*	Diru, Mawujeram
12.	*Wongangawa*	Third grade *manda*, may be the same as *feske*	Wongangawa, Ngauna, Kugunga, Babillo, Bugduma

Note: *Manda* is the general word for this type of salt in Kanuri; while *mangul* is a particular type of *manda*. In Hausa *mangul* is the generic term for Mangari salt, while *manda* is a specific variety, which is black in contrast to the white or grey-white colour of most *mangul*. In this table the names used at the source of production, i.e. Manga terms, are used.

Sources: Report of Mahomet Lawan, 1941, Mai Prof. 2/2 3664, Local Salt Production. Bornu Province, Reports of J. Becklesfall, 28 March 1907 and W. Browne, 19 May 1906, both in SNP 7/8 2281/1907. Salt from Bornu Province – Samples for transmission to the Imperial Institute for Report; and Classification of the various salts produced at Manga saltings, SNP, 15/1 Br Rpt. 5, May 1903. All in Nigerian National Archives, Kaduna.

Table 4.2 *Sources of Mangari and Muniyo salt and natron, c. 1895–1910*

I. *Mangul* (Kanuri: *manda*)	II. *Kanwa* (Kanuri: *kilbo*)
Dirsille	(Distinctions between *jar*
Lagai	and *farin* often not made in
Faske	sources)
Cheri	Gamdou
Koremaram	Gourselik
Garrua	Badumuni or Gadamuni
Madda	Bune
Dabilia	Chillima (Silimma?)
Dara	Keleno
Chocknapchumni	Kalakama
Shedanno	Adebour
Diru	Dierera
Newujeram	Gazafa (Kabba)
Wongangawa	Bondem-kata
Ngauna	Kassamari
Karagua	Dari
Babillo	Kenoukam
Chillima (Silimma?)	Bouboukoa
Bugduma	Djemba (Zumba?)
Ngibia	Legarari (*jar*?)
Nglabunglawa	Wadoram
Dubkunerum	Adeberdana (*jar*?)
Malakar	Yani Souarni (*jar*?)
Sikutkudwa	Kaiatwa (*jar*)
Kasga	III. *Kige*
Yamia	Ajiri
Zumba	Bitur (Bizar)
Djemba (Zumba?)	(Mobbeur country)
Gamgoua	(Shores of Lake Chad)
Gourselik	Dakindiri
Adebour	Kadzell
Souarni	
Guidjigaoua	IV. *Gwangwarasa*
Audoro	Aoumba
Maine-Soroa	Tatoukoutou
Tatoukoutou	Maine-Soroa
	Mailleri
	Zumba

Sources: Reibell (1931), 250–256; Foureau (1902), 574–588; Lahache and Marre (1911), II, 555–569; Classification of Various Salts Produced at Manga Saltings, SNP 15/1 Br. Rpt. 5, May 1903; Browne and Becklesfall reports, SNP 7/8 2281/1907; Mahomet Lawan report, 1941, Mai Prof 2/2 3664., in Nigerian National Archives, Kaduna; Barth (1857–59), III, 45, 63, 67.

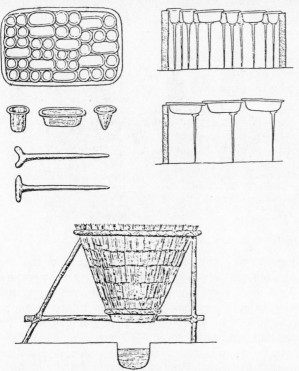

Figure 4.1 Furnace accessories for the production of *manda*

concentrate salt efficiently. The technique required the presence of brine to wash the salt-earth and the availability of fuel for use in boiling. The brine came from the depressions, while firewood, and sometimes grass, was gathered in the surrounding countryside. As Foureau noted in the 1899–1900 production season, workers carefully stripped bushes and trees so that the trunks remained, thereby guaranteeing the regeneration of the fuel supply in the next rainy season.[40]

The filtering devices (*chagadi*) were made of braided straw mats placed on three legs which raised the filter off the ground. Sand was used in the bottom of the filter, and pots were placed underneath to catch the brine. Filtering devices were often 1.5 m in diametre and 1 m high. The vessels at the salines near Nguru were about 38 cm in diametre and 50 cm deep.[41] The brine was stored in large pots, 1.2 m by 0.6 m in size, until enough brine had been filtered to make possible a firing of the oven.[42] Usually the filtering process lasted a whole day.[43]

The filters helped separate some of the sodium sulphate out of solution, thereby increasing the concentration of sodium chloride and sodium carbonate. Sodium sulphate was also deposited in the collecting basin under

67

Illustration 4.2   Manga filtering devices for *manda* salt

the filter and in the storage reservoir next to the furnace. Garde found that the production of *manda* at Gourselik, which he considered the most important saline in Mangari in 1908, benefited from the elimination of some of the sodium sulphate from the brine.[44] Foureau made the same observation in 1900, when he was at Gourselik.[45] At Karagou, located east of Gourselik, the *manda* was less pure than that produced at Gourselik, even though there was less sodium sulphate in the depression; at least less sodium sulphate separated out in the filtering process.[46] At times in Chocknapchumni, Cheri and other places, no filters were used.[47] The water from the local depressions was sufficiently concentrated for the brine to be boiled directly, without leaching the salt out of the earth. This kind of salt, known as *Allah wuse* – 'God provides' – was not necessarily any purer than salt made after filtering, but it was easier to make. At some places *Allah wuse* was made only at the end of the season when the depressions were almost dry and the remaining water was highly charged with salt.

The boiling operation was a delicate procedure and consequently only an experienced person undertook it. The boiling had to be continuous but at a low heat – the operation usually lasted 24 hours. The boiler master used a long spatula to stir the brine as new brine was added to keep the moulds full. The stirring was necessary to maintain a uniform mixture of salts so that the sodium carbonate and sodium sulphate did not precipitate out before the sodium chloride. The boiler master eventually added a few pinches of finely-ground millet to facilitate precipitation if the salt did not crystallise spontaneously.[48]

The ovens varied greatly in construction. Smaller ones required wooden legs which were only a few centimetres in diameter, while the largest ovens needed much thicker wood. Earth was built up around the legs, which helped retain heat and also provided additional support for the vessels, which were

68

Illustration 4.3 Manga *manda* ovens

placed on clay pedestals. It is probably true, as Gouletquer and Kleinmann have hypothesised, that there was a development from smaller ovens to larger ones.[49] In the early twentieth century both types were common,[50] but the use of ovens of various sizes may only indicate the availability of wooden supports of various dimensions; the size of trees and bushes invariably limited the size of the oven.

Despite the efforts of the boiler master to maintain a uniform mixture of the different salts, the finished product consisted of layers of salt mixtures. Sodium carbonate and sodium sulphate precipitate before sodium chloride, so that the first layer (at the top of the salt cone) has a greater concentration of these first two salts. Foureau tested the *manda* produced at Gourselik in 1900 and observed that the top of the cone contained all three salts with a residue of sand; in the middle of the cone sodium chloride was dominant but with a noticeable proportion of sodium sulphate and 12 parts per 100 of sodium carbonate; the base of the cone – which was the last layer to precipitate in the mould – had some sodium sulphate and a weak proportion of sodium carbonate (5 parts per 100), but sodium chloride was dominant.[51] Foureau also found that the *faske* – a better quality salt made in elliptical moulds – had a higher proportion of sodium chloride. Only brine was used, with no salt-earth, which thereby reduced the amount of sodium carbonate, in the final product.[52]

It is clear from the numerous studies of the Mangari salt industry that a number of technological advances had been achieved by the end of the nineteenth century. First, the filtering and boiling were effective methods of concentrating brine, thereby increasing the rate of production over solar evaporation alone. The size and shape of these boiling and filtering devices almost certainly had undergone some evolution; the problem is establishing when the changes took place. Furnace construction in particular had a profound influence on the production of salt, because furnaces are more efficient than open fires. The construction of large, earthen furnaces capable of holding 150 moulds or more, in which the moulds were raised off the naked fire, must have developed after an earlier stage in which simpler devices were used. Gouletquer and Kleinmann, in their study of the salines of Manga in 1973, presented an hypothesis on the origin and development of the industry which attempts to trace the evolution in the size of furnaces.[53] According to their research – based in part on a preliminary survey of potential archaeological sites and in part on a comparison with archaeological work on prehistoric salt sites in Europe – the production of salt through the use of furnaces and filtering devices is relatively recent, perhaps less than 180 years old in the area of Maine-Soroa, at least. The lack of appreciable quantities of debris suggests the relatively late development of the industry. If this hypothesis is correct, archaeological work should uncover the following evolution in the size of furnaces. There should be evidence of *manda* production which used naked fires, with the boiling pots sitting directly on the fire, a procedure for which there is no evidence in tradition nor in direct observation. The use of supports to raise the boiling pots off the fire is a necessary development in the evolution of furnaces. When the supports become larger in order to accommodate bigger pots, it becomes necessary to build reinforcement banking out of earth. There is no direct evidence for this stage either. Only fully-developed ovens or their remains have been found in Mangari.

Another development in the Manga industry was the attempt to control the composition of the salt mixture in the finished product. Local knowledge of the process of precipitation had not evolved to the point where a true scientific understanding of the chemistry of salt existed, so that the salt workers were not able to take full advantage of the differences between the various salts.[54] None the less, salt workers were aware of the distinctions between the three basic salts in the Mangari region. Relatively pure sodium chloride came from neighbouring Kadzell, where *kige* was made in a similar manner to the manufacture of *manda*; only plants were burned and their ashes filtered before boiling. Crystals of sodium chloride (*yergal*) were gathered wherever they formed; it was recognised that these crystals were pure and as a consequence were highly valued. A distinction was also made between sodium carbonate and sodium chloride; sodium carbonate, either as soda or trona, was well known, since the *ungurnu* from the eastern shores of Lake Chad was a mixture of these two compounds, with virtually no other salt in evidence. Finally, sodium sulphate was so heavily concentrated in a few of the depressions, that it crystallised into an almost pure form.[55] It was collected for use in tanning. The sodium sulphate which precipitated out in the filtering process, in the collecting pots, and in the reservoirs for the ovens was discarded as an impurity, thereby increasing the concentration of sodium chloride. The problem was developing techniques to separate the three salts from each other.

When possible, brine was used to make *faske*, without adding the salt-earth which contained greater concentrations of sodium carbonate. As the samples of *mangul* and *faske* which have been analysed clearly demonstrate, the product was still relatively impure. Distinctions were made on the basis of the sodium chloride content, but it was not possible, given the technology, to produce large quantities of relatively pure sodium chloride. To do so would have required a more thorough scientific knowledge than was available. First, it would have been necessary to prevent the cones from boiling dry in order to take advantage of the different rates of precipitation among the three main salts. Secondly, it would have been necessary to alter the temperature of the solution in order to allow for variations in precipitation; sodium chloride remains in solution over a much greater range in temperatures than sodium carbonate, for example. Nevertheless, the removal of sodium sulphate from solution was a major advance and perhaps accounts for the reason why *manda* production began in the first place. The salt-earth could be used for many purposes without additional processing, but the manufacture of *manda* concentrated sodium chloride, admittedly to an imperfect extent, and hence *manda* could serve as a substitute for other salts which also contained a high degree of sodium chloride.

Production of salt in Kadzell involved a different process from that used in making *manda* in Mangari and Muniyo. The salt, *baboul* or *kige*, was made from the ashes of a bush, *Salvadora persica* (Kanuri: *babul, kaligu*; Arabic: *arak, siwak*), which is found throughout the central Sahara and sahel. It grows abundantly in the pastures of Egei, Borku, and Tibesti, for example. Its coloured, currant-like berries ripen in April and have a peppery flavour which drying partly eliminates. Used in Borku and by the Teda of western Tibesti as a food, it is highly nutritious and eaten as a famine food; nomads of southern Borku travel to Egei to gather the berries. Usually the berries are pressed together in round loaves to facilitate handling and preservation. For the Jagada nomads of southern Borku, a common dish is camel's milk diluted with water and mixed with dum flour or siwak seeds.[56] This bush grew throughout Kadzell, eastern Mangari, the area south of the Komodugu Yo near Lake Chad and also to the east of the lake; only in this region was it used to make salt. Other plants were also burned to produce salt, including three varieties of grass (Kanuri: *pagam, kalaslim*, and *kanido*) which were found near Lake Chad, and the bush *Capparis aphylla* (Kanuri: *tundub*), which was found as far south of the Komodugu Yo as Kukawa.[57]

The crucial variable was the availability of water for filtering, the bushes themselves being common. *Kige* salt was produced at Bitur and Ajura, near Yahdia and Maine-Soroa in the same area where *manda* was produced.[58] This was the furthest west that *kige* was made. There were also sites near Kukawa, south of the Komodugu Yo in the heart of Borno.[59] Moll reports that production was also extensive in the area south-east of Lake Chad; salt was also made in Barowa, Bagirmi and in Sara country.[60] None the less, *kige* production was most extensive in the arid region of Kadzell, where temporary

71

camps were established during the dry season. There may have been as many as 100–200 salt-camps in the Kadzell region at the end of the nineteenth century.[61] These camps were located at wells which could be used as a source of water for filtering the ashes.

The equipment used in making *kige* was similar to that used in Mangari and Muniyo to make *manda*, but first the bushes and clumps of grass were burned, and the ashes placed in a filter similar to the ones used in the production of *manda*. The brine was then boiled in small ovens or in single pots over a fire:

> The solution from which the salt is obtained is prepared by treating with water the ashes of burnt branches and leaves of the *kigu* tree. This solution is put into large conical pots about 20 inches high and 16 inches diameter at the base. Usually two of these pots, sometimes three, are placed in a roughly-made furnace consisting merely of a hole in the ground with convenient supports for the pots, and a wood fire is lighted. The solution is concentrated by boiling, the pot being continually replenished as its contents evaporate. When the solution has attained a certain degree of concentration, which is marked by the formation round its rim of small salt crystals, the fire is allowed to go out, and the contents of the pot cool. In doing so they solidify and form a cone of salt which is extracted by breaking the pot. The salt solution requires to be boiled about 24 hours before it is sufficiently concentrated to deposit the salt on cooling.[62]

One variety, *labatura*, was cylindrical rather than cone-shaped. The cones varied in size; some were 25 cm in diameter and 50 cm deep. In general, however, the size of the cones was larger than those used in the manufacture of *manda*. The cones weighed from 5 to 6 kg.[63] The *kige* cone had a black bottom, but the centre and top were white. Mahomet Lawan, who studied the industry in 1941, thought the bottom was black because it was burnt, but in fact boiling the salt dry resulted in almost pure NaCl or KCl, except for the mother liquor, containing a variety of salts and impurities which remained at the bottom.[64] The purity of the salt varied considerably. The *kige* made in the Kadzell region was highly charged with sodium chloride or potassium chloride; the quality was so good that it was a superior salt, the rival of any produced in the central Sudan.[65] The product made on the southern shores of Lake Chad, however, had much lower concentrations of sodium chloride; samples ranged from 34.1 per cent to 68.3 per cent sodium chloride.[66]

The antiquity of *kige* production is open to speculation. It may well be, as Gouletquer and Kleinmann have suggested, that *kige* was made before the development of the *manda* industry.[67] Unlike *manda* production, the pots of brine in the manufacture of *kige* are placed directly on the open fire. From 3 to 5 cones were usually made at one time, but in the most western areas of *kige* production, the example of the *manda* ovens appears to have stimulated the development of relatively small ovens for use in making *kige*.[68] Even these 'ovens' are not true ovens, since the cones were still on the fire (Figure 4.2). In general, however, the technique of boiling is a simple one, which suggests an ancient and obscure origin. Because of the wide geographical distribution of the *kige* technique, moreover, Gouletquer and Kleinmann suggest that *kige*

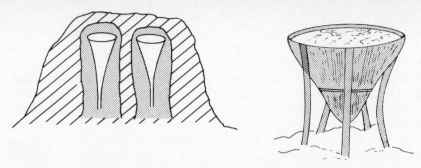

Figure 4.2   Sketch of oven and filter for *kige* manufacture at Bitur

producion may have inspired the development of the *manda* technique.[69] Whatever the case, it is clear that at the end of the nineteenth century there were two distinct procedures for making salt – one involving ovens for the manufacture of *manda* and the other involving the boiling of brine on an open fire in the manufacture of *kige*. There has been some exchange between the two techniques, beside the development of quasi-ovens near Maine-Soroa. The moulds for *kige* are generally larger than those for *manda*, except in the area around Maine-Soroa where there is an overlap between the two techniques. In the Maine-Soroa area, the moulds for *manda* production are similar in size to the *kige* moulds and larger than the moulds that are used for *manda* in Goudoumaria and other parts of Mangari, where *kige* production is not found. When these influences spread is uncertain. Both the evolution towards a *kige* oven and the use of *kige*-sized moulds in *manda* production were in evidence in 1906. Browne's diagram of *kige* manufacture at Bitur (see Figure 4.2) shows a boiling device for two cones, in which the earthen supports appear to have been made in a fashion similar to the construction of *manda* ovens.[70] Cone sizes for *manda* varied, as already noted, but the large ones which corresponded to *kige* moulds were sometimes found in the first decade of the twentieth century.[71]

These problems of tracing the spread of different techniques highlight the difficulty of establishing the antiquity of *manda* and *kige* production in the absence of archaeological investigation. As already noted, Heinrich Barth, who travelled through the salt region of Mangari in the 1850s, did not report the production of *manda*, although he observed *kige* production in Kadzell.[72] Because Barth was such a skilled observer who noted with accuracy the manufacture of salt elsewhere, his omission of *manda* cannot be dismissed as a simple oversight. He reported salt for sale in the market of Kabowa, but this could well have been *kige*.[73] He does not mention the existence of *manda* in any of the markets in Borno or the Sokoto Caliphate. His colleague, James Richardson, who died in February 1851 on the road between Goure and Kukawa, having passed through Mangari, reported that the inhabitants of Mandemnia were 'occupied in making salt', but it is unclear whether the salt was *kige* or *manda*.[74] It was certainly being made when Nachtigal was in Borno in the early 1870s, even if it was not being produced in Barth's day. In 1891 Monteil compared salt-making in Dallol Fogha to salt-making in Borno – both involved the washing of brines through filters. The comparison implies a similarity in the use of salt-earth, which characterises *manda* production but not *kige* production.[75]

In December 1823, however, Clapperton reported that Hausa merchants purchased 'trona or natron, common salt and beads' in Borno, 'which together with coarse tobes [gowns], are also carried by Bornouese adventurers to Haussa'.[76] It may well be that this 'common salt' was *manda*; certainly Clapperton's distinction between natron and salt in the export trade is convincing proof that either *kige*, Bilma salt or *manda* was being exported, and since both Hausa and Borno merchants engaged in the traffic it appears to have amounted to substantial quantities. Late in the century, *kige* was not exported west to the caliphate; there simply was not enough made. The Tuareg had been taking Bilma salt to 'Haussa' – but not through Borno – since the eighteenth century. *Manda* is the likely candidate for Clapperton's 'common salt', but the circumstantial evidence is far from convincing proof. Whether or not Clapperton observed the *manda* trade, by 1899 all the major distinctions in the types of *manda* – which suggests a fully developed industry – were noted by Foureau.[77] Round cones (*mangul*), rectangular loaves (*pieske*), high-quality cones (*karianu*), tube-shaped moulds (*kubule*), and *Allah wuse* were all available. Subsequent reports, especially those of Browne and his associates on the British side of the new colonial border, confirm Foureau's observations.[78] Barth most surely would have commented on such variety, if there had been any in his day.

NATRON PRODUCTION IN THE BORNO SAHEL: MANGARI, MUNIYO AND KANEM

The production of natron in the Borno sahel required virtually no technological improvements, unlike the manufacture of *kige* and *manda*. The industry depended upon the natural environment; solar evaporation of the sahelian depressions left the natron deposits of Mangari and Muniyo, while the seepage phenomenon of Lake Chad concentrated trona in Kanem. As Vischer noted in 1906:

> Everywhere on the south-east coast of Lake Chad, in the basin of Lake Chad itself, large flat pools collect during the rainy season. During the subsequent months they dry up, and leave a natron deposit resembling an ice-crust, and in this form they enter the market. The natron crust often forms on the water itself.[79]

In Mangari and Muniyo, production was confined to the belt of territory where *manda* was made, although larger quantities of natron came from the western depressions. Although natron also came from Guelele, near Teguidda n'tesemt, the Air Massif, and Kawar, the proximity of Mangari and Muniyo to the markets of the savanna gave the output of the Borno sahel an advantage.

The earliest reference to natron production dates to the second decade of the nineteenth century. A former Hausa trader between Kano and Asante – one Sergeant Frazer of the Second West Indian Regiment in Sierra Leone – provided the first description of natron production in the Mangari–Muniyo region:

> The congwa [*kanwa*] is procured in Bornou, during the dries, from a place where water lodges to the depth of about nine inches in the rainy season; it is like fine flour, and lies from twelve to fifteen inches thick along the ground, from whence it exudes so profusely, next morning at the spot as much may be gathered as will fill ten baskets. There is also a sort of red congwa, which is dug out of the ground in lumps, and tastes exactly like the white.[80]

The reference to both white and red natron makes it clear that Frazer's description is of Muniyo or Mangari, rather than Kanem.

According to the research of the early colonial officials in French and British Borno, natron was worked at several dozen locations in Mangari and Muniyo. The natron (*kwaras kwaras*) was scraped from the ground or from the edges of the retreating lakes. The amounts produced at individual sites could be considerable, as Barth observed when he visited the natron lake at Keleno, near Magadjiri in Muniyo, in 1853. He found that a

> large provision of natron, consisting of from twenty to twenty-five piles about ten yards in diameter, and four in height, protected by a layer of reeds, was stored up at the northern end of the lake. The whole circumference of the basin, which is called 'abge' [*tabki*] by the inhabitants, was one mile and a half.[81]

Late in the season a crust about one inch thick formed very quickly on the surface, while during the main production season at the end of the rains, larger pieces were obtained. Barth found that natron production was on a comparable scale at Bune, located 40 km further east in Muniyo, where six foot deep pits were dug on the shores of a natron lake which had dried up.[82] A survey of other production sites in 1915 revealed that there were at least 52 major natron workings, although it is significant that by then neither Bune nor Keleno was listed.[83] As was the case in the manufacture of *manda* salt, depressions came into production for a number of years, only to lose their importance as the salt was removed. Pieces of white natron came from the edges of the lakes, while the natron-earth came from the ground wherever a natron deposit was found. The impure natron-earth (*gari*) was packaged in mats. Because of the impurities, distinctions were made between different kinds of 'white' natron (Hausa: *farin kanwa*): white, grey and black.

The other major types of natron were red natron (*jar kanwa*) and relatively pure sodium sulphate (*gwangwarasa*). In contrast to *farin kanwa*, the red natron was obtained from the brine in the depressions. As Mundy observed production in 1903, *jar kanwa* was almost invariably worked when water is lying on the deposit and therefore very often in the rains. The reason is that in the dry season a kilbo kime [*jar kanwa*] becomes a sticky peat like bog very difficult to work on and injurious to the naked foot, whereas with some water lying on it, it can be more easily worked and is apparently also purer in quality, the natron working to the surface.[84]

Early in the century, *jar kanwa* was found at Yamia, Yani Souarni, between Guidjigaua and Adebour, and only a few other places. Finally, *gwangwarasa*, used in tanning, came from very few sites – including Zumba, Maine-Soroa, and Tatoukoutou in the first decade of the century.[85] It was worked in the same fashion as white natron, moreover.

Natron could be found in many places to the east of Lake Chad, including isolated locations in the Bahr al-Ghazal, and in parts of Kanem. Natron-earth, which was gathered in a manner similar to the collection of *gari* in Muniyo and Mangari, came from Lechgour, in the Chittati region of Kanem, on the northern shore of Lake Chad.[86] It may well be that at various times in the past natron was collected elsewhere in Chittati and Foli. Certainly the geological conditions were appropriate for its production. It seems that very little, if any, of this natron was exported over considerable distances, in contrast to the natron of Mangari and Muniyo.

Trona (*ungurnu*), which was found in the western Kanem province of Foli, in a region between Rig Rig and Liwa, was produced in great quantities and for export. Technically, *ungurnu* is a particularly pure form of trona and soda, with trona predominating, but in the central Sudan it was considered a form of natron. It differed in appearance from the natron of Mangari and Maniyo, as Barth observed in 1850, because *ungurnu* was always

in large pieces like stone, and is carried in nets, while that coming from Muniyo consists entirely of rubble, and is conveyed in bags, or a sort of basket. The former is called 'kilbu tsarafu' [in Kanuri], while the latter is 'kilbu boktor'.[87]

Barth was unable to learn more about *ungurnu* than its Kanem origins, but it is instructive that he recognised – and described – the differences between the types of natron, while he did not record the existence of *manda* salt. *Ungurnu* production, at least, was an important industry in the 1850s, and other material on the kola trade between Asante and the Hausa cities indicates that *ungurnu* was a major item of export even earlier.[88]

The Tilho expedition of 1906–09 found that *ungurnu* was being produced at Kelbouram, Bedara, Liwa, Tergouna and Anjia, while Vial and Luxeuil reported in 1938 that natron came from the canton of Liwa: Njile, Liwa, Arou, Sol, Mayala and Bedara; and from the canton of Ngelea: Keya, Ouadani, Amis (not identified), Soundourom (Soutarom?), Diklia, Gadi Bol (Gadi Ndia?), Bodoufanana (Fanana), Boula Kouloufourom (not identified) and Anjia (Table 4.3).[89] Variations in the level of Lake Chad, and consequently the extent of seepage through the north-east littoral, affected these depressions and determined which were exploited. Exploitation can begin as early as December, once the water from the rainy season has evaporated from the

Table 4.3   *Trona deposits of foli*

Name of deposit	Area of deposit (ha)
Canton of Liwa	
Liwa	50
Bedara	22
Gadi-Yala	15
Arou	15
Njile	29
Moussoro	80
Njikar	38
Soundourom	11
Makairoua	8
Mayala	14
Canton of Ngelea	
Gadi Ndia	39
Kaya	27
Diklia	30
Kaourou Ndia	11
Anjia	14
Fanana	4
Sol	19
Sol Ndara	6
Ouadani	30
Ouadani Ndia	25
Ngollom	22
Soulia	41
Ndea	12
Djara	65
Labia	37
Choua	80
Total: 26 deposits	744

Source: Bouquet (1974), 132

depressions, but because the level of Lake Chad reaches its maximum in January, thereby raising the level of the water table in the region of Foli, the depressions can become submerged again. The annual crest of Lake Chad also fluctuates with long-term changes in the level of the lake, so that in years when the lake is at its greatest extent, production in the depressions can only begin in the middle of March. Mosrin observed the lake under these conditions, and not until the waters had evaporated some 50 cm in the lake itself was it possible to begin extracting *ungurnu* in the depressions. This delay cut the production season from seven months to four months, the season ending in July.[90] As has been described in Chapter 3, however, the reserves of trona and soda are so considerable that the amount of *ungurnu* produced was not affected seriously. Recent studies of the *ungurnu* deposits by Mosrin, Couty and Bouquet have shown that there are twenty-nine depressions which have been worked more or less regularly since 1949, and many of these sites are the same as recorded by the Tilho expedition, Freydenberg and other early observers (Table 4.3). Mosrin calculated that a surface area of 744 ha consisting of twenty-six deposits was mined more or less regularly from 1949 to 1965. The conditions at another 456 deposits were insufficient for exploitation, although some of them may have been worked at some time in the past. The productive deposits were all located in the cantons of Liwa and Ngelea. Mosrin's survey of twenty-six deposits revealed an average area of 28.6 ha.[91]

The extraction of the trona involves the removal of the top layer of the depression, which is cut into slabs ranging from 5 to 10 cm thick by 60–80 cm long and 40 cm wide – roughly elliptical in shape.[92] Freydenberg, who studied the Lake Chad region and its geology, observed the process in 1909.

> The blocks of natron which crystallise under these conditions are 5–10 cm thick; they are not found everywhere. To find them, the local people probe the ground with an iron rod; when they feel some resistance, they probe around it to see whether the slab is of the desired size. They then lift it out of the mud, cut the natron with an axe and extract the block by means of wooden levers. The block is then shaped into its final form and cleaned of the slime which dirties it. The blocks that are thus prepared are buried in sand in the shade of a tree in order to dry them. This drying process lasts about two weeks, after which the blocks are loaded on oxen and carried to market.[93]

This top layer, *dugulum* or white natron, was exported south of Lake Chad and was considered inferior in quality to the *ungurnu* below the surface, although in fact the chemical composition of the two layers is very similar. The slabs of *dugulum* weighed 10–20 kg in the early part of the century. More recently, slabs of 25–38 kg have been extracted. The *dugulum* slabs, if they were extracted in perfect condition, were considered the best quality, called *biu*; if the slabs needed repair because of holes, they were filled with small pieces, held into place by a mortar made of moistened salt from the pits. A third quality (*doctor*) was made by reconstituting a slab from the debris; again salt mortar was used to hold the pieces together.[94]

Once the slabs had been removed to a depth of about 1 m, the dark sediment under the surface layer of *dugulum* was then extracted. This dark sediment – 'black' natron – was considered better quality than the *dugulum*, and its primary market was across Lake Chad in Borno and beyond. The sediment was composed of several layers. The top (*tougour*) contained small pieces weighing less than 1 kg each, including *fona fona* (*gali*), clear crystals but fragile, and *kaourou koulfou* – the heart of the natron – which was compact and hard. The two layers (*gombul* and *gobkoro*) below the *tougour* had larger and larger pieces which increased with depth. The bottom layer, *gobkoro*, contained large masses of crystallised *ungurnu*, which were cut into slabs like the *dugulum* layer. The very dark *gobkoro* slabs were particularly sought after, for they were very dense and could weigh as much as 15–30 kg.[95]

By comparison with other production sites, only the salines of Bilma and

Illustration 4.4 Loading blocks of trona

Fachi appear to have been capable of as intensive output as the mining of *ungurnu* in Foli. The technological level of the industry in each of these sites was relatively low. Natural conditions had created huge reserves of common salt, soda and trona which were processed without the necessity of filtering, boiling or other processing which required capital investment. Only the iron tools used in the extraction of the salts were needed in the production process. In terms of output alone, however, the Foli works were even more productive than Bilma and Fachi, because at Bilma and Fachi the salts were mixed in order to make *kantu*. The technology of the Bilma–Fachi industry made possible only the limited production of the relatively pure *beza*; the additional processing sacrificed quality for quantity. In Foli, by contrast, there was little additional processing other than repairing broken or incomplete slabs. The natural salt, being almost pure trona and soda, was mined for its own sake. Because of the absence of sodium chloride in the deposits, *ungurnu* did not satisfy the same market demand, and the quantity was sufficient for there to be no need to dilute it. *Ungurnu* was the only salt in the central Sudan which was comparable to the rock salt of Ijil, Amadror, Taoudeni and other Saharan sources. Like these other salts it was shaped into blocks or bars; only *ungurnu* was not sodium chloride, as the desert salts were.

SALT AND NATRON IN THE WESTERN DALLOLS

The production of salt and natron in the various tributary valleys of the Niger River in what is today north-western Nigeria and western Niger bore many

79

similarities to the salt and natron industry of the Borno sahel. Because the salt occurs as an efflorescence as the water of the rainy season evaporates, the salts are a mixture of different compounds which could only partially be separated under indigenous technology. In the two major locations, Dallol Fogha and Dallol Bosso, salt and a mixture of salt and natron were produced through a process of filtering and boiling, in which the product was formed in distinctive moulds. In other places, including many minor sites, natron was scraped from the ground and distributed for livestock use and, more rarely, for mixing with tobacco and for use as medicine. These places included Bunza, Zaura, Suru, the Kulwa marsh, and other places scattered along the Sokoto River, as well as a few locations near Ilorin, Kano and Zaria.[96] Natron was also worked in small quantities near Dosey, north of Sokoto, and in the upper reaches of the Dallol Bosso, which connects with the valley of Teguidda n'tesemt.[97]

The most important centre of production was Dallol Fogha.[98] Barth may have failed to notice salt production in Mangari, but when he visited Dallol Fogha in June 1853, he passed at least four salt-hamlets and learned of more. The one where he stayed, near Kawara-Debe, was situated on an artificial mound of rubbish, which

> was of considerable size, measuring about 200 yards in length and the same in breadth, with an elevation of 50 feet toward the bottom of the valley, and about 20 toward the edge of the bank, the whole of this mound bearing evident proof of its artificial character, consisting as it did of nothing but the soil of the valley itself, from which the saline particles had been extracted. The salt is here prepared in the following manner. The earth is taken from the bottom of the vale and put into large funnels made of straw and reeds, when water is poured upon the earth, and strained through the funnels, after which it is caught in vessels placed underneath, and then boiled, and the sediment formed into the shape of a small loaf.[99]

Elsewhere in the Fogha, grass was burned to produce salt-ash, which was then filtered and boiled. Fogha salt was greyish-yellow and 'of a much better quality than the bitter salt of Bilma'.[100]

The process of salt-making required the removal of the top layer of earth, which accounts for the debris observed by Barth, before the salt-earth could be carried to the salt-hamlets (*tunga*), where it was filtered and boiled. The filters (*koko*), roughly 1–1.5 m in diameter were made of palm fronds, placed on three or four wooden supports which were raised about 1 m off the ground. Each filtering device in Dallol Fogha held 50–60 kg of salt-earth, when filled three-quarters full.[101] As in Mangari, salt-earth was washed with brine from the basin. Earthen pots collected the more concentrated brine under the filters, after which the concentrated brine was boiled on a wood fire. Unlike the Mangari industry, there were no ovens; the boiling pots were put directly on the fire, as was done in the production of *kige*. Furthermore, the brine was not allowed to boil dry. Instead it was removed while still moist and then placed in moulds. Rochette identified two moulds: the large cylindrical moulds (*dila pese*), made of palm tresses, were 80 cm long and 20–25 cm in diameter,

80

weighing 12–15 kg. The smaller moulds (*pese*), also cylindrical, weighed 8–10 kg. Tercel noted that the salt blocks weighed only 2.5–4.0 kg.[102] Although Barth did not provide information on some of the details of the industry, his account is sufficiently detailed to indicate that the technical aspects of production were relatively unchanged from 1853 to the early twentieth century.

When Faure compared the industry in the two separate parts of Dallol Fogha (the lower valley, 40–60 km below the confluence with the Dallol Maouri, and the upper valley around the seasonal lake of Bara), he found that the debris at one site in the south was a mound 15 m high, several dozen metres wide, and 100 m long. A radio-carbon dating was obtained from the exterior base of this mound which indicates that it is at least 370 years old ($\pm$ 110), which suggests a date around 1600.[103] This mound is almost the same size as the one reported by Barth at Kawara-Debe, located in the northern production zone.[104]

The techniques of production were the same for both parts of Dallol Fogha, only the brine was more concentrated in the north. Consequently, less firewood and fewer man-hours were required in producing salt there. In 1963 Faure estimated that more than twice as much firewood was needed in the south, 9,400 bundles of wood as compared with 3,990 bundles in the north, to produce an estimated 500 tonnes of salt in each sector.[105]

Similar techniques to those of Dallol Fogha were also used in Dallol Bosso, although on a smaller scale. Dallol Bosso, located further west than Dallol Fogha, was divided into two areas of production. In the upper portion of the Dallol at Tounga Amarzia, Birni, Souda, Barbe, Loudoudie, and Bagaouamou, natron was made through a process of filtering and boiling. The moulds produced bars which weighed about 25 kg. In the south, at Diankoto, Guiladjie, Alfa Koara, Belande, and Koudie, salt was made in a similar fashion, producing bars which weighed 5 kg. each. Production lasted from January through May.[106] Monteil noticed the production of both salt and natron through the use of these techniques in 1891.[107] Besides the smaller scale of production, the Dallol Bosso industry differed from that of Dallol Fogha in that natron was actually produced in the same way as salt, possibly because Dallol Bosso was so far from the other major sources of natron – the Borno sahel and Kawar. Consequently, local natron could benefit from the lower cost of transport to supply some of the western markets which Borno natron also supplied.

Barth's observation, the earliest description of Dallol Fogha salt production, is important in its own right but also because of Barth's failure to identify a comparable industry in Mangari. There is an obvious basis for comparing salt production in the two regions. Pales, for example, has suggested that the filtering devices in Dallol Fogha were probably the inspiration for the filters of Mangari, but his reasoning is based on the inaccurate information that the workers in both regions were Hausa, which is true for Dallol Fogha but not for Mangari.[108] None the less, the similarity in filters is striking, but the terminology is not the same. The filters are called *koko* in Dallol Fogha and *gamba* in Mangari. Pales' explanation also does not take account of the filters used in *kige* production; hence it must be concluded that it is not possible to establish an influence of the Mangari–Kadzell filters on the Dallol Fogha industry or *vice versa*. Gouletquer and Kleinmann have admitted a possible connexion too, but they have pointed out an important difference in the techniques.[109] The salt of Dallol Fogha is not allowed to boil dry, as it is in Mangari. Rather, the salt is removed when it is a thick paste and put into moulds. This technique, together with the absence of ovens in Dallol Fogha, makes it very difficult to draw any connexions between the industries of the two regions, despite the established antiquity of the Dallol Fogha industry and the lack of evidence for an early salt industry in Mangari.

SALT FROM BRINE IN THE BENUE TROUGH

The brine springs of the Benue trough were scattered over a wide area; many were relatively unimportant and only supplied local demand (Table 4.4). The largest were at Awe, Keana, and Akwana, although the proximity of a number of smaller sites near Awe and Keana enabled Abuni, Kanje, Ribi, Azara and Arufu to contribute significantly to the total output of the Benue industry. Other small sites – Nassarawa, Lafin Gishiri, and the sites in the Gongola basin – were marginal; the fact that they were worked at all attests more to the scale of demand in the region than to their potential. At some places, such as Jebjeb and Barkar, only a few square metres of salt flats were workable, so that production took place only every other year. At Bomanda, the alluvium covered an area of approximately 260 ha, which allowed the output of more salt there than at any of the other sites in the Gongola River region. Jebero, which was deserted in 1905, may have produced as much as Bomanda at some time in the past because of the presence of fairly good brine springs.[110]

A number of sites, including Keana and some neighbouring locations, depended upon springs found at the bottom of pits, wells, or lakes which had to be drained of rain-water before the processing of brine could begin.[111] Production at these sites involved a larger labour input than at sahelian and desert sites, where because of the rainy season the length of the working year was much less, perhaps only a third to one half as long. At Keana, for example, a pit approximately 80 m long and 40 m wide and some 17–20 m deep had to be cleared of water. Once drained – which took 3–5 days – the brine was allowed to seep in, but if a late rain struck then the pit had to be emptied again. Salt-making could not begin until eight days after the draining. There were also two smaller pits and three other brine springs that were worked, but less labour was involved in preparing these sources for production. In some years drainage did not begin until early to mid-January and rains began in March,[112] although the normal season was four months. The Keana pit was the biggest, but at other Benue sites water had to be drained or, at least, production could not begin until some evaporation of rain-water

Table 4.4 *Sources of brine for salt-making, Benue–Cross River basins*

I. Benue Basin

A. Gongola River–Bomada Region

1.	Ayabe	11.	Langa (Ranga)
2.	Bage	12.	Mutum Daya
3.	Barkar	13.	Nafada
4.	Bomanda	14.	Pero Hills
5.	Gyakan	15.	Pindiga
6.	Gujba	16.	Takulma
7.	Jarowo	17.	Todi
8.	Jebero (Jabrin)	18.	Tumu
9.	Jebjeb	19.	Wuza
10.	Jende	20.	Zanga

B. Awe–Keana–Akwana Region

1.	Abuni	9.	Karkure
2.	Akiri	10.	Keana
3.	Akwana	11.	Lankaku
4.	Arufu	12.	Lengrel River
5.	Awe	13.	Moi Igbo
6.	Azara	14.	Nassarawa
7.	Dofa	15.	Ribi
8.	Kanje	16.	Northern Tiv country,

II. Cross River Basin

A. Ogoja Region

1.	Abatchor	7.	Igbekureku	13.	Okpoma
2.	Akrafo	8.	Ijegu		
3.	Aloda	9.	Itegaokudu		
4.	Echimoga	10.	Okircha		
5.	Gabu	11.	Okpene		
6.	Ibeku-Rekor	12.	Okpodo		

B. Abakaliki Area

1.	Abakaliki	7.	Isiagu
2.	Ameka	8.	Iyi-Oku River
3.	Amori	9.	Nkaliki
4.	Enyibichiri	10.	Okpuru
5.	Ike	11.	Obegu
6.	Ikwo		

C. Afikpo Area

1.	Achara	4.	Okpesi-Uku
2.	Eseukwu	5.	Uburu Lake
3.	Okayi		

D. Ikom Area

1.	Abunerok Abia	6.	Nbenyan
2.	Aiyawaba	7.	Nsanakang
3.	Danare	8.	Okuni
4.	Ikom	9.	Odukpani
5.	Mbakang		

Sources: Beltaro and Bojarski (unpublished, 1971); Afigbo (1976): Abubakar (unpublished, 1974); Wilkinson, 26 October 1939, Lafia Div 2/1 351; Falconer, Report No. 5, 22 February 1905, SNP 7/10 3513/1904, Nigerian National Archives, Kaduna; Duffill to author, 1 April 1976.

Illustration 4.5 Keana salt works

had occurred.[113] Only at Awe and possibly at Ribi was it not necessary to drain the rain-water.

Because the brines were weak, methods were often employed which concentrated the salt. At Awe, the extensive flats around the town eventually dried up after the rains had stopped, so that the sun could dry

> the wet salt-impregnated earth causing the salt to crystallise on the surface, this top layer of earth is scraped away and taken into the town to be filtered, then a new layer of earth is brought from near by to replace the original layer, this is sprinkled with the water from the oozing trickles and pools, allowed to dry, scraped off when the salt has come to the surface, and carried into the town. This process is gone through as often as the season permits. The first heavy rains usually put an end to the working for that year.[114]

As was the case at other sites, the peak season lasted four months, with reduced production continuing for another four months, but heavy rains could shorten the season considerably.

In the washing and filtering stage of the operations, scrapings from the marshes (Hausa: *fadama*) were put in filtering pots, which were usually mounted in twos or threes above a split bamboo, palm frond, or other trough-

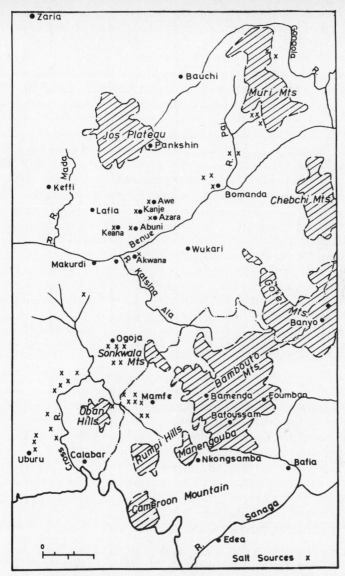

Map 4.2   The brine springs of the Benue–Cross River region

like fixture. The scrapings were washed with the natural brine, and the concentrated solution was allowed to drain into boiling pots. Filtering and boiling continued until the boiling pot was full of salt. This operation necessitated the use of large quantities of firewood, as well as pots to replace those broken in the fire during the final stage of the boiling process.

Further south, brine was often boiled directly, without any intermediary stage of solar evaporation and filtering. This method was less efficient, for it required more firewood, which meant that it could only be used in areas with many trees. At sites near Moi Igbo, south of Makurdi, for example, firewood was plentiful, which also suggests that the scale of production was very small. In Ogoja, too, no filtering process seems to have been followed. At Uburu, however, the technique was similar to that at Keana, Awe and other Benue sites,[115] and it appears that Uburu output was on roughly the same scale.

Finally, output was determined by the rate of flow from the brine springs. In March 1965, late in the season, Kanje was actually dry, and work had ceased. At Azara, the springs were producing 38 litres per day, and consequently the sprinkling process was confined to only a few calabashes at a time. Only at Awe (and Uburu Lake) did the springs produce sufficient water to maintain operations at a peak until the rainy season ended production. The discharge at Awe was greater than at any other Benue site. Two boreholes were drilled at Awe in 1905, which appear to have increased brine output dramatically – it rose to 10,200 litres per hour at one (although the weakest) spring. The weak brine flooded the marshes around the town, thereby cutting down on the size of the drying flats. It is likely that the complaints of the Awe workers that production decreased as a result of this drilling are true. The constraint at many sites was the lack of brine from the springs.[116] This was not a problem at Awe, where the shortage of firewood and drying flats for solar evaporation was the main problem.

OTHER SALTS

The demand for salt was so great that a variety of other salts were also available in the central Sudan. Sea salt was brought up the Niger River from the lagoons of the delta, where fishing and salt-making communities were long established.[117] Elsewhere along the Guinea Coast, sea salt was also exported into the interior, where it competed with the salt and natron of the central Sudan.[118] Vegetable salt was produced from *acha* (*Digitaria exilis*, also known as *fonio* or 'hungry rice'), guinea corn stalks, used indigo, and even dried dung.[119] Techniques of production were similar to the methods used in filtering brine and boiling the brine dry. As Shea has noted, local plants and dung were burned to produce ashes which

> are deposited in a clay pot which has holes on the bottom, and a grass mat or some fibrous material is placed over the holes, forming a sieve which prevents the ash from falling through. This pot is then placed over another, and water is poured onto the ashes in the top pot. This water filters through the ashes, and passes through the sieve into the pot beneath where the ash water is gathered. This water which is collected in the bottom pot contains the salts which have been filtered out of the ashes. The water can then be evaporated out to produce dry salts, but frequently it is poured directly into stews for flavouring. It is this ash water which is (also) used as a mordant in indigo dyeing in many areas, and it was probably one of the earliest mordants used in the dyeing process in West Africa.[120]

86

In the Hausa textile industry, ash water was largely replaced by *katso* ashes, the burned residue of indigo in the bottom of pits. Elsewhere, vegetable salts were processed in different ways. In southern Jema'are, for example, salt obtained from *acha* ash was 'mixed with some grains of *acha* and fried until it forms a kind of pulp', [121] while Rohlfs noted in 1867 that 'the ashes of the runo tree' were used to make salt near Bauchi. [122] Vegetable salt, known as *tomguli* in Mbamga and *mbiyanghab* in Sah, was produced in large quantities in Mambila, particularly in the villages of the Donga and May Gertogal river valleys – including Ndum Yaji, Antere, Inkiri, Sah, and War Kaka. These areas were rich in elephant grass, whose ashes were filtered to make salt. [123] Similar salts were made to the south of Lake Chad. [124]

European salt was processed for the Nigerian market, especially by the Kakanda, who lived along the Niger between the confluence with the Benue and the town of Eggan. They operated to Lagos in the nineteenth century and were probably responsible for introducing imported salt in adulterated form. It was ' "Cooked" by the trader into cylinders about 6 inches in diameter which is then sold in slices of about 1 inch thick'. [125] *Gishirin kakanda* – European salt – was 'often pressed into earthen moulds and then baked hard by building a fire over and around the mould. When cold, the lump is dug out of the mould, which is always pyramid-shaped, and the cake is sold as *gishirin kantu* either as the whole mould or in slices. The process of manufacture of *gishirin kantu* can be watched in any large market-place' – McCulloch observed its manufacture in Kano and Malamfashi. [126]

Perhaps there is no more instructive example of the low technological level of salt production than this adulteration of European salt – pure sodium chloride – which had to satisfy local taste and compete with the impure indigenous salts. The 1832 expedition to the confluence of the Niger and Benue took salt as one of the commodities to be traded there, and it was found to be in considerable demand:

> The greatest profit was on salt; we cannot say at what per centage, but it was very great. It is, indeed, the article which must bring the most sure return, as it is for immediate consumption, and the natives have no other means of supply than that from Bishi [Abushi, the Benue port for Akwana, Awe and other salines], which is dear and bad; so that they ate our beautiful white salt like sugar. [127]

Subsequently, salt was always a major export north along the Niger River. Baikie estimated that 2,000 bags of European salt, about 40 tonnes, was imported in 1862; he thought the market could take 100 tonnes. [128] Whether or not these early imports were adulterated is unknown, but it seems likely in the light of later evidence. Greater profits could be generated, apparently, by sacrificing quality for quantity, as the producers at Bilma and Fachi already knew. Because technology had not developed to a point which pure sodium chloride could be produced in substantial quantities, consumers were willing to accept mixtures; indeed the taste for salt developed in response to the technological capabilities of local industry. Distinctions were made between the various salts, but people responding to this cultural adaptation considered common salt only one among many varieties, and ironically not as 'good' as other salts. The desire in the central Sudan was for a relatively pure sodium chloride which was mixed with varying amounts of other salts. Imported European salt was not an acceptable substitute unless its purity was reduced. Vischer, who studied the Borno industry in 1905–06, considered the local salts 'substitutes' for salt; in fact his Euro-centric view prevented him from realising the extent of the cultural barrier which separated his world from the societies which he had come to govern.

THE LOW LEVEL OF TECHNOLOGY

The salt producers attempted to utilise the process of solar evaporation to maximum advantage, but they made relatively minor advances in technology. No area of salt production has received more attention than the process of graduation, whereby brines are concentrated through solar evaporation, boiling or both, and there were some improvements in these techniques in the central Sudan.[129] By comparison with the long, open buildings – graduation houses – or the improved furnace techniques at some European works in the late eighteenth and early nineteenth centuries, these changes in the central Sudan are not very impressive. Whereas graduation can be improved through the circulation of brine over bundles of straw, porous clay, a dense mass of thorns, rope or other materials that effectively increase the surface area for atmospheric evaporation, solar evaporation alone – without the aid of artificial techniques – was usually sufficient in the central Sudan. Even where fires were used for boiling the brine, solar evaporation was so efficient that there were few attempts at fuel conservation. Boiling devices were relatively simple; only in Mangari were ovens used.

Because of the rapid rate of solar evaporation in the sahel and desert, there was little need to develop technology to improve output through increased graduation. With the exception of Teguidda n'tesemt, none of the sahel and desert sites relied on man-made techniques. Natural basins provided sufficient brine for production purposes. At Teguidda, the series of decantation basins made increased production possible; this innovation represented a true technological breakthrough and seems to have been inspired by the ancient irrigation networks and saline works associated with copper production at Azelik in the Middle Ages. At the Benue sites, graduation was increased through the use of flats where the brine was allowed to evaporate until a concentrate could be removed to the boiling houses. Access to drying flats, not brine, was the main determinant of output. Considering the shorter production season in the Benue Valley, it is no wonder that evaporation was the key variable. Despite these exceptions, salt production in the central Sudan is noteworthy for the lack of artificial graduation to increase solar evaporation. The overwhelming quantity of salt was produced without efforts to improve the rate of evaporation by solar means.

The most advanced techniques to increase graduation by boiling were developed in Mangari, and while current knowledge can date the origins of the Mangari ovens only to the early nineteenth century, it is possible that ovens were used in preceding centuries. These ovens involved several improvements in technology; the boiling pots were removed from the open fire, thereby increasing fuel efficiency. The scale of production – as many as 150 pots in a single oven – resulted in larger work units and greater specialisation. It is likely that this scale also resulted in increased output. Elsewhere, boiling operations were simpler. Although the design of the boiling apparatus in Kadzell, Dallol Fogha and the Benue sites differed, the salt was boiled on an open fire, with a resulting loss of efficiency in fuel consumption. The Benue salines combined different techniques of graduation – man-made drying flats and boiling – to increase yields; this combination of techniques represented a particularly significant advance in technology. Still, there was no attempt at drilling to increase the rate of flow of brine, and boiling could have been made more efficient through the development or the spread of ovens. Dallol Fogha relied on natural evaporation in the valley before the brine was transferred to the boiling villages; this procedure was similar to the one followed in Mangari and Muniyo, but no ovens were used. The Kadzell salines depended upon brine from wells which was then placed directly on an open fire, without atmospheric graduation. No containers were developed for solar evaporation, as was done at Teguidda, where the sandstone shield provided a natural floor for the decantation basins.

The fact that different salts precipitate out of solution at different temperatures and concentrations was a factor in production in the desert sites and some places in the sahel, but this knowledge was not the basis of a scientific understanding of salt production. While it was readily observed that crystals of different salts – most notably sodium chloride but also sodium sulphate and other salts – formed on the sides of containers or evaporating depressions, the salt workers did not exploit this knowledge to advantage. It was impossible to separate fully the different salts with the available technology, although at Fachi and probably Bilma workers were aware of the principle of crystallisation and tried to remove the *beza* from solution at the most opportune moment. They even flushed the *beza* in solution to wash off the less-pure *minto*. Such attempts at purification hardly affected price, however. [130] Crystals were collected, and concentrations of specific mixtures were altered through the transfer of brine, but more refined techniques were not developed. The mother liquor (that residue of impurities and various minor salts in a particular solution) was not separated; in other salt manufactories, workers discovered that a purer salt could be obtained by not letting a solution boil or evaporate dry. The mother liquor could then be separated, so that the heavily-laden brine that was siphoned off would be purer. [131]

The relative technological backwardness of the central Sudan salt industry – due perhaps to the natural advantages of solar evaporation –

explains why there was such variation in the types of salt available on the market. The impurity of the salt was a measure of the low level of technological development; just as the sophistication of consumer distinctions was a consequence. Producers failed to apply the innovations introduced at one saline to another; the ovens of Mangari may have been adapted for the production of *kige*, but only at those sites immediately adjacent to the Mangari salt works. The advantages of ovens were lost to the salt workers of the Benue basin and Dallol Fogha. Similarly, the knowledge of salt chemistry – especially the distinctions between sodium chloride, sodium sulphate and sodium carbonate – was not utilised, probably because a recognition of these distinctions could not have been adopted into the productive process in a manner that would have increased output. Quality would have improved, but in a situation in which almost any salt found a ready market, even when the salt was very impure, there was little advantage in improving quality. As the production techniques at Bilma and Fachi – where high quality *beza* was mixed with impurities to make *kantu* – demonstrate, or as the adulteration of imported European salt to 'satisfy' consumer preferences makes clear, salt workers chose to sacrifice quality for quantity. Such a choice invariably lessened the possibilities that technology would be harnessed in order to increase production. Whatever other reasons there were for the technological backwardness of the industry (and political insecurity, the poverty of large sections of the population, and climatic irregularities were not insignificant obstacles to improvements in production) market demand for salt – any salt – had a negative impact on the development of the salt industry.

The relationship between market demand for salt and the level of technological development of salt production had an important influence on the purity and quantity of salt. The wide variety of uses for the various salts resulted in the diversification of demand; impure salts were needed in textile production, dyeing, medicinal formulae, livestock care, and tobacco consumption, and the expansion of these markets probably retarded the development of demand for purer salt for cooking. Salt workers had a ready market for whatever salt they produced, and price differentials do not appear to have been sufficiently pronounced to have encouraged the production of better quality salt, especially pure sodium chloride. Those who could afford relatively pure sodium chloride provided some incentive for improving the techniques of production, but this portion of central Sudan society was too small to influence the market sufficiently to shift production strategies away from the production of greater quantities of salt and natron to increased output of *beza*, the diversion of the Benue salts away from local markets, and the maintenance of imported European salt in its pure form. A more prosperous class of merchants, craftsmen and farmers who could afford to pay more for salt might have spurred salt workers and merchants to produce more salt in which sodium chloride was dominant, but this situation had not developed by the end of the nineteenth century.

It can be concluded, therefore, that the natural advantages of solar evaporation pre-empted further technological change, and furthermore, that market demand was not discriminating enough to require the further purification and separation of the different salts. Despite experiments with various methods of increasing solar evaporation, the level of technological development remained low. The many and varied – indeed often ingenious – uses of salt were a direct consequence of this retarded technology. The presence of different mixtures that ranged widely in purity is striking proof of the failure to develop salt technology.

What do these conclusions tell us about the history of technology in the central Sudan? They suggest that technological development in general was retarded, although not static. The salt industry experienced several changes – the development of ovens, the construction of decantation basins, and the use of filters. In general, however, the industry expanded or contracted as workers were able to apply well-established technology to a greater or smaller number of salines. Workers could extend the industry, but they could do little to increase productivity. The mobilisation of labour, not technology, was the key variable (after climatic and geological conditions), and the availability of workers depended on political factors and the social organisation of the workers themselves.

A comparison of the salt industry with other sectors of the central Sudan economy demonstrates that technology was generally retarded. Agriculture, for example, depended on simple tools – short-handled hoes, primitive irrigation devices and crude harvesting blades.[132] Manure was applied to some gardens as fertiliser, and livestock grazed on fields after the harvest to supply additional manure. But there was little – and usually no – effort to improve seed. The absence of ploughs, wheeled vehicles and other labour-saving instruments further highlights the low level of technology. Storage facilities were equally simple; the use of mortar and pestle to grind the grain dramatically illustrates the point. There were no mills and no attempt to process grain into flour, except on a daily basis. The rhythmic pounding of millet kept women busy, but it was as inefficient as the agricultural techniques employed by men.

The textile industry was also technologically backward, although the spread of *laso* dyepits in the nineteenth century and the introduction of women's looms represented some improvement in technology.[133] The types of cotton that were grown were low-yielding varieties which quickly gave way to new strains in the colonial period. Farmers even picked the plants a second and third year, despite the great decline in output that such practices involved. Carding and spinning were hand tasks with simple tools; invariably output was inefficient, and these stages in textile production were major bottlenecks in the industry. The most common loom was narrow; strips of cloth had to be sewn together. Only in dyeing were any significant changes in the scale of production achieved. The development of bigger pits, made possible by using the residue (*laso*) from the dyeing process as a cement, increased output and resulted in the concentration of textile production between Kano and Zaria, probably on a scale previously unknown in the central Sudan. Still, one is struck by the labour intensity of textile production, and consequently this industry had the same basic problem – the low level of technological development – that characterised agriculture and salt production.

Finally, transport was no better off than these other sectors. Donkeys, oxen, and camels were used to transport large quantities of goods, often over considerable distances. But livestock movements followed transhumant cycles which meant that animals were more readily available in some seasons than in others. Roads were poorly developed; there were no carts or other wheeled vehicles. The ability to move goods was dependent, therefore, on the size of the animal population and the necessity of deploying this population over a vast region that was characterised by poor communications. Invariably, the low level of technology meant that market forces were very imperfectly developed. Weaknesses in the transport sector strongly retarded the expansion of agriculture, textile production and salt output, as well as virtually every other sector in the central Sudan economy.[134]

A comparison of salt technology with agricultural techniques, textile production and transportation indicates that a fundamental component of central Sudanese society was a poorly-developed technology which crippled intellectual and entrepreneurial activity. People made little effort to develop or apply new technology that would have increased productivity. The weaknesses of one sector inevitably retarded other sectors of the economy, which thereby discouraged technological innovation in general. All sectors remained labour intensive; there were few economies of scale that could have been achieved in any sector. As a result, the control of labour – through a variety of means – was of fundamental importance to this social formation. Technological developments that would have increased the level of productivity would have shifted the relationships of production away from a concern for the control of labour to a greater interest in the control of the instruments of production. People were what mattered, however, and this preoccupation with the organisation of labour further crippled intellectual and entrepreneurial innovation. Production could be expanded through the exploitation of more labour; that is, production could be extended. Production was not expanded through technological change; that is, it was not intensified.

The fact that the salt industry suffered from a failure to improve technology is indirect proof that the potential demand for salt based on a calculation of average annual consumption of 4.5 kg per person exceeded the supply. Despite the great number of locations where salt was produced, the combined output of these sources had to satisfy a wide geographical region with a very large population. Estimates of this population are mere guesses, but Hill's haphazard figure of 10 million people for the Sokoto Caliphate alone is a useful figure in calculating the possible volume of salt demand.[135] Human consumption of 45,000 tonnes, together with livestock consumption and industrial uses, suggests a big market indeed. While local production of vegetable salts would have accounted for some, if not a lot, of this volume, the salt industry would still have had to be on a level of tens of thousands of tonnes of salt per year to satisfy this large market, even if many poor people consumed little or no salt. As is apparent in the discussion that follows in Chapter 5, this volume was not attained.

5

The volume of salt production

Any effort at quantifying the volume of trade and production in the pre-colonial and early colonial periods of African history, especially for indigenous sectors like the salt industry, must be undertaken with extreme caution.[1] Yet an attempt is made here to establish parameters on the size of the trade. There is no sure way of determining which figures are representative of output at particular salines, and there is almost no possibility of reconstructing a series of production figures. None the less, the need for reasonable estimates is clear; the nature of the data, when analysed carefully, allows some assessment of the relative importance of different salines, a rough idea of the number of manhours per tonne of salt produced, and an indication of which sectors were most important in the commerce of the central Sudan. In order to assess the volume of salt production, it is necessary to work backward from early colonial and more contemporary estimates. Fortunately, a number of scientific studies are available which supplement the scattered trade statistics and general observations of earlier observers. These different sorts of data are here combined as a means of establishing preliminary estimates of the scale of production, although it may never be possible to derive more accurate figures.

In general, the salt sources in the sahel and Sahara produced greater quantities of salt than the brine springs of the Benue trough. The usual assumption – based in part on a comparison with the great desert salines of the western Sudan, including Taoudeni and Ijil – is that the production of salt in Kawar and Fachi supplied the bulk of the salt trade. This statement is true with respect to salts with high sodium chloride content and may have been true in particular periods or certain years in the past, but if all salts are taken into consideration, far more salt was probably produced in the sahel – at least in the late nineteenth century – than in the desert (Table 5.1). Indeed output in the Borno sahel alone surpassed that at all other sites combined, at least in normal years at the end of the nineteenth century, and if Kanem output of trona is included in the estimate, then the ascendency of the Borno sectors is even more striking. It is unclear whether or not the Borno sahel produced as much salt and natron before the end of the nineteenth century, but since Kawar and Fachi were once part of the Borno state, until the late eighteenth century when their dependence became only nominal at best, the salt industry of the central Sudan can be considered to have been largely an industry centred on Borno. The output of Teguidda n'tesemt, Amadror, the western

94

Table 5.1   *Estimates of central Sudan salt production*

Source	Estimated volume (tonnes)
Kawar and Fachi (all types)	2,300–5,400
manda (Mangari)	1,000–4,000
kanwa (Mangari, Muniyo)	1,000–4,000
ungurnu (Kanem)	1,000–1,500
kige (Kadzell and Chad shores)	200–400
Dallol Fogha	500–700
Dallol Bosso	200–300
Benue basin sites	
(Awe, Keana, etc.)	1,300–2,000
vegetable salt	
(other than *kige*)	no estimate, large
Amadror	100–300
Taoudeni (for sale in the	
Central Sudan)	no estimate, small
Teguidda n'tesemt	400–600

Dallols, the Benue brines, and the other, minor sites supplemented the Borno industry, but the combined volume of all these other sites probably never amounted to more than a quarter to a third of the total output of the central Sudan salines. The production of vegetable salts would have lowered the Borno share somewhat more, but the dominance of Borno is still clear.

KAWAR AND FACHI

Estimates for Kawar and Fachi production are most complete for the first decade of the twentieth century, but unfortunately at that time the industry was suffering severe dislocation in the wake of Rabeh's conquest of Borno, insecurity in Kanem, and the subsequent European intervention in the area. Although the French began to provide convoys for caravans crossing from Agades to Bilma in the early twentieth century, the 1890s had been such a chaotic time that it is doubtful if the trade ever recovered to its former height. First, Tuareg and Daggera transporters had fewer camels than they had owned earlier, in part because the French began to commandeer them and in part because of highway robbery in the Kawar and Fachi region.[2] Nevertheless, figures assembled by the French provide an important departure for a quantitative analysis of Kawar–Fachi output (Table 5.2). These data show that the volume of the main caravans alone was of the order of 2,000–2,300 tonnes per year.

French estimates of the annual level of exports just before their arrival range from 10,000 to 25,000 camel loads, but the upper amount seems preferable in light of the first exact figures, which derive from the early customs post at Djadjidouna.[3] In the fiscal year 1903–04 it was reported that

Table 5.2 *Volume of salt and dates ex-ported from Fachi and Bilma, 1903–14*

Year	Export (tonnes)
1903/4	2,270
1905	n.a.
1906	1,254
1907	1,591
1908	1,881
1909	1,425
1910	n.a.
1911	2,232
1912	2,472
1913	2,375
1914	1,900

Sources: The tonnage was computed from the count of the number of camels returning from the oases loaded on the average with 95 kg each. The figures for the years 1911–14 are from Baier (1980b), 237; the figure for the season 1903–04 is calculated from Baier (1980b), 125, where it is reported that 17,930 loads of salt and 184 loads of dates were recorded at Djad-jidouna, which Baier estimates represented 75 per cent of the trade. The figures for 1906–08 are from Prévôt. 1909, Archives de Bilma. The figure for 1907 includes 175 camels taken to Nguigmi, while the 1908 figure includes 80 camels on this southern route.

duty was paid on 17,930 loads of salt and 184 loads of dates, and because of the ease with which caravan movements could be detected in Damergu, it is reasonable to assume that most traffic passing this way was counted. The main branch of the salt route passed through Damergu, with a lesser one going to Kel Gress country in the west. The Djadjidouna figures represent something like 75 per cent of the yearly trade, which suggests a total of 23,900 loads or 2,270 tonnes.[4] In 1907, the French provided armed escorts for caravans, and the amount of salt rose steadily, reaching a peak in 1912, when tax collectors at Bilma recorded a total of 26,017 camels, a figure which translates into about 2,470 tonnes of salt and dates. Since the date trade represented only a fraction of the trade in salt, it can be assumed that the combined figure for both salt and dates is a close approximation for the production of salt. As the information from 1907–08 indicates, some salt was transported south to Nguigmi, and some salt was also consumed locally, exported to Kanem, or sold to Tubu nomads.[5]

Estimates earlier in the nineteenth century are based on the size of the large annual caravans, and they do not take into account the numerous, smaller expeditions which took place during safer times. Nachtigal, whose 1870 estimates for the two main caravans accord well with later figures, suggests that perhaps as many as 70,000 camel loads were exported when smaller caravans were included.[6] This would mean that perhaps 6,300 tonnes were produced, slightly less if allowance for date exports is made. Nachtigal attributed 50,000 camel loads to small caravans which visited the oasis at times other than when the main autumn and spring caravans arrived, a figure which Baier considers high by a factor of ten.[7] The autumn, spring and intervening rainy season are the only times when it pays to take camels, millet, fodder, and water across the Tenere, and in the various French reports the rainy season expeditions were always small. The 1870s was not a time when conditions were particularly safe, and the main reaction of the Tuareg was to join the annual autumn caravan, not strike out on their own in small groups.[8]

The volume of salt actually produced at Bilma, as distinct from Kawar and Fachi combined, probably varied between 1,000 and 3,000 tonnes per year. The 1,000 tonne figure is certainly low; it represents the amount which could be carried by approximately 10,600 camels, assuming a load of 95 kg. Figures from the last several decades show that even in the reduced state of production which had prevailed in contemporary times a figure of 900–1,000 tonnes is easily attained.[9] In the past, when Bilma was the main source of salt for the Tuareg caravans – perhaps amounting to two-thirds of their exports – the total must have been higher, although not high enough to fill Nachtigal's guess.

Faure's calculations on the amount of debris at Bilma, the rate of evaporation and the area of the salt works led him to estimate the volume of production at 1,000 tonnes per year. The average output, as recorded at Bilma between 1953 and 1960, supports this estimate; 1961 was a bad year with only 545 tonnes exported.[10] Despite the importance of Faure's scientific study of the Bilma industry, his calculations of volume are open to a number of criticisms. First, his estimates for the amount of debris, rate of evaporation and surface area of production all contain room for considerable error. In order not to over-estimate volume, Faure reached his conclusion on the basis of minimum figures for each variable. Thus he used 250 grams per litre (g/l) rather than 400 g/l for the capacity of production, based on a surface area of 5,000 m². On the basis of these figures, evaporation would result in the loss of 10,000 m³ of water and the precipitation of 3,750 tonnes of salt and debris. Faure then estimated that actual production of salt and debris was probably closer to 2,000 tonnes per year, and he allowed for equal volumes of salt and debris, which accounts for his estimate that 1,000 tonnes of salt were produced.[11] If, however, the debris to salt ratio was significantly different, with a greater amount of salt produced per unit of debris, then the production figure would be higher. Furthermore, if his figure of 3,750 tonnes is more accurate, then again more salt could be produced. It may also be the case that the salt workers made a slightly less pure salt in the past – thereby using more debris – which would also increase the volume of salt exported, even if its

Table 5.3   *Volume of salt exports from Fachi,*
1907–76

Year	Volume (tonnes)	Year	Volume (tonnes)
1907	635	1949	650
1909	636	1950	700
1932	280	1951	550
1935	240	1952	350
1936	225 (partial)	1953	900
1937	460	1954	370
1938	540	1955	500
1939	450	1956	600
1942	640	1957	750
1943	500	1960	600
1944	750	1962	900
1945	650	1972	1,500
1947	440	1974	700
1948	750	1976	1,000

Sources: Fuchs (1983), 55; Périé, Monographie du Poste
de Bilma, 1941, Archives de Bilma; Faure (unpublished,
1965), 143.

quality was not as good. Faure's estimate, which reflects the caution of a
scientist, may also have been influenced by the official figures for salt
exports during the 1950s, when it is known that production was actually lower
than in the past.

The Fachi portion of the annual trade was of the order of one fifth to one
third of the total. Fuchs, who has undertaken the most thorough study of the
salt industry at Fachi, has uncovered records (Table 5.3) that show that the
production of salt at Fachi varied from a low of 240 tonnes in 1935 to an
estimated 1,500 tonnes in 1972.[12] The earliest figures are for 1907 and 1909,
when 635 and 636 tonnes respectively were exported. Custom returns from the
1930s, when the trade had recovered somewhat from the disastrous aftermath
of the Tuareg revolt during World War I, range from 240 to 540 tonnes per
year, a level which was maintained into the 1960s. During the 1940s the
volume averaged 625 tonnes per year, about the same level as in the first
decade of colonial rule. Output dropped off slightly in the 1950s, declining to
an average of 590 tonnes per year between 1950 and 1957, although a peak of
900 tonnes was reached in 1953. Scattered returns since then suggest an
average output of 940 tonnes per year, which indicates what the maximum
level of production was in the past, since production techniques have not
changed significantly since the nineteenth century. These figures also demonstrate that the desert industry had not collapsed in recent years; rather
production had actually expanded. Faure's study of the salt industry at Fachi
led him to conclude that output could easily have reached 600–700 tonnes in

peak years, and the returns reported by Fuchs confirm his analysis.[13] An average of 600–700 tonnes per year seems a reasonable estimate, therefore.

Production at the northern sites in Kawar was much lower than at Fachi, let alone Bilma. At some distant time in the past, output may have been considerable, if traditions of the gradual southern movement of the salt industry can be taken to mean that the relative importance of the northern salines had declined from a once-higher level. The figures for Djado, assembled by Périé, show an output of 24 tonnes in 1936, 10.5 tonnes in 1937 and 10 tonnes in 1938,[14] and the incomplete report of Barbaste from Djado in 1938 supports the official figures of Périé. Barbaste indicates that production averaged 4–5 tonnes per month, during the five-month production season of 1937 – a total of 20–25 tonnes. In 1938, output was up slightly. The returns for four of the five months total 49 tonnes.[15] Although this amount is small by comparison with Fachi and Bilma, it does indicate that 50–60 tonnes of salt could be produced at Djado in relatively stable times.

In 1961 75.4 tonnes of *beza* were produced at Seguidine, in northern Kawar, which only required the labour of six men and their families.[16] This figure suggests that with a greater labour input, the volume of salt could be increased substantially, and it may well be that at some time in the past Seguidine production was much greater. The scattered reports from the nineteenth and the early twentieth centuries do not indicate that production in modern times was ever greater. First, the population of northern Kawar was small. Unless nomads directed their slaves in production, then the labour necessary for a substantially larger output was simply not there. Secondly, there is no indication in the accounts of Denham, Barth, Rohlfs, Nachtigal or others of a substantial export trade.

There are no reports on output at Dirku and other sites in Kawar, but output was probably small in the nineteenth century. None the less, the total production of all the salines in Kawar and at Fachi could have been much more substantial than the early colonial reports indicate. Insecurity invariably kept the actual output well below the potential, but even in moderately safe times it may well have been possible that the total volume of salt production was of the order of 2,000–6,000 tonnes. Undoubtedly in some years the figure fell below even the 2,000 tonnes figure, as it has in the twentieth century.

THE BORNO SAHEL

The combined output of the salt industry in the Borno sahel probably exceeded 4,000 tonnes per year, although geological conditions and the political situation seriously affected the amount produced. Again, the attempt at quantification will focus on the early years of the twentieth century as the best means of suggesting the possible level of production in the past. Projections backward in time must be treated especially carefully because each of the four sectors of the Borno industry had a different history. The production of trona in Kanem, for example, was probably very old, considering the extensive reserves which exist and the relative ease of exploitation. Projections for this sector could be lower than the amount actually produced in the past. For the production of *manda* in Mangari, by contrast, the estimates for the early twentieth century are likely to be much higher than the amount produced a half century or more earlier. Natron in Mangari and Muniyo may have been collected in substantial quantities before 1900, so that estimates for this sector may be a relatively accurate indicator of past potential. The problem with natron collection, however, is that it was diffused over a considerable area, and it is impossible to gauge the extent to which the various sources were actually exploited. Finally, *kige* production was probably relatively constant for a long time into the past. At least it seems to be an old industry which depended upon a relatively fixed number of wells in the sahel. There was probably considerable fluctuation in the amount of *kige* which was made in the short term, but over the course of the past several centuries output was probably not much greater than a few hundred tonnes per year.

The extraction of trona in Foli could have been extensive in the past. Since the reserves can permit the production of as much as 120,000 tonnes per year, it is certainly clear that the potential for large-scale extraction was there.[17] The limiting factors were the availability of labour and transport. The number of potential workers in the region in the late nineteenth century probably totalled 10,000 or so. Unless Kanembu, slaves, Yedina or other people were involved in production in the past – for which there is no evidence – then the quantity produced depended upon the *haddad* population – those people who belonged to an endogamous caste of artisans, and then only a part of that population, since many *haddad* were engaged in other occupations. It seems reasonable to assume, however, that several hundred – perhaps as many as a thousand – men were available. This number of people could have produced as much as 1,000–2,000 tonnes of trona.

The earliest reports on the volume of the trade date from the first decade of the century. British custom returns indicate that 400–1,000 tonnes were imported across Lake Chad each year between 1906 and 1912 (Table 5.4), although the way the returns were recorded is ambiguous, which may mean that this total is on the low side by as much as 200–350 tonnes per year.[18] It is also certain that additional supplies were smuggled past the British custom posts. In addition, at least 100–200 tonnes of trona were exported south from the Lake into the Logone and Chari basins and these amounts were not reflected in Borno imports.[19] Hence it is likely that trona production alone could reach 1,000 tonnes, and possibly as much as 1,500 tonnes. My earlier estimates of the quantity of trona exported to the middle Volta basin, one of its main markets, are in line with these estimates. An analysis of the kola trade suggests that at least 200 tonnes were exported west.[20]

More recent figures are much higher than those from the first decade of the century. Mosrin's study of the industry in 1965, based on his experience as an administrator in the region after 1949, revealed that at least 26 depressions had

Table 5.4   *Volume of trona imported into Borno, 1906–12*

Year	Total number of slabs[1]	Slabs (15 kg)[2]	Other slabs[3]	Total (tonnes)
1906	37,996	23,748	14,248 (56 lb.)	718
1907	24,250	15,157	9,093 (84 lb.)	574
1908	21,634	13,522	8,112 (84 lb.)	512
1909	34,379	21,487	12,892 (14 lb.)	404
1910	61,571	38,482	23,089 (14 lb.)	734
1911	58,137	36,336	21,801 (42 lb.)	960
1912	27,351	17,095	10,256 (70 lb.)	582

1. The report lists the total number of slabs of trona, and a bracketed figure showing the number of slabs at a specific weight. I assume that the bracketed figure represents odd-sized slabs which were either larger or smaller than the average slab. I have subtracted the bracketed figure from the total, although it is possible that the bracketed figure refers to additional slabs of an odd size, and that the figure which I am interpreting as a total only represents slabs of the average size.
2. The report does not indicate the weight of average-sized slabs, but on the basis of other reports 15 kg seems a reasonable estimate.
3. I have left the weight in pounds, as given in the report, but I have converted the total to tonnes. I wish to thank R.J. Gavin for access to this document and for the discussion about its interpretation.
Sources: Hewby, Borno Annual Report, 1912, SNP 10/14 182p/1913, Nigerian National Archives, Kaduna.

Table 5.5   *Trona production in Foli, 1961–67*

Year	Trona slabs (number)	Trona slabs (tonnes)	Trona in pieces (tonnes)	Total (tonnes)
1961	88,828	3,375	2,237	5,612
1962	101,056	3,840	3,484	7,324
1963	102,188	3,883	6,180	10,063
1964	82,668	3,141	4,524	7,765
1965	76,283	2,898	5,779	8,677
1966	171,434	6,514	3,500	10,014
1967	130,675	4,966	5,440	10,406

Source: Bouquet (1974), 133

been worked on a more or less regular basis in this period.[21] According to Bouquet's figures for 1961–67,[22] the average annual output in Foli was 8,552 tonnes (Table 5.5). Five sites produced 75,352 slabs of trona in 1965, approximately 2,640 tonnes, while in 1967 eight sites produced 114,475 slabs – about 4,000 tonnes – and another 5,240 tonnes of trona pieces, for a total of 9,240 tonnes (Table 5.6).[23] The figures for the individual sites do not correspond completely with the totals for 1961–67, but they are close enough

Table 5.6   *Trona production by deposit, 1965, 1967*

Deposit	1965		1967	
	Trona slabs	Pieces of trona	Trona slabs	Pieces of trona (tonnes)
Liwa	22,262	—	60,000	500
Bedara	26,713	—	17,500	1,800
Gade-Yala	15,000	—	—	100
Gadi Ndia	6,417	—	—	—
Kaya	—	—	16,800	1,240
Diklia	4,960	—	14,075	1,000
Kaourou Ndia	—	—	1,600	500
Andia	—	—	3,000	50
Fanana	—	—	1,500	50
Total	75,352	—	114,475	5,240

Source: Bouquet (1974), 132

to indicate that production was concentrated at relatively few sites, despite the availability of other depressions which were exploitable.

Perhaps the most accurate method of measuring the output of the Mangari *manda* industry is to combine the reports of Ronjat, made in 1905,[24] with the information of Browne, Seccombe, Gall and others, completed in 1906. Ronjat reported on 22 *manda* salines, which had 270 furnaces.[25] He estimated the output of these furnaces at 2,700 tonnes, based on his observation that each work unit produced salt every three days for five months, an average of 40 cones per unit. He calculated the volume of 540,000 cones at 5 kg each to reach his figure of 2,700 tonnes of salt. Browne and his associates examined the salines on the British side of the border – there is no overlap in the reports, unless some places had different names or the French and English ear was muddled on the pronunciation of the place names. They reported that 18 salines produced an estimated 289,000 cones of salt, that is 1,445 tonnes. The combined estimate is 4,145 tonnes, although it is likely that there is considerable error in the estimate. First, the calculations for the number of salt cones may be too high, since not all the salines produced for the full five month season. Secondly, the size of the cones varied because of the different moulds used. In this case it is impossible to tell whether the average of 5 kg per cone is too high or too low. Thirdly, there may well have been other salines, particularly in Goudoumaria and Maine-Soroa, which were unrecorded in the surveys by Ronjat and the British officials. There were also the relatively minor salines in the area of Ouacha, one of the small Sosebaki states between Muniyo and Damagaram. Figures collected by Battistini in 1916 indicate that Ouacha and Katchibare produced 32 tonnes of salt in 1914 and 54 tonnes in 1915, which hardly affects the total for the region as a whole but does demonstrate that not all the salines were recorded in Ronjat's survey of the

Table 5.7. *Manda production*

Year	Tonnes	Number of cones
1903	1,130	250,000 (10 kg)
1905	2,700	540,000 (5 kg)
1906	2,000–3,000	
1906		2 million
1906	1,310	289,000 (10 kg)
1915	761 (partial)	
1915	1,056	
1936	935	
1937	1,265.2	
1942	4,000	
1959	2,000	
1963	1,000–2,000	

Sources: Mundy, 1903, Nigerian National Archives, Kaduna; Ronjat, 1905, Archives Nationales du Niger, Niamey; Chambert, 1908, Niamey; Vischer, 1906, Kaduna; Browne, 1906; Becklesfall, 1906, Kaduna; Dunstan [Cd. 4719], Public Record Office, London; Janouih, 1916, Niamey; Rapport sur l'exploitation des salines et mares de natron, 1915 A O F 11 G. 16, Paris; L'administrateur adjoint commandant le cercle du Manga, 12 juillet 1936, Niamey; Chazelas au Gouverneur Général, 2 sept. 1938, Niamey; Niven, 16 Jan. 1942, Kaduna; Reignaut, as cited in Faure (unpublished, 1965), 40. Faure (unpublished, 1965), 40, 46

French sphere.[26] A figure of 4,000 tonnes should perhaps be considered as a capacity figure, therefore, in the absence of more reliable data (Table 5.7). Indeed one figure in 1942 placed *manda* production at 4,000 tonnes per annum, but the source of this estimate is unknown.[27]

These figures can be checked against a few scattered estimates of the volume of the *manda* trade and later estimates of total output. About 376 tonnes of *manda* were imported into Kano in 1904, which probably represents Kano City consumption.[28] In 1907 649.3 tonnes were recorded. It is known, however, that more of this type of salt was consumed in rural Kano than in the city, because it was cheaper than Kawar imports,[29] which suggests that total Kano imports may have reached 1,000 tonnes. *Manda* was also distributed in Borno and to the south, but no figures have as yet been located.

Natron production in Mangari and Muniyo is more difficult to assess, but a good guess seems to be of the order of 1,000–4,000 tonnes, and perhaps more. The largest quantities were needed for livestock, which used vast amounts of powdered *kanwa* (*gari*), but the numerous other uses suggest that production was very large indeed. Barth's 1853 description of natron stores at Keleno

Lake, only one of many locations, that 'A large provision of natron, consisting of from twenty to twenty-five piles about ten yards in diameter, and four in height, protected by a layer of reeds, was stored at the northern end of the lake', supports this conclusion.[30]

Barth met numerous, often small, caravans while travelling between Borno and Kano and between Borno and Zinder: in one day in 1851 he recorded over 500 loads on the road to Gumel from Kano. Some of these loads probably were trona but many must have been from Mangari and Muniyo. Later, in the early 1880s, Flegel reported over 100 tonnes of natron transported by steamer down the Niger from the confluence, most of it destined for Lagos and points west as far as Sierra Leone.[31] There are no estimates for the quantities carried by canoe, but it is certain that large amounts were being shipped down river by this means. *Kanwa*, either from east of Lake Chad or from Muniyo and Mangari, also went overland to Ilorin, Lagos, and elsewhere. At Ilorin, in 1904, 483.3 tonnes were recorded, while 654.5 tonnes were tallied in Zaria in one month, probably much of it for re-export south and west, and 267.7 tonnes were noted at Kano. For the year ending 31 December 1907, it is possible to follow the trade in natron and trona at scattered points. At Kano 608.6 tonnes of loose natron and 40 tonnes of trona were recorded. In Nassarawa Province, 41.7 tonnes of loose natron, 17.3 tonnes of stone natron (probably trona), and 81.3 tonnes of imported European salt were recorded, virtually all through the town of Keffi, but smaller amounts came through Abuja, Loko and Lafia.[32] These amounts are relatively unimportant in themselves, except an an indicator of local demand for various salts in these towns, but there was undoubtedly a large transit trade as well, if the information from other years is indicative of a general pattern. In 1912, 170.8 tonnes of natron were shipped down the Niger River past Idah; another 211.8 tonnes went by rail through Offa; and 345.4 tonnes were counted going by caravan through Bude Egba, on the Ilorin–Ogbomoso road. These figures amount to a total southern trade of 728 tonnes.[33]

The most complete survey of the production sites was made in 1915, when 743 tonnes was the recorded level of output: 41 tonnes from the area west of Muniyo, 500 tonnes from Muniyo, and 202 tonnes from Mangari,[34] but earlier reports establish that the volume of trade was much greater than these figures suggest. In fact, the ease of extraction and the great number of depressions made it difficult to estimate output. It must be concluded, therefore, that the magnitude of production was of the order of a few thousand tonnes.

Sodium sulphate, *gwangwarasa*, was available in workable quantities at only a few sites in Mangari, although sodium sulphate crystals could be collected at many places. Its use in tanning meant that there was a steady but relatively small demand which is difficult to quantify, especially since other salts could be used in tanning if enough *gwangwarasa* was not available. In the middle of World War II, however, the French regime promoted the production of sodium sulphate for use in sanitation among its troops.[35] Consequently, there are some figures on the amount of *gwangwarasa* available in Mangari. The head of the department of pharmacology in the AOF kept statistics which show that 3 tonnes were procured in 1944, 9 tonnes in 1945, 16 tonnes in 1946, 15 tonnes in 1947, 14 tonnes in 1948 and 8 tonnes in 1949.[36] These figures cannot be taken as an exact equivalent to the amount of sodium sulphate produced for tanning – in part because *gwangwarasa* was still needed even during the years when these figures were recorded and in part because the colonial needs may well have stimulated demand to such an extent that the production of Na_2SO_4 was increased. None the less, they do provide a rough guide to *gwangwarasa* production.

Because the salt-camps where *kige* was made were widely scattered in Kadzell, Kanem, and other areas bordering Lake Chad, an assessment of total output must be based on a projection from the known output of a relatively few salt-camps. The most complete survey, conducted by Ravoux in 1932, covers twenty-two camps in Kadzell.[37] Ravoux estimated that 419 workers were able to make 2,000 cones. Cones were of two sizes, a large one which weighed about 18 kg and a smaller one which appears to have weighed about 12 kg.[38] There is no information on the proportions of production of each size cone. Assuming an average of 15 kg, then Ravoux's twenty-two camps produced about 30 tonnes. It is likely that there were another hundred camps which produced *kige*, since Ravoux did not cover all of Kadzell, some salt-camps were located in British territory, and others were in Kanem and on the east shore of Lake Chad.[39] It may well be that there were many more than 100 camps in the past when the industry was flourishing. It is likely that this number of camps could produce about 150 tonnes of salt, an estimate which can be checked against two reports from the 1930s. In both 1935 and 1936 estimates were made of the scale of the *kige* industry; both calculated an output of 150 tonnes for taxation purposes.[40] It seems reasonable to guess that total production at the turn of the century may have been of the order of 200–400 tonnes.

The figures for the total production of *kige, manda, ungurnu*, and natron from Mangari and Muniyo should be considered as the range of probable output in normal years; possibly the upward end of this range is even a maximum. The period from which some of the figures are derived (1914–30) was a time when the Kawar and Fachi industry was in dramatic decline, which could have encouraged the expansion of output in the sahel, where transport problems were less serious. It is also possible that the early colonial years were a time of expansion in the production of *manda* and natron, although *kige* production may have begun to fall as slaves and former slaves refused to work in the salt-camps. Even with these qualifications taken into consideration, however, it is clear that the Borno sahel was the centre of a large-scale industry, probably ranging from 3,200 to as much as 9,900 tonnes for all types of salt.

The volume of salt production

THE WESTERN DALLOLS, TEGUIDDA N'TESEMT, AMADROR AND TAOUDENI

The various estimates of the amount of salt produced in Dollol Fogha indicate a level of output ranging from 500 to 700 tonnes per year. Bovill estimated that 700 tonnes were produced in c.1921, and a report of 1938 records 500 tonnes.[41] Faure's survey of the salines in 1963 led him to examine Dallol Fogha carefully, and he concluded that the southern and northern parts of the valley could each produce 500 tonnes.[42] Production in Dallol Bosso was less, but still substantial. In 1935, the five major salt villages made 127.5 tonnes of salt, while seven natron villages made 172.5 tonnes of natron cones, for a total output of 300 tonnes.[43] Later estimates in Dallol Bosso reveal a greater range in output. In 1949–50, only 87 tonnes of natron were produced, while in the following year the total was 290 tonnes.[44] There is no report on salt made in Dallol Fogha for these two years. It is clear from these reports that total output for both Dallols was considerable, perhaps exceeding 1,000 tonnes per year. When compared with other locations in Borno and the Sahara, it can be seen that the Dallols were a major source of salt.

Estimates of the quantity of salt produced at Teguidda n'tesemt range from 100 to 600 tonnes per year. Thérol, who visited Teguidda in 1909, calculated that 5,000 bars of salt were made each year; the bars weighed 20–25 kg.[45] There were also smaller pieces used as money which he did not include in his calculation. His figure of 100–125 tonnes per year may well be the figure used later by Mauny, Lambert and Abadie.[46] Cortier, who was in Teguidda in the same year as Thérol, calculated an output of 600 tonnes, based on bars of 30–35 kg.[47] He tried to elicit an estimate from the owners of the salt works, but they pretended ignorance since they apparently feared, with reason, that salt production would be taxed. A report for 1915 places the level at 116 tonnes, although it is suggested, because of a possible error, that this figure should be 139 tonnes.[48] Faure, who studied the industry in the early 1960s, estimated that the 700 units of production could produce about 400 tonnes per year.[49]

Finally, some rock salt also came into the central Sudan from Taoudeni, north of Timbuktu, and from Amadror, in southern Algeria. It is not possible to calculate the proportion of Taoudeni production which fed the central Sudan market. Total output for Taoudeni has been of the order of 1,500–4,800 tonnes in the twentieth century, which appears to indicate the level of production earlier, but only a small fraction of this amount ever reached the central Sudan.[50] Amadror, on the other hand, produced relatively modest amounts of salt, perhaps a couple of hundred tonnes, and much of this may have been taken to Damergu, Agades and other southern points. Régnier estimated 2,000 loads, representing 200–240 tonnes, as a capacity figure.[51] More recently, Museur has estimated that 70–110 tonnes have been exported to Niger each year in the second half of this century.[52] In the nineteenth century, 160–200 tonnes may have been the volume of exports.

106

Table 5.8   *Salt production at some Benue Valley locations: 1920, 1941*

Place	1920 (measure 15 lb)	1920 (tonnes)	1941 (measure $2\frac{1}{2}$ lb)	1941 (tonnes)
Awe	11,400	76	11,244	12 (75)
Azara	5,500	37	7,680	9 (51)
Ribi, Kanje, Abuni, Akiri	3,790	25	3,845	4 (26)
Total	20,690	138	22,769	25 (152)

The measure for the 1941 assessment was probably 15 lb, not 2.5 lb, as reported. The figures in parentheses are based on a 15 lb measure and are preferred.

Sources: Ward's Assessment Report, Awe, 1920 (Lafia Div 2/1 60); and Report on Salt Industry, Awe District, 1941 (Lafia Div 2/1 542), both in Nigerian National Archives, Kaduna.

THE VOLUME OF THE BENUE BRINE SPRINGS

Figures for the Benue sites are comparable to the output of the various sahel and Sahara sources. Early colonial estimates suggest that production was of the order of several hundred tonnes for Keana, Awe, Azara and neighbouring sites. In 1904, Lugard, apparently basing his estimate on geological reports, stated that the amount of salt produced in the area of Awe was about 400 tonnes per year.[53] The most complete data are for 1920 and 1941, although the size of the measure used is in question (Table 5.8). The 1920 measure was weighed at 15 lb (6.8 kg), for assessment purposes, but the 1941 measure was calculated on the basis of only $2\frac{1}{2}$ lb (1.1 kg). There seems to have been considerable evasion in tax reports for the two years, although there probably was a decline in output in the 1920s, 1930s and 1940s. The 1920 and 1941 figures represent an output lower than that potentially achievable during the nineteenth century.

By the 1960s reported output had increased dramatically (Table 5.9). The figures for 1967–71 represent output after pumps were in use to drain the sources, although pumps only worked occasionally and were not really a significant factor. Unless there has been an absolute and drastic decline since the nineteenth century in the quantities of natural brine being produced, which seems unlikely in light of the geological evidence, these figures could very well correspond to the minimum level of output in the past.

Unomah has estimated production at Awe, Azara, Ribi, Kanje and Abuni at 8,900 tonnes per year, with a capacity of 22,700 tonnes per year, but this estimate cannot be accepted. Unomah's figures on the number of salt plots are too high, and he assumes that the plots at all centres had the same yields. He claims there were 4,250 drying flats at the various sites: 2,000 at Awe, 1,250 at Azara, and 1,000 at the less important saltings of Ribi, Kanje, Abuni and Akiri.[54] He estimates that each plot could produce 2–5 tonnes per year, but it is unlikely that the best plots could produce more than 1.6 tonnes per year, and

Table 5.9. *Salt production at some Benue Valley locations, selected years*

Year	Awe	Azara	Ribi, Kanje Abuni, Akiri	Total
1920	76	37	25	138
1941	75	51	26	152
1967	310	250	211	771
1968	325	240	253	818
1969	380	230	290	900
1970	410	237	311	958
1971	430	240	313	983

Sources: Table 5.8; and NR/4 file, Awe District Office, cited in Unomah (1982), 173.

since the brine springs at some sites actually went dry late in the season many plots could not have reached maximum output. Only at Awe was the flow of brine not a problem, although the salt content of the Awe brine was relatively low. In order for the Benue saltings to produce the amount of salt calculated by Unomah, it would have required a work force of 224,000 for a five month season, and this number of people was simply not available. It appears that Unomah is off by a factor of ten; the Awe complex probably produced an amount closer to 890 tonnes, rather than 8,900 tonnes. It seems likely that these sources accounted for an output of the order of 1,000 tonnes.

In 1939, when production at Keana had apparently declined considerably, only five to six tonnes were reported, with 33 more from Akwana, and seven from Arufu. This was at a time when other Benue sites produced 376 tonnes.[55] Later, in 1951, there were 245 drying terraces in operation in Keana, and these produced an estimated 14,700 measures in six weeks.[56] Since these measures (*tasa*) weighed 3 lb each, approximately 20 tonnes were made. The introduction of pumps at Keana may not have had a significant impact, although pumps did compensate for the loss of labour. In the past, five other brine springs were exploited, besides the 40 by 80 metre pit. Unfortunately, data have not been found for later years, after pumps were introduced. Unomah estimates that Keana accounted for one quarter of Benue area production, which was true for 1920. This would suggest an output of about 250 tonnes, and probably somewhat less at Akwana and Arufa.

One way to estimate the quantity of salt produced at Keana is to calculate an average amount per salt plot based on production in 1982. Each plot can yield a maximum of 300 kg per month in a four month season and a correspondingly smaller amount (100 kg) per month for the less productive four months following the main season. Today not all workers make salt in the least productive months, but it is possible that full capacity was maintained in the nineteenth century. In 1982 about half the total number of plots were in production in the intensive season and perhaps only a third in the less intensive season. Calculating on this basis, the Keana saline could produce approximately 500 tonnes. By extrapolating backwards and assuming that all plots were at maximum production, one can calculate that Keana had a capacity of 1,230 tonnes.[57] It is unlikely that such a capacity figure was ever attained, but any estimates exceeding that amount must be discounted. Most especially, Adefuye's figure of 50,000 tonnes must be rejected, but even Unomah's revision of 3,000 tonnes is too high.[58] A more realistic figure would be 400–800 tonnes, depending upon rainfall, political conditions and the ability to mobilise labour, and the actual amount produced could easily have fallen to a few hundred tonnes or less. The capacity figure – which must not be used as anything more than a rough guide – is almost certainly high. It is based on the assumption that plots were uniform in size, which they were not, and that output per plot was the same. As is often the case in estimates of this sort, calculations are based on figures from the most productive units, which are then used as averages for all units. It is likely that true capacity was considerably less than 1,230 tonnes.

Geologists Phoenix and Kiser were probably wrong when they estimated that all sources in Lafia Division probably never produced more than a few hundred tonnes of salt.[59] Instead 1,300–2,000 tonnes must be considered a realistic estimate for all sites. This opinion is supported by a comparison of filtering devices in use at Keana and in Mangari. Keana pots were considerably smaller than the mat filters of Dara, Maine-Soroa, and other Mangari sites and even smaller than those along the north shore of Lake Chad. In Keana two or three pots were rigged to drain into the boiling pot, which produced one block of salt at a time. The ovens of the north contained 80–150 moulds, each forming 5 kg cones. At the three Dara ovens or the ten ovens at Maine-Soroa, boilings took place every 7–10 days for a five to eight month season, for an average of fifteen boilings and a production of 1,200–1,500 cones, weighing 5–7 tonnes, per oven. This represents potential output, since it is likely that workers carried the salt to market and were otherwise away from camp during breaks between cycles. Nevertheless, it is clear that in places with three ovens, like Dara, or ten ovens, like Maine-Soroa, more salt could be produced than with the comparable filtering and boiling devices of the Benue salines. The huge works at Ngibia, with 40 ovens, produced more than many of the Benue sites.[60]

Benue basin salts were less important than some of the sites further north. Any of the major locations exceeded or matched Benue output, including Mangari, Muniyo, the Chad basin, Kawar and Fachi. The Dallols probably had an output of a slightly smaller order of magnitude. Some sites within these large complexes even exceeded output at Awe, the biggest producer near the Benue. Among the northern sites, the Mangari–Muniyo region appears to have processed the most salt, particularly *manda* in Mangari and natron in Muniyo. In terms of capital investment, these two areas exceeded all other locations, although filtering devices – but no ovens – were built along the northern shore of Lake Chad and in Dallol Fogha. The investment in desert sites (except Teguidda n'tesemt) was smaller, and at these locations relatively less processing was required.

EUROPEAN SALT

The salt trade as a whole can be compared with the level of imported European salt, which began to spread into the central Sudan in the nineteenth century and was very large by the first decade of the twentieth century. All along the frontier between the forest and savanna, central Sudan salt came into competition with imported European salt. The scale of the import trade at Calabar and the Niger Delta – some 7,300 tonnes – suggests that European salt – mostly from Britain and Germany – found a ready market in the interior. The expansion of this market is difficult to assess, but Manning has shown that European salt was a major export north from Dahomey in the 1890s, and it is likely that European salt was also shipped north through the Yoruba states.[61] When European salt first crossed the forest–savanna divide is unclear, and it is probable that European salt only displaced sea salt, not salt from the central Sudan. Hence the penetration of the central Sudan market with European salt, which began as a trickle in 1832, and increased to a steady flow in the 1860s, only reached flood proportions at the end of the century.

Salt was brought up the Niger on the vessels of the various European expeditions, the Royal Niger Company, and the indigenous river traffic. At least 40 tonnes – and perhaps as much as 100 tonnes – were sold at the confluence in 1862. By 1903, 4,214 tonnes were transported north between June and December.[62] In 1906 the total for the river and overland trades accounted for the import of 10,371 tonnes of salt into northern Nigeria (Table 5.10),[63] at a time when the total volume of salt imports into all of Nigeria was 32,525 tonnes.[64] In a remarkably short period, the volume of imported European salt rose to a substantial level. The volume of the European trade demonstrates that the central Sudan market was far from saturated with salt; the local industry simply could not supply the quantities which could be purchased, especially since imports favoured those areas most distant from the major sources of central Sudan salt, i.e., the southern portions of northern Nigeria. The estimates for salt production for all the central Sudan sites suggest a range of 8,000–15,700 tonnes, which is about equal to the volume of European imports by 1906. It is possible that the various calculations for the specific sites are too low, but even so the amount of imported European salt still accounted for a large portion of the total market. Considering that no allowance has been made for the production of vegetable salts, other than *kige*, the total volume of locally-produced salt was probably much higher. Still, the impact of European imports was sudden but apparently without dramatic effect on the level of local output. There is no evidence that any of the salt sites began to produce less salt in the first decade of colonial rule, not even the Benue brine springs that were most vulnerable to

110

Table 5.10   *Imports of European salt into northern Nigeria, 1903–07*

Year	Niger River (tonnes)	Overland (tonnes)	Total
1903 (June–Dec)	4,214	—	—
1904	—	—	7,863
1905	—	—	7,769
1906	6,267	4,104	10,371
1907	4,350	5,586	9,936

Sources: Estimates, Customs Department, 1903; SNP 18/1 G. 61; Annual Report of the Customs Department, 1907; SNP 7/9 330/1908; Northern Nigeria Blue Books, 1906 and 1907. All in Nigerian National Archives, Kaduna.

the invasion of imported European salt. If the central Sudan industries had been meeting the full market demand for salt, then the introduction of large quantities of European salt would have driven some of the local salt off the market. That this was not the case reflects two factors. First, European salt only competed for the culinary market, not the industrial, medicinal and other uses for salt. The market for non-culinary purposes still required the production of large quantities of local salts and thereby served as a cushion for the culinary market as well. Secondly, many people could not afford European salt, even when adulterated, and they continued to use locally-produced salts. Culinary tastes also required local salts, which served to maintain the existing market.

There was a large, unsatisfied market for sodium chloride, which the expansion of European imports demonstrates. The fact that local industry could not satisfy this market is worth noting, for it helps substantiate the conclusion presented in Chapter 4 that technological backwardness deriving from the market situation prevented the evolution of techniques that could have produced better quality salts. Clearly the demand for purer sodium chloride grew very rapidly when European salt became available in large quantities. The central Sudan industry was not able to develop this demand through the evolution of better production techniques, and by the time the demand was developed it was too late for technological innovation. The modern production of salt in Britain and Germany could fully satisfy any potential demand at a relatively low price. The central Sudan industry was permanently subjected to technological stagnation. It continued to supply the market for industrial, medicinal and other uses, but there was no prospect in the colonial period of technological changes leading to a modern chemical industry based on the resources of the salt deposits.

PRODUCTIVITY OF THE SALINES

Because the technology of production was relatively undeveloped, the salt industry of the central Sudan was highly labour intensive, although there were significant variations in the level of productivity among the various salines. In terms of man-hours per tonne of salt, the most productive sites were Foli, Bilma, Fachi and Teguidda n'tesemt, and the least productive were those sites where filtering and boiling of brine were necessary. A comparison of the different sites reveals that Foli could export several thousand tonnes of trona, probably involving only 500 workers.[65] Bilma required the labour of about 200–300 workers to produce approximately 1,000–2,000 tonnes of salt in a year.[66] Fachi was behind Bilma in productivity; about 300 workers could make 600–700 tonnes of salt.[67] At Teguidda n'tesemt, the level of output appears to have been about the same; 200 workers made 600 tonnes of salt.[68] Efficiency dropped sharply from the figures which characterised these more productive sites. While each worker could produce several tonnes of trona in Foli, 4 tonnes in Bilma, 3 tonnes in Teguidda n'tesemt, and 2–3 tonnes in Fachi, the corresponding figures for the sahel locations dropped below one worker per tonne in Dallol Fogha and even less in Dallol Bosso.[69] In Mangari and Kadzell, productivity was even lower. Janouih's survey of 1916 suggests that it took six or seven workers to make a tonne of *manda*, although later reports indicate a level of efficiency of two to three workers per tonne.[70] There are no comparable estimates for the Benue sites, but the ratio of output to worker was low, particularly if the labour required to drain the salt wells and pits is taken into account. Halad Keana has estimated that a woman, together with her assistants, could produce as much as 1.6 tonnes of salt per season at Keana, but his estimate is based on ideal conditions and is probably high.[71]

These estimates – based on a thorough analysis of data on both output and number of workers – can be checked against a report of 1915, which attempted to assess volume of production, number of workers, amount of tax, and value of salt for most of the salines of the central Sudan (Foli and the Benue sites are not included, and the information for Dallol Fogha is incomplete). Rough as the calculations for 1915 are, it is still apparent that Bilma and Fachi were three times as productive as the natron sites of Mangari and Muniyo and five times as productive as the *manda* industry (Table 5.11).

It can be shown, moreover, that volume was lower than usual at Bilma and Fachi because of drought and because the French requisitioned camels for the conquest of Tibesti. Consequently, the Tuareg did not travel to Bilma in their usual numbers, and in the following year they revolted over French exactions.[72] The reported output for Teguidda n'tesemt – 116 tonnes – is probably too low; a reassessment of volume based on the value of the salt produced in 1915 suggests a figure of 139 tonnes. Either figure indicates a level of productivity of about one tonne per worker, not as high as for Bilma and Fachi, and low by Teguidda standards anyway. The figures for Mangari and Muniyo are consistent with my calculations from other data, and they are

Table 5.11. *Productivity of the salines, 1915*

Saline	Number of workers	Output (tonnes)	Workers/tonne of salt
Bilma and Fachi	900	1,000	0.9
Manda sites (Muniyo and Mangari)	4,732	1,056	4.5
Natron sites (Muniyo and Mangari)	2,068	703	2.9
Teguidda n'tesemt	145	116 (139)	1.3 (1.0)

Source: Rapport sur l'exploitation des salines et mares de natron, 1915, Archives Nationales du Niger, Niamey.

consistent with each other. The production of *manda* involved a labour input comparable to that for the collection of natron, plus an additional input for the filtering and boiling of brine.

Since each of the salines had a different production season, a more accurate comparison must also take account of the number of months in which salt was actually produced. And the labour involved in preparing the salines, making pots, and gathering firewood must also be included, because these ancillary activities were part of the production process. Furthermore, slack hours in the production schedule have to be allowed for, which only highlights the relative productivity of the various salines. Foli appears to be even more productive than the other sites, while the Benue brine springs are shown to be less productive than an analysis based on output per year alone would suggest. The environmental conditions of the various sites provide a logical explanation for this discrepancy. Foli, with its tremendous reserves of trona, could be exploited more efficiently than the weak brine springs of the Benue valley, whose rate of flow even dwindled in the course of the season, so that the minor springs often went dry, thereby curtailing production entirely.

The calculation of productivity is only a rough guide. Considering the difficulty of estimating output and the unreliability of data on population, all figures must be taken with a grain of salt. There are a few estimates, made by direct observers, which can be used to check the general impression of relative productivity, but these estimates too suffer from the same defects in data. There simply are no reliable figures on the number of workers, scale of output, time involved in production, or variations between different years to allow a proper statistical comparison. None the less, the correlation between the natural environment – which provides some parameters – and the results of the different observations is sufficiently accurate to sustain the conclusion that the salt industry, even for the most productive salines, was labour intensive. By comparison with modern salt production, the number of available workers was the most significant variable in the factors of production. Modern salt works, and even European workings that were

113

contemporary with the late nineteenth century central Sudan industry, were far more dependent upon the technological input; labour was not an important constraint. Salt production in the central Sudan fitted into a pattern in which most economic activity was labour intensive. Farmers used the most rudimentary tools – short-handled hoes and axes; the carding and spinning of cotton depended upon hand methods, while weaving was most often practised on narrow looms; land transport relied on head porterage and livestock, without the use of carts or other vehicles, let alone railways. It is not clear whether or not the salt industry was more labour intensive than these other sectors, but certainly the competition for labour between various sectors must have been a constraint on the expansion of salt production.

6

The mobilisation of labour

The salt industry was seasonal, and the number of months in which salt was produced varied. Rainfall interfered with production in the sahel and savanna, while temperature was the most significant factor in the desert. The productive cycle was different depending upon these factors. In the sahel and savanna, salt and natron were made in the dry season, as the geology of the salines makes clear. Efflorescence occurred with the variations in the water table which resulted from the fluctuations between the rainy and dry seasons. The seepage phenomenon of Lake Chad 'pushed' the trona to the surface of the Foli depressions, which were workable once the water from the rains evaporated. Only the brine springs were not directly affected by the season. The brine maintained its salinity throughout the year, although some springs went dry late in the season, but rain-water prevented production until several months after the last rain. At Teguidda n'tesemt, the rains – scanty as they were – flooded the valley, and the salt could not be worked until most of this water had evaporated. Hence the salt season there coincided with the work cycle in the savanna. The other desert sites, by contrast, were unaffected by the rains. At Fachi and in Kawar, there was hardly ever any rain; production varied with temperature. The hottest months lasted from the end of the savanna dry season through the rainy season; consequently production took place out of step with the savanna cycle.

Two patterns characterised the productive cycle, therefore. In Kawar and Fachi, production was concentrated in the summer months, but salt was produced during the dry season everywhere else, despite variations in the length of the season. Except for Kawar and Fachi, this concentration of production fitted neatly into the labour requirements of the agricultural economy which dominated the central Sudan. In the rainy season, people could farm, but in the relatively labour-free months of the dry season, labour was available to undertake other activities – in this case the production of salt. The salt industry benefited from a situation in which the opportunity costs of labour were at their lowest. There was little else to do, so workers engaged in other activities, even if the returns were modest, because the alternative was to do nothing but wait for the rains. And most people could not afford to do nothing.

As Watts has demonstrated, large portions of the central Sudan population were caught in the grip of poverty, and famine always threatened to strike, although in the nineteenth century famines tended to be relatively localised. People had to supplement their agricultural output through other activities, often because poverty and indebtedness forced them to sell part of their crops at harvest time when prices were lowest.[1] While the opportunity costs of labour may have been relatively low during the dry season, people still had to work. Some people *chose* to make salt, collect natron, or extract trona, but others were *forced* to do so, either because they were slaves or because their social and economic conditions assigned them to a class or caste which needed the extra income to survive. Other alternatives existed. People could engage in a craft, herd livestock, or undertake irrigated agriculture, and these choices were made in proximity to many of the salines. People pursued these activities for the same reasons that some workers made salt: they either had to because of slavery or other constraints, or they found that these activities were more rewarding, either because of cultural factors or opportunities, or both.

The Manga agricultural villages were located either in Muniyo or in the valleys to the south of the salt region, where the drainage system of the Komodugu Yo and Komodugu Gana basins provided better farm land for rainy-season agriculture. Such villages as Wuelleri, in Mashena territory (western Borno), or the Manga town of Bundi – near Nguru – with its 8,000–9,000 people in 1851 were better situated for agriculture than the salt district.[2] In December 1852, Barth found the agricultural districts of the Manga

> undulated in downs of red sand, famous for the cultivation of groundnuts and beans, both of which constitute a large proportion of the food of the inhabitants, so that millet and beans are generally sown on the same field, the latter ripening later, constituting the richest pasture for cattle and camels. Of grain, negro millet (Plennisetum typhoideum) is the species almost exclusively cultivated in the country of Manga, sorghum not being adapted for this dry ground.[3]

In 1903, there was even a Manga quarter as far south as Adia, a Bedde town which Mundy found to be the largest town in Borno.[4]

In 1938, Marwick studied the village of Dara, 20 km north of Geidam, which was a small Manga village of 165 people, including three work units of 11, 13 and 15 people who made *manda* at the saline of Silimma.[5] The population included 51 men, 61 women, 30 children, and 23 'infirm'. The crops consisted of millet and ground nuts; there were 126.9 ha in millet, producing 32.3 tonnes; and 29 acres of ground-nuts, producing 1.7 tonnes. Marwick did a careful study of the size of holdings and output per holding for both millet and ground-nut farms. Even the largest holding – that of the village chief – only had 9.7 ha under millet and 0.8 ha in ground-nuts; the average millet farm was 3.8 ha, with an output of 960 kg per holding, or about 100 kg of threshed grain per acre, while the average ground-nut farm was 0.19 ha, producing 27 kg of decorticated nuts. The inhabitants also owned

1,958 gum arabic trees, which added to the agricultural output of the village.

Considering this modest agricultural setting, it is not surprising that people had to supplement their harvests with a dry-season occupation. Even in normal times, the amount of food could fall short of family needs, and the variations in rainfall from year to year left no alternative but to find other employment. According to Patterson, who considered the plight of the Manga peasantry in 1917,

> The first thought [of the Manga] is easily to provide himself from his profits on the work on salt with a year's supply of corn, for the rainfall in Manga Dist[rict] is lower than in other parts of the District [Geidam] and the crops of *gero* [millet] on the sand dunes are much below the average in Bornu, only in an exceptionally good year will the inhabitants of this area be exempt from the necessity of eking out home grown corn with supplies bought in the Sern [southern] parts of the District. The uncertainty of the corn harvest has made the bean crop a more important one in this region than elsewhere in the District.[6]

As Patterson observed, many Manga peasants had to pursue a strategy of supplementing agriculture with salt production. His comments came at a time that demonstrated this point with considerable tragedy, for only a few years earlier (1913–14) a disastrous drought devastated the central Sudan. While this particular drought was more serious than most, it highlights the thin line between subsistence and starvation that many peasants faced throughout the central Sudan.[7] Even in good years, surplus production could always be taken north to the salt camps, where there was a steady demand for foodstuffs. As Géry found in his study of Adebour and neighbouring sites in 1946, many workers lacked provisions or the means of buying them, so that they were forced to pay in salt.[8] Some of these provisions were obtained locally. Certain of the salines were ringed with an area of gardens (*kriyo*) where there was fresh water close to the surface and irrigation was not necessary, and there was dry-season farming at many other places, including Myrria, to the immediate west of Muniyo, Guidimouni, Bune and other places in Muniyo itself, and in Mobbeur country along the Komodugu Yo, to the east of the salines.[9] There appears to have been little, if any, movement of labour between salt production and irrigated agriculture. People did what their fathers had done. As one man put it to Mahomet Lawan in 1941: 'My father and grandfather solely depended upon salt making and I hope my son too will do the same thing, much less [sic] myself.'[10] Salt production was a full-time activity, and even when irrigated agriculture was practised near the salt camps, as at Cheri and some other sites, those who owned irrigated plots concentrated on farming. The work of salt-making precluded the involvement of part-time labour, which is all that the farmers could have offered. It is possible that farmers participated in the collection of natron, since that activity only required scraping the ground of the natron crust.

Farming and salt production were also complementary in Kanem, where the trona deposits of Foli were located. The Foli pans were a desolate wilderness, hardly the place for a permanent population. While there was flooding in the rainy season, the water was tainted with the salt deposits and not suitable for agriculture. Most trona workers came from the area near the lake where they farmed the valleys along the shore. It may be that they created polders in places that were lower than the level of the lake and that were separated from the lake by dykes. It is difficult to say when the first polders were developed. The Tilho mission (1904–08) did not notice any, but there were polders in 1913. Several were noticed in 1924, and in 1949 twenty-three were identified. Farmers constructed earthen mounds 2–3 metres high and about 2 m deep that separated the depressions from the lake. The water subsequently evaporated at the rate of 2 m per year. As the years passed, farmers had more and more land available for agriculture.

While the land belonged to the Kanem aristocracy, the actual labour was performed by *haddad* (an artisan caste known as Danawa) and former slaves. It is likely that this system of land reclamation was already established in the nineteenth century and that the Danawa from these polders also engaged in the extraction of trona.[11] Other Danawa lived in the vicinity of Ngouri, 120 km to the east, and they may have migrated to the trona deposits during the dry season. The inhabitants of Ngouri and surrounding villages numbered about 6,500 in 1871, when Nachtigal visited the area.[12] He estimated that about 3,000 Danawa lived in or near Ngouri and another 3,500 lived in other parts of southern Kanem, including the lake district. Ngouri itself had 600 houses.[13] Later estimates are consistent with these population figures. Le Rouvreur, for example, cites eighteen Danawa villages in the Ngouri area, with a population of 3,810 in 1962.[14] These Danawa were first and foremost farmers, despite their occupational identification as artisans. They reputedly had a stronger inclination for work than other people in Kanem, or at least Trystram is of this opinion: 'it is rare to find a ouaddi [valley] with *haddad* inhabitants which has land that lies fallow. In many ouaddis, where the *haddad* are the agricultural workers, practically the whole of the ouaddi is cultivated.'[15] They grew bulrush millet and beans, and the surplus was sold to nomads.[16] But the Danawa were faced with the same dilemma as the Manga of Borno and Muniyo. They needed to supplement their harvests, which they could do through any one of a number of dry-season occupations. As artisans, the Danawa wove and dyed textiles, made iron implements, worked in leather, and fashioned pots. They were also hunters, both of game and ostriches.[17] The extraction of trona was only one of many alternatives.

Kawara-Debe, one of the settlements in Dallol Fogha which Barth visited in 1853 and 1854,[18] again was not an unusual savanna village in terms of its agricultural economy. The principal crops were millet, sorghum, maize, sugar cane, rice, ground-nuts, cotton, sweet potatoes and acha.[19] When Rochette studied the village in 1964, he found a pattern of agriculture which used the uplands and the valley in a complicated system of crop management. Although there were a few large landowners in the village, the more typical situation was small peasant holdings. Rochette provides the example of a man who worked seven fields, which totalled 4.54 ha. On one of the *tunga* (salt-camp) mounds, he had 1.5 ha in millet and sorghum, while on the intermediate ground on the opposite bank of the valley he cultivated another 2.3 ha of millet on land owned by another man. He also had an adjacent plot (3,100 m^2) in ground-nuts. In the basin of the valley itself, the man had three fields: 180 m^2 in sweet potatoes, 500 m^2 in maize, and 1,000 m^2 in sugar cane. He also worked two flats where he grew rice; one 250 m^2 and another 1,250 m^2. In the rice flats, he subsequently planted manioc and potatoes once the rice was harvested.[20] Rochette measured the output from these fields and gardens; there was a surplus beyond the needs of the man and his family, but the agricultural output of the village as a whole was far from sufficient to feed the number of workers involved in salt production. Food had to be imported from neighbouring Djerma and Maouri country, where salt was not produced.[21] Not only was the local agricultural cycle complementary to salt production, but a much larger area than Dallol Fogha was integrated into an economy which required the movement of foodstuffs. The output of the salines tied into this economy because the salt workers needed provisions – and had the resources to buy them. Even so these same workers were also farmers in the rainy season, although most came from elsewhere. The fact that the migrants did not bring food from their own granaries demonstrates that people had to work to supplement their agricultural output. Migration seems to have been a strategy adopted by those farmers who were relatively poor. They moved because they had to, a point which helps substantiate Watts' analysis that many peasants struggled against famine.[22]

Even Teguidda n'tesemt fitted into the pattern in which salt production complemented the agricultural cycle. Brackish water prevented agriculture during the rainy season, although in the fourteenth century and earlier there had been irrigated agriculture nearby at Azelik. In more recent centuries, people retreated to In Gall, 80 km to the south-east, where oasis agriculture is possible. In 1972, there were 10,083 date palms at In Gall, and some irrigated agriculture was practised as well.[23]

In the Benue basin, the crops were different and the farming season longer, but there too the salt season officially began after the crops were harvested. Formal ceremonies marked the new season; at Keana the first requirements in preparing for salt production involved draining the pits and wells, which had to be a communal effort, undertaken by the men, and the men were not available until the crops were in. The ceremonies reflected the community spirit, as well as providing an occasion for celebration and an expression of religious belief. The draining operations, which took several days at Keana, usually began in December.[24] The main salt season also ended well before the time for planting.

Only in Kawar and Fachi, where agriculture was not a major activity, was the relationship between agriculture and salt production not important. Some dates were harvested, and a little irrigated agriculture was practised, but these activities were not allowed to interfere with work at the salines, whose most active period coincided with the agricultural demands of the gardens and date trees. In fact the possibilities for gardening and date cultivation were limited by natural conditions. In 1941, there were 8,970 date palms at Bilma and 8,500 at Fachi, although the total number for all of Kawar and Fachi was about 53,000 trees.[25] In Bilma and Fachi, there were idle months during December, January and February when agriculture was at a stand-still and the salines were not productive. The inhabitants of these oases did not have the alternatives available to the farmers near the savanna and sahel salines. In local tradition, the Tuareg have been blamed for this unhappy state of affairs at Bilma and the Tubu at Fachi. It is claimed that the Tuareg prohibited agriculture in Kawar as a means of controlling the population and safeguarding their trade in grain to the oases. The Tubu limited production at Fachi in order to promote Bilma.[26] Whether or not these traditions have any basis in fact will be examined below in Chapter 9, but the traditions serve to confuse the ecological limitations on agriculture and the corresponding under-employment of the desert population with the political situation.

The complementary nature of salt production and the agricultural cycle disguises a human problem. As should be clear from the analysis of the ecological conditions of the salines, most salines were not located in a pleasant environment and seldom were they located adjacent to sufficient agricultural land to feed all the workers. Usually people had to move with the seasons. This phenomenon – labour migration – is often ascribed to the colonial period in relation to the establishment of a capitalist sector (mining, modern plantations and the like), as if a similar pattern had never existed before. In fact the movement of people for economic purposes such as salt production was widespread in the pre-colonial era, at least in the central Sudan. People moved because they were told to or because they had to. The opportunity cost of labour may have been low, but many people still had to work, even if it involved leaving their families for months at a time and living in temporary camps. Only in the Benue basin, and perhaps in Dallol Bosso, was there sufficient arable land to support all – or at least most – of the workers needed in salt production. Even in these cases, some people came to the salines for brief periods in search of work, at least in the early twentieth century and probably in the nineteenth century too. In the case of the other salines, except Bilma and Fachi, migrant workers travelled from their home villages, where they farmed, to camps and villages at the salines. This kind of labour mobility was the only recourse open to people seeking to avoid a fate similar to the one accepted by the people of Kawar and Bilma – under-employment in the dry season.

THE MIGRANT WORKERS OF MANGARI

In Mangari and Muniyo free, migrant labour produced the salt and natron.[27] Most sites, particularly the many small ones, were temporary settlements.

120

Only a few of the production centres, including Adebour, Cheri, Bune, and Gourselik, were inhabited permanently, and even then the resident population was relatively small. In 1946, the permanent population of some of these villages was as follows: Adebour had 234 inhabitants, Cheri had 182, Bousayram had 167, and Dassorom had 105.[28] In 1903 Mundy claimed that there were only two villages in the Manga salt district which were really permanent, Adebour and Cheri, 'and even they more than quadruple in size during the salt-collecting season, which really becomes busy in April, reaches its height about the end of May and begins to dwindle rapidly by the end of July'.[29] Actually, Mundy was a few months off in his assessment of the busy period, as the workers had to return home in time for the first rains in order to plant their crops.

The majority of workers, most of whom were Manga, except in the far west where Hausa were also found, moved into the salt camps during the production season from November to March and stayed until April or May. Many came from villages further south, so that the general pattern was a north–south migration similar to the transhumance of others along the desert-edge. As Vischer noted in 1906,

> The last storm of the rainy season has hardly passed before thousands of the Manga leave their homes in the north of Bornu and make for the salt-pits. In the course of a few days the lowlands are studded with villages, and everywhere a scene of busy life is presented to the eye.[30]

In 1903, when 'the repopulation of the Manga district is going on rapidly', Mundy encountered an estimated 3,000 men, besides women and children, leaving Hadejia for Mangari.[31] Browne found that the workers at Bugduma. which had 60 ovens in 1906, fell into two groups, which demonstrates that production units were formed at the home villages of the migrant workers, not at the salines. The workers in the camp on the north-west of the depression came from Maine-Soroa, while the workers on the south-east were from Borum. At Ngibia, the workers were from all parts of Borno, including Zumgo, Karigi, Jer, Guai, and Wadi. There were about 150 compounds and 25 ovens, which suggests a population of 250–300.[32] Since workers migrated in groups that were organised in their villages of permanent settlement, they maintained a corporate identity that facilitated co-operation in making salt.

The pattern of migration observed in the first years of the colonial occupation appears to have originated at some point in the nineteenth century, an hypothesis that will be examined below. Certainly the pattern continued well into the colonial period, which demonstrates that the phenomenon was not limited to the first decade of the twentieth century. In 1936, for example, migrants still moved by the thousands. Only a few were from the vicinity of the salines. The rest came from Nigeria after the millet and ground-nut harvest.[33] Géry reported a similar pattern in 1946. The migrants – poor peasants who arrived at the salt-camps without provisions of millet – came north for six months, or longer.[34] They had to buy their food from Kanuri merchants who brought millet, ground-nuts and beans to the camps to buy salt.[35] Géry found that 60 per cent of the 1,000 workers at Ari Kombomiram were from Nigeria, while the others came from villages elsewhere in Niger.[36]

In the first decade of colonial rule, the population of the Manga district of Nigeria appears to have numbered tens of thousands, although there was no census of the region at that time, and later computations did not distinguish between Manga and Kanuri. In French Niger, however, there are statistics on the size of the Manga population of Muniyo. In 1913, a census of the Manga district revealed a population of 28,029.[37] Later tabulations which were taken each year between 1925 and 1929 show a sedentary population of 23,000–24,000, virtually all of whom were Manga.[38] Urvoy reported 32,000 Manga in Goure and Maine-Soroa for 1942.[39] It is likely, therefore, that the total Manga population was well over 50,000, which indicates ample human resources for the salt and natron industry of Mangari and Muniyo.

Work units consisted of 10–20 people, mostly men, who carried brine, scraped salty earth for the filters, made the filters and furnaces, fetched firewood, and packaged the finished salt cones for transport.[40] A headman was in charge of the furnace, other workers (*kandine*) made the moulds for the salt boiling, while male and female workers (*bagazao*) did the rest. At Ari Kombomiram, a major location near Cheri, for example, there were ten furnaces in operation in the early 1940s, and these were organised into work units of approximately ten people each. At one furnace there were five *kandine*, including the furnace master, and five *bagazao*. This unit included eight men and two women, who were the wives of the furnace master and one of the workers.[41] The salt season lasted from five to eight months, depending upon the year and the site. In a seven month season, a work unit could stage twenty-seven boilings, which would produce fifty cones each time, for a total of 1,350–1,400 cones.[42]

In 1905 and 1906, there were probably 4,600–8,250 workers involved in the production of *manda* at 43 sites. The number of furnaces was of the order of 440, although information on the number of furnaces or the size of work units is available only for 29 sites (Table 6.1). Another 12 locations produced 98,000 cones of salt, which indicates that 70 furnaces were probably in operation.[43] Ronjat's survey of 22 sites in 1905 revealed 270 work units, which were groups of 10–20 workers, each centred on a furnace. The number of workers, therefore, was probably of the order of 2,700–5,400 people. One year later on the British side of the border, surveys showed that 209,000 cones of salt were made at sixteen sites, while the number of ovens at six locations alone totalled 103.[44] The British figures suggest a total of 173 ovens, or 1,730–2,600 workers, assuming 10–15 workers per oven. While it is possible that there was some movement between different locations in the course of the two separate seasons, there is virtually no overlap in the two reports with respect to the salines. Despite the possibility of error in combining the two estimates, these

Table 6.1   *Work units in the production of manda salt, 1905–06*

Site	Number of work units (furnaces)	Number of workers (estimate) (15 workers/furnace)
Bugduma	60	900
Adris	50	750
Gourselik	25	375
Ngibia	25	375
Maibirim I	20	300
Karamoua	20	300
Maramaram	19	285
Karagou	16	240
Tairi	14	210
Kila Kamanghana	14	210
Darouram	13	195
Ouakatgi	12	180
Matafaram	12	180
Abgue	10	150
Doumaoua	10	150
N'Gariram	7	105
Maibirim II	7	105
Diru	6	90
N'Goriani	5	75
Babilla	4	60
Kurugu	4	60
Dokoraram	4	60
Kourkouroa	4	60
Kongolimaram	3	45
Nawujeram	3	45
Kadellaoua	2	30
Billama Boucar	2	30
Kogoua	1	15
Yadhia	1	15
Total	373	6,625

Sources: Lt. Ronjat, Etude faite sur les mares salines du Mounyo, 1905, Archives Nationales du Niger, Niamey; Browne, 1906, Nigerian National Archives, Kaduna.

reports provide the most detailed information on the size of the work force. Since other small sites were not included, there is also the possibility of underestimation.

Ten years later, in 1915, Janouih examined thirty sites in Mangari and estimated that 4,690 workers were involved in the production of 707 tonnes of salt (Table 6.2). Janouih did not include a number of small sites in his survey.[45] There is some overlap between Janouih's report and the earlier

Table 6.2   *Work units in the production of manda salt, 1915*

Site	Number of workers	Furnaces (estimate)	Tonnes
Dietkorom	500	33	80
Fanamiram	340	22	90
Kakorom	300	20	32
Miamia	285	19	39
Adebour	280	18	30
Boumboumkoa	275	18	37
Ari Goudorom	260	17	33
Bitoamaram	260	17	22
Yani Souarni	250	16	20
Zatoukoutou	245	16	34
Ari Kombomiram	230	15	28
Dirighia	225	15	28
Bugduma	195	13	50
Gamgaouo	110	7	17
Kangaroua Tiari	110	7	16
Guidjigaoua	105	7	17
Gourselik	80	5	15
Kogoua	80	5	15
Abatilori Kilbou	70	4	10
Frainé Delaram	65	4	6
Mina Dabalia	65	4	8
Kousouloua Kilboua	55	3	6
Kilborom	50	3	12
Fanamiram	50	3	10
Cheri	45	3	13
Forsarimaram	45	3	15
Kangaroua	40	2	8
Maibirim	30	2	5
Tchabaram	25	2	7
Zoumba	20	1	4
Total	4,690	304	707

Janouih noted that there were many other small sites.
Source: Janouih, Rapport sur les salines, 24 fév. 1916, Archives Nationales du Niger, Niamey.

studies of Ronjat, Browne and the other British agents, but not as much as might be expected. It is possible that different names were used for some of the sites, but it is still likely that many new depressions were brought into production in the intervening ten years. Only five sites (Bugduma, Gourselik, Maibirim, Karagou, Tairi-Kangarou Tiari and possibly a few others) appear on the two lists. Notably absent from the 1905–06 list are Dietkorom, Adebour, Cheri, and other large sites which are known to have been in operation from the early part of the century through the 1940s. Many sites

124

appear to have been left off the earlier lists because Ronjat surveyed Muniyo, thereby missing eastern Mangari where many sites were located, while the British reports only covered the border region, missing many of the same sites. These gaps only serve to highlight the major conclusion suggested by the reports. Thousands of workers were involved in production. The reports taken alone must be considered minimum figures, even if there is some exaggeration of the size of the work force or the number of furnaces at the locations actually included in the lists.

Another report for 1915, which was probably based in part, at least, on Janouih's study, estimated the number of workers in the production of *manda* and natron at 6,800.[46] For *manda* alone, this report indicates a working population of 4,235 in Mangari, 442 in Muniyo, and 55 in the Sosebaki salines west of Muniyo; that is a total of 4,732 workers. The number of natron workers included 1,479 in Muniyo, 500 in Mangari, and 89 in the Sosebaki area: a total of 2,068. While there may have been some overlap between workers in *manda* and natron production, this report – backed by Janouih's more thorough estimates for specific sites – probably represents an accurate indication of the size of the labour force. Furthermore, it is the only report which attempts to estimate the number of natron workers.

Twenty-one years later still, the *manda* sites were again surveyed. Fifty-five sites were listed, many of which were included in the 1915 survey (Table 6.3). The 1936 report indicates that there were forty-eight sites with three or fewer furnaces, and this list does not include additional sites south of the Nigeria–Niger border. The report indicates that the larger sites had decreased significantly in size, with the exception of Adebour, Bugduma, Fanamiram, and Yani Souarni. Most notably, Dietkorom, which had had 500 workers in 1915, only had eight furnaces and probably only 100 workers in 1936. The 1936 report suggests that approximately 2,490 workers were involved in production, a considerable drop in the number of workers. Depressions which had once been enormous – Gourselik and Cheri, for example – were reduced to only four furnaces between them. The geological and climatic cycle of the salt country had taken its toll. In 1905 Gourselik had been a major site, with approximately 25 furnaces. Ten years later, the number of furnaces was greatly reduced, perhaps down to five, since there were only 80 workers at the site. By 1936 Gourselik was reduced to insignificance, with only one furnace. The 1936 report provides confirmation of Faure's analysis of the geological cycles of salt production in Mangari.[47] The mobilisation of labour through migration was a flexible method of adjusting to different conditions. Workers were free to move from one saline to another as the natural cycle based on geology and climate brought particular depressions into a condition that was worth exploiting.

Although free migrant labour characterised the production of *manda*, slavery was on the increase in the Manga region as a whole, just at the point of colonial conquest. Some of the new slaves, at least, began to be used in salt production by the end of the nineteenth century, although slavery was still

Table 6.3. *Work units in the production of manda salt,*
Mangari, 1936

Site	Furnace	Number of workers (estimate) (15 workers/furnace)
Bugduma	18	270
Adebour	16	240
Fanamiram	15	225
Karagou Koura	15	225
Yani Souarni	12	180
Dietkorom Manda	8	120
Kangaroua Gana	6	90
Abatilori Dibinoa	3	45
Katafourorom	3	45
Maibirim I	3	45
Djenafout	3	45
Maina Dalaram	3	45
N'Gario	3	45
Katokouto	3	45
Cheri	3	45
Gangaoua	3	45
Bitoamaram	3	45
Abatilori Kilboa	2	30
Doumbokoa	2	30
Bagaram	2	30
Dirguia	2	30
Fofio	2	30
Gadoroa	2	30
Karajou Gamdoua	2	30
Alkamaram	2	30
Kellakam	1	15
Mina Dabalia	1	15
Gourselik	1	15
Kassaoron	1	15
Koussouloa	1	15
Kairiri	1	15
Afounorom	1	15
Allosseram	1	15
Ari Korgorom	1	15
Damagaram	1	15
Djajibolom	1	15
Foussamaram	1	15
Katkomguia	1	15
Gourjiou Guirgui	1	15
Kolo Dibia	1	15
Kololoua	1	15
Koudoua	1	15
Kossa	1	15
Mandaoua Kilboa	1	15
Melaram	1	15
Ouangangoua	1	15

Table 6.3.   (*Cont.*)

Site	Furnace	Number of workers (estimate) (15 workers/furnace)
Ouadorom	1	15
Rakaoua	1	15
Yabari	1	15
Gokordi	1	15
Ari Gadourom	1	15
Gazorom	1	15
Miamia Koura	1	15
Goudourom	1	15
Zumba	1	15
Total	166	2,490

Source: L'Adjoint des s.c. chef de la subdivision de Mainé-Soroa, 29 mai, 1936, Archives Nationales du Niger, Niamey.

marginal to the principal form of labour – migrant peasants. When slaves were used, they worked alongside their masters. Laforque noted as late as 1913, for example, that some salt workers owned slaves:

This work is done by groups of 10–20 people, generally a whole family together with its clients or former captives. Every body in the group has his or her own particular role. While the men look after the washing, the filtering and the manufacture of the moulds, the women and children go into the basins to look for earth to wash, carry water and fetch straw and brush for the furnace.[48]

Laforque referred to the slaves as 'clients' or 'former captives', but since he was writing in 1913, by which time the French had adopted a policy of discouraging slavery, he probably observed slaves, whatever transitional status they may have held. His comments seem to indicate that some slaves, at least, were present in the salt industry a few years earlier, since it is unlikely that masters would only involve former slaves in production. Laforque's comments indicate, therefore, that slaves only supplemented family labour, which appears accurate in light of other descriptions of the work force. The people of Dara, for example, were hardly wealthy enough to have owned many, if any, slaves, and the destitute migrants who took neither food nor money with them certainly could not have owned slaves.[49]

None the less, it is important to recognise that Laforque described the organisation of labour at a time when the adjustments to colonialism had been under way for over a decade. By extrapolation backward, it is possible to discern that slaves were used in production, but the terms of employment in 1913 were not the same as those in 1900. The introduction of colonialism heralded the decline of slavery through the curtailment of enslavement and the slave trade. Many slaves fled at the time of the conquest or shortly

127

thereafter; those slaves who stayed almost certainly benefited from the pressures put on slave owners by these desertions. The terms of labour shifted more in favour of the slaves as a result, and in this sense Laforque is correct in distinguishing between 'clients' or 'former captives' and slaves. The period 1900–13 was a transitional era in the organisation of production.

Slaves were well treated, or so Chambert observed in 1908. Slaves were part of the family and content with their lot. Some, however, who wanted their freedom,

> fled, and their master did all he could to recapture them as he would have tried to catch a runaway horse, simply because of his subject's commercial value. If he succeeded in bringing the slave back to his house, then he tied him up in his house and beat him or at least made as if to beat him, for one mustn't damage too much the instrument that had to be used the next day. In any case the slave had to scream loudly in order to attract the attention of the villagers; in that way the latter learned that the runaway slave had been found.[50]

Chambert's observation disguises the relationship between master and slave in the pre-conquest decades by suggesting that the punishment meted out to fugitives was a sham for public consumption. Most people were not fooled, as Chambert apparently pretended to be. Slaves were usually acquired for their labour – in salt production and agriculture among other activities – and those who fled did so in order to escape this exploitation. Chambert not only must have known this simple truth, but he also was probably reporting on the conditions of the early colonial era when it was easier for slaves to flee than it had been before the temporary collapse of political authority during the conquest. Chambert's observation confirms my analysis of Laforque's description of the relations of work and the changed status of 'slaves'. Because colonialism altered the relations of production and the nature of slavery, care must be taken in using the reports of colonial officials in uncovering what slavery was like in the years before 1900.

One of the ways in which the relations between master and slave changed was in the ease with which slaves could acquire their freedom through self-purchase. Hence some of the 'clients' reported by Laforque may well have been individuals who had already become free or who were in the process of buying their freedom. Even as late as 1941 this process of transition to new forms of labour mobilisation was still apparent, although colonial officials were seldom careful in distinguishing the differences between slaves, former slaves and those individuals who were working for their freedom. As one official saw it, 'the extended family comprises not merely free members but also their slaves. The status of the slaves varies, but the most common status is that of "client" of the "gens" in Roman law.'[51]

Despite the methodological difficulties of using colonial data, it is still safe to say that by 1900 more and more of the inhabitants of Mangari appear to have been able to afford slaves, in part because they took salt directly to market, where it was possible to purchase slaves at a low price, and in part because the ruling elite was more prosperous as a result of profits from the salt industry and could therefore invest in slaves. Most holdings were modest, but some commoners had five, six or even ten slaves who cultivated for their masters, and perhaps worked in the salines.[52] In 1908 Chambert reported that slaves had come from the south – Borno, Bagirmi and other places. At Maine-Soroa, Kabum, Sara and Wula slaves were common.[53] In 1903 Mundy found that slaves were still being transferred through Borno to Manga country from Dikwa: 'Slaves find their way up to Kabi in considerable numbers and it will not be possible to stop the trade entirely until the slave market at Kabi can be stopped.'[54] Not until the end of 1906 did 'the raw slave-traffic into French Manga which flourished so during the latter part of last year and the earlier part of this year, seem to have decreased'. Even then there was 'a large number of Mangas in Marrua and Mandara, now waiting to return to their country with slaves'.[55]

MIGRATION TO DALLOL FOGHA AND DALLOL BOSSO

When Barth visited Dallol Fogha in 1853, salt was still being produced, even though it was July. The workers had set aside supplies of salt-earth which lasted 1–2 months into the rainy season. Near Kalliul (Kawara-Debe), a Fulani town, were at least seven or eight *tunga*.[56] Barth actually spent the night in one, yet he was surprised when he returned the following August, 1854, to find the population of Kawara-Debe so small. By August 'the numerous salt-manufacturing hamlets were destitute of life and animation, and overgrown with vegetation', but the town was 'only scantily inhabited, although . . . the hamlets for manufacturing salt are almost deserted at this time of year, as no salt can be obtained as long as the bottom of the valley is covered with water'.[57] Barth does not explain the situation further, but it appears that migration was an important factor in the production of salt in the 1850s, as indeed it was during the colonial period.

Dallol Fogha was different from Mangari in a number of important respects. Unlike Mangari, there was a substantial local population because the agricultural potential of the valley was considerable. Permanent communities dotted the whole length of the Dallol. In the 1850s, Barth listed eight towns, besides Kawara-Debe.[58] Three of them – Bengu, Bana and Bara – still existed in the early twentieth century as centres of salt production, as well as farming. The lower Dallol Maouri, which joined the Fogha at the point which separated the salt district into its northern and southern sections, was close enough for the Dendi town of Yelou, located in Dallol Maouri, to have satellite salt-camps in Dallol Fogha.[59] Furthermore, Fulani cattle herders sought out the valley for its pastures and water, and their presence constituted a potential source of labour as well, if only because of the availability of their slaves for work.[60]

The local population was not able to provide all the necessary labour for salt production. Kawara-Debe only had a population of 255 in 1932, for example, and other permanent settlements were of similar size.[61] It is unlikely that the population of Kawara-Debe or the other villages in the valley was much larger in earlier decades, and Barth's comments from 1853–54 suggest a similar demographic structure then. Only a few of the inhabitants of the neighbouring areas, including Dallol Maouri, worked the salines.[62] The Maouri and Djerma brought firewood and foodstuffs to sell in the salt *tunga*, but they did not make salt.[63] Some local people, including slaves, appear to have moved to the *tunga*, but the great majority of workers, at least by the early years of French colonial rule, were Hausa migrants from the east, particularly from Kebbi.

Loffler first noticed the importance of migrant labour. In 1905 the permanent residents were fewer than the migrant population, which included Hausa, Djerma and Maouri, who either stayed long enough to acquire their provisions of salt for the year or worked the whole season until the beginning of the rains.[64] In the 1909 salt season, numerous migrants came to work the salt, although it is not clear how many people were actually involved.[65] The cartographer for the Tilho expedition shows what appear to have been 70 *tunga* on his map of Dallol Fogha, however, and this number can be used to estimate the total in 1909.[66] If later information on the size of settlements can be used, then the *tunga* had populations ranging from 23 to 129, with an average of 84 people, which suggests a total migrant population of 5,880. In 1915, it was estimated that 5,000 workers were involved in production, while in 1924, when the migrants included Fulani, Hausa, Djerma, Maouri, Dendi and Tienga, the population was officially estimated at 4,000–6,000, a quarter of whom were thought to have come from Nigeria.[67] That is, the pool of migrants from which the workers were actually drawn amounted to 1,000–1,500 people. It is possible that some of the Nigerians were also merchants, so that the number of workers would have been less than one quarter of the total population. This estimate for the working population can be checked against the tax returns. Each *koko* (filtering unit) was assessed 5 francs; total revenues amounted to 9,410 fr, which indicates that there were 1,882 *koko* (Table 6.4). Assuming that a worker could handle 2–3 *koko*, these tax returns suggest that the number of workers was of the order of 630–940. Using Faure's ratio of *koko* per worker (2.67), there were 705 workers.

A similar pattern prevailed in 1938: the population of the Dallol swelled to 4,000–5,000 because of the arrival of Hausa from Nigeria, who made the salt, and Djerma and Maouri, who brought firewood, particularly during the most productive months, from January to March.[68] In 1938 there were 1,449 *koko*, which indicates that the number of Hausa workers must have been of the order of 500–700, assuming that an individual could work 2–3 *koko*. Faure estimated that 580 workers in the southern Fogha produced 500 tonnes of salt, while the 213 workers recorded in the upper Fogha also made 500 tonnes.[69] There were 570 *koko* in the upper basin, but unfortunately he did not provide a figure for the number of *koko* in the south. His figures do suggest 2.67 *koko* per worker, which would mean that there were about 1,550 *koko* in the south, for a total of approximately 2,120 *koko* for the whole valley.

Table 6.4.   *Salt 'tunga' in Dallol Fogha, 1924*

Location	Tax returns (francs)	Number of koko	Number of workers (estimated)
Bengu	2,000	400	150
Tounouga	600	120	45
Bana	1,625	325	122
Yelou	1,100	220	82
Bara	1,265	253	95
Kawara-Debe	1,995	399	149
Sabon Birni	825	165	62
Total	9,410	1,882	705

The number of *koko* is estimated on the basis of the rate of taxation; 5 fr per *koko*, while the number of *koko* per worker is assumed to be 2.67 (see Faure, unpublished, 1965, fn 77).
Source: Commandant de cercle de Dosso, rapport de tournée, Dallol, Gaya, fleuve, Fogha, 1924, Archives Nationales du Niger, Niamey.

Because of the small population of the permanent settlements in Dallol Fogha and the unwillingness of the neighbouring Djerma and Maouri to work the salines, other sources of labour had to be found. Before 1900 this labour included local slaves and probably free Hausa migrants from the east. By 1905 migrant workers virtually monopolised salt making, but before then there is not enough information to reach a conclusion. It may be that Hausa migrants came to dominate salt production in the colonial period because there was a local association between salt production and slavery, which would explain the failure of Maouri and Djerma to do more than bring firewood and food for sale to the salt workers.

In Barth's day, Kawara-Debe was a Fulani town, but later traditions credit immigrants from Birnin Debe, a Kebbi town destroyed in the *jihad,* with founding the settlement.[70] These immigrants, the Toulmawa, also founded other villages in the upper region of Dallol Fogha. Yet Barth only refers to the Fulani and their slaves at Kawara-Debe, although the village was much reduced in size when he was there in 1853 and 1854 because of the revolt of the Dendi against the Sokoto Caliphate. The Dendi stronghold at Yelou, in the lower Dallol Maouri, was only 12 km away. As a result of numerous raids on Kawara-Debe, the Fulani had 'lost the whole of their slaves, who, under such circumstances, had run away in a body'.[71] It is possible that the connexion with Birnin Debe is associated with the enslavement of its inhabitants at the time Muhammad Bello took the town in the *jihad.* The people of Birnin Debe may have been involved in salt manufacturing in the Dallol Fogha at the time, for Birnin Debe was only a half day's march to the east. Or refugees, who first settled with the Dendi at Yelou before moving on because of friction there, may have moved into Dallol Fogha to settle and work the salt.[72] None the

131

less, the Fulani, as representatives of the caliphate, established control over the northern part of the valley, which was a centre of Fulani transhumance anyway. Fulani cattle herders from Gwandu came to Dallol Fogha to graze their herds in 1905, and probably in the nineteenth century as well.[73] Further west in Dallol Bosso, the Fulani also used slaves to make salt; hence slavery seems to have been common in both valleys.[74]

In the southern section of Dallol Fogha, the Tienga, who were the main population at Tounanga, Bana and in the area of Yelou, also owned slaves who made salt. Marsaud, who studied the customary rights of the Tienga in 1909, distinguished between 'captifs de case' and 'captifs en guerre' because the domestic slaves were not supposed to be sold.[75] The 'domestics' worked in the fields, in exchange for food and housing. The distinction was important because the 'captifs en guerre' fled or were set free at the time of the French occupation, but they probably worked in the salt villages and farmed before 1900. After that time, domestic slaves still did, although Marsaud insists on the voluntary nature of slavery and its relatively mild form:

> but these people are slaves virtually only in name. Generally speaking the Tiengas treat them gently and have them live in the same conditions as they do. The master doesn't prevent his slave from earning money if the slave can do so; i.e., the slave can purchase his freedom through his work if he wants to. In short it seems that slavery will gradually end of its own accord with slaves becoming in the near future workers working for their employers in return for a wage.[76]

As was the case in my use of colonial observations to analyse the organisation of labour in Mangari, Marsaud's observations must be used carefully. As he himself noted, recent war captives fled or otherwise acquired their freedom at the time of or shortly after the French conquest. Those slaves who stayed behind were able to work towards their freedom and in general experienced better terms of employment than they had previously had, even if those terms were still relatively bad. Marsaud referred to the payments made to salt workers as 'domestic wages', in which slaves were expected to turn over 60 per cent of their output to their masters.[77] In this assessment and others, the French administrators attempted to deny the significance of slave labour in production, but it was a long step from slavery to the status of wage-earner, and that step was not taken in the production of salt. Workers received a portion of their output, which served as an incentive for their labours, but these portions were certainly not wages.

The organisation of production in Dallol Bosso appears to have been similar to that in Dallol Fogha, although the only substantial information is Loyzance's report of 1947. Slaves and other workers migrated to the temporary camps – also known as *tunga* – in order to work the salt and natron. In 1947, five families – slaves by origin – worked the natron at Fondegna Tunga, near Birni. The main centre was at Tungare, where ten families – about 100 people – set up camp each November. They came from the Fulani village of Barbe and collected natron in three depressions near

Tungare. Another six families, also from Barbe, were installed at Loga, while some former slaves of the Tuareg from Tagazar worked natron at Bitelako. As late as the 1970s, Barbe had 40 ex-slave families, while there were only 20 free Fulani families. At Birni Silinke, there were another 24 ex-slave families and at Souda Peul eight. Finally, salt was made near Dionkete, Boulongeuy, Sangabouti, Bangou Beri, Kalleyel, Kaban Tafi, and Watingori. Each of these depressions was near a village, but the workers moved to temporary camps during the production season.[78]

SLAVERY AND KIGE PRODUCTION

The production of *kige* and *manda* presents an interesting contrast. While *kige* was made by filtering the ash of *baboul* and other plants and then boiling the brine dry, *manda* was made from salt-earth left on the ground after the rain-water had evaporated. *Manda* techniques used large ovens, but more often than not *kige* was made one cone at a time on an open fire. The two adjacent regions – Mangari and Kadzell – even relied on a different means of mobilising labour for the salt work. As discussed above, free peasants migrated into the *manda* salines during the dry season. In Kadzell, by contrast, slaves made almost all the *kige*, although by the end of the nineteenth century, some Manga were also manufacturing *kige* in areas adjacent to the *manda* zone.[79] The importance of slavery in a district next to a region where slavery was of only minor significance is striking. It may well be that the difference related to the fact that nomads controlled Kadzell, while salt production in Mangari and Muniyo depended upon sedentary farming communities. Those nomads who owned slaves and who passed through Kadzell with their herds could instruct their slaves to make salt, especially since slaves had another purpose – they maintained wells for their masters. In short, the presence of slaves in Kadzell was necessary to the transhumance of the nomads. The correlation between slave labour and *kige* production on the one hand, and migrant peasant labour and *manda* production on the other hand, reflected the political history of Borno in the nineteenth century. It may well be that before the nineteenth century this correlation did not apply.

An examination of the organisation of labour in the transitional years of the early colonial period reveals that slavery was essential to the production of *kige* salt in the nineteenth century, although it is not possible to uncover the full meaning of what it meant to be a slave before the conquest. As late as 1941 the workers were still identified as 'ex-slaves', forty years after the imposition of colonial rule. The relations between these servile workers and their former masters are clear in the period after 1900 and hence are worth examining for what can be learned about the era when slaves provided almost all the labour in the manufacture of *kige* salt.

In the nineteenth century – and probably earlier still – the nomadic population, including the Koyam, Segurti, Kanembu, and Tubu, settled slaves along the routes which they followed in their transhumance across Kadzell,

133

while Kanembu and Shuwa Arabs also owned slaves along other routes south of the Komodugu Yo. Slaves were concentrated in Kadzell, but they were found throughout the Lake Chad basin. The Kanembu, for example, acquired large agricultural holdings south of the Komodugu Yo. In 1919, Patterson found that salt manufacturing was 'almost entirely confined to the domestic slaves of inhabitants along Lake Chad',[80] and further south still the Shuwa Arabs had a few salt-camps such as the ones at Djimtilo and Mani, near the lake.[81] Riou, who made the most thorough survey of the Kadzell camps, learned in 1941 that the salt workers had to be distinguished from their former owners, as he reported of Segurti ex-slaves: 'for the most part these ex-slaves are salt workers quite distinct from the genuine Segourtis and are more like other ex-slaves who regardless of their former masters: Tubu, Kanembu, Mobbeur ... have common characteristics and constitute one of the elements of the population of the Nguigmi [*cercle*] which is designated by the name Karia'.[82] Even the Dietko, a remnant nomadic population from earlier times, had had some slaves employed in salt manufacturing.[83] Only the Mobbeur and a few Kanuri were the exceptions to the pattern that slaves employed in *kige* production belonged to nomads. The Mobbeur, who inhabited the Komodugu Yo Valley, had also sent their slaves north into Kadzell to make salt.[84] In 1941 the Mobbeur sometimes worked alongside their ex-slaves in the production of salt. They relied on their families and kin, but also used 'domestiques',[85] which was a French euphemism for former slaves.

Barth found salt being made between Baroua and Nguigmi along the shores of Lake Chad in the early 1850s. At one place he saw 'a considerable salt manufactory, consisting of at least twenty earthen pots. Large triangular lumps of salt were lying about, which are shaped in moulds made of clay. Several people were busy carrying mud from an inlet of the lake which was close at hand, in order to make new moulds.'[86] He observed other sites as well; at one there were about 40 workers, although it must have been difficult to tell since the workers attacked Barth's caravan, apparently thinking that they were being raided.[87] Barth thought these salt-camps and villages belonged to the Yedina, and he may well have been right.[88] Later reports, however, mention these same locations as the sites of slave villages of the Kanembu and others. Nachtigal, for example, passed along the same route from Nguigmi to Baroua in 1870, which took him through a number of salt-camps on his journey southward along the shore of Lake Chad. The slaves in these villages belonged to the ruler of Kadzell, the Kazelma, who lived in Nguigmi. One of the villages – Kinjalia – meant 'village of slaves'. Even Baroua had some salt-camps. There were also two hamlets between Baroua and Kinjalia.[89] Freydenberg, who studied the Lake Chad basin in 1905, reported that slaves of the Kanembu of Nguigmi made *kige*, which 'was made in great quantities in the region of n'Guigmi, at Djimtiloh and at Assala, and is consumed throughout Bornou'.[90]

The preoccupation of these Kanembu dependants with salt continued well into the colonial period. In 1941 Riou found that 'for the most part these

Kanembu are former slaves who live in the bush around wells during the dry season, where they manufacture *baboul* salt. They all own a few goats and cows and during the rainy season grow finger millet on the dunes.'[91] By 1941, these people were indeed 'former slaves'. While their masters still maintained some measure of domination over them, it is not clear from Riou's reports what obligations slaves had to their masters in the pre-colonial era.

The Kanembu district near Lake Chad, south of the Komodugu Yo River, became more important than it had been, after al-Kanemi assumed the effective leadership of Borno in 1810. With the destruction of Birni Ngazargamu, the old capital of Borno, and the establishment of a new capital at Kukawa, the eastern districts became heavily populated with slaves. Slave settlements included Gorgaram Shehuri, which belonged to the new rulers, and Kinjarwa (which means 'slave village'), but there were many more. The Chad shore was a prosperous district, with large herds of cattle and irrigated agriculture in the dry season. Crops included tobacco, indigo, cotton, maize, ground-nuts, beans, and tomatoes. The Kanembu slaves worked these gardens with the aid of *shadif*, which raised water onto the farms from low-lying areas where water still remained. Slaves either engaged in irrigated agriculture or they made salt at such places as Yebi Tasmsugwa near Ngurutuwa, or the places observed – and photographed – by Boyd Alexander in 1905. According-ing to one colonial report, 'slaves [were] a large and well treated class in Kanembu'.[92] These were not the only concentrations of slaves in Borno. The Koyam of Ngemzei had owned 'large numbers of slaves' before Rabeh invaded Borno in 1892.[93] Tegetmeier also reported a similar reliance on slave labour in 1925.[94] Falconer found that 'slaves of Mongonu and Musara prepare salt ... from the ash of three varieties of grass, "pagam, kalaslim and kanido", which are found in the immediate neighbourhood of the lake'.[95]

It has been possible to establish the location of 107 salt-camps or small villages where *kige* was made in Kadzell and Borno, near Lake Chad. Of these, the social status is known for the inhabitants of 75 camps, and the ethnic identity is known for 73 (Table 6.5). While there is some possibility of overlap in the various reports, especially since camps could move from year to year, it is known that many of the camps were relatively permanent, attached to wells which were maintained by nomads or by the settled population on behalf of nomads. The Manga, who lived at 14 camps (19.2 per cent), were all in the area bordering Mangari country, either in western Kadzell or north of the main production area for *manda*. These people appear to have been mostly free peasants, and it is likely that they had had few slaves in the period before 1900. Former slaves are known to have been the only inhabitants of 53 camps and may have been a majority of the population of eight others. These figures can be extrapolated backward as a rough guide to the role of slavery in the past. In all likelihood, the number of free peasants, as represented by the Manga population, increased between 1900 and 1941, while the number of people of servile origin (former slaves) decreased either through flight or because of the impossibility of importing new slave recruits. Hence the

135

Table 6.5   *Social status of workers in kige camps*

Ethnic group	No. of villages	Per cent	Free	Mixed	Slaves	Unknown
Kanembu	19	26.0	—	—	19	—
Segurti	3	4.1	—	—	3	—
Mobbeur	19	26.0	—	8	11	—
Tubu	15	20.5	—	—	15	—
Kanuri	1	1.4	—	—	1	—
Dietko	2	2.7	—	—	2	—
Manga	14	19.2	14	—	—	—
Subtotal	73	99.9	14	8	51	
Unknown	34		—	—	2	32
Grand Total	107					

Sources: Ravoux, 10–30 août 1932; Riou, 18–26 jan. 1941; Riou, 2–16 juillet, 1941; Riou, 13 fév–1 mars, 1941; Riou, 17 nov–1 déc 1940; Fischer, 1930's; Rapport de tournée du chef de subdivision de Mainé-Soroa, 10–27 fév. 1936; Cagnier, Rapport de tournée 1935; all in Archives Nationales du Niger, Niamey. J.D.H., Kanembu District Notebook, 1926, Nigerian National Archives, Kaduna; J.D. Falconer (1911), 267; Nachtigal (1980), 103–104; Dunstan, Mineral Survey, 1906–7 [Cd. 4719], Public Record Office, London.

composition of the salt-camps in 1941 probably represents a conservative assessment of the ratio of slave to free in 1900. Taken together, former slaves were found in 61 camps (81.3 per cent in 1941). In terms of ethnic identity, Kanembu and Mobbeur owned the most camps, and these were inhabited entirely by former slaves in the case of the Kanembu and mostly by former slaves in the case of the Mobbeur. The Tubu also had significant holdings – 15 camps – again inhabited by ex-slaves. The Segurti and Dietko, two small groups of nomads, had 5 camps between them, and as was the case with the other nomads, these were servile. The Shuwa Arabs are not represented in the sample, which is weighted heavily towards *kige* production in Kadzell, where the Shuwa did not graze. It is known, however, that the Shuwa did make salt to the south of Borno.[96] Furthermore, the Kanembu share (26 per cent) is too low for the same reason. First, Kanembu in Kanem had also owned slaves who made *kige*, and secondly, the Kanembu to the south of the Komodugu Yo are under-represented in the sample.[97]

The total work force for *kige* production is virtually impossible to estimate. There were no major centres, only small camps which were widely scattered. The most complete survey was done by Ravoux in 1932, but he only examined twenty-two *kige* camps (Table 6.6). Ravoux counted 419 workers, which meant an average of 19 workers or approximately two labour units per site. The largest had only fifty workers. These twenty-two camps produced 2,000 salt cones, or about 91 per site. On the basis of other reports, however, it seems likely that there were at least another hundred and perhaps many more camps

Table 6.6 *Kige salt production in Kadzell, cantons of Deoua and Diffa, 1932*

Name of camp	Number of workers	Number of salt cones
Toumaya	11	60
Kadedja Koura	40	130
Korilla	50	140
Kaoua	20	95
Koussouloua	14	60
Ibram Diato	10	70
Kourouloua	12	85
Kouroua	10	65
Guissiria	14	75
Gadegami	10	65
Kala Kemaguena	20	75
Korea	30	140
Toubori	12	70
Kirieoua	13	55
Koutto	40	195
Katiella Gonbol	40	225
Mustapha Zarami	14	70
Kintiendi Assembe	20	110
Mamadou Dovdoumibe	10	75
Alla Garno	8	45
Mela Boudoumirom	13	55
Korsouloua	8	40
	—	—
Total	419	2,000

Source: Ravoux, Rapport de tournée, 10–30 août 1932, cercle de Nguigmi, Archives Nationales du Niger, Niamey.

where *kige* was made, so that the total number of workers was probably of the order of 2,500, who could have made at least 12,000 cones, or 150 tonnes.[98]

Riou also conducted a detailed survey of other *kige* camps in 1940 and 1941 (Table 6.7). There is almost no overlap in the names of these camps, and the itineraries of Ravoux and Riou indicate that they covered different parts of Kadzell. Unlike Ravoux, however, Riou did not try to distinguish between general population and salt workers, although it can be assumed that virtually the whole population of these camps and villages was engaged in *kige* manufacture. That 'ex-captifs' could still be identified with their former owners, if only by ethnicity, demonstrates that the transition from slavery to freedom was a gradual process in Kadzell. The slaves involved in *kige* manufacture were only freed in 1922.[99] It is likely that the terms of the master-slave relationship shifted more in favour of the slaves with the imposition of

137

Table 6.7. *Population of kige camps, 1940–41*

Camp/Village	Ethnicity	Status	Population
Lari	Kanembu	ex-slave	104
Metime	Kanembu	ex-slave	23
Woudi	Kanembu	ex-slave	42
Ferewa	Kanembu	ex-slave	46
N'guibouloa	Kanembu	ex-slave	30
Kournawa	Kanembu	ex-slave	21
N'galewa	Kanembu	ex-slave	153
N'Dibo	Kanembu	ex-slave	29
Kantanawa	Segurti	ex-slave ⎱	52
Silawa	Segurti	ex-slave ⎰	
Magadam	unknown	unknown	36
Worio	unknown	unknown	31
Billi Djedi	Tubu	ex-slave	44
Kossouloa	Tubu	ex-slave	62
N'Gagam	Mobbeur	ex-slave	unknown
Bangaley	Tubu	ex-slave	64
Moussari	Dietko	ex-slave	unknown
Dagourgo	Manga	free	215
Diawtya	unknown	ex-slave	73
Goma	Tubu	ex-slave ⎱	158
Maderde	Tubu	ex-slave ⎰	
Waragou-Kingoa	Tubu	ex-slave	41
Kandiloa	Manga	free	31
Total			1,255

Source: Riou, Rapports, 1940, 1941, Archives Nationales du Niger, Niamey.

colonialism. Otherwise, it is hard to imagine why the slaves would have chosen to stay where they were.

These surveys demonstrate that a number of different work regimes for the production of *kige* operated in the late nineteenth century. Most important, nomads owned slaves who were settled at wells in Kadzell during the dry season to make salt; sometimes the slaves also grew crops on the dunes near these wells. To the south of the Komodugu Yo, nomads and other livestock herders also directed slave labour in the production of salt. This pattern, which was probably common well into the past, long before the first direct evidence, explains the activities of most Kanembu, Segurti, Tubu, Dietko, and Shuwa Arabs. A second pattern characterised the Komodugu Yo Valley, where the Mobbeur lived. The slaves of these Mobbeur farmers moved north into Kadzell to make salt at temporary camps. In some cases, the slaves may have lived to the north of the Komodugu Yo Valley all year round, growing some crops on the dunes in the rainy season. None the less, migration was involved for at least some of the slaves. Finally, Manga participation in *kige* production, which followed the pattern for Manga industry in general, involved the migration of peasants to temporary salt-camps; some Manga moved into Kadzell, others moved to northern Mangari, beyond the region of *manda* production, and still others made *kige* in eastern Mangari, near Maine-Soroa. The Manga appear to have begun making *kige* later than the nomads and Mobbeur. Traditions record the eastern movement of the Manga into the *kige* area only in the last half of the nineteenth century, which accords well with the general eastward drift of the Manga as the exploitation of *manda* depressions expanded in the nineteenth century.[100] For the Manga, *kige* manufacture was an extension of the *manda* industry. These various patterns suggest that the use of slave labour was the older, established method of labour recruitment, but that the migration of free peasants began to compete with slavery in the second half of the nineteenth century.

SLAVE LABOUR AT THE DESERT SITES

Despite the penetration of Manga peasants into the *kige* industry, the organisation of labour in Kadzell fitted into a wider pattern of desert-side economy and society.[101] In many parts of the sahel and southern Sahara slaves constituted a major part of the work force. They lived in agricultural communities along the transhumant corridors of their masters, and other slaves helped in the management of livestock.[102] It might be expected, therefore, that the production of salt at the desert sites would also rely extensively on slavery. At Teguidda n'tesemt, the workers were mostly slaves from In Gall, who moved to the salines after the surface water of the rainy season had retreated.[103] The rest of the year they worked the gardens and date groves at In Gall. Nomads also gathered salt-earth at Guelele, near Teguidda n'tesemt,[104] and it is probable that this too was a task for slaves. In Kawar, the nomadic population of the northern oases, including Djado and Seguidine, relied on slave labour,[105] and they sent slaves south to Bilma, and perhaps occasionally to Fachi, to work the salt for their own consumption and trade. Most salt produced at Bilma, and also at Fachi, was produced by local people, and many, if not most, of these were slaves.[106] Slavery at Teguidda, Bilma and Fachi, moreover, differed from the usual pattern along the desert-edge and in the southern Sahara. The owners were not nomads but the sedentary population of the oases.

The history of slavery in the Teguidda region is very old. Ibn Battuta, who was at Azelik in 1353, when the major export was copper, not salt, found that slaves were the principal workers in the copper-ore pits:

> the mineral is dug up and brought to town where it is smelted in houses. This task is performed by slaves of both sexes. Once the red copper has been obtained it is formed into long bars of a span and a half, some of them thin, others thick.[107]

The salt made at Guelele for use in the smelting process may also have been the work of slaves, and the elaborate irrigation system which was maintained in support of agriculture at Azelik almost certainly depended upon slave labour.[108] Tradition even has it that a slave discovered the salt of Teguidda n'tesemt, although it does not appear that the Teguidda salt was actually exploited for commercial purposes in the fourteenth century.[109]

The inhabitants of Azelik were forced to evacuate the copper works, probably sometime in the fifteenth century, when the new centre at Agades successfully challenged the supremacy of Azelik in the region. War ravaged Azelik, and the site was permanently abandoned. The refugees eventually settled at In Gall, where their descendants – the Inusufa and Imesdraghen – have lived ever since.[110] The salt has been worked at Teguidda n'tesemt for several centuries at least. Cortier, who visited Teguidda in 1909, recorded a somewhat garbled tradition which recounts the exploitation of salt over seven generations, which he estimated traced the salines back 200–250 years, roughly to the last half of the seventeenth century.[111] Bernus and Gouletquer think that the production of salt there is older than that, but began after the early sixteenth century. There is extensive debris at Teguidda, but unlike the debris at Bilma and Dallol Fogha, it has not been used to date the saline, for some of the debris is re-introduced into the basins each year and thereby the remaining debris does not appear to contain a continuous, undisturbed base that might yield useful radio-carbon material. Not only is the antiquity of the saline in question, but there is no way to tell whether or not slaves were used in the seventeenth, eighteenth or nineteenth centuries.[112] In 1907, Gadel reported that the 200 salt workers at Teguidda were 'virtually slaves of the people of Ingall',[113] and Cortier, who visited Teguidda in the same year, recovered traditions about the importance of slavery in the history of Azelik and noted that slaves were assigned the work of making salt and guarding the houses at Teguidda.[114] No one else other than these slaves from In Gall – estimated at 145 in 1915 – was allowed to make salt at Teguidda.[115]

Edmond and Suzanne Bernus, who have recorded a number of traditions concerning the history of In Gall and Teguidda n'tesemt, have established that the legacy of slavery continues to survive in the production of salt. Their work, undertaken in 1970, includes considerable detail on inheritance and work patterns. One family owned four *abatol*, the series of basins where the evaporation of the brine takes place, which were worked by 'un serviteur et sa fille', while an ex-slave, his wife and daughters worked the six *abatol* of another patron. The 'serviteur' lived permanently at Teguidda and only occasionally went to In Gall.[116] The population of In Gall was 1,880, while Teguidda had another 380 people.[117] While this last figure may be a low estimate, it does show that most people lived at In Gall; as Bernus and Bernus observed:

> In effect the inhabitants of Tegidda, starting with the chief, have long established permanent residence at In Gall... and the only ones who stay at Tegidda are those who work on the salt fields, domestic servants, former slaves or freed slaves, junior members of the family, widows or old men. Other people merely come for periods of varying duration and virtually the whole of the population is to be found

140

at In Gall during the rainy season when fewer than a hundred people remain at Tegidda to watch over the salt works and occasionally to dispose of the rest of the season's production.[118]

Their work confirms some of the details of earlier reports. Teguidda was not entirely abandoned after the end of the salt season. Some people stayed behind to take care of the village and the salt works, but essentially the production of salt was based on the migration of workers from In Gall. Since the French conquest prompted a transition from slavery to other forms of labour, the actual number of *iklan*, people of slave status, in 1970 was relatively small.[119] Slavery had declined in the past eighty years. Now 'clientage' is a more apt term to describe the relationship between workers and proprietors, but the older pattern of labour mobilisation can still be reconstructed. What is not clear is the extent of slavery in the past and the proportion of slaves to freed slaves, who may well have constituted a category that is not subsumed in such terms as 'anciens captifs' and 'serviteur'.

At Fachi, Bilma and other places in Kawar, most of the workers in agriculture and salt production were also slaves. In 1906 Gadel reported that slaves had been imported from the south in order to work the salines and the irrigated gardens of Bilma.[120] In 1865 Rohlfs discovered that the Tubu brought slaves from the south for sale in Bilma,[121] and of course slaves were usually available for purchase from passing caravans along the major slave route through Kawar to North Africa.[122] As Périé noted in 1941 with reference to the past, the Tubu sometimes captured slaves in the south – Damergu, Mangari – or in the west – the Air Massif – for use in Kawar, but other people in Kawar, including the mixed Tubu–Kanuri population (Guezebida and Djadoboy) and the Kanuri, also obtained slaves. Indeed slaves were the 'workers for all the races'.[123] Slaves were so essential to salt production that they were recognised as a distinct unit. In Muslim ceremonies slaves even danced as a group, thereby publicly acknowledging their dependence.[124]

Slaves apparently worked alongside their masters in both Bilma and Fachi, or at least under their close supervision. According to Rottier, who reported on Kawar in 1924:

> the slaves [*serviteurs*] of the Kanuri are attached from father to son to their master who used them for working the land or the salines and assures their subsistence. For work on the land, generally speaking, the slave who cultivates a garden for his master has the right to cultivate another garden, whose produce belongs to him and is used for his own subsistence and that of his family. Occasionally a slave is able to buy his freedom by agreement with his master in return either for a sum of money or for undertaking to pay his master a certain sum each year based on the produce of his labour. Generally speaking, the situation of the slave is not bad. Quite often a master at his death frees a slave who has been particularly loyal and may even include him in his will.[125]

The extent to which slaves were 'part of the family' in the nineteenth century is difficult to assess. The institution of slavery had already been modified by the

141

time Rottier was in Kawar. In 1906, Vischer discovered that the French prohibition of slavery was a serious problem, which was confirmed by Gadel in the following year when he had to deal with 'a great number' of slaves requesting their liberty.[126] Many of the slaves may not actually have left Bilma and Fachi, however. As Gadel noted, it was impossible to escape without a camel, provisions and knowledge of the route. The difficulty of leaving was not an unimportant aspect of slavery in the desert; slaves had little choice but to stay with their masters, and thereby they had to find ways to accommodate themselves to their status.

The French regime discouraged full emancipation, but it appears that slavery declined in importance none the less. According to Prévôt, 'the descendant of a captive is free in the third generation. Most of the families in the oasis have this origin. They are called Toubbous or Kanouris according to the race of their former patrons.'[127] This custom of gradual emancipation between generations may have reflected the image rather than the reality of slavery in Kawar, but it was certainly a view which the French encouraged.

> Though legally free since our occupation, most of them remain in the families of their masters and they are the ones who ensure the relative prosperity of the country by providing the labour necessary for cultivation and for the exploitation of the salt fields.[128]

Indeed 'since the French occupation the number of slaves has been rapidly diminishing and slaves are tending to disappear; bit by bit free men are starting to do the work that previously had been done by their slaves'.[129] Those slaves who did not leave their masters in 1906, at the time of the French occupation, continued to live with their masters – by 1943 all were virtually free. The same was true for Fachi.[130] Moreover, workers from Aney and Arrigui also came to Bilma during the salt season to work in the salines; at least they did so by the 1940s. It may be that these workers were also slaves or former slaves. This migration, although not very large by comparison with the population movements in the savanna and sahel, appears to have compensated for the decline in the slave population. It is not clear if the migration of people within Kawar was characteristic of labour mobility in the past. Despite the apparent change in slave status, ex-slaves were still responsible for the irrigated gardens, date trees and salines, which suggests the possibility that the workers from elsewhere in Kawar were continuing an established pattern. The ex-slaves at Bilma were still responsible for communal work – much as they had always been – including repair of the town walls and maintenance of the wells. At Fachi, the head (*mai*) of the oasis re-allocated salt flats in 1939 in order to increase production. The ex-slaves had refused to work the salines, and production had dropped accordingly. Backed by the colonial regime, the *mai* granted some unused flats to ex-slaves, which appears to have prompted many saline owners to work out better arrangements with those ex-slaves who agreed to work the salines. Once slaves had also been responsible for the upkeep of the defensive fortresses (*gassar*, Arabic: *qasr*) which were located at every village in Kawar and also at Fachi.[131] The end of slavery altered the relations of production; slaves had to be given better terms.

The slave population of Kawar and Fachi identified with the ethnicity of their masters. They were either Kanuri or Tubu. This division reflected the distinction between the sedentary customs of the Kanuri and the nomadic lifestyle of the Tubu, although there was some geographical separation too. The Tubu tended to live in the north of Kawar, at Dirku, Seguidine, Djado and other places, while the Kanuri were concentrated at Bilma and Fachi, with only a few families at Dirku. Tubu slaves did some of the same tasks as Kanuri slaves. They maintained wells, practised some irrigated agriculture, and generally performed any work that needed to be done.[132] Only the ethnicity of their masters differed. The Tubu came to Bilma, and perhaps Fachi too, in search of salt, but they did so on an irregular basis and on a relatively minor scale. It was possible for the Tubu to rent a saline for a brief period, during which time their slaves made salt.[133] As Gadel noted:

> There is also the custom that if slaves from villages of the north come to manufacture salt at Bilma, they receive a portion of the salt as a wage, but if they sell the salt to the Touareg at a profit they must collectively give the chief of the village forty cubits of cloth strips.[134]

In effect, a distinction was made between production for personal consumption and production for trade with the Tuareg. This participation of the Tubu in production, albeit on a small scale, appears to have been an old arrangement, for Denhan noted that the Tubu were collecting salt at Bilma in 1823, although he did not comment on the social status of the workers.[135]

In 1906, Gadel found that slaves constituted 27.4 per cent of the population of Bilma, but only 20.5 per cent of Kawar as a whole (Table 6.8). Gadel had no figures for Fachi. In 1907, Colonna di Leca reported slightly higher figures, 28.2 per cent according to his categories (Table 6.9). Prévôt stated in 1907 that slaves ('l'élément captif') were very numerous, 1,000 in a population of 3,500 or 28.6 per cent.[136] It may well be that Colonna di Leca's and Prévôt's figures are based on the same census. For Bilma, Colonna di Leca shows a slave population of 140 (28.6 per cent of the population), compared with Gadel's figure of 131, while the slaves at Fachi (117 in a population of 659) constituted 17.8 per cent. There are several problems with Colonna di Leca's figures. First, the sex ratio of 'free' adults suggests the possibility that many women were slaves or of slave origin, since the women outnumbered the men to a considerable extent (37.3 per cent male and 62.7 per cent female at Bilma; 39.4 per cent male and 60.6 per cent female at Fachi) a ratio of 59 males for 100 females at Bilma and 65 males for 100 females at Fachi, when the 'importés' and children are excluded. Either there was a regular out-migration of males, or female slaves were imported as concubines and wives, or both. It is likely that at least some of the women were slaves, which would suggest that the actual number of people of servile origin was higher than the slave category

Table 6.8. *Population of Kawar, 1906*

Place	Slave population	Total population	% Slave
Bilma	131	478	27.4
Emi-Madama	15	100	15.0
Chimidour	40	350	11.4
Dirku	100	300	33.3
Tiguimami	30	150	20.4
Arrigui	100	250	40.0
Gaser	10	130	7.7
Achenouma	20	300	6.7
Emi-Tchouma	15	130	11.5
Aney	50	300	16.7
Total	511	2,488	20.5

Source: Gadel (1907a), 375.

Table 6.9. *Population of Kawar and Fachi, 1907*

Location	Men	%	Women	%	Children	%	Importés	%	Total
Kawar (Emi-Madama; Chimidour; Dirku; Tiguimami; Arrigui; Gaser; Achenouma)	246	14.1	447	25.6	500	28.7	550	31.6	1,743
Bilma	82	16.7	138	28.2	130	26.5	140	28.6	490
Emi-Tchouma; Aney	58	14.9	103	26.4	110	28.2	119	30.5	390
Fachi	123	18.7	189	28.7	230	34.9	117	17.8	659
Total	509	15.5	877	26.7	970	29.6	926	28.2	3,282

There were also 170 people at Djado. Mouret (1908b), 173, reports the population of Fachi as 661.
Source: Colonna di Leca, 1907, Archives de Bilma.

alone would indicate. As such, the number of recorded slaves is probably an excellent indicator of available labour. It is significant that the number of recorded slaves was greater than the number of free males in both Fachi and Bilma, because men did more work in the salines than women and children. The usual work unit consisted of four men and an old woman or child and, while these units may not have been composed entirely of slaves, most of the labour was in fact slave labour.

In 1915 the work force in the salines of Fachi and Bilma was estimated at 900, a figure which seems slightly high in comparison with the earlier population estimates.[137] Since the total population of the two villages was only

1,149 in 1907, the 1915 estimate makes virtually no allowance for infants, the infirm and the otherwise unemployed. It is likely that the 1915 report is a capacity figure: the number of able-bodied people, including children, who were available for salt production. The actual work force probably consisted of a couple of hundred slaves and the people who owned them.

This interpretation that slavery was the principal means of mobilising labour at Kawar and Fachi is different from Grandin's analysis of production at Bilma and is most notably at odds with Vikør's discussion of Bilma.[138] Grandin, who examined the salt industry in 1946, emphasised the importance of the family as the basic unit of production, although, as explained above, freemen increasingly had to assume the responsibilities of slaves after the French conquest, and by the 1940s there were few slaves left. Hence Grandin's analysis of the situation in 1946 is useful as a study in its own right but also as an indication of the changes which had occurred over a forty year period. According to Grandin,

> Exploitation is essentially based on the family. During the salt season, all the kin – young and old – are employed in the basins. However the numerous proprietors employ a certain number of workers in addition to their families according to the arrangement and importance of their salines. This exploitation is characterised by payment to salt workers according to specific rules. A real contract (customary contract) exists between proprietor and worker. Work for the 'maitre' ends each day after *zawell* [2.00 p.m.], the rest of the day belongs to the workers. Friday is consecrated to God. Payment of workers is made in the product of the salines.[139]

In earlier times four-fifths of the work force had to be drawn from the adult population of free males and slaves, who were probably mostly males, at least in Colonna di Leca's tabulation. Some women probably worked alongside the men, however. The distinction between *fochi* and *kantu* – the small mould and the large column – normally reflected a sexual division of labour. Women made *fochi*, while the major share of production – involving the men and only incidentally some women – went into the manufacture of *kantu*, the main trade salt.

Vikør makes the mistake of projecting Grandin's analysis backwards in time, thereby underestimating the importance of slavery. He too argues that the basic work unit was the family, although he admits that extra workers were sometimes employed alongside the family members when necessary.[140] According to Vikør, 'slaves appear into [sic] the oases incidentally.... [they] do not form the human basis for the production; this was done by the salt-basin owners and their families'.[141] Other information makes it clear that slave labour was crucial to production. Grandin received some of his information on the Bilma industry from an 'ancien captif' from Fachi, who had been freed by his master and was living in Bilma in 1946. The man was an expert on salt production at Fachi; his job had been making moulds for *kantu* production.[142] Mouret also reported slaves at Fachi, but Colonna di Leca's material is conclusive.[143] While the percentage of slaves at Fachi (17.8 per

cent) was lower than at Bilma, the same observations apply to Fachi as to
Bilma: the number of slaves was probably disguised because the slave wives of
freemen appear not to have been included in the list. The crucial factor
appears to have been the number of slaves in relation to the number of free
males, which was almost equal. There may have been fewer slaves at Fachi,
but their contribution to salt production, as well as irrigated agriculture, was
essential. As Fuchs has demonstrated for Fachi, the ending of slavery, which
occurred gradually after the French conquest, was reflected in declining
output. Between 1906–09 and the 1930s, production fell from 600–700 tonnes
to less than half that level. Fuchs attributes this decline to the emancipation of
slaves. Only in 1939, as a result of state intervention on behalf of ex-slaves, did
production figures start to rise again.[144]

In the past, especially in the nineteenth century, the slave population of
Kawar and Fachi was periodically depleted as the result of raids and warfare.
The Awlad Sulayman, who moved from North Africa to Kanem in the 1840s,
were a particular menace, although Tuareg and Tubu raids also occurred,
despite the interest of most Tuareg and Tubu in the safety of the oases.[145]
Nachtigal, who passed through Kawar in 1870 and stayed in Borno until 1872,
provides excellent information on the seriousness and frequency of these
raids. The Awlad Sulayman – those 'pitiless hereditary enemies of the
oasis' – repeatedly attacked Kawar, 'dragging away to their homes as fine
plunder the women and children of the inhabitants'.[146] One raid in 1872, for
example, carried off many captives – one tradition remembers the number at
1,500[147] – although through the intervention of the Borno government many
of the free people were returned. But slaves were fair booty, so that in this and
other raids the capture of slaves resulted in a net loss of population – and salt
workers.

While it is not possible to chronicle the history of slavery in the production
of salt with any detail, certain broad patterns are clear. The Tubu probably
had slaves settled in Kawar for centuries. Perhaps the Guezebida and
Djadoboy, mixed populations of Tubu and Kanuri, represent the descendants
of ancient slave communities, although, however likely this may be, there is no
direct evidence. Traditions do claim that the Borno government once settled
slaves in Kawar, which suggests that irrigation and salt production were
promoted as a result, and the Tuareg settled war captives there after defeating
Borno in c. 1759.[148] By the nineteenth century, most slaves were owned by
local merchants and nomads who could be identified either as Kanuri or
Tubu. It does not appear that the Tuareg kept their own slaves in Kawar,
except perhaps for a time after 1759. They were content with the privileges of
commercial access and tribute won after the Bilma war.[149]

TRONA PRODUCTION IN FOLI

The extraction of trona from the depressions of Foli also relied on servile
labour, but not the labour of slaves. The workers belonged to a caste of

artisans attached to the various fractions of the Kanembu. Barth referred to them as the 'peculiar tribe', these artisans whom the Kanembu called Du or Danawa.[150] The Awlad Sulayman described them as *haddad*, blacksmiths, because in their society blacksmiths formed a distinct caste, and *haddad* has been used as a generic term for the caste of artisans, hunters, and salt workers. In Tubu they were known as *aza*, only among the Tubu they dug wells, farmed the scattered oases, and were blacksmiths.[151] 'Peculiar' is an apt description, because this caste was found in many different societies in the southern Sahara and sahel east of Lake Chad. A few were found among the Kanembu on the western shores, but otherwise the lake marked the western boundary of the *haddad* caste in the savanna.[152] Despite the cultural and linguistic labyrinth to the east of Lake Chad, the caste structure crossed all boundaries. The *haddad* spoke the language of their superiors, whether it was Kanembu, Tubu, Arabic, Yedina, or Kreda. They practised many of the same customs of these dominant societies; yet they were set apart through strict endogamy and a common tradition that transcended all ethnic groups. The Danawa were Kanembu, but they were different, 'neither slaves nor nobles'.[153] In the 1850s, Barth described them as follows:

> [they] go almost naked, being only clothed with a leather wrapper round their loins, and are armed with bows and arrows and the goliyo [throwing knife]. They are very expert bowmen, and when attacked, withdraw into the dense forests of their districts (to which seems to apply the general name of Bari), and know well how to defend their independence in politics as well as in religion – for they are pagans.[154]

Barth and Nachtigal identified this region as Bari,[155] but Danawa were found in Foli too. They may have been pagans in the 1850s, but they were Muslims only a few decades later. It is likely that Barth was wrong on this point; he appears to have interpreted too literally the charges of his informants among the Awlad Sulayman, who probably doubted the Islamic credentials of the *haddad*.

Those Danawa who worked the trona deposits were attached to the Kankena fraction of the Kanembu and lived in the region of Mattegou and Kamba, south-east of Kouloa. The Kankena and two associated fractions of Kanembu, the Kadjidi and Korio, had been in the vicinity of the lake since at least the 1840s.[156] Freydenberg, who surveyed Foli in 1905, thought that the Kankena (Kinguina) were the proprietors of the deposits, but it is more likely that he observed Kankena workers at the salines and attributed ownership to them. *Haddad* from Faraguimi and Hedimirum worked the depressions to the west of the main deposits between Wanda and Kamba; Freydenberg did not identify these people with a particular fraction, but they may have been Kankena too.[157] Certainly in the area of Kouloua, the Kankena *haddad* exploited the salines, but the *haddad* of the Kadjidi and Korio may have supplied some workers too. The Kadjidi were centred near Bol, which was always one area where the Yedina came to buy trona, while the Korio were in the vicinity of Kaira, which was also convenient to the deposits.[158]

Vial and Luxeuil estimated the number of workers extracting trona in 1938 to be of the order of 500 – 200 in the region of Bol and 300 in the region of Rig Rig.[159] In 1938 work units consisted of three men, one who cut out the slabs with an iron tool, a second who collected the debris, and a third who relieved the others. Workers were given a portion of a depression that measured about 7–8 metres square.[160] A unit could produce about 50 slabs (15–20 kg each), so that in a season lasting from December to June, it was possible to produce one tonne per unit.[161] Vial and Luxeuil thought that 280 tonnes were produced in 1938, but this figure is probably low, and it is probable that work units produced more than a tonne each during a season. Since 1938, the number of workers has increased. *Haddad* from the areas adjacent to Foli and also from Ngelea have continued to work the deposits, but *haddad* from Ngouri appear to have joined them.[162]

In the 1960s there were 3,823 Danawa in the *préfecture du lac* in a total population of 88,911, or 4.34 per cent of the total population.[163] Since only men extracted trona, it is clear that a sizeable proportion of the Danawa population was involved in the industry. It may well be that Danawa from other parts of Kanem, particularly the Ngouri region of southern Kanem, where the Danawa constituted 75 per cent of the population, migrated to the trona depressions.[164] Otherwise it is difficult to explain how 1,000–2,000 tonnes of trona could have been exported. In the past slaves may have worked the deposits alongside the Danawa, and the *haddad* of the Yedina islanders may have journeyed inland to the depressions too, but there is no evidence on the contribution of either group.

The presence of an occupational caste in the production of trona is in sharp contrast with the organisation of labour at every other saline in the central Sudan. The reliance on slaves and peasants elsewhere can be understood in terms of differences in political economy. Labour could be tied to the salines through slavery, or migrant workers could be allowed to move into the salt-camps in order to supplement their agricultural output. Why these particular alternatives were not pursued in Foli seems to relate to the development of a unique political economy in Kanem and areas to the east, where forms of dependency had become solidified in the course of centuries to include a caste structure for artisans, as well as slave and peasant categories. There was nothing exceptional about the nature of trona production that determined the employment of *haddad*, but there was something exceptional about the political economy that resulted in the formation of an artisan caste that included salt workers.

SEXUAL DIVISION OF LABOUR

In many of the salines, men and women worked together, but there was a clear division of labour based on gender. In Mangari, women gathered salt-earth and carried water, while the men made the filters, moulds, and ovens, boiled the salt, and gathered firewood.[165] A similar division characterised Dallol Fogha, Teguidda n'tesemt, Kawar and Fachi.[166] At Bilma, the separation of tasks was expressed in the right of women to make small blocks (*fochi*), which consisted of the same mixture of salt as the large *kantu*, but which belonged to the women.[167] Apparently, *fochi* were made in the late afternoon, after the work day was over. In Foli, the extraction of trona was a task for men; apparently women did not participate in production at all.

At the brine springs in the Benue Valley, the sexual division of labour was enshrined in tradition. Salt 'cooking' was women's work.[168] Men drained the pits and wells, but women made salt. As Ward noted in 1920, 'the work is entirely confined to the women', although Ward qualified his observation by stating that women 'employ men to assist them in digging out the dry earth to be used in the fadama [salt flats], for carrying it when impregnated with salt into the town, and for carrying the salt water to the compounds'.[169] At Keana, for example, it took 150 men several days of hard work to drain the huge pit before production could begin, and men could fetch firewood and carry brine-encrusted soil.[170] Even though it is claimed that 'women do the job', as Makwangiji Jibirin of Awe has said, it is clear that men did much of the work.[171] In fact, women were in charge of production and responsible for filtering and boiling the salt in the compounds. They did indeed make the salt, but they depended upon additional labour.

Before the colonial period, most of this necessary labour was actually done by slaves, with women supervising the work. Only with the introduction of colonialism and the end of slavery did free women become directly involved in all stages of the work.[172] It may well be that many of the slaves were women; hence tradition may reflect a sexual division of labour which really disguised a more fundamental division based on slavery. The only work that free men did was the draining of the salt pits and wells in order to expose the brine springs. For this work, all males – slave and free – appear to have been involved. Because the production of salt depended upon exposing the brine springs as soon as possible, male involvement at this stage was essential as a means of overcoming a bottleneck in the initial stage of the productive cycle.

The tradition of the sexual division of labour reflects an ideology which reveals stages in the historical development of salt production. As the *tafida* of Kanje stated in 1976: 'The reason why this salt is neglected today is because women no longer want to work here. They do not want hard labour, this is why the salt is here [in the ground]. Otherwise, in the past, if you came here, you would see women all over working. But now they refuse. They prefer to sit at home and prepare food.'[173] The *tafida* was contrasting the present attitude of women, who have successfully liberated themselves from the hard work of salt-making through the imposition of the Islamic custom of wife seclusion, with a system of labour dating to the early colonial period. A price which is not competitive with imported salt and the refusal of the men to do a task which has always been considered women's work have also contributed to the decline in salt work. The men blame British colonialism, because the attempts at increasing the flow of brine at Awe and the survey of the other brine springs were interpreted locally as the first step in the modernisation of the industry. Men do not have to work at salt-making because the British promised that they would do the work.

The battle between the sexes which is apparent in the conflict over labour disguises the older pattern of slavery. As Makwangiji Jibirin reported in 1976: 'all the salt you see here [Awe] used to be processed by slaves, [but] there are no slaves now. Slaves used to do it. When the slave trade was abolished, women took up the job.'[174] Alhaji Aliyu, the aged chief of Ribi, and his young assistant, Galadima Salihu, also claim that slaves once did the job; 'they worked strenuously' but then salt truly became the work of women.[175] The same was true at Kanje, where slaves 'cooked the salt'. Women at Keana had as many as twenty people working for them.[176] In poorer households, free women worked alongside the slaves, but at the most productive basins slaves probably contributed the major labour input.

Both men and women owned slaves, but men appear to have owned the most. A rich woman could buy a slave, but men were able not only to buy slaves but also to capture them. As the *tafida* of Kanje remembers: 'When our grandparents caught slaves they made them work in the salt flats. They used to buy them and make them do the salt work.'[177] At Azara, Magajiya Yaboinya, Masha, Ajala Nene, Anyala and Wajo – all women – are remembered as particularly wealthy salt producers who owned from five to twenty slaves each. At Awe, Magajiya Gishiri Mariamu, another producer, had nearly fifty slaves. She had so many dependants that she founded her own village (Nassarawa) outside Awe.[178] Slaves were purchased from merchants coming from the north: Awe tradition remembers that slaves came from Bauchi, Borno, Katsina, Sokoto and Kano.[179] But the wars of Bayero and Dan Karo – two adventurers who raided the Benue Valley, particularly the area to the south around Wukari – also produced slaves for the market. It may be that the salt towns shunned these slaves, who could escape to their homelands quite easily, and anyway, there was no problem of slave supply. Even the large caravans of men like Madugu Mohamman Mai Gashin Baki, which travelled through the salt towns from Adamawa and other southern regions, brought slaves who could have been sold.[180]

A reconstruction of developments at the Benue salines reveals three periods in the history of production. Traditions that salt-making is women's work indicate that before the nineteenth-century expansion of salt production a sexual division of labour, in which women did most of the work, characterised the salt industry. These traditions, collected early in the colonial era when the memories of slavery were vivid, had the function of justifying the subjugation of women to a degree which may never have existed, but the older traditions probably reflect an earlier era, before the expansion in slave supply had made the use of slaves practical.[181] In the nineteenth century, salt production expanded because slaves were introduced to supplement the labour of women. Slaves could do 'women's' work without altering the accepted division of

150

labour based on gender. The northern immigrants who took control of the salt sites – the Zamfara settlers at Kanje, the Katsina settlers at Awe, and the Kambarin Beriberi at Ribi and Azara – displaced the earlier Jukun and Alago communities.[182] In the early days of northern domination the work probably also fell on the shoulders of women, many of whom must have been of local origin,[183] but the increase in slave holdings shifted the pattern of labour mobilisation from a gender-based division to one based on slavery.

In the colonial period, the demise of slavery led to a struggle between the sexes, as women tried to get their men to participate in production, even if only to collect firewood and carry salt-laden earth. Men reasserted the tradition that salt-making was work related to cooking and therefore the province of women. Women then had to seek alternative sources of labour to replace slaves. The employment of migrant workers alleviated the labour shortage to some extent, and for a time labour migration came to assume an important role in production. By 1920 much of this labour came from the Jos Plateau. As Ward noted at Awe, 'in recent years this work has largely been done by Yergamawa who come down in large numbers and receive payment of course in salt. A man will probably work for a week and receive in payment as much salt as he can carry away.'[184] By 1937, the women 'employ[ed] Munchi [Tiv] labour at 1d a day to carry in the salt-bearing earth from the marshes, in addition to what the women can carry, in order to avoid being forestalled by the rains'.[185] At Awe, some women came from Baure, Kafinmoyi, Tunga, Kekura and other villages nearby. The village women stayed in the homes of the different title-holders, whose salt flats they worked. Migrants also came from further afield – Keffi, Lafia, Wase, Bauchi, Pankshin, Langtan and Dengi. These migrants included both men and women. At Azara, migrants were Angas, Birom, and Ankwe. The origins of the work force at both Azara and Awe indicate that most migrants came from the plateau, perhaps revealing a time when migrant labour was a principal means by which salt was acquired for trade in the plateau.[186] Ultimately, however, the industry has declined into insignificance, and because of the poverty of the area men and women now work collectively. The traditional division of labour is maintained in theory, and women pool their labour in joint activities as a means of maximising their labour under conditions that are socially more agreeable.[187]

CONCLUSION

The many thousands of workers, perhaps 25,000, who were employed in the production of salt and natron in Kawar, Fachi, Muniyo, Mangari, Kadzell, Foli, Teguidda n'tesemt, the Dallols and the Benue Valley at the end of the nineteenth century, were involved in a wide range of social relations that affected the organisation of production. Mobilisation of the labour force included the migration of free peasants (the Dallols, Mangari, Muniyo), the migration of an inferior caste of artisans (Foli), the migration of slaves (Teguidda n'tesemt), the use of a sedentary slave population (Kawar, Fachi,

Kadzell), and the substitution of slaves for gender-based division of labour (Benue salines). In many of these cases, the dominant form of labour was supplemented by other forms. Slaves were used in Mangari and Muniyo, even though free peasants made most of the salt, and free peasants were found in Kadzell, where slaves constituted most of the work force. Slave and free worked side by side in Kawar, Fachi, and Teguidda n'tesemt, while it is unclear whether slaves or free peasants were more common in Dallol Fogha. This complexity reflected the different social structures of the various societies that included the populations of the salines. The salt industry, in its several forms, had its own requirements that helped shape the social structure, but there was nothing intrinsic about the salt industry that isolated it from society as a whole. While an attempt has been made to factor out the relations of production for purposes of analysis, it should be recognised that patterns of labour mobilisation, varied as they were, changed over time in the context of larger issues of political economy.

Free migrant peasants were concentrated at those sites which were relatively close to populated areas in the savanna and sahel. At these places it was possible to control the salt locations and allow labour to respond to market conditions. This situation characterised Muniyo, Mangari and Dallol Fogha, at least at the end of the nineteenth century. The domination of salt production in Foli by the *haddad* caste of Kanem occurred under demographic and geographical conditions similar to those in Mangari, Muniyo and Dallol Fogha, but the presence of a caste structure that was absent in other areas determined that members of the caste would be employed in salt production. Free peasants were confined to agricultural tasks and were not involved in the mining of trona. The contrast between the forms of labour mobilisation in Foli and in Muniyo, Mangari and Dallol Fogha demonstrates the extent to which the recruitment of salt workers fitted into larger patterns of society.

In the Sahara and at those places in the sahel which were relatively remote from populated districts, slaves were forced to stay in places which were otherwise economically unfavourable. Thus in Kawar and Fachi, the resident population included slave workers, and nomads also assigned their slaves work in the pits at the appropriate times of the year. In Kadzell, production sites were also the locations of wells, which were maintained and owned by nomads concerned with transhumant migration and livestock management. The slaves of Kadzell had a double purpose, therefore. They repaired the wells and they made salt. The organisation of the salt industry depended upon whether it was more feasible to own the workers or the salt sites and whether or not labour could be mobilised without the coercion inherent in the institution of slavery. The question of proprietary rights to the salines was therefore closely related to the means of labour mobilisation; this subject is examined in Chapter 7.

7

Proprietorship: the rights to salt and natron

The rights to the salt and natron produced in the central Sudan were embedded in social and political institutions. Even where freehold existed, the property relationship was severely bound by cultural constraints and developed in specific historical circumstances. Sometimes, proprietorship and political authority were confused, and it is not clear whether a portion of the product was paid as a form of tax or tribute or whether the owner, who was also an official, was collecting his share of the output as a personal right. In Mangari and Foli, for example, officials had proprietary rights to the salines. but they also collected tax from the local population. In the Benue basin, by contrast, the salt flats belonged to individuals who held political titles, but most of these titles lacked political significance. A title indicated that an individual controlled one or more flats. He may or may not have had a voice in the political decisions affecting the salines. In Bilma and Fachi, where title to the salines was clearly established, there was no confusion between political rights and ownership, although sovereignty over the salines was confused. The Tuareg, the Tubu and the Borno government vied for political influence in Kawar and Fachi. Their rivalry affected tributary relationships but not ownership of the salines. These different situations reveal the problem of analysing the question of proprietorship. It is as important to analyse the various rights of individuals and groups, so that these rights can be correlated with the organisation of labour and the returns which workers could expect from their output, as to identify whether or not specific groups or individuals actually owned or otherwise controlled the salines.

FREEHOLD: INDIVIDUAL RIGHTS TO PROPERTY

Around 1900 – and for an unknown period before then – salines were considered private property at Bilma, Fachi, and Teguidda n'tesemt. Individuals had full title to these salines, which meant that they could be bought and sold, inherited, and rented. At these desert sites, property took the form of salt basins, and individuals also owned date trees which could be bought and sold. The relative scarcity of arable land and the limited space for salt production promoted the development of a market for these immovable items. The desert sites depended upon a restricted area which did not change and could not be enlarged substantially. As the abandoned area around Azelik (near Teguidda n'tesemt) and the ruins of Kalala in Kawar demonstrate, additional labour could bring more land under cultivation or could increase salt production, but such expansion was still limited. At Fachi, there were more flats that could have been developed, but political constraints and the lack of enough workers prevented expansion, at least in the nineteenth century. These examples establish that political factors acted as constraints on the exercise of proprietary rights to salt basins, agricultural land, and date trees. The destruction of Azelik in the fifteenth century and the withdrawal from Kalala sometime before the early nineteenth century took place in specific historical circumstances. In these cases, Azelik fell to the Tuareg of Agades, while Kalala could no longer be occupied once the Tuareg became dominant in the Bilma trade. The Tubu prevented the people at Fachi from working some of the salt basins. The struggle for power in the desert could and did affect the ownership and control of salt workings. In particular the rise of the Tuareg confederation altered the social and political relations of production at both Kawar and Teguidda n'tesemt. This chapter examines what is known about proprietary rights at the turn of the twentieth century and how this situation arose. Chapter 9 will consider the interaction between the trade and politics of the desert-edge.

At the end of the nineteenth century, no one could construct a warehouse or open a saline at Kalala – where the Bilma salines were located – without the permission of the *mai*, the chief of the village, and the *bulama*, an official who represented the Bilma salt producers in their dealings with the Tuareg. Traditionally – that is, in the nineteenth century, at least – the request was accompanied by a payment of 5 to 50 silver coins (Maria Theresa thalers), depending upon the wealth of the applicant and probably depending also upon the proposed site of the new warehouse or salt basin. The payment could be made in coin, millet or cotton cloth, but never in salt or dates. This sum was remitted to the *mai*, who gave part to the *bulama*. Another payment, which was considered a gift, was made upon acceptance of the application. This gift consisted of a man's gown, imported from the savanna, or 20 Maria Theresa thalers.[1] This authorisation gave the applicant the right to work a saline with a surface area of about 15 m^2. The new proprietor could apply for an additional basin, but each new request had to be accompanied by another payment comparable to the initial one. The property continued to belong to the owner, even if it was not used.

The role of the *bulama* in granting rights to warehouse sites and salines originated in the subjugation of Kawar to the Tuareg, which appears to have occurred in c. 1759.[2] At that time, the Tuareg defeated Borno, and the conditions of peace were unlimited access to Kawar, nominal authority over the economic affairs of the oases, and the right to collect tribute. The *bulama*, who was, in origin at least, a slave, was installed at Bilma to represent the Tuareg. Grandin states that the *bulama* was subordinate to the Kel Gress, while Jean suggests that the Kel Ewey had real authority at Bilma and the Itisen at Fachi.[3] Both Tuareg fractions were part of the Agades Confederation, but relations between them were often belligerent. Indeed, in the eighteenth century the Kel Ewey had driven the Kel Gress from the Air Massif to Adar, a region to the south-west. The Itisen have been traditional allies of the Kel Gress. None the less, all three groups, and other Tuareg, traded to Bilma and Fachi, and it seems likely that the *bulama* dealt with all the Tuareg. His functions were commercial and legal. He received the order from the Tuareg for the quantity of salt which would be needed for the large autumn caravan, and he set the quota for each salt proprietor. He also determined when the salt season would begin and end. Hence, his responsibilities in granting land for housing and sites for salt basins were closely associated with broader powers which were ultimately derived from Tuareg influence.[4]

At the time of the Tuareg conquest, five Kanuri families, who were either already resident in Kawar or who were the remnants of the defeated Borno army that was supposedly settled in Bilma, were allowed to purchase (or keep) approximately 2 hectares of salines, which were then divided between these families. One of these families was most likely the Amarma, from among whom the *mai* was usually selected. According to traditions collected by Grandin, each of these families paid the equivalent of 100 Maria Theresa thalers in textiles to acquire freehold. The area, known as Lugorum, was exempt from annual tribute, unlike the remaining area of the salines – another 13 ha.[5] The owners of other salines had to pay an annual tribute (*tawail*) to the Tuareg when the large autumn caravan left Kawar. This tribute was paid through the office of *bulama*. The *bulama* also owned salines, and it may be that he was exempt from this payment.

In 1906 there were approximately 70 families at Bilma who owned the 1,000 salines, an average of 14 salines per family. Both women and men owned salines; the largest holdings consisted of 20 basins. Productivity varied considerably. The favoured owners had 3–4 basins in the most productive part of the salines,[6] but many salines had more than one owner because of the division of the salines through inheritance.[7] If a saline was abandoned and the owner disappeared without issue, it returned to the chief, who could give it out once again.[8]

Salines could be rented. Grandin reports that contracts allowed the workers to retain total output – less tributary payments to the Tuareg – for the first three years of exploitation. In the following years, the lessee divided the salt equally with the owner. If the owner died and the inheritors did not want to maintain the contract, a mediator estimated the value of the saline, and the worker was entitled to half the value as a severance payment.[9] Owners also allowed workers to use a saline in return for a payment. The Tubu from other parts of Kawar came to Bilma, for example, and their slaves gathered salt for a fee.[10] Whenever the salt was sold, only the proprietor, or the head of the family if more than one person owned a saline, was allowed to handle commercial transactions. The proprietor or head of the family then divided the proceeds into shares and distributed the shares to the independent workers and joint owners.[11]

At Bilma, the *bulama* and the *mai* supervised ceremonies which legitimised the proprietary rights of the salt basin owners and re-established political allegiance. The *mai* sent for the *bulama*, who chose a fast day, which was always on a Monday, determined through astrology, sometime in April. The *mai*, as the political official under the sultan of Kawar at Dirku and originally owing allegiance to Borno, represented territorial authority, as well as being a major owner of the salines. He sanctified the quotas set for each proprietor and determined the date of the salt season, after which salt could only be made with special permission or on payment of a heavy fine. The *bulama*, as the commercial agent with the Tuareg and also a proprietor, had the more important role in the ceremonies, probably in recognition of – if not because of – his vital economic functions. The ceremony began at the time of the morning, mid-day, or evening prayer. All the men retired to the mosque to recite selected verses of the Quran and the *fathia*. Then they ate a meal of couscous which had been prepared at the *bulama*'s house. He then led the men to the salines, where the start of the season was officially recognised. The *bulama*, aided by the other men, made seven columns of *kantu*; when they had finished they drank a bowl of millet porridge (*fura*).[12]

The situation at Fachi was similar to that at Bilma. The Tuareg collected tribute, which was payable at the time of the annual caravan, but the Tubu of Kawar retained nominal political authority, as they did at Bilma. The chief (*mai*) of Fachi came from one of four Kanuri families – Abjibo, Aquadre, Adada and Alogol. Although these four families (123 men and 189 women) accounted for much of the total population of 659 in 1908, the salines were owned individually, and each family possessed its date trees and a small garden as well. The few Tubu who lived at Fachi did not possess any salines. Salt flats could be inherited, rented, sold or loaned to relatives.[13]

The Tubu owned the salines in other parts of Kawar, although traditions keep alive a memory of a time when the Kanuri inhabited the northern oases and presumably controlled salt production. At Djado, for example, the people of Djaba worked the salines.[14] These people – the Djadoboy – have a mixed ancestry, part Tubu and part Kanuri, which appears to reflect the historical change in ownership or former slave status, or both. Similarly at Dirku, where some Kanuri families still live, the salines belonged to the local people, the Guezebida, also of mixed descent, but it is not clear if the Kanuri of Dirku once had proprietary rights to the salines.[15] The salt and natron workings in northern Kawar were not as developed as at Bilma and Fachi, which may be why ownership does not appear to have been as clearly defined there. There was no investment in permanent basins, and consequently it may have been possible for anyone to work the salines, as long as a fee was paid to the dominant political group. Since Dirku was the capital of Kawar, such a payment there would have been made to the Tubu chief.

In 1909 Cortier heard that production of salt at Teguidda n'tesemt was limited to the inhabitants of the village,[16] but in fact the salines belonged to the people of In Gall. Thérol learned in 1907, the owners of the Teguidda salines

156

had lived at In Gall since they were forced to abandon Azelik, that is since the fifteenth century.[17] The connexion with Azelik is instructive, for it suggests that ownership has remained within a single community for several hundred years.[18] None the less, the chief did not own the salines, as Cortier thought. Holdings were extremely diffused; sometimes several people owned shares in a single saline, as was also common at Bilma and Fachi.[19]

Edmond and Suzanne Bernus provide the most detailed information on proprietary rights at Teguidda n'tesemt and In Gall. Although their material dates from 1970, it appears to be typical of earlier periods,[20] particularly since the situation at Teguidda was comparable to that at Bilma. Bernus and Bernus recorded traditions of inheritance that involved the transfer of property over several generations, which suggests that the pattern of proprietary rights has existed since at least the end of the nineteenth century. Although it is not known how these rights have changed since then or how old private ownership is, their information supports Thérol's observations of 1907 that the people of In Gall have owned the salines for many centuries.

The unit of ownership was the *abatol*, the series of decantation basins which constituted a single unit of production. The means of acquiring *abatol* were diverse. They could be bought and sold or inherited under one of several practices. The owners included the descendants of the original inhabitants of In Gall – all of whom came from Azelik. These people were divided into four groups, Isherifen, Isawaghen, Inusufa and Imesdraghen. Inheritance resulted in the division of the salines over the past several centuries, although purchase counteracted this fragmentation. The laws of inheritance provided that all children of an owner should receive a share; males received a double portion. Frequently, men divided their holdings among their children before they died, in order to avoid disagreements among the offspring of different wives. This custom was known as *eighelal*. Another form of inheritance (*elkhabus*) was confined to females. The owner of a saline provided for his daughters and their female offspring in perpetuity by making a public declaration in the presence of a Muslim cleric and witnesses. The female descendants then had the right to the proceeds from the saline, but they could not sell or transfer the holding. Salines or shares in salines also formed part of marriage compensation, given by the family of the husband to the wife. The property was transferred at the time of marriage, at the birth of a child, or when a new child was named. A share in a saline was also given to a slave at the time of his or her emancipation.[21]

Bernus and Bernus provide a number of examples of holdings and the method of inheritance.[22] One woman and her widowed sister owned twelve *abatol* between them, which they worked together. Another man, who was Inusufa by origin, owned six salines, but upon his death these were divided among his two sons and two daughters, the sons receiving two salines each and the daughters one each. The *imam*, who was Isawaghen by origin, owned six salines, which were located in five different parts of Teguidda n'tesemt. He had acquired these *abatol* in the following manner: his father had given him three

157

before he died (his sisters had received two); he also inherited one *abatol* from his mother (his sisters had received shares in another *abatol*); and he had bought two salines. The first he had purchased before 1940 from a former judge; the other had belonged to a sister, but when she died without issue, he and his two sisters inherited the saline. He subsequently bought out his two sisters. Besides his own holdings, his wife owned six salines in common with other members of her family. Four of these had been inherited from her father, and the proceeds were divided among his three boys and two girls according to the custom of giving double portions to the males. The *imam*'s wife had also inherited a saline from her mother, which she shared with her sister until her death, whereupon the two children of her deceased sister inherited that portion. Finally, the *imam*'s wife and her sister had inherited another saline as *elkhabus* through the female line, and with the death of her sister her niece assumed an equal share. Another man, Kenji, owned five *abatol*; his wives owned another two, and his brother-in-law four. Kenji managed all eleven salines, and he also worked another 17 *abatol*, which belonged to four different people.[23] The Sultan of Agades, who was recognised as the sovereign of In Gall and hence Teguidda n'tesemt, also owned some salines.[24] Each of the major groups had their own mark which was put on the moulds of salt. The Inusufa used +, the Isherifen ⊥, the Isawaghen Δ|, and the Sultan of Agades 0|||0.[25]

The traditions of Kawar, Fachi and Teguidda n'tesemt demonstrate the role of inheritance in the accumulation of property within the communities of Bilma, Fachi and In Gall. Holdings were relatively small, although individuals could invest in additional shares in a saline or purchase salines outright. These patterns of inheritance and investment were similar to the proprietary control over agricultural land and date trees, and hence rights to salines cannot be separated from other forms of property. The role of women as proprietors related to their position in society as well. Rights came as part of marriage compensation or inheritance practices that were designed to provide for free women in society. These practices guaranteed that the dominant free families continued to own and control the salines – as well as other property – and thereby helped maintain community solidarity in the larger desert political economy of which they were a part. Despite this solidarity, however, it does not appear to have been possible for individuals to amass enough property to attain a monopoly of salt production. The oasis communities remained dependent upon the Tuareg nomads who dominated the desert. This dependence was expressed in real terms through tribute payments. The Sultan of Agades – as representative of the Tuareg confederation – even owned salines at Teguidda, but never a major share, and no other outsiders seem to have owned salines. The Sultan's involvement was symbolic, despite some income, for it demonstrated the reality of political power. The In Gall proprietors could not benefit from the salines unless they accepted the overlordship of the Tuareg. But this relationship of dominance also had its reciprocal dimension, for the Tuareg required the services of the In Gall community, as well as those at Fachi and Bilma, to organise the production of salt, as well as other commodities.

PROPRIETARY RIGHTS AND TITLES IN THE BENUE VALLEY

The proprietors of the Benue brine springs were those individuals with titles. The heads of the various towns and villages where the salines were located appointed men to these titled positions, which had salt flats (Hausa: *fadama*) attached to them. In effect, ownership of the salines was communal (except at Ribi); salt flats could not be bought or sold but remained tied to titles that were distributed as political patronage within the free community, often within the same families from generation to generation.[26] Unlike farmland, which was also divided into individual parcels but which seldom, if ever, came on the market, salt flats were a scarce resource that acquired value. The expansion of the flats was difficult; hence competition for political titles was extreme.

The Benue salt flats belonged to men, even though the work was managed by women. At Keana, where the local Alago population had exclusive control of production, 'the claims are passed on from father to son and no Hausa or other settler in the town is allowed to participate'.[27] In 1913, 509 Alago men had claims to salt sites. At Awe, Varvill interpreted these rights in 1937 in terms of ownership; the men 'rented' the salt flats to their wives and other women:

> The marshes are not open to all comers. They are subdivided into plots which are the outcome of many years of private ownership. To describe these plots, however, as private property, far less as freehold property, is misleading. The owner is not an individual but an official. In Awe and elsewhere the right to each section of the marsh is vested in an office and inalienable from it. But, as the offices are the hereditary property of certain families, each section normally passes from one generation to the next, in one family. Occasionally the Sangari [head of the town] may find no suitable person of the right years to present to an office, or he even may be strong enough to pass over the true candidate in preference for a favourite, but in general the office – and plot of marsh – will remain in the correct family.[28]

Although Varvill's observations were made in 1937, he was interpreting a pattern that dated back to the late nineteenth century and probably the nineteenth century as a whole. His confusion between freehold and the attachment of flats to titles highlights the problem of analysing proprietorship in the context of the political structure of the Benue basin, but the antiquity of the practice of gaining access to salt flats through the acquisition of political titles is not in question. In 1920 Ward had made similar observations for Akiri, Azara, Ribi, Kanje and Abuni, as well as Awe: 'The salt working rights in each town were originally in the hands of the chief who parcelled them out to the chief Sarakuna [office holders].'[29] At Awe there were 120 such titles in 1937,[30] while the smaller sites had correspondingly fewer officials. In 1941 the total number of holdings at the Benue sites, except Keana, was 123; by this time the

Table 7.1 *Scale of production, Benue sites, 1941*

Place	Cooking pots	Output (*mudu*)	*Mudu*/pot	Capacity equivalent (pots)
Azara	317	7,713	24.3	1,881
Akiri	140	2,069	14.8	505
Kanje	33	178	5.4	48
Abuni	88	463	5.3	113
Awe	2,801	11,377	4.1	2,801
Ribi	155	963	6.2	235
Arago	45	281	6.2	69

Source: Report on Salt Industry, Awe District, 1941, Nigerian National Archives, Kaduna.

Table 7.2. *Size of holdings at brine springs, Awe District, 1941 (Mudus of 2.5 lbs.)*

Place	0–25	26–50	51–75	76–100	101–200	201–300	301–500	501–1,000	Over 1,000
Azara	—	1	1	2	16	4	1	3	1
Akiri	—	—	—	3	2	—	4	—	—
Kanje	6	—	1	—	—	—	—	—	—
Abuni	—	10	—	1	—	—	—	—	—
Awe	—	—	—	—	15	21	2	5	1
Ribi	—	4	9	1	1	—	—	—	—
Arago	2	7	—	—	—	—	—	—	—

Source: Report on Salt Industry, Awe District, 1941, Nigerian National Archives, Kaduna.

number at Awe had shrunk from 120 to only 43, although the reasons for this drop are not clear.[31]

The work unit was based on the cooking pot in which the brine was boiled dry. In 1941, the Awe holdings were much more extensive than the combined output of Azara, Kanje, Abuni, Ribi and Arago. Among these sites, Awe accounted for almost 50 per cent of production (Table 7.1). Based on these figures, it is clear that the cooking pots at Azara and Akiri were larger than those at the other sites. If the average quantity of salt per pot for Awe (4.1 *mudu* per pot) is applied to the other sites, then a figure is derived which represents the equivalent capacity of the cooking pots for these sites. This calculation assumes that the *mudu* (2.5 lbs.) used by the tax assessors was the same for all sites, although it is likely that there was some variation in the measure.[32] The large pots at Azara could produce about two-thirds the quantity of salt produced at Awe, while the combined capacity of all the other sites was virtually the same as the output for Awe alone.

Clearly the largest holdings were at Awe and Azara (Table 7.2), although the wives of four men at Akiri also produced over 300 *mudu* of salt. The *sarki* of Azara had the largest holding, capable of producing 1,700 *mudu*, while the flats of the *sangari* of Awe produced 1,216 *mudu*. The eight holdings that produced between 500 and 1,000 *mudu* had a combined output of 4,970 *mudu*; the ten largest holdings taken together produced 7,886 *mudu*, which represented 34 per cent of total production. The seven holdings in the 301–500 *mudu* range accounted for 2,827 *mudu*; while the 25 holdings in the 201–300 bracket made 5,220 *mudu*. The holdings over 200 *mudu* accounted for 15,933 *mudu*, or 69 per cent of total output (23,044 *mudu*). These 42 holdings represented only 34 per cent of the total number (124) of salt titles. None of the holdings at Awe, and only four at Azara, produced less than 100 *mudu*.[33]

At Keana there were 274 proprietors with titles in 1948, down considerably from the 509 titles reported in 1913. These proprietors controlled 475 salt flats; the largest holding belonged to the *osana*, the chief of Keana, who had fifty. The average holding was about $1\frac{1}{2}$ flats per title, if the *osana's* holdings are excluded. No one else owned more than eight, and only a few people had as many as five or six.[34] Eladoga Oji remembers when some women had 40–50 pots, with as many as 20 people – mostly slaves – working for them. The scale of these holdings – which appear to date back to the first decade of the twentieth century – indicates access to a larger number of salt flats in the past than the 1948 survey reveals. Other than the *osana*, the two most important officials were the *osikigu* and *inole*. These officials supervised the distribution of brine, and both owned slaves who worked in the flats. The *osikigu*, a male title, and the *inole*, a female title, were responsible for the safety of the workers, who often stayed in the salt flats overnight.[35]

The system of titles, which was common to all the sites, whether Jukun, Alago or Hausa, was a means of apportioning the salt flats, and as Varvill noted in 1937, the system achieved the same purpose as freehold but did not actually involve the ownership of private property.

> As might be expected, the great majority of them [titles] carry no administrative or other duties whatsoever – beyond periodic salutations to the chief. Nevertheless for economic reasons they are much sought after. At Awe the marshes are in the control of the Muslims – no other means of classifying these heterogeneous communities is possible. That of Akiri is controlled by the Jukun. At Azara and Ribi there are separate Muslim, Jukun and Arago [Alago] marshes, while at Kanje and Abuni the small deposits are controlled by Muslims.[36]

The Alago controlled the flats at Keana, while the owners of marshes at Bomanda and other places are not known. Although the titles generally stayed in the same families, there were exceptions. In the 1930s the *sangari* of Awe installed an Ankwe favourite in the position of *makwangiji*, but the family of the former office holder complained to the British, and the holding reverted back to the 'correct' family.[37] Similar cases of re-apportionment probably occurred in the past, and it is likely that the consolidation of positions in particular families only came about as the result of a protracted struggle between the heads of the towns and the rest of the community. At Awe, the

161

position of *sangari* rotated between three families; the two which did not hold the title possessed the minor posts of *chiroma* and *bunu*. The *sangari* had the largest holding – 299 flats in 1941 – but these went with the title, so that upon the succession of a new *sangari*, the three titles rotated, together with the number of salt flats.[38]

The title system preceded the consolidation of Muslim control in the early nineteenth century. Before then, Jukun and Alago controlled most, if not all, of the sites. Whether the use of titles had other significance in the eighteenth century and earlier is not clear, but it seems safe to say that the Jukun were responsible for the development of title holding. At Kekura, the Jukun village which predates Awe, there were at least 23 titles associated with salt production. The Jukun claim to have exploited salt at Awe before Hausa and other immigrants arrived, and they still do, although on a small scale. It also seems likely that a similar system was in use at Bomanda and other brine springs which were once in the Jukun domain.[39]

Community ownership of the salines, as structured through the title system, was symbolised through ceremonies that opened the salt season. At Keana, a festival initiated the communal effort required to drain the salt pits. The young men of the town gathered before the palace of the *osana*, who directed the draining of the salt pits and allocated salt flats. Another official, the *osikigu*, organised the dances of the three performers in the masquerades of Keana – Inaiko, Agbassa, and Ikashi – who made public appearances at the salt festival and at the deaths of important officials. Once the pits were drained, the *osuza* or *osikigu* roped off the entrance to the pits until the weak brine formed in sufficient quantities to be collected for salt making. Thereafter, the salt season was officially open. These ceremonies maintained the Alago monopoly of production – the ceremonies were Alago ceremonies, and titles could only be held by Alago.[40]

At Awe, a traditional ceremony (*adashe*) was associated with the Jukun, not the Hausa, who dominated production in the nineteenth century. This association recognised the prior rights of the Jukun to the Awe salt but, more important, it upheld the system of titles which was the basis of proprietorship. From a Jukun perspective, the ceremonies placated the spirit of *agu*, whose shrine was located in Kekura, the Jukun village near Awe. On the first day, ceremonies were held at three places, where the *adashe* danced. Drums were beaten, and the village boys struck the ground with sticks outside the compound of the *tsiye*, where the *agu* shrine was located. A young boy and girl – both virgins – made the first salt. Dressed in white and carrying containers for the brine and whips to hit anyone they encountered on the road, they went to the salines alone; everyone else stayed in his house. This first brine was boiled in the house of the *tsiye*. Among the titled officials involved in the ceremony, the *kuma*, *kundu* and *awe* took part in the initial activities; the *adashe* danced and went to the various places where the ceremony occurred; while the *tsiye* was in charge of the shrine. Initially the Hausa title holders did not participate in the ceremony; they recited Quranic verses on their own. At some time in the nineteenth century (Unomah dates the change at about 1850) the Muslims started an *adashe* festival of their own. This truncated version of the original Jukun festival lasted only one day, instead of seven. Six boys and six girls – again virgins – went to the basin to gather the first salt, only now officials with Hausa titles – *sarkin gishiri, madaki* and others – presided over the day's activities. Despite these changes, the ceremony had the same function as the earlier Jukun version; it helped to legitimise the system of titled proprietorship.[41] Similar ceremonies were held at Azara, Abuni, Akiri, and probably at the other salines.

The title system differed considerably from freehold property. As the dispute over the transfer of salt flats to an Ankwe immigrant at Awe demonstrates, community pressure could be brought to bear to prevent individuals, even the head of the town, from redistributing salt flats to people other than those who had a traditional claim to the flats. The free community at the various brine springs maintained a collective right to salt flats. These rights were apportioned in unequal segments, but the male heads of houses could expect to receive access to flats, and this access was passed on to their male children, or at least those males who in turn became heads of households. Local custom prevented the Alago of Keana from passing titles to non-Alago, but elsewhere Muslims, Jukun, and Alago had flats at the same springs. One function of the heads of the towns was to control distribution of titles, thereby undermining any tendency toward the development of freehold, but each chief had different powers. The Keana chief seems to have maintained the tightest control over distribution by granting titles only to Alago. Because chieftaincy rotated at Awe, it may have been possible for settlers to buy their way into the system, as the temporary transfer of the *makwangiji* holdings to an Ankwe man appears to demonstrate.[42]

THE SALT FIEFDOMS OF BORNO

The proprietorship of the Borno salines ultimately rested with the state, as represented by the *mai* before c. 1810 and thereafter by the al-Kanemi dynasty. Authority was exercised through titled officials. As Chambert interpreted the system in 1906, 'the devolution of authority or proprietorship over a salting was in some sense the equivalent of the investiture of a fief; the chief of the territory did so according to his whims and especially according to his interests'.[43] In Mangari and Muniyo, most officials claimed to be Kanuri, not Manga, even though their families had lived in Mangari for many generations.[44] Virtually all officials, who often used the Borno titles *kachella, lawan*, etc., were connected with the old aristocracy of the Saifawa dynasty. Because Mangari and Muniyo were once close to the Borno capital at Birni Ngazargamu, state influence over the salines had been strong, but the power of the title-holders increased with the movement of the capital to Kukawa. In the nineteenth century, the *muniyoma*, who lived at Goure, the *kachella* of Maine-Soroa, and the *lawan* of Goudoumaria each claimed those salines which were near their towns. Other officials appointed directly from Kukawa exercised control of smaller areas, sometimes only a depression or two. Most of these were found in southern Mangari and Muniyo. These officials were known as *kuma ngorbe* (chief of the salt basin) and sometimes more simply as *ngorma*.

A similar system of titled officials prevailed in Foli. The *alifa* of Kanem, who lived in Mao, controlled the Foli depressions. Before 1845 Borno also exercised sovereignty over Kanem, but thereafter Kanem was under Wadai control or was effectively independent. Allah was credited with supreme authority, with the *alifa* as His representative. In fact, however, the *alifa* delegated control to at least one official, the *mai*, although it may be that there were two of these officials, one located at Liwa and the other at Ngelea. The effective proprietorship rested in these lower appointments, not with the *alifa*.

As Chambert explained the devolution of authority in Mangari and Muniyo, local officials rented the salines each year and thereby acquired the right to fabricate *manda* and collect natron.

> The tax farmers [*fermiers*] of one or more depressions were given command of the surrounding countryside and levied tax on it. Mounyo [Muniyo] was not divided into native administrative districts but by the very existence of these tax farmers and their privileges there were annual and indeed renewable divisions [*groupements*]. The *koumangorbe*, or simply the *ngorma* (head of the salt depression), as the local inhabitants called him, exercised authority and often dispensed justice... over all the villages which provided workers.[45]

The French wanted to turn the officials into 'fermiers' (tax-farmers), and consequently organised public auctions at Goure and other centres. Chambert presided over the first one at Goure, which took place on 19 November 1906.[46] A great gathering of local people assembled in front of the post, as Chambert inaugurated a new era in the Mangari salt industry, or so he thought. In fact, the French assumed the role of the central government and, while public auction replaced court intrigue as the means of acquiring rights over the salines, the essential nature of proprietorship had not changed.

The system which Chambert imposed was devised out of necessity. Ronjat's report on the salines in 1905 distinguished between the salines under the direct authority of the *muniyoma* at Goure and other salines which belonged to 'other lesser chiefs who generally came from Bornou and who had installed themselves in the Addia side of the territory and have not yet recognised the suzerainty of Mounyo'.[47] Because they did not pay tribute to the *muniyoma*, the French had some trouble establishing their influence, which they tried to do from Goure. These officials received special exemptions as a means of securing their submission so that they would continue to organise the annual migration of workers to the salines. As noted in Chapter 6, workers were free to migrate, but they had to negotiate with the *ngorma* for the right to settle at a particular site. It is likely, although available data are unclear on this point, that migrants established relatively permanent clientship relations with particular *ngorma*, both in the nineteenth and in the twentieth century.

164

Table 7.3. *Proprietors of the Mangari salines, 1905–06*

Title	Occupant	Furnaces (number)	Depressions (number)	Location of depressions
Kaigama	Tiari	n.a.	5	Kilgoua Gana, Kilgoua Koura, Banaoua, Kalhoua, Badjiram
Lawan	Kombari	n.a.	5	Abba Tilori, Mandabaram, Yani Souarni, Kangaroua, Dietkorom
Kaigama	Magaltoumi	n.a.	3	Boumboukoa, Ngadoua, N'Galmaram
Lawan	Aissagam	n.a.	2	Maibirim III, Kata Fournouroum
Lawan	Goudjia	n.a.	1	Douroua
Lawan	Mama	n.a.	1	Ari Kombomiram
Muniyoma		105	4	Abque, Adris, Gourselik, Maibirim I
Lawan	Adjimi	25	4	Kongolimaram, N'Goriani, Darouram, Dokoraram
Lawan	Dimorim	48	3	Karamgaouna, Karagou, Ouakatgi
Lawan	Kellema	20	4	N'Gariram, Kourkouroa, Maibirim II, Billama Boucar
Lawan	Goni	23	3	Kogoua, Doumaoua, Maramaram
Chitima	—	14	1	Taeri
Guerema	Digadgi	2	1	Kadellaoua
Kaigama	Fendami	12	1	Matafaram
Kachella	Abdu	89 +	11	Gunga, Wogungawa, Yadhia, Silimma, Diru, Nganua, Nawujeram, Bugduma, Ngibia, two natron lakes (no names)
Kachella	Mahmoud	8	2	Kurugu, Babilla
Totals:	16 officials		51	

Mundy, Bornu Report, No.5, 1903, Kaduna, notes that Lawan Kambare of Budum had five salines and Kachella Arri of Alanguruti had six. I assume that Kambare is to be identified with Ronjat's Kombari, who had five salines in 1905, and Kachella Arri is to be identified with Ronjat's Tiari, who had five salines in 1905, as opposed to six in 1903.
Sources: Ronjat, 1905, Archives Nationales du Niger, Niamey; Browne 1906, Nigerian National Archives, Kaduna.

The size of holdings – both under the new regime and the old – varied considerably (Table 7.3). Some officials held five or six locations which were very large. The *muniyoma*, for example, held the works at Abque, Adris, Maibirim, and Gourselik, which in 1905 employed approximately 1,500 workers.[48] Others also held more than one site and employed from 200 to 1,000 workers each, while some holdings were much smaller, located at one site and needing only twenty or thirty workers. When the eastern part of Mangari was controlled from Birni Ngazargamu before 1806, officials generally lived in the capital, and it is likely that salt-camps were originally granted as political rewards.[49]

The holdings of the *muniyoma*, while consisting of only four sites, were in fact considerable because the salines were so large. Consequently, he appointed officials to oversee their operation, who were effectively recognised as title-holders of a similar status to other proprietors. The salines at Abque, in western Muniyo, were placed under a man from Kollari, one of the villages from which many of the workers came.[50] Gourselik was also provided with an official, who was the chief of the town. This man managed the saline, assigning workers to different areas to strip the salt-earth from the ground.[51]

The adjudication system, which the French imposed as an attempt to rationalise the pre-colonial system of political appointments, had the effect of concentrating the salines in fewer hands. At the annual auction in November 1935, 29 natron depressions and 61 *manda* salines were rented out. Mai Musa of Goudoumaria acquired 32 sites, 17 producing natron and 15 salt; the *manda* sites had 44 furnaces. Only one other official, Lawan Gadji, was able to win a contract – for one natron site. In Maine-Soroa, holdings were more diffused. Grema Ari acquired the large *manda* site of Fanamiram, with its 15 furnaces; Chetima Mustapha took the largest site, Bugduma, with its 18 furnaces; Lawan Gadji – probably the same man who took the natron depression in Goudoumaria – won Yani Souarni and 12 furnaces, another natron site, and a small *manda* depression (one furnace). Five other small salines went to less successful bidders (Grigri took Gangaoua and three furnaces; Grema Mainema obtained a natron site; Lawan Mama took the one furnace at Miamia Doura; Aissa Gana had one furnace at another site; and Makinta got three furnaces at yet another place), but the overwhelming majority of salines went to a single man, Kachella Liman of Maine-Soroa. He acquired seven natron depressions and 38 *manda* sites, the largest being Adebour (16 furnaces) and Dietkorom (8 furnaces). Altogether he had the rights to 68 furnaces.[52]

To a great extent the auction involved considerable luck, as well as knowledge of the output of previous years. Conditions could change substantially from year to year, so that a saline which produced large quantities of *manda* one year might not be able to support as many ovens the next year. None the less, the concentration of holdings in relatively few hands guaranteed officials the probability of a good season. While the largest producing sites might change, these men were in the best position to reduce their risk. This situation would have been the same in the pre-colonial period; only then political intrigue, rather than competition at public auction, would have dominated the attempts to acquire sites. Furthermore, the possession of sites probably did not change as often – certainly not every year, as was theoretically the case under the colonial system.

Chambert's description of the salines as 'fiefs' provides indirect proof that the Mangari depressions were once held under longer-term tenancies than was the case during the colonial period.[53] Similar tenancies were common elsewhere in Borno, and in the British sphere some were still in operation during the early colonial years. A North African merchant had acquired one in the region near Lake Chad, which he subsequently sold.[54] While this one was in an area where *kige* was produced, and not *manda*, the case is instructive.

166

First, it demonstrates that someone who was nominally a foreigner could obtain tenancies, and secondly, it establishes that they could be bought and sold.

During the period when Birni Ngazargamu was under siege and finally destroyed (1806–8), the *manda* district was in chaos. The old proprietors were dispersed; some died or fled in the *jihad*, while others lost their rights to the new appointments of al-Kanemi. The officials at Maine-Soroa, who acquired the control of an extensive region in the saline district, trace their settlement to the decade after 1810.[55] The region under Goudoumaria also appears to have been reorganised after the fall of Birni Ngazargamu, for the Goudoumaria royal family also settled there in the early nineteenth century.[56] The holdings further west in Muniyo continued to be the domain of the *muniyoma*, although change is also suggested for these salines. Soon after 1822, the capital of Muniyo was moved from Bune – the site of a saline – further north to Goure.[57] Finally, the 'lesser chiefs' of Borno, who held the tenancies to the southern salines, were directly under the Kukawa government, not Muniyo, and this devolution of authority appears to have developed as a result of direct grants from the al-Kanemi dynasty.[58]

In the 1850s, Barth, despite his failure to mention *manda* production, commented on the size of these holdings in the region where the Manga lived. Kachella Said, who lived at Zurrikulo, was responsible for twelve villages which were probably the homes of salt workers, and undoubtedly there were salines in the *kachella*'s domain.[59] Chejessemo – where Shecheri (Cheri ?) was located – was another district, while the *galadima* of Nguru also possessed a territory from where many workers must have come.[60] Some domains were so small that they amounted to little more than a single estate, such as the one Barth found at Chelugiwa.[61] It seems likely that these tenancies were also characteristic of the pattern before 1800. Undoubtedly, there were tenancies in the region of the salines other than those reported by Barth, but his examples tell us something about the pattern that developed in the nineteenth century. Title-holders lived in their districts, not in the capital of the state. In earlier times it would have been easy for title-holders to maintain residence at Birni Ngazargamu and only visit their districts from time to time. Only in the nineteenth century did it make sense to establish tenancies centred at Maine-Soroa, Goudoumaria and the other smaller districts because of the distance from Kukawa. Such a change invariably resulted in greater decentralisation of administration.

Control of the trona depressions of Foli appears to have been exercised in a manner similar to that for the salines of Mangari and Muniyo. The depressions were part of the domain of the *alifa* of Kanem, located at Mao.[62] The *alifa* delegated authority to lesser officials in Foli, who were the effective proprietors. These officials had the title of *mai* or *maina*. Both the *mai* and the *alifa* came from the ruling house of Kanem – the Magoumi. In the early colonial period, the French attempted to rationalise the proprietorship of the Foli deposits, just as they instituted reforms in Mangari and Muniyo. In the case of Foli, the situation was complicated by the insecurity of the last decades of the nineteenth century. A *mai* was appointed, and the French confirmed this delegation of authority by establishing two *cantons*, one centred at Liwa and the other at Ngelea.[63] Until 1936, the *mai* exercised proprietorship over the Foli depressions:

> It is the Mai who apportions the ground to be worked to the Haddad when the level of the lake falls. The presence of the Haddad for this heavy labour is not surprising: it confirms the explicit condition in which the group finds itself in local society. The parcels are square, 7 to 8 m a side, marked off by stakes driven in the ground.[64]

In 1936, the French abolished the position of *mai* and split the depressions between the *cantons* of Liwa and Ngelea. The depressions of Liwa, Moyala, Bitara, Guedi, Sountoro, and Arou were in the *canton* of Liwa, while Kaya, Anza, Dikelea, Kadiboul and Woddeni were under Ngelea.[65] When Mosrin became *chef de circonscription du lac* in 1949 – a position he held until 1957 – the *canton* chiefs were considered to be the proprietors of the depressions, although even then some trona was forwarded to the *alifa* in recognition of his traditional claim.[66]

Just as the French interpreted the proprietorship of the Foli depressions in terms of tax-farming in the same manner that they applied the concept to Mangari, it appears that the pre-colonial situation also had many similarities. First, the salt workers did not own the salines but had to submit to the authority of an official whose position depended upon the state. The *alifa* of Kanem recognised the Kukawa dynasty only nominally before 1845 and thereafter only in theory. The decline of Borno – despite the partial recovery under the al-Kanemi dynasty – left Borno influence east of Lake Chad at a low ebb. The autonomy of Muniyo and Damagaram in the west were developments which highlight the similarity in the delegation of authority over the salines in Mangari, Muniyo, and Foli. Theoretically, all the salines were still the property of the royal dynasty, and effective proprietorship devolved on the titled officials appointed by the government. In fact, the al-Kanemi dynasty ruled over a decentralised regime, and most of the salines came under the hegemony of autonomous provinces.

Rights to the salines were enshrined in public ceremonies which marked the opening of the salt season. These ceremonies were simple in Mangari and Foli. Muslim clerics recited prayers at the sites before the first salt was made and received in payment a portion of the salt.[67] These payments – like other gifts to clerics – were considered a form of alms, although the involvement of *malam* or *faki* also helped to legitimise the proprietary rights of the titled officials who controlled the salines. In Foli, for example,

> The Mai, assisted by a faki [Muslim cleric], opens the season by sacrificing an ox on the shore of the depression. This practice of the Muslim clerics is similar to the sacrifices for rain demanded by the farmers. What is involved here is the

absolution of the sins of the village in order that the natron might be plentiful and that there not be any accidents in the pits.[68]

Both the titled official *(mai)* and the cleric *(faki)* were present in order to confirm the relationship between workers and proprietors. The *mai* was able to meet the workers, who acknowledged their dependency and accepted the traditional arrangement whereby a portion of output was set aside for the *mai*. The *faki* sanctified this relationship.

The situation in Kadzell resembled the other regions. The right to make *kige* salt belonged to officials appointed by the Kukawa regime. The French changed the nature of these appointments, in part to rationalise the system of proprietorship and in part because Kukawa was in British territory. As Boyle reported in 1911 'the salt pans along Chad are annually let to the highest bidder and must form a considerable source of revenue – some reaching as high as £25'.[69] The area along the shore of the lake near Nguigmi was part of the domain of the *kazelma*, who was an official located at Nguigmi. Baroua, Kinjalia and other salt-camps belonged to this official in the 1870s.[70] The salt-camps near the mouth of the Komodugu Yo were under the chief of Diffa, who appointed a *kachella* to tour the camps in his tenancy. This *kachella* was known as the 'chief of the well', since *kige* production was concentrated near wells which supplied the water for filtering the *baboul* ashes.[71] Maine-Soroa alsc assumed authority over eastern Mangari, where some *kige* was made. The right to these camps appears to have been an extension of the rights over the *manda* depressions. Other fiefs between Maine-Soroa and Nguigmi had similar proprietary claims attached to them.[72]

Although proprietorship of the *kige* sites was vested in territorial officials, at least in most cases that are recorded, the nomads of Kadzell had rights of access because their slaves maintained the wells where salt was made. The nomads recognised the authority of tribal officials, also appointed by the state, who protected their rights to transhumance. It may be that many of the more remote *kige* sites in Kadzell were actually under the jurisdiction of tribal officials rather than fief holders. In any case two sets of officials governed the *kige* sites, one set through control of land and the other through control of people. Sedentary Mobbeur and Manga, who moved to the salt-camps during the production season, appear to have received permission to work the salt from the territorial officials. Similarly, the settled Kanembu near Lake Chad owed their right of access to fief-holders. But in virtually all cases, except the Manga, the limiting factor was ownership of the labour force that maintained the wells. Unlike land, which was plentiful and would have had little value even if a system of freehold had developed in the *kige* region, the wells were valuable, even though they were not bought and sold. But wells required a labour input to maintain the flow of water, and the number of sites was limited. The nomads concentrated their capital in the ownership of slaves who stayed at the wells, and their presence made the manufacture of *kige* possible.

169

PROPRIETORSHIP OF THE DALLOL SALINES

Most of Dallol Fogha, Dallol Bosso, and the numerous smaller salines of the river valleys north-east of the Niger River were incorporated into the Sokoto Caliphate in the nineteenth century, although at certain times rebellions challenged this authority. Proprietorship was invested in officials who collected a fee in salt for the right to exploit the salines. In Dallol Fogha, the 'sedentary population' owned the salt *tunga*, the temporary villages where migrant workers settled during the salt season,[73] which suggests that officials granted *tunga* sites to subordinates and other permanent residents in the towns along the valley. These subordinates became the chiefs of the *tunga*. In the late nineteenth century, Dallol Fogha was divided into five units, each of which paid tribute to Birnin Kebbi, and ultimately to Gwandu, the twin capital of the Sokoto Caliphate responsible for the western districts. These divisions included Dioumdiou and Koma in the north; the region near Laina; Bara; Kawara-Debe; and Yelou.[74] In the 1850s, Yelou and the southern basin were in revolt, but Kawara-Debe had a Fulani governor, who was subordinate to Birnin Kebbi.[75]

The proprietors of the *tunga* came from the Tienga population, in the lower Dallol Fogha, and the Toulmawa (of Kebbi origin), who predominated in the northern basin. It may well be that other people of different ethnic origins also had proprietary rights. There were Dendi and immigrant Hausa at Yelou and other places in or near Dallol Fogha. Perron lists the various settlements in the region and gives some account of their origins. The diversity of the population is striking and attests to immigration during different historical periods.[76] The Tienga, the oldest inhabitants of the valley, claim to have come from Tiengakouey. The Toulmawa, Hausa in origin, trace their home to Birnin Debe, which was destroyed by Muhammad Bello in the *jihad*. They moved west to Yelou and from there to Koma in Dallol Fogha. Their principal place of residence, Kawara-Debe, kept the name of their abandoned home.[77] The Dendi, the descendants of the Songhay, lived along the Niger near the confluence with Dallol Fogha. There is no known association between the Dendi and salt production, but Tienga and Dendi sometimes inhabited the same villages. Nupe, Kanuri and numerous groups of Hausa may have been connected with salt production, but most of these people are more likely to have been involved with trade. Finally, Fulani pastoralists grazed their herds in Dallol Fogha.

In Dallol Bosso, the proprietors of the salines were the Fulani pastoralists who maintained villages in the valley. The Fulani have followed a nomadic way of life in Dallol Bosso for centuries, but they were able to take advantage of the *jihad* in the early nineteenth century to consolidate their position. As a result their slaves made salt in the valley. Whether or not salt was worked before this time – and under what conditions – is unknown, but the Fulani were able to assign salt production to their slaves, most of whom were settled in such villages as Barbe and probably Birni Silinke, Souda Peul and other villages in the vicinity of Birnin Gaoure.[78]

DIVISION OF SALT

There is very little information on the distribution of the proceeds from salt production between proprietors and workers. Except for one saline in Mangari, vitually no distinction is made between different types of tasks, nor is it clear what differences were made between the work of slaves and of free peasants. Nor is it possible to calculate the relative importance of salt in the total income of workers and proprietors, although it is likely that the proceeds from salt production were a significant part of the total income for both workers and proprietors alike.

At Bilma, the amount of salt to be produced was set according to the order placed by the Tuareg at the time of their spring caravan. The *mai* and *bulama* assigned a quota to each proprietor, which was supposed to be filled by the end of the salt season, before the arrival of the large autumn caravan from Agades.[79] If the proprietor failed to meet his quota, he was penalised, unless he received special permission to work beyond the closing date. The penalty amounted to 90 per cent of the *kantu* produced after the end of the season.[80] In effect, proprietors had to organise production on the basis of this quota. The only time that labour was a problem was during the peak season when *kantu* was being made. If it appeared that additional labour was necessary to meet the deadline, workers had to be recruited at Bilma or among the migrants from elsewhere in Kawar. Contracts with these workers involved specific payments and rights to the salines. These arrangements appear to have been similar to the work regime for wives, slaves, and other dependants.

Workers worked for the proprietor from early morning until the time of the 2:00 p.m. prayer; the rest of the day and Fridays belonged to the workers, and at this time they were entitled to any *kantu* which they could make, if they were men, and to the *foshi* – the smaller blocks of salt – if they were women. Workers also received 3–4 containers of *minto*, from which they could make *kantu* or *foshi*, and they had the right to any *beza* produced during the height of the *kantu* season. Since virtually all *beza* was collected before the manufacture of the columns of *kantu* began, the amount of *beza* collected at this time was not significant. The workers could profit from their access to the salines, but they had to sell their salt through the proprietor. Workers were also entitled to sixty strips of white cloth and a wrapper of blue cloth; the first for the man and the second for his wife. It is not clear who fed the workers during the work period, but it is likely that provisions were the responsibility of the proprietor. The *kalla baktuma* – the specialist who broke the salt crust on the salines before the production of *kantu* began – received special compensation. Each proprietor paid him 10 per cent of the *kantu* and *beza*.[81]

The amount of salt which was actually distributed among workers and proprietors cannot be calculated. It appears that proprietors kept approximately half the proceeds, if allowance is made for the salt made by the workers in their own time and the cloth provided at the end of the season. It may well be that this proportion was even less if allowance is made for food. In addition, the proprietors were subject to tribute payment to the Tuareg, except for those owners with salines in the Lugorum – that special district that dates back to the Bilma war of c. 1759 – who were exempt from payment. The several hundred proprietors accounted for 1,000–2,000 tonnes of *kantu*; individual owners could have amassed as much as 50–100 tonnes, although there was considerable variation in earnings between the large proprietors, such as the *mai* and *buluma*, and the many small owners.

At Teguidda n'tesemt, the proceeds were divided among the members of the work unit, depending upon whether the workers were part owners, employees or slaves. In the case of part owners, each received a portion in accordance with his share in the *abatol*. In the case of employees and slaves, the exact ratios are not known. Faure provides an approximation: one third of the salt belonged to those who collected the salt-earth, another third to the water carriers and a third to the owners of the salines.[82]

In Mangari the proprietor appears to have kept about one-quarter of the *manda* salt produced, although the proprietors of natron sites may have taken a higher percentage of output. In 1905, the *lawan* of Karamgaoua collected 35 pieces of cloth, valued at 174 frs, and 100 salt cones, valued at 25 frs, from each *case de sel*, for a total of 299 frs per furnace. If the estimate for Karamgaoua is converted to the equivalent in salt, then the *lawan*'s share was 800 cones of salt. Other salines were valued at 200–1,000 frs each, presumably based on a similar ratio of cloth and salt.[83] In 1912, Laforque claimed that the *fermiers* received one-fifth of the production but in previous years the workers had surrendered one cone in four.[84] In 1914 it was calculated that the *kachella* of Maine-Soroa, who had the salines of Adebour, Fanamiram, Ari Kombomiram, Dietkorom, Bitoa and Kaboboa, received at least 250 cones of salt per furnace.[85] This quantity – based on an oven producing 50 cones per firing – was the same as the amount allocated to the furnace master for each furnace, which seems too low. The workers – assuming ten per furnace – received an average of 90 cones each for a seven month season during which time a furnace could produce a total of 1,350–1,400 cones; that is the workers received two thirds of total production, while the owner and furnace master received one-third. According to this calculation, the proprietor's share was approximately 18 per cent. The distribution was determined as follows: the salt from every third firing was set aside for the furnace master which amounted to about nine firings for the season, with the last firing of the season also going to the furnace master. This amount – 500 cones – was divided in half; the furnace master kept one share, and the rest was sent to the *kachella* of Maine-Soroa. In 1926, the chief of Guidimouni was charged with keeping nine-tenths of the natron collected there; the women who did the work were left with the rest until colonial intervention reversed the proportion.[86]

In 1936, one estimate indicates that one-third of the salt went to the *adjudicataires* – that is, those who won the rights to the salines in public auction.[87] Returns for 1936 show gross proceeds at 198,000 frs for Goure and Maine-Soroa. Of this amount, 21,500 frs were spent on the salaries of the agents of the *adjudicataires*, gifts to attract workers, and expenses associated with building the furnaces. Two-thirds of the production – 132,000 frs – went to the workers; while the *adjudicataires* took 19,474 frs. The officials in Maine-Soroa and Goure were left with a profit of 25,000 frs.[88] It appears that the third set aside in 1914 had to cover the salaries of agents and other expenses, for the 1936 figures indicate that the proprietors only received 12.6 per cent. The problem with both assessments is that they were based on information from the proprietors, who were attempting to increase their tax base while underestimating their own earnings.

Observations made in 1937 at the salines of Adebour, Cheri, Bugduma, Yani Souarni, Karagu and Gourselik reveal a slightly different method of accounting:

> The workers are paid in the following way. They fire a furnace for the master and a furnace which the workers share according to the tasks which they perform. The young man who stokes the furnace is entitled to a cone of salt. The workers who turn the brine while it is being boiled are entitled to two or three cones; the one who produces the best cones getting a little more as a bonus. One cone of salt is worth 2–3 pence.[89]

The boiler master received approximately 2–3 times as much salt as the other workers, but the *patron* received 50 per cent of total production. Excessive returns for the proprietors are also noted in other reports. Géry found that at Ari Kombomiram, near Cheri, 1,350 cones of salt could be produced at a furnace in a season. Of these the *kachella* of Maine-Soroa received 384, the furnace master 192, and the nine other workers from 48 to 120 cones, depending upon the job. In addition 36 cones were given to local *malams*, and the agent of the *kachella* also received 36 cones (Table 7.4). There were also three special firings (*djoubouk*) in which the owner received two-thirds of the output. Since there were ten furnaces at Ari Kombomiram in 1945, the *kachella*'s share was about 3,840 cones of salt, which was approximately 28.4 per cent of total output.[90]

In 1932 the *kige* workers at Diffa had to pay one salt cone to the *kachella*, who represented the chief of Diffa in the salt-camps. This payment was for the right to work the salt.[91] In 1936, workers gave the *canton* chief two *kige* cones per year, which represented approximately 8 per cent of output. In that year 600 workers made an estimated 15,000 cones in Kadzell or 25 each.[92] Both these estimates appear to be very low. It is likely that other payments were made to the owners of the slaves who made the salt. Boyle's report of 1911 claims that the holders of the salt pans along Lake Chad near Nguigmi paid as

Table 7.4. *Division of salt, Ari Kombomiram,*
1946

Recipient	Cones (number)	
Proprietor (*kachella*)	384	28.4
Furnace master	192	14.2
Two principal *kandine*	120 each (240)	17.8
Seven workers (average)	66 each (462)	34.3
Malam	36	2.7
Proprietor's agent	36	2.7
Total	1,350	100.1

Source: Géry (1952), 317.

much as £25 for the right to make salt there, which Boyle thought was a good return.[93]

In 1938 Vial and Luxeuil reported that the *canton* chief of Rig Rig received two slabs of trona out of every ten extracted from the Foli depressions.[94] He forwarded one of these to the *alifa*. In the *canton* of Bol, a representative of the chief also collected two slabs out of ten, keeping one and passing the other on to the chief. It does not appear that the *alifa* received a share of the production in this *canton*. Another slab was collected at Baga Sola, the lake port for the trade to Borno. When Mosrin was *chef de la circonscription du lac* in 1950, these ratios were still the same: two slabs were collected in the depressions and a third at the point of embarkation. Mosrin reduced the payment to one-tenth.[95] Traditionally, the *mai* collected the payment, and Bouquet has confirmed the fact that 30 per cent was standard in the past.[96] These figures are to be compared with estimates that farmers in Kanem had to pay between one-sixth and a half of their crop as tax and other dues.[97] Nicolaisen, in his study of the *haddad* attached to nomadic camps, indicates that the payment in agricultural produce for the right to farm in Kanem was as high as 50 per cent of the crop.[98]

Information on the distribution of salt in Dallol Fogha also suggests that proprietors took a significant proportion of output. In 1909, Marsaud found that the Tienga owners in southern Dallol Fogha took a third, if the migrant workers came with their own tools, and three-fifths, if the proprietors supplied the equipment:

> the owner of the land allows a stranger to work it in return for a third of the salt produced. But if the stranger doesn't have any of the tools necessary for the manufacture of salt, then he has to agree to conditions similar to those which govern share-cropping in France. The owner gives him all the necessary tools but keeps three-fifths of the produce of his labour.[99]

It may well be that slaves and other dependants worked under a proportional distribution analogous to those workers who lacked equipment.

In the Benue salines, Ward found that 'each owner of a salt working hires out his area to his wives or other women, who pay him a certain number of measures of salt which is fixed annually before the working commences. Anything over and above this fixed number belongs to the women.'[100] According to what he learned in 1920, the heads of the various towns – Awe, Akiri, Azara, Ribi, Kanje and Abuni – received a portion of the proceeds from each establishment. Varvill found that the 'majority of proprietors have not the staff to work the whole of their shares in the marsh [at Awe]. A part, therefore, in each holding is commonly sublet to a tenant for a rent and his women-folk will work the salt.'[101] According to Varvill's calculations at Awe, Akiri, and Azara, the title-holders received one-quarter of the salt, which consisted of a sum paid by the women and the rent from flats which were sublet. The title-holder was expected to hire extra workers and pay tax out of his share. The women kept three-quarters of the salt, but they had to buy firewood and food, and they were expected to set aside salt for family consumption. Jukun women at Awe paid 3–5 *mudus* of salt when they rented a flat from a Hausa owner.[102] At Keana, each woman also had to give salt to the *osikigu* and *inole* – the two officials responsible for security and brine distribution – and pay the *osana* 1–2 *mudu* (approximately 1–3 kg) each.[103]

Varvill's calculation of the earnings of six households in 1937 provides some idea of the proportion of salt retained by the title-holders and the women.[104] The *bunu* of Awe had four wives, three of whom made salt. Each of these paid him 20 measures of salt (valued at £1). The *bunu* also sublet two holdings for the equivalent of 15 measures (£0.75) and he loaned another flat to a brother – forgoing a rent of 8 measures (£0.40). Although Varvill had reservations about the amount of salt the women produced, he estimated that they cleared 80 measures each (£4.00). The *bunu* earned 83 measures of salt (£4.15), but he had to pay tax of £1.35; hence he cleared £2.80. Approximately one-third of his estimated income went to the colonial state. The *tara* of Awe, who had one wife, received 30 measures (£1.50) from her, and he sublet several flats for 60 measures (£3.00), out of which he paid tax of £1.75. His tax was one-quarter of his earnings. His wife realised a return of 128 measures (£6.40). Varvill's assessment of six households at Awe, Azara and Akiri suggests that the average earning of title-holders (£3.47) was less than the average for their wives (£4.39) (Table 7.5). It is probable that Varvill's scepticism about the estimates of total output – and hence the share kept by the women – is valid, and it may be that the title-holders disguised the amount of salt they received. None the less, the relative proportions of salt which the title-holders and the women shared is probably an accurate indication of the distribution of profits. Varvill did not attempt to assess the amount of income of casual labourers and firewood sellers, although he did note that a woman could spend 6d. per day on wood, which was not always readily available.

Of the declared income of the title-holders at Awe, Varvill's estimates show that they paid as much as 39 per cent of their income in tax. Obviously, Varvill saw nothing wrong in this assessment; he agreed with general colonial policy which held that families, rather than men and women separately, were taxable.

175

Table 7.5. *Income from salt production, Awe District, 1937*

Title-holder	Women employed	Women's income	Title-holder's income	Total
Galadima (Akiri)	3	£10.00	£2.40	£12.40
Magayaki (Azara)	2	10.50	3.00	13.50
Tafida (Azara)	2	10.50	3.00	13.50
Tara (Awe)	1	6.40	4.50	10.90
Bunu (Awe)	3	12.00	4.15	16.15
Chiroma (Awe)	3	12.00	3.75	15.75
Total	14	61.40	20.80	82.20
Average		4.39	3.47	

Source: Varvill, 1937, Nigerian National Archives, Kaduna. These calculations do not include expenses – taxes for men and firewood for women.

Whatever injustice this decision may have invoked, the tax still represented 16 per cent of earnings for men and women combined. Varvill and other colonial officers did not consider the possibility that the distribution of salt between title-holders and their wives may have changed in order to circumvent this tax. Women may have received a greater share of salt during the colonial period than they did in the past because men were taxed on the basis of their income and women were not.

CONCLUSION

Because of the lack of information, many questions concerning the reapportionment of salt have to remain unanswered; consequently, the relationship between proprietors and workers is not as clear as one would like. There are no accounts for different salines, even for individual years. Colonial reports in particular are suspect because of local efforts to avoid taxation, the lack of trained personnel to conduct surveys, and variables in weights, measures and methods of enumeration. Furthermore, the only data that do exist were collected during the transitional era of the early colonial period, and conditions were different in the nineteenth century. Indeed slaves and former slaves won for themselves better terms of employment after 1900, and it is likely, therefore, that their share of production increased under the colonial administration. The intervention of the state to prevent extreme exploitation, as one French official did at Guidimouni in 1926, demonstrates that worker–proprietor relations were uncertain. Whether or not the chief of Guidimouni had traditionally kept nine-tenths of the output, as he was accused of doing, cannot be determined. However much was kept at Guidimouni and other salines, it seems safe to conclude that the estimates of the early colonial period establish that proprietors had always collected a substantial proportion of output, probably ranging from 20 to 35 per cent or more.

176

Despite variations in the methods of control – freehold, title-holding, or fiefdoms – the proprietors were seldom engaged directly in production, not even on the managerial level. Management and labour were often delegated to others – slaves, women, clients, *haddad*. The fief-holders of Borno were a separate class from the workers, whether the workers were slaves, free peasants or members of the *haddad* caste. Many of the proprietors at Bilma, Fachi and Teguidda n'tesemt worked alongside their slaves, but the largest owners, including the *bulama* and *mai* at Bilma and the Sultan of Agades at Teguidda n'tesemt, left the work to others. Even the sexual division of labour at the Benue salines disguised the separation between workers and pro-prietors, because many slaves were used in production during the nineteenth century. Men held the rights to salt flats, while their women made the salt. Among the larger holdings, however, most of the labour was actually done by slaves. Small-scale production based on family units did not characterise the salt industry at any of the major sites in the central Sudan; rather people worked for others who benefited from the control of the salines.

In the nineteenth century, proprietorship of the salines was ultimately derived from the intervention of political authority in the economy, even though intervention varied with the different salines. At Bilma, Fachi and Teguidda n'tesemt, the Tuareg were politically dominant and had been at Bilma since c. 1759 and Teguidda since the fifteenth century. When the Tuareg achieved hegemony at Fachi is unclear, but it must have been in about 1759 if not earlier. Ownership of the salines at these sites depended upon recognition of Tuareg domination; either established rights were reconfirmed, as was the case for a portion of the salines at Bilma and probably also at Fachi, or permission to expand or begin production had to receive Tuareg permission in exchange for a fee and annual tribute. Those who owned the salt basins therefore had to accommodate themselves to Tuareg hegemony, even though attempts could be made to temper Tuareg influence through recognition of traditional ties to Borno and the Tubu, in the case of Bilma and Fachi, or to historic connexions with medieval Azelik, in the case of Teguidda. As was also true of irrigated gardens and date trees, salines were fixed assets that were recognised as freehold property. Proprietary rights developed and were maintained in this form because of the nature of political intervention.

At the salines in the sahel – Foli, Mangari, Muniyo and the Dallols – the state intervened through the medium of appointed or hereditary officials whose authority allowed them to collect a significant proportion of salt output as a tax or rent. While the situation before 1800 is unclear for lack of information, the relationship between the state and proprietorship in the nineteenth century is well established. Lesser officials under the *alifa* of Kanem controlled access to the Foli trona depressions; the *muniyoma* of Goure and other officials – both local, hereditary rulers at Goudoumaria and Maine-Soroa and titled nobles appointed from the Borno capital – controlled depressions in specific areas of Mangari and Muniyo; while in the Dallols subordinate officials within Tamkalla and Kebbi, two emirates of the Sokoto

Caliphate, determined who could work the salt deposits. Before the nineteenth century, a similar pattern seems to have existed, except that Kebbi controlled Dallol Fogha and the officials who regulated the Mangari and Muniyo salines resided in the old capital of Birni Ngazargamu and were probably appointed in a different manner from their nineteenth-century successors. Changes in political history – the rise of the Sokoto Caliphate and the decline of Borno – were responsible for these transformations in proprietorship.

Finally, ownership of the Benue salines was also derived from political authority, as symbolised in the title-holding system that prevailed in the nineteenth century. Titles were awarded to individuals by the head of the town; at most of the brine springs these political officials established themselves as a result of the *jihad* that created the Sokoto Caliphate. At Keana, where the existing political structure was maintained, access to salt flats also depended upon political recognition through the receipt of titled positions. Before the nineteenth century, a similar system of titles also existed, although it is not clear how it operated in practice. The continuation of these practices at Keana provides confirmation for this conclusion for that saline; the traditions of the Jukun at Awe and other places establish the case for the other salines. The Muslim take-over early in the nineteenth century resulted in changes in titles and different ceremonies that legitimised proprietary rights. These changes demonstrate conclusively that proprietorship was an extension of state authority and that, as access to political power was transformed, so was the composition of the proprietary class.

As is clear from a comparison with the findings of Chapter 6, the nature of labour recruitment varied with the salines, and these variations can now be correlated with differences in the nature of proprietorship. Slavery was the dominant mode of recuitment in the desert and Kadzell, where political power was concentrated in the hands of nomads; migrant labour, slavery and *haddad* caste labour were found in the sahel, where state officials controlled the salines; and women (together with slaves) made the salt at the Benue brine springs, where proprietorship was registered through politically-appointed titles that were issued to men. The full significance of these correlations remains to be analysed, but for now it is only necessary to emphasise that the interaction between labour recruitment, proprietorship and the political economy was intimate. The relations of production have to be analysed within the context of the larger social formation that characterised the central Sudan economy and society. Only then can the significance of the differences in proprietorship and in the organisation of labour be fully appreciated. Access to the salines depended upon political developments, and consequently the relations between proprietors and workers changed. First, it is necessary to examine the development of the salt marketing networks that enabled the movement of salt from the salines to the markets of the central Sudan, in order to consider the relationship between commerce and the political sphere.

178

8

Salt marketing networks

As is clear from the discussion of salt distribution in Chapter 2, salt flowed into every nook and cranny of the vast marketing network which criss-crossed West Africa. Salt is included in virtually every list of commodities found in local markets. While it is not always possible to ascertain the origin of this salt, information is sufficiently complete to demonstrate that salt or natron from greater Borno (Kawar, Mangari, and Foli) was marketed from the northern tributaries of the Zaire River in the east to the Volta basin in the west. In these distant places, central Sudan salts had to compete with more readily available local sources of supply, like salt from Daboya in Gonja and Uburu in the Igbo country, as well as sea salt, imported European salt, and a wide variety of vegetable salts. These other salts were used especially in cooking, so that *manda, foga, kige, kantu* and other central Sudan salts with a high concentration of sodium chloride were not found south of Hausa country, the Bariba states or the Benue basin. The only salts that were exported that far were natron and trona, because there were no satisfactory substitutes available locally. To examine the salt trade at its greatest extent, therefore, it is necessary to distinguish between *gishiri* and *kanwa*; *gishiri* (*manda foga, kige, kantu, beza, awai,* etc.) had a more restricted market that was confined to the Sokoto Caliphate, Borno and their immediate neighbours, while *kanwa* (*jar kanwa, farin kanwa, ungurnu*) was exported more widely. A full examination of the salt trade, moreover, would require a consideration of other sources of salt in these distant places, which is beyond the scope of this study. Because salt was only one item traded in local markets, the study of salt more properly belongs in an examination of long-distance and regional trade in general. Consequently, many aspects of the salt trade are not considered in this chapter; the concern here is with the wholesale marketing of salt and natron – how salt and natron were transferred from the major sources of production to the principal market-places of the central Sudan.

Several interlocking networks were responsible for the transfer of salt from the production sites to the major wholesale markets of the Sokoto Caliphate. First, Tuareg caravans moved salt from Kawar, Fachi, Teguidda n'tesemt and Amadror to the Hausa cities and towns. Secondly, the Yedina, who inhabited the islands of Lake Chad, transported Kanem trona across the lake to Borno, where they sold it to Kanembu middlemen at the Borno port of Baga Seyoram (Baga Kowa). Thirdly, a variety of merchants – including itinerant Hausa

179

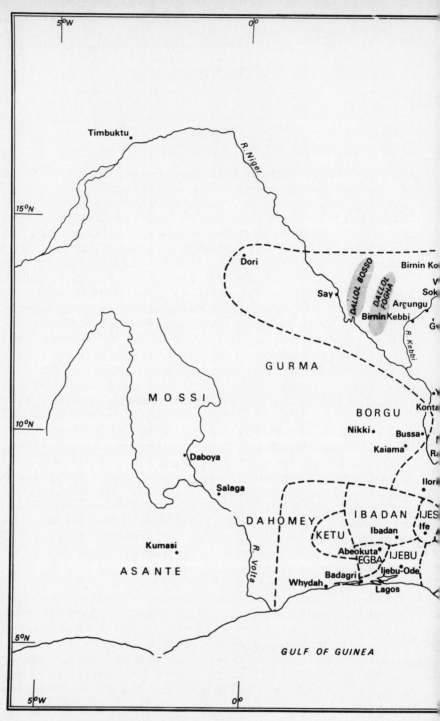

Map 8.1 Commercial centres of the salt trade

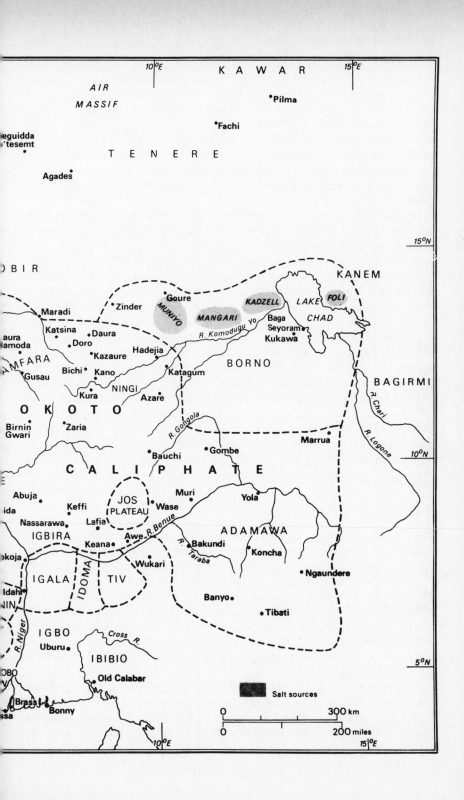

traders from the caliphate, Borno merchants settled in Mongunu, Kukawa and other towns near Lake Chad, and Manga traders from the salt districts of Muniyo and Mangari – transported the various salts of Borno westward. These networks converged on the central provinces of the caliphate, especially Kano, Katsina, Zaria and Sokoto, where large depots handled the distribution of salt locally and facilitated the re-export of natron, trona and some salt further afield. In the context of the re-export trade, Hausa merchants from the caliphate also engaged in the distribution of salt and natron from Dallol Fogha and Dallol Bosso in the west and salt from the Benue salines in the south.

Despite the concentration of salt distribution in the central emirates of the caliphate, not all salt and natron passed through the Hausa depots. The Tuareg consumed some salt themselves and distributed salt locally in the sahel, while the Yedina also carried natron south to the Chari River for re-export to Bagirmi, Kotoko and areas further south. Salt and natron also had to satisfy the Borno market, which was done without resort to the salt depots of the caliphate, and additional supplies were sent directly south of Borno to Bauchi, Gombe, and Adamawa – emirates in the caliphate which could import salt and natron directly, thereby bypassing Kano, Zaria and other centres. The Benue salines also had a separate distributional network that did not rely on merchants from the Hausa cities to the north, although these salines also exported salt north to Zaria, Kano and other emirates and relied on Hausa merchants from those emirates. Benue salt was sold to people on the Jos Plateau, and an older marketing network controlled by the Jukun was responsible for the export of salt south of the Benue. Finally, salt and natron from the Dallols also entered local trade, despite the vital role played by Hausa caravans passing through the salt markets. Merchants from Borgu, Nupe and Yoruba country came north to buy salt and natron too.

THE TUAREG TRADE

The Tuareg who were loosely organised into a confederation under the Sultanate of Agades controlled the distribution of salt from the desert salines, at least since the last several decades of the eighteenth century. The structure of the trade from then until the early twentieth century seems to have remained largely unchanged, although undoubtedly the importance of various Tuareg fractions and the role of different merchants did change. What follows is an analysis of the trade during this period in essentially static terms. Wherever possible, variations in the longer pattern are assessed, but because of the lack of data it has not been possible to examine the trade in terms of short-term changes.

The major groups in the trade were Kel Ewey, Kel Gress, Itisen, Kel Fadey, Kel Tagama, and their vassals.[1] They operated between the Air Massif and Kawar and carried almost all the output of Bilma and Fachi, while the Kel Gress – besides playing a major role in the trade from Bilma – also managed the transport of Teguidda salt to the savanna. The Kel Ahaggar and Kel Ajjer, who were not part of the Agades Confederation but formed a federation of their own in the Ahaggar, to the north-west, were responsible for the movement of Amadror salt south. Although they were independent, they maintained an alliance with the Kel Ewey that enabled them to take salt to Agades, Zinder and other towns in the south.

The organisation of the desert salt trade had to overcome the difficult problem of transporting large quantities of salt over considerable distances. Such organisation required access to camels, and as a consequence those nomads who owned the most camels dominated the trade. The Bilma–Fachi trade required the services of tens of thousands of camels per year, and because the major route crossed the desolate Tenere, which lacked fodder and water, the expeditions had to be carefully managed. At least 26,000 camels were needed to transport 2,500 tonnes of salt and dates; if maximum output of 5,000 tonnes were achieved, twice that number of camels would have been necessary. It is likely that some camels were pressed into service for more than one trip per year; there were two principal caravan seasons per year, one in February or March when as many as 1,500–3,000 camels were used, and the October trade, when 20,000–30,000 camels – a caravan that could stretch 25 km across the sands – made the trip.[2] Sometimes there was a third, equal in size to the February–March one, in mid-July. Other, small caravans travelled south from Bilma to Lake Chad and on to Borno or Kanem, and some also went south and south-west from Fachi to Mangari and Damagaram. These caravans included Tubu, Dagera, Koyam and other nomads.[3]

The Teguidda n'tesemt trade, which accounted for 400–600 tonnes of salt, required 4,000–6,000 camels. Because the distance from Teguidda to the savanna markets was not as far as from Bilma to the Hausa savanna, camels could make the journey more than once in a year. Still, the Teguidda trade also tended to concentrate on a single large-scale movement.[4] The Amadror trade, with its 100–300 tonnes, needed 1,000–3,000 camels. Although the earliest references to this trade only date to the 1860s, it is likely that Amadror salt had long found its way to the central Sudan. Again a single large caravan was responsible for most of this volume. It came south from the Ahaggar Mountains each year.[5]

Although different fractions of the Tuareg controlled the three principal trades, individuals or small groups could travel with any of these large caravans, if political relations were cordial, so that there was some flexibility in the composition of caravans over the years. Tubu and Arab nomads sometimes joined the autumn caravans leaving Bilma and Fachi, although most Tubu concentrated on the trade south from Bilma and avoided contact with the Tuareg.[6] Similarly, others could join the caravan to Amadror, perhaps in conjunction with other trade across the Sahara to North Africa.[7] The bulk of the salt followed established patterns that tended to be stable for long periods. Hostilities between Tuareg fractions, such as the war between the Kel Gress and the Kel Ewey in 1854,[8] could disrupt trade for short periods,

Table 8.1. *Composition of a Bilma salt caravan 1905*

Name of fraction	People	Camels	Horses
Kel Ewey			
Anastafidet	30	70	11
Touraoua	13	20	3
Mouzou	5	8	
Kel Timia	37	60	
Kel Ouadigui	40	185	
Tabellaoua	4	13	
Kel Aagourou	32	85	
Ilesdeyen	5	16	
Kel Eloc	6	14	
Kel Agaraguer	2	10	
Kel Zangufan	40	70	
Kel Assode	13	37	
Kel Abracan	8	21	
Total	235	609	14
Kel Tafidet			
Kel Tafidet	113	250	
Kel Tafidet	27	130	
Kel Agazar	23	66	
Iguermaden	10	30	
Total	173	476	
Azamieres			
Azamieres	73	189	5
Iguedinaouen	51	130	5
Kel Faras	44	123	
Izayaken	8	70	1
Imarsoutanes	72	223	3
Total	248	735	14
Ikaskasan			
Affagourouel	139	641	3
Kel Lazaret	90	472	3
Iguerzaouen	40	165	2
Ibadaran	12	100	1
Kel Ouilli	14	75	1
Isherifen	50	200	8
Kel Taguei	4	20	1
Kel Takreza	14	50	—
Albourdatan	147	552	8
Kel Agalel	30	100	—
Kel Tamat	2	4	—
Imezouregs	50	250	4
Total	592	2,629	31

Table 8.1. (*Cont.*)

Name of fraction	People	Camels	Horses
Kel Mouzouk	17	50	1
Immakitanes	4	3	—
Kel Tadek	30	110	—
Ifadalen	25	100	1
Ikaraden	4	8	1
Izagaran	73	150	10
Grand Total	1,401	4,870	72

With the caravan were 18 Arab traders and 11 Kanuri and Hausa pilgrims.
Total Kel Ewey caravan probably numbered 6,000 camels.
Gadel connected the title of *tambari* with Immakitanes and the Agoalla title with Kel Tadek, Immakitanes and Izagaran.
The intermediary for the Sultan of Agades was a Mouzou. All the groups met with the Sultan before going on to Bilma; caravans usually formed 2–3 groups.
Source: Gadel, Rapport sur une tournée en Air ou Azbin, 1905. Rapports, 1904–08, Archives de la République du Sénégal, Dakar.

but major changes in the flow of trade in the long term were relatively rare. Raiding was a problem, especially since slow-moving, heavily-laden camels made an easy target. The size of the caravans inhibited raiding to some extent, but on several occasions, at least, enemy nomads successfully seized camels and cargoes. Raid and counter-raid were a way of life in the desert.

The Bilma and Fachi trade was concentrated in the autumn, when the large caravans that left the Air Massif in October arrived. There were usually two of these caravans; one under the direction of the Kel Ewey and the other headed by the Kel Gress. In 1824 Clapperton learned that the Bilma caravan at Kano had 3,000 camels, and since the Kel Ewey were the main suppliers of the Kano market, this estimate probably represents a portion of the Kel Ewey caravan for that year.[9] In 1850, Barth estimated that the Kel Ewey caravan, which was divided into more than thirty sections, totalled 3,700–3,800 camel loads. Barth was only able to observe eleven of these sections and obtain particulars on four others.[10] The Kel Gress caravan, which travelled separately, 'was said to consist of not less than 10,000 camels'.[11] Rohlfs, who was at Bilma in 1866, learned that the Kel Ewey came with 3,000–4,000 camels.[12] Henri Gadel, who witnessed the Kel Ewey caravan in 1905, was able to compile a list of sections in this caravan (Table 8.1).[13] The forty sections totalled 1,401 people, 4,870 camels and 72 horses, which suggests a carrying capacity of 463 tonnes of salt based on a load of 95 kg per camel. Each section averaged 123 camels, managed by 35 people or one person for every three or four camels. In fact, however, Gadel's figures contain many anomalies. The Affagourouel managed 641 camels – one driver per five camels, while the Mouzou had only eight camels, with five people. It is likely that the larger sections – Affagourouel, Kel Lazaret, Albourdatan – were subdivided but were not recorded as such.

Merchants of the Bilma trade included the major leaders of the Tuareg fractions, individual Tuareg with a camel or two, and traders resident in Zinder, Bilma, Dirku, Agades and other towns, who hired camels for the annual expeditions. Annur, who was the head of the Irolangh (the family of the *amenokal* – the highest official – of the Kel Ewey), had 200 camels in the 1850 caravan, and he headed a larger caravan of 2,000 camels, which consisted of subordinate groups.[14] Barth also mentioned Elaiji, Annur's brother, also of the Irolangh, Hamma of the Kel Tafidet, Haj Makhmud of the Kel Tagrimmat, Amaki of the Amakita, Mohammed dan Aggeg of the Imasagh-lar, Barka and Tambarin Hasoma of the Iserararan, and Mohammed Irogagh and Wuentusa of the Ikazkezan. Each of these men owned camels and dealt in salt, but many other Tuareg invested in the trade. According to Nicolaisen, a Tuareg who did not want to go to Bilma let a kinsman or a friend trade for him with his camels.[15] The payment for this was a large cone of salt (*kantu*) which constituted one-sixth or one-seventh of a camel load.

Mohammad Boro, an Adarawa merchant and former official (*sarkin turawa*) at Agades, also operated an elaborate commercial empire that included salt as a principal commodity. From his headquarters in Sokoto, Boro used his large family as the basis of his firm. With houses in Agades, Kano, and Zinder, he imported goods from North Africa, as well as salt from Bilma and Fachi.[16]

> Though he holds no office at present, he is nevertheless a very important per-
> sonage, not only in Agades, but even in Sokoto, where he is regarded as the
> wealthiest merchant. He has ... not less than about fifty sons with their families;
> but he still possesses such energy and enterprise, that in 1854 he was about to
> undertake another pilgrimage to Mekka.[17]

Muhammad Boro had been *sarkin turawa* in the 1840s, if not earlier. In 1850, he accompanied the Kel Gress–Itisen caravan to Bilma, together with some of his sons, after which he returned to Sokoto 'for Sokoto is his real home'.[18] Boro was associated with the Adarawa community in Sokoto; these merchants imported kola from Asante and shared the northern trade to Adar with the Kel Gress.[19] Boro's close connexion with these Tuareg demonstrates how savanna merchants became attached to Tuareg nomads, first as clients, then as wealthy traders on their own.

Other important merchants in the Tuareg trade lived at Zinder, the capital of Damagaram, the virtually autonomous western province of Borno. Zinder was for the Kel Ewey what Sokoto was for the Kel Gress. It developed as a major staging point in the transport of salt to the Hausa market. Salt was sold from the houses of Tuareg merchants, who often had homes in Damagaram and Air, and who sent servants to nearby markets. According to Baier, 'if salt was left over when the Tuareg left for the north at the beginning of the rains, they entrusted it to female servants or concubines who stayed at the southern encampment to sell salt on the master's account'.[20] These fully-fledged landlady-brokers are the only known example of women in a trade that was otherwise the exclusive prerogative of men. The Tuareg also arranged marriage partners for servile men who were salt traders, and in this way generated a distributional network based at Zinder. In short, the mechanisms that the Tuareg used to penetrate the savanna economy were not overtly economic in nature. Marriage alliances and the use of female brokers were effective methods of converting social relations into an advantageous economic position.

Among the more important savanna merchants who dealt in salt at the end of the nineteenth century was Musa Abdallah, known as Malam Yaro. Malam Yaro's father was a Kanuri scholar from Kulumfardo (a later town named after the old Koyam centre), who had moved to Zinder after the destruction of Kulumfardo and had become a successful merchant. Yaro 'gave millet to Tuareg traders in Zinder who took it to Bilma to exchange for salt; upon their return, they divided the profit from the transaction with him'.[21] Yaro married a prominent noblewoman of the Kel Tafidet and used this connexion to get the camels he needed. In 1905, he hired 476 camels to transport salt from Bilma and Fachi.[22] Such marriage alliances between sedentary merchants and nomads may have been just as common as marriages between nomads and local women. Certainly Yaro's situation is a further example of the ways in which social relations along the desert-edge could be manipulated to commercial advantage.

Merchants from Bilma and Dirku also invested in salt; they travelled with the Tuareg caravans through the Air Massif in order to sell their goods in the caliphate,[23] or they organised their own expeditions via Zinder. Abdallah Indimi, the headman of Bilma in 1906, who dressed in a wide Hausa shirt and a huge turban of shiny blue cloth, 'was a trader like his father, and had inherited from him houses in Kano, Zinder, Kuka, and Tripoli'.[24] His house in Kukawa was destroyed at the time of Rabeh (c. 1892), and consequently,

> He had spent the last years at Tripoli and Anay .... He knew every trader of the great Arab community from Tripoli, Ghat, Ghadames and Murzuk; he had been to Tibesti and fought the Tuareks. As soon as possible he hoped to make the pilgrimage to Mecca like his father, Hadji Mohammed Tahir .... Abdullah Indimi calls himself a Kanuri, as do most of the wealthier people. Like the local village chiefs, they seem to have little authority over the men, who trade or rob as much as they please. In the days of former prosperity, the frequently passing caravans brought wealth and life into the oasis, which served as a convenient half-way station to the traders. Now, but a single caravan in the year arrives

from Bornu, and another is sent by the local traders to Murzuk with dates and wares from Bornu.[25]

In 1904 Abdallah Indimi organised one caravan of 120 camels, which travelled from Bilma to Zinder.[26] It is significant that Abdallah Indimi described himself as Kanuri. Son of a man who had made the pilgrimage to Mecca and wealthy in his own right, Indimi was part of the merchant class of the savanna, even though he had assumed political office in Bilma. The position of *mai* at Bilma was reserved for the descendants of the Kanuri population, and it may well be that Indimi's family had long lived there. In any case, Indimi was no ordinary resident of the oasis; he was involved in the trans-Saharan trade and had wide connexions in the savanna. As the *mai* he also owned salt basins.

Another of the principal merchants in the salt trade was the holder of the Agades title, *kokoy geregere*, 'master of the Sultan's courtyard', who was usually identified by the Hausa title, *sarkin turawa*, chief of the Arabs.[27] By the middle of the nineteenth century, this official was responsible for the collection of caravan taxes for the Sultan, and consequently he was involved in commercial operations to North Africa and Bilma. The *sarkin turawa* or his representative accompanied the Kel Ewey or Kel Gress caravan to Bilma and was responsible for commercial negotiations there.[28] He arbitrated in any disputes which occurred in the grand caravan. According to Barth, the *sarkin turawa* collected one *kantu* of salt per camel-load – that is one-eighth of the load.

> After having brought the salt caravan to Sakatu, the Serki-n-Turawa annually has to go to Kanu, where he receives a small portion of the 600 cowries, or duty levied on each slave brought to the slave-market, after which he returns to Agadez with the Kelgeris that have frequented the market of Kanu. This long annual journey, which brings the Serki-n-Turawa much more in connection with the Tawarik than with the Arabs, makes him at the same time a sort of intermediator between Agades and Sakatu.[29]

He also levied 10 *mithkal* (a measure of gold) on every camel-load which crossed the Sahara. Both Muhammad Boro, who was *sarkin turawa* in the 1840s, and Ashu, who held the position in 1850, were very rich, no doubt as a result of their office.[30] As was the case with the *mai* of Bilma, who identified with savanna society, the *sarkin turawa* was also associated with the savanna, even though he worked for the Tuareg. The *sarkin turawa* appears to have been Hausa (unlike the *mai*, who was Kanuri), and more exactly, one of the Adarawa, who formed a major portion of the commercial population of Sokoto and traced their ancestry to the province of Adar, north of Sokoto.[31]

The Tuareg brought grain and manufactured goods to the salt markets at Bilma and Fachi. In 1906, Vischer observed the arrival of a Tuareg caravan of over 8,000 camels and 1,000 men.

> The Asbinawas bring millet and grass from Air, wood for camel saddles, Manchester cloth, Hausa tobes [gowns], and all the luxuries which can be found in the Kano market. Men, women and children arrive from all the villages to buy

their provisions for the year, which the Tuareks give them in exchange for salt and dates .... The great encampment with the many thousand camels, the stacks of grass and piled-up loads, looked like an immense fair. The oasis, of course, could never support all these animals, so the Asbinawas, before they leave Air, feed up their camels on the fattest grazing-grounds, and then, having chosen only the fittest animals, load about a third of the number with grass, which is used for fodder on the way. Great quantities are buried in the sand at intervals to be used on the return journey, for on that desolate stretch of desert water is very rare, and not a blade of grass grows between the interminable sand-dunes.[32]

In 1909 Prévôt estimated that the gardens at Bilma could produce 40 tonnes of grain per year, but the population required 250–300 tonnes (500 g per person per day). The difference had to be imported; in addition, a comparable amount of grain was needed in Fachi, and both oases served as markets for nomads from elsewhere in the central Sahara.[33] The smaller caravans of private merchants also dealt in grain, but they tended to concentrate on manufactured goods, kola nuts and other luxuries. Abdallah Indimi's caravan of 1904, with its 120 camels from Zinder, included 30 loads of millet, 90 loads of tanned leather, women's textiles and men's gowns, while the caravan of the Zinder merchant, Koloa, consisted of 34 loads of tanned leather and 56 loads of millet.[34]

THE LAKE CHAD TRADE

The trade across Lake Chad represented a different pattern of desert-side exchange from the Tuareg trade. Salt, dried fish, and livestock were the staples of production in the lake basin, and these were exchanged for grain and manufactured goods. Yedina also sold wheat, cattle, hippopotamus hide and meat, as well as dried fish and trona.[35] In exchange they purchased millet, which was a major import into the trona district of Foli, cloth, onions, kola nuts, tomatoes, peanuts, tobacco and Maria Theresa thalers.[36] Because trade flowed east and west across the lake, the Yedina were able to maintain a vital intermediary role similar to that of the Tuareg in the desert, only they used to advantage their monopoly of boats rather than camels.

Establishing a chronology for the Lake Chad trade presents even more difficulties than the reconstruction of the Tuareg desert trade. Almost certainly the traffic across the lake is very old, but virtually nothing is known about it until the nineteenth century. Even then changes in its volume and organisation are largely unknown. This section examines the information available on the structure of the trade; although the antiquity of this structure is unclear, it is certain that people living on the islands in Lake Chad have long been involved in transport services and other economic activities that have tied them to the mainland.

The Yedina paddled to the lake-side markets of Foli to buy trona. Such ports as Kindell, Bol, Ouda (Wanda), Hedimirum, and Kinjiria were the centres of the trade. The *haddad* salt workers carried the trona slabs to the shore of the lake – a distance of a day or more – on oxen. At Kindell and Forom, there were 500–600 houses for storing trona in 1903.[37] These centres, located in the central region of the lake, developed as important markets for grain where Arabs and Tuareg nomads came to revitalise their supplies and sell booty seized in raids. From these markets, the Yedina took the trona west to Baga Seyoram, the main port for Borno, or south to Jimtilo, at the mouth of the Chari River.[38] As Alexander observed in 1904:

> Potash [trona] is the great monopoly of Kowa and upon this the Lowan waxes rich, for all the supply goes first through the Kowa [Baga Seyoram] market and has to pay a toll.[39]

In 1904, Baga Seyoram was located 14 miles from the shore of the lake, so that the actual port was Baga Kowa:

> here the principal trade is done in potash [trona] and dried fish, which are brought up by Kanembus from the Buduma [Yedina] fish-market, some fourteen miles distant on Lake Chad. The latter place is called by the Budumas Kowa Baga, which means market for Kowa.[40]

The Yedina (known as Buduma by the Kanuri) transported the trona across the lake on large rafts (*kadei*) made of long bundles of papyrus laid layer upon layer and lashed together with rope, which were, according to P. A. Talbot, who travelled on one in 1911, 'so stable that even the sudden violent storms of the lake seldom ... sink them'.[41] These rafts were also used to transport cattle from the mainland to the islands and between the islands. In 1851, Barth observed one of these rafts which was 'about twenty feet long, but seemed tolerably broad; and one of them contained as many as eleven people, besides a good quantity of natron and other things'.[42] The standard ones in operation in 1903 had crews of two or six men and could handle 20–60 slabs of trona, approximately one-quarter of a tonne to one tonne.[43] Some were 12 metres long. In 1904 D'Huart learned that these rafts were purchased in the north-east of the lake, near Kindill,[44] which was also a natron port. The Yedina organised expeditions which could involve as many as forty vessels; a fleet of this size could transport from 10 to 30 tonnes.[45] If the estimate that upwards of 1,000 tonnes were being produced is accurate then a very considerable number of people must have been involved in transport.

Because of Yedina independence and the importance of the trona trade across the lake, the Borno government attempted to maintain cordial relations with the leaders of the various Yedina fractions, especially the powerful Gouria. Only in this way could supplies of trona be restocked. The Borno official at Baga Seyoram, who had the title *lawan*, sent presents of cloth to the island headman of the Yedina – almost certainly the head of the Gouria.[46]

> A standing truce prevailed at the shore-markets between Kanembu and Budduma: the former thus obtained sole control of exchange of cloth, millet etc. from inland with salt and wheat from the island.[47]

190

This arrangement had existed at least since 1851, when Barth witnessed a similar trade between Kanembu and Yedina:

> The Kanembu inhabitants of many neighbouring villages carry on trade with the islanders almost uninterruptedly, while elsewhere the latter are treated as most deadly enemies. Two parties of Kanembu happened to be here with argum or millet, which they exchanged for the natron.[48]

There was no problem of communication since the Yedina spoke Kanuri, of which Kanembu was a dialect. Hence they could speak with merchants on the west side of the lake and the *haddad* producers on the east side of the lake.[49] The Kanembu, for their part, purchased considerable quantities of trona, so that they could supply the market even when the lake was low and the Yedina did not come to Baga Seyoram.[50]

Not all the trona went across the lake to Borno, but most did. The Yedina also supplied the Kotoko ports at the mouth of the Chari River with trona for re-export further south still. And Freydenberg learned in 1904 that caravans came to Foli around the northern side of the lake and from Bagirmi south of the lake. The Borno caravans took trona to Kabi, while the Bagirmi merchants took it to Chekna, the capital of Bagirmi.[51]

THE BORNO TRADE

The transport of salt and natron across Borno required an elaborate network of routes and markets, which connected the various sources of salt in Borno with the Hausa cities and towns to the west and with markets in Mandara and the Benue River basin in the south. While it is clear that salt has been exported throughout this region for a long time, probably many centuries, the early history of this trade is as difficult to reconstruct as the trade across Lake Chad and the trade from the desert salines. The political dislocation of the *jihad*, which struck Borno between 1806 and 1812, had profound economic repercussions (examined in more detail in Chapter 9). The following analysis outlines the major changes in the nineteenth century as they affected the organisation of the salt trade. Because this trade was closely associated with the commerce in other commodities and depended upon the production of goods other than salt and natron, the analysis must be considered preliminary. None the less, certain broad patterns are clear. These include the following: first, the scale of the trade was very large, since it involved something like 3,000–9,500 tonnes of salt and natron. The number of merchants, commercial assistants, and transport animals had to be very extensive to handle this volume, no matter what fluctuations in volume occurred from year to year. Secondly, the merchant community included Hausa merchants from the central emirates of the Sokoto Caliphate, merchants from eastern Borno, and Manga traders from the salt districts of Mangari and Muniyo. The composition of these three communities is analysed in some detail. Thirdly, the relative importance of the three communities changed in the course of the nineteenth century. Merchants from the caliphate commanded an increasingly larger share of the trade, especially because many traders from Borno emigrated to the Hausa emirates. The Manga entered the trade as the production of *manda* increased, until they formed a significant group of merchants by the end of the century. These changes required extensive adjustments in the commercial infrastructure of Borno. The arrival of more and more merchants from the caliphate at the same time that the resident merchant community suffered a decrease in numbers through emigration placed severe strains on the Borno economy. Many caliphate merchants operated in itinerant caravans rather than depending on resident brokers and landlords, a development which reflected the disintegration of the Borno economy. Borno suffered a steady decline, albeit one that was punctuated with periods of partial recovery in certain sectors and the re-organisation of the commercial infrastructure. The history of the salt trade provides some insights into this economic change, but the following reconstruction is necessarily incomplete since it only concentrates on the movement of salt and natron.

In the nineteenth century, the arc of the salt network stretched from Baga Seyoram to Kukawa and along the southern edge of the salt districts as far as Gumel, 340 km to the west, and extended to Zinder, 200 km further north-west. Trona from Kanem was re-exported from Baga Seyoram westward, while the hundreds of salt-camps in Kadzell, Mangari, Muniyo and the Kanembu districts along the lake formed a large and continuous belt of territory from which salt could be purchased. While the main orientation of this trade was from east to west, the many towns on this axis also exported salt and natron south. The merchants who operated along this axis included Hausa traders from the west, who journeyed to Borno to sell kola nuts, textiles, and other goods, and Borno merchants who travelled west to the Hausa cities and south to Mandara and the Benue basin. At one time, Borno merchants dominated this trade, but in the nineteenth century there were more Hausa merchants active along this route than merchants from Borno. Many of the 'Hausa' merchants were, in fact, of Borno origin, most especially the Kambarin Beriberi and other traders who considered themselves Beriberi (the Hausa name for Kanuri). Of the Borno-based merchants in the nineteenth century, the Manga were the most important. These merchants were from the salt districts of Mangari and Muniyo and either exported the product of their own labour or purchased supplies at the salt-camps for re-sale in the west or south. Other Borno merchants exported salt too, but there were no important groups comparable to the Manga.

According to Barth, who observed the trade as he travelled west in 1851:

> The intercourse on the road ... was exceedingly animated: and one motley troop followed another – Hausa fataki [*fatake*, merchant], Bornu traders or 'tugur-chi', Kanembu, Tebu, Shuwa Arabs, and others of the roving tribe of the Welad Sliman [Awlad Sulayman], all mixed together – while their beasts of burden formed a multifarious throng of camels, oxen, horses, and asses.[52]

Barth made important distinctions in his assessment of the trade. The Hausa merchants who lived in the caliphate included kola merchants, cloth dealers and others whose interest in the Borno market was only part of a larger business. The 'Bornu traders or "tugurchi"' are more difficult to identify. Some were Manga from the salt districts of Mangari and Muniyo, but others were residents of the various towns along the commercial axis. The final group – Kanembu, Tubu, Shuwa Arab and Awlad Sulayman – consisted of various nomads who participated in the savanna trade in much the same way that the Tuareg did further west. Some undoubtedly traded in salt produced at the *kige* camps of Kadzell and the Chad shores. Others may have acted as transporters for resident merchants of the salt markets.

The Hausa merchants commanded an increasingly important part of the Borno trade in the course of the nineteenth century.[53] Hausa traders had travelled to Borno – no doubt to buy salt and natron – at the end of the eighteenth century and in the first part of the nineteenth century. In 1824, Clapperton joined one caravan that eventually included about 500 people travelling from Kukawa to Kano; when it left Kukawa there were 27 North African merchants and about fifty Borno traders in the troop, but as the caravan passed by the markets south of Mangari the number swelled to at least 500 people.[54] At least eight caravans had left Kukawa for Kano that season.[55] Hausa and Borno merchants mixed together; the Hausa came to Borno to buy 'trona or natron, common salt, and beads; which together with coarse tobes [gowns], are also carried by Bornouese adventurers to Haussa'.[56] By 1846, Madugu Mohamman Mai Gashin Baki – an important caravan leader from Kano who centred his trade first at Bauchi and later in Adamawa – was trading to Borno; on one journey to Kukawa, where he sold galena that he had brought from Bauchi, he purchased five pack oxen loaded with trona, which he took back to Bauchi.[57] A decade later, in Barth's time, the Hausa trade, not only south to Bauchi but mostly west to Kano and other towns of the central districts of the caliphate, was of major proportions. Even so, most Hausa traders did not go any further than Gumel, the most western market on the Borno axis, where Borno merchants from Muniyo, Mangari and Baga Seyoram came with their supplies:

> Gummel is the chief market for the very extensive trade in natron, which . . . is carried on between Kukawa and Muniyo on one side, and Nupe . . . on the other; for this trade passes from one hand into another, and the Bornu people very rarely carry this merchandise further than Gummel. Large masses of natron, certainly amounting to at least one thousand loads of both qualities . . . , were offered here for sale – the full bullock's load of the better quality [*ungurnu*] for five thousand, an ass's load of the inferior sort for five hundred kurdi [cowries].[58]

In his trip from Kano to Gumel, Barth passed a number of caravans – all loaded with natron (and probably salt too). On one day – 12 March 1851 – he counted over five hundred loads, including 'a very numerous caravan with natron, coming from Kukawa'; 'now and then a motley caravan of horses, oxen and asses, all laden with natron, . . . coming from Muniyo', forced his own party off the road.[59] Barth could tell the origin of each variety of natron

193

because *ungurnu* 'which is obtained in the neighbourhood of the Tsad, was all in large pieces like stone, and is carried in nets, while that coming from Muniyo consists entirely of rubble, and is conveyed in bags, or a sort of basket'.[60]

By the end of the century, when accounts based on oral data are particularly rich in detail, Hausa merchants more often than not bypassed Gumel and continued on to the Mangari markets or the trona depots further east. Merchants either travelled through Damagaram to the centres of Muniyo and Mangari or they followed the main east–west axis further south. Malam Miko Hamshak'i, whose father was the famous caravan leader, Madugu Kosai, remembers trips to Mongunu, near Kukawa; he even went to the lake – Baga Seyoram – to buy trona, and sometimes took his supplies to Mandara, further south, in order to buy slaves. His caravan also went directly to the Manga centres – particularly Adaburda, Cheri, and Zumba.[61] Alhaji Bak'o Madigawa, another Kano merchant who was trading in the 1890s as a young man, travelled via Jema' are and Azare to Borno, going as far as Kukawa to obtain trona.[62] This pattern was also followed by other important merchants, such as Madugu Isa na Garahu, who led his own caravans to Borno to buy trona and red natron.[63] These three accounts are representative of the activities of the largest Kano merchants at the end of the nineteenth century. Each of these men either led his own caravans (Madugu Isa and Madugu Kosai) or travelled in a separate caravan (Bak'o's family went with one of several Kambarin Beriberi leaders).

The smaller merchants from rural Kano and Katsina also made the Borno trip, sometimes travelling with the big caravan leaders but often forming their own, smaller expeditions because it was not necessary to travel in the large caravans that were characteristic of the trade to Asante or southern Adamawa. Traders from Garko, near Kano, went to the markets north of Geidam in Mangari – Garsali and Kumagana are remembered as sources of red natron.[64] Other merchants from rural Kano – such as those at Gumawa – went to the same places, but in their own caravans, and they also went on to the trona markets further east.[65] Some of the kola merchants at Dunkura and Kumurya only traded in Mangari natron, which they also obtained near Geidam, and trona from either Baga or Mongunu.[66]

Hausa merchants from other parts of the caliphate also participated in this trade. Those from Gummi, in Sokoto province, for example, followed a route to Kano, where they sold kola before continuing to western Borno. These merchants bought both white natron from Muniyo and trona from Kanem, which they re-exported to Asante. Unlike the Kano merchants, however, the Gummi traders bought their trona supplies at the western end of the Borno commercial axis. Perhaps because of the distance from their homes, they did not travel to Lake Chad.[67] Their style of business was similar to that reported by Barth for the trade at Gumel in the 1850s. Katsina merchants, by contrast, often went to Damagaram and across to the markets of Muniyo, which was a shorter journey than the route followed by the traders from Kano. The

Damagaram trade also had the advantage of less competition in acquiring Muniyo natron, but that route lacked access to trona supplies.

The lack of a central depot for salt and natron – impossible because of the size of the salt districts – militated against the necessity of merchants staying in one place for more than a few days – indeed for more than a market-day. Merchants moved on to the next town along the main east–west axis, or they travelled into the salt districts of Mangari or Muniyo to buy directly from the salt-camps.

These traders stayed in temporary campsites (*zongo*) while they were buying natron and salt.[68] Such caravan leaders as Madugu Isa of Zinder (originally from Mai Jirgi, near Tassawa) took their caravans to the salt lakes of Muniyo, where Isa led the bargaining for natron. He initiated the negotiations by giving a gift to the proprietor of the saline and then set the price of the natron in terms of millet. All the caravan members followed this exchange rate.[69]

Merchants who had more goods to sell than most caravan members stayed with landlords (*fatoma*), however. Such *fatoma* were found at markets near Maine-Soroa, including Kua, where merchants came to sell kola nuts and textiles and to buy natron.[70] At Dumbula, one of the largest markets in Mangari, each quarter had a designated chief who served as a *fatoma*. Hausa merchants came in groups of at least twenty. The *fatoma* provided lodging and brokerage services; food was prepared for these strangers, but they always ate separately from their Manga hosts.[71] Baga Seyoram controlled trona distribution to such an extent that brokerage services developed more fully there, but trona was also sent to Mongunu, Kukawa and other markets away from the lake. Itinerant merchants could buy supplies at one of several markets, so that itinerant trading competed with resident brokerage services even in this trade.

The Borno traders continued to handle a large portion of the natron and salt trade, even though their range of operations shrank steadily in the course of the nineteenth century. In the 1820s, Clapperton met Borno traders at Kulfu, in northern Nupe, which was then the terminus of their trade to the south-west.

> The Bornou caravans never go further than this place, though generally some of their number accompany the Houssa merchants to Agolly in Yourriba, Gonja, and Borgoo, from which they bring Kolla or Gora nuts, cloth of woollen, printed cottons, brass and pewter dishes, earthenware, a few muskets, a little gold, and the wares brought from Yourriba. They carry their goods on bullocks, asses and mules; and a great number of fine women hire themselves to carry loads on their heads; their slaves, male and female, are also loaded. The Bornou merchants, during their stay, stop in the town in the houses of their friends or acquaintances, and give them a small present on their arrival and departure, for the use of the house.[72]

As Barth noted, by the 1850s Gumel was the last stop for many Borno traders, although by then many other merchants who had once been based in Borno had emigrated west. They settled in or near Kano, Katsina and other Hausa towns, where they became involved in the import trade in salt and natron.

This shift – evident in the increasing number of Hausa merchants travelling to Borno, their deeper penetration of the state, and the emigration of Borno merchants – was part of a wider pattern of economic adjustment related to the decline of the political fortunes of Borno and the consolidation of the Sokoto Caliphate (see Chapter 9). These changes in commercial patterns were related to the expansion of *manda* production in the nineteenth century. It may be that *manda* was produced on a large scale in the eighteenth century; if so the commercial patterns of the nineteenth century represented a sharp break with previous practice. Whether the *manda* industry was recovering its eighteenth-century position or whether it was an entirely new industry is not clear, but in either case Hausa merchants became more involved in trade to Borno than ever before, and merchants in Borno were gradually reduced to middleman functions. The Kanembu brokers at Baga Seyoram and the trona wholesalers in Mongunu, Kukawa and other towns provided useful services for the itinerant Hausa traders from the west, but they commanded a steadily decreasing share of the export trade itself. As the activities of Madugu Mohamman Mai Gashin Baki demonstrate, even as early as the 1840s, Hausa merchants were penetrating the Borno salt trade from the south. Where once Borno merchants had probably monopolised the distribution of salt and natron in the Benue basin, they came to face stiff competition from wide-ranging Hausa merchants like the Kano-born Mai Gashin Baki.

The trade south of Borno, which Hausa traders had moved into but did not dominate the way they did the trade to the west, continued to be an important outlet for salt and natron throughout the nineteenth century.[73] One route passed south from Kukawa through Izgu and Sorau to Yola, the capital of Adamawa on the Benue. Another linked Kukawa and Mora through Dikwa. Various towns and villages to the south of Borno – Madagali, Sakun, Midlu, Gulak, Kamale, Muchala and Lamurde – have traditions that Kanuri traders brought *manda* and natron, among other goods.[74] Four kinds of salt were common in Mandara, at least at the end of the nineteenth century if not earlier. These included *kige*, which marks Mandara as the south-eastern limit for this salt, *manda* from Mangari, *gwangwarasa* (thenardite for tanning), and trona. The principal merchants in this trade included merchants from Mongunu, as well as from other parts of Borno, including Mangari, and Kotoko from the Chari River Basin. Kanembu, Tubu, and other Borno merchants brought the trona. Despite the importance of Borno participation in the Mandara trade – and the proximity of Mandara to Borno would have made it difficult for any other merchants to dominate its market – Hausa traders were still present. They came to buy slaves, and they brought salt as a principal item of exchange. The activities of these Hausa merchants – who included such Kano merchants as Madugu Kosai and his son Miko Hamshak'i – further demonstrate the extent to which Hausa merchants had become pre-eminent in the trade of the central Sudan.[75] Borno merchants continued to be active in the trade to Bauchi; in 1866 they brought *kige* and probably natron south to the Gongola River and on to Bauchi.[76] The intensity of this southern trade can be shown by the number of Kanuri residents in the towns along the trade routes to the Benue River. Immigrants were found at Otobono, Gabchari, Maimadi, and Jadda, which were towns between Bauchi and the Benue. Other immigrants had settled in the Wase area.[77]

The major change in the composition of the nineteenth-century merchant community in Borno was the emergence of the Manga as a factor in the natron and salt trade (although not in the trona trade). As has been demonstrated in Chapter 6, the Manga moved into the salt district east of Muniyo in the early nineteenth century, even giving their name to the district. By the end of the century, they not only made salt and collected natron; they exported these too. Probably the Manga of Muniyo had long sold natron west, but this earlier trade – assuming that it existed – is lost to history. It may well be that the natron trade of eighteenth-century Katsina, when that city was the major long-distance trade centre in the Hausa country, followed a route through Damagaram to Muniyo – as the nineteenth-century trade did.[78] If so, the Manga surely played a major role. None the less, the Manga had established themselves anew by the end of the nineteenth century, and from bases in Mangari as well as Muniyo. Consequently, they followed the main commercial axis across Borno to Kano and Zaria. F. Cargill recognized the difference between Manga and other merchants from Borno in 1907:

> Beriberis bring to Kano stone potash [*ungurnu*], cattle, ostrich feathers and ivory and buy Kano cloths and gowns (black and white) and Arab goods. Mangawa bring in mangul [*manda*] salt and red potash [natron] and buy black Kano cloths and gowns. Both Beriberis and Mangawa use bullock transport.[79]

It is not clear how Cargill was using the Hausa term *beriberi*, which could either refer to merchants from Kukawa and other districts near Lake Chad or to the residents of Kano Emirate who traced their origin to Borno. In either case, the Manga stood out as important traders in salt and natron who had entered a profitable trade that had long been dominated by others. As Patterson observed in 1917, it was a short step from producer to merchant:

> in many cases the producers, instead of selling the salt at the *Tubkis* in Manga District go themselves to Bauchi and Kano Provinces to dispose of it...Practically every salt maker who can afford to do so keeps one camel or more, and from being primarily a salt maker the Manga becomes an all round trader of great importance. His first thought is easily to provide himself from his profits on the work on salt with a years [sic] supply of corn, for the rainfall in Manga District is lower than in other parts of the District and the crops of *gero* [millet] on the sand dunes are much below average in Bornu. Only in an exceptionally good year will the inhabitants of this area be exempt from the necessity of eking out home grown corn with supplies bought in the southern parts of the District.[80]

In 1924 J. B. Wellman noticed the same pattern in Manga commercial life, a pattern that was at least several decades old:

As soon as they can afford it, the majority of people invest in a donkey, pack-ox or camel and start trading in salt . . . In the slack time of the dry season a man may make two or three journeys to the salt pans in the north where he buys 'mongul' or potash [natron] and returns home with his loads. These he stores in his house until after the millet has begun to sprout, when he packs up and sets off for Kano, trades the salt or potash [natron] there at 350-400 per cent profit and returns to his village in time for the harvest. Some make a journey before the rains begin.

While Wellman claimed that some purchased more animals and 'abandon[ed] farming altogether and live[d] entirely by trading',[81] it is doubtful that even the most successful Manga merchant actually relinquished his right to land or his control over the output of farms. More likely, Wellman either observed or was told that some Manga no longer engaged directly in agricultural labour.

Kambar, a salt merchant in Maine-Soroa who was born in about 1885, was probably one of the Manga to whom Patterson and Wellman referred. He took salt and livestock to Kano, making three trips a year.[82] So too did the family of Koyar (born in 1882). They lived in Kadjikwini, where they made salt which they took to Kano to buy cloth. Koyar himself made several trips a year to Kano, where he camped outside the city and sold salt in the villages. In Kano he needed an interpreter because he did not speak Hausa. So he stayed with a *fatoma*, 'who housed them and provided corrals for their animals. The patron provided food for them, but never ate with them . . . . He was the broker in the sales of salt and received a percentage of the sale.' The Hausa called these Manga merchants *masu mangoul* (those in possession of salt).[83] Caravans were also organised at several villages in Borno where there were camels, oxen and donkeys. These caravans toured the salt district and then travelled to Myrria or Kano. According to Ronjat, the camels took loads of 30 pieces of salt at 5 kg each; oxen 20; and donkeys 12. Most of the people at the salt-camps also owned oxen and occasionally they joined these Borno caravans, which consisted of 300 animals or more.[84]

Manga merchants also distributed *manda* salt and natron in Borno, Bedde country, Mandara, Marrua and probably Adamawa. Besides going to Kano, for example, Kambar went to Yelwa, continuing the commercial contacts established by his father.[85] Another Manga merchant who was born in Kabia around 1888 and traded to Kano did the same; as his father had done before him, he travelled to Kano, Bedde country and Yelwa.[86] In 1906 Hewby reported that a 'large number of Mangas in Marrua and Mandara were now waiting to return to their country with slaves' which they had purchased as a result of *manda* and natron sales.[87] By the turn of the century, Manga merchants such as these and the many more who travelled to Kano were well on their way to establishing themselves as a corporate commercial group similar to the Agalawa, Tokarawa and others.

The other outlet for the products of Manga industry – and indeed for the salt and natron of the small Sosebaki towns on the frontier between Hausa and Kanuri countries – was via Damagaram, especially the towns of Myrria and

Zinder.[88] To the extent that the natron trade was centred on Zinder, the Borno trade overlapped with the southern end of the Tuareg network, so that Zinder occupied a unique place in the larger salt trade of the central Sudan. It served as a depot for the natron of Muniyo and the salt of Bilma and Fachi and therefore had some similarities with the great salt depots of Katsina, Kano and Zaria, even though Zinder was not part of the Sokoto Caliphate. Despite this special situation, the pattern of trade was similar to that of the main commercial axis of Borno; only the merchants were different. The Hausa merchants who followed the route through Damagaram came from Katsina, and the destination of the Manga and other traders travelling west was also Katsina.[89]

The trade at Zinder was in the hands of resident landlord-brokers who served as intermediaries for the people from Katsina. At the end of the nineteenth century Dan Bade and Dan Maleka were among the brokers who controlled the market. Both of these men, who came from Tassawa, on the route of Katsina, settled in Zinder around 1880. Dan Bade, who lived at Zongon Tudu, north of the city walls, had a monopoly of the supply of water skins for the trans-Saharan caravans. Dan Maleka did local trading and employed weavers during the dry season, but in each case the men derived a major portion of their income from the trade with Katsina Emirate, whose traders brought tobacco and kola nuts to Damagaram in order to buy salt, natron and livestock.[90]

Merchants had been plying the routes between Zinder and the south at least since 1851, for Barth 'met a considerable natron-caravan coming from Zinder, the ass and the bullock going on peaceably side by side.'[91] The trade was partly directed towards Nupe, for there was a good route from Katsina to Nupe that bypassed Kano. Again Barth noted this trade, although he was not the first to do so. Near Tassawa he found 'encamped the natron-caravan of al-Wali, which in a few days was to leave for Nupe'.[92] Fifteen years earlier, Daumas had learned that direct communication existed between Katsina and Nupe; large caravans journeyed that far to buy slaves, and while Daumas did not learn of the commodities exported to Nupe in exchange, it is likely that natron and perhaps salt too were important items.[93] At the end of the century, Madugu Isa, who was of Borno origin but came from Mai Jirgi, near Tassawa, successfully moved into the natron trade between Zinder and Nupe. He led expeditions eastward to Muniyo, where grain was sold and natron bought. The caravans went to Nupe and Ilorin, and Isa even lived for seven years in Nupe, where he and his three brothers provided brokerage services for the Zinder–Nupe trade. He married daughters to two other caravan leaders in the trade – Madugu Sharubutu and Madugu Ilias. Not all members of his caravans made the complete journey to Nupe or Ilorin. Some stopped in Kano to buy cloth, while others stayed in Zaria, buying cotton or selling transport services for local trade. The main caravan bought Nupe textiles, beads, iron-work and swords in Nupe but also took European textiles, kola nuts and English salt.[94]

As the activities of the Manga and the Zinder-based traders demonstrate, the export trade of Borno had changed considerably in the course of the nineteenth century. Clapperton's observation that Borno caravans came as far as Nupe in the 1820s establishes that Borno still commanded a major share of the transport business in salt and natron, although by then the metropolitan districts of the old Saifawa dynasty had been abandoned and many Borno merchants had moved west to the Sokoto Caliphate. By the 1850s, when Barth studied the trade, most Borno traders went no further than Gumel, leaving much of the transit business to Hausa merchants and to those immigrants from Borno – by then assimilated to Hausa society – who had settled in or near the Hausa towns. Zinder, even though Damagaram was nominally part of Borno, was pulled into the economic orbit of the caliphate, and as the careers of the relocated Tassawa merchants make clear, a similar process of 'Hausa-isation' was also taking place there. The Zinder–Nupe trade looks like the Borno trade described by Clapperton, but the base of operations and the identification of the merchants as Hausa rather than Kanuri was different. Finally, the entry of the Manga in the transport business introduced a new element from Borno, which suggests that the salt districts were beginning to reach a level of prosperity that could support a merchant class. The emergence of a group of Manga merchants indicates that a new commercial community was developing in Borno, after almost a century of relative decline. It took that long to replace those merchants who had emigrated in the first two decades of the nineteenth century.

SALT DEPOTS OF THE SOKOTO CALIPHATE

On his way to conquer the central provinces of the Sokoto Caliphate, Frederick Lugard reported that 'by far the most important trade of Northern Nigeria is that in "potash" [natron] and livestock. This "potash" (which consists of carbonates of soda) is of two kinds, slabs of rock [*ungurnu*] and loose or powdered [from Muniyo].'[95] He also should have added salt from both Bilma and Mangari to his list. Upon the British occupation of Kano, Lugard found out even more: the merchant community was divided into several sections, according to the type of business, and salt and natron traders were among the most visible, which is not surprising in the light of Lugard's earlier information on the importance of the salt trade. The salt merchants included those who dealt in Bilma salt and hence were connected with the Tuareg network, those who imported salt and natron from Borno, and the kola traders to Asante, who exported natron in large quantities and hence were also dealers in their own right.

The key merchants in this business were landlord-brokers of Kano city and the many other towns in the central provinces of the caliphate. The generic term for landlord-broker in Hausa is *mai gida*, literally a house owner or landlord, who ran a hostel (*masauki*) for visiting merchants. The institution has been described in detail elsewhere: Abner Cohen has analysed the cattle and kola trade of the Hausa in the Yoruba towns of southern Nigeria during the twentieth century;[96] Polly Hill has discussed the institution in the context of the cattle and kola trade of the Hausa in twentieth-century Ghana;[97] Stephen Baier has examined the operation of landlords (and landladies) in Zinder at the turn of the century; and I have discussed the institution in the context of the nineteenth-century kola trade.[98] This research has demonstrated how *mai gida* hosted itinerant merchants, extended credit in commercial transactions, served as bankers, translators and mediators, and provided a host of other services that facilitated long-distance trade in pre-colonial and colonial times.

The development of a commercial infrastructure at these salt depots was closely related to other changes in the organisation of trade between the salines of the desert and the salt districts of Borno. Salt and natron were major imports into the Hausa country in the eighteenth century; traditions first note the importance of the trade in the fifteenth century. As with other sectors of the salt industry, the pre-nineteenth-century period is extremely sketchy. Katsina was the major commercial town of the eighteenth century, and Usman has drawn attention to the role of salt in its economy. Elsewhere I have discussed the concentration of the eighteenth-century kola trade at Katsina, and this trade invariably overlapped with the distribution of salt and natron.[99] Kano, Birnin Zamfara, Alkalawa and other towns participated in similar commercial patterns, and it is safe to conclude, despite the absence of details, that a wholesale trade in salt and natron was well established at these centres too.

In the nineteenth century there were major changes in the organisation of the Hausa economy, including the structure of the salt trade. To a great extent, the salt trade mirrored these more general changes. First, the distribution of salt continued to be widely dispersed among the many towns and villages of the Hausa country; there was no centralisation of distribution and no monopoly situation arose. Secondly, Kano Emirate, including Kano City and the numerous towns to its immediate south, developed into a metropolitan district in which the wholesale trade in salt and natron was particularly well developed. In effect, Kano replaced Katsina as the leading centre of economic activity, not only for salt but for other commodities as well. Although similar developments occurred throughout the caliphate, it was in Kano that the commercial infrastructure developed to the greatest extent.

Because of the scale of the natron and salt trade in the caliphate, the functions of landlord (*mai gida*) and broker (*dillali*) were distinct, although landlords often served as brokers or relied on their own agents, as indeed was the case for wholesale trade in general, at least at Kano, Zaria, and other major centres. Hoskyns-Abrahall's comments on trade in Kano City in 1926 would have applied to the nineteenth century too: 'Brokers form a large group, and deal in ... practically everything of local manufacture as well as imported goods.'[100] Imam Imoru, describing trade as he knew it during the last several decades of the nineteenth century, observed:

> There are many *dilali* [brokers] in Hausaland.... People give to him their things for him to sell.... There are *dilali* of cloth (*tufafi*), of horses, of cattle, of slaves, of cotton. These last are sellers of bags of raw cotton (*tadula*). There are *dilali* of goats, of kola.... There are *dilali* of *kanwa* [natron], of *gishiri* [salt], of *bak'i* [dyed cloth]....[101]

Brokers tended to specialise in particular commodities and consequently established ties of clientage with landlords; the landlords controlled the trade, for they determined which brokers received the business of visiting merchants. The landlords also guaranteed credit for the transactions of their clients and were often major importers and wholesalers themselves. Brokers had to hustle for business, maintaining their reliability because landlords directed itinerant merchants their way, but being available for other traders that they might find who did not have landlords. Brokers were used at both ends of transactions; they acted for buyers and sellers, receiving a commission for their services.[102]

The landlords of the natron and salt trade were known as *fatoma*, which was originally a Kanuri term but was borrowed into the Hausa language to distinguish the brokerage firms of the salt merchants from other landlord-brokers in the Hausa economy. The term was even used in connexion with the Tuareg trade, and because of the close association between salt imports and textile exports, the term was also used to refer to textile brokers, as Shea has noted.[103] These *fatoma* provided the same services as other landlords, and hence the comments of Fremantle on the landlords of Zaria, in 1913, where the distinction between *mai gida* and *dillali* was as important as at Kano, are instructive:

> The householder not only acts as general guide, and helper in the transaction, but is responsible for payment whether from or to the lodger. If the latter cannot obtain payment, or the buyer disappears, he looks to the householder who in turn has the right to throw responsibility on the dillali. The dillali in turn asks the householder of the delinquent. Similarly if goods turn out wrong, the householders concerned have to give their services to arrange matters to the satisfaction of their clients.[104]

In Zaria and Kano the *dillali* and householder split the commission, which amounted to 5 per cent on most goods, 10 per cent on livestock. Only the term used for the natron and salt landlords was different; the use of a Kanuri word reflected the evolution of the trade from a Borno-based commerce in the eighteenth century to a Hausa-based commerce in the nineteenth century.

Fatoma were wholesalers, as well as landlords. The use of a term other than *mai gida* indicated that the development of wholesaling, based on long-distance trade, transcended other types of brokerage. Hoskyns-Abrahall recognised this distinction in 1926, although apparently he was not aware of the details of terminology.

> Of salt and potash [natron] sellers the latter are the more wealthy class. Salt-sellers are of two kinds: the broker who expects to get 1d profit per bag of salt; i.e. $\frac{1}{2}$d from the native merchant owner and $\frac{1}{2}$d from the buyer, and the buyer outright

202

who divides up his bag as a rule into sixty lots at 1½d, and may reasonably expect to get a profit of from 1/6 to 2/- thereon . . . . Potash [natron] sellers are mostly wholesale middlemen and make a nett [sic] profit of 6d per load. During the six months that this market is open, an average of one thousand loads pass through each man's hands. A few of the wealthy buy outright and hold for a good market, when they should make a profit of 25 per cent.[105]

Salt brokers collected a commission from both buyer and seller because they acted as the sole agent. More often, these brokers split their commission with the *fatoma*, who are not referred to in Hoskyns-Abrahall's account of the salt trade. The salt buyers were retailers or small wholesalers. In his account of the natron trade, Hoskyns-Abrahall was describing the *fatoma* and their brokers. The 'wholesale middlemen' who handled 1,000 loads, or about 28–30 tonnes, per year lived in Zangon Beriberi or other wards near the city market-place, or they lived in Fagge, the commercial ward outside one of the main city gates. Without realising the full implications of his report, Hoskyns-Abrahall inadvertently described the brokerage system for the salt trade and the role of *fatoma* in the natron trade. In fact, both trades relied on *fatoma* and brokers.

Although some *fatoma* had clients dealing in both salt and natron, Hoskyns-Abrahall correctly observed that the two trades were separate, or rather the Tuareg salt trade and the Borno trade in *manda* salt and various types of natron were separate. Almost all the salt, whether from Bilma or Mangari, was consumed locally, while much of the natron from Borno was re-exported. The same merchants dealt in natron and *manda* salt because these both came from Borno, often brought in the same caravans. Bilma salt was separate. Those merchants who handled its distribution were connected with a different marketing network – that of the Tuareg. Barth recognised this distinction at Kano in 1851:

> the salt trade . . . is entirely an import one, the salt being almost all consumed in the province. Of the three thousand camel-loads of salt, which I have computed as comprising the airi [*ayari*, caravan] with which I reached Katsina, we may suppose one third to be sold in the province of Kano, therefore that hereby a value of from fifty to eighty millions [of cowries] annually is drained from the country. But we must not forget that the money which is paid for this requisite (and not only for that consumed in Kano, but also in other provinces) is entirely laid out by the sellers in buying the produce of Kano, viz., cloth and corn [millet]. Here, therefore, is an absolute balance – a real exchange of necessaries and wants.[106]

Barth's account is a classic description of desert-side trade between nomadic and sedentary economies. The same observations could be made for Sokoto, Katsina and other parts of the caliphate. In January 1827, Clapperton met a caravan of 500 camels laden with Bilma salt near Sokoto, while at Kwara (Quarra), on the Kano–Sokoto road, he reported that 'during the dry season, a number of Tuaricks who come with salt from Bilma, lodge in huts outside the walls'.[107] Again the exchange involved the sale of salt and the purchase of grain, textiles and other manufactures needed in the desert. The caravan at

Kwara had almost 50 tonnes of salt; Barth's estimate for Kano's share of the 1851 caravan was almost 100 tonnes, which appears to be low. In 1904, British customs officials recorded 280.5 tonnes of Bilma salt imported into Kano, which also was probably a low figure since it was easy to bypass customs posts.[108]

The salt sellers of Hoskyns-Abrahall's account obtained their supplies from Tuareg merchants who delivered Bilma salt to one of several depots in the Kano area: Fagge (the ward outside Kofar Mata gate into Kano city), Bichi, Bebeji, Kura or Tofa. Upon delivery, the camels were taken to grazing lands, which served as a base of operations in hiring out camels to transport agricultural and other commodities within the emirate. When Barth was travelling near Kano in 1851, he met 'the first strings of empty camels belonging to the airi [*ayari*, caravan] with which we had been travelling. They were returning from Kano, where they had carried the salt, in order to retrace their steps to good pasture-grounds, while their masters remained in the capital to sell their merchandise.'[109] The main pasture for these camels was near Bichi, located 25 km north-west of Kano and the site of Tuareg-owned plantations.

In Kano, many of the merchants stayed in the compounds of *fatoma* in Zangon Beriberi or other wards which were adjacent to the city market. The family of Alhaji Mahaman Alhassan was lodging Tuareg traders in the 1870s, and perhaps as early as Barth's day. Alhassan, who was born in Zangon Beriberi in the 1870s, was related to the Kanuri of Bilma through his mother's family and had connexions with the Tuareg trade. Other *fatoma* in Zangon Beriberi also accommodated Tuareg dealers.[110]

Fagge was located outside the walls of Kano City where merchants bringing salt and natron could unload their camels, oxen and donkeys without taking their animals into the crowded, narrow streets of the city itself. It this ward, the Tuareg and Borno trades overlapped; there were *fatoma* for both trades – and both were called *fatoma*, even though the Tuareg word for landlord-broker (*tanbara*) was known. The head of the ward has been drawn from both the Beriberi and Buzu (Tuareg) communities. Of the thirteen ward heads, four have been Buzu and nine Beriberi. In the nineteenth century, the title for the ward was *sarkin zongo* (head of the *zongo*, i.e. caravanserai); later the title was changed to *galadima* of Fagge.[111] According to Malam Mahmudu Dayyidu, whose family has run a lodging place in Kano since the days of his great-great grandfather Umaru,

> Fagge was founded because of the expansion of trade, because it was no longer possible to accommodate everyone in the city. The *bak'i* [strangers] used to stay in small huts built for them in Fagge until they finished *ciko*, that is until they returned from Kura, where they bought dyed cloth. Tuareg also stayed in the Kano area selling transport services; they kept their proceeds and goods with their *fatoma*. The amounts they deposited were written down in Arabic on an *atakaku* [wooden board]. Cowries were used at that time.[112]

204

Dayyidu's family had their lodging place in Bakin Zuwo ward, even though many of their clients stayed in Fagge.

Other Tuareg journeyed beyond Kano to Bebeji, 'a considerable place [in 1851], with a market much frequented, at which the Tuaryg [sic] sell a considerable portion of their salt',[113] and to Kura and Tofa, where it was possible to buy dyed cloth. Both Kura and Tofa were major centres of the textile industry and catered particularly to the Tuareg trade. Indeed Kura was the most important dyeing centre for cloth exported north into the desert. The type of cloth made there was known as *yan kùra* and was used for turbans and for women's clothes.[114] In his assessment of 1909, Frewen found that there were 19 salt merchants in Kura town alone; in neighbouring Gora District there were 51 salt dealers.[115] In both cases, the number of resident merchants indicates how important these heavily-populated areas to the south of Kano were to the business of the Tuareg.

The trade in salt and natron from Borno – recognised as a distinct trade by Hoskyns-Abrahall – was on a larger scale than the Bilma commerce. In the 1850s Barth fully appreciated this fact when he assessed the value of imports from Borno in the economy of Kano:

> Another important branch of the commerce of Kano is the transit of natron from Bornu to Nupe..., which here always passes into other hands, and in so doing leaves a considerable profit in the place. The merchandise is very cheap, but the quantity is great, and it employs a great many persons.... Twenty thousand loads, at the very least, between pack-oxen, sumpter-horses, and asses, of natron must annually pass through the market of Kano, which, at 500 kurdi [cowries] per load, merely for passage-money, would give 10,000,000 kurdi.[116]

This amount probably totalled 700 tonnes in the re-export trade alone. Barth witnessed the departure of one caravan for Nupe; it consisted of 200–300 donkeys loaded with natron.[117] Early colonial reports indicate that Barth's estimate was a reasonable one. In 1904, caravan officials were able to establish that at least 376 tonnes of *manda* salt and 268 tonnes of natron were brought into Kano Emirate, while in 1907, when officials were more diligent, they tabulated 608.6 tonnes of natron from Muniyo, 40 tonnes of trona from Lake Chad, and 649.3 tonnes of *manda* salt.[118] These figures must be considered only partial estimates of the total trade, but they do indicate that the scale of operation was of at least the same order as that identified by Barth fifty years earlier.

The salt and natron trade from Borno – because it was bigger than the Bilma trade and because savanna-based merchants controlled its transport – had a more elaborate infrastructure than the Bilma trade. Hoskyns-Abrahall's description of the Kano market in 1926 grasped this essential difference; his reference to the wholesale middlemen who averaged 1,000 loads of natron per year and other wealthy merchants who bought imported natron on speculation was based on some knowledge of the *fatoma* of such wards as Fagge, Zangon Beriberi, Bakin Zuwo, and Alkantara. These

205

places specialised in either Borno natron and salt or Bilma salt or both. There were also other depots in the city; all the wards inhabited by kola merchants, including Madabo, Bakin Ruwa, Madigawa, and Marraraba, were centres of the natron trade, for these merchants re-exported natron west to Asante.

The *fatoma* either served as the brokers in the natron trade or instructed assistants to act for them as their agents. The assistants received the commission (*la'ada*) in such situations. As was the case with other landlords, the *fatoma* provided accommodation and food, receiving only presents from their clients when they arrived and when they left. Otherwise the itinerant merchants paid nothing other than the commission on transactions. According to Alhaji Aminu Dahiru, whose family ran an establishment in Bakin Zuwo ward, the *fatoma* had other opportunities to make a profit:

> When the *bak'i* [strangers] stayed for a long time and did not sell their livestock and goods, the *fatoma* would buy them out. Later the *fatoma* would send their assistants to Zaria or Kaduna with the livestock or natron, where they would be sold. This enabled the *bak'i* to leave when they wanted to.[119]

Fatoma might also sell the manure left by the animals of their clients. Dahiru's account demonstrates that Hoskyns-Abrahall's observations on the commercial practices of the large natron wholesalers applied to the period before the 1920s. Although Dahiru refers to a re-export trade to Kaduna – a colonial town – it is clear from comments in his and other interviews that *fatoma* had long been engaged in the direct purchase of natron and salt, as well as importing on their account and acting as brokers in other transactions.

Zangon Beriberi ward, as the name suggests, catered for the Borno trade. *Beriberi*, the Hausa name for Kanuri, identified both the direction of trade and the origins of the *fatoma* who lived there. *Zango* (or *zongo*) was a resting place for caravans, and caravans indeed did come to this ward on a regular basis. Individual *fatoma* in the ward could accommodate merchants with up to 100 animals: the houses had 10–30 rooms for clients. Some *fatoma* had five compounds and rented compounds to merchants who wanted to stay in Kano longer than most itinerant traders did. The larger *fatoma* could take care of 30–60 merchants at one time; some of these clients stayed as long as two months. There were at least ten, and perhaps twenty, *fatoma* in this ward alone, and others, such as the famous Alhaji Baba Gade-Gade, had compounds that bordered on Zangon Beriberi; in this case Gade-Gade was actually located in Alkantara ward. Others had to set up business in Bakin Zuwo ward, which also adjoined Zangon Beriberi.[120] Merchants competed for clients, although they tried to attract those traders with whom they had done business previously. According to Alhaji Audu Mohammad, the grandson of the famous *fatoma*, Ari Tugu, who had moved to Kano from Borno sometime after the middle of the nineteenth century, a *fatoma* enticed clients

> by giving them gifts; if they enjoyed his gift, then they went to his place. He also attracted their attention by good food and sometimes he gave them cloth and

money [cowries]. Clients used to discuss among themselves the hospitality of the *fatoma*.[121]

Many other natron and *manda* dealers were merchants associated with the kola trade, most especially Agalawa, Tokarawa and Kambarin Beriberi merchants who lived in or near Kano, Katsina and Zaria.[122] While their main commercial investment was in trade to Asante for kola, they had subsidiary interests in salt and natron because Borno was an important market for kola and because natron was a major export to Asante. They dealt in *manda* too because it was easy to buy both natron and *manda* in the same markets in Borno. Although Agalawa, Tokarawa and Kambarin Beriberi merchants did not specialise in marketing salt and natron to the extent that the *fatoma* of the central caliphate did, they still imported such large quantities that their operations invariably affected the market. On occasion they could sell natron locally, especially when other kola merchants wanted to obtain some for re-export to Asante, and they always sold their *manda* imports.

Some Tokarawa merchants served as intermediaries in the Tuareg trade, although Bilma salt was seldom, if ever, exported to Asante. These merchants purchased or took on credit salt and natron from the Tuareg caravans. Those who were settled at Bichi, for example, carried salt and natron to Kano City or to Tofa in the southern part of Kano Emirate.[123] Agalawa also bought natron from the Tuareg, some of which they took to Asante. The Tuareg did not sell their supplies through the market; instead they went directly to the large kola dealers, such as Tambarin Agalawa Yakubu in Madabo ward in Kano City. Merchants such as Yakubu also imported natron directly from Borno, but if the price was right they supplemented these supplies with Tuareg imports. Often the Tuareg purchased kola with the proceeds from their natron sales, so that no money actually changed hands.[124] Some Tokarawa such as those at 'Yan Bundu near Bichi, even went to Agades to buy salt, taking textiles, sugar and tobacco north for the exchange.[125]

The other group in the caliphate wholesale trade identified themselves as Beriberi who, like the Kambarin Beriberi, originally came from Borno.[126] Unlike the Kambarin Beriberi of Gummi, they are not associated with a single emigration. It is most likely that their more diffuse origins involved numerous such migrations which are now forgotten. None the less, Beriberi were found throughout the central provinces of the caliphate – in rural and urban areas. H. Q. Glenny, reporting for the important commercial district near Rano, south of Kano city, found that immigrants from Borno were numerous in the district in 1909: 'They have been established there for two or three generations. Most of them combine farming with a trade. The salt and potash [natron] trades are mainly in their hands. Lodging house keepers [*fatoma*] are mostly Beri-beri.'[127]

Other merchants simply identified with Kano – these merchants were known as Kanawa. The father of Alhaji Sule Na Aba, for example, took natron, which he bought in Borno, to Lagos, along with knives, pepper and other goods. In Lagos he bought kola and textiles. Some of the kola he sold in Kano, where he bought local textiles (black gowns, trousers, and turbans) and beads. These items, along with kola, were then taken to Borno. This pattern was developed by the 1880s. He took 10–20 donkey loads of trona at a time. Some merchants carried trona and natron as far as Ilorin, directly from Borno, but his father stayed in Kano and sent his clients to Lagos.[128]

Junior kin provided much of the necessary labour for the salt and natron trade. Junior kin worked for their fathers, uncles or other members of the same ethnic fraction, often as apprentices. Their assignments involved more menial tasks than those of their patrons, but they worked alongside their patrons and could expect to establish themselves as independent merchants eventually. Junior kin received irregular compensation for their labour. They were housed, clothed and fed as family members, but they did not receive wages or a share of the profits. The early career of Alhassan Dantata, the wealthy Kano businessman who invested heavily in ground-nut buying after 1911, is a case in point. Born into an Agalawa family at Bebeji, near Kano, he left his home at an early age to join a caravan to Asante. He apprenticed himself to another Agalawa merchant, even though his father also traded in kola. After learning the caravan trade, Dantata established himself as a landlord-broker in Ghana, before returning to Kano during the ground-nut boom after 1911. Although Dantata did not work for his father, many sons did. Merchants like Dantata's patron relied on this system of apprenticeship as a means of satisfying their need for commercial agents and caravan assistants. One consequence of this system of apprenticeship and labour mobilisation was that there were relatively few family firms that survived a single generation. Junior kin were just as apt to work for someone else as for their own father. Merchants could trace their connexion with trade through their parents and grandparents, as virtually all Agalawa, Tokarawa, Kambarin Beriberi and Beriberi did, but membership of the larger commercial community was more important in the establishment of a successful business than personal inheritance.

Although Kano City was the largest single market for natron and salt, there were many other depots near the city.[129] Wherever Agalawa and Tokarawa were located, for example, the quantity of natron and *manda* was extensive. *Manda*, which was distributed locally, was consumed in Hadejia, Katagum and rural Kano especially. Natron also had a large market, besides being re-exported. In addition, all the major textile centres which catered to the Borno trade imported large amounts of natron and *manda*. The Kano market did not dominate the trade simply because the trade was too large to be centralised. Numerous merchants from many towns dealt in natron and *manda*. The routes were open, there being no natural barriers or political restraints on the free movement of caravans. The routes to Borno and Damagaram were relatively safe, despite periodic trouble from Bedde and other bandits. Even though the route through Hadejia was unsafe for a fairly long period in the middle of the century because of the rebellion of Buhari, it was not difficult for merchants to bypass such trouble spots. Unlike the trade to Adamawa and Asante, where large, well-organised caravans were necessary to assure safe passage, merchants could travel to Borno in groups of ten or fifteen, at least for most of the nineteenth century.

In the southern part of Kano Emirate, the trade in natron and salt from Borno was concentrated at the major textile centres that catered to the Borno market. According to Shea, these were the major centres for the production of *kore*, a type of cloth that was originally made in Borno but came to be a mainstay of Kano exports in the nineteenth century. Centres of textile production for Borno included Dal (and its predecessor Tsakuwa), which was located south-east of Kano City in Wudil District, and Zarewa, Fellatan, Belli, Rogo, Dan Guzuri and Makarfi, which were all located in the region straddling the border between Kano and Zaria Emirates. Many of the dyers and textile brokers (also known as *fatoma*) who lived in these centres were immigrants, or descendants of immigrants, from Borno who had moved to Kano in the nineteenth century. These textile *fatoma* often dealt in cattle, grain, natron and salt, as well as textiles.[130]

Parts of Kano Emirate, particularly the north-eastern districts and the area south of Kano City, were located on the major trade routes between Borno and the south-east. As F. W. Bell found in his assessment of Dutsi district in 1911,

> The District is exceptionally well supplied with markets, the principal of which are situated on the main trade routes and at convenient distances along the borders. The former serve as halting places for Caravan traders and the latter are much frequented by people from adjoining Districts. The bulk of the trade is in salt, potash [natron], skins, cattle, sheep and goats from the East; Beri-Beri traders on all the main routes being numerous. A considerable amount of the traffic however passes through the District to markets further West where better prices are obtainable.[131]

The 'Beri-Beri' merchants are not identified further; they undoubtedly included Manga and Kanuri traders from Borno who were involved in the export trade in natron and *manda*, but part of the local merchant community included families of Borno origin who were involved in the trade. As Glenny had found in his assessments of the districts north-east of Kano, merchants from Borno were active in trade; in the Ringim area, he observed that 'most trade is by Beriberi driving westward pack oxen laden with salt, potash [natron], and grain, to return home with black cloths, and gowns, caps, hardware, and kolas'. Further to the north-east, in the region adjoining Hadejia, Beriberi settlers dominated commerce: 'Donkeys, here as elsewhere where Agalawa are not numerous, mostly belong to Beriberi being employed in the salt and grain trade.'[132] One *fatoma* in Kibiya was Musa Mai Mangawa, a Kanuri who died in about 1950, and who had owned slaves. As his name suggests, he accommodated Manga merchants who brought their *manda* and natron supplies to Kibiya.[133]

Although the discussion here has concentrated on Kano Emirate because of its importance in the salt and natron trade, other parts of the caliphate also had their depots. Katsina City and the towns to its south-east, Sokoto and its subordinate towns of Gummi and Jega to the south, Zaria and the many towns to its north – these centres and others fitted into the pattern described for Kano. The Tuareg and Borno trades overlapped to some extent in that merchants sometimes dealt in the imports of both trades, and *fatoma* in particular willingly served any salt merchant from the north or east. Language determined the choice of *fatoma* in many cases; if Tuareg and Borno merchants could not speak Hausa they needed a *fatoma* who spoke Tamachek or Kanuri, but most traders understood Hausa anyway. The Borno network was more complicated than that for the distribution of Tuareg imports, in part because the places where the Tuareg caravans stopped served as depots in themselves and in part because the savanna-based trade of the Borno industry involved more widely-based merchants who travelled in smaller groups. The Borno trade was larger and more diffuse; consequently the infrastructure had to be more elaborate.

At Katsina there was an official (*zanua*) who was responsible for the supervision and taxation of the salt and natron trade. This title – Kanuri in origin – was also associated with the regulation of the immigrant Borno population, at least at the town of Dutsi, south-east of Katsina.[134] The Tuareg caravans at Katsina camped outside one gate; the quarter adjacent to the gate was similar to the commercial ward of Fagge at Kano. It was easier to unload camels outside the walls at both cities, and consequently the wholesaling of Bilma salt was concentrated at these locations. In Katsina City Gambarawa ward was the principal commercial district; such merchants as Madugu Sha'ibu, late in the nineteenth century, imported natron from Damagaram and also provided accommodation for visiting Manga traders who came from Muniyo.[135] In rural Katsina, natron was also a major commodity of trade. The Tokarawa merchants of Jani, for example, bought natron in Zongon Daura, which served as a distributional centre for Muniyo natron. From Jani, these merchants exported natron to Asante.[136] The Doro merchants, especially the Agalawa at Gabankare, also traded in natron.[137] At Shibdawa, the pattern was the same: the resident Agalawa went to Borno or Damagaram to buy natron for re-export further west.[138] Other merchants, particularly those at Dutsi who were descended from immigrants from Borno, also engaged in the import trade.[139]

The northern part of Zaria Emirate, including the towns of Kudan, Hunkuyi, and Zaria city, was to all intents and purposes a continuation of the extensive network of market towns extending from Kano City southward.[140] In each of these centres, particularly in those places where there was an extensive textile-dyeing industry, Borno merchants found resident *fatoma*, often of Borno origin, with whom they could reside. The pattern of exchange was similar to that at the Kano textile centres; visiting merchants entrusted their natron and salt to their *fatoma* and concerned themselves with buying textiles for the Borno market. Some of the natron was subsequently re-

210

exported, but a lot was consumed locally. In 1904, British returns show that at least 654.5 tonnes of natron entered Zaria Emirate, which was two and half times as much as recorded for Kano Emirate. The returns do not accurately reflect the relative importance of the natron trade in the two emirates; both figures are certainly too low; only Kano's figure is very much so. Caravan officials had difficulty catching all of the trade because it followed myriad routes and because it was not easy to distinguish between imports and the transit trade south. In the same year that 267.7 tonnes were tabulated for Kano Emirate and 654.5 tonnes were recorded in Zaria, 483.3 tonnes of natron were identified at Ilorin, far to the south-east.[141] Virtually all of the Ilorin trade had to come through Zaria and much of it through Kano as well. Furthermore, the Nupe market lay on the road before Ilorin and probably consumed several hundred tonnes a year. The Ilorin and Nupe markets together suggest that at least 700 tonnes had to pass through the depots of northern Zaria and southern Kano, while in addition many hundreds of tonnes were consumed in the vicinity of these central depots.

THE RE-EXPORT TRADE IN NATRON

As early as the last decade of the eighteenth century, natron was available in the coastal markets of the Bight of Benin.[142] How much older this trade was is impossible to say at this time, but it is clear that by the early nineteenth century natron was found from Asante in the west through a broad region directly south of the central Sudan.[143] The re-export trade followed three principal routes. First, natron was taken from the Hausa depots directly south, through southern Zaria, to the lower Benue basin; this trade was connected with the distributional network for the Benue salines and supplemented the natron trade through Bauchi and Adamawa. The dividing line between the trade through Bauchi and Adamawa and the trade from the Hausa depots was the Jos Plateau; to the east of the plateau it was easier to bypass the central emirates of the caliphate, but to the west it was not. Secondly, natron flowed south-west from Kano and Zaria through Nupe, northern Yoruba country (Oyo before c. 1830; Ilorin thereafter) and westward through Borgu to the Volta basin. Thirdly, natron crossed the caliphate from Kano and Katsina to Sokoto, Gummi and Jega and supplied the markets of northern Borgu westward as far as the Volta basin. This route enabled merchants to deal in salt from Dallol Fogha, as well as other products.

The description provided by Sergeant Frazer, the former Kano merchant who exported white and red natron from Borno to Asante before 1820, makes it clear that the re-export trade was very profitable: 'It is bought in Bournou for fifty cowries an ass load, and sold in Goingia [Gonja] for 3,000.'[144] At this time natron was 'found abundantly in Dagwumba [Dagomba]; in the Ashantee market, a lump the size of a duck's egg, was sold for 2s'.[145] In 1826, Clapperton learned that natron, glass beads and a few slaves were the principal exports to Asante.[146] At that time the merchants travelled through

211

Kulfu, in northern Nupe; later they visited Rabba, the Nupe capital on the Niger. This route facilitated the distribution of natron over a wide area. Women traders obtained natron and other goods at Kulfu, which they took west as far as Nikki in Borgu, independently of the Hausa traders:

> They take back principally natron, beads made at Venice of various kinds, ... and unwrought silk of various colours, principally red ...; it and natron are as good as cowries.[147]

Similarly, Clapperton, who followed the movements of another caravan that had been in the Oyo capital while he was there, subsequently found the same merchants in Borgu, 'where they sold what natron they had remaining after they left Yourriba', before returning to Kulfu.[148] In 1830, the local merchant community at Rabba, which included 'a great number of Arabs', dealt in considerable quantities of natron,[149] so much so that merchants from as far away as Wawa in Borgu bought from these 'Arabs'.[150] Whether or not North African traders were actually present is open to speculation. The observer, Richard Lander, was not particularly astute and he may only have noticed the presence of Muslims, whom he called Arabs. None the less, at Jaguta, west of Ilorin, the Landers 'met with a party of Nouffie [Nupe] traders from Coulfo [Kulfu], with asses carrying trona for the Gonja market'.[151] Although the Landers referred to 'trona', they could have meant either natron from Muniyo or trona from Kanem; both were exported west, although trona was more important late in the century and may have been earlier too.

Natron followed routes from Katsina, Kano and Zaria to Nupe from the 1850s until the early twentieth century.[152] At Kano in February 1851, Barth witnessed the departure of one caravan which consisted of 200–300 donkeys and he estimated that the re-export of natron netted the Kano government 10,000,000 cowries in 'passage money' alone.[153] Late in the century both Muniyo natron and trona continued to be important in this trade.[154] Sarkin Kanwa M'azu, a *fatoma* in Kano at the end of the century, provided accommodation for Yoruba and Nupe merchants who came north to buy natron,[155] but the dominant pattern still involved the transport of natron south by Hausa merchants. At Dan Mak'eri village, near Dandi, local Agalawa merchants took natron to Ilorin, passing through Zaria on their trip south-west. These traders usually dealt in white natron, which they obtained in Hadejia, Gumel or other markets south of Muniyo. The Agalawa from Kumurya, near Rano in Kano Emirate, pursued similar practices: natron was a major item in their commercial dealings.[156] On the southern trade to Ilorin and Lagos, Katsina merchants – especially *'yan bojuwa* (merchants with head-loads) – bought natron in Kano.[157] In 1906 and indeed for some time before then, there were 'numbers of Hausas ... at Ebute Metta', and 'a large business [was] done by them in Abeokuta and Ibadan'. The main trade was in cattle and natron.[158]

By the end of the nineteenth century, the south-western route that fed natron to the Volta basin, Borgu and the Yoruba country probably accounted

Table 8.2. *Value of seaborne natron imports and exports through Lagos, 1870–1901*

Year	1870	1871	1872	1873	1874	1875	1876	1877	1878	1879	1880	1881	1882	1883	1884	1885
Imports £																
River Niger	15	43	137	434	534	not on schedule			58	2,867	—	657	2,177	22,635	123	14,455
Oil Rivers	4	—	8	—	—	—	—	—	12	601	208	607	—	286	2,567	—
Exports £																
Sierra Leone	—	—	50	—	—	—	—	—	—	—	—	—	—	—	36	257
Porto Novo	—	—	—	—	—	—	—	—	—	—	—	—	—	—	370	822

Year	1886	1887	1888	1889	1890	1891	1892	1893	1894	1895	1896	1897	1898	1899	1900	1901
Imports £																
Niger	262	179	1,478	1,381	3,801	265	1,137	—	358	—	—	1,900	3,418	5,471	—	—
Oil Rivers	40	6,582	—	—	—	—	—	582	—	175	984	—	—	—	395	37
Exports £																
Sierra Leone	32	21	47	115	50	16	69	96	32	50	138	—	70	5	17	9
Porto Novo	—	500	—	—	322	33	—	—	444	1,479	1,260	1,009	1,870	2,143	1,509	1,226
Oil Rivers	—	—	—	—	—	—	60	—	—	75	708	2,156	1,987	1,536	1,376	1,392
Gold Coast	65	—	—	—	—	80	154	210	106	—	—	—	84	21	25	55

Source: Lagos Blue Books, Nigerian National Archives, Ibadan.

for the greatest volume of natron in the re-export trade. The 483.3 tonnes tabulated at Ilorin in 1904 represented a part of this commerce, although certainly not all.[159] The trade had grown tremendously in the last several decades of the nineteenth century. Merchants started to import kola by sea, and they continued to rely on natron as a staple in the export trade.The value of the seaborne trade in natron from Lagos (Table 8.2) rose from almost nothing in the early 1880s to about £400 in 1884, over £1,000 in 1885, over £3,000 in 1897, peaking at around £3,700 in 1899.[160] These figures demonstrate the importance of kola imports, as well as natron exports, since the two trades were linked. Most of the exports were for the coastal market, particularly that at Porto Novo, near which Adams first noticed natron for sale at the end of the eighteenth century. By the end of the nineteenth century, some natron found its way as far as Sierra Leone and the Gold Coast, while the rest – a sizeable portion by the late 1890s – went to the Niger Delta.

By this time, the overland trade to Asante followed a northern route through Jega and the western parts of the caliphate. Merchants from Kano and Katsina joined caravans that followed this western route. Merchants, such as those at Utai, invested heavily in natron, which was the most important item they traded to Asante. At Damergu village, the resident Agalawa merchants went to Gumel and Borno to buy natron, while those at Tsaure Fankurun (near Kura), Makwa Yamma, Kuiwar Gabas, Gala, Sumaila, Garfa, and Guzai went to Hadejia, but all of them took the natron to the middle Volta.[161] Katsina merchants sold white natron in Katsina to the Fulani for their herds, but they took red natron and trona to Gonja. Alhaji Gambo Turawa estimated that natron was so important in the Asante kola trade that about two-thirds of all loads were made up of natron.[162] Madugu Sha'ibu of Gambarawa ward in Katsina, who traded to Asante in the last third of the nineteenth century, took *kanwa* – often red natron – to Asante. His caravan obtained the natron in Damagaram. They also bought *kanwa*, which had been brought by Manga traders, in Katsina.[163]

In the commercial community at Sokoto, Kambarin Beriberi and Gobirawa merchants dealt in salt and natron. Hungumawa ward was a major centre of the Kambarin Beriberi; they imported kola from Asante but also travelled to Borno to buy natron. They do not appear to have dealt in *manda* salt. These merchants were related to the Kambarin Beriberi in Kano, particularly those in Madigawa and Marraraba wards, and sometimes the Sokoto merchants only went as far as Kano, choosing to buy natron from their associates there.[164] Among the Gobirawa merchants, Madugu Dodo was particularly important at the end of the nineteenth century. He too pursued the Asante–Borno trade in kola nuts and natron, and he and his followers were responsible for importing considerable quantities of natron, some of which met local Sokoto demand.[165]

The towns of Gummi and Jega, located in the Zamfara River valley south of Sokoto, were perhaps more important commercially than Sokoto – Gummi because it was the home of the Kambarin Beriberi and Jega because it was a major staging point for caravans travelling to and from the west.

Malam Basharu na Mahu of Gummi traded to Asante in the last few years of the overland trade at the turn of the century. He worked under his father, Alu: again, one of the commodities they dealt in was natron. They bought it in Nguru (i.e., southern Muniyo), not selling any before reaching the middle Volta basin. Muhammad Sani, also from Gummi, who traded in the last decades of the nineteenth century, took trona to Gonja. His father often bought trona in Kano, rather than travel to Borno, but he sold some in Gummi and did not keep it only for the Asante trade.[166]

Jega also served as a natron market. Kambarin Beriberi and other merchants were able to buy natron there because Tuareg brought in their camels, but other merchants went to Kano to buy natron. Malam Garkuwa dan Asiri, who was twenty when the British arrived at Jega in 1903, was involved in this trade. He took natron – which he bought in Jega – to Asante, along with other goods (red and white thread, medicines). The natron had been imported from Sokoto, although other traditions indicate that Kano was the main centre of supply.[167] Occasionally, at least, these same merchants travelled to Borno directly.

The re-export of natron from the depots of Kano and Zaria southward to Bauchi, southern Zaria, the Benue Valley and beyond involved shipments along an elaborate network of routes. Lander first noted the trade in January 1827 at Katab, when he mentioned 'trona' in a list of items in the market.[168] Five years later, Allen and Thomson, in their expedition to the confluence of the Niger and Benue, found that 'trona, which is a kind of alkali, is brought from Haussa'.[169] In 1879, Flegel reported that natron was shipped down the Niger from the confluence in quantities that amounted to at least 100 tonnes.[170] By this time natron was a regular import at Lagos. It came down the Niger, either directly from the confluence or indirectly through the 'Oil Rivers'. Its value in 1870, only £19, rose to £3,468 in 1879, when Flegel noted shipments of 100 tonnes.[171] Reported values fluctuated wildly for the next two decades, but there is substantial evidence that the trade continued on a large scale, at least until the 1890s when overland shipments via Ilorin may have competed successfully with the river trade (Table 8.2).

The Niger trade demonstrates the importance of natron in the economy of the Benue basin and the area further south. The recorded values reaching Lagos were a small portion of the total trade. Ralph Moor, reporting to the Colonial Office in 1899, noticed the value of this trade in the Aro trade system of Igboland. One of the complaints of the Aro that arose from the imposition of colonial rule was that the Aro monopoly of natron imports came to an end: 'Since the establishment of the Government their [the Aro] monopoly in the trade of potash [natron] has been broken and all natives are enabled to carry it out through the territories.'[172] The importance of natron in the Igbo market continued after the colonial conquest. A Niger company report of 1920 referred to the natron trade at Oguta as a crucial part of its business in obtaining palm products:

Our salvation as far as kernels were concerned was native Potash. This is in demand and our women traders can place it for cash any time and make a profit, thus enabling them to buy fairly cheap kernels. We get this from Lake Chad way through our Yola Agent. He buys all he can through the dries [and] generally ships us down a few thousand pairs in the high water.[173]

By then natron followed the river from Yola, as it may have earlier too, although earlier much of the trade passed through southern Zaria, down the Niger, or overland through Idoma country to Igboland.

The intermediate trade between the depots and the Benue basin is not as easy to document, but it was surely important. Some Sumaila traders operated between Nguru, Hadejia, Sumaila and Bauchi and did not trade in kola nuts at all. Dandi village, near Ringim, was one centre of such activity by the Agalawa; Madugu Dagajiro sometimes took textiles and natron to Asante, although he also traded in slaves and livestock. He purchased natron in the markets south of Muniyo – Magatari and Gumel – and bought trona further east in central Borno. But Madugu Dagajiro also took natron to Bauchi and Ningi, where he purchased galena (lead sulphide).[174] Merchants changed routes if they could make a profit. The dominant current flowed south and west, but individual caravans could shift direction and thereby fill the demand for natron over a wide region off the major course of trade.

DISTRIBUTION OF THE BENUE AND DALLOL SALTS

Much of the trade of the Benue salines and the Dallols can be understood in the context of salt distribution from the Hausa depots. Merchants who came from the central caliphate passed through the outlying salt districts and purchased salt. In this way the Benue salines and the Dallols benefited from the operation of the far-flung Hausa commercial system. The re-export trade of the central depots encouraged production of salt elsewhere, because merchants tended to re-export natron and wanted salt for the same markets. Dallol Fogha and the Benue sites in particular served to limit the re-export of Bilma salt and Mangari *manda*, but they did not compete with the sources of natron.

Hausa merchants, many of whom came from Kano and other towns to the north, purchased salt at the Benue brine springs, some of which they took north to Kano, Zaria, Bauchi and Gombe but most of which they sold further south.[175] These merchants brought cattle, horses, textiles, metal goods and beads. As late as 1902 they came in caravans of 200 people and 300 donkeys. Their major stops were at Keana, Awe and Azara – the largest salines. The principal routes south from the salines followed the Katsina River (not to be confused with Katsina City, far to the north) to Katsina Ala and then proceeded overland to Obudu, Ogoja and Calabar or from Ibi, a major crossing point on the Benue, to Wukari and then either through eastern Tivland to Takum or to Donga and Tissa to Takum.[176] Much of Tiv country was supplied from Awe and Keana, although salt from Ogoja also came north.[177] Akwana salt – and perhaps salt from Keana and Awe – reached Bamenda, although the brine springs of the Cross River basin and imported European salt also served the same market.[178] Southern Idoma country was the effective limit of the Benue salines; this area received its salt from Uburu and sometimes from Ikom. Besides the Hausa merchants who travelled these routes, local Jukun traders – Abakwariga – also dealt in salt. As their northern origins suggest (the Abakwariga claim descent from Hausa and Borno traders who settled in Kwararafa before 1800), these Jukun were associated with earlier distributional patterns in the Benue basin, which predate the expansion of trade during the nineteenth century.[179]

The Benue trade also had an autonomy of its own. Much of the salt from the brine springs was taken north into the Jos Plateau. Several parallel relay networks passed into the hills. The Ron (Challa) of the Daffo area received salt from the Benue salines along a commercial corridor running from the lowlands south of the plateau to the north-east section of the plateau. Along this corridor, salt, palm oil and slaves travelled northward, while cattle and, to a lesser degree, horses moved southward. Iron implements, pottery, baskets and agricultural produce were also traded.[180] According to David Tambo,

> Certain groups to the south of the Ngas and Birom brought salt which they had obtained from their own southern neighbours, and exchanged it for iron items, which they then took back and resold. In effect, they were middlemen in a trade where iron moved south and salt moved north. for the Ngas, the Chip were the main middlemen in this trade, while for the Birom, it was the Ron (Challa).[181]

The Kulere of Richa were intermediaries in the salt trade with the Ron, while Daffo obtained its salt from Alago merchants who brought it to Monkwor or Mbaka, both of which were located at the foot of the escarpment.[182] Despite these local patterns of trade, the Benue salines had been brought fully into the orbit of the Hausa commercial system.

The same observations can be made for the distribution of salt from the Dallols. While some salt was brought into the central parts of the caliphate, most was exported west and south, often by merchants from the caliphate. In March 1852 Barth met a small caravan of 100 merchants from Zaria who had taken locust-bean cakes, used as a condiment in cooking, to Sokoto: 'The return freight which these petty merchants bring back from Sokoto generally consists of the salt of Fogha.'[183] As for the western trade, Baikie learned in 1862 that Dallol Fogha salt 'supplies the whole caravan road to Gonja'.[184] Kebbi merchants, among others, took salt to Nupe, Ilorin and the middle Volta basin in exchange for kola. In the eighteenth century these merchants – known as Zoromawa, the pottery, blacksmith and trading caste in Kebbi – traded south to Nupe and probably took salt with them.[185] In the nineteenth century, however, the kola traders from Kano, Katsina and elsewhere were the main exporters of Dallol Fogha salt. In 1905 Loffler found that Tounouga and Gaya were major markets in this exchange; caravans brought textiles and leather goods from the east to exchange for salt.[186] Monteil had earlier (1891) met a caravan near Say that was engaged in this transit business.[187] Such merchants as Madugu Isa na Garahu travelled through Dallol Fogha on his trips to the middle Volta; he stopped there to buy salt.[188] Other traders from the west and south also came to the Dallols, particularly the Wangara merchants of the various Bariba towns (Nikki, Bussa, Kiama). Because Dallol Bosso produced natron, rather than salt, it was especially attractive to these merchants. People came from as far away as Yoruba country and Nupe, as well as Borgu.[189]

The relationship between the salt depots of the Hausa emirates and the various salines varied; the pattern fell on a continuum from near domination to marginal involvement. Virtually all Bilma, Fachi, Amadror, and Teguidda salt went south; local consumption represented only a small portion of total output for these desert salines. Consequently, the Hausa depots were essential for the distribution of 2,500–6,000 tonnes of salt, depending upon the year. Similarly, the salt of the Borno axis tended to go west, although the Borno market absorbed a sizeable portion of total output and a lot of salt bypassed the Hausa depots and went directly south to Mandara, the Benue basin, Adamawa, and areas to the east. None the less, it is likely that the bulk of Borno salt – with the exception of *kige* – found its way to the central emirates of the caliphate, and, therefore, the wholesale depots exercised an important influence on the flow of the Borno salt trade. At least half of the output of *manda* and *kanwa* went west, while probably more than two-thirds of trona production was re-exported west; that is, 2,000–4,000 tonnes of salt, natron and trona passed through the Hausa depots. The other salines – Dallol Fogha and the Benue workings – exported most of their output elsewhere, although some of this salt – perhaps a few hundred tonnes – was also brought into the central emirates. The bulk of Benue salt was consumed locally, taken onto the Jos Plateau or exported south, while most Dallol Fogha salt was sold along the routes to the Volta basin or was consumed locally. Dallol Bosso natron does not appear to have entered the central emirates at all.

With the partial exception of the Dallols and the Benue, therefore, it is clear that salt – particularly salt and natron from greater Borno – fuelled the long-distance trade of the Hausa commercial network. And salt from the Dallols and the Benue entered into the same network, even though most of it was not brought through the central emirates. Hausa merchants from Kano, Katsina and Sokoto, many of whom carried salt from the central emirates, stopped at the Dallols and the Benue salines, where they purchased additional supplies for export west and south.

Beyond the Sokoto Caliphate, the salt trade can be subdivided into four sectors, each identified with the final destination of salt exports. These included the middle Volta trade, known in Hausa as the Gonja trade, in recognition of the important market of Salaga, which was part of Asante before 1874 and independent thereafter. This western sector absorbed the salt from Dallol Fogha, which supplied the western caliphate and the route to

Asante with a salt comparable in purity and use to *manda* and *kantu*, the principal salts of Mangari and Bilma respectively. As I have demonstrated elsewhere, this trade expanded during the nineteenth century; the quantity of kola imported from Asante rose from a minimum of 70–140 tonnes per year in the early part of the century to at least several hundred tonnes per year at the end of the century, and perhaps much more.[190] Since natron was a major export to the west, the volume of exports appears to have expanded too. The second and third sectors, also dominated by Hausa merchants from the central emirates, were the trades to the Yoruba states via Ilorin and to Igbo country overland through Idoma and south along the Niger River. In both networks, non-Hausa merchants purchased salt and natron, and particularly the latter, at one of several markets: Ilorin for the Yoruba country, Idah or other river markets for the Niger River trade, and Katsina Ala or other trans-Benue markets in Tiv or Jukun country. It would appear that this trade also expanded in the nineteenth century, probably on a modest basis before 1880 and then quite dramatically thereafter. By the first decade of the twentieth century, as has been discussed in Chapter 5, the level of exports amounted to at least 500 tonnes per year, and perhaps several hundred tonnes more. The final sector was the Cameroon or southern Adamawa trade, which depended upon exports from the Benue Valley or directly from Borno and Foli. The growth of this trade is difficult to assess, but it probably totalled a few hundred tonnes, at least, by the end of the nineteenth century. The trade appears to have expanded after the middle of the century, along with the general extension of Hausa commerce south-eastward.

CONCLUSION

There is no doubt that the governments of Borno and Sokoto encouraged trade because it provided a source of revenue through taxation of the trade itself and through taxation of the production of commodities that entered into the trade. To isolate salt from this general preoccupation of governments with taxing commerce would distort a discussion of the importance of salt as a source of revenue, and, in the absence of quantifiable custom returns which would allow an evaluation of the relative importance of salt and other commodities, only a few general observations can be made.

All trade was subject to taxation, including import duties that were often collected at the borders of Borno and the caliphate as *fito* or *garama*, re-export duties at the major commercial centres such as Kano, and periodic, usually annual, gifts (*gaisuwa*) to political authorities.[191] Strictly speaking, *fito* was a fee for ferrying goods across rivers, but often rivers served as the usual barrier at which to collect tax. Between Borno and the caliphate, this tax was often collected at the first major town across the border. *Gaisuwa* was a form of tribute that varied with the wealth of the giver; it symbolised political subordination and the recognition of patronage, and it was usually given in kind, often in the form of clothing.

The amount of revenue derived from the salt trade cannot be estimated, but Barth's report that the revenue from the duties on natron re-exported through Kano in 1851 amounted to 10 million cowries demonstrates that the salt tax was an important source of funds.[192] Political officials at every major town along the trade routes from Borno and the desert benefited from such taxes; indeed the protection of trade and markets was a major concern of the state because of this revenue.

9

The trade and politics of salt

While my reconstruction of the salt industry and its trade has concentrated on the nineteenth century, salt has obviously played a major role in the economy of the central Sudan for many centuries. The broad outlines of this role can be described as follows. As the account of al-Idrīsī makes clear, the salt of Kawar, and probably Fachi, has been an object of trade since medieval times; as I have argued in Chapter 4, al-Idrīsī's 'alun' probably refers to the various salts of Kawar, not just alum alone.[1] Certainly the amount of debris at Bilma indicates such as antiquity for the trade. Because Kawar also offered a good route between North Africa and Lake Chad, these oases were an obvious target of political ambitions. Kanem took the oases early, and the later ascendancy of Borno only shifted the locus of power. As early as the late sixteenth century Borno expeditions reached Kawar and Fachi, which then enters the historical record for the first time.[2] There is every reason to believe that the quest for salt was an important concern of Borno, as it must have been for Kanem before the fifteenth century. It is hard to imagine that a state would not take advantage of existing resources such as the trona of Kanem, the salt of Kawar and Fachi, and the natron of Muniyo, but until archaeological work is undertaken, it is not possible to substantiate this hypothesis, however logical it may be.

The other salines cannot be dated to the medieval period. Teguidda n'tesemt was not worked until after the fifteenth century, and its predecessor at Azelik was known for its copper, not its salt. While salt must have been available at Guelele and in the wells around this desert complex, there is no evidence for an export trade in the medieval era. With the destruction of Azelik in the fifteenth century, the old Songhay-oriented regime slipped into obscurity; its successor was centred at In Gall and eventually organised the elaborate salt industry at Teguidda n'tesemt. It can safely be said that whereas Kawar salt production is ancient, the Teguidda works are relatively modern.[3]

The only other saline for which there is early information is Dallol Fogha, where radio-carbon dates indicate the presence of a salt industry in c. 1600.[4] The close association between Dallol Fogha and Kebbi confirms this dating, and the tradition that salt production was first introduced by the Tienga suggests that production may have begun even earlier, probably during the period of Songhay ascendancy in the sixteenth century or earlier still.

Otherwise the historical record is silent, and archaeologists have done little work to fill the void. Geological conditions may be such that the origins of many salines may never be dated. Gouletquer and Kleinmann may well be correct that *manda* production in Mangari and Muniyo is very recent, dating only to the beginning of the nineteenth century, but until proper excavations are completed their hypothesis can only be noted.[5] Other evidence suggests a greater antiquity, but there is no real proof. The same can be said about the Benue salines. While it is clear that salt was made well before the nineteenth century, it is not known how old the industry is. Unomah, on the basis of oral traditions, has divided the history of the lowland salt industry into three periods; the Wadu period before 1700, the Kwararafa (Jukun) period (1700 to the 1820s) and the Bauchi (Sokoto Caliphate) period of the nineteenth century.[6] As for the various sources of natron – Muniyo, Foli, Dallol Bosso – traditions do not even allow us to confirm its production before the nineteenth century, although there is every reason to suppose that natron was indeed produced well before then. Adams' observation of natron in the market at Ardrah in the 1790s pushes the date back slightly, but earlier sources are silent altogether.[7]

In the absence of substantial evidence on the salt trade before 1800, its role in the political history of that period must be considered tentative.[8] None the less, it seems likely that the control of salt and natron sources and the trade routes to these sources strongly influenced political decisions. Indeed, three major developments in the political history of the central Sudan had a crucial impact on the course of the trade. First, the Agades Sultanate emerged as a confederation of nomadic tribes centred in the Air Massif, Adar and Azawaq. This confederation was in fact an uneasy series of shifting alliances between tribes, and the Agades Sultanate served more to mediate disputes than to provide the political structures needed to govern a centralised state. The changing arena of desert politics affected which group dominated trade, but taken as a whole the Tuareg still brought the south-central Sahara, including Teguidda n'tesemt, Fachi and Bilma, under their control. In the case of Teguidda that control was exercised directly and as early as the fifteenth century, while in the case of Fachi and Bilma the Tuareg only emerged in a dominant position after c. 1759.[9] In both cases, moreover, political hegemony extended to the salt trade, which was monopolised by Tuareg caravans.

Secondly, the fortunes of the Borno state were closely linked with the salt industry. When Borno was at its strongest, from the sixteenth century to the middle of the eighteenth century, it incorporated within its territory Kawar, Fachi, Muniyo, Mangari (then called Gourbei), Kadzell and Foli – that is all the major centres of salt production in the central Sudan except Teguidda n'tesemt, the Dallols, and the Benue brine springs. The loss of Bilma and Fachi after the middle of the eighteenth century still left Borno in control of major salt deposits, but these losses amounted to a serious reorientation of the salt trade. This adjustment continued in the nineteenth century. The *jihad* in Borno (1806–12) resulted in the destruction of the capital and led to the political disintegration of the state. Despite the efforts of Sheikh al-Kanemi, the reformed state was more decentralised than in the pre-*jihad* period.[10] Greater autonomy in the salt districts resulted in further economic decline that altered the structure of the salt trade.

Thirdly, the consolidation of the Sokoto Caliphate in the nineteenth century established the central Hausa emirates, particularly Kano, as a focal point for economic development. Expansion of agriculture, textile and leather production, and commerce had serious repercussions for the central Sudan as a whole. The salt trade was an important part, albeit by no means the only or most important part, of this expansion. The distribution of salt depended upon a commercial infrastructure that was centred in the Hausa country; its growth was to a large extent at the expense of Borno and involved a close association with Tuareg salt merchants. The caliphate also expanded into the Benue salines, Dallol Fogha and Dallol Bosso, and merchants from the central emirates were more active than ever before in the distribution of salt from these sources. In broad outline, therefore, changes in the salt trade reflected the transformation of the central Sudan economy from a Borno-centred system before the middle of the eighteenth century to a caliphate-centred system in the nineteenth century.[11]

DESERT-SIDE POLITICS BEFORE 1800

In the period before 1800, the basic rivalry that affected the salt trade along the desert-edge was between Borno and the Tuareg, for Borno dominated the political history of the central Sudan in the sixteenth and seventeenth centuries until the Tuareg threatened this position in the eighteenth century. Nur Alkali has divided Borno history into three periods between 1500 and 1800.[12] In the sixteenth century, the state expanded to include territory or tributaries from Kanem in the east to the Hausa country in the west and from the Gongola River basin in the south to northern Kawar in the north. A capital was established at Birni Ngazargamu on the banks of the Komodugu Yo River. This first period was important for the salt industry because it was at this time that Borno came to control the major salt districts. The capital was close to the salt deposits of Mangari and Muniyo, and westward expansion brought all the salt sources of these districts under Borno control. Northward expansion incorporated Kawar and Fachi into the state and established alliances with the nomads frequenting these oases that guaranteed the domination of the salt industry there.[13] The reconquest of Kanem brought the trona deposits of Foli under state supervision as well.

The second period was one of consolidation in the seventeenth century. Titled officials were appointed to govern the major regions of the empire: a *galadima* was appointed for the west, and an *alifa* (*khalifah*) was assigned the administration of Kanem. Another official, the *yerima*, was given responsibility for the area north of the Komodugu Yo River. It may be that the *yerima* title already existed before this period, but this tripartite division, as it emerged in the seventeenth century, had important repercussions on the

223

organisation of the salt industry. The *yerima* oversaw the administration of all the salt districts except Foli, which was in the *alifa*'s territory. In both cases, a system of territorial land grants, which Alkali calls 'fiefs', was imposed in order to collect taxes and administer land.[14] Office holders acquired title either through inheritance or appointment, but in either case they were responsible for taxation and the regulation of the peasant population. Their powers extended to the supervision of salt production, although the details of how this supervision affected the salt industry are not known. It can be assumed, however, that the various depressions of Muniyo, Gourbei, and Foli were divided among a number of functionaries. The *galadima* administered the region traversed by most of the trade routes to the west and included a number of towns that must have served as salt markets. One of his tasks was to guarantee the safety of these routes and thereby promote commerce, including the trade in salt and natron.

The *galadima, alifa* and *yerima* had many other functions besides those connected with the salt industry, but, as Alkali has demonstrated, the development of effective administration was a major achievement of the Saifawa dynasty in this period. Centralised administration had important consequences for the salt industry because of more general economic and demographic changes. The growth of population along the Komodugu Yo and Komodugu Gana Rivers, the expansion of textile and leather production in the capital district, and the increased scale of livestock production in the Chad basin present a picture of a dynamic economy that had close links with the salt industry.

The third period analysed by Alkali was one of *status quo* that culminated in stagnation and gradual decline. The administrative structure became increasingly complex, and, while Alkali does not elaborate on the nature and significance of this complexity, it is clear that by the end of the eighteenth century the state was much weaker than it had been a century earlier.[15] One reason for this weakness was a result of another administrative device of the state, a system of titled officials who were responsible for nomadic tribes. Borno had secured the allegiance of several groups of nomads, including the Koyam, centred in Kadzell and Koutous, the Tubu of Kawar, and the Kanembu and Segurti of Kanem. These nomads received the protection of the state but in turn were responsible for safeguarding the territory north of the Komodugu Yo, particularly the trans-Saharan route through Kawar, which was vulnerable to attack from the west. Until the middle of the eighteenth century this route, and several less important ones that connected Fachi and Kawar to Muniyo, were the main avenues for the salt trade of Bilma and Fachi. As long as the nomads could control this territory, the Borno state benefited from the desert salt industry, but this control evaporated in the second half of the eighteenth century as the Tuareg successfully routed the Borno nomads in a series of encounters. The rivalry between the Tuareg and the Borno nomads was as much a struggle for power among nomads as it was a conflict between the desert and the sown. The stakes were high – control of the salt trade of Bilma and Fachi and domination of the trans-Saharan trade.

Besides their interest in controlling the salt trade, the Tuareg had three aims in this centuries-long power struggle.[16] First, they jostled among themselves for the best pastures in the Air Massif, Adar, Azawaq, Damergu and neighbouring parts of the sahel. By the eighteenth century the Kel Ewey dominated the Air Massif, the Kel Dinnik controlled Azawaq, and the Kel Gress and Itisen were centred in Adar. Secondly, the Tuareg struggled to improve their position in the savanna to the south. At various times different Tuareg fractions sided with one Hausa state in a war with another; each fraction sought a commercial corridor into the savanna, so that they could exchange the products of the desert for those of the savanna. Thirdly, the Air Massif lay astride a major caravan route to the northern Sahara and the Mediterranean world. This route, which connected with Ghat, Tuat and other northern oases, was in competition with other routes further east and west. For our purposes here, the major competitor was the Borno road through Kawar to Murzuq. Steady pressure on Borno for control of Kawar related as much to this trans-Saharan rivalry as it did to the desire to dominate the salt trade, although the two aims were not incompatible.

Inter-Tuareg competition, Tuareg–Hausa relations, and the trans-Saharan trade affected the orientation of the commerce in salt. The Tuareg rivalry determined the composition of the salt caravans and led to the intervention of the Sultan of Agades as a mediator between fractions so that hostilities could be contained during the commercial season. Tuareg–Hausa relations were significant because the Hausa country was the major market for the Tuareg caravans. Specific fractions could become allies of one or another Hausa state, but each fraction had to maintain access to the savanna. The trans-Saharan factor is important because changes in Fezzan and Hoggar could well bring about reorientations of trade and thereby affect the relative wealth and power of the various fractions.

Although there is no direct evidence that a concern for the salt industry affected political decisions in Borno before the middle of the eighteenth century, there is much circumstantial evidence that salt had been a major consideration since at least the fifteenth century. The separation of Borno from ancient Kanem in the fifteenth century led to a realignment of political power in the Chad basin. Whereas the old state had been centred to the east of Lake Chad, Borno was located to its west. This separation had far-reaching consequences, for the centre of political power was now in a much more fertile agricultural region close to the even more fertile Hausa country. The promotion of the salt trade was compatible with other economic developments that were pursued by Borno.

The agricultural potential of the region west of Lake Chad and the desert-side exchange based on livestock and salt production provided Borno with a sound economic base. As Alkali has argued, the Chad basin was particularly suitable for livestock breeding.[17] The export of horses and cattle and the production of leather goods, which were also exported, were well-developed commercial sectors for several centuries before 1800. Textiles were also manufactured in the districts near Birni Ngazargamu, and locally made cloth strips (*gabaga*) circulated as currency. The salt trade fitted into this commerce because salt came from regions through which livestock herders passed, some nomads employed slaves in salt production, and those who owned transport animals were involved in distributing salt. By controlling Kawar, Fachi, Muniyo, Kadzell and Kanem, Borno was able to dominate the major commercial patterns of the central Sudan. The export of slaves and other goods to North Africa and the production of textiles in the districts adjacent to Birni Ngazargamu undoubtedly contributed substantially to the economy too, but these sectors also had links with the salt trade. Kawar stretched along the main route to North Africa, so that its security had the double effect of encouraging salt production and the trans-Saharan trade. The textile industry supplied livestock herders and salt producers, and the textile workers bought salt and other goods in return. Because the state had access to North Africa and extensive areas in the south and west which could be raided for slaves, it was possible to manage the economy in such a way that slaves could be exported or settled within Borno as a means of expanding agricultural and, perhaps, salt production. When slave raiding was managed carefully and desert-side trade in salt, grain, and other commodities functioned smoothly, the Saifawa aristocracy was able to maintain control of an extremely wide area.

The central location of the Komodugu Yo Valley was recognised as early as the end of the fifteenth century, when Birni Ngazargamu was established on the southern bank of the river. Birni Ngazargamu became the centre of a densely populated metropolitan district, whose location must have been crucial to the salt industry of the sahel.[18] The town was within a 100 kilometre radius of perhaps two hundred places where salt could be produced, so that the capital could oversee production and trade and the metropolitan district could supply many of the agricultural and craft commodities needed in the salt-camps. The northern side of the Komodugu Yo in effect consisted of a broad belt which stretched from the Sosebaki states in the west to the shores of Lake Chad. The region was subdivided into Muniyo, Gourbei (Mangari), Kadzell, and the islands and eastern shore of the lake. Only the lake itself was not under the political control of Borno, but even so the state was able to influence trade across the lake.

While there is at present no evidence that salt was produced in this belt at the time Borno was founded – indeed the first evidence for salt production dates only to the nineteenth century – geological conditions are such that it is extremely likely that salt was in fact being processed in the sixteenth, seventeenth and eighteenth centuries. What is clear is that the potential output of this belt greatly exceeded that of the desert sites of Kawar and Fachi, even though the quality of the salt was poorer. The sources may be silent, and because of this handicap the early organisation of the sahel industry is unknown, but it seems reasonable to speculate that salt has been a major export from the Borno sahel since the fifteenth century.

In the sixteenth and seventeenth centuries, the Tubu commanded considerable influence in Borno, especially since they controlled Kawar.[19] Borno–Tubu affairs were regulated through an appointed tribal official who resided in Birni Ngazargamu. Until the middle of the eighteenth century, when Borno was relatively strong, the Tubu served as agents in the north in the peculiar manner which the nomads of the desert have often assumed with savanna states. A symbiotic relationship was maintained which recognised the independence of the nomads – they retained autonomy over their own affairs and their political jurisdiction extended over relatively specific areas of the Sahara. In return they sent horses and salt to Borno. The nomads were given access to the savanna, probably maintaining extra-territorial rights which exempted them from certain taxes, gave them access to grazing lands, and provided them with privileges of trade, often granting them virtual monopolies over some commodities, such as salt.

Before the eighteenth century, the Tubu imported slaves and settled them in the oases to grow dates and make salt. The Djadoboy and Kanuri elements in northern Kawar are probably remnants of these early slave communities. Nomadic herds provided the transport services for the trans-Saharan trade and the trade with the savanna in salt and dates. There were natural limits on this expansion, for pastures in Kawar were not particularly good. The crucial factor, therefore, was the ability of Borno to maintain its hegemony over as wide an area as possible. Specifically, the Tuareg of Air had to be contained and Kanem had to be controlled or kept isolated. A strong state in North Africa, particularly one able to control Murzuq to the north of Kawar, was also an important factor. Otherwise, nomads from elsewhere could undermine the Tubu position in Kawar.

The Tuareg steadily weakened the Tubu, something they accomplished progressively from the late seventeenth century through the eighteenth century. Tuareg influence gradually expanded, first at the northern oases, but spreading south, culminating in the Bilma war between the Tuareg and Borno in c. 1759. Raiding and tribute collection were the governing elements of desert politics. Raids were continuous, directed against enemies who could be successfully challenged, and then tribute relationships were established whenever possible. These relationships were periodically upset. Drought, political factors elsewhere, including the relative success or failure of nomads in other areas, and the fortunes of war in the savanna, could alter the balance of power, and then new raids from a different quarter began, until other tributary relationships were established. By the nineteenth century, the Tubu only retained control of salt production in the northern parts of Kawar, and by that time most Bilma salt was not shipped southward to Borno. The Tuareg had undermined the once powerful position of the Tubu.

The other early merchants in the salt trade from Kawar and Fachi were the Koyam, or nomadic Kanuri, some of whose traditions indicate that they once lived at the Kawar oases.[20] In the seventeenth and the eighteenth centuries, and perhaps earlier, their transhumance was centred in Kadzell and Koutous, to the immediate west of Lake Chad. In this area there were a number of centres which served as bases for Borno political control. Termit was an oasis between Fachi and Muniyo, and Kidouboulaouan and Oumouroudon-Aouzouguer were villages on a route through Termit between Fachi and Muniyo. In the middle of the seventeenth century, Kulumfardu (founded early in the reign of Mai Ali, perhaps in 1647) became a famous religious centre of the Koyam.[21] Its mosque was built of burnt brick, as were buildings at Birni Ngazargamu, a fact which demonstrates the close links with the Borno capital and the importance of the town as a Muslim centre.

Borno relied on the Koyam as the first line of defence against the Tuareg, since they inhabited the region closest to the Air Massif and Damergu, where the Tuareg led their nomadic life. As early as the late sixteenth century, the Koyam were a factor in containing the Tuareg. At that time, Mai Idris Alooma ordered them to raid the Tuareg 'day and night' in order to keep the Tuareg away from Borno.[22] In the seventeenth century raids and counter-raids appear to have been common, and for the time being Borno's control north of Muniyo and Kadzell remained relatively secure.

This was probably a time of relative economic prosperity, if rainfall conditions can be taken as an accurate indicator of agricultural output and the ability of such marginal places to sustain population. Nicholson's study of climatic change indicates that relatively wet times prevailed into the eighteenth century, and it seems more than a coincidence that Borno's power in the desert was at its height during this period.[23] A wetter climate in the Borno sahel meant that more people could live in the salt-producing provinces and in the southern desert regions to the north of Gourbei and Muniyo.

Tuareg–Borno hostility accelerated during the second half of the seventeenth century. Wars occurred in c. 1657, 1667, 1669, 1684, 1688 and in the early 1690s. The 1667 war was particularly destructive; according to Medicon, who reported the battle in North Africa, the Tuareg laid waste an area approaching the Borno capital, and Mai Ali (1639–77) then led retaliatory raids of equal severity.[24] Kulumfardu was destroyed in the 1680s by Tuareg raids at the time of a severe drought which marred the general climatic pattern of the sixteenth, seventeenth, and early eighteenth centuries.[25] Despite the incursions of the Tuareg, Borno seems to have been able to contain the threat until the middle of the eighteenth century, but the Koyam suffered extensively because they were in the front line of attack. The destruction of Kulumfardu in c. 1688 did not end Koyam influence, but it must have demonstrated the difficulty of holding Koutous and protecting central Borno.

The middle of the eighteenth century marked a turning point in the trade of Kawar and Fachi, which came to depend upon Tuareg caravans that crossed the Tenere from Agades and the Hausa centres to the south. This route effectively bypassed Borno and meant that salt exports flowed in a wide arc around Borno. The Kawar and Fachi inhabitants needed grain and manufactures, but they now came to depend almost completely upon merchants who were not citizens of Borno. According to Hausa tradition, the Tuareg began selling salt as early as the fifteenth century, but this was probably not from Bilma or Fachi. This salt may have come from northern Kawar or Teguidda n'tesemt instead.[26] None the less, this early tradition, seen in retrospect, highlights the beginnings of a major shift in desert trade.

According to other legends, the Tuareg first obtained salt from Murzuq, but later they obtained supplies at Djaba and later still at Seguidine. The southern progression of Tuareg influence continued thereafter; exploitation of the salines moved south to Guisibi and then Dirku, in central Kawar. Finally, the Tuareg came to concentrate their trade at Bilma, probably in the eighteenth century.[27] These traditions are indirect proof that the Tubu and Koyam controlled the Bilma trade and directed it south to Borno before the Tuareg period. Tuareg involvement in the northern Kawar trade would have taken them very far north, half-way across the desert. They may well have redirected some of the trans-Saharan trade away from Borno by providing a direct link with the Hausa towns. It may be that Borno attacks on Agades in this period were meant to undermine this trade, both salt and trans-Saharan, by making the route unsafe – perhaps it was not possible to trade every year along the Seguidine route. By the time the Tuareg went to Dirku, which is further south but was probably not the main source of salt, Dirku produced natron, not *beza* and *kantu*. It was possible to obtain high quality red natron and large quantities of cheaper natron, both white and red, and salt could still have come from Seguidine, too, but only when the Tuareg secured the right to transport salt from Bilma were they able to break into the big market. The Tuareg achieved this objective and became the main transporters of Kawar and Fachi salt by c. 1759 when they won the Bilma war.

The Bilma war (1173 AH, 1759 AD), is described in the Asben Record of Abu Tali Annaju: 'It is related that after one Bornu expedition to Ahir the Kelowi pursued the retreating Kanuri to Balma. Some three or four hundred of the Bornu army were captured and installed by the Kelowi as their subjects at Balma to work the salt. This is said to be the origin of the rights of the Kel-Ahir in Balma, in acknowledgement of which an annual present is sent to Agades.'[28] The struggle continued. In 1765 the Kel Ewey were set upon and massacred by the Kanuri: 'The Sultan Muhammad of Agades retaliated by attacking Bornu. He marched to the gates of Kukawa [Birni Ngazargamu] and took two thousand cattle, exacting a promise that Asben caravans should not be interfered with again.'[29] In another campaign that can be dated to c. 1787–92, the Koyam suffered a humiliating defeat. Their centre at Gaskeru, the successor of Kulumfardu, was destroyed and many Koyam were massacred.[30]

The timing of the Bilma war appears to be very significant in terms of the changing political fortunes of Borno. It came at the end of one of the worst droughts in Borno history, the Great Drought which lasted from the late 1730s to the 1750s.[31] This drought, which is reported in many places in West Africa, was perhaps the most severe in the last half millennium. While the

229

generally wetter conditions of the previous two and a half centuries did return, the Great Drought probably had a devastating effect on Borno economy and society. Research must be directed towards uncovering the impact of such a disaster, but it seems likely that the Borno sahel, where the salt industry was centred, suffered the most. Why the Tuareg fared better in the drought than nomads in Borno is still unclear, but they definitely emerged in a superior position. They not only acquired a near-monopoly over Kawar and Fachi salt, but they apparently forced the desert inhabitants to abandon agriculture, except for date production.[32] This commercial advantage effectively tied the Kawar and Fachi salt industry to the Tuareg and probably contributed to a decline in trade southward to central Borno. The Tubu, who – in the nineteenth century at least – controlled production of salt in parts of Kawar, lost their position as transporters, as did the Koyam of Kadzell. The Tuareg now used the desolate Tenere as a staging ground which they crossed for commerce as well as war.

The traditional hostilities between Borno and the Tuareg over control of the routes of Tenere and Koutous spilled over into Damergu, Mangari, Muniyo and even Air and central Borno, with the result that Borno influence contracted from the late seventeeth century onward. Termit and other villages between Air and Fachi and between Fachi and Muniyo had to be abandoned. In this period several important developments occurred, including the incorporation of Kanuri people – the Dagera – into Damergu, the abandonment of Koyam centres in the area north and north-east of Gourbei, and the gradual reduction of the Koyam to insignificance. Agadem, north of Nguigmi, was abandoned, for example, and even Kalala near Bilma was evacuated.[33]

Unfortunately, little is known about Muniyo in the period before the eighteenth century, except that Borno established its authority over the area by defeating a series of smaller states – Sosebaki and others that are referred to in Borno tradition as the 'So'.[34] The hilly region of Muniyo was initially settled by the Dagera, but their connexion with the salt industry is unknown and by the eighteenth century, most Dagera were living to the north.[35] By then, the Manga, who also spoke Kanuri, were the main population of Muniyo, and they definitely worked the salt industry. According to Lange, the Manga probably incorporated many of the earlier Dagera. Traditions indicate that 'Manga' is not an ancient ethnic or regional term of the Kanuri, for the earliest references to the name are in the late seventeenth century,[36] and the name may not have assumed its ethnic connotation until the eighteenth century. It is tempting to see a connexion between the emergence of the Manga and the Great Drought of the mid-eighteenth century. While traditions do not associate the disappearance of the Dagera from the salt region with drought conditions, it seems possible that the ethnic transformation was somehow related to the evacuation and resettlement of Muniyo under climatic pressures. By the middle of the eighteenth century the capital of Muniyo was Birni Gafata, perhaps an old Dagera centre. This town was located north-west of the major production sites, and many Manga claim to have migrated from there and villages in its vicinity. By the end of the century and continuing into the nineteenth century, Bune was the capital. It was an important production site for natron and a Manga town.[37]

The political struggle between Borno and the Tuareg resolved the issue of who would control the salt trade. By the 1760s, Niebuhr learned in North Africa that Hausaland obtained its salt from the 'city of Asben', i.e. Agades.[38] Imhammed reported the main features of the trade as he observed them in the 1780s, and his remarks – when corrected for obvious errors – could well apply to the trade for the next 120 years:

> Among the few circumstances which characterize the trade of Cashna [Katsina], as distinguished from that of Bornou, the most remarkable is, that the merchants of the former kingdom [Katsina] are the sole carriers to other nations, of a scarce and most valuable commodity, which is only to be obtained from the inhabitants of the latter [Borno]. For though the salt of Bornou supplies the consumption of Cashna, and the Negro kingdoms to the south, yet its owners have abandoned to the commercial activity of the merchants of Agades, the whole of that profitable trade.[39]

Imhammed learned that the salt came from Bilma, 45 days' march across the desert, in 'immense caravans'.[40] Imhammed's report indicates that Katsina controlled Agades, which is not true, but an Agades–Katsina commercial axis certainly did exist. In 1798, Hornemann found that the merchants were Kel Ewey, and he traced the caravan route across the Tenere on the map he constructed of the central Sudan. The route went through Fachi, which was also supplying salt to the trade at this time.[41]

THE DECLINE OF BORNO

The political and economic system of imperial Borno broke down as the result of drought and holy war. Economic decline began with the Great Drought of the eighteenth century and accelerated with the loss of Kawar and Fachi to the Tuareg in c. 1759. Continued Tuareg inroads after 1760 further weakened Borno, and defeat at the hands of Mandara (1781) was another blow. A second drought, but not as serious as the Great Drought, struck either in the 1790s or the first years of the nineteenth century.[42] Borno had survived earlier climatic and political catastrophes, and it might have recovered from this series too, but for the meantime Tuareg successes north of the Komodugu Yo River and their control of Kawar and Fachi went unchecked. Probably because the Koyam had been massacred, there was no counter-offensive to the Tuareg challenge. Eventually, Kanembu, Shuwa Arabs or other nomads might have filled the gap, providing Borno once more with a strong nomadic force that could contain the Tuareg, but this eventuality never occurred.

The *jihad* of the Borno Fulani – allied with the emerging Sokoto Caliphate – struck Borno from 1806 to 1812 and dealt a major blow that prevented recovery. Indeed, the open hostility of the Borno Fulani removed vital support from this nomadic population – the very forces needed to replace the Koyam. Borno had initially established its hegemony in the Chad basin in a situation where there was no other large state, except a distant and weak Kanem, which was eventually conquered, and a more distant Songhay far to the west. In the early nineteenth century, the Sokoto Caliphate emerged as a formidable rival, and now Borno found itself yet again on the defensive. The Borno Fulani were eventually defeated; they moved south to promote the *jihad* in Adamawa.[43] None the less, the tributary Hausa states and the borderlands between the Hausa and Borno fell to the forces of the *jihad*. The new emirates of Hadejia, Katagum and Jama'are were the principal benefactors. Damagaram, Muniyo and Kanem gained greater control over their internal affairs because the reformed regime of Sheikh al-Kanemi simply lacked the resources to secure the total submission of these provinces.[44] The new regime accepted greater decentralisation in the provinces as a necessary political reform. Still economically weak and facing a much stronger army in the west, Borno was no longer in a position to dominate the desert-side trade and use its geographical position advantageously. Where once it had been possible to exploit the salt industry for political ends, now even the salt trade became dependent upon the Sokoto Caliphate.

A major blow to the old order was the destruction of Birni Ngazargamu in 1808, when the *jihad* armies gained a temporary victory.[45] Ngazargamu, reoccupied briefly, was permanently abandoned in 1809, and the populated districts around it were evacuated. As Denham reported in 1823, the 'whole neighbourhood of Gambarou [the river-side town near Birni Ngazargamu] was once in a superior state of cultivation' but 'the whole country [had] been abandoned ever since the Felatahs [Fulani] commenced their inroads' – which Denham dated to 1809.[46] Denham counted 'thirty large towns which the Felatahs had completely razed to the ground at the time they destroyed the capital', and he learned of another ten which he did not see.[47] Such a major depopulation of the central provinces most certainly affected the salt industry. The Koyam had suffered at the hands of the Tuareg in the last decades of the eighteenth century; now the capital itself was in ruins. The salt districts were deserted, and there were few people in the immediate vicinity of the depressions who were available to work the industry.

Under the leadership of al-Kanemi, a new capital was eventually established at Kukawa, which was located further east, close to Baga Seyoram, the main port in the Lake Chad trona trade, but this location left Mangari and Muniyo more autonomous than had been the case before 1808. Initially, the Manga opposed the emergence of al-Kanemi as the strong man of Borno. Al-Kanemi's rise was at the expense of the old dynasty, from which the political leaders in Muniyo derived their positions. Rebellions flared in 1824 and in 1846, although it is doubtful that the region had always had 'an independent outlook', as Johnston and Muffett argue.[48] The pre-*jihad* province was centred at Bune, which was not particularly remote from the capital at Birni Ngazargamu. As an important source of natron, Bune was strategically located in the hilly region on the north-western frontier of the salt-producing country. It remained the capital until the 1820s. Certainly the new capital of Goure, established by Muniyoma Koso (c. 1822–54), was more remote than Bune.[49]

The 1824 revolt was led by a Muslim cleric, Fanama, who objected to the usurpation of the Borno throne by al-Kanemi. According to Denham, the Manga

> had never thoroughly acknowledged the sheikh's [al-Kanemi's] supremacy, and the collecting of their tribute had always been attended with difficulty and bloodshed. They had, however, now thrown off all restraint, and put to death about one hundred and twenty of the sheikh's Shouaas [Shuwa Arabs], and declared they would be no longer under his control, as the sultan of Bornou was their king; and headed by a fighi [cleric] of great power, had begun to plunder and burn all the sheikh's towns near them. It was reported, and with some truth, that they could bring 12,000 bowmen into the field.[50]

In 1822 Muniyo also had to contend with an invasion from Damagaram in the west, although both Damagaram and Muniyo were part of Borno.[51] The difficulties with Damagaram in the west and the al-Kanemi regime at Kukawa in the south-east probably influenced Muniyoma Koso's decision to move his capital from Bune to Goure, which was located north of the salt district.

Another revolt occurred in 1845–46. The Manga established a stronghold at Maidonomari, in southern Mangari, and rose at the same time that Wadai invaded Kanem. The central government was able to crush the revolt and the town was abandoned. When Barth passed through the region in December 1854 he found the district 'exhausted by recent exactions and contributions, the greater part of the population having even sought safety in a precipitate flight'.[52] Despite this loss, Koso continued to rule Muniyo until his death in 1854. He remained loyal to Kukawa during the 1845–46 revolt, but he demonstrated an inability or an unwillingness to contain the Manga peasantry.

A more serious reversal struck Muniyo in 1876, when Damagaram invaded the Muniyo hills and annexed the salt districts. From 1876 until the French conquest in 1903, Muniyo was part of Damagaram.[53] This struggle for power between two provinces which were supposedly part of Borno demonstrated the weakness of the central government. In contrast to the days of Birni Ngazargamu, the salt-camps lacked the protection of the state. Salt and natron were still produced, and the trona trade across Lake Chad still had to pass through central Borno, but conditions were much less secure than they had been during the sixteenth, seventeenth and eighteenth centuries. The trona trade was relatively unaffected because Kukawa, the nineteenth-century capital, was only 25 kilometres from Baga Seyoram, but trade from the Manga districts was beyond state control.

Borno virtually ceased to function as the overlord of the provinces north of the Komodugu Yo. It not only had no voice in the affairs of Kawar and Fachi, which continued under Tuareg domination, but Damagaram had emerged as autonomous in the north-west. In 1892, the final collapse of Borno took place, when an invading army under Rabeh ibn Fadl moved on Kukawa from south of Lake Chad.[54] Thus the Borno state which had once ruled most of the Chad basin and the major trans-Saharan route through Kawar experienced defeat after defeat. Despite the efforts of al-Kanemi and his successors to revitalise the state, a steady decline can be seen which began with the Great Drought of the mid-eighteenth century and continued uninterrupted through the nineteenth century.

THE EXPANSION OF MANGA INDUSTRY

The *jihad* in Borno dislocated the salt industry in Muniyo and Gourbei and ushered in a period of readjustment in the districts north of the Komodugu Yo River. The basis of production changed dramatically because of the evacuation of the districts around Birni Ngazargamu and because the transference of the capital to Kukawa undermined the established system of proprietorship over the salines. The system of labour migration described in Chapter 6 and the control of the salines described in Chapter 7 date to the period after the *jihad*. Because the dislocation of the *jihad* was so severe and because contemporary documentation concentrates on purely political and religious issues, it is difficult to reconstruct the economic history of these salt districts for the period before 1800. Nevertheless, it is clear that a dramatic change occurred in the early nineteenth century.

Before the *jihad*, the region that came to be known as Mangari was called Gourbei, which is a Kanuri term for valley or depression. As late as 1909 part of Mangari was still known locally by that name. When the region was known as Gourbei it belonged to the Koyam, and tradition has it that the Koyam had occupied Gourbei for 250 years before they were forced to evacuate it.[55] The old Koyam capital had been further east, at Kulumfardu, and later at Mir, both of which were located in Kadzell, but it seems possible – although tradition is silent on this point – that the management of salt production was in the hands of the Koyam. Who were the workers? Were they slaves or free migrants? It is impossible to reach any conclusions, except that the Manga claim that before they moved into Mangari, they were only farmers. Since natron and some salt was also found in Muniyo, it is certain that many ancestors of the Mangari inhabitants did more than farm, but the tradition may indicate that before 1800 they did not migrate to Gourbei to produce *manda*.

As Gouletquer and Kleinmann's analysis of production techniques suggests, *kige* production is older than *manda* production.[56] The manufacture of *manda* relied on ovens, a more sophisticated technique than the use of open fires, which was the technique for making *kige*. This comparison suggests a possible evolution from *kige* production, which used weak brines from wells and the ashes of salt-laden plants, to *manda* production, which used the brine derived from surface evaporation of depressions and ponds. It may well be that the Koyam – or more likely their slaves – used the brines from the depressions of

Mangari before the Manga became involved in production in the nineteenth century. Whether or not ovens were developed at this time is unclear, but there is every reason to believe that a type of *manda* salt was made. Both *manda* and *kige* were made in the vicinity of Maine-Soroa at the end of the nineteenth century, and some Manga salt workers had shifted to the manufacture of *kige* late in the century, which indicates a reversal of an older pattern. Where it is likely that *manda* production was initially an extension of the *kige* industry in order to increase the quantity of salt (despite the greater impurity of *manda* when compared to *kige*), by the end of the nineteenth century, salt workers were shifting from the poorer salt to *kige*. The expansion of Manga industry in the nineteenth century, first into *manda* production and later into *kige* production, suggests that a similar movement, only from *kige* production to *manda* production, may well have occurred in an earlier period.

Many of the workers in Gourbei must have come from the central districts of Borno around Birni Ngazargamu, whether the Koyam and their slaves worked the salines of Gourbei or not. Because of the proximity of the heavily-populated capital district to the depressions of Gourbei, it stands to reason that seasonal migration characterised labour mobilisation in the eighteenth century and earlier, just as migration was common in the nineteenth century. The silence of the historical record prevents confirmation of this hypothesis, but given the ecological setting and the demography of the region, this conclusion seems probable. The salt depressions could not support a large population under the technological conditions that existed before 1800, and the system of fiefs, in which title-holders lived in the capital, lent itself well to the exploitation of salt deposits that varied from year to year and shifted among the depressions of Gourbei.[57] It is also possible that many of these migrant workers were slaves; the Borno state engaged in slave raiding and the export trade across the Sahara on a major scale. Slaves settled near Birni Ngazargamu would have been available for dry-season employment, just as they probably were at the *kige* camps of Kadzell to the north and north-east of Birni Ngazargamu.

The Manga moved into the void created by the *jihad* and the destruction of the Saifawan capital. They were already involved in the collection of natron at the many salines in the Muniyo hills, but now they were able to move east into Gourbei, which soon took the name of Mangari to reflect their new role in the production of *manda*, and south into the districts west of the Birni Ngazargamu ruins, where there was relatively good agricultural land. This resettlement of central Borno (although the immediate vicinity of Birni Ngazargamu did not become a centre of population) resulted in the conditions which made possible the migratory pattern that characterised the salt industry late in the nineteenth century.

The traditions of origin for many of the permanent residents in the area of the salt-camps establish a long history of migration, although there is a sharp distinction between workers and the political elite. The elite – who had access to patronage and therefore proprietorship of the salines – usually claim

235

to have come from Borno, i.e. the south, while the workers maintain that they came from Muniyo. Workers who have been long settled at Adebour and Maine-Soroa, for example, cite Birni Gafata, Bune and other old centres in Muniyo as their ancestral homes. The only tradition that predates the *jihad* comes from the Manga in the Alanjuori District of Borno, who claim to have come from the north in c. 1760 to work the salt pans at Ngajigawa, until they were driven out by the Fulani. These Manga appear to have moved south before the *jihad*, perhaps at the time of the Great Drought in the middle of the eighteenth century. The other traditions date from the early nineteenth century. The Manga living north of Geidam, for example, reported in 1909 that they had settled at Madinga, Maine-Soroa and Abashiri about eighty years earlier, c. 1830. These traditions establish that the Manga were the people of Muniyo who moved east and south to escape famine, political oppression and insecurity.[58] The opportunities present in the salt district served to pull them east and south-east, while the political situation in Muniyo encouraged an exodus. The relative importance of these 'push' and 'pull' factors is difficult to assess, but it is clear that the combination prompted the movement of a substantial population.

The fullest traditions of origin were collected by Landeroin between 1906 and 1909. At Toungouri, 60 km east of Goure, people say the Manga originally came from Kaoura, which no longer exists but was situated near Tchangari (50 km SW of Goure). Their ancestors had lived there a long time, but during the reign of Muniyoma Koso (c. 1822–54), they left Kaoura because of the exactions of the government.[59] At Goudoumaria, the elders claimed that their ancestors were originally from Baga, Kaoura or western Muniyo. They first moved to Kadellaba, near Goudoumaria, which was uninhabited when they arrived. At Tamsah, between Cheri and Goudoumaria, the inhabitants say they originally came from Toungoure (16 km SSW of Goure), which they evacuated during a drought in the reign of Koso. At Maine-Soroa, the ruling family was descended from a certain Adem Lafiami, Manga in origin, who had lived in Ngaragou, south-west of Cheri. His father was a contemporary of Muniyoma Ibrahim, who ruled at the time of the *jihad* (i.e. 1806–12). Adem Lafiami moved to Maine-Soroa, where he was given the title of the town, perhaps after the final abandonment of Birni Ngazargamu, the ruins of which were only a few kilometers away. Other traditions tell a similar story for other settlements in Mangari.[60]

Gouletquer and Kleinmann, in their preliminary survey of archaeological sites in Mangari, confirm these traditions. Katiella Abdou of Maine-Soroa claims that *manda* had been produced for only 155 years before 1973; that is *manda* production began in the area of Maine-Soroa around 1818, when the town was settled by Manga coming from Muniyo.[61] As Gouletquer and Kleinmann point out, this tradition accords well with the information collected by Landeroin in the first decade of this century. It appears that there was a gap in the production of salt in Mangari around the time of the *jihad*, which is not surprising, considering the prolonged struggle in the region of Birni Ngazargamu. In effect Manga traditions recount the reoccupation of the salt district. The annual migration of free Manga appears to date from this time.

Only gradually was the fief system re-established as a method of control over the salines, and even then the Kukawa government was left with relatively minor salines – and only a few at that – in the southern part of the salt district. The important salines – and by far the greatest number – were controlled from Goure, Goudoumaria, and Maine-Soroa. This more decentralised system of fiefs, controlled from the provinces rather than from the capital, altered the organisation of production. As Alkali has demonstrated, the Saifawa dynasty had distributed fiefs as a way of administering territory.[62] Members of the royal family, well-placed slave officials, and nobles had competed for fiefs, many of which had been in the region of Birni Ngazargamu and must have extended into the salt district. Besides access to a portion of taxes collected in these fiefs, officials had also settled slaves – often in large numbers – in their fiefs. Although there is no direct evidence that slaves had lived in the salt district or that slaves on the fiefs adjacent to the salt districts actually had worked the salines, it is likely that they had been involved in production. In the nineteenth century there were fewer fiefs in this area – and hence fewer slaves.

The few fief-holders that were directly under the Kukawa government do not appear to have expanded their slave holdings in the vicinity of the salt districts, probably because they did not have access to enough slaves and the greater distance from the capital made supervision of the fiefs more difficult. The officials at Goure, Goudoumaria, and Maine-Soroa had slaves, but apparently not enough to work the salines. The decentralised provincial administration at Goure, Goudoumaria, and Maine-Soroa was a pale reflection of the elaborate fief system of the eighteenth century.

Because this new distribution of political and proprietary control prevented the assignment of a slave population to the salines, migrant peasants worked the deposits. There were relatively few influential title-holders who owned slaves, and there was no longer a wealthy merchant class in the area. The conquest of Muniyo by Damagaram in 1876 weakened the local proprietor-political elite further, thereby enabling the Manga peasantry to continue their role in production. The court intrigue that had determined who controlled the salines under the Saifawa regime was gone. The Koyam had lost their influence in the region and were not able to re-establish their earlier position, and the Fulani were forced to evacuate the area after they failed to consolidate their early victories over the Saifawa dynasty. The spread of the Manga into Mangari and the territory west of old Birni Ngazargamu completed the peasantisation of salt production, even though slaves were once again becoming a factor in production by the end of the century.

KANEM AND THE SALT TRADE OF LAKE CHAD

The political decline that allowed the emergence of a new economic order in Mangari also affected the course of trona production in Kanem. Because the al-Kanemi regime drew support from the Kanembu inhabitants of Kanem,[63] many Kanembu moved to the western shores of Lake Chad, which left Kanem less easy to defend in case of invasion. Kanem was still distant from the capital, even though Kukawa was closer than Birni Ngazargamu had been. Despite Kanembu support, the emergence of the al-Kanemi regime had the effect of depleting the human resources of Kanem, rather than tying Kanem more tightly to Borno. To a certain extent, history was repeating itself. Centuries earlier, the Saifawa dynasty had moved from Kanem to Borno, with the result that Kanem became a minor province. In the early nineteenth century, al-Kanemi organised a similar evacuation, albeit for different reasons.

Invasion came from two fronts, the Sahara and Wadai. The Tuareg, Tubu and the Awlad Sulayman raided Kanem at various times; the Tuareg took what they could and then left, but the Awlad Sulayman came to stay.[64] Wadai was an even more serious threat than the nomads. In 1846, Wadai invaded Kanem, proceeded south across the Chari River and marched on Kukawa. Although Wadai was defeated at Kusseri,[65] for the rest of the century Kanem owed allegiance to Wadai or was effectively independent of the Kukawa government. Borno attempted to use the Awlad Sulayman as a counterforce to Wadai, and sometimes this policy worked and sometimes it did not. In any event, political authority remained relatively segmented.

In the context of this political situation, the Danawa who worked the trona of Foli and the Yedina transporters who inhabited the islands of the lake were able to consolidate their autonomy from the aristocracy. The Yedina merely continued an existing tradition of independence, and the Danawa, using their corporate status as *haddad*, increased their autonomy. The Kanem government exerted more control over Foli in the eighteenth century, but the Yedina were probably just as independent then as they were in the nineteenth century.

Even as late as the fourth decade of the nineteenth century, the rulers of Kanem, centred at Mao, held sway over a relatively well-populated district near the trona pans of Foli. There were more than 300 villages in Foli, according to traditions collected by Landeroin in 1901. The *kachella* of Foli collected taxes from these villages and forwarded them to Mao. The population of the district included slaves and 'vassals', who were probably Danawa.[66] One of the principal places, for example, was known as Kindjiria, a name which had the same connotation as in Borno – it referred to a slave settlement. It stands to reason that some of this population, at least, was engaged in the trona pans, although there is no direct evidence of their involvement.

The Wadai invasion of 1846 destroyed many of the Foli villages. The Magoumi *kachella* withdrew to an island (Kamba) in the lake, while the slaves and Danawa scattered. Some refugees settled at Wanda (Ouannda) and others at Kindjiria, while still others found their way to the Danawa concentration of Bari.[67] Foli was on its way to becoming a deserted wilderness. Because the *kachella* refused to recognise Wadai overlordship, a combined Wadai–Mao expedition swept through the region too. Later Awlad Sulayman and Tubu raids plagued the few survivors.[68]

The Danawa were already concentrated in southern Kanem, particularly in the area around Nguri (Bari), where refugees from Foli sought sanctuary. In contrast to the Danawa and *haddad* settlement in other parts of Kanem, the Danawa of Bari lived in their own villages; they constituted most of the population near Nguri, and a sizeable minority in other parts of southern Kanem.[69] Further north they formed only a small portion of the total population.

In the predominantly nomadic north, among the Arabs and Daza, the *haddad* represented less than 5 per cent of the population. These *haddad*, and others further south who were associated with nomads, lived in tents that were pitched behind those of their patrons. A few *haddad* were hunters and gatherers, but most were blacksmiths. By contrast, among the semi-nomadic Kanembu population centred on Mao, the Danawa were usually integrated into the villages of the Kanembu, often in groups of ten or twenty persons. These Danawa performed the menial tasks connected with agriculture and cattle keeping, as well as some artisan tasks. In this area of central Kanem, they constituted perhaps 10–15 per cent of the population and occasionally were numerous enough to live in separate hamlets close to the villages of their patrons. The number of craftsmen in this population was lower than might be expected from the general pattern of Danawa domination of artisan activities, and those Danawa who were engaged in a craft were usually of Daza rather than Kanembu origin.[70] Blacksmiths in particular were often Daza, both in central and southern Kanem.

Because of their numerical strength and their concentration, the Danawa of southern Kanem had become quasi-autonomous, at least by the middle of the nineteenth century, if not earlier.[71] The Kanembu lineages of Mao maintained ties of political and economic domination as represented through tribute payments (sections of the Kogona and N'gijim lived there),[72] but the close, personal dependence that characterised Danawa–Kanembu relations near Mao and *haddad*–nomad relations further north and east did not exist.

The Danawa of southern Kanem trace their ancestry to a number of different origins. Conte has established several patterns in these traditions.[73] Some are descendants of hunters and gatherers from northern Kanem and from the Manga region north of Kanem and are therefore distantly related to the *haddad* population among the nomads there. Others claim to have come as hunters from Lake Chad.[74] The two hunting traditions are distinguishable by the use of different techniques; those from the lake used bows and arrows, while those from the north used nets. Whether or not the correlation between technology and origins reflects a real historical difference is unclear. It may be that the Danawa merely explain their preferences in hunting techniques with

239

reference to myth. A third group of Danawa trace their ancestry to vassal groups of the Bulala, who played an important role in Kanem until defeated by the Tunjur Arabs in the middle of the seventeenth century. The Bulala themselves were descended from the medieval Kanem state; the civil war that resulted in the movement of the Saifawa to the west of Lake Chad and the foundation of modern Borno left the disputed territory in the hands of the Bulala, who also claimed descent from the old aristocracy of Kanem. When Borno defeated the Tunjur in the seventeenth century, Kanem came under its political sway; thereafter the seat of Borno power was at Mao. Its representatives in southern Kanem were the Kogona.[75] The dependants of the Bulala – who came to be known as N'gijim – continued to occupy the Dibinenchi and Nguri areas. Their vassals, who lacked aristocratic connexions and were thereby classified as *haddad*, were identified as Darka. Other Danawa have more diverse origins and represent the incorporation of political refugees who were forced to flee the repeated invasions that dominated the history of the Kanem region and who had to barter their autonomy against protection. Finally, slaves, many of whom were acquired in the nineteenth century, were assimilated. Kanembu raiding parties pushed south to Bagirmi and beyond, returning with captives. Some of these slaves and their descendants found their way into the ranks of the Danawa.

At the end of the nineteenth century, four autonomous but allied lineages of Danawa dominated the Nguri area, from where some of the salt workers of Foli probably came. These included the Haddad Rea, Adia and Bara, all of whom claimed hunter ancestry, and the militarily influential Darka, who claimed mixed Bulala and *haddad* ancestry.[76] The Darka in turn had five Kanembu lineages and their *haddad* subservient to them – a striking reversal of the usual pattern of dominance and subordination in which Danawa were subordinate to the Kanembu. As a result of some forgotten turn of events related to the military success of the Darka – perhaps associated with the Wadai invasion of Kanem in the 1840s, resistance to the Awlad Sulayman in the 1860s or an even older tradition of military strength – the relative autonomy of these allied Danawa had become assured. The subservience of the local Kanembu demonstrated this autonomy both symbolically and in real terms. This Darka-led alliance of Danawa took advantage of the weakened position of Borno in Kanem, but the Danawa were unable to free themselves entirely from a socio-political structure divided between free Kanembu and dependent Danawa. In the Nguri area, the Kogona section of the Kanembu – related to the family of the ruling *alifa* in Mao – served as a police force; they controlled the collection of tribute. The N'gijim Kanembu – descended from the medieval Bulala – owned more fertile land and commanded more armed men than anyone else in southern Kanem and thereby helped guarantee continued respect for the established social and political structure.[77]

In the second half of the nineteenth century the Danawa of the Nguri region suffered a series of calamities, including strife among the allied Danawa, the cyclical movements of Lake Chad, exposing and then inundating once more very fertile soil, and, finally, successive waves of invaders, especially from 1870 to 1899. This turmoil resulted in a repeated influx of small groups of refugees, generally of servile origin, who preferred to opt for the relative stability of life with the allied lineages. Despite internal disagreements within the alliance, the Bari region was protected from external invaders by the dense tree covering of its valleys and the strategic advantage offered by Danawa poisoned arrows.[78]

Whether or not the Danawa of Bari engaged in the production of trona, they provided sanctuary for other Danawa and fugitive slaves who had to flee the Foli depressions to escape the raids of the Awlad Sulayman, Tubu and others. Fugitive slaves fitted into Danawa society as new recruits; their assimilation was assured since they were fugitives from Kanembu masters and hence had already acquired the cultural tools of Kanembu society. They now became *haddad* because they lacked affiliation with aristocratic Kanembu lineages. The settlement of Danawa and slave refugees from the lake region enabled the Darka alliance to sustain its autonomy. The effect on the trona district is unclear, but it seems likely that the population movement was not one-way. Some of the Danawa and slaves who had come from the lake shore probably returned to the trona deposits, since they knew the trona business and had contacts there.

The relationship of the Yedina islanders in Lake Chad to the trona trade fitted into the decentralised pattern of political life. The Yedina had long used the islands in Lake Chad as sanctuaries to maintain their independence from Borno, Kanem and other states of the mainland. Hornemann's report in 1798 that the island dwellers were a 'heathen and savage race' attests to a reputation that they reinforced during the nineteenth century.[79] Denham learned that the Yedina were 'a people who live by plundering on the main land, and carry off any thing they can pick up'.[80] He heard that they kidnapped Borno people, demanding ransom in slaves for free captives. They also kidnapped slaves in Bagirmi, taking them to their island homes: 'These islands lie on the eastern side of the Tchad ...; the two largest are named Koorie and Sayah. They have a language of their own, although resembling that of Kanem.'[81] The theft of cattle and kidnapping of people earned them a reputation that has led Martin Verlet to call them the Normans of the Great Lake.[82] Like the society of the camel nomads of the desert, Yedina political structure was also segmented; they raided each other as well as people on the mainland. There were four main fractions; Goudja, located on islands in the northern archipelago, the Maibokla near the divide in the middle of the lake, the Gouria in the southern archipelago, and the Madjigodjia off-shore from Bol in the southern archipelago. As early as 1851, Overweg recognised several of these distinctions. When he crossed Lake Chad in 1851, he found that the Gouria had already established their hegemony over the central lake district. 'A great number of Kanembus' were living on the islands that formed the great divide between the northern and southern parts of the lake; they were forced to evacuate the mainland during the Wadai invasion of Kanem in 1846,[83] and many of the Danawa who worked the trona deposits came from their population.

In 1851 there were ten villages on the island of Belarigeh, which was the principal centre of the Madjigodjia, who were already subservient to the Gouria.[84] Nachtigal included the four main fractions, as well as mentioning the Marganna and Dschillua, in the early 1870s,[85] while in 1902, Destenave estimated the population of the three largest fractions at 17,000; the Gouria, numbering 10,000, inhabited 19 islands; the Madjigodjia, numbering 2,000, lived on three islands; and the Boudja [Goudja], 5,000 strong, occupied four islands.[86] By the 1870s, when the Gouria dominated the trona trade, Otte Kami was their leader, and his son Koremi was in power in 1902 (the dates of their reigns are otherwise unknown). The Madjigodjia and the Kanembu of Djabo (the peninsula that juts into the lake from Kanem) both paid tribute. It was to this chief, Koremi, that the *lawan* of Baga Seyoram must have sent presents at the time of the British occupation of Borno.[87] In addition there were other lake dwellers – identified in early reports as Kouri – who lived on islands in the extreme southern part of the lake. They had the same origins as the northern islanders – they were refugees from the mainland – but were not associated with the trona trade.

THE DEPENDENCE OF BORNO ON THE SOKOTO CALIPHATE

The extensive commercial diaspora in regions south and west of Borno which linked Borno with other parts of the central Sudan also experienced a major re-adjustment as a result of the *jihad*.[88] Initially this diaspora was centred on Borno, but gradually it became submerged in a Hausa-dominated mercantile system. Settlers left Borno for towns and cities along the trade routes which radiated south to the Benue River valley and west as far as the Volta River basin. Settlement was especially heavy in the Hausa towns, which were in a relatively more fertile and wetter area than much of Borno.

The dislocation of the salt trade during the *jihad* accelerated the process of commercial decline and the greater dependency of Borno on the Hausa economy. The Hausa cities and towns, particularly Kano, Katsina and Zaria, became the western market centres for the Borno desert-side corridors of trade, while Borno markets, including Kukawa, became intermediary points. Many merchants and craftsmen who were involved in this trade shifted their operations to the Hausa country, while numerous Hausa traders now included the Borno market in their business. The process took approximately 150 years to complete, but by the end of the nineteenth century Borno had become an economic satellite of the central Hausa country. In general economic terms, this process of change amounted to the greater integration of Borno and the Hausa country, but from the perspective of Borno, it is possible to see the developments from 1750 to 1900 as a process of increasing dependency.

242

The scale of emigration from Borno was considerable. In the absence of quantifiable data, it is impossible to measure this demographic shift with accuracy, but the impression from oral traditions and contemporary observations is that the movement was steady throughout the nineteenth century. Almost certainly, many people left during the turmoil surrounding the *jihad* in Borno. The fall of Birni Ngazargamu in 1808 occurred at a time when the Hausa emirates had already succumbed. The hostility of the Saifawa government to the caliphate probably had little effect on the decision by refugees to seek new homes in or near the Hausa towns. Merchants who were already engaged in trade to the west would have found it easy to establish themselves near Kano, Zaria or Katsina.

Many of these merchants may have heeded the call to emigrate to the Muslim camp. The Kambarin Beriberi settlement at Gummi demonstrates that immigrants were welcomed during the *jihad*. They contributed to the construction of the defensive walls of Saifawa, where Usuman dan Fodio established an early capital. By settling in Gummi, in the Zamfara River valley, and later at Kano, Sokoto, Katsina and other places, the Kambarin Beriberi were able to invest in the lucrative trade with Asante, exporting Borno natron in order to buy kola nuts.[89]

Other Kambarin Beriberi moved into the Benue River valley. They settled at Lafia, Kambari and other towns where they found themselves in a similarly advantageous position to handle Borno salt and natron exports, as well as other goods, and they could buy locally-made salt too. Whether many of the Borno settlers in the Benue Valley actually dealt in salt and natron is not clear, but in 1867 Rohlfs met a party of 'Kanuri from Lafia' at Zaranda, west of Bauchi, who were carrying sacks of 'dirty grey' salt, presumably from the Benue salines.[90]

Those Borno immigrants who became brokers in the cloth and salt trade of the central depots also reflected this economic shift away from Borno. The number of these immigrants cannot be calculated easily, but virtually every major textile centre between Kano and Zaria – there were well over thirty – had its community of Borno immigrants who acted as cloth and salt brokers. As Shea has demonstrated, Borno settlers were a particularly significant element in the local population of Dal, Zarewa, Fellatan, Belli, Rogo, Dan Guzuri and Makarfi – precisely where *kore* textiles were made for the Borno market.[91]

In the context of increased trade in general, this demographic shift is even more impressive. Many Hausa merchants, not just those of Borno origin, took kola nuts, cloth, and other goods to Borno in order to buy salt and natron.[92] Significantly, reports of Borno immigrants dot the historical record for the rest of the century. No comparable movement of people to Borno from the Hausa towns as settlers has been registered. Zinder attracted Hausa immigrants, but then Damagaram expanded because of its commercial links with the caliphate, despite its nominal loyalty to Borno and the occasional raids exchanged between Zinder and the caliphate. Zinder's position as the savanna base for the Kel Ewey, the gateway across the Sahara for the caliphate, and the transit centre in the exchange between Muniyo and Katsina was due to its geographical proximity to the caliphate, not its formal relationship with Borno.

The entry of Manga peasants into the natron and *manda* trade between Mangari and the Hausa towns was a further manifestation of the commercial hegemony of the caliphate. Manga merchants competed with itinerant traders from Kano, Zaria and elsewhere who travelled to the salt markets of Borno. They relied on resident *fatoma* in the caliphate, and few, if any, of these Manga merchants travelled further west. The profitable re-export trade and the local distribution of salt and natron were left in the hands of the *fatoma* and other Hausa businessmen. Furthermore, the Manga trade to the west bypassed the centre of nineteenth-century Borno. Kukawa lay far to the east of the Mangari–Muniyo region, and only the Lake Chad trona trade had to traverse central Borno. Mangari and Muniyo had become economic provinces of the Sokoto Caliphate.

Another consequence which accelerated the growing dependence of the salt industry on the Hausa economy was the collapse of the Borno textile industry, which had been centred in the Birni Ngazargamu area before 1808. In the nineteenth century textiles from Kano and northern Zaria supplanted Borno production. Indeed many textile workers emigrated to Kano and Zaria, some perhaps as slaves captured during the early *jihad* campaigns but others as freemen, probably as part of the exodus related to the changing political situation. The textiles for which Borno was once famous could not compete with the very same fabrics which were now produced more cheaply and on a larger scale in the Hausa centres.[93] Cloth had to be imported from the Hausa emirates, and these imports had to be purchased with local resources, particularly salt, natron and livestock.

The currency system, which had been based on units of copper (*rottl*) and strips of cloth (*gabaga*) that were manufactured in Borno, gave way to the use of cowrie shells – the currency of the Sokoto Caliphate. By 1848 the *gabaga* was officially replaced by cowries, although in some parts of Borno, including Mangari and Muniyo, there was resistance to this new currency as late as the 1850s,[94] and cowries and *gabaga* appear to have circulated alongside each other. The import of shells, which came from the caliphate, cost Borno additional resources which only aggravated the economic dislocation that resulted from the movement of the textile industry to the caliphate. Cloth had been one of the main items of purchase by salt workers as well as being a standard of value in the salt districts. Once this link was severed, merchants from the Hausa region were able to penetrate the salt markets in greater numbers than ever before. Their presence filled the vacuum left by the emigration of the Borno merchant community, and the cloth and cowries that they brought satisfied local demand for textiles and currency.

THE IMPACT OF THE CALIPHATE AT THE BENUE AND DALLOL SALINES

In contrast to the salt deposits of Borno which were increasingly brought within the commercial orbit of the Sokoto Caliphate but never incorporated politically, the Benue salines, including Awe, Azara, Keana and the other salines on the northern side of the Benue, were formally annexed; the only exceptions being several small workings that remained under Tiv control. Keana was placed directly under Bauchi, while Awe, Azara and the other salines recognised Wase, which was a sub-emirate under Bauchi. At some sites the old proprietors lost their control of salt production, as recent Muslim immigrants seized the opportunity presented by the Bauchi *jihad* to usurp political power in the salt-producing towns and villages and thereby gain control over production and marketing of salt. Some of the Jukun and Alago, who had controlled the salines, were dispersed and consequently lost all access to production; other Jukun and Alago remained in the area, but with greatly reduced rights of access. The Jukun of Awe were allowed rights at Kekura and retained limited rights at Awe itself. A similar division occurred at Ribi, the small site controlled by the Alago before the *jihad*. The Alago of Keana maintained their hold of that town, however.[95]

Unomah dates the outbreak of the *jihad* in the area to about 1812, when Bauchi forces moved west from Wase with the aim of bringing the salt district, Lafia and Shendam into its orbit.[96] At that time the salt region was part of Kwararafa; indeed the effective capital was situated at Wuse (not to be confused with Wase), close to Azara. Wuse had been a Jukun settlement at least since the eighteenth century. It became a refuge for the *aku*, the political and spiritual head of the state, in the early nineteenth century, when Chamba marauders ravaged the Jukun country south of the Benue. Shortly after the Jukun court had retreated to Wuse, Madaki Hassan of Bauchi established himself at Wase, to the east of the salt district. The Jukun court was defeated and moved across the Benue once again, re-establishing itself at Wukari, while the Jukun and Alago towns sought to make peace with the *jihad* army. Acceptance of tributary status did not prevent local Muslims from seizing power in the district. Kambarin Beriberi took over at Azara and Ribi; Zamfarawa took Kanje; and Katsinawa took Awe. Only the Jukun of Akiri and the Alago community at Keana maintained their old rulers and kept control of the salines, although the Jukun retained limited access at Awe, Azara, Ribi and perhaps Abuni.[97] It is not entirely clear how Akiri and Keana accommodated themselves so successfully when the others did not. The Jukun of Akiri may have supported the expulsion of the *aku* from Wuse, thereby securing a special status. Keana, as one of the three most important salines and the most distant from Wase, is a special case. It welcomed the opportunity to escape Kwararafa overlordship and recognised Bauchi directly. The Wase forces were preoccupied in other parts of the salt district, and as a consequence of good timing in its peace bid and some luck in its geographical position, Keana escaped the revolution that transformed the rest of the region.

The caliphate also conquered Dallol Fogha, which had been part of Kebbi until the *jihad*. With the fall of Birnin Kebbi, the western marches of Hausaland were laid open to the armies of the holy war. The old Hausa aristocracy re-established itself at Argungu and harassed the capital districts of Sokoto and Gwandu throughout the nineteenth century, but the salines were taken with the aid of local Fulani. Muhammad Bello, the son and successor of Usuman dan Fodio, destroyed Birnin Debe, a town midway between Birnin Kebbi and Dallol Fogha that interfered with consolidation of the western marches. Refugees from Birnin Debe subsequently settled at Kawara-Debe in Dallol Fogha, which was placed under Fulani administration. Resistance flared among the Dendi population of the region, so that the southern part of Dallol Fogha was sometimes independent. The stronghold of this opposition was Yelu, located in southern Dallol Maouri, only a few miles from the salt district.[98] None the less, the salines of Kawara-Debe and the northern Dallol remained in caliphate hands.

Dallol Bosso was also part of the caliphate in the nineteenth century, although again local resistance made caliphate control doubtful at times. Fulani cattle herders had shared the grazing lands of Dallol Bosso with various Tuareg nomads in the eighteenth century, and the local Djerma population had to accept the presence of both groups. The *jihad* offered an opportunity for the Fulani to consolidate their position. From a base north of Birnin Gaoure, Boubacar Louloudji led a campaign to secure the valley. Boubacar Louloudji was allied with the Fulani of Say, one of the emirates in the caliphate, on the Niger River. From 1816 to 1830, the situation was confused. Boubacar was established at Tamkalla, but the Djerma farmers held out for twenty years. Not until 1849 were the Fulani, under Boubacar's son Abdoul Assane, able to control the region between Dallol Bosso and Dallol Fogha.[99]

Caliphate policy was not preoccupied with salt, although the trade was taxed and brought in considerable revenue. In both the Dallols and the Benue Valley, conquest was left to local leaders who sought to establish their own influence. Loyalty to the central administration was advantageous because of military and diplomatic support. Bauchi played such a major role in the Benue Valley that the salines were recognised as dependencies of Bauchi Emirate – Keana directly under Bauchi, the rest indirectly through Wase. Dallol Fogha came within the jurisdiction of Kebbi because independent Kebbi had controlled the valley in the eighteenth century. Tamkalla was a new emirate fashioned out of Fulani transhumant patterns; Dallol Bosso was the most fertile part of its territory. As is clear from the political history outlined above, effective control of the salines fluctuated in the course of the nineteenth century. Parts of the Dallols were in open rebellion at mid-century, while the loyalty of Wase to Bauchi was not always strong and Wase's influence at the Benue salines was sometimes marginal. None the less, salines were an important resource in all these cases, and a desire to control them was certainly an important motivation, if only locally.

THE HEGEMONY OF THE SOKOTO CALIPHATE

The caliphate came to dominate the salt trade because of the size of its market and the activities of its merchants, and hence the history of salt ultimately fits into the general economic history of the caliphate. The *jihad* of 1804–08 united the central Hausa country into a single state for the first time. Despite political insecurity from raiding and banditry, this political consolidation enabled the concentration of population on a larger scale than ever before. The highest densities were found in Katsina Emirate (south of the city), in the closely-settled zone of Kano Emirate (including a belt that stretched to northern Zaria Emirate), and in the Sokoto–Rima River basin. These areas already possessed a considerable population before 1804. Some of this population was dispersed, at least temporarily, but the number of people increased significantly over pre-*jihad* levels because of immigration, both slave and free. Increased population invariably meant a larger market for salt and natron. While quantifiable data on the growth of the market are lacking, it seems reasonable to conclude that the market did indeed grow, probably substantially.

The expansion of the market related not only to increased population but also to an improvement in the relative prosperity of that population. Watts is undoubtedly correct in thinking that much of the peasantry faced the perennial danger of famine, in part because so many peasants barely eked out an existence at subsistence level and, I would add, because much of the slave population was first to suffer when times were difficult, but also in part because localised drought was a common occurrence in the nineteenth century.[100] Despite the general level of poverty, however variable and unpredictable, the number of relatively prosperous commoners (*talakawa*), including craftsmen, merchants, clerics, and pastoralists, increased, and the size of the bureaucracy, including slaves and aristocrats, also expanded. These sections of the population could afford to buy salt and natron on a regular basis. When combined with the occasional purchases of the poor, the total market for salt and natron was substantial and grew in direct correspondence to demographic expansion. As demonstrated in Chapter 5, several thousand tonnes of salt and natron were annually imported into Katsina, Kano and Zaria Emirates around 1900. Without the existence of a relatively prosperous and large population, these amounts would not have found a market.

Many Borno refugees and other immigrants from the desert-edge were among the people who contributed to the expansion of population in the central emirates. Some of these settlers were directly connected with the production or distribution of salt and natron. Many others were indirectly associated with changes in trade, either because they came from the districts around Birni Ngazargamu and fled upon its destruction, or because they were Agalawa and Tokarawa whose ancestors were slaves or freed slaves of the Tuareg.[101] The direction of immigration followed the salt routes. Either people came from the north and were associated with Tuareg commercial activities in the savanna, or they came from Borno along routes from the trona, *manda* and natron markets. Many of these immigrants engaged in the salt and natron trade in their new homes, and a substantial number became prosperous enough to buy or import slaves for use in commerce and agriculture. When taken together, the merchants who traded in salt and natron – the *fatoma* wholesalers, kola merchants, and others – owned considerable numbers of slaves. The scale of these holdings is impossible to estimate, but oral data indicate that hundreds of merchants owned anywhere from a score to several hundred slaves each.[102] These merchants were not only important in terms of their role in the salt trade, therefore, but they also represented the general pattern of increased prosperity and contributed to the demographic expansion of the emirates.

Other sectors of the caliphate economy were closely linked to the expansion of the salt trade and reinforced the concentration of commercial capital in the Hausa emirates, particularly Kano, Zaria and Katsina. The textile industry, for example, grew dramatically in the nineteenth century, in part because cloth was a major export to the salt markets of Borno and the desert, and in part because commerce was expanding in general. As Shea's data have established, Kano alone developed a large export-oriented dyeing industry that included an estimated 15,000–20,000 dye pits employing 50,000 or so dyers by the end of the century.[103] This industry extended into northern Zaria, where several thousand more pits were located and thousands of additional dyers lived. Textile brokers, also known as *fatoma*, organised the production of dyed cloth and often imported salt and natron on a considerable scale. Specific centres catered to the Tuareg trade, while others made cloth destined for the Borno market.

The development of the textile industry demonstrates two important changes in the regional economy of the central Sudan, and these changes affected the structure of the salt trade. First, the decline of Borno textile production in the face of competition from the Hausa emirates shifted the focus of the textile industry from a district that was adjacent to major sources of salt to a region that had become the largest market for salt and natron. Secondly, expansion of Hausa textile production resulted in the greater integration of commercial patterns. Whereas Borno had made its own cloth before 1800 and the Tuareg had bought their cloth from Hausa craftsmen, after 1800 both industries were concentrated in the same region. Dyeing centres could shift production from one trade to the other, depending upon market demand. This advantage helped destroy the Borno industry and probably kept textile prices lower than they otherwise would have been. This competitive advantage worked to the benefit of the economy as a whole, for cheaper textiles resulted in an expanded domestic and export market. The salt traders facilitated this expansion because they were major purchasers of textiles. In effect, the salt trade and the distributional network for Hausa textiles overlapped.

The consolidation of the Sokoto Caliphate was also linked to the concentration of the salt trade in the Hausa emirates. The extension of the *jihad* south-eastward into the Benue River basin and further south into Adamawa opened up a vast region to Hausa trade. Salt from the Benue salines and natron from Borno were exported along these new commercial corridors, as merchants went south to buy ivory, slaves and, by the end of the century, kola nuts. Hausa merchants became more common in Nupe, Ilorin, and other emirates that were newly incorporated into the caliphate, and again the link with the salt trade is well established. While *manda* and *kantu* were not exported to these emirates in appreciable amounts, natron and trona were. Hundreds of tonnes, perhaps more, of natron and trona fed these markets by 1900, and as this trade spread to Lagos in the 1880s, the scale of exports increased to accommodate markets as far away as Sierra Leone. The expansion of trade south-west through the Bariba states to the middle Volta basin and Asante can be linked to the general growth of long-distance trade after 1800. The volume of natron exported along these routes was only a small portion of the total trade in salt and natron, but given the importance of the kola traders who operated along the routes to Asante, the inclusion of natron and trona in their assortment of exports reflects the links between the salt industry and other sectors of the central Sudan economy. The incorporation of the Benue salines, the Dallols and the western portions of Borno where some of the salt markets of Muniyo were located is further evidence of the close association between the centralisation of the salt marketing network in the Hausa emirates and the consolidation of the Sokoto Caliphate as an empire. These salines competed locally for a share of the regional market.

Until the middle of the eighteenth century, the Borno state had a near monopoly of salt production in the central Sudan, for most of the major salines were under its domination. These salines included Kawar and Fachi in the desert and the districts of Muniyo, Gourbei (Mangari), Kadzell, and Foli in the sahel. Only the desert site of Teguidda n'tesemt, the sahel sites of Dallol Fogha and Dallol Bosso and the Benue Valley brine springs were outside of Borno, but in each of these cases the production of salt was more limited and held a competitive advantage only locally. For much of the Hausa country and all of Borno, virtually the only sources of mineral salts were the Borno salines. The importance of these salines did not diminish after the middle of the eighteenth century, but Borno lost control of Kawar and Fachi, which effectively destroyed the state's monopoly position. Thereafter, the Tuareg established their hegemony at Bilma and Fachi, the two most important salines in the desert region of Borno. This transformation resulted in a significant shift in the economic control of the salt industry from one in which a state asserted political domination of salt production to one in which transporters and merchants established a monopoly over the trade of these salines. For the next century and a half, the Tuareg controlled the desert salines, including Kawar, Fachi and Teguidda n'tesemt, and Borno was left with its sahelian sites. While desert and sahel produced somewhat different salts, there was nevertheless competition between the two sectors. By the end

249

of the nineteenth century, no state had a monopoly or near monopoly of salt production. By that time the salt industry of the central Sudan was effectively divided into four sectors, including the desert salines controlled by the Tuareg, the Borno sahelian locations, the Benue brine springs, and the two Dallols (Fogha and Bosso). In addition, significant quantities of imported European salt had entered the market, which in effect added a fifth source.

The Sokoto Caliphate did not try to impose a monopoly over salt production because many of the sites in the desert and Borno were far beyond the borders of the empire. Perhaps if the caliphate had been successful in the *jihad* against Borno, a new monopoly situation would have arisen in which a state could have dominated all the major sources of salt in the central Sudan. In any event, the caliphate came to control the salt trade because of its economic importance in the region. Instead of limiting production for monopoly purposes, the caliphate expanded into the Dallols and the Benue basin, and its political domination actually encouraged production, despite local political upheavals in both regions at different times in the nineteenth century. Neither the rebellion in the lower Dallol Fogha nor the marauding raids of Dan Karo and Bayero in the Benue Valley at the end of the century reversed this trend towards greater output.[104] From the perspective of the caliphate government, greater production in all sectors of the economy promoted trade and the prosperity of the Muslim state. As I have already argued in Chapter 8, the taxation of trade – through the periodic gifts (*gaisuwa*) of merchants, transit duties at rivers (*fito*), and general duties on imports (*garama*) – was an important source of revenue for the state and its officials.

CONCLUSION

While this chapter has examined the interaction between the salt trade and political history, it is possible to delve deeper into the relationship between state and economy, as this relationship is revealed by a study of salt. As is clear from the discussion in Chapter 7, the Tuareg, Borno and the Sokoto Caliphate intervened in the economy in a manner that determined proprietary rights over the salines, and the study of commercial networks in Chapter 8 demonstrates that trade was shaped by political interference. Earlier chapters have revealed constraints on political intervention, including the technological backwardness of the industry, which placed limits on the scale and intensity of production, and climatic irregularities that could disrupt production. Labour mobilisation also affected production, and unlike climate and technology which were largely or completely beyond the control of political authorities, the recruitment of labour could be regulated, however imperfectly. The question of labour mobilisation, therefore, also draws attention to the relationship between the state and the economy. This chapter has examined trade and politics, but when this analysis is considered in combination with the technology of production, forms of labour mobilisation, the nature of proprietorship, and the commercial structures of the trade, then it is possible to determine the ways in which the economy changed as a result of state intervention. In the following chapter the dynamic elements in this political economy – state intervention, proprietary relationships, forms of labour recruitment, and ethnicity – are examined.

10

The social organisation of trade and production

ETHNICITY AND THE RELATIONS OF PRODUCTION

In examining the relations of production of the salt industry, it has been necessary to discuss ecology, technology, chemistry and various other factors that affected how people interacted in the utilisation of the salt resources of the central Sudan. The existence of a regional market in which different salts competed has allowed me to consider the industry as a single unit of analysis, even though there were many salines and the markets for these did not overlap entirely. The principal purpose of this regional approach has been to demonstrate how people responded to market demand and how the forces of production varied in the region as a whole. A regional approach is implicitly comparative, since very different relations of production characterised the different salines that form the basis of this analysis.

Seen from the perspective of the region as a whole, it might seem as if ethnicity was the fundamental organising principle that brought the forces of production together. The saline workers, the saline proprietors and the salt merchants usually belonged to different ethnic groups or different ethnic fractions. The ethnicity of the workers varied the most; each saline or set of salines had its own ethnic association. Unravelling the development of this complex cultural mosaic has been essential in reconstructing the social relations of trade and production and how these relations changed. The problem with focussing on ethnicity alone is that such a focus distorts the dynamics of the social formation. Ethnic identities changed. Uncovering why they changed shifts the analysis away from a static examination of social relations based on ethnicity back to a dynamic analysis of the forces of production.

This chapter explores the interface between class and ethnicity in the context of the salt trade. The aim is to explain the forces of production of the industry and thereby to contribute to an understanding of the historical development of the political economy of the central Sudan. Ethnic relations are analysed as a means of uncovering the forces of production. The analysis uses as a starting point the theoretical framework of Frederik Barth, whose study of ethnicity has concentrated on the interaction between people across ethnic boundaries. According to Barth, 'ethnic groups are categories of ascription and identification by the actors themselves, and thus have the characteristic of organising interaction between people'.[1] An ethnic group is largely self-perpetuating biologically, shares fundamental cultural values that are realised in overt cultural forms, makes up a field of communication and interaction, and has a membership which identifies itself, and is identified by others, as constituting a distinguishable category of people.[2] It is argued here that ethnic groups and fractions of ethnic groups characterised the organisation of trade and production in the central Sudan salt industry, but that these groups have to be analysed in the context of the relations of production, thereby exposing the meaning of ethnicity in the context of class relationships. An examination of the interface between class and ethnicity exposes the forces of production – why certain people controlled the means of production and why others provided the labour force necessary for that production.

The study of the salt industry has indeed revealed a complex cultural mosaic. Salt workers of diverse ethnic identities, including Manga, Mobbeur, Segurti, Kanuri, Ingelshi, Hausa, and Alago, sold the product of their labour to merchants who had still other ethnic identities, including Tuareg, Yedina, Hausa and Kanembu. These merchants in turn often sold their supplies to other merchants in an exchange that once again involved cross-cultural interaction. As Curtin has pointed out, such cross-cultural trade has been common in history.[3] One can add that cross-cultural interaction was even more widespread, for the salt proprietors themselves were sometimes ethnically distinct from the workers, and merchants frequently catered to markets in which consumers were of yet other ethnic groups.

On the most general level, this mosaic included Hausa, Kanuri and Tuareg, whose significance as ethnic labels extends far beyond the history of salt. In the nineteenth century Hausa was the language of the caliphate and of the commercial networks that radiated outward from the caliphate. Before then Hausa had a more restricted meaning as a term that applied to the various Hausa states of Kano, Katsina, Gobir, Kebbi, Zazzau and Zamfara. Kanuri was the ethnic label for Borno, although sometimes it was used to apply only to the ruling aristocracy of the Saifawa state. In this sense Kanuri referred to the Borno nobility in the same way that Fulani referred to the Muslim aristocracy of the caliphate. This use of both 'Fulani' and 'Kanuri' confused ethnicity and class, for not all Fulani were rulers and Kanuri was also used as a convenient term to refer to the people who spoke the language of Borno, whether or not they spoke the Kanembu dialect, Kanuri proper, Manga, or some other variant. As such, Kanuri had a political and historical significance connected with the Borno state. Tamachek, as the language of the Tuareg, was the specialised tongue of the desert, and as such was a language that served the trade of the desert-edge and corresponded with the ecological division between sedentary and nomadic life.

The meaning of these ethnic terms changed over time, as is evident in the correspondence of Hausa and Kanuri with the political fortunes of the Sokoto Caliphate and Borno. The conception of Hausa changed with the creation of the Sokoto Caliphate; it became associated with the dominant culture of the

253

caliphate, and the Hausa language became the language of communication for most of the caliphate. Kanuri, by contrast, had a more restricted meaning in the nineteenth century than it had earlier, when it was the ethnic term associated with the Borno empire. With the decline of Borno in the early nineteenth century, the number of people who identified as Kanuri also decreased. In both cases, moreover, Hausa and Kanuri ethnicity incorporated numerous sub-ethnic groups or ethnic fractions, so that in both cases ethnicity was broadly-based and heterogeneous. These ethnic groups were not small, closely-knit groups of people but were the product of cultures that were associated with the expansion of political states. In the context of this political history numerous other ethnic groups maintained separate identities as a means of establishing their autonomy from the dominant political cultures. Moreover, ethnic fractions within Hausa and Kanuri societies used ethnicity as a means of controlling interaction within the dominant cultures. In short, ethnic consciousness was a vital force in the organisation of relations between people.

Ethnicity had meaning in terms of conflict, as people struggled to protect economic rights, occupational privileges and political position. The result of this struggle was the emergence and maintenance of a cultural mosaic. As social and economic realities changed, so did the cultural mosaic. Ethnic groups were constantly forming, disbanding and reforming, depending upon political and economic factors. As Frederik Barth has argued,

> categorical ethnic distinctions...entail social processes of exclusion and incorporation whereby discrete categories are maintained *despite* changing participation and membership in the course of individual life histories....One finds that stable, persisting, and often vitally important social relations are maintained across such boundaries, and are frequently based precisely on the dichotomized ethnic statuses. In other words, ethnic distinctions do not depend on an absence of social interaction and acceptance, but are quite to the contrary often the very foundations on which embracing social systems are built.[4]

The boundaries between ethnic groups had meaning precisely because people interacted across those boundaries, whether those boundaries also coincided with political frontiers (the Agades Confederation, Borno and the Sokoto Caliphate or the Hausa states before 1804) or with ecological divisions (desert–savanna and Lake Chad–savanna).

When people remained beyond ethnic frontiers, they changed their ethnic allegiance, sometimes as a result of commercial opportunities and sometimes because of political problems. Immigrants in the Sokoto Caliphate who came from Borno or the desert-edge stopped being Kanuri or Tuareg and became Hausa. When slaves were brought into the desert to join nomadic groups, they became Tuareg, and those slaves who were settled in the caliphate or Borno usually became Hausa or Kanuri. Such flows across ethnic boundaries by individuals or small groups demonstrate that ethnicity was dynamic; ethnicity was modified in accordance with political and economic forces. Ethnic boundaries provide insight into what people thought was important in terms of their identity. Ethnic groups were constantly being made, unmade and remade, depending upon the relationship of people to the control of the means of production.

FROM POLITICAL ECONOMY TO CLASS ANALYSIS

The previous chapter outlined the major changes in the political history of the central Sudan over several centuries before 1900 as these affected the salt industry. The composition of the aristocracy experienced two major alterations in this period. First, the Kel Ewey, Kel Gress, Itisen and Kel Dinnik secured their places along the desert-edge in the eighteenth century, and the balance of power that was attained guaranteed the continuation of aristocratic control of the desert-side resources. The Kel Ewey, centred in the Air Massif, the Kel Gress and Itisen, re-established in Adar, and the Kel Dinnik, located in Azawaq, maintained an uneasy truce that was more or less mediated through the Sultanate of Agades. Effective political and economic power was concentrated in the hands of the noble lineages of these Tuareg fractions. Subsequent political and economic changes altered the relationship between these fractions and permitted the participation of other fractions in the desert-side political economy, but later changes did not alter the nature of class relationships among the Tuareg.

Secondly, the *jihad* of 1804–12 revolutionised class relations in the savanna regions of the central Sudan. It brought to power a Fulani elite in the caliphate which largely replaced the former Hausa aristocracy, and it resulted in serious changes in the composition of the Borno nobility. The Fulani elite represented an entirely new aristocracy, since its members were drawn from the ranks of immigrant pastoralists and clerics who had previously been only marginal to the political process. This elite was actually composed of Torodbe – the sedentary Fulani clerical class of diverse, often humble origins – and the nomadic clan leaders who controlled much of the pastoral activities of the rural Fulani. The amalgamation of these two groups took several decades, but in the process of class solidification, they succeeded in spreading caliphate rule over a very large area. Not only were existing relationships transformed but these were extended throughout much of the central Sudan. In Borno, the *jihad* resulted in the emergence of a new dynasty – that of al-Kanemi – but some members of the old aristocracy continued to have influence. The change in Borno involved the decimation of the old aristocracy and its replacement by new recruits. Class relationships continued as before; only the personnel were partially different.

The replacement of the Hausa aristocracy by the Fulani leadership and the augmentation of the Borno aristocracy with the family and supporters of al-Kanemi altered the composition of the aristocratic classes, but the basic relationship between aristocracy and peasantry remained unchanged. That relationship was based on tributary collections that were generated from within the central Sudan. The new aristocracies of the nineteenth century modified

255

these relationships in that they relied more on enslavement and the threat of enslavement than had been the case before the *jihad*. Subsequently, the incidence of slavery increased, and slaves became a vital source of labour in production, particularly in agriculture. Slave-based production was not new, but the relative importance of slavery with respect to the independent peasantry increased. While larger numbers of slaves made possible the greater exploitation of labour by the aristocracy and by merchants, this intensification of slavery did not alter the essentially regional orientation of the economy. Regional markets and local demands continued to direct the relations of production.

The Tuareg aristocracy, the Fulani regime of the Sokoto Caliphate and the al-Kanemi government of Borno had varying interests in the salt trade. The Tuareg monopolised salt distribution from the desert sites, and hence the Tuareg leaders were directly interested in salt trade and production as well. As has been demonstrated in Chapter 9, they intervened in the organisation of production in order to assure their commercial position. Tuareg 'merchants' included the nobility, vassals, former slaves (*irewelen*) and slaves, although the nobles seldom went to Bilma and Fachi. The trip was left to vassals, *irewelen* and slaves, who were the workers of the salt trade. The Borno aristocracy was interested in salt because of tribute collections related to proprietary rights to salines, but only a portion of the aristocracy had a direct interest in salt production. This relationship was similar to other class interests of the aristocracy, including those in agriculture, livestock production, trade and craft industries. The Borno aristocracy depended upon tributary relations with the other parts of Borno society but otherwise was not directly involved in the salt trade, as the Tuareg nobles were. Finally the Fulani aristocracy of the Sokoto Caliphate had very little direct interest in salt. The government encouraged and taxed trade – any trade, including salt – but only locally in the Benue Valley and at the Dallols was there any interest in the tribute that could be raised from the production of salt. Even at these salines, the proprietors of salt flats were not really part of the dominant aristocracy of the caliphate. They had more in common with merchants than with the Fulani nobility.

Aristocratic rule allowed extensive autonomy for members of the dominant classes. The Tuareg of the desert, the Borno nobility and the Fulani rulers of the caliphate acted in their own interests and struggled amongst themselves for power within the central Sudan. This struggle directly affected the history of the salt trade, as has been documented with such instances as the Bilma war of c. 1759, the *jihad* in Borno, and the struggle of the Borno aristocracy to retain control of the salt districts. Despite these tensions between and within the three aristocracies, all sections of the dominant class recognised and promoted acceptance of a broad ideological framework that derived from Islam. One can speak of the hegemonic function of Islam, to alter a phrase of Eugene Genovese.[5] Governments and individuals were judged in terms of their Islamic credentials, and while there was extensive disagreement as to what was considered legitimate and who was pious, there was common agreement that adherence to Islam was the standard by which actions should be judged.

Among the Tuareg, certain tribal fractions – particularly the leaders of these fractions – were devoutly Muslim and were widely recognised as upholders of the faith. While the sharp division between warrior and cleric was not as pronounced among the Tuareg as it was among the Moors of the western Sahara, the reliance on Islam as a guide to legitimacy was just as clear.[6] The Tuareg aristocracy justified its ascendancy not only in terms of real power – control over camels, ability to mobilise dependants, domination of water and grazing rights – but also in terms of Islamic credentials. Vassals, slaves and other dependants were viewed as inferior because they were not considered to be as good Muslims as the aristocracy considered itself. Religion reinforced class distinctions within Tuareg society.

In both the Sokoto Caliphate and Borno, the *jihad* intensified the association between Islam and the aristocracy, in the caliphate because the Fulani leaders – especially Torodbe – were the champions of the new theocracy and in Borno because al-Kanemi represented Islamic reform in the face of Fulani aggression. The bitter diplomatic correspondence between Muhammad Bello and al-Kanemi on the legitimacy of the Fulani war with Borno demonstrates the significance of Islam on the ideological level.[7] Both sides argued on the basis of Islam that they were right to pursue their policies – the caliphate, its invasion of Borno, and Borno, its resistance to that invasion. While the two sides did not reach an acceptable compromise, they did succeed in strengthening the commitment to rule on behalf of aristocratic, Islamic class interests.

The merchant class – whether it was Hausa, Kanuri or Tuareg – accepted the legitimacy of Islamic class rule. For merchants, Islam and trade went together, and historically the merchant community had supported the Islamic clerics with their alms and had provided recruits from among their sons for the clergy. In the nineteenth century some sections of the merchant class were closely associated with the clergy, most especially merchants of Borno origin and merchants of Mande origin. Clerics and merchants often came from the same families. But other sections of the merchant class, including the Agalawa and Tokarawa, only gave alms. Clerics were not recruited from their ranks until the twentieth century.[8] Despite these differences, all merchants accepted the general principles of commercial life – allegiance to Islam, support of the Muslim clergy, and reliance on clerics for advice.

Salt workers too supported clerics and recognised the hegemonic power of religion. They gave alms to clerics, and, as has been demonstrated for Mangari and Foli, Muslim clerics were essential to the ceremonies that legalised tributary relations and opened the salt season. In Foli, the aristocracy may not have considered the *haddad* artisans Muslim, but the *haddad* considered themselves Muslims, as their recognition of Muslim clerics demonstrates.[9] The question of who was a good Muslim and who was not puzzled many people in the central Sudan in the nineteenth century, not just al-Kanemi and

Muhammad Bello. Each class identified with Islam but what that meant in practice differed.

The Manga revolts against the al-Kanemi government demonstrate how different classes interpreted their actions within an Islamic framework.[10] Even though al-Kanemi represented Islamic reform within Borno, the Manga peasants did not readily accept al-Kanemi's claim to Islamic legitimacy. Instead, they chose to oppose the dynastic pretensions of the al-Kanemi regime. Their leaders in these popular uprisings were Muslim clerics who were in tune with the aspirations of the peasantry. The Manga were in fact asserting their claim to work the salt districts of Gourbei, which could only be achieved with the decline of central government control. Yet they struggled for their autonomy by demanding the reinstatement of the Saifawa dynasty. As a restorationist movement, the rebellions were justified in the name of Islam and dynastic legitimacy, which confirms the importance of the hegemonic power of Islam and aristocratic rule; only in the context of the first half of the nineteenth century the Manga peasantry was struggling against the new noble class by posing as champions of the old noble class. For the Manga salt workers, the result was the establishment of a new order in the salt districts.

The hegemonic umbrella which derived from religious culture was based on the implementation of *Shari'a* law, the influence of Muslim clerics, and the perpetuation of an Islamic political tradition. This agency of class rule was clearly established before the *jihad* of 1804–12. The *jihad* legitimised the transfer of power to a new elite throughout much of the central Sudan; the class structure of central Sudanese society was transformed in accordance with political change. In the Benue basin, the subordination of local society to Islamic rule came about as a direct result of military expansion. In the Dallols, incorporation into the caliphate placed local society more directly under aristocratic control than had been the case, at least since the height of Kebbi rule in the sixteenth century.

The social formation that encompassed the Agades Confederation, Borno and the Sokoto Caliphate was inwardly directed. Its links with the outside world – particularly with the capitalist world – remained marginal for the whole of the nineteenth century, although it is possible to detect some pressures on the central Sudan region as early as the late eighteenth century.[11] Capitalist penetration was blunted by the great distances from the Guinea Coast and from the Mediterranean. Beginning in the late eighteenth century, slaves were exported through Oyo and ivory, hides and skins and other goods were shipped across the Sahara. This trade marked the first links between the economy of the central Sudan and the European world. In the nineteenth century, these contacts intensified, and by the end of the century the demands of the world market had encouraged a number of economic changes on the periphery of the central Sudan economy. Shea butter exports from Nupe, ivory shipments from Adamawa, and the export of ostrich feathers, civet, and hides and skins from the desert-edge became important locally, while such sectors as kola imports and textile and natron exports were indirectly related to the penetration of capitalism into other parts of West Africa. In terms of long-range developments, this penetration of capitalism presaged major structural changes in the relations of production, but, despite the growing influence of capitalism, there was little direct effect on most sectors of the central Sudan economy even as late as the end of the nineteenth century.

Nowhere is the regional orientation of the economy more evident than in the case of the salt industry, which experienced few changes that can be associated with capitalist penetration, despite the rapid expansion of European salt imports towards the end of the nineteenth century. Before 1900 changes in the salt industry derived from alterations in the regional political economy, not from the expansion of capitalism. Because of the absence of links to capitalism, we can say that primitive accumulation characterised the salt market. Merchants and aristocrats found ways to extract surplus from salt workers, either through the profits of long-distance trade or from the various taxes on production. In neither case did accumulation lead to the consolidation of sufficient amounts of capital for any alteration to take place in the relations of production. The salt trade remained a regional trade. Salt merchants invested their modest returns in other commodities and sometimes purchased slaves for use in agriculture and trade, but no really large entrepreneurs emerged within the salt industry. The profits of the salt trade were dissipated over a vast region, with producers, merchants and aristocrats sharing in the proceeds in a fashion that only reinforced the existing social relations of production.

The composition of the merchant class changed over the several centuries before 1900. Individuals from non-mercantile backgrounds joined the merchant community, and new routes were developed beyond the central lands of Borno and the Hausa cities. In broad outline, this expansion resulted in the consolidation of a Hausa-dominated commercial diaspora and the gradual absorption of an earlier Borno-centred network. In the seventeenth century, the merchant community was either tied to Borno or connected with Juula commercial settlements in the western Sudan. After 1800, Hausa became the commercial language of an enlarged network, as merchants from the caliphate came to dominate the trade of the central Sudan. Such changes affected the salt trade, as has been demonstrated in Chapter 8. Individuals could participate in this expansion if they saw themselves as Muslims and spoke Hausa. Acceptance of Islam and fluency in Hausa were prerequisites for membership in the merchant class.

The *jihad* forced a restructuring of the merchant class. Kanuri, Hausa and Tuareg merchants had to adjust to new political realities that included the consolidation of the caliphate and the political and economic decline of Borno. These adjustments resulted in the expansion of a Muslim, Hausa diaspora under the aegis of the caliphate. Either merchants saw themselves as Hausa or they established business connexions with Hausa brokers. In either case, the creation of an avowedly Islamic government reinforced merchant

259

preoccupation with Islam, which had long facilitated cross-cultural trade in West Africa. The consolidation of an enlarged and reconstituted merchant class is best symbolised by the histories of Agalawa, Tokarawa, Kambarin Beriberi, Beriberi and other commercial groups. Agalawa and Tokarawa personified the Tuareg–Hausa link. Tuareg in origin, these merchants were some of the most important Hausa merchants of the nineteenth century. The Kambarin Beriberi and Beriberi represented the old Borno merchant class, which had been displaced in the *jihad* and in the period of economic decline that befell Borno after 1812. Despite their Borno origins, they too identified as Muslim Hausa. The take-over of the Benue salines – done in the name of Islam – was a further victory for the enlarged merchant class. Merchants from Borno or from Katsina, Zamfara, Kano and other Hausa centres seized power at most of the salines. They then organised production for their own benefit.

The salt workers, as producers, were caught in a squeeze between merchants and aristocrats. They were forced to pay tribute in a variety of forms to those who controlled access to the salines, on the one hand, and they had to accept relatively low prices for their salt from the merchants, on the other hand. Undoubtedly tribute payments and prices varied, but the profits to be made from salt production were derived from proprietary rights and from the ability to move salt great distances, with a corresponding mark-up in price. The producers themselves achieved only modest returns for their labour. Much of the history of production was based on individual or collective efforts to lessen this squeeze between merchants and aristocrats. Depending upon political and climatic conditions, workers strove to become merchants and thereby transfer their allegiance from one class to another, or they emphasised cultural and other distinctions which strengthened their corporate, and hence class, solidarity.

The class identity of workers was complex because peasants, slaves and artisans all produced salt. Each saline or system of salines had its own set of workers. Consequently, the methods of extracting surplus from the working population varied. These differences have been examined in Chapters 6 and 7 but are briefly summarised here. It is important to point out that the methods of exploiting labour arose out of historically specific conditions, but in each case workers had to struggle to retain a portion of their output. Whether workers were slaves, free peasants or members of the *haddad* caste, they surrendered a major part of the product of their labour to merchants and aristocrats.

In Mangari and Muniyo, Manga peasants migrated to the salt basins to make *manda* in the nineteenth century; before then it is probable that slaves were used in at least some parts of the salt district. By the end of the nineteenth century, slaves were being used once again, but only as a supplement to the dominant form of labour – the peasantry. In neighbouring Kadzell, slaves were almost the only source of labour for *kige* production, although some Manga and Mobbeur peasants worked alongside them. Slaves and migrant peasants also made salt in Dallol Fogha, at least in the nineteenth century and probably earlier still, while in Dallol Bosso slavery seems to have been the only source of labour. In the desert sites, slaves were also the major source of labour, but many worked alongside their masters. How far back in time slavery was dominant is not clear, but it seems likely that slave labour was the basis of salt production in the desert for many centuries. In Foli, artisans provided the labour, not only in the nineteenth century but probably earlier still. Slavery was confined to other sectors of the economy, but the nature of the caste structure of Kanem society was such that artisans were servile in status. Surplus was extracted through the state and its officials because workers were identified with the *haddad* caste. Finally, in the Benue basin, much of the labour was also derived from the output of slaves, despite the fact that the work was supposed to be only for women. The sexual division of labour that assigned salt production to the same sphere as cooking disguised the real basis of the social organisation of labour. Before the Muslim take-over in the early nineteenth century, women may have provided most, if not all, of the labour, but in the nineteenth century slaves performed much of the labour in making salt. Many of these slaves were probably women, and they were all under the supervision of women.

Workers did not constitute a single class, although the relations between workers, proprietors and merchants involved class antagonisms. Because the salines were geographically dispersed, there was virtually no communication between the salt workers of the different salines. The salt workers of Bilma probably knew very little about the people of Fachi; they certainly knew nothing about the workers at the Benue brine springs. That both sets of workers sometimes acted on the basis of class interests derived from their relations to the means of production, not their consciousness as a class. The varying status of salt workers further demonstrates the complexity of class relations. Slaves, artisans, peasants, and small-scale proprietors who worked their own holdings had similar problems in dealing with political authorities and visiting merchants, but their class positions differed. Whenever several forms of labour were employed at the same salines, these differences became important factors in the relations of production. The absence of a single class of workers does not mean that class relations were not significant, however.

ETHNICITY AND THE SALT TRADE

The structure of trade in the Sahara and across Lake Chad was dependent upon a sharp cleavage between merchants and producers that was reinforced by clear ethnic distinctions. The desert and the lake required specialised transport which shaped various aspects of the economy and society; camel nomads and island-dwellers monopolised the salt and natron trade of Kawar, Fachi, Teguidda n'tesemt, Amadror and Kanem. The organisation of trade in these sectors was tied directly to the control of the means of transport. Those who owned the camels and the lake boats had advantages that were mani-pulated to their fullest, and the producers of salt had no way of breaking out of

261

this commercial stranglehold. Because of the need to work the salines for long periods each year, the working population had to be sedentary, although at both Teguidda n'tesemt and the Foli trona depressions, workers lived elsewhere when salt and trona were not being produced – at In Gall in the case of the Teguidda workers and elsewhere in Foli and southern Kanem in the case of the trona workers. Invariably the different needs of transportation and production were reflected in the different ways of life of nomads and sedentary people, and these differences corresponded with ethnic distinctions.

The residents of In Gall (Ingelshi) were the descendants of the sedentary society of medieval Azelik and ultimately were associated with Songhay, as reflected in the continued use of an archaic Songhay dialect as the language of production.[12] At Kawar and Fachi, the resident working population was Kanuri, in contrast to the local nomadic element of Tubu.[13] Again the cultural identification was with sedentary, savanna society that derived from medieval times. Just as Azelik was once an outpost of the Songhay empire before the sixteenth century, Kawar and Fachi were the northern limits of Kanem and Borno. Subsequent immigration to In Gall, Kawar and Fachi reinforced this pattern; immigrants became Kanuri or Ingelshi if they joined the sedentary population but they identified as Tubu or Tuareg if they were brought into nomadic society.

Although the functional importance of the nomad–sedentary division is apparent, the actual situation at any point in time was the product of a struggle between people, not a mechanistic consequence of ecological constraints imposed on human behaviour. Even when the connexion with Songhay was severed with the destruction of Azelik and the incorporation of the region into the Tuareg confederation centred on Agades, the Songhay language survived; although it was a relic of the past, it was a useful tool in maintaining a distinction between the inhabitants of In Gall and the dominant Tuareg society of the desert. The Songhay heritage protected the rights of access to the salines for the descendants of the Azelik survivors – Igdalen, Inusufa and others who settled at In Gall and became known collectively as Ingelshi.[14] Slaves or other dependants of the Tuareg could have been brought in as a new labour force. The dilemma for the inhabitants of In Gall was how to prevent such an intrusion. The Tuareg lacked the technological knowledge that would have made possible the construction of decantation basins. This technology derived from the earlier works at Guelele. Instead the Tuareg and Ingelshi reached an accommodation that allowed the Ingelshi to continue to provide the labour for salt production.[15] This arrangement necessitated Ingelshi acquiescence to Tuareg domination and Tuareg acceptance of Ingelshi monopolisation of production. Once the Teguidda salines came into production in the sixteenth or seventeenth century, the free inhabitants of In Gall were recognised as proprietors of the decantation basins, in return for tribute payments to Agades. Political authority at In Gall guaranteed that tribute was paid while at the same time community solidarity was maintained among the producers. Much of the actual work on salt production (as indeed was the case in date-palm cultivation and irrigated agriculture at In Gall) was left in the hands of slaves. The working population was servile, but the organisation of production depended upon the maintenance of ethnic boundaries.

The identification of salt production at Bilma, Fachi and Dirku with the Kanuri served a similar function to the maintenance of an archaic Songhay community at In Gall, although the link with Kanuri society in the savanna was stronger and more continuous than the connexion between the Ingelshi and the Songhay population of the Niger Valley. Borno depended upon the trans-Saharan trade through Kawar, even in the nineteenth century, after real political control had evaporated; the destruction of Songhay in 1592 severed the need for a link between the Songhay state and the trans-Saharan trade through the Teguidda area. Because of this close tie to Borno, the cultural autonomy of the Kawar community was much stronger than in the case of the Ingelshi. The Kanuri language, as spoken in Kawar and Fachi, was more similar to the Kanuri of Borno than Ingelshi was to Songhay, and Kanuri customs seem to have been very close to those in Borno, at least in the nineteenth century.[16]

These pockets of Kanuri culture in the desert had a double function which reflects historical change. On the one hand these Kanuri were distinct from the Tubu nomads who inhabited Dirku and northern Kawar; on the other hand Kanuri ethnicity confirmed the division between the oasis dwellers and the Tuareg who dominated the salt trade in the late eighteenth and the nineteenth centuries. Even in northern Kawar, the Guezebida and Djadoboy were mixed populations of Tubu and Kanuri origin, which suggests that the division between nomad and sedentary oasis dweller may have been more pronounced in northern Kawar in the past. The evolution of culture in this context is as difficult to unravel as it is for the Ingelshi, but the significance is just as clear: ethnicity reinforced class differences in a specific historical and ecological context. At a time when Tubu and Koyam dominated the export trade in salt, the Kanuri salt workers had also distinguished themselves from merchants on the basis of ethnicity, although then class and ethnic divisions were maintained within the context of the Borno state. At that time – and indeed later too – the division between nomad and sedentary farmer was a fundamental division within Borno society. Koyam were nomadic Kanuri, one of many nomadic groups that lived in northern Borno and Kanem; the Tubu were allies of the state who controlled the trans-Saharan route through Kawar and provided transport for the trade with North Africa. This corporate structure, through which the Saifawa dynasty controlled the Chad basin and the desert to the north, continued after the collapse of Borno authority in Kawar. The 'Kanuri-ness' of the salt workers was as essential to the control over the salines once Borno authority ended as it had been earlier, only the reasons for that control changed. The Tuareg recognised the association between Kanuri residents and salt production in forcing a tributary relationship upon the oases. The *bulama*, a Kanuri titled official, was established as the intermediary between the nomadic Tuareg and the Kanuri oasis dwellers.

From the perspective of the Kanuri residents, the maintenance of a Kanuri identity was a crucial aspect of guaranteeing their rights over the salines.[17]

Another struggle shaped the social organisation of trade and production in Kanem, only in this case the Yedina islanders – that is the commercial intermediaries and not the producers – were the perpetuators of a cultural cleavage between themselves and the *haddad* salt workers. In the desert, the oasis inhabitants had to protect their interests against the nomads, who dominated desert life. Cultural distinctiveness was one weapon in maintaining special rights over the natural resources of the salines. In the Chad basin, the Yedina had to protect their monopoly of transport across the lake, which required their political independence from Borno and Kanem. Hence it was in their interest to assert a cultural identity that distinguished them from the inhabitants of Borno and Kanem. The Yedina spoke their own language and had their own customs, while the producers of trona were part of the dominant society of the mainland. Refugees who fled to the islands had to become Yedina because incorporation into island society required such acculturation.[18]

Both Yedina and Tuareg used ethnicity to maintain their autonomy, but the results of their manipulation of identity were different. The Tuareg were able to transform their control over camels into commercial and political power. In the fifteenth century they destroyed Azelik and brought the area of the Teguidda salines under their political control, and in c. 1759 they absorbed Bilma into their commercial orbit. Camels provided transport not only for goods but also for warriors, and both at Azelik and Bilma the Tuareg exploited their military capabilities to achieve commercial advantages. They also intervened in savanna society through raiding and war, as well as trade. Over time, and especially in the nineteenth century, individual Tuareg and some Tuareg fractions as collectivities established plantations and branch firms in the savanna and sahel. They had access to the trans-Saharan trade and the savanna trade as well. Such opportunities accentuated class divisions within Tuareg society, but these divisions were usually subordinated to ethnic solidarity. Indeed, ethnicity reinforced the hierarchical status that enabled the Tuareg aristocracy to control manpower in a climatic and political setting that necessitated periodic expansion and contraction.[19] In good times, dependants and clients could be called on to perform economic and political services; in bad times they could be let go as conditions warranted. Nomads in general had an ecological advantage over sedentary populations in the movement of goods along the desert-edge because they had camels and because they controlled the commercial corridors, but they had to fight both amongst themselves and with the savanna states to decide which specific nomadic groups could realise that advantage at any given time.

By contrast, the Yedina were not able to develop their political influence to the extent that the nomads could. The Yedina were subject to ecological constraints that gave them a niche in the transit trade in trona but prevented them from extending their influence beyond the shores of the lake. Through their monopoly of lake transport and raids that could not be countered from the mainland, the Yedina were able to maintain their political independence, but at a price. They remained in the lake, unable to expand their commerce and industry beyond the needs of local consumption, except for fish, and consequently could not escape economic dependence upon Borno. Whereas the Tuareg were able to invest in trade other than in salt and could establish slave plantations along the desert-edge, the limitations of the ecological setting of the Yedina prevented more than a modest involvement in the regional economy.

Despite the ethnic solidarity of the Tuareg and the self-contained world of the Yedina, both societies were hierarchical. Ethnicity was manipulated to exploit the advantages of an ecological niche – transport could be monopolised. Because of the necessity of mobilising a whole society to maintain the monopoly, ethnic distinctions from the surrounding populations were emphasised. None the less, ethnicity was maintained primarily in the interests of the Yedina merchants and the Tuareg aristocracy. Ethnic identity and language reinforced the control of these classes over the means of production in sectors other than the salt trade and over the transport monopoly in the salt trade. Ethnicity helped the elites of the Tuareg and Yedina societies to mobilise people as workers. Membership in the ethnic group was essential to participation in trade, and membership depended upon social links with a patron or master.

The interface between ethnicity and class involved tension. An individual who could acquire a few head of cattle or some trade commodities could break away from Tuareg society, settle in the savanna and begin life as a petty merchant in the Hausa countryside. The Agalawa and Tokarawa recount traditions that demonstrate just such disaffection with Tuareg society. In the case of the Agalawa and Tokarawa, individuals and small groups changed their ethnic identity and at the same time changed their class allegiance. They stopped being servile members of Tuareg society, where they had been slaves or *irewelen*, and became Hausa merchants.[20] A different pattern characterised the flow of people across the ethnic boundary that separated the Yedina from mainland society. The inhabitants of the Chad islands do not appear to have been able to maintain their population through biological reproduction. It was always necessary to recruit new members through slave raids and by welcoming political refugees from the mainland.[21] In both cases, but for different reasons, people crossed ethnic frontiers. Where people entered their adopted society varied considerably. Agalawa and Tokarawa broke ties of dependency that were servile, even slave, in order to become merchants. They changed class. Immigrants to the Chad islands usually had to accept subordination, if they came freely, and many arrived as captives or purchased slaves. The Yedina also recognised the *haddad* artisan caste as a distinct category of society. Control of the islands required the tight management of resources, for the size of the islands (and the corresponding amount of land available for crops and grazing) fluctuated unpredictably. Ethnic loyalties guaranteed a social mechanism for organising labour, but class relationships determined access to resources.

ETHNIC FRACTIONS AND THE HAUSA DIASPORA

In the context of the salt trade, the broad configuration of ethnicity is revealing only to the extent that it helps illuminate the division between and within classes. Finer distinctions than Hausa, Kanuri or Tuareg were made within the merchant community and between producers and the larger societies of which they were a part. These finer distinctions have been referred to as 'ethnic fractitions' by Guy Nicolas, although Nicolas's analysis is not concerned with the salt trade.[22] Nicolas developed the concept of ethnic fraction to help explain social differentiation within a complex, heterogeneous and rapidly expanding society such as that of the Hausa over the past several hundred years, but the concept is also useful for a cultural mosaic like that of the central Sudan, where no single ethnic group predominated. In the context of Hausa society, fractions of ethnic groups were somewhat analogous to clans, although there was no common ancestor. While people tended to marry within the fraction, they could marry members of other fractions with whom they had established 'joking relations' (*abokin wasa*). Nicolas concentrated on the fractions he observed in Maradi; there were many more within broader Hausa society and still more in Kanuri and Tuareg societies.

Hausa ethnic fractions derived their identities from traditions that were manipulated to create and maintain a sense of corporate loyalty. These traditions referred to the medieval Hausa states (Kano, Katsina, Zazzau, Gobir, Zamfara, etc.) or to some non-Hausa origin. All these fractions shared the Hausa sense of identity and value system, no matter what their origin. They were always 'Hausa' or had become 'Hausa'. Behavioural and classificatory rules resulted in the cultural conversion and integration of immigrants, which allowed the emergence of a heterogeneous society that was in sharp contrast to the usual picture of an ethnic group as a homogeneous, closed system. I have described the institutional manifestation of this process of integration and identification elsewhere as *asali*, an institution of ethnic identity based on the recognition of common origin.[23] Nicolas identified some of the more important immigrant *asali* groups as Fulani, Beriberi and Buzu (Tuareg), but Arab (Larabawa), Agalawa, Tokarawa, Adarawa and other fractions were also common.

The natron and *manda* dealers in the Sokoto Caliphate who considered themselves as ethnic fractions included the Agalawa, Tokarawa, Kambarin Beriberi and Beriberi. Some of the activities of these merchant groups have been examined in my earlier study of the kola trade between the central Sudan and Asante. All four groups of merchants were immigrant in origin. They each fostered a sense of corporate identity based on these origins and on their occupation in trade, especially kola and natron importing. The use of group consciousness and social relationships followed a commercial pattern already well established in the central Sudan. By emphasising their distinct origins, using recognised facial and body markings, and practising endogamous marriage customs, these groups were able to dominate kola importing and

assume a major role in other trade, including the trade in natron and *manda*.
The Agalawa, Tokarawa, and Kambarin Beriberi

> traced their origins to the desert-side trade of the Tuareg and Borno economies,
> probably within a few decades of 1800. The closely related Agalawa (s. Ba'agali)
> and Tokarawa (s. Tokarci) were *bugaje* in origin, that is their *asali* [origins]
> claimed a previous servile status in Tuareg society. The Agalawa lived in
> sedentary, agricultural communities in Katsina and Kano emirates, which were
> the by-product of Tuareg trade with the Hausa economy, while the Tokarawa
> were the descendants of low status nomads who abandoned livestock herding
> and cattle trading for life in the savanna. The Kambarin Beriberi were refugees
> from Borno, and they were part of a much larger emigration of Borno traders,
> many of whom used the same name. The Kambari in the Hausa heartland
> became specialist kola traders, unlike their counterparts who largely settled in
> the Benue basin. The choice of a new home for both groups coincided with the
> main orientation·of Borno's staple export trade in natron.[24]

The Beriberi also claimed a Borno origin, although they lacked a specific
association with the kola trade. Their settlement in the area of the Hausa
towns was closely associated with trade between Borno and the caliphate, as
has been demonstrated in Chapter 8.

The location of the Agalawa and Tokarawa coincided with the main
orientation of the Tuareg salt trade, while both groups of Borno immigrants
had a direct connexion with the natron and *manda* trade. It is not surprising,
therefore, that these four groups played such a major role in the distribution of
salt and natron. What is surprising is that the Agalawa were not important in
the distribution of Bilma and Fachi salt, at least in the nineteenth century, and
that while some Tokarawa did distribute Bilma and Fachi salt, this aspect of
their business was clearly secondary to the kola trade. Instead, both Agalawa
and Tokarawa merchants shifted their investments to the Borno trade in
natron and *manda* because of the requirements of the kola trade.

Despite their connexion with the Tuareg, the Agalawa and Tokarawa
virtually severed their links with the Tuareg trade. Their movement across the
ethnic frontier between Tuareg and Hausa society resulted in an entirely new
ethnic and economic status.[25] By contrast, the Kambarin Beriberi and
Beriberi developed an existing commerce by extending their established
interests in the export trade of Borno. None the less, the expansion of their
commerce also required a change in ethnic status, but for reasons that were
different from those of the Agalawa and Tokarawa. The Kambarin Beriberi
and Beriberi maintained links across the cultural boundary that separated
Hausa and Kanuri societies; they took advantage of their knowledge of the
Borno market and retained existing contacts with merchants in Borno. They
changed their ethnicity but not their class allegiance.[26] In most cases, the
Agalawa and Tokarawa ended personal and business connexions with the
Tuareg, although they owed a tremendous debt to their heritage because they
had learned about long-distance trade from the Tuareg. Because the Agalawa
and Tokarawa changed their class affiliation at the same time that they

267

changed their ethnicity from Tuareg to Hausa, they were free to search out new commercial opportunities. To have maintained established contacts with the Tuareg commercial network would have required a continuation of patron–client relations with their former masters. Such contacts lacked the flexibility that the merchant class had to have. Merchants had to be free to follow new routes and to make new contacts. The Kambarin Beriberi and Beriberi had that flexibility because they were already part of the merchant class. The Agalawa and Tokarawa had to acquire that flexibility by ending their servility.

The commercial activities of these merchants help explain the development of ethnic fractions within Hausa society. In effect the Agalawa, Tokarawa, Kambarin Beriberi and Beriberi provided links between the dominant societies of the central Sudan. Although all four groups were Hausa fractions, their origins enabled them to act on the periphery of Tuareg and Borno societies. The emergence of such groups as the Agalawa and Tokarawa is evidence of the strong, historical connexion between the Tuareg and the Hausa. They are a product of the desert-side economy of the central Sudan.[27] The Beriberi and Kambarin Beriberi demonstrate a similar interdependence of the Borno and Hausa economies. The ethnic overlap in all four cases facilitated trade between different parts of the central Sudan and provided a mechanism of integration across political and cultural boundaries.

This type of economic interaction and the corresponding development of ethnic fractions can also be discerned for the Benue salines, where the older ethnic affiliations of the Jukun and Alago were absorbed into the expanding political economy of the caliphate.[28] By the twentieth century, Jukun and Alago had become ethnic fractions in what had emerged as a dominant Hausa society.

Hausa fractions included Katsinawa, Zamfarawa, Kambarin Beriberi, and Kanawa, who settled at the various salines early in the nineteenth century. Itinerant merchants who came from Kano, Zaria, Bauchi and other parts of the caliphate who used similar *asali* identifications reinforced this system of social organisation and indirectly helped legitimise Hausa usurpation of most of the salines.

Once Dallol Fogha and Dallol Bosso were incorporated into the caliphate, the local populations had to refashion their identity in the context of caliphate society too, and that meant *vis à vis* Hausa ethnicity. The indigenous Dendi and Tienga found themselves transformed into ethnic fractions alongside immigrants from Borno, Kebbi and elsewhere.[29] In each case these ethnic fractions provide a key to the history of the area, for it is possible to decipher the history of each and their relationship to the economy. The Kebbawa refugees from Birnin Debe who settled at Kawara-Debe to produce salt in Dallol Fogha are only one example of such population movements. The Birnin Debe community maintained its corporate identity, which then became the basis of its claim over the Dallol Fogha salines.

The Hausa commercial system expanded through the assimilation of ethnic fractions. Reference to ethnic fractions was one way that merchants, craftsmen and others established and maintained social relations throughout the central Sudan. These relations could be put to advantage whenever merchants travelled away from their homes, and the institution of *abokin wasa*, which functioned as joking relationships between fractions, provided a ready network of contacts outside each fraction. Identification with a fraction was exclusive but not hostile to other members of the merchant class, for people were explaining their location in society by reference to tradition. As Muslims and Hausa, they could interact with other merchants whenever class interests were paramount, as they often were during long commercial expeditions or when itinerant merchants needed accommodation and broke-rage services. These positive implications of ethnicity served class needs. Identification by origins also helped aspiring merchants to acquire the credit and other resources necessary to compete in the market, and consequently ethnic fractionalism also reveals the tension between different parts of the merchant class. The Agalawa and Tokarawa, for example, could develop as important sections of the merchant community, despite servile origins, because they maintained a sense of group loyalty in a commercial setting in which they were new-comers. As individuals they would have had difficulty competing with established merchants who had long-standing contacts along the trade routes. Because of group solidarity, they were able to benefit from each other's contacts and expertise and thereby rapidly gain a foothold in long-distance trade. The Kambarin Beriberi and Beriberi had other difficulties to overcome. They shifted the locus of their operations from Borno to the caliphate and, while they knew the Borno market, they had to establish relations with the Fulani aristocracy of the caliphate in order to acquire new homes. Ethnic solidarity allowed them to promote their legitimacy as established merchants, despite their recent immigration from a state with which the caliphate had been at war. Immigrants from Borno had few difficulties maintaining their class identity as merchants, but they did have to overcome the disadvantages of large-scale emigration.

THE SOCIAL BASIS OF PRODUCTION IN BORNO

Borno society also had its ethnic fractions: these had originally developed in the context of the Saifawan state before 1804, but as a consequence of political decline in the nineteenth century ethnicity had to be redefined. Regional differences and the nomad–sedentary dichotomy were strongly reflected in the delineation of fractions. The Dagera, Manga, Mobbeur, Kanembu and other groups were identified with specific provinces, while Shuwa Arab, Koyam, Tubu, Segurti, and Dietko maintained a corporate identity as nomads.[30] Whereas ethnic fractions of diverse origin were found in most Hausa towns, many fractions in Borno tended to be found only in their province of origin, and when migration did occur – as among the Manga and Kanembu in the nineteenth century – the migrants tended to concentrate in specific areas. Hence some Manga moved out of Muniyo to occupy Gourbei and the area immediately to the south, and it is instructive that the area subsequently became known as Mangari. Similarly, many Kanembu followed al-Kanemi to Borno, and the province adjacent to Lake Chad from the Komodugu Yo River south to Baga Seyoram was reinforced as a Kanembu province.

The class and ethnic status of the salt workers in Borno varied with the province in which the salines were located. Manga were the sole workers in Muniyo and Mangari, although the western extension of this salt district lay in the region of the small Sosebaki towns, such as Wacha, which continued in local hands. The workers were predominantly peasants. In Foli, the workers were Danawa, which represented a special case, since the Danawa were in reality a caste in Kanembu society. As a caste, their status was low, and their caste affiliation took precedence over their ethnic identification as Kanembu. Class and ethnicity, which reinforced each other among the Manga peasantry, were interpreted in combination as caste in Kanem. The Danawa were artisans and Kanembu; that is they were workers engaged in craft production, hunting, fishing and trona extraction whose ethnicity was identical to that of the dominant aristocracy. Finally, in Kadzell, there were a variety of ethnic fractions, but the workers were mostly slaves. Of the known salt-camps, the Kanembu and Mobbeur each accounted for 26.0 per cent, the Tubu 20.5 per cent, the Manga 19.2 per cent, the Segurti 4.1 per cent, the Dietko 2.7 per cent and the Kanuri 1.4 per cent (Table 6.5). If the region south of the Komodugu Yo River is included, the percentage of Kanembu camps would have been much higher. Kadzell differed from Foli, Mangari and Muniyo because of the transhumance of nomads across Kadzell and the proximity of the settled Mobbeur of the Komodugu Yo Valley to the salt district.

The term Manga came to designate the inhabitants of Muniyo and Mangari. Lethem, who studied the Manga in 1919, learned from the *galadima* of Nguru that 'Manga' not only identified the people of these districts but also implied an inferior status and origin when compared to the aristocracy of pre-nineteenth-century Borno. But 'Manga' also had an occupational meaning, for it signified the workers engaged in salt and natron production.[31] Landeroin learned the 'Manga' was synonymous with *talakawa* in Hausa; that is that they were commoners.[32] Their status was defined as non-royal and non-nomadic; they constituted the peasantry of Muniyo and later Mangari.[33] In short, these traditions blur the distinctions between class and ethnicity, because the Manga as an ethnic fraction were associated with a particular class – the peasantry.

The antiquity of the name – and hence their emergence as a fraction – is unclear. There is a province of that name in northern Kanem, which appears to be very ancient, but there does not seem to be any connexion with the Manga of Borno, although some sources credit the Manga with a connexion with Kanem.[34] Palmer, for example, speculated that the Manga were originally slaves of the Kanem ruling class and were incorporated into Borno at an early date.[35] As with much of Palmer's material, however, the source and validity of this claim are unknown. Abadie, equally unclear about his source, postulates the movement of the Manga from Borno in the fifteenth century.[36] The first reference to the Manga dates back to the seventeenth century. A *mahram* (decree) of the fifteenth century which exempted a group of Fulani from taxation lists the son of one Ahmad Manga as a witness to the *mahram*'s reconfirmation in the seventeenth century. A later witness with the title *mangalma* is mentioned in the *mahram*'s reconfirmation during the reign of Mai Dunama Idris b. Ali (c. 1694–1704). In several reigns during the eighteenth century, officials with the title *mangalma* or the name Manga were also witnesses, including Mangalma Duwa b. Fakama, Mangalma Ahmad Wai, and the slave officials Mangalma b. Fugama and Mangalma Tufu in 1717, and Manga Muhammad al Kabir in 1791.[37] It may well be that these titles and names indicate the existence of a Manga province.

The social structure of Kanem differed substantially from that of Borno. Whereas the Manga constituted a peasantry engaged in salt production during the dry season, the Danawa formed a caste apart from Kanembu society. The class structure of Kanem consisted of sharp cleavages between the Kanembu aristocracy and its free dependants, on the one hand, and the *haddad* caste, on the other hand. The Kanembu also owned slaves, who were also distinguished from the *haddad*. The Danawa were free but dependent, and were defined most clearly in opposition to the Kanembu lineages that claimed a royal connexion.[38] Intermarriage between Kanembu and Danawa was strictly prohibited, and ownership of cattle, a principal form of wealth, was reserved for the Kanembu. With the partial exception of the four politically autonomous Danawa lineages of the Nguri–Yalita area, the Danawa found themselves in a situation of political and economic vassalage to their Kanembu overlords. The Danawa had to pay tribute, and they were excluded from corporate political involvement in the state. They were also denied ownership of cattle and land. Nor did they control their own labour, in that they were confined to certain occupations, and they did not have the right to marry outside their group. One of the main functions of the *haddad* caste was to control and integrate smaller groups of people who lacked an aristocratic connexion. According to Conte

> in the pre-colonial period endogamy was not the monopoly of any professional caste but rather a boundary-enforcing function in both main social strata as well as lineage-based status groups within these strata. The pre-colonial economic system had as its main pinion a rigid social stratification system allowing little vertical mobility.[39]

In the nineteenth century, the economy of Kanem relied to a great extent on this hierarchical structure that separated producers, owners, merchants, and nomads. This segmented structure was a necessity of political insecurity. The range of occupations among the Danawa was so wide that some observers thought that they did virtually all the work in Kanem. While the Danawa were also farmers, their classification as artisans set them apart from the basic economic–cultural division of the region, that is the division between nomads

271

and sedentary farmers. The Danawa were fishermen, hunters, potters, blacksmiths, salt workers, textile workers, tanners and well-diggers. These occupations were specifically identified with production; they were not allowed to become merchants.

'Caste' suggests a social stratification not associated with ethnicity, and this distinction does present a problem in analysing society east of Lake Chad. Ethnic groups included Kanembu, Arab, Yedina, Tubu, and others further east – all of whom made the distinction between an artisan caste and the rest of society. Each group of *haddad* spoke the language of the ethnic group with which it was connected – Kanembu, Yedina, Arab, or Tubu. The *haddad* status crossed ethnic boundaries. The various groups of *haddad* were organised into fractions within the different ethnic groups of the region, but they were not ethnic fractions *per se* because the distinctions that were recognised within each ethnic group were not ethnic differences but class differences. Elsewhere ethnic boundaries reinforced class relations; either ethnicity set classes off from each other or ethnic fractions in combination constituted a class. The trans-ethnic dimension of the *haddad* status has impressed most observers – which is why they have referred to the *haddad* as a caste. Economic and political power was in the hands of nomads – Arab, Tubu, Kanembu – or the islanders of Lake Chad – Yedina and Kouri – and livestock production and management were the basis of economic and political power. *Haddad* were effectively isolated from the power struggles between nomadic groups. For many reasons, therefore, *haddad* were often excluded from the observations of the political and economic structure encompassing the region of Lake Chad, Kanem and Lake Fitri. Whether or not it was nineteenth-century observers, indigenous Borno chronicles, or early colonial accounts, the *haddad* were not perceived as an important subject. They simply worked hard.

Manga and Danawa had sole access to the means of production, but at a price. Both Manga and Danawa kept a portion of their output, which they could then sell, but they worked under conditions in which they did not own or control the salines. They had to pay a share of their output to the proprietors of the salines. Their identity as corporate groups protected their right of access, even though that identity placed them in a subordinate social category which allowed the extraction of surplus from the product of their labour. This kind of dependency was perceived as *métayage* by the French, whose reforms of proprietary rights were designed to bring local custom into line with French tradition. The French were perceptive in their analogy, although they hardly succeeded in recreating rural French society. Both the Manga and Danawa were involved in a system of 'share-cropping', but they were free to undertake activities other than making salt or cutting trona slabs. The Manga could deal in salt, make textiles, or practise dry-season farming, while the Danawa could hunt, fish or pursue a craft. When they chose to work the salines, they had to accept the terms of proprietorship; salt was not a free good and access depended upon social status and a contract with a political authority. Manga and Danawa status implicitly accepted dependency. Labour was mobilised through the agency of the state, as interpreted by the officials in control of the salines. The workers received their share, but state power guaranteed that officials took more than any single worker.

Work units rather than individuals were taxed; the proportion extracted by the proprietors was 30 per cent of output in the trona trade, where units consisted of three men, and comparable proportions in *manda* production, where units varied from 10 to 15 people. The discrepancy between individual shares and the amount kept by the proprietor and his agent was most pronounced in the *manda* trade, where the proceeds had to be divided among more people and the furnace master kept a larger share than other workers. At Ari Kombomiram, with its ten workers, the proprietor and his agent together took over 31 per cent output, while the furnace master was left with only 14.2 per cent, the two *kandine* with about 9 per cent each, and the seven labourers with less than 5 per cent each (Table 7.4). By contrast, trona workers each kept about 23 per cent of total output, while they surrendered 30 per cent to the proprietor. The Danawa secured better terms than the Manga, even though the position of the Danawa in society was lower than that of the Manga.

The method of surplus extraction reinforced the social basis of labour. Because workers had to pay for access to the salines as a unit, the organisation of production was left in their hands. Consequently, people came together in the work place on the basis of previous social relations – membership in an ethnic fraction, in the case of the Manga, or the *haddad* caste, in the case of the Danawa. Knowledge of salt production and clientship relations with the proprietors were thereby retained within the ethnic fraction or caste. People could not sell their labour as individuals; social relations remained an essential lever in the recruitment of the work force.

SLAVERY AND ETHNIC RELATIONS

Slavery was an important means of mobilising labour both in trade and in production. As has been discussed in Chapter 6, slaves were used at the desert salines, in Kadzell, at the Benue salines, and in the Dallols. By the end of the nineteenth century, some slaves were also involved in *manda* production, and I have speculated that slaves once performed a more important role in the Borno salt industry than they did in nineteenth-century Mangari and Muniyo. Similarly, slave labour was vital to the functioning of trade. Caravan workers, crewmen, and commercial agents were recruited from the ranks of slaves whenever merchants could afford to do so.[40] Slavery was seldom the sole method of labour recruitment. Merchants, for example, relied on dependent clients and junior kin too, and the Tuareg distinguished between slaves, freed slaves and the descendants of slaves, whose obligations varied considerably. The status of slaves also differed depending upon the size of slave holdings. When slaves worked alongside their masters, they could transform their relationship into one of clientage, whether or not they were actually given

273

their freedom. When slaves worked on their own or in the company of other slaves, they experienced more directly the exploitation of labour by one class over another.

The relations of slavery were inherently exploitative. The status of servility determined the relation of an individual to the means of production; a slave did not own the means of production nor did he have legitimate access to the means of production. Indeed the slave himself was owned and hence an intrinsic part of the productive process. Furthermore, servility determined the relation of an individual to the product of his labour; as a slave, he did not have the right to any part of that product. Servility also determined the relation of an individual to other members of society, and this relationship was essentially one of class antagonism. A slave could work alongside his master and a slave could be assigned tasks that allowed considerable freedom of movement and scope for independent judgement, but a slave owned by a merchant was still not part of the merchant class and a slave owned by a small-scale producer of salt was not a peasant producer, however much he was treated as a member of the family. The consciousness of slaves as a class was not well developed, but the relationship between slaves and their masters was still essentially one based on class. Slaves were wanted for their labour power, which could be exploited for the benefit of their masters.

Slaves were identified with their masters, no matter what the origins of the slaves had been. At the *kige* camps of Kadzell, for example, where only the Manga and some Mobbeur camps contained free workers, virtually all labour depended upon slaves, but the slaves were recognised as Kanembu, Segurti, Tubu, Kanuri, Mobbeur or Dietko, depending upon the ethnic fraction of their masters (Table 6.5). Because slaves were property, they were perceived as an extension of their masters; they did not have an identity of their own. Similarly, the slaves of Kawar and Fachi may have come from areas to the south of Borno, but their place in the social structure of desert society was alongside their masters. If their masters were Tubu, they became Tubu; if their masters were Kanuri, they became Kanuri.

The ethnicity of slaves depended upon who was attempting to identify the location of the slaves in society. Viewed from across an ethnic boundary, slaves were considered part of the other ethnic group, but viewed from within an ethnic group or ethnic fraction they were outsiders and units of work. The Hausa, for example, had difficulty distinguishing the various social categories within Tuareg society. Most Hausa could see who was a Tuareg noble; individuals with wealth and power were easy to single out. What was more difficult, and often impossible, was to differentiate between vassals, freed slaves, descendants of slaves and slaves – all of these were *buzu* to the Hausa, and Agalawa and Tokarawa were *buzu* in origin, even though the actual origin of individual Tokarawa and Agalawa was more specific.[41] Ethnicity was in the eye of the beholder. It served a function that arose from the attempts of people to manipulate social relations for purposes related to controlling the means of production.

274

The Yedina, for example, relied extensively on slave labour, particularly in fishing and poling boats. Dried fish was a major staple in the lake-side trade, especially with Borno.[42] As Alexander learned in 1904, the chiefs of various Yedina fractions – he mentioned the Gouria and Madjigodjia – owned large numbers of slaves who 'do all the heavy work of fishing and poling and are cruelly treated by their masters, who starve and beat them'.[43] Olive MacLeod also found that 'slaves do the hard work and the distant fishing'.[44] Many of these slaves were purchased in the southern markets of Kotoko; Sara, Nielim and Ham were common origins for slaves at the time of the European conquest. Slaves were also obtained from the Mobbeur and Tubu in Borno.[45] Slave raids had long been a source of labour. D'Huart reported in 1904 that

> a considerable number of captives [had been] amassed from the shores of Borno by the ancient Buduma [Yedina] pirates. Little by little, profiting from the decadence of their ancient masters, these groups of autonomous villages have only conserved a relationship which is a very loose vassalage with the Buduma.[46]

The autonomy of these slaves suggests that they had entered the ranks of the *haddad*, and hence may well have been a source of labour in the trona depressions too. As was the case in Kanem, the *haddad* were despised and exploited by the Yedina to the extent that Freydenberg thought that they were held in semi-captivity.[47] Like the *haddad* of the mainland, the island *haddad* did much of the work in certain sectors of the lake economy. For example, the Goudja, the Yedina in the northern part of the lake, did not fish; that work was left to *haddad* and probably slaves. Even more significant was the perception of slaves and *haddad* by the Yedina. For them, assimilated slaves entered the ranks of the *haddad*. For outsiders, they simply became Yedina, or more accurately Buduma (people of the reeds), the derogatory term used for the Yedina in Borno and Kanem.

As a method of labour recruitment, slavery was a means of bringing people across ethnic boundaries. The identification of slaves with their masters thrust upon slaves an ethnic association that was not theirs by choice and was not even fully recognised in society. Slaves were outsiders, unwilling pawns in a social formation that used ethnicity as a means of explaining class relationships. To the extent that slaves were accorded the same ethnic identification as their masters, slavery was more than a method of labour recruitment; it facilitated the development and maintenance of ethnic identification. The adoption of the master's ethnic identity by slaves helped shape the basic social relations of production and the methods of surplus extraction and distribution. The extension of the master's ethnicity to his slaves was a means of dealing with class relations and the recognised status of the slaves. Slavery, therefore, was instrumental in shaping the development of ethnicity because slaves were instruments of labour that could be exploited in the promotion of ethnic interests.

The importance of slavery in the perpetuation of ethnic identities can be seen with reference to salt production in Kadzell and at the desert salines. Although slaves did much of the work in Kadzell and the desert salines, their sphere of reference and social interaction was within the ethnic fraction of their masters. They had little contact with other slaves and consequently little opportunity to develop a common identity as slaves. Unless they escaped, slaves were locked into a social structure in which they could only hope to reduce their marginality in society through acculturation. To the extent that they could reduce their marginality, they became recognised members of an ethnic group or fraction.

At the Benue brine springs, where slaves performed much of the 'women's work' associated with salt production, slaves are barely remembered in tradition (see Chapter 6). Who controlled the salines depended upon ethnic associations. Hausa adventurers – merchants in their class allegiance – annexed many of these salines for the caliphate, so that most of the salt towns were subsumed in caliphate society, which meant the adoption of the Hausa language for commercial purposes and identification with the Muslim culture of caliphate society. Keana remained Alago because of its submission in the *jihad*, and hence cultural differences between the Keana producers and the Hausa merchants who came to buy the product of its saltings remained strong. Alago also kept some rights to the salines at Ribi, while the Jukun retained control of Akiri and continued to have access, although this was limited, at Awe, Azara and Ribi. The slaves are largely forgotten. Who did the work? Women, but when pressed people admit that slaves actually prepared the salt flats, carried the brine, fetched the firewood, and did most of the other work. But it was women's work that they did. The ethnicity of the slaves is not remembered as being important. After all, they only worked. Ethnicity related to control of the means of production, not who was exploited.

Long-distance trade provided distinct advantages for those slaves who were assigned to caravan duty because trade could promote assimilation. Because of the ease of escape, only those slaves who could be trusted were allowed to engage in trade, and such trust invariably came only after slaves were fully acculturated. Tuareg nomads, Hausa *fatoma*, and Yedina islanders faced a similar problem – whom to trust with goods. When clients and junior kin were not available or a merchant's operation was large enough to require additional assistance, slavery was a logical means of recruitment, despite the risks. Many of the nomads who accompanied the annual caravans to Bilma and Fachi were slaves, descendants of slaves or dependent clients. The proportion of each varied with the section of the caravan. None the less, slaves often did the most onerous tasks on the trip. Hausa traders took slaves on journeys for the same reasons; slaves unloaded livestock, fetched water and fodder, and constructed temporary shelters for their masters. And of course they tended the livestock on the road.

To the extent that slaves performed menial tasks associated with long-distance trade, they remained workers, distinct from their masters in terms of their interests and their relationship to the means of production. But when slaves became agents, trustees of estates, or otherwise were assigned positions of responsibility they could aspire to the ethnic status of their master and might be recognised as members of the merchant class. This process of assimilation occurred on the level of the individual, however, and consequently the basic class antagonisms between masters and their slaves continued. Furthermore, such movement across ethnic and class boundaries only took place in the context of the continued acquisition of slaves and the presence of enough slaves to perform the menial tasks that were assigned to slaves as a class. Slaves may not have recognised themselves as a class, but they certainly knew that they were exploited and that the nature of the exploitation was ultimately based on coercion. The fact that a few slaves slipped across ethnic and class boundaries did not alter the status of the majority of slaves, who remained essential to the productive process because of their labour power.

Those slaves who were employed as agricultural workers on the farms and plantations of the merchant class supported the interests of their master's ethnic fraction (and of course the interests of the master too), but the social relations of production were based on class. In order to feed their clients, which was part of the arrangement in accommodating merchants, the *fatoma* required large stores of grain and other foodstuffs. For this purpose, *fatoma* managed farms and plantations outside Kano and other towns. Holdings were often scattered; some *fatoma* owned a number of separate farms (at Kano, some had five; one had twenty farms), although all were in relatively easy reach of the towns. Many of the farms at Kano were near Fagge, immediately outside the walls of the city and convenient to the temporary huts of the Tuareg and other merchants there. And these lands were worked by slaves – a common pattern among the merchant community of the caliphate and other parts of West Africa. Audu Madobi, one *fatoma* in Zangon Beriberi ward, employed about 40 slaves on his farms; other *fatoma* owned from 20 to 50 slaves.[48]

Some of the kola traders operated even more extensive plantations than the *fatoma*. One of the wealthiest Agalawa merchants, Tambarin Agalawa Yakubu of Madabo ward in Kano, owned hundreds of slaves – family tradition credits him with 500 – who worked his farms and plantations. Yakubu owned at least four farms within the walls of Kano and another three immediately outside the city, and he also had two large farms and a plantation at Rijiyar Lemo, west of the city. Finally he managed farms at Rantan, near Kura, and probably at several other villages as well. Because of the scale of Yakubu's holdings, it was necessary for him to sell some produce on the market. Unlike the *fatoma*, who mainly supplied their own establishments, the kola traders began to invest in commodity production.[49]

Because the Tuareg, especially the Kel Ewey, Kel Gress and their associates, maintained an elaborate commercial infrastructure in the savanna to handle their business, they invested heavily in land, slave labour, and grain production. Throughout Katsina, Kano, Damagaram, Maradi, southern Adar and Tessawa, individual Tuareg merchants owned plantations that provided grain supplies for the desert-side trade.[50] Not all the inhabitants of these plantations were slaves, however. Some – perhaps many – were *irewelen* (freed slaves or people of slave ancestry). Their obligations to their former masters were less onerous than those of slaves; they were expected to pay a small tribute and to house the Tuareg while they were visiting. As in other sectors of Tuareg desert-side society, the existence of these estates provided a safety-valve during periods of climatic and political crisis. Nomads could retreat to the estates when necessary, assured of accommodation unless conditions were equally bad in the south. In good times, slave plantations were simply a good investment.[51]

The range of uses to which slaves were put demonstrates that slavery fitted into a social formation in which ethnicity was a crucial factor in determining who had access to the means of production. Slaves were assigned tasks because they were units of labour. Those who worked for merchants might be successful in inserting themselves into a commercial organisation that allowed identification with their master's ethnic fraction. They could change class and become members of their master's ethnic group. Other slaves found themselves alongside salt workers – slave and free – and were considered by outsiders to be ethnically identical with the dominant fraction involved in production. Other slaves were farmers and, while they became 'Hausa' or 'Tuareg' to outsiders, they were merely slaves to their masters and whatever ethnic identification they had related to their origins. The slaves themselves often retained memories of their birth or ancestry as a means of accommodating themselves to a society that emphasised *asali* connexions.

Slavery reinforced and contradicted ethnic allegiances. It reinforced ethnicity in the sense that it served as a method of recruitment across ethnic boundaries. In a social formation in which identity was conceived in terms of distinctions between groups of people on the basis of language and culture, slaves had to be identified with something. Individuals, slave or free, could not exist without an ethnic attachment. Hence outsiders looked across an ethnic boundary and *saw* a uniform ethnic group, without hierarchy or class. For the Tuareg, there were nobles, vassals, freed slaves, descendants of slaves and slaves, but for the Hausa there were only nobles and *buzu*. In reality, however, people also recognised class distinctions. A Tuareg noble talked about ethnic, even racial, differences – all blacks were meant to be slaves and workers; all Tuareg were light-skinned and nobles – but Tuareg nobles, often black-skinned, interacted with the aristocracy of the Sokoto Caliphate, courted Hausa merchants and knew that all successful merchants and influential aristocrats owned slaves. Ethnicity had meaning in terms of access to the means of production. From the perspective of the Tuareg noble, slaves were Hausa and not Tuareg, because to be Tuareg meant that people had rights to the means of production. Yet many slaves became Tuareg and were accepted as such. The Hausa perception of Tuareg society – a view from across the ethnic boundary – was not inaccurate. Other than the nobility, all Tuareg were *buzu*, which also meant that all *buzu*, i.e. those of servile status, were indeed Tuareg. Ethnicity and class were interconnected, but people needed to know how they were connected only when it mattered.

11

Conclusion

Four major conclusions need to be emphasised as a result of this study of the central Sudan salt industry. First, the limits of a poorly developed technology had a profound influence on the industry. Technology was relatively simple, but salt workers and merchants were able to manipulate the natural conditions of their environment to a significant degree to produce 10,000–20,000 tonnes of salt and natron per year. Secondly, transport was the fundamental bottleneck that constrained the industry. While 20,000–30,000 camels and many times that number of oxen and donkeys were used to transport salt, the reliance on animal transport prevented the expansion of production beyond the 10,000–20,000 tonne level. Thirdly, salt production and trade were confined to regional markets; the weak links with capitalism meant that there was virtually no impact on the industry from the external world before 1900. Finally, the salt industry fitted into a larger social and economic formation within the central Sudan. To isolate salt allows an analysis of one sector of this formation, but care must be taken not to generalise about the formation as a whole on the basis of salt alone.

Salt workers exploited the geological conditions of their environment, sometimes adapting their techniques of production so as to improve or increase production, but essentially they employed relatively simple technology to take advantage of natural conditions. The desert salts of Kawar, Fachi and Amadror derived from ancient lakes; the sahelian sites and Teguidda n'tesemt depended upon efflorescence, as the sun caused surface water to evaporate; the Foli trona deposits formed as a result of the seepage phenomenon on the shores of Lake Chad; and the Benue salts came from brine springs. These geological conditions affected the technology that was employed in production: efflorescences could be scraped from the ground or filtered and boiled dry or solar evaporation could take its effect. Salt could be processed through the burning of plants that were high in salt content; the seepage phenomenon of Lake Chad produced large deposits of trona that could be mined in slabs; desert sources relied entirely on solar evaporation; while the brine springs combined solar evaporation with filtering and boiling.

Because of these diverse geological conditions and the various methods of production, salt output consisted of a variety of chemical mixtures, including combinations of sodium chloride, soda, thenardite, trona and smaller amounts of other salts. The uses of these salts depended in large measure on

279

the relative proportions of the compounds and the degree of impurities in the mixtures. While it is possible to isolate these salts scientifically, local knowledge of chemistry was rudimentary and made only certain kinds of distinctions. On the general level, natron and salt were recognised as different, although in reality this difference largely depended upon the relative amounts of sodium chloride and sodium carbonate in particular mixtures. All major salts were known, since trona deposits were relatively pure, sodium chloride from the Benue brines had low concentrations of other compounds, and thenardite formed on the filtering devices in Mangari, but these facts were not collected together to form the basis of a scientific understanding of the salt deposits. There was really no reason to do so, for market conditions did not require the refinement of production techniques. Rather, consumers experimented with the available salt supplies to discover as many uses as possible for the different salt mixtures.

Transport capacity was limited. Despite Tuareg camel caravans, Yedina lake boats, and the donkeys and oxen of savanna merchants, there simply were not enough animals to enable a significant increase in the scale of production over a level of 10,000–20,000 tonnes per year to take place. The potential market for salt was much larger than this, and to a great extent salt needs had to be met from impure plant ash – and in many cases salt was not used at all. Political and climatic factors temporarily reduced the available transport still further, although the reliance on numerous salines scattered over a wide area usually meant that transport was interrupted only locally and for relatively brief periods. The number of sources also eased the transportation bottleneck somewhat, in that each saline had its own area of distribution. For the region as a whole, these areas overlapped. Transport services were extensive enough to create a single, regional market for salt. None the less, the rapid expansion in the volume of the salt trade after 1900, when transport facilities were greatly improved and it was possible to import large quantities of European salt, demonstrates that the market for salt was far from saturated before 1900 and that transport was a major – probably *the* major – reason for the limited size of the market. Within a few years after 1900, European imports alone quickly doubled the volume of the central Sudan salt trade.

The difficulties of transport resulted in a situation that allowed the Tuareg and the Yedina to maintain a monopoly in their sectors of the salt trade – the Tuareg in the desert and the Yedina across Lake Chad. In both cases, the monopoly functioned beyond the borders of the two major states of the central Sudan – the Sokoto Caliphate and Borno. Both the Tuareg and the Yedina maintained confederations amongst themselves that facilitated their commercial operations, but their monopolies depended ultimately on ecological factors – the particular requirements of travel in the desert and on the lake. In a market situation like that for the central Sudan salts, a state theoretically could have organised the salt trade as a monopoly, and there is some evidence that Borno did achieve a quasi-monopoly position, at least, before the middle of the eighteenth century, but in general the sources of salt were too dispersed for a state to establish or to maintain a monopoly. Instead, as the activities of the Tuareg and Yedina demonstrate, the particular circumstances of ecology and political economy in the central Sudan were such that groups of transporters achieved a monopoly situation, but only in portions of the trade. Within the savanna, the distribution of salt depended upon the movements of many small and large merchants. Undoubtedly, the operations of these savanna merchants and the Tuareg while they were in the savanna greatly facilitated the transport of other goods, both because goods were exchanged for or alongside salt and because merchants used their livestock to carry other commodities when they were not trading salt. Although these services were essential to the economy of the central Sudan, the transportation system was still inefficient.

The structure of the salt trade reveals the relative autonomy of the central Sudan as a region. The trade had little connexion with world markets, even though some European salt was imported into the region by the end of the nineteenth century. Virtually the whole of the domestic product was sold within the central Sudan, and the capital that financed the trade was also generated locally. While some trona and natron were exported to the middle Volta basin and Asante, which were outside the region, the amounts were relatively small in comparison with the whole trade, and even these exports were exchanged for kola nuts, a consumer good produced within the Asante state. To the south, natron and trona sales financed the import of textiles, cowries and other goods, and here more than anywhere else some links with the world economy can be discerned. But in the context of the total trade, these links were weak.

A comparison with the trans-Saharan trade of the nineteenth century establishes more clearly the regional orientation of the salt trade.[1] The trans-Saharan trade in slaves, ivory, ostrich feathers and tanned skins increased in value in the course of the nineteenth century, rising from an estimated value of £60,000–£100,000 per year early in the century to a high of £200,000–£220,000 per year in the decade of 1872–81, based on Tripoli prices. Thereafter, the value declined, although even in the 1880s and 1890s the total value of exports (£120,000–£146,000 per year) was probably greater than during any decade before the 1860s. Slaves constituted the most valuable export until the 1870s, when ivory and ostrich feathers surpassed slaves in value. Tanned skins became a major export in the 1880s. Since the trans-Saharan trade was obviously linked with external markets, it provides an excellent gauge of the ties to the world economy. Slave exports were mostly intended for Ottoman and North African markets, but ivory, ostrich feathers and tanned skins were destined for Europe. The shift in this trade, which occurred in the 1860s and 1870s, paralleled the transition from slaves to 'legitimate' goods on the West African coast. These estimates for the value of trans-Saharan exports are important not only because they provide a gauge for external links with the world economy but also because they establish when the pull of European capitalism began to be felt for the first time. External links were relatively modest anyway, but links to capitalist Europe had virtually no impact on the central Sudan economy until the 1860s.

The relative scale of the external trade is put in proper perspective by a comparison with the value of the salt trade. Based on Kano prices for Bilma salt, Mangari natron, *manda* salt, and trona in 1904, it can be estimated that the approximate value of the central Sudan salt trade was of the order of £98,000–£219,000 at a time when 2,300–5,400 tonnes of *kantu*, 1,000–1,500 tonnes of natron, 1,000–3,000 tonnes of *manda*, and 1,000–1,500 tonnes of trona were traded in the central Sudan.[2] These estimates do not account for variations in price in the nineteenth century or at different places in the central Sudan, and hence they serve as only the roughest of guides to the value of the salt trade. Since salt from the Benue salines, the Dallols, and Teguidda n'tesemt is excluded from these estimates, it can be assumed that these figures – conservative as they probably are – suggest the general order of magnitude of the trade. In any event, a range of £100,000–£200,000 does suggest several conclusions.

The salt trade was probably more valuable than the trans-Saharan trade in most years and was possibly much more valuable in many years, despite the fact that the trans-Saharan trade involved commodities that were much higher in unit price than salt. In short, one sector of the regional economy – salt – was at least as valuable as the export trade across the desert. It is generally assumed that the external trade via the Sahara was more valuable than the trade to the Guinea Coast until 1900,[3] but still allowance should be made for trade to the south in any attempt to evaluate the whole of the external trade of the central Sudan. Slaves were exported south for most of the nineteenth century; from the 1880s, shea butter and ivory were sent down the Niger River from Nupe and Adamawa respectively. The value of this trade increases the total for the whole export trade of the Sokoto Caliphate and Borno, but even so the salt trade remains of comparable proportions.

Clearly, commodities other than salt were important to the economy of the central Sudan. Textiles, leather goods, livestock and agricultural commodities were traded widely. Salt is only used as an indicator of the vitality of the regional economy. An examination of the textile trade, for example, would reveal a similar commercial structure; the trade in locally-produced cloth was probably more valuable than exports to North Africa and the Guinea Coast.[4] As late as 1900, this regional economy maintained its inward focus. The merchants and aristocrats of the Sokoto Caliphate and Borno had vague indications of economic adjustments to come, but most of their attention was directed towards controlling the patterns of trade and production within the central Sudan. The capitalist world order had little meaning as yet. A study of the salt trade demonstrates the extent to which the regional economy governed the actions of merchants and aristocrats alike.

Salt production and trade cannot be isolated from the larger social and economic formation of the central Sudan, but a study of this sector does provide numerous insights into how the forces of production were brought to

282

bear on one particular resource. The production of salt depended upon the labour of artisans (the Danawa), peasants (the Manga), slaves (in Kadzell and the desert), and women (at the Benue salines). Migrant labour was often necessary, since peasants and artisans in the Dallols, Mangari, Muniyo and Foli lived in farming villages during the rainy season and only set up salt-camps during the dry months. The relations of production were based on slavery or tribute. The proprietors of the salines either extracted surplus product from the workers because they owned the slaves who produced the salt or because they commanded the political power to force workers to pay a sizeable proportion of their product as a tax or rent. These relations were common in the central Sudan as a whole, although the specific relationships at the various salines departed from the general pattern to different degrees. Slaves worked in camps entirely by themselves in Kadzell, while they usually worked alongside their masters at the desert salines. In the Benue basin, they did 'women's work', a fiction that disguised slave–master relations under the rubric of gender-based relations of production. Women owed a portion of output to their husbands, who held the political titles that gave access to the salt flats, but slaves actually did much, if not most, of the work. The migrant peasants of Mangari and the Danawa artisans of Foli paid a share of their labour for the right to work the salt depressions. They were free to extract salt or not, but they could only work in places where they had agreed to tributary payments that derived from access to state power.

Tributary and slave relations characterised many other sectors of the central Sudan economy, not just the salt industry. Agriculture, in particular, was based on the extraction of surplus through slavery or tributary payments. A comparison between these sectors demonstrates that slave-holdings were sometimes much greater in agriculture than in the salt industry. Indeed, slave-holdings were characteristically small in salt production. There were certainly no large enterprises comparable to the slave plantations of the Sokoto Caliphate and Borno. Among free peasants and the artisan caste of Kanem, tributary payments in salt production appear to have been very similar to agricultural taxes. Salt production was seen as one of many types of dry-season activity and was taxed accordingly.

Merchants relied on clientage, kinship, and slavery as their means of labour recruitment. They formed bonds within specific ethnic fractions that enabled the establishment of patron–client relations to take place. These relations sometimes governed business transactions between independent traders, but more commonly merchants recruited junior kin from within their ethnic fraction who became apprentices and assistants in trade. Slave labour supplemented this dependent labour force; sometimes slaves too became clients, despite their servile status. Many other slaves performed agricultural and other menial tasks that supported the operations of merchants. These observations apply to the salt trade but can be made about trade in general in the central Sudan, if not about other parts of West Africa too.

The class relationships that characterised the organisation of trade and production were interpreted in terms of ethnicity, and it is the interface between class and ethnicity that unveils the forces of production in the central Sudan. Although no attempt is made here to extend the analysis to other sectors of the central Sudan economy, it can be suggested that a similar conclusion probably applies to the larger social formation of which the salt industry was a part. Manga, Kanuri, Ingelshi, Hausa and Tuareg had meaning in terms of the way people related across ethnic frontiers. These frontiers often coincided with access to the means of production, and to the extent that this pattern was true for the salt trade, this study has attempted to decipher how, when and why ethnicity changed in the context of the history of salt production and trade. Many questions remain unanswered in reconstructing the interface between class and ethnicity over the period of this study, but the broad outlines of the social relations of production are reasonably clear. In some cases ethnicity reinforced class antagonisms, while in other cases, class antagonisms were contained by ethnic relations. The Manga, for example, emerged as an ethnic fraction within Borno because of their identification with the salt districts of Muniyo and Mangari, where they were farmers and salt workers. Their consciousness as an ethnic group helped channel their class interests as a dependent peasantry. Buttressed by this consciousness, they moved into Gourbei in the early nineteenth century and redeveloped that district – subsequently known as Mangari – as a source of salt. To achieve this transformation, the Manga had to struggle against the al-Kanemi regime and aristocratic rights to the salines. By contrast, the Tuareg contained class antagonisms by exploiting a sense of ethnic solidarity that was essential in the maintenance of a commercial monopoly along the desert-edge. Resources in people were carefully managed to allow the expansion and contraction of this sector as climatic and political factors changed. To participate in the desert-side trade in salt, grain, textiles and other goods, individuals had an advantage if they were Tuareg, no matter whether they were slaves, freed slaves, descendants of slaves or vassals. Class differences were important, but they were interpreted within an ethnic context, not only across ethnic boundaries.

Ethnicity had meaning in relation to the access of people to the means of production. Individuals established an identity on the basis of ethnicity, but knowing that says little about the organisation of trade and production as such. Only when ethnicity is analysed in the context of the social and economic relations of production is it possible to discern how ethnicity evolved in specific historical situations. The salt industry fitted into a complex cultural mosaic, in which the salt workers, the salt merchants and the salt proprietors represented only scattered pieces in the social formation as a whole. Despite the incomplete picture that is formed by a study of the salt trade, one is still left with a valuable if partial view of the social formation that characterised the central Sudan. Regional in its focus, labour-intensive in its exploitation of resources, and vulnerable to the penetration of capitalism – all these factors aptly characterise the salt industry and demonstrate clearly why an era came to a crashing end with the imposition of colonialism.

Notes

Archival references, unless otherwise stated, are to the Archives Nationales du Niger, Niamey (if French) or to the Nigerian National Archives, Kaduna (if English). The Public Record Office, London, is referred to as PRO. Interviews are from the Lovejoy Collection unless otherwise stated.

1. Salt in the history of the Central Sudan

1 Carter (1975), 13; Kaunitz (1956), 1141–1144; Multhauf (1978), 4; Dauphinee (1960), 382–453; McDougall (unpublished, 1980), 1–6.
2 Estimates for human consumption of salt range from 0.7 to 7.5 kg per capita per year. I have adopted Multhauf's estimate of 4.5 kg; see Multhauf (1978), 3–6; also see McDougall (unpublished, 1980), 2–3.
3 Multhauf (1978), 210–227.
4 Multhauf (1978) provides the most convenient survey, but see Kaufmann (1960) and Nenquin (1961).
5 Chiang (1976), 516–530; Multhauf (1978), 88–89; Needham (1965) Vol. 4, pt. 2. Also see Kondo (1975), 61–65, on Japan; Gutman (1977), 88–96, on Mexico; and Godelier (1977), 127–151, on New Guinea, for comparisons with other areas.
6 Multhauf (1978), 54, 79, 80.
7 Multhauf (1978), 126–140.
8 Mollat (1968); Bridbury (1955); De Brisay and Evans (1975); Gilmore (1955), 1011–1015; Hauset (1927), 270–287; Jeannin and Le Goff (1968), 307–322.
9 Alexander (1975), 81–83; Gouletquer (1974a), 2–14; Gouletquer and Kleinmann (1972), 17–49.
10 Mosrin (unpublished, 1965), in Bouquet (1974), 132.
11 McDougall (unpublished, 1980), 46; also see Mauny (1961); Vikør (unpublished, 1979); and Sundström (1974).
12 Lovejoy and Baier (1975), 573–574.
13 Alkali (unpublished 1969); Unomah (1982).
14 Latham (1985); Minutes of Evidence before Select Committee on the African Slave Trade, PP 1850 IX(53).
15 McDougall (unpublished, 1980); Roberts (1980), 169–188; Curtin (1975); Lovejoy and Baier (1975), 551–581.
16 Le Rouvreur (1962), 448–450; Capot-Rey (1959), 188–192; Tubiana (1961), 196–243.
17 Capot-Rey (1959), 189–192.
18 Abir (1965),1–5; Abir (1966), 1–10.

19 McDougall (unpublished, 1980); also see McDougall (unpublished, 1976).
20 McDougall (unpublished, 1980); Carl and Petit (1954); Clauzel (1960); Du Puigaudeau (1940); Duchemin (1951), 853–867; Pales (1950).
21 Glanville (1930), 52–56; Curtin (1975); McDougall (unpublished, 1976); McDougall, (unpublished, 1980), 212–217.
22 McDougall (unpublished, 1980), 214–215.
23 Museur (1977), 49–80; Régnier (1961), 234–261.
24 McCulloch (1929), 21.
25 Hill (1977), 18.
26 Scientific tests on animals show that horses require 2.7 kg per year and milk cows 10.3 kg per year (Multhauf, 1978, 3), but these studies were done in North America. My estimate is deliberately low. All livestock require salt, however; see Bell (1960), 454–469.

2. Consumption of the Central Sudan salts

1 The confusion is especially noticeable in numerous colonial reports, but also see Baier (1980b).
2 Whitting (1940), 175.
3 Rattray (1913), II, 254.
4 McCulloch (1929), 18. Also see Ferguson (unpublished, 1973), 285.
5 McCulloch (1929), 19; Ferguson (unpublished, 1973), 285–288; Isiaku dan Amadu and Malam Alassan dan Ibrahim, Kano, 16 November 1969; Dan Tsoho Koki, Kano, 5 July 1973; Haruna Bakin Zuwo, Kano, 3 and 4 July 1973; and Mahmudu Koki, Kano, 8 and 14 July 1973
6 The bags were called *sukulmi*; see Ferguson (unpublished, 1973), 387.
7 Bargery (1934), 558.
8 Bargery (1934), 558.
9 Forde (1946), 56; Ferguson (unpublished, 1973), 389.
10 See the discussion in Flegel (1985).
11 Anon, 'Uburu and the Salt Lake', (1958), 84–96; Sutton (1981), 59–61; Interviews with Kagbanyiche Adzara, Daboya; Wasipewura Safo, Daboya; Imam of Daboya and Yagbumwura, summer 1969 (Daaku collection).
12 Sutton (1981), 43–61; Alagoa (1970), 325–326; Latham (1985); Return of traders from Accra to Salaga, November 1881, December 1881; Rowe to Kimberley, 16 January 1882 (PRO).
13 Mahmudu Koki, 14 July 1973.
14 Haruna Bakin Zuwo, 3 July 1973; Dan Tsoho Koki, 5 July 1973; Ferguson (unpublished, 1973), 69, 249, 258, 285–288; Dalziel (1937), 268.
15 Dalziel (1937), 268, 270, 447, 457, 483, 484, 550. Botanical names have been revised according to Hutchinson, Dalziel and Hepper (1954–72).
16 Ferguson (unpublished, 1973), 83–84.
17 Dan Tsoho Koki, 5 July 1973.
18 Ferguson (unpublished, 1973), 286.
19 Abdalla (unpublished, 1981), 87–110.
20 Abdalla (unpublished, 1981), 136–174.
21 Dalziel (1937); Hutchinson, Dalziel and Hepper (1954–72).
22 Seetzen (1810), 274.
23 Bowdich (1819), 333.
24 Misrah (1822), 11.
25 Adams (1823), 90; Clapperton (1829), 59.
26 Pochard (1943), 181–182; Moll (1913), 125.
27 McCulloch (1929), 22.

28 McCulloch (1929), 22.
29 Noel (1920), 554. Also see Cline (1950), 31.
30 Dan Tsoho Koki, 5 July 1973.
31 Haruna Bakin Zuwo, 3 July 1973; Mahmudu Koki, 14 July 1973; Isiaku dan Amadu and Malam Alassan dan Ibrahim, 16 November 1969.
32 Noel (1920), 554; Dan Tsoho Koki, 5 July 1973; also see Couty (1966), 119–129.
33 Dan Tsoho Koki, 5 July 1973; Ferguson (unpublished, 1973), 250–251.
34 Dan Tsoho Koki, 5 July 1973; Dalziel (1937), 180, 288, 341, 421, 427.
35 Noel (1920), 554; Haruna Bakin Zuwo, 3 July 1973; Dan Tsoho Koki, 5 July 1973.
36 Ferguson (unpublished, 1973), 142.
37 Dan Tsoho Koki, 5 July 1973; Haruna Bakin Zuwo, 3 July 1973; Dalziel (1937), 16, 31, 205, 316, 432, 486.
38 McCulloch (1929), 18.
39 McCulloch (1929), 18; Dan Tsoho Koki, 5 July 1973; Dalziel (1937), 2, 26, 27, 135, 302, 434, 440, 446, 461.
40 McCulloch (1929), 68.
41 McCulloch (1929), 21.
42 Dan Tsoho Koki, 5 July 1973.
43 Dalziel (1937), 42, 297, 311.
44 Denham, Clapperton and Oudney (1966), 661.
45 Although Clapperton noted that 'smoking tobacco is a universal practice, both of negroes and Moors' (1966, 661), it was not common by the end of the century.
46 Clapperton (1829), 59, 129; Lander and Lander (1858), II, 22; and Denham, Clapperton and Oudney (1966), 661.
47 Seetzen (1810), 274; Daumas and de Chancel (1856), 240; Cline (1950), 30; Richardson (1854), I, 260; Denham, Clapperton and Oudney (1966), 208; Barth (1857–59), I, 312.
48 Adams (1823), 90; Verger (1964), 349–369.
49 Bowdich (1819), 333.
50 Haruna Bakin Zuwo, 4 July 1973.
51 Natron, probably not *ungurnu*, however, was taken to Timbuktu, and perhaps as far as Segu, before 1820, as reported by Setafa, the emissary of the King of Segu, who was in Sierra Leone in the 1820s. Setafa reported that Hausa merchants brought natron to Timbuktu, where the 'Congwa is used for many purposes; it is mixed with their food, is taken as medicine, and is sometimes pounded and put into snuff; it has a bitter taste'; see Misrah (1822), 10–11. Also see Stewart (1979), 412.
52 Moll (1913), 125.
53 Bowdich (1819), 333.
54 Khamed Ibrahim as Khamed el Moumine, Abalak, 28 and 29 January 1976.
55 Leo Africanus (1956), II, 472.
56 Gansser (1950), 2,938–2,939, 2,943, 2,952.
57 Denham, Clapperton and Oudney (1966), 660; Rattray (1913), II, 244–246; Ferguson (unpublished, 1973), 314–315.
58 Gansser (1950), 2954; Dalziel (1926), 225–236; Ferguson (unpublished, 1973), 308.
59 Denham, Clapperton and Oudney (1966), 660; Dalziel (1937), 540.
60 Shea (unpublished, 1975), 151–152. I am also indebted to Shea for additional information.
61 Dalziel (1937), 442, 546.
62 Denham, Clapperton and Oudney (1966), 523.
63 Haruna Bakin Zuwo, 3 July 1973; Dan Tsoho Koki, 5 July 1973.
64 Lander and Lander (1858), II, 22.
65 Bowdich (1819), 325, 333.
66 Freydenberg (1911), 54; Le Rouvreur, cited in Bouquet (1974), 129.

67 Dalziel (1937), 113, 325, 418, 422, 428.
68 Bernus and Gouletquer (1976), 53.
69 Jeffreys (1940), 37–38.
70 Jeffreys (1940), 38.
71 Bernus and Gouletquer (1976), 61–64; Gouletquer, S. Bernus, Ahalla, Mahoudan and Fani (1979), 80–106; and E. Bernus, Ahalla, S. Bernus, Ag Arias (1979), 107–113.
72 See the text of Ibn Battuta in Bernus and Gouletquer (1976), 66–68.
73 Dalziel (1937), 39, 250.

3. The chemistry and geology of the Central Sudan salts

1 Multhauf (1978), 126–140.
2 J. Y. Gac to author, 21 January 1980. Also see Garde (1910), 262.
3 Margin, Rapport sur la production en sel et natron du canton de Birni, 1936; Loffler, Ancien cercle du Djerma, 1905.
4 Faure (unpublished, 1965); Maglione (1968, 1969, 1970a, 1970b, 1971); Garde (1910) 262–263; Falconer (1911), 151, 158–159, 265–267; Soula (1950), 21–56.
5 Faure (unpublished, 1965), 78–79.
6 Faure (unpublished, 1965), 82, 87.
7 Faure (unpublished, 1965), 111.
8 Faure (unpublished, 1965), 112.
9 Faure (unpublished, 1965), 111–114.
10 Faure (unpublished, 1965), 114.
11 Lange (1982), 21–23.
12 Faure (unpublished, 1965), 120–121.
13 Faure (unpublished, 1965), 121–122.
14 Faure (unpublished, 1965), 133–138.
15 Faure (unpublished, 1965), 138–139, 145.
16 Faure (unpublished, 1965), 144, 146.
17 Barth (1857–59), I, 312; Dupire (1962), 69.
18 Gouletquer (1974c), 47; Faure (unpublished, 1965), 48; Bernus and Bernus (1972); Bernus and Gouletquer (1976), 15–17.
19 Faure (unpublished, 1965), 37; Gouletquer (1974c), 51; Soula (1950), 8–9.
20 Faure (unpublished, 1965), 37; Soula (1950), 13–15.
21 Soula (1950), 24.
22 For a discussion of the cycle of efflorescence, see Faure (unpublished, 1965), 37–38, 42–44; Soula (1950), 9, 13, 26.
23 Faure (unpublished, 1965), 44.
24 Compte rendu, Miria, Babantapki, Droum, Kissambana, Guidimouni, 1926.
25 Barth (1857–59), I, 558–586; II, 24–71; III, 584–591.
26 Faure (unpublished, 1965), 44–45.
27 Faure (unpublished, 1965), 40.
28 Nicholson (1979), 44; Watts (1983), 98–99.
29 Vischer (1910), 301
30 Couty (1966), 78–79; Bouquet (1974), 185.
31 Faure (unpublished, 1965), 31.
32 Lambert (1938), 49.
33 Faure (unpublished, 1965), 31.
34 Perron (1926), 369.
35 Faure (unpublished, 1965), 32.
36 Faure (unpublished, 1965), 30; Barth (1857–59), III, 642.

37 Faure (unpublished, 1965), 36.
38 Dunstan, Reports on the Results of the Mineral Survey, 1907–08 and 1908–09; Falconer to H. Excell., 13 March 1908; SNP 7/10 3285/1909. For the other sites, see Barth (1857–59) III, 639.
39 Maglione (1968), 388; Mosrin (unpublished, 1965) as cited in Couty (1966), 71.
40 Maglione (1968), 390.
41 Maglione (1968), 265–267; also see Bouquet (1974), 130 and Pias (1962), 75 ff. as cited in Couty (1966), 68.
42 Maglione (1968), 390, 393–394. Also see Maglione (1969, 1970a, 1971).
43 Maglione (1968), 388–395; also see Bouquet (1974), 132.
44 Maglione (1968), 394.
45 Maglione (1970b), 81–94; Maglione (1968), 82, 84, 92.
46 Roche (1968), 73; Couty (1966), 67.
47 Bouquet (1974), 132, citing Mosrin (unpublished, 1965).
48 Verlet and Hauchecorne (1974), 32; Bouquet (1974), 27–29.
49 Verlet and Hauchecorne (1974), 32; Bouquet (1974), 28.
50 Beltaro and Bojarski (unpublished, 1971).
51 Beltaro and Bojarski (unpublished, 1971).
52 Beltaro and Bojarski (unpublished, 1971).
53 Falconer, Report No. 6, 1905; Falconer (1911), 266–267.
54 Falconer (1911), 265–266; Falconer, Report No. 3, 1905; Phoenix and Kiser (unpublished, 1942); Beltaro and Bojarski (unpublished, 1971).
55 Falconer, Report No. 8, 1905; Falconer, Report No. 6, 1905; Falconer (1911), 266; M.B. Duffill to author, 1 April 1976.
56 Wilkinson, Salt Rights and Industry, Keana, 1939.
57 Simpson (unpublished, 1949).
58 Beltaro and Bojarski (unpublished, 1971).

4. The technology of production

1 Soula (1950), 23.
2 Bouquet (1974), 70–75.
3 Bouquet (1974), 130.
4 Vikør (1982), 115–144; 170–175; Vikør (unpublished, 1979); Fuchs (film, 1978a; film, 1978b), Fuchs (1983), 52–74 and Fuchs (1984), 123–138.
5 Faure (unpublished, 1965), 58–71.
6 Baier (1980b), 123.
7 Coste, Monographie du Djado, 1935 (Archives de Bilma).
8 Faure (unpublished, 1965), 72–76.
9 Denham, Clapperton and Oudney (1966), 211.
10 For salt production in Kawar see Dixon Denham and Walter Oudney in Denham, Clapperton and Oudney (1966), 208–216; Abadie (1927), 274–275; Grandin (1951), 488–533; Vischer (1910), 259–269, 298–299; Nachtigal (1980) 67–71; Rohlfs (1868), 24ff; Lavers (unpublished, 1965), 139–145; Lavers (unpublished, 1976); and report of Capitaine Prévôt on Kawar, 1909, in Gentil (1946), 24–55.
11 Rohlfs (1868), 26–27.
12 Vischer (1910), 268–269.
13 The best analysis is Grandin (1951), 501–510, 529–533. Also see the 1906 Prévôt report on Bilma and Mouret's 1907 report on Fachi in Gentil (1946), 24–69.
14 Grandin (1951), 501.
15 Faure (unpublished, 1965), 106.

16 Grandin (1951), 501–508; Vikør (unpublished, 1979), 47–54.

17 Vikør (unpublished, 1979), 47–49; Grandin (1951).

18 Grandin (1951), 505; Vikør (unpublished, 1979), 48–49; Fuchs (1983), 68–69.

19 Denham, Clapperton and Oudney (1966), 215.

20 Denham, Clapperton and Oudney (1966), 215.

21 Grandin (1951), 505–6.

22 Abadie (1927), 75; Vikør (unpublished, 1979), 50.

23 Vikør (unpublished, 1979), 50.

24 Grandin (1951), 502.

25 Grandin (1951), 501; Vikør (unpublished, 1979), 47; Faure (unpublished, 1965), 105–109.

26 This discussion is based on the translation of al-Idrīsī in Vikør (unpublished, 1979), 170–172. Also see Lange (1982), 21–24.

27 al-Idrīsī, as translated in Vikør (1979), 172.

28 al-Idrīsī, as translated in Vikør (1979), 170–172. Lange (1982), 21–22. I have preferred the spellings of the names in Lange to those in Vikør's translation.

29 Fuchs (film, 1978a; film, 1978b); (1983), 52–74.

30 Fuchs (1983), 54; Mouret's report on Fachi, in Gentil, (1946), 56–69, Mouret (1908b), 183; Vikør (unpublished, 1979), 50–51.

31 Faure (unpublished, 1965), 54; Lhote (1933), 734.

32 Bernus and Bernus (1972), 30–46; Bernus and Gouletquer (1976), 55–56; Faure (unpublished, 1965), 49–54. Also see Abadie (1927), 275–277.

33 Faure (unpublished, 1965), 49, 51.

34 Bernus and Gouletquer (1976), 54.

35 Barth (1857–59), I, 312.

36 Chudeau (1909), 283–284.

37 For the Muniyo and Mangari natron and salt sites, see Gouletquer and Kleinmann (unpublished, 1973); Gouletquer (1974b), 572–577; Lahache and Marre in Tilho (1910–11), II, 533–588; Barth (1857–59), III, 45–70; Reibell (1931), 250–258; Foureau (1902), 570–588; Abadie (1927), 278–280; Soula (1950); Géry (1952), 309–320. Reports of W. H. Browne (1906), J. Becklesfall (1907), and Seccombe (1907), in Salt from Bornu Province – Samples for transmission to the Imperial Institute for Report (an earlier report by Vischer has not been located, but see Vischer (1910), 300); B. A. Marwick, Geidam Assessment Report, 1938; Mahomet Lawan, Touring Notes, in Local Salt Production, c. 1941; letter of H. Vischer, 13 December 1904, Geidam, in Confidential Papers on the Anglo-French Boundary from Niger to Chad; G. C. R. Mundy, Borno Report No. 5, May 1903; J. B. Wellman, Village Life on the Manga of Nguru, 1924; Janouih, Rapport sur les salines, secteur de Mainé-Soroa, 24 fév. 1916; Géry, Rapport de tournée, chef de subdivision de Mainé-Soroa, 1944; L'Adjoint des s.c. chef de la subdivision de Mainé-Soroa à Monsieur l'Administrateur commandant le cercle du Manga, 29 mai 1936 in Les Salines, 1905, 1936, 1938; l'Administrateur adjoint commandant le cercle du Manga à Monsieur le Gouverneur du Niger, Gouré, 12 juillet 1936; Battistini, Rapport annuel sur les salines, Magaria, 1 mars 1916; S. C. Boraud, Rapport de tournée effectuée dans le canton de Yamia du 6 octobre 1933 au 19 octobre 1933; Ronjat, Etude faite sur les mares salines du Mounyo. Leur exploitation – leur rapport – les ressources, qu'elles peuvent fournir au cercle du Gouré, 1905; Capitaine Chambert, Rapport sur une tournée pacifique dans l'est-sudest de Gouré, 23 sept. 1908; Compte rendu de tournée dans les cantons de Miria, Babantapki, Droum, Kissambana, et Guidimouni, 20 juin 1926, cercle de Zinder; L'Adjoint des s.c. chef de la subdivision de Mainé-Soroa, 29 mai 1936; Rapport politique, 2ᵉ trimestre, année 1914, cercle de Mainé-Soroa; Monographie du cercle du Manga, 24/7/41.

38 For the *kige* industry, see Nachtigal (1980), 103–104; Foureau (1902), 640–642, 662–665; Schultze (1913), 85–86; Vischer (1910), 297–298; Gouletquer and Kleinmann (unpublished,

1973), 8–12; Falconer (1911), 267; Boyle, French Circle of Ngegmi, 1911; J. R. Patterson (1919), in Mobber District Notebook; J. D. H., Kanembu District Notebook; Laforque, Monographie du cercle de N'Guigmi en 1913; Ravoux, Rapport de tournée effectuée du 10 au 30 août 1932, cercle de Nguigmi; Tournée administrative du 5 avril au 29 avril 1934, cercle de N'Guigmi; Fischer, Rapport de tournée administrative, cercle dans le Kadzell, 2–12 sept. 1934; Cagnier, Rapport de Tournée, canton de Komadougou, jan. 1935; Rapport de tournée du chef de subdivision de Mainé-Soroa, 10–27 fév. 1936; Riou, Rapport de tournée, 17 novembre au 1 decembre 1940, dans le canton de la Komadougou; Riou, Rapport de tournée, rive ouest du Tchad, Kadzell, Komadougou, 13 fév. au 1 mars 1941, cercle de N'Guigmi; Riou, Rapport de tournée dans la région ouest du cercle de N'Guigmi, 14–18 mars 1941; Riou, Rapport de tournée; Kadzell et secteur ouest de la Komadougou, 2–16 juillet 1941.

39 L'Adjoint des s.c. chef, Mainé-Soroa, 29 May 1936.
40 Foureau (1905), 521. Also see Soula (1950), 18.
41 Dunstan, Mineral Survey, 1906–07 [Cd. 4719], 20, (PRO); Géry (1952), 312.
42 Mahomet Lawan, Local Salt Production, c. 1941; and Browne, Salt from Bornu Province, 1906.
43 Garde (1910), 156.
44 Garde (1910), 156.
45 Foureau (1905), 661.
46 Garde (1910), 158.
47 Seccombe report in Becklesfall, 28 March 1907; and Dunstan, Mineral Survey, 1906–07 [Cd. 4719], 20 (PRO).
48 Géry (1952), 311–312. Also see Mahomet Lawan, Local Salt Production, c. 1941, who described the use of 'a pinch of castor flour' to counteract 'effervescence during the heating of the brine'.
49 Gouletquer and Kleinmann (unpublished, 1973).
50 See, for example, Foureau (1905), 575–588, whose discussion includes pictures. Foureau's account, based on his observations during the 1899–1900 season, is the earliest report on the Mangari industry. Other reports from the first decade of the twentieth century confirm Foureau's observations.
51 Foureau (1905), 661
52 Foureau (1905), 661.
53 Gouletquer and Kleinmann (unpublished, 1973), 33–34. Gouletquer has also elaborated on his preliminary findings in a letter to me, 3 May 1982.
54 For a comparison with these improvements and the development of modern chemistry, see Multhauf (1978).
55 Soula (1950), 15.
56 Cline (1950), 30.
57 Schultze (1913), 85–86; Falconer (1911), 267; Gouletquer and Kleinmann (unpublished, 1973), 8–13; Moll (1913), 127; Patterson, Mobber District Notebook, 1919; Alexander (1908), I, 342; Couty (1966), 78–79; Portères (1950), 48, 60.
58 Browne, Salt from Bornu Province, 1906.
59 Alexander (1908), I, 341, which includes a picture of *kige* production.
60 Moll (1913), 127; Nachtigal (1874), 15.
61 See Boyle, French Circle of Ngegmi, 1911; Ravoux, Rapport de tournée, cercle de Nguigmi, 1932; Tournée administrative, cercle de N'Guigmi, 1934; Fischer, Rapport de tournée administrative, cercle dans le Kadzell, 1934; Cagnier, Rapport de tournée canton de Komadougou 1935; Riou (17 nov. 1940; 13 fév. 1941; 14 mars 1941; 2 juillet, 1941); and Rapport de tournée, Mainé-Soroa, 1936.
62 Patterson, 1919, Mobber District Notebook; also see Alexander (1908), I, 341–342; and

Vischer (1910), 297–298.

63 Browne, Salt from Bornu Province, 1906; Moll (1913), 127.
64 Mahomet Lawan, Local Salt Production, c. 1941.
65 For the purity of *kige* see Table 3.5.
66 Portères (1950), 48, 60.
67 Gouletquer and Kleinmann (unpublished, 1973), 34.
68 Browne (Salt from Bornu Province, 1906) noted that pots were supported in an oven, which was open, on clay pedestals, similar to but smaller than the ones used to make *manda*. He noted that there were five partitions in each oven.
69 Gouletquer and Kleinmann (unpublished, 1973), 34.
70 Browne, Salt from Bornu Province, 1906.
71 Foureau (1905), 947.
72 Barth (1857–59), II, 259–260.
73 Barth (1857–59), I, 568.
74 Richardson (1854), II, 332.
75 Monteil (1894), 198.
76 Denham, Clapperton and Oudney (1966), 616.
77 Foureau (1905), 661.
78 Browne, Salt from Bornu Province, 1906; Seccombe report in Becklesfall, 28 March 1907.
79 Vischer (1910), 301. Also see Schultze (1913), 85; Vischer (1910), 287; and Reibell (1931), 278.
80 Misrah (1822), 15–16.
81 Barth (1857–59), III, 64.
82 Barth (1857–59), III, 45.
83 Janouih, Rapport sur les salines, 1916.
84 Mundy Bornu Report 5, May 1903.
85 Foureau (1902), 579, 587; Lahache and Marre in Tilho (1910–11), II, 563; Soula (1950).
86 Freydenberg (1911), 53.
87 Barth (1857–59), I, 533.
88 Lovejoy (1980), 123–124.
89 Landeroin in Tilho (1910–11), II, 336–337; Vial and Luxeuil, as cited in Couty (1966), 72. Also see Le Rouvreur (1962), 100.
90 Mosrin (unpublished, 1965), as cited in Couty (1966), 90.
91 Mosrin (unpublished, 1965), as cited in Couty (1966), 71–72; and Bouquet (1974), 132.
92 Couty (1966), 86–91; Bouquet (1974), 129–133; Pochard (1943), 183 (based on observations from 1936); Le Rouvreur (1962), 100–101; and Freydenberg (1911), 54–55. It should be noted that Freydenberg appears to have been mistaken in stating that there were two types of depressions, rather than different layers.
93 Freydenberg (1911), 55.
94 Bouquet (1974), 130; Couty (1966), 89. Also see Alexander (1908), II, 97; Moll (1913), 125; MacLeod (1912), 215–216; and Bruel (1935), 241–242, who cites Moll (1913), who cites Freydenberg (1911).
95 Bouquet (1974), 130.
96 Falconer (1911), 268; Falconer to His Excellency, 13 March 1908; Ferguson (unpublished, 1973), 387; Barth (1857–59), I, 312; Abadie (1927).
97 Faure (unpublished, 1965), 36; Margin, Rapport sur la production en sel et natron du canton de Birni, 1936; Loffler, Ancien cercle du Djerma, 1905.
98 For a discussion of Dallol Fogha, see Rochette (1965b), 169–203; Lambert (1938), 49–51; Abadie (1927), 277–278; Perron (1926), 368–372; Pales (1950), 28–29; Tercel, Epuise sommaire sur le Fogha, 10 sept. 1938.
99 Barth (1857–59), III, 64.
100 Barth (1857–59), III, 164.

101 Rochette (1965b), 197; Pales (1950), 29.
102 Rochette (1965b), 197; Tercel, Epuise sommaire sur le Fogha, 10 sept. 1938.
103 Tercel, Epuise sommaire sur le Fogha, 10 sept. 1938.
104 Faure (unpublished, 1965), 31; Barth (1957–59), III, 64.
105 Faure (unpublished, 1965), 32–33.
106 Margin, Rapport sur la production en sel et natron du canton de Birni, 1936.
107 Monteil (1894), 200.
108 Pales (1950), 30.
109 Gouletquer and Kleinmann (unpublished, 1973), 33–34.
110 Falconer, Geological Survey, No. 6, 1905; Falconer, Geological Survey, No. 5, 1905; Flegel (1880), 226.
111 Phoenix and Kiser (unpublished, 1942); also see Beltaro and Bojarski (unpublished, 1971); and Tattam (unpublished, 1942). For an early, brief description, from 1832, see Allen and Thomson (1848), I, 377. For 1867, see Rohlfs (1872), 74.
112 Keana (unpublished, 1983), 20–27. Also see Nzekwu (1964), 262–278; and Adefuye (unpublished, 1976).
113 Fremantle (1920), 53–54 appears to be an account of Akwana, but there is a slight possibility that he was describing Awe production.
114 Ward, Awe Assessment Report, 1920; Varvill, Salt Tax Re-assessment, Awe District, 1937; Report on Salt Industry, Awe District 27 October 1941; Unomah (1982), 151–178; Fremantle (1920), 53–54.
115 Fremantle (1920), 53. Also see the anonymous article, 'Uburu and the Salt Lake', 84–96; and Beltaro and Bojarski (unpublished, 1971). Howard Wilkinson, Salt Rights and Industry, Keana, Lafia Emirate, 26 October 1939, noted the existence of seven workable salt deposits in Tiv Division, all in the northern part. One was near Nyam in the Nbaikuran area of Mbaduem, a second in the Mbatoho area of Mbagwem, near Makuri, three more in Mbakin and Mbayon area of Nagohor, a sixth between Mbakper and Mbamar areas in Njiriv, and the seventh between the Mbaiger and Mbagusu areas in Yonov. The output was unknown, but a 'good white salt, albeit rather coarse', was produced. The Nyam deposit was about 260 ha in extent, which suggests that potential output could have been very large. One of these sites may be identified with Moi Igbo, noted in Beltaro and Bojarski. Moi Igbo appears to have acquired its name from the Jukun office holder apparently responsible for salt production and taxation; see Fremantle (1920), 53–54; and Simpson (unpublished, 1949).
116 Phoenix and Kiser (unpublished, 1942).
117 Afigbo (1974), 8, 24–25; Northrup (1972), 217–236.
118 Sutton (1981), 43–61; Alagoa (1970), 325–326.
119 Portères (1950) has the fullest discussion of vegetable salts; also see Schultze (1913), 85, 180; Shea (unpublished, 1975), 149–154; Hamman (unpublished, 1975), 40; and Aku (unpublished, 1974), 13.
120 Shea (unpublished, 1975), 152.
121 Aku (unpublished, 1974), 13.
122 Cited in Aliyu (unpublished, 1973).
123 Hamman (unpublished, 1975), 40.
124 Moll (1913), 127.
125 Forde (1946), 56; Rohlfs (1872), 85; and Ferguson (unpublished, 1973), 389.
126 McCulloch (1929), 68.
127 Allen and Thomson (1848), I, 406. It should be noted that large quantities of European salt were imported along the Guinea Coast by the eighteenth century. According to Latham (1985), 'several hundreds of bushels of salt were a common feature of the cargo of Liverpool ships sailing for Calabar in the 1770's'. By the 1820s salt was a major export in the Calabar

293

palm oil trade, and by 1845 the port received 2,984 tonnes of salt. Although not much, if any, of this salt reached the central Sudan, the expansion of this trade does demonstrate that the frontier for European salt must have been moving steadily inland, even before the Niger River was opened to European merchants.

128 Baikie to Lord Russell, 22 March 1862 (PRO).
129 Multhauf (1978), 54, 79–80, 126–129; 137–139.
130 Fuchs (1983), 68.
131 Multhauf (1978), 126–129, 137–139.
132 Watts (1983).
133 Shea (unpublished, 1975).
134 Many of these points have been made more generally for West Africa by Hopkins (1973), 50, 73–75.
135 Hill (1977), 18.

5. The Volume of salt production

1 The danger of exaggeration is clear in two earlier studies of the Benue Valley salts. Thus Unomah (1982), 166, has claimed that 10,000 tonnes of salt were produced annually at Awe, 6,700 tonnes at Azara, and 6,000 tonnes at neighbouring sites in the nineteenth century, if not earlier, and Adefuye (unpublished, 1976) has estimated over 50,000 tonnes were produced yearly at Keana. As will be apparent below, even 10,000 tonnes of salt for the whole of the central Sudan is a lot of salt.
2 For an excellent discussion of this trade, see Baier (1980b), 122–128.
3 Baier (1980b), 125.
4 Rapport commercial, cercle de Zinder, 2e trimestre 1904, as cited in Baier, 1980b, 125. Also see Gadel (1907c), 52. Bilma exported 15,000 loads via Zinder, 800 via Tessaoua, and 1,500 by Guidambado. M. de Jonquières claimed that Bilma exported 40,000 loads per year; loads of 150 kg suggest a volume of 6000 tonnes, which seems exaggerated.
5 Prévôt, Rapport, 1909, (Archives de Bilma); The import of salt from French territory (28,510 cwt: or 1,271 tonnes) in 1907 probably represented part of the Bilma trade (Northern Nigeria Blue Book, 1907). Also see Barth (1857–59), III, 601.
6 Nachtigal (1980), 69.
7 For Baier's criticism of Nachtigal, see (1980b), 125.
8 Other figures are also too high; Abadie (1927, 274–275) estimated that 100,000 loads were produced in Kawar and another 10,000 loads at Fachi. 80,000 loads was estimated by Muhammad al-Hashā'ishī (1912).
9 Faure (unpublished, 1965), 108; also see Baier (1980b), 237.
10 Faure (unpublished, 1965), 108.
11 Faure (unpublished, 1965), 107–108.
12 Fuchs (1983), 55.
13 Périé, Monographie du poste de Bilma, 1941, (Archives de Bilma); Faure (unpublished, 1965), 143; Fuchs (1983), 55.
14 Périé, Monographie du poste de Bilma, 1941.
15 Barbaste, Rapport: tournée de la Djado, 1938, (Archives de Bilma).
16 Faure (unpublished, 1965), 64.
17 Mosrin, cited in Bouquet (1974), 132.
18 Hewby, Borno Provincial Report, 1912.
19 Moll (1913), 125; also quoted in Bruel (1935), 243.
20 Lovejoy (1980), 123.
21 Mosrin, as cited in Bouquet (1974), 132.
22 Bouquet (1974), 133.

23 Bouquet (1974), 132.
24 Ronjat, Etude faite sur les mares salines du Mounyo, 1905.
25 Dunstan, Mineral Survey, 1906–07 [Cd. 4719] (PRO). Also see the reports and references in SNP 7/8 2281/1907, 'Salt from Bornu Province', especially those by Becklesfall (1907), Seccombe (1907), and Browne (1906). An earlier report by Vischer has not been located, but he did estimate that two million cones were produced; Vischer (1910), 300.
26 Battistini, Rapport annuel sur les salines, Magaria, 1916.
27 Niven, 16 January 1942.
28 Annual Report, Northern Nigeria, 1904, 297; F. Cargill, Annual Report, Kano, 1907.
29 Cargill, Annual Report, Kano, 1907.
30 Barth (1857–59), III, 63.
31 Barth (1857–59), I, 530–539; and Flegel (1883–85), 139; Lovejoy (1974), 569.
32 Summary of Caravan Statistics of Nassarawa Province for the Year Ending 31 December 1907; Cargill, Annual Report on Kano Province for 1907; Annual Report, Northern Nigeria, 1904, 298.
33 I wish to thank R. J. Gavin for information on 1912, which he obtained from the Northern Nigeria Blue Book.
34 Rapport sur l'exploitation des salines et mares de natron, 1915.
35 Soula (1950), 3–4. I have been unable to locate Soula's report of 1946, on which his thèse de doctorat d'Etat en Pharmacie was later based. Nor have I seen the earlier report of Aude (unpublished 1942).
36 Soula (1950), 87.
37 Ravoux, Rapport de tournée effectuée du 10 au 30 août, 1932, cercle de Nguigmi.
38 Assessment Report, Magumeri District, 1934. There appears to be an error in this report, which estimates the weight of the cones at 260 lb. I have assumed that the figure should be 26 lb, or approximately 12 kg. To the south-east of Lake Chad, however, the cones weighed only 5–6 kg; see Moll (1913), 127.
39 See Boyle, French Circle of Ngegmi, 1911; Laforque, Monographie du cercle de N'Guigmi, 1913; Tournée administrative du 5 avril au 29 avril 1934, cercle de N'Guigmi; Moll (1913), 127; Alexander (1908), I, 341; Fischer, Rapport de tournée administrative, cercle dans le Kadzell, 1934; Cagnier, Rapport de tournée, canton de Komadougou, 1935; Riou, Rapports, 1940–41; Patterson, Mobber District Notebook, 1919.
40 L'administrateur adjoint commandant le cercle du Manga, 12 juillet 1936; L'Adjoint des s.c. chef de la subdivision de Mainé-Soroa, 29 mai 1936.
41 Bovill (1922), 57; Tercel, Epuise sommaire sur le Fogha, Gaya, 10 sept. 1938. An earlier report gives a figure of 2,900 tonnes, which seems completely out of line. I assume there has been an error in copying; see Lamarche, Rapport sur les salines, 20 mars 1916.
42 Faure (unpublished, 1965), 32, 35.
43 Margin, Rapport sur la production en sel et natron du canton de Birni, (subdivision de Niamey), 30 jan. 1936.
44 Urfer, Rapport sur le recensement du canton du Tagazar, 1951.
45 Thérol, Notice sur Teguidda n'Tessoum, 1907.
46 Mauny (1961), 333; Abadie (1927), 277; Lambert (1935), 370.
47 Cortier (1914), 151.
48 Rapport sur l'exploitation des salines et mares de natron, 1915.
49 Faure (unpublished, 1965), 55. A 1955 report from In Gall indicates a level of 3,600 tonnes; very likely this estimate contains a decimal error.
50 Clauzel (1960), 80; Meunier (1980), 135.
51 Régnier (1961), 234–261.
52 Museur (1977), 59.
53 Lugard, Northern Nigeria Annual Report, 1904.

54 Unomah (1982), 166.
55 Wilkinson, Salt Rights and Industry, 26 October 1939.
56 Roberts, Report on Lafia Division, 6 Sept. 1951.
57 Based on the figures in Keana (unpublished, 1983), 39–41.
58 Unomah (1982), 166; Adefuye (unpublished, 1976).
59 Phoenix and Kiser (unpublished, 1942).
60 Browne, Report of 19 May 1906. Also see Abadie (1927), 270, and the account of Ba Kambar in Horowitz (1972), I, 162.
61 Latham (1985); Manning (1985); Minutes of Evidence before Select Committee on the African Slave Trade, PP 1850, IX (53) (I wish to thank John Latham for this reference).
62 Baikie to Lord Russell, 22 March 1862 (PRO); Estimates, Customs Department, 1903.
63 Northern Nigeria Blue Book, 1906.
64 Annual Report of the Customs Department, 1907. Total imports were 31,215 tonnes in 1907.
65 Vial and Luxeuil (cited in Couty, 1966, 87 fn) reported that 500 workers produced 280 tonnes of trona in 1936–37, which suggests a level of productivity of almost 2 workers per tonne, but they also stated that it took three workers to produce a tonne. The length of the season is unknown. As Couty (87 fn) argues, however, these figures are not possible, at least data for 1961–64 suggest as much. At this time, when an average of 6,900 tonnes was produced, the ratio of 2 or 3 workers per tonne would require a labour force of 14,000–20,000, but the total number of *haddad* – the only source of labour – in the area of Foli was less than 4,000. It seems more likely, therefore, that productivity was much higher than indicated by Vial and Luxeuil, although the level of output per worker cannot be calculated. Unfortunately, Couty, whose study of the industry is quite extensive, does not provide data on productivity.
66 Cortier (1914, 158–159), estimated that a good saline at Bilma – one which measured 20 by 30 m – could produce 400 *kantu* (17 kg each) and 30 bags of *beza*, based on a labour force of twelve workers. This estimate suggests an output of 6.8 tonnes of *kantu* per saline, but the workers could easily manage a number of salines.
67 The output of salt at Fachi was probably of the order of 600–700 tonnes per year in peak years. In 1909 output was estimated at 636 tonnes; Faure (unpublished, 1965), 143. Fuchs (1983), 54, estimates output per basin at 2.6 tonnes, with a range of from 1.5 to 8.0 tonnes. Workers operated 5–7 basins, which suggests an output of 3.25–4.8 tonnes per worker, based on units of four workers. This calculation is higher than that used in the text.
68 Gadel (Rapport sur une tournée en Air, 1905), estimated the number of workers would be 200 in 1907; Cortier (1909, 151), estimated output at 600 tonnes in 1909.
69 Faure (unpublished, 1965, 31–32), made a more careful study of the number of salt workers in 1963. In the lower Dallol, there were 580 salt workers, who made 500 tonnes of salt, while in the upper Dallol 213 workers made another 500 tonnes. Faure's estimate suggests an output of 1.26 tonnes per worker, but the total number of workers (793) is considerably less than earlier estimates, which appear to have included merchants, firewood sellers, and others indirectly associated with the industry but not actually engaged in production. Tercel (Epuise sommaire sur le Fogha, 1938), estimated that each *koko* (filtering device) produced 2–3 kg of salt per day, with most production occurring from January to March. Tercel does not indicate the number of workers per *koko*, however. In Dallol Bosso, approximately 1.25 tonnes of salt were produced per family – the size of the family is unknown. In 1951, P. Urfer estimated that 232 families were producing natron in upper Dallol Bosso, west of Hamdalleye in the Tagazar. Each family produced an average of 50 bars (25 kg) so that total production was 11,600 bars (290 tonnes), although in 1949–50, the previous year, the average was only 15 bars per family, or a total of 3,480 bars (87 tonnes) (Rapport sur le recensement du canton du Tagazar, Cercle de Niamey, subdivision de Filingue, 1951).
70 Janouih's survey (Rapport sur les salines, 1916) of thirty *manda* salines reveals that it took

4,690 workers to produce 707 tonnes of salt; that is it took between six and seven workers to produce one tonne in the course of the season, but these workers did everything – gather firewood, collect salt-earth, carry brine, etc. Estimates for individual sites suggest a range of from six workers per tonne to over nine workers per tonne. In 1905 Ronjat (Etude faite sur les mares salines du Mounyo) reported 270 *cases de sel* in Muniyo, which produced an average of 40 cones of salt per unit every three days for five months, or 540,000 cones (each weighing 5 kg), 2,700 tonnes. Ronjat's figures suggest a level of productivity of two workers per tonne, if *cases* consisted of fifteen workers each. Other estimates in 1936 suggest a range of two to three workers per tonne. The *adjoint* of Maine-Soroa (1936) estimated a five month season, with firings every ten days. Furnaces varied in size from 40 to 170 cones, but an average of 60 cones (each weighing 6 kg) and fifteen workers per furnace for the 166 furnaces suggests that 2,490 workers produced 900 tonnes of salt, or that it took 2.76 workers to produce each tonne.

Information on the productivity of *kige* output is confusing but indicates, nonetheless, that it took a number of workers to produce a tonne of salt. In 1932 Ravoux counted 419 workers, who made an estimated 2,000 cones (Rapport de tournée, 10 au 30 août 1932, cercle de Nguigmi), but this calculation suggests a phenomenal ratio of 21 workers per tonne of salt, which seems hard to believe. The *adjoint* of Mainē-Soroa estimated that 600 workers made 150 tonnes of *kige*, or 4 workers made one tonne, which seems more reasonable.

71 Keana (unpublished, 1983), 39–41. It should be noted that Roberts' report (1951) cannot be trusted. It is unlikely that Roberts actually witnessed production, and it is even possible that he never visited Keana. His figures appear to have been manufactured to please his superiors.
72 Rapport sur l'exploitation des salines et mares de natron, 1915; Baier (1980b), 118–121.

6. The mobilisation of labour

1 Watts (1983), 89–122; For a similar situation in the production of gold in the western Sudan, see Curtin (1973), 623–631.
2 Barth (1857–59), I, 551, 556.
3 Barth (1857–59), III, 35–36.
4 Mundy, Bornu Report No. 5, 1903.
5 Marwick, Assessment Report, Geidam District, 1938.
6 Patterson, Assessment Report, Geidam District, 1917.
7 Watts (1983), 285–297.
8 Géry (1952) 310.
9 Soula (1950), 15–19; Mobber District Notebook, Vol. II; Reed, Mobber District Notebook, 1928; Hall, Mobber District Notebook, 1933; Tegetmeier, Mobber District Notebook, 1933; Reynolds, Mobber District Notebook, 1924; Patterson, Mobber District Notebook, 1919; Mundy, Bornu Report No. 5, 1903; Compte rendu de tournée dans le canton de Goudoumaria, 1937; Compte rendu de tournée dans les cantons de Miria, Babantapki, Droum, Kissambana et Guidimouni, 1926; Saunders (unpublished, 1980).
10 Mahomet Lawan, Local Salt Production, c. 1941.
11 Bouquet (1974), 99–100.
12 Nachtigal (1877), 53.
13 Nachtigal (1881), 446.
14 Le Rouvreur (1962), 379. Nicholaisen (1968), 92, reported 25,000 Danawa. Lebeuf (1959, 36), reported 14,000 Danawa in the Massakori area, which apparently included Nguri.
15 Trystram (1958).
16 Bouillié (1937), 87.
17 Le Rouvreur (1962), 377–385.
18 Barth (1857–59), III, 163–166; 545–546.

19 Rochette (1965b), 184–186.
20 Rochette (1965b), 189–190.
21 Esperet, Monographie de la subdivision de Gaya, 1917; Tercel, Epuise sommaire sur le Fogha, 1938.
22 Watts (1983), 82–147.
23 Bernus and Bernus (1972), 47–60.
24 Sarkin Awe and Elders, 4 June 1974 (Webster, unpublished, 7); Tsumbu of Kekura, 30 June 1974 (Webster, 41); Kindabi Awe, 21 July 1974 (Webster, 69); Adefuye (unpublished, 1976); Wilkinson, Salt Rights and Industry, Keana, 1939; Keana (unpublished, 1983).
25 Périé, Monographie du poste de Bilma, 1941, (Archives de Bilma); also see Fuchs (1983).
26 Rohlfs (1872), 26–27; also see Vikør (unpublished, 1979), 138–139; Fuchs (1983), 53.
27 Géry (1952), 311; Wellman, Village Life of the Manga of Nguru, 1924; Chambert, Rapport, 1906; Rapport politique, cercle de Mainé-Soroa, 1914; and Salifou (1971), 175.
28 Géry (1952), 310.
29 Mundy, Bornu Report, No. 5, 1903. Also see Géry (1952), 310, who reported in 1945 that Adebour had 234 permanent residents while Cheri had 182. Also see Vischer's letter of 13 December 1904, in Confidential Papers on the Anglo-French Boundary.
30 Vischer (1910), 299–301.
31 Mundy, Bornu Report No. 5, 1903;
32 Browne, Salt from Bornu Province, 1906.
33 L'Adjoint des s.c. chef de la subdivision de Mainé-Soroa, 1936; also see Compte rendu de tournée du chef de la subdivision de Mainé-Soroa, Goudoumaria, 1937.
34 Géry (1952), 310.
35 Testimony of Koyar, born c. 1882, in Horowitz (1972), II, 497.
36 Géry (1952), 313.
37 Horowitz (1972), III, 747; although Horowitz states that the figure is for Maine-Soroa, it appears more likely that it was a figure for the whole Manga region.
38 L'Administrateur du cercle du Manga, 1929.
39 Urvoy (1942a), 28.
40 Ronjat, Mares salines, 1905; L'Adjoint des s.c. chef de la subdivision de Mainé-Soroa, 1936; Mundy, Bornu Report, No. 5, 1903; and Rapport politique, cercle de Mainé-Soroa, 1914.
41 Géry (1952), 312–315; Marwick (Assessment Report, Geidam, 1938), found that workers from Dara, who made *manda* at Silimma, operated three furnaces in units of eleven, thirteen and fifteen workers.
42 This is based on observations made at Adebour, Fanamiram, Dietkorom, Bitoa, and Koboboa; see Rapport politique, cercle de Mainé-Soroa, 1914. Thirty-nine men at Silimma produced 4,386 cones at their three furnaces in 1938, giving an average of 1,462 at each one; see Marwick, Assessment Report, Geidam, 1938.
43 Ronjat, Mares salines, 1905; Browne, Salt from Bornu Province, 1906.
44 Dunstan, Mineral Survey, 1906–7 [Cd. 4719], (PRO).
45 Janouih, Rapport sur les salines, secteur de Mainé-Soroa, 1916. It should be noted that the tonnage cited in my preliminary article (1978b, 647) is here corrected.
46 Rapport sur l'exploitation des salines et mares de natron, 1915.
47 For Faure on the cycles of Mangari, see above, Chapter 3. In 1905 Gourselik had 25 work units, which appears to correspond to the number of furnaces (Ronjat, Mares salines, 1905). Ten years later, the number of furnaces was greatly reduced; perhaps down to five, since there were only 80 workers at the site (Janouih, Rapport sur les salines, secteur de Mainé-Soroa, 1916).
48 Laforque, cited in Monographie du cercle de N'Guigmi, 1913.
49 Géry (1952), 310; Marwick, Assessment Report, Geidam, 1938.
50 Chambert (1908), 272.

51 Monographie du cercle du Manga, 1941.
52 Account of Lawan Gaptia, born c. 1888, and son of Katiella Abdu, in Horowitz (1972), II, 422.
53 Chambert (1908), 272; see also report of Lawan Gaptia, in Horowitz (1972), II, 422, 522, who notes that slaves came from Mandara.
54 Mundy, Bornu Report, No. 5 and 8, 1903.
55 Hewby, Report on Bornu Province, 1906.
56 Barth (1857–59), III, 163–164, 166.
57 Barth (1857–59), III, 545, 546.
58 Barth (1857–59), III, 165.
59 Commandant de cercle de Dosso, rapport de tournée, Dallol, Gaya, Fleuve, Fogha, 1924.
60 Loffler, Monographie: Ancien cercle du Djerma, 1905.
61 Cantons, chefs de canton de la subdivision de Gaya, 1932.
62 Loffler, Monographie: Ancien cercle du Djerma, 1905.
63 Esperet, Monographie de la subdivision de Gaya, 1917.
64 Loffler, Monographie: Ancien cercle du Djerma, 1905.
65 Marsaud, Monographie du secteur de Gaya. Droit coutumier Tienga, 1909.
66 Map in Tilho (1910–11) of western region.
67 Rapport sur l'exploitation des salines et mares de natron, 1915; and Commandant de cercle de Dosso, rapport de tournée, Dallol, Gaya, fleuve, Fogha, 1924.
68 Tercel, Epuise sommaire sur le Fogha, 1938.
69 Faure (unpublished, 1965), 31–32.
70 Barth (1857–59), III, 163; but contrast with Perron (1924), 63–64; Esperet, Monographie de la subdivision de Gaya, 1917.
71 Barth (1857–59), III, 165.
72 Loffler, Monographie: Ancien cercle du Djerma, 1905; Esperet, Monographie de la subdivision de Gaya, 1917; Perron (1924), 63–64.
73 Loffler, Monographie: Ancien cercle du Djerma, 1905. For a later report, see Rochette (1965b).
74 Loyzance, Canton de Birni N'Gaouré, recensement, 1947.
75 Marsaud, Monographie du secteur de Gaya. Droit coutumier Tienga, 1909. Also see Perron (1924), 59, 76.
76 Marsaud, Monographie du secteur de Gaya. Droit coutumier Tienga, 1909.
77 Marsaud, Monographie du secteur de Gaya. Droit coutumier Tienga, 1909.
78 Loyzance, Canton de Birni N'Gaouré, recensement, 1947; Beauvilain (1977), 136.
79 Nachtigal (1980), 103–104; Patterson, Mobber District Notebook, 1919; Fischer, Rapport de tournée administrative, cercle dans le Kadzell, 1934; Cagnier, Rapport de tournée, canton de Komadougou, 1935; Ravoux, Rapport de tournée, cercle de Nguigmi, 1932; Kiou, Rapports, 1940–1941.
80 Patterson, Mobber District Notebook, 1919; Alexander (1908), I, 342.
81 Monod, as cited in Portères (1950), 48.
82 Riou, Rapport, 13 fév–1 mars 1941.
83 Riou, Rapports, 1940–41.
84 Ravoux, Rapport de tournée, cercle de Nguigmi, 1932.
85 Ravoux, Rapport de tournée, cercle de Nguigmi, 1932.
86 Barth (1857–59), II, 260.
87 Barth (1857–59), II, 315.
88 Barth (1857–59), II, 260; III, 604.
89 Nachtigal (1980), 103–104. This is confirmed later by Chambert (1908), 283.
90 Freydenberg (1911), 23.
91 Riou, Rapport, 13 fév–1 mars 1941.

92 J. D. H., Kanembu District Notebook, I, 1926; and Alexander (1908), I, picture, 342.
93 Tomlinson, Report of 1918.
94 Tegetmeier, Yerwa Assessment Report, 1925.
95 Falconer (1911), 267.
96 Monod, as cited in Portères (1950), 48.
97 Patterson, Mobber District Notebook, 1919.
98. Boyle, French Circle of Ngegmi, 1911; Patterson (1919), in Mobber District Notebook; J. D. H., Kanembu District Notebook; Laforque, Monographie du cercle de N'Guigmi, 1913; Ravoux, Rapport, 1932; Tournée administrative du 5 avril au 29 avril 1934, cercle de N'Guigmi; Fischer, Rapport, 1934; Cagnier, Rapport, 1935; Rapport de tournée du chef de subdivision de Mainé-Soroa, 1936; Riou, Tournée, 1940; Riou, Rapports, 1941.
99 Riou, Tournée, 17 nov–1 dec, 1940.
100 Nafyn, Rapport de tournée, canton de Laouan-Yerimari, 1934.
101 Lovejoy and Baier (1975), 551–581.
102 Baier and Lovejoy (1977), 391–411.
103 Gadel (1907c), 51; Thérol, Notice sur Teguidda n'Tessoum, 1907.
104 Bernus and Gouletquer (1976), 53–54.
105 Rottier (1924), 82; Le Sourd (1946), 11; Gadel (1907a), 374.
106 Gadel (1907a), 375; Prévôt in Gentil (1946), 23; Rottier (1924), 82; and Colonna di Leca, Rapport, 1907 (Archives de Bilma).
107 Ibn Battuta, as cited in Bernus and Gouletquer (1976), 67.
108 Bernus and Gouletquer (1976), 60; and Bernus, Ahalla, Bernus and Ag Arias (1979), 107–113. It should be noted that Bernus and Gouletquer do not state that slaves were used, but in the light of Ibn Battuta's observations, it seems highly likely.
109 Bernus and Gouletquer (1976), 53–61; Thérol, Notice sur Teguidda n'Tessoum, 1907.
110 For an excellent reconstruction of the history of Azelik, see Bernus and Gouletquer (1976); and Gouletquer, Bernus, Ahalla, Mahoudan, and Fani (1979), 80–106.
111 Cortier (1914), 150–151.
112 Bernus and Gouletquer (1976), 56.
113 Gadel (1907c), 51.
114 Thérol, Notice sur Teguidda n'Tessoum, 1907.
115 Cortier (1914), 150; and Rapport sur l'exploitation des salines et mares de natron, 1915.
116 Bernus and Bernus (1972), 66–68.
117 Bernus and Bernus (1972), 23.
118 Bernus and Bernus (1972), 23.
119 Bernus and Bernus (1972), 24.
120 Gadel (1907a), 375; also see Prévôt in Gentil (1946), 23. Carbou (1912, 34), learned that many of the slaves seized by the Awlad Sulayman in Kanem were sold to Kawar.
121 Rohlfs (1872), 27.
122 Rottier (1924), 82.
123 Périé, Monographie du Poste de Bilma, 1941 (Archives de Bilma).
124 Grandin (1951), 500 fn.
125 Rottier (1924), 82.
126 Vischer (1910), 255; and Gadel (1907a), 375.
127 Prévôt, in Gentil (1946), 23.
128 Prévôt, in Gentil (1946), 23.
129 Rottier (1924), 82.
130 Prévôt, in Gentil (1946), 23; Fuchs (1983), 60–61.
131 Rottier (1924), 82; Grandin (1951), 502; Fuchs (1983), 53, 60–61.
132 Rottier (1924), 82. Le Sourd (1946, 11), also notes Tubu slaves at Dirku.
133 Prévôt, in Gentil (1946), 23.

134 Gadel (1907a), 374.
135 Denham, Clapperton and Oudney (1966), 215.
136 Prévôt, in Gentil (1946), 23.
137 Rapport sur l'exploitation des salines et mares de natron, 1915.
138 Grandin (1951), 507–508; Vikør (unpublished, 1979), 53–56.
139 Grandin (1951), 508.
140 Vikør (unpublished, 1979), 53–54.
141 Vikør (unpublished, 1979), 56; and (1982), 119.
142 Grandin (1951), 507.
143 Mouret, in Gentil (1946), 68. In Gentil, the report is anonymous, but see the original archival source, or Mouret (1908b), 173–187. Also see Colonna di Leca, Rapport, 1907 (Archives de Bilma).
144 Fuchs (1983), 60–61.
145 See Cordell (unpublished, 1972, 1979) for a general history of the Awlad Sulayman. For Tubu raids on Fachi, see Fuchs (1983), 53.
146 Nachtigal (1980), 52. Also see the excellent discussion in Fisher's footnotes, Nachtigal (1980), 53 fn. and Cordell (unpublished, 1972).
147 Abadie (1927), 133–134.
148 Palmer (1936), 66.
149 In my earlier report on the Borno salt industry (1978b, 641), I overstated my case that slaves were important in the production of salt in Kawar. It may be, as I stated, that the number of slaves 'approached several thousand' at the height of Borno power in the sixteenth and seventeenth centuries, but it cannot be proven. Furthermore, the implication that slaves were that numerous later is wrong. My mistake is based on misunderstanding the productivity of the Bilma salines. It was not necessary to have that many workers to produce 2,000 tonnes of salt. Although slaves were probably used to produce natron and salt elsewhere in Kawar, their numbers need not have been large either. It is more likely that there were never more than a few hundred slaves involved in production.
150 Barth (1857–59), II, 608.
151 Le Rouvreur (1962), 377–85; Carbou (1912), I, 49–72, 209–212. Lebeuf (1959), 9.
152 J. D. H., Kanembu District Notebook, I, 1936 refers to 'Dugu' among the Kanembu of Borno who engaged in crafts.
153 Bouillié (1937), 86.
154 Barth (1857–59), II, 608. Compare with Nachtigal (1881), 446–447.
155 Barth (1857–59), II, 608; Nachtigal (1881), 480.
156 Bouillié (1937), 33; Carbou (1912), I, 45–46.
157 Freydenberg (1911), 33.
158 Carbou (1912), I, 46; Bouillié (1937), 55.
159 Vial and Luxeuil (1938), cited in Couty (1966), 87.
160 Bouquet (1974), 129.
161 Vial and Luxeuil (1938), as cited in Couty (1966), 87.
162 Le Rouvreur (1962), 76, 378; Conte, (1979).
163 Couty (1966), 87 fn. Also see Le Rouvreur (1962), 378.
164 Conte (1979), 75.
165 Laforque in Monographie du cercle de N'Guigmi, 1913; Also see L'Adjoint des s.c. chef de la subdivision de Mainé-Soroa, 1936.
166 Grandin (1951), 505; Bernus and Bernus (1972), 38–39.
167 Grandin (1951), 509.
168 Eladoga Oji, Keana, 21 December 1975 (Aliyu Collection); Ayitogo Onyapa, Keana, 18 December 1975 (Aliyu Collection); Galadima Salihu, Ribi; Makwangiji Jibirin and Malam Bala Ismaila, Awe, 26 April 1976; Varvill, Salt Tax Re-assessment. Awe, 1937; Ward,

Assessment Report, Awe, 1920.
169 Ward, Assessment Report, Awe, 1920; also see Nzekwu (1964), 266.
170 Keana (unpublished, 1983), 21–22.
171 Makwangiji Jibirin, Awe, 26 April 1976.
172 Tafida Yakuba Abawa, Kanje, 26 April 1976; Makwangiji Jibirin and Malam Bala Ismaila, Awe, 26 April 1976; Eladoga Oji; Keana, 19 July 1975 (Ojobo Collection); Osabwa Aklo, Keana, 15 December 1975; Otaki Agbo, Keana, 20 December 1975 (Aliyu Collection); and Odapu Onyapa, Keana, 20, 22 July 1975 (Ojobo Collection).
173 Tafida Yakuba Abawa, Kanje, 26 April 1976.
174 Makwangiji Jibirin, Awe, 26 April 1976.
175 Alhaji Aliyu and Galadima Salihu, Ribi, 26 April 1976.
176 Eladoga Oji, Keana, 19 July 1975 (Ojobo Collection); but note that Keana (unpublished, 1983, 20–27) reports that there were few slaves at Keana.
177 Tafida Yakuba Abawa, Kanje, 26 April 1976.
178 Unomah (1982), 168.
179 Makwangiji Jibirin and Malam Bala Ismaila, Awe, 26 April 1976.
180 For Madugu Mai Gashin Baki, see Flegel (1985).
181 Ward, Assessment Report, Awe, 1920.
182 On the origins of the various towns, see Makwangiji Jibirin and Malam Bala, Awe, 26 April 1976; Sarkin Zaure and Alhaji Ali, Kanje; Galadima Salihu and Alhaji Aliyu, Ribi, 26 April 1926; and Tafida Yakuba Abawa, Kanje, 26 April 1976.
183 Fremantle (1920, 53–54) describes production at Akwana, where Jukun women did most of the work.
184 Ward, Assessment Report, Awe, 1920.
185 Varvill, Salt Tax Re-assessment, Awe District, 1937.
186 Unomah (1982, 167) states that seasonal migration characterised the pre-colonial period too, but it is likely that his informants were referring to the early colonial period when slave labour was no longer available.
187 Keana (unpublished, 1983), 20–27.

7. Proprietorship: the rights to salt and natron

1 Grandin (1951), 496.
2 The Bilma war occurred in 1173 AH, 1759 AD, according to the Asben Record of Abu Tali Annaju; see Palmer (1936), 66. Also see Prévôt, 1909, in Gentil (1946), 29–31, 34.
3 Grandin (1951), 497–498; Lange (1982), 21–24; Jean, Rapport sur l'Oasis du Kaouar, 1906 (Institut Catholique de Paris).
4 Grandin (1951), 497–498.
5 Grandin (1951), 495.
6 Grandin (1951), 496; Jean, Rapport sur l'Oasis du Kaouar, 1906 (Institut Catholique de Paris).
7 Cortier (1914), 159; Gadel (1907a), 373.
8 Grandin (1951), 497.
9 Grandin (1951), 497.
10 Prévôt, in Gentil (1946), 23.
11 Grandin (1951), 497.
12 Grandin (1951), 499–500, 502.
13 Colonna di Leca, Rapport, 1907 (Archives de Bilma); Mouret (1908b), 176–183; Fuchs (1983), 53.
14 Barbaste, Rapport; tournée de la Djado, 1938 (Archives de Bilma).
15 Coste, Monographie du Djado, 1935; Barbaste, Rapport, 1938; Lejeune, Carnet mono-

graphique du canton du Kawar, 1952 (all in Archives de Bilma).
16 Cortier (1914), 150.
17 Thérol, Notice sur Teguidda n'Tessoum, 1907.
18 Bernus and Gouletquer (1976), 11–12.
19 Bernus and Bernus (1972), 61.
20 Bernus and Bernus (1972).
21 Bernus and Bernus (1972), 61–73.
22 Bernus and Bernus (1972), 65–73.
23 Bernus and Bernus (1972), 36.
24 Bernus and Bernus (1972), 45.
25 Bernus and Bernus (1972), 45.
26 Galadima Salihu and Alhaji Aliya, Ribi, 26 April 1976.
27 Norton-Traill, Assessment Report, Keana District, 1914.
28 Varvill, Salt Tax Re-assessment, Awe District, 1937; see also Salihu Usa, Awe, 17 July 1974 (Webster, unpublished, 59.)
29 Ward, Assessment Report, Awe, 1920.
30 Varvill, Salt Tax Re-assessment, Awe District, 1937.
31 Report on Salt Industry, Awe District, 1941.
32 Report on Salt Industry, Awe District, 1941.
33 Report on Salt Industry, Awe District, 1941.
34 Keana Native Salt, 1948; Natron-Traill, Assessment Report, Keana District, 1914; Keana (unpublished, 1983).
35 Eladoga Oji; Ayitogo Onyapa; Oyokpa Oga (Aliyu Collection).
36 Varvill, Salt Tax Re-assessment, Awe District, 1937.
37 Varvill, Salt Tax Re-assessment, Awe District, 1937.
38 Varvill, Salt Tax Re-assessment, Awe District, 1937.
39 Mohamadu of Kekura, 10 June 1974 (Webster, unpublished, 12); Tsumbu of Kekura, 30 June 1974 (Webster, 41).
40 Adefuye (unpublished, 1976).
41 Jifi Acho of Kekura, 11 June 1974 (Webster, unpublished, 20); Kindabi of Kekura, 21 July 1974 (Webster, 69); Agwa of Tsohongari, Awe, 14 July 1974 (Webster, 53-55); Sarkin Awe and elders, 4 June 1974 (Webster, 7); Tsumbu of Kekura, 30 June 1974 (Webster, 41); Unomah (1982).
42 Varvill, Salt Tax Re-assessment, Awe District, 1937.
43 Chambert (1908), 298. On feudalism in Borno, although not specifically applied to Mangari and Muniyo, see Cohen (1966), 101–103; and Nur Alkali (unpublished, 1978).
44 Monographie du cercle de Manga, 1941.
45 Chambert (1908), 279–280.
46 Chambert (1908), 280.
47 Ronjat, Etude faite sur les mares salines du Mounyo, 1905.
48 Ronjat, Etude faite sur les mares salines du Mounyo, 1905; Géry (1952), 308.
49 Brenner (1973), 16.
50 Ronjat, Etude faite sur les mares salines du Mounyo, 1905.
51 Garde (1910), 156.
52 L'Adjoint des s.c. chef de la subdivision de Mainé-Soroa, 1936.
53 Chambert (1908), 298.
54 J. D. H., Kanembu District Notebook, I, 1926.
55 Gouletquer and Kleinmann (unpublished, 1973), 33; Tilho (1910–1911) II, 424.
56 Landeroin in Tilho (1910–1911), II, 423–424.
57 Barth (1857–59), III, 55.
58 Ronjat, Etude faite sur les mares salines du Mounyo, 1905.

59 Barth (1857–59), II, 42.
60 Barth (1857–59), II, 43.
61 Barth (1857–59), II, 44.
62 Trystram (1958); Couty (1966), 82; Bouquet (1974), 129.
63 Trystram (1958); Couty (1966), 82.
64 Bouquet (1974), 129.
65 Le Rouvreur (1962), 101.
66 Couty (1966), 82–83; Vial and Luxeuil, cited in Couty (1966), 83 fn.; Bouquet (1974), 129.
67 Géry (1952), 316.
68 Bouquet (1974), 129.
69 Boyle, French Circle of Ngegmi, 1911.
70 Nachtigal (1980), 103–104; Chambert (1908), 283.
71 Ravoux, Rapport de tournée, cercle de Nguigmi, 1932.
72 Riou, Rapports, 1940–41.
73 Loyzance, Canton de Birni n'Gaouré, recensement, 1947; Marsaud, Monographie du secteur de Gaya. Droit coutumier Tienga, 1909; Loffler, Monographie; Ancien cercle du Djerma, 1905; Perron (1924), 55; Lambert (1929).
74 Loffler, Monographie: Ancien cercle du Djerma, 1905.
75 Barth (1857–59), III, 164–5.
76 Perron (1924), 51–83. Also see M. B. Alkali (unpublished, 1969).
77 Perron (1924), 63–64; Also see Barth (1857–59), III, 158 on Birnin Debe ruins.
78 Loyzance, Canton de Birni N'Gaouré, recensement, 1947; Robaglia, Rapport de tournée dans le sud-est de la subdivision de Niamey, 1941; Beauvilain (1977), 136, 141–144.
79 Grandin (1951), 502.
80 Grandin (1951), 502.
81 Grandin (1951), 508–510.
82 Bernus and Bernus (1972), 35, 39, 54.
83 Ronjat, Etude faite sur les mares salines du Mounyo, 1905.
84 Laforque, in Monographie du cercle de N'guigmi, 1913.
85 Rapport politique, cercle de Mainé-Soroa, 1914.
86 Compte rendu, Miria, Babantapki, Dorum, Kissambana, Guidimouni, 1926.
87 L'Adjoint des s.c. chef de la subdivision de Mainé-Soroa, 1936.
88 L'administrateur adjoint commandant le cercle du Manga, 1936.
89 Compte rendu de tournée du chef, Mainé-Soroa, 1937.
90 Géry (1952), 316–317.
91 Ravoux, Rapport de tournée, cercle de Nguigmi, 1932.
92 L'Adjoint des s.c. chef de la subdivision de Mainé-Soroa, 1936. Also see L'Administrateur adjoint commandant le cercle du Manga, 12 juillet 1936.
93 Boyle, French Circle of Ngegmi, 1911.
94 Vial and Luxeuil, cited in Couty (1966), 83 fn.
95 Mosrin (unpublished, 1965), cited in Couty (1966), 83.
96 Bouquet (1974), 129.
97 Trystram (1958); Conte (1984), 108–113.
98 Nicolaisen (1968), 95.
99 Marsaud, Monographie du secteur de Gaya. Droit coutumier Tienga, 1909.
100 Ward, Assessment Report, Awe, 1920.
101 Varvill, Salt Tax Re-assessment, Awe District, 1937.
102 Salihu Usa, Awe, 17 July 1974 (Webster, unpublished, 59).
103 Odapu Onyapa, 17 Dec. 1975 (Aliyu Collection).
104 Varvill, Salt Tax Re-assessment, Awe District, 1937.

8. Salt marketing networks

1 Baier (1980b), 122–128; Vikør (unpublished, 1979) and (1982), 115–144; Bernus and Bernus (1972). See also Spittler (1984), 139–160.
2 For a list of caravan sizes, as estimated by various observers, see Vikør (1982), 134.
3 Fonferrier (1923), 304.
4 Bernus and Bernus (1972); Thérol, Notice sur Teguidda n'Tessoum, 1907.
5 Lhote (1969), 1022–1027; Museur (1977), 50.
6 On the Tubu trade at Bilma, see Nachtigal (1980), 69; Prévôt in Gentil (1946), 23; Barth (1857–59), I, 396 and III, 601; Rohlfs (1868), 26–27; Hornemann (1964), 112; Cline (1950), 35; Denham, Clapperton and Oudney (1966), 215; Gadel, Rapport sommaire, 1905.
7 Baier (1978).
8 Barth (1857–59), I, 289.
9 Denham, Clapperton and Oudney (1966), 654.
10 Barth (1857–59), I, 453.
11 Barth in Petermann (1851), 142; and Barth (1857–59), I, 340.
12 Rohlfs (1868), 27.
13 Gadel, Rapport sur une tournée en Air ou Azbin, 1905 (Archives de la République du Sénégal).
14 Barth (1857–59), I, 392.
15 Nicolaisen (1963), 217.
16 Barth (1857–59), I, 370.
17 Barth (1857–59), I, 322.
18 Barth (1857–59), I, 338, 343.
19 Lovejoy (1980), 62–64.
20 Baier (1980b), 47–48.
21 Baier (1980b), 68.
22 Gadel (1907c), 30; also see Baier (1980b), 46–47, 68–69, 77, 100, 106, 110; Salifou (1972).
23 Barth (1857–59), III, 616.
24 Vischer (1910), 251, 255.
25 Vischer (1910), 225, 265.
26 Lefebvre, Etude sur la question de Bilma, 1904 (Archives de la République du Sénégal).
27 Barth (1857–59), I, 369. Vikør (1982) is wrong in translating the Hausa title as 'chief of the whites' – chief of the Arabs would be more exact, which reflects the importance of the trans-Saharan trade.
28 Noma (1969), 186.
29 Barth in Petermann (1851), 150–151.
30 Barth (1857–59), I, 345, 343, 338, 370; III, 129; also see Le Sourd (1946).
31 Lovejoy (1980), 62–64.
32 Vischer (1910), 268.
33 Prévôt, Rapport, 1909 (Archives de Bilma).
34 Lefebvre, Etude sur la question de Bilma, 1904.
35 J. D. H., Kanembu District Notebook, 1926.
36 J. D. H., Kanembu District Notebook; 1926; P. F. M.-S., Kanembu District Notebook; Destenave (1903d), 720; Mundy, Bornu Report No. 5, 1903; Alexander (1908), II, 55, 68.
37 Destenave (1903d), 720; Freydenberg (1911), 54.
38 Tilho (1910–1911), II, 336–337; J. D. H., Kanembu District Notebook, 1926; MacLeod (1912), 215.
39 Alexander (1908), I, 304.
40 Alexander (1908), I, 302.

41 Talbot (1911b), 272–273, and picture; also see Alexander (1908), II, 100 for a picture.
42 Barth (1857–59), II, 66.
43 Mundy, Bornu Report, No. 5, 1903.
44 D'Huart (1904), 173.
45 Mundy, Bornu Report, No. 5, 1903.
46 Alexander (1908), I, 305.
47 P. F. M.-S., Kanembu District Notebook, 1935.
48 Barth (1857–59), II, 66.
49 Alexander (1908), II, 96.
50 Mundy, Bornu Report, No. 5, 1903.
51 Freydenberg (1911), 54.
52 Barth (1857–59), I, 563.
53 Seetzen (1810), 274, 335.
54 Denham, Clapperton and Oudney (1966), 610–611; 615.
55 Denham, Clapperton and Oudney (1966), 422.
56 Denham, Clapperton and Oudney (1966), 616.
57 Flegel (1985).
58 Barth (1857–59), I, 539.
59 Barth (1857–59), I, 530, 533.
60 Barth (1857–59), I, 533.
61 Miko Hamshak'i, 8, 10 September 1969.
62 Bak'o Madigawa, 1 December 1969.
63 Abubakar Salga, 28 December 1969.
64 Adamu Isma'ila, 23 January 1970.
65 Mato, 29 January 1970.
66 Ibrahim dan Yaro, 27 January 1970; Iliyasu, 27 January 1970.
67 Umaru Musa, 8 March 1970.
68 Audu, Unguwar Agalawa, Makwara Yamma, 1 April 1970.
69 Baier (1980), 52–53.
70 Ba Kambar, b. 1888, in Horowitz (1972), II, 397.
71 Krilama, born in 1887 in Goudoumaria, in Horowitz (1972), II, 392, 394.
72 Clapperton (1829), 137–138.
73 For this discussion of the trade to Mandara and the south, I am indebted to information supplied by Steven Morrisey; see his forthcoming Ph.D. Thesis.
74 Madziga (1976), 64–79.
75 Miko Hamshak'i, 10 September 1969; also see Abubakar (1979), 109, 115.
76 Aliyu (unpublished, 1973); and Rohlfs (1872), 43.
77 Aliyu (unpublished, 1973), citing E. B. NacNaghten, Short Description of Towns, Ibi, 6 Oct. 1898. Also see Low (1972), 75–77, although Low does not equate Borno emigration with the *jihad.*
78 Usman (1983), 191–192.
79 Cargill, Annual Report on Kano Province, 1907.
80 Patterson, Assessment Report, Geidam, 1917.
81 Wellman, Village Life of the Manga of Nguru, 1924.
82 Horowitz (1972), I, 1b.
83 Horowitz (1972), I, 1c, 61, 108, 113–114.
84 Ronjat, Etude faite sur les mares salines du Mounyo, 1905; see also Becklesfall, Salt from Bornu Province, 1907.
85 Horowitz (1972), I, 1b.
86 Horowitz (1972), I, 1c, 87, 164; Chambert (1908), 272; Mundy, Borno Report No. 5 and 8, 1903.

87 Hewby, Report for Bornu Province, 1905, 1906.
88 Baier (1980b), 47–55.
89 Muhammad Lawan Barmo, 5 January 1970; Musa Urwatu, 3 January 1970; Ahmadu Aci, 4 February 1970.
90 Baier (1980b), 51.
91 Barth (1857–59), I, 527.
92 Barth (1857–59), I, 429.
93 Daumas and de Chancel (1856), 266.
94 Baier (1980), 52–53.
95 Lugard, Northern Nigeria Annual Report, 1902.
96 Cohen, A. (1971), 266–281.
97 Hill (1966), 349–366.
98 Baier (1980b), 27, 29, 47–48, 51, 55, 59, 69; Lovejoy (1980), 81–83, 127–131; also see Shea (unpublished, 1975), 232–240.
99 Usman (1981); Lovejoy (1980), 51–73.
100 Hoskyns-Abrahall, Kano City, Re-assessment, 1926.
101 Ferguson (unpublished, 1973), 180.
102 Ferguson (unpublished, 1973), 180.
103 Shea (unpublished, 1975), 232–233.
104 Fremantle, letter of 19 May 1913 (Nigerian National Archives, Ibadan).
105 Hoskyns-Abrahall, Kano City, Re-assessment, 1926.
106 Barth (1857–59), I, 515–516.
107 Clapperton (1829), 226; and Denham, Clapperton and Oudney (1966), 672.
108 Lugard, Northern Nigeria Annual Report, 1904.
109 Barth (1857–59), I, 486.
110 Mahaman Alhassan, 30 Aug. 1973; Umaru Sumaila, 19 August 1973.
111 Nasiru (unpublished, 1973), 25, 33.
112 Mahmudu Dayyidu, 8 July 1973.
113 Barth in Petermann (1851), 195.
114 Bawa Halidu, 17 December 1970 (Shea collection); and interview of 22 February 1971 in Kura, arranged by Alhaji Gambo (Shea collection); Shea (unpublished, 1975), 56, 78–80.
115 Frewen, Assessment Report, Kura District, 1909; Frewen, Assessment Report, Gora District, 1909.
116 Barth (1857–59), I, 515.
117 Barth (1857–59), I, 503.
118 Lugard, Northern Nigeria Annual Report, 1904; Cargill, Annual Report on Kano Province, 1907.
119 Aminu Dahiru, 8 July 1973.
120 Suda Sha'aibu, 22 July 1973; Audu Mohamman, 14 August 1973; Umaru Sumaila, 19 August 1973; Halilu, 16 August 1973; Aminu Dahiru, 8 July 1973.
121 Audu Mohamman, 14 August 1973.
122 Lovejoy (1980), 91, 123–124.
123 Muhammadu Kasori, 1 February 1970.
124 Musa na Madabo, 1 February 1970.
125 Abubakar Usmanu, Yan Bundu, 21 March 1970.
126 Lovejoy (1980), 75–83, 89–95; (1973), 633–657.
127 Glenny, Assessment Report, Rano District, 1909.
128 Sule na Aba, 30 November 1969.
129 Foulkes, Assessment Report, Dan Buram District, 1912; Webster, Assessment Report, Dan, Iya District 1912; Cargill, Annual Report on Kano Province, 1907.
130 Shea (unpublished, 1975), 56, 81, 83–84, 236, 237.

131 Bell, Assessment Report, Dutsī District, 1911.
132 Glenny, Assessment Report, Wombai District, 1909; Glenny, Assessment Report, Barde's District, 1909.
133 Sarkin Bugu, Tarai, Rano District, 8 October 1971. Borno traders came to Bunkure, Rano District where they brought salt and stayed with *fatoma*; Isiyaku Bunkure, 30 September 1971; also see account of Dan Ladi Marini, Rurum, Rano District, Kano Emirate; also at Tofa, Dawakin Tofa District, Kano Emirate, Borno traders came with salt; see account of Badan Ladi, 28 October 1971; for Rogo, see account of Uban Gila, November 1971; Sarkin Bugu of Tarai listed Musa Mai Mangawa as an important *fatoma* at Kibiya (8 October 1971); Garba of Limawa, Kumbotso District, Kano Emirate (27 October 1971) also noted that Manga used to come there (all in Shea Collection).
134 Usman (1983), 192.
135 Musa Urwatu, 3 January 1970; Muhammad Lawan Barmo, 5 January 1970; Ahmadu Aci, 4 February 1970.
136 Bala Idi, 5 February 1970.
137 Mamman of Gabankare, 5 February 1970.
138 Inusa, Sule and Ali of Shibdawa, 6 January 1970.
139 Usman (1983).
140 Abubakar of Kudan, 1 December 1975; Usuman of Kudan, 1 December 1975; and Yusufu of Hunkuyi, 6 December 1975; Shea (unpublished, 1975), 83–84.
141 Lugard, Northern Nigeria Annual Report, 1904.
142 Adams (1823), 90.
143 Bowdich (1819), 333 for Asante in 1817.
144 Frazer in Misrah (1822), 16. It should be noted that I. B. Sutton (1981, 43–61), has misunderstood my earlier discussion of Borno salt, which included modern Ghana in the area of distribution (1978b, 637). As is clear from the article, my reference is to both natron and sodium chloride. In a footnote she states: 'Lovejoy's contention that Borno salt was traded all over Ghana in the eighteenth and nineteenth centuries [is] unlikely. No Ghanaian source is cited in support of this statement. Most evidence, admittedly imprecise for this period, seems to indicate that Hausa and Moshi [Mossi] traders bought salt at various points along the Volta, for distribution elsewhere, rather than bringing salt in. Sea salt had a more than local importance and wider distribution than implied in this article, at least in Ghana.' As is clear from a fuller analysis of the central Sudan salt industry, sea salt and central Sudanic salts could compete in the same markets. Trona and natron in particular had little competition from sea salt, and hence it should not be surprising that these salts were taken to the Volta basin. 'Ghanaian' sources have been cited for this trade at various points in this book, but also see several reports cited in Johnson, *Salaga Papers* (n.d.), and the following interviews from the Daaku Collection: Mumuni of Salaga; Baba of Salaga; Respondent 'X', Kpandai; Nyaba Abukari, Salaga. Paul Lubeck also collected similar traditions at Yendi. Imam al-Juma' a Hajj Abdullah b. Hajj al-Hasan, Yerdi, interviewed 3 August 1968 states that Hausa traders brought natron, along with other goods. Also see the account of Mohammad b. Khalid b. Ya'qub b. Muhammad Bawa Mai Kanwa b. Mahmoud, 10 July 1968. Ya'qub came to Yendi in search of his father, who was a trader – which is confirmed in his nickname, 'Mai Kanwa' (dealer in natron). Abu Bakr Baba Galadima b. Sarki Muhammad b. Musa b. Mallam Muhammad b. 'Abdullah, interviewed 17 July 1968, mentions natron as traded in Dagomba; and Al-Hajj Idris Kambangna b. Ya Na Imam 'Abdullah b. 'Abd al-Mu'min b. Zakariyya, interviewed 20 July 1968, includes natron in the list of goods traded (all in Lubeck Collection). Ferguson, in Report on Mission to Atabubu, 1891 (PRO), reported that traders from Hausa and Marawa brought horses, donkeys, bullocks, shea butter, cloths, saddles, leather goods, natron and small metal work. Altham noted that Mossi caravans brought slaves, sheep, cattle, horses, leather-work, cloths, hats,

salt, and swords from the north, and he quotes a French report from Wagadugu that salt was one of the commodities traded south to Yeji and other places in the middle Volta basin (in Further Correspondence relating to the Northern Territories, 1898, PRO). In addition to these 'Ghanaian' sources, virtually every kola merchant interviewed in connexion with my study of the trade to Asante listed various types of natron as important exports. For a discussion of Dallol Fogha salt in this trade, see above, pp. 217–218.

145 Bowdich (1819), 333.
146 Clapperton (1829), 68.
147 Clapperton (1829), 136–137.
148 Clapperton (1829), 133.
149 Lander and Lander (1858), II, 66.
150 Lander and Lander (1858), II, 22.
151 Lander and Lander (1858), I, 152.
152 Barth (1857–59), I, 439, 479.
153 Barth (1857–59), I, 503, 515; also see Hastings (1926), 156. A report by Krause (1888), 'the transit duty on natron [at Kano] amounts to ten million cowries', does not appear to be an independent estimate and probably derives from Barth's earlier estimate.
154 Ferguson (unpublished, 1973), 182.
155 Umaru Sumaila, 19 August 1973.
156 Hawwa Sule, Dan Mak'eri, 11 February 1970; Ibrahim dan Yaro of Kumurya, 27 January 1970.
157 Habu Muhammadu of Katsina, 6 January 1970; Husaini Danjaji of Kano, 26 August 1969.
158 Birtwistle, Kano, Trade with, 1913. Also see H. Libert, in Birtwistle, Hausa trade with Lagos, who reports on *zongo* between Ebute Metta and Yaba where Hausa caravans stopped. (Both Birtwistle references are to Nigerian National Archives, Ibadan.) Also see Glenny, Assessment Report, Rano District, 1909.
159 Lugard, Northern Nigeria Annual Report, 1904.
160 Lagos Blue Books; I wish to thank R. J. Gavin for this material.
161 Bature of Utai, 23 January 1970; Baladari Ali, 20 March 1970; Umaru Mahamma, of Tsaure Fankurun, 4 May 1970; Audu, Makwara Yamma, 1 April 1970; Alhaji of Kuiwar Gabas, 1 April 1970; Miko Hamshak'i, 10 September 1969; Husaini Danjaji, 26 August 1969; Audu Ba'are, 1 January 1970; Gambo of Katsina, 3 February 1970; Isma'ila, Habību and Musa Alhasan of Kawo, 29 January 1970; Isa Madigawa, 1 January 1970; Baba Dayidu, 4 September 1969.
162 Gambo of Katsina, 2 February 1970.
163 Ahmadu Aci, 4 February 1970; Musa Urwatu, Katsina, 3 January 1970; Muhammad Lawan Barmo, Katsina, 5 January 1970.
164 Lovejoy (1973), 633–657; (1980), 81.
165 Sa'idu Ladan na Madugu, Sokoto, 23 February 1970.
166 Basharu na Mahu, Gummi, 7 March, 1970; Muhammadu dan Amarya, Gummi, 5 March, 1970.
167 Bawa Ibrahim, Jega, 26 February 1970; Garkuwa dan Asiri, Jega, 26 February 1970; Audu Isa of Jega, 26 February 1970.
168 Clapperton (1829), 294.
169 Allen and Thomson (1848), I, 404.
170 Flegel (1883–85), 139.
171 Lagos Blue Books.
172 Ralph Moor to C.O., No. 141 of 9/9/99 in CSO 1/13 of 1899, cited in Afigbo (1974), 72.
173 Ekechi (1981), 49, quoting from Enugu Archives, OWDIST (9/6/3, No.45/1920), Report on Owerri Division, for January-June 1920.
174 Kallo Muhammadu, Sumaila, 13 February 1970; Umaru, Garfa, 13 February 1970; Idi

Abubakar, Garfa, 13 February 1970; Malam Idi Magani, Guzai, 13 February 1970; Muhammadu Jibirin, Gala, 13 February 1970; Garba Husaīnī, Dandi, 11 February 1970. Galena, often referred to incorrectly as antimony, was used as a cosmetic, particularly as eye shadow.

175 Foulkes (Assessment Report, Dan Buram District, 1912) found that Awe salt was brought to Minjibir, while Cargill (Annual Report on Kano Province for 1907) states that Awe salt was brought to Kano in bags: 'It is preferred to any other kind of salt but only small quantities are brought.' Also see Low (1972), 223; Rohlfs (1872), 74.

176 Dorward (1976), 579.

177 Adesue Aba, Tse Aba, 11 July 1975; Iba Aive, Mbabur, Ushongo, 29 July 1975; Malu Abuur, Lessel, Mbagwa District, 6 August, 1975; Rev. J. E. I. Sai, Harga, Shitire District, 10 September 1975; Gbise Gbise Ako, Mbayongo District, 12 September 1975; T. G. Iarva, Sai, 13 September 1975; Gberindyer Naiko, Mbaibon, Mbateuem Ukem Division, 17 September 1975; Mhambe Shie, Mbaakav, Mbaterem District, 18 September 1975; Ingough Yade, Mbadwem, 22 September 1975 (all in Kpurkpur Collection).

178 Chilver (1961), 248–249.

179 Ada Ogbona, Edumoga District, 13 July 1975; Aba Ogo, Edumoga District, 25 July 1975; Michael Ochagwu, Edumoga District, 16 August 1975 (all in Agbo Collection). On the Abakwariga, see Adamu, M. (1978), 37—45.

180 Tambo (unpublished, n.d.).

181 Tambo (unpublished, 1976).

182 Tambo (unpublished, n.d.).

183 Barth (1857–59), III, 98–99. Also see Burdon, Sokoto Tour, Report No. 8, 1903.

184 Baikie, to Lord Russell, 22 March 1862 (PRO).

185 Muhammad Bello Alkali (unpublished, 1969), 42.

186 Loffler, Monographie: Ancien cercle du Djerma, 1905.

187 Monteil (1894), 198. Also see François (1905), 158–159.

188 Muhammad Bello Alkali, 23 February 1970.

189 Loffler, Monographie: Ancien cercle du Djerma, 1905.

190 Lovejoy (1980), 114–118.

191 Lovejoy (1980), 106–109.

192 Barth (1857–59), I, 515.

9. The trade and politics of salt

1 Al-Idrīsī, as translated in Vikør (unpublished, 1979), 170–172; Lange (1982), 21–22.

2 Palmer (1936), 227, 250, 241; Lange (1977), 107–111, 122, 127–128.

3 Bernus and Gouletquer (1976), 53–64.

4 Faure (unpublished, 1965), 31.

5 Gouletquer and Kleinmann (unpublished, 1973), 34.

6 Unomah (1982), 152.

7 Adams (1923), 90.

8 The analysis here expands upon Lovejoy (1978b).

9 Gouletquer and Kleinmann (1976), for Tuareg domination of Teguidda; for Kawar, see below. There is no adequate study of Tuareg history in this period, but see Lovejoy and Baier (1975), 572–573.

10 For the political history of Borno, see A. Smith (1972), 164–182; Hunwick (1972), 205–212; Adeleye (1972), 497–508; Lange (1977); Urvoy (1949); Alkali (1983a), 127–139; Alkali (1983b), 57–77; Tijjani (1983), 127–139; Brenner (1973); Alkali (unpublished, 1978).

11 Lovejoy (1980), 75–100; Adamu (1978) Shea (unpublished, 1975).

12 Alkali (1983a), 103.

13 Urvoy (1949, 91–92) states that Borno was the theoretical sovereign of Kawar and Fachi, but that the Tubu were really in control, especially from the end of the seventeenth century. For an interpretation that Borno controlled Kawar from 1600 to 1800, see Adeleye (1972, 469), who assumes that when the Air Tuareg achieved mastery of the Bilma salt trade in the mid-eighteenth century they secured exclusive commercial relations with Kawar but not political rights, which remained in the hands of the Tubu and nominally Borno. It is clear, however, that Borno had a strong influence, and perhaps real political power, from the early sixteenth century through the seventeenth; see Martin (1969), 15–27; Le Sourd (1946), 1–54; Hunwick (1972), 208–212; and Lavers (unpublished, 1976). For the best study of early Kawar history, see Lange (1977), 107–111, 122, 127–128. Also see Lange (unpublished, 1977); A. Buchanan in Palmer (1936), 126 fn. Elsewhere Palmer (1936, 18), states that 'in about 1574–5, Mai Idris Alooma of Bornu made an expedition against Aghram and took Jawan, Ahannama and Bilma in the Kawar Oasis, which had by that time all reverted to the Tubu'. Dierk Lange has been most helpful on the problem of Borno control of Kawar in this period.

14 Alkali (1983a); and Alkali (1983b), 69–74. Also see R. Cohen (1966), 87–105.

15 Alkali (1983a), 103.

16 Lovejoy and Baier (1975), 572–573.

17 Alkali (1983b), 57–77.

18 A. Smith (1972), 182; Hunwick (1972), 205.

19 Urvoy (1949), 91–92; Adeleye (1972), 469.

20 Grandin (1951), 491.

21 Le Sourd (1946), 28; Palmer (1929), 46–47; Tilho (1910–11), II, 396–397. Kulumfardu of the seventeenth century should not be confused with a later community founded in Muniyo, probably by refugees from the earlier centre.

22 Palmer (1936), 240.

23 Nicholson (1978), 5–10.

24 Palmer (1936), 65; La Roncière (1919), 80, 86; and Tilho (1910–11), II, 397, 399.

25 Nicholson (1978), 5–10.

26 *Kano Chronicle*, in Palmer (1928); III, 111. For a discussion of economic change in the central Sudan in the fifteenth century, see Lovejoy (1978a), 173–194.

27 Colonna di Leca, Rapport, 1907 (Archives de Bilma).

28 Palmer (1936), 66.

29 Palmer (1936), 86; also see Jean (1909), 121; Prévôt in Gentil (1946), 29–31, 34; and Barth (1857–59), III, 51.

30 Tilho (1910–11), II, 399.

31 Lovejoy and Baier (1975), 570–574; Nicholson (unpublished, 1976), 125–145; and Nicholson (1978), 9–10.

32 Grandin (1951), 519 fn.

33 Le Sourd (1946), 28; Grandin (1951), 491–493; Grall (1945), 14.

34 Hunwick (1972), 208; Landeroin in Tilho (1910–11), II, 425–426.

35 Salifou (1971), 32; Monographie du cercle du Manga, 1941.

36 Palmer (1929, 46) states that the Manga were probably in origin slaves of the Kanem rulers who were incorporated into Borno at a comparatively early date, but he provides no proof for this speculation. Nachtigal (1881, I, 539-30) notes that Manga is not an ancient name among the Kanuri, as Barth also observed in the 1850s (1857–59, III, 36). Dierk Lange has been most helpful in providing information and insights on the Dagera.

37 Barth (1857–59), III, 45, 61; Monographie du cercle du Manga, 1941.

38 Niebuhr (1790), 986.

39 Lucas in Beaufoy (1967), I, 169.

40 Lucas in Beaufoy (1967), I, 158.

41 Hornemann (1964), 64; Walckenaer (1821, 449), based on the account of Haj Kassem.

42 Lovejoy and Baier (1975), 570 574. In personal communication, Dr Nicholson explains that meteorological evidence indicates that there was a continued degradation of conditions which accelerated rapidly toward 1800; see also Nicholson (1978) 9–10, and Alkali (unpublished, 1978), 395–405.

43 Abubakar (1977), 43–47; Brenner (1979), 162–164.

44 Salifou (1971); Brenner (1973), 26–47; Low (1972).

45 Brenner (1973), 26–35.

46 Denham, Clapperton and Oudney (1966), 363–365.

47 Denham, Clapperton and Oudney (1966), 363.

48 Brenner (1973), 45, 60, 61, 72; Johnston and Muffett (1973), 148.

49 Salifou (1971), 50; Barth (1857–59), III, 54; Monographie du cercle du Manga, 1941.

50 Denham, Clapperton and Oudney (1966), 359; also see 365–366, 371, 379.

51 Salifou (1971), 50.

52 Barth (1857–59), III, 37; Salifou (1971), 44, 74–75.

53 Salifou (1971), 60, 74–75, 127.

54 Brenner (1973), 123–130.

55 Landeroin in Tilho (1910–11), II, 423.

56 Gouletquer and Kleinmann (unpublished, 1973).

57 Alkali (1983a), 107, 111, 115–118; Alkali (1983b), 70–71.

58 Maps of Administrative Divisions in Bornu Province, 1909; field notes, Geidam; and Monographie du cercle du Manga, 1941.

59 Landeroin in Tilho (1910–11), II, 423.

60 Landeroin in Tilho (1910–11), II, 423–424; Nafyn, Rapport de tournée, canton de Laouan-Yerimari, 1934.

61 Gouletquer and Kleinmann (unpublished, 1973), 33.

62 Alkali (1983b), 70–71; (1983a), 107–108, 122 fn; Brenner (1979), 163.

63 Brenner (1973), 35, 37–39.

64 Cordell (unpublished, 1972, 1979).

65 Brenner (1973), 65–66.

66 Landeroin in Tilho (1910–11), II, 389.

67 Landeroin in Tilho (1910–11), II, 389; Conte (1979), 285.

68 Landeroin in Tilho (1910–11), II, 389.

69 In recent times, the Danawa have constituted 75 per cent of the population near Nguri and as much as 20 per cent in other parts of southern Kanem; Conte (1979), 280.

70 Conte (1979), 280, 285.

71 Nachtigal (1881), 446; Barth (1857–59), II, 608; Conte (1979), 281.

72 Conte (1979), 285.

73 Conte (1979), 285–286. Lange (1977: 151–153) discusses the problem of *haddad* origins and their possible connexion with the Zaghawa, but he does not note their association with trona production.

74 Nachtigal (1877), 43–44; Carbou (1912), I, 52–53.

75 Conte (1979), 285.

76 Conte (1979), 285.

77 Conte (1979), 286.

78 Conte (1979), 288.

79 Hornemann (1964), 119.

80 Denham, Clapperton and Oudney (1966), 232. Also see p. 267.

81 Denham, Clapperton and Oudney (1966), 398.

82 Verlet is undertaking a full-scale study of the Yedina.

83 Overweg (1855), 297.

84 Overweg (1855), 296–297. For the identification of Overweg's Belarigo island with the

Madjigodjia, see D'Huart (1904), 173, who reported that the Maibolloas, Rabokas and Madjigodjia inhabited the islands of Koun, Kourouadji and Belarigeh.

85 Nachtigal (1877), 81.

86 Destenave, Reconnaissance effectuée dans les îles du Tchad, 1902 (Archives Nationales, Paris).

87 Destenave, Reconnaissance effectuée dans les îles du Tchad, 1902; and Alexander (1908), II, 96; and Verlet (1967), 191–193.

88 For a discussion of Borno merchants in the south and west, see Lovejoy (1973), 633–651; Lovejoy (1980); Gavin (unpublished, 1973); Aliyu (unpublished, 1973); Abubakar (1979), 105–124; Wellman, Village Life of the Manga of Nguru; Mundy, Bornu Report No. 5, 1903.

89 Lovejoy (1973), 633–51; and Lovejoy (1980).

90 Rohlfs (1872), 59. Also see Adefuye (1982), 117.

91 Shea (unpublished, 1975), 30–85, 232–234; Abubakar, Kudan, 1 December 1975; Usuman, Kudan, 1 December 1975; Yusufu, Hunkuyi, 6 December 1975.

92 There is no comprehensive study of commerce between Borno and other parts of the central Sudan, but see Gavin (unpublished, 1973); Lovejoy (1980); Works (1976), 181–206; Brenner (1971), 137–150; Lavers (unpublished, 1965).

93 Shea (unpublished, 1975), 33, 56, 75, 80–84.

94 Lovejoy (1974), 577–578. Cloth strips were still recognised as currency in Muniyo as late as the 1850s, when 100 cowries were worth one *gabaga*. Some taxes, however, were assessed in cowries; see Barth (1857–59), I, 568; III, 53, 58.

95 Unomah (1982), 163–165. I am indebted to M. B. Duffill for much of this information.

96 Unomah (1982) 163; Webster (unpublished, n.d.); Tafida Yakubu Abawa, Kanje, 26 April 1976; Makwangiji Jibrin and Malam Bala Ismaila, Awe, 26 April 1976; Aliyu and Galadima Salihu, Ribi, 26 April 1976; Omana Ozegya, Keana, 18 December 1975 (Aliyu Collection); Osabwa Aklo, Keana, 15 December 1975 (Aliyu Collection); Eladoga Oji, Keana, 19 July 1975 (Ojobo Collection).

97 Varvill, Salt Tax Re-assessment, Awe District, 1937.

98 Perron (1924); Barth (1857–59), III, 165.

99 Beauvilain (1977), 54–55.

100 Watts (1983), 92–104.

101 Lovejoy (1980), 75–90.

102 See Lovejoy (1978c), 358–361. For additional confirmation of the importance of the plantation sector, see interviews with Abubakar of Kudan, 1 December 1975; Sha'aibu, Kano, 23 June 1970; Gwadabe of Kano, 21 June and 10 August 1971; Amadu of Kano, 29 June 1971; Inuwa of Kano, 4 August 1971; Abdu Mai Kano of Kura, 23 September 1971; Na Kurma Sarkin Baba of Dal, 7 October 1971. It can also be noted that Baba of Karo was of Borno origin, and her family had an extensive plantation on the Kano–Zaria frontier (M. Smith, 1954). It should be noted that many of the interviews in the various collections of oral data that were conducted under my supervision between 1974 and 1976 contain references to plantations in the Zaria and Kano areas. A full study of this sector will be undertaken in the near future.

103 Shea (unpublished, 1975); Lovejoy (1978b), 356.

104 Tafida Yakuba Abawa, Kanje, 26 April 1976; Muhammadu Iya, Awe, 26 April 1976.

10. The social organisation of trade and production

1 F. Barth (1969), 10.
2 F. Barth (1969), 10–11.
3 Curtin (1984).
4 F. Barth (1969), 9–10.

5 Genovese (1972, 25–49), speaks of the 'hegemonic function of the law' in discussing slavery in the southern United States.
6 Stewart (1976), 73–93.
7 Tijjani (1979), 261–277; Last and Al-Hajj (1965), 231–240; Willis (1979), 38 fn; Brenner (1979), 167–170.
8 Lovejoy (1980), 94–96.
9 Barth (1857–59), II, 608; Bouquet (1974), 129; Géry (1952), 316.
10 See above, Chapter 9.
11 Lovejoy (1984); (1980), 141–148; Watts (1983), Chapters 2 and 3.
12 Bernus and Gouletquer (1976), 10–11; Lacroix (1975), 1–2.
13 Jean, Rapport sur l'Oasis du Kaouar, 1906; Colonna di Leca, Rapport, 1907; Prévôt, Rapport, 1909; Cline (1950).
14 Bernus and Bernus (1972), 23–24.
15 Bernus and Gouletquer (1976), 58–60.
16 Vikør (unpublished, 1979), 21.
17 Grandin (1951), 495–500.
18 Not all the lake dwellers were Yedina. The Kouri lived in the southern part of the lake but do not figure in the trona trade. An analysis of the distinction between Yedina and Kouri is beyond the scope of this study. For the Kouri, see D'Huart (1904), 168–171; Destenave (1903d), 717.
19 Lovejoy and Baier (1975), 551–581.
20 Baier and Lovejoy (1977), 397.
21 Verlet (1967), 190–193.
22 Nicolas (1975), 399–441.
23 Lovejoy (1980), 75.
24 Lovejoy (1980), 77.
25 Lovejoy (1980), 75–81; Lovejoy and Baier (1975), 551–581.
26 Lovejoy (1980), 81–83; (1973), 633–657.
27 Lovejoy and Baier (1975), 551–581.
28 Unomah (1982).
29 Perron (1924), 51–83; Périé and Sellier (1950), 1015–1074.
30 Horowitz (1972); Bovin and Schierup (unpublished, 1975).
31 Lethem, Assessment Report, Machena District, 1919.
32 Landeroin in Tilho (1910–11), II, 422.
33 Monographie du cercle du Manga, 1941.
34 Barth (1857–59), III, 36.
35 Palmer (1929), 46.
36 Abadie (1927), 137.
37 Palmer (1936), 36–37, 43–44, 48.
38 Conte (1979), 280–281.
39 Conte (1979), 291.
40 Lovejoy (1980); Baier (1980b); Duffill and Lovejoy (1985).
41 Lovejoy (1980), 80.
42 Redmond (unpublished, 1976).
43 Alexander (1908), II, 93.
44 MacLeod (1912), 227.
45 Alexander (1908), II, 68.
46 D'Huart (1904), 172.
47 Freydenberg (1911), 159.
48 Audu Mohamman, 14 August 1973; Suda Sha'aibu, 22 July 1973; Ibrahim Isa, 17 July 1973.
49 Lovejoy (1978c), 360–361; (1980), 92–93.

50 Baier and Lovejoy (1977), 396.
51 Baier and Lovejoy (1977), 400–401.

11. Conclusion

1 Lovejoy (1984).
2 Lugard, Northern Nigeria Annual Report, 1904, 297; Lovejoy (1984).
3 Johnson (1976), 95–117; Baier (1980b).
4 Shea (unpublished, 1975).

Glossary

abatol	series of decantation basins at Teguidda n'tesemt
Agalawa	Hausa merchants of Tuareg (servile) origin
alifa	political official in Kanem
alum	potassium double sulphate; potassium aluminium sulphate
baboul	type of bush which was burnt to make salt
Beriberi	Hausa merchants of Borno origin
beza (Hausa)	purest salt from Bilma and Fachi
bulama	Bilma official
canton (French)	French administrative district
cure salée (French)	annual livestock migration to salt-licks and brine wells
Danawa	Haddad caste of Kanem
dillali (Hausa)	broker
efflorescence	formation of salt crust on surface as a result of solar evaporation
fadama (Hausa)	salt flat (Benue basin)
fatoma (Hausa)	commercial landlord
gallo (Hausa)	Taoudeni salt
gari (Hausa)	impure, loose natron
gishiri (Hausa)	salt
gwangwarasa (Hausa)	sodium sulphate, thenardite, Glauber's salt
haddad (Arabic)	artisan caste of Kanem and neighbouring areas
imam (Hausa)	leader of Friday prayer
jihad	holy war, specifically 1804–12 in the central Sudan
kachella	Borno political title
kaigama	Borno political title
Kakanda	Nupe traders
kalvu (Kanuri)	natron
kantu (Hausa)	type of Bilma and Fachi salt
kanwa (Hausa)	natron
kazelma	Borno political title
kelvu (Kanuri)	salt
kige (Kanuri)	type of Borno salt
lawan	Borno political title
mai (maina)	Borno political title
mai gida (Hausa)	landlord
malam (Hausa)	Muslim cleric
manda (Kanuri)	type of Borno salt
mangul (Hausa)	type of Borno salt; same as *manda*
mithkal	gold unit of account
muniyoma	Borno political title

natron	mixture of sodium sulphate (thenardite), sodium carbonate (soda) and sodium chloride
potash	potassium carbonate (but used erroneously for natron)
soda	sodium carbonate (Na_2CO_3)
talakawa (*Hausa*)	commoners
thenardite	sodium sulphate (Na_2SO_4)
Tokarawa	Hausa merchants of Tuareg (servile) origin
transhumance	nomadic livestock migratory pattern
trona	$Na_3H(CO_3)_2 \cdot 2H_2O$
ungurnu (*Hausa*)	trona
yerima	Borno political title
zango (*zongo*) (*Hausa*)	caravanserai

Note: African names are used in their singular form, even when the reference is plural. This applies throughout, with the exception of passages quoted from published works.

Bibliography

I. ARCHIVAL REFERENCES

Archives Nationales du Niger, Niamey

L'Adjoint des s.c. chef de la subdivision de Mainé-Soroa à Monsieur l'Administrateur commandant le cercle du Manga, 29 mai 1936; in Les Salines, 1905, 1936, 1938. Mares de sel et natron; cuvettes de Baboul.

L'Administrateur adjoint commandant le cercle du Manga au Gouverneur du Niger, Gouré, 12 Juillet 1936; in Les Salines, 1905, 1936, 1938.

L'Administrateur du cercle du Manga à Lt. Gov., Gouré, 5 fév. 1929.

Cantons, chefs de canton, villages, chefs de villages, de la subdivision de Gaya, cercle de Dosso, 1932.

Commandant de cercle de Dosso, rapport de tournée, Dallol, Gaya, fleuve, Fogha, 1924.

Commerce avec les colonies étrangères, secteur de Gouré, 1909.

Compte rendu de tournée dans les cantons de Miria, Babantapki, Droum, Kissambana et Guidimouni, 20 juin 1926.

Compte rendu de tournée du chef de la subdivision de Mainé-Soroa dans le canton de Goudoumaria, 1 fév.–16 mars 1937.

Extract, undated, no author, on Dallol Bosso (c. 1905), in Les Salines, 1905, 1936, 1938.

Monographie du cercle du Manga, 24 juin 1941.

Rapport de tournée du chef de subdivision de Mainé-Soroa, 10–27 fév. 1936.

Rapport de tournée du commandant de cercle du Manga, 21 mars 1931.

Rapport économique, subdivision de Gaya, cercle de Dosso, 1926.

Rapport politique, 2ᵉ trimestre, année 1914, cercle de Mainé-Soroa.

Tournée administrative du 5 avril au 29 avril 1934, cercle de N'Guigmi.
  Rapport sur le recensement.

Arnal, Rapport de la tournée, 12–19 jan. 1934, sud-est du canton de Gouré.
  Rapport de la tournée, 10–18 fév. 1934.
  Rapport de la tournée, 16–24 mai 1934.

Battistini, Rapport annuel sur les salines, Magaria, 1 mars 1916.

Boraud, S. C. Rapport de tournée effectuée dans le canton de Yamia du 6 october 1933 au 19 octobre 1933.

Cagnier, Rapport de tournée, canton de Komadougou, jan. 1935.

Chambert, Rapport du cercle de Gouré sur une tournée pacifique dans le Mounyo, 1 sept. 1906.
  Rapport sur une tournée pacifique dans l'est-sudest de Gouré, 23 sept. 1908.

Charlier, Tournée effectuée dans le canton de Gouré, 26–31 mars 1932.

Chazelas au Gouverneur Général, 2 sept. 1938, in Les Salines, 1905, 1936, 1938.

Dario, Monographie du cercle d'Agadez par le Capitaine Dario, reproduite par le Capitaine Bonaccorci, 1913.

Esperet, Monographie de la subdivision de Gaya, 1917.

318

Fischer, Rapport de tournée administrative; le recensement des populations du sud du Manga, 17 nov–5 dec. (1930s?).

Rapport de tournée administrative, cercle dans le Kadzell, 2–12 sept. 1934.

Géry, R. Rapport de tournée, chef de subdivision de Mainé-Soroa, 14–29 fév. 1944.

Janouih, Rapport sur les salines, secteur de Mainé-Soroa, 24 fév. 1916.

Joubert, Les Coutumes et le droit chez les Kel Tadeles, cercle d'Agadez, 1938.

Laforque, in Monographie du cercle de N'Guigmi en 1913, par le commandant de cercle.

Lagarde, Rapport sur la tournée effectuée par le Lt. de Réserve Largarde, Mainé-Soroa, 8–22 mai 1941.

Lamarche, Rapport sur les salines, secteur de Gaya, cercle de Niamey, 20 mars 1916.

Lambert, Roger, Les salines du Dallol Fogha (Niger), 26 juin 1929; in Les Salines, 1905, 1936, 1938.

Loffler, Monographie: Ancien cercle du Djerma, 1905.

Loyzance, A. Canton de Birni N'Gaouré, recensement, historique, politique, religion, économie, santé, greniers, 2 juin 1947.

Margin, Rapport sur la production en sel et natron du canton de Birni (subdivision de Niamey), 30 jan. 1936.

Marsaud, Monographie du secteur de Gaya. Droit coutumier Tienga, 1909.

Nafyn, Rapport de tournée, canton de Laouan-Yerimari, 12–19 jan. 1934.

Ravoux, Rapport de tournée effectuée du 10 au 30 août, 1932, cercle de Nguigmi.

Riou, Tournée effectuée du 17 novembre au 1 décembre 1940, dans le canton de la Komadougou.

Rapport de tournée, canton de N'guigmi, 18–26 jan. 1941.

Rapport de tournée: Rive ouest du Tchad, Kadzell, Komadougou, cercle de N'guigmi, 13 fév–1 mars 1941.

Rapport de tournée: dans la région ouest du cercle de N'Guigmi, 14–18 mars 1941.

Rapport de tournée; Kadzell et secteur ouest de la Komadougou, 2–16 juillet 1941.

Rabaglia, Rapport de tournée dans le sud-est de la subdivision de Niamey, 13–27 sept. 1941.

Ronjat, Etude faite sur les mares salines du Mounyo. Leur exploitation – leur rapport – les ressources, qu'elles peuvent fournir au cercle du Gouré, 1905.

Séré de Rivières, Rapport de tournée d'ensemble recensement du canton du Tagazar, 1944.

Tercel, Chef de subdivision. Epuise sommaire sur le Fogha, subdivision de Gaya, cercle de Dosso, 10 sept. 1938.

Thérol, Notice sur Teguidda n'Tessoum, 1907.

Urfer, P. Rapport sur le recensement du canton du Tagazar, cercle de Niamey, subdivision de Filingue, 1951.

Archives de Bilma

Barbaste, Rapport: tournée de la Djado, juin, juillet, sept. 1938.

Coste, Monographie du Djado, 1935.

Colonna di Leca, Rapport, 1907.

Dufour, Rapport politique, 1919.

Gadel, H. Rapport, 1907.

Gamory-Dubourdeau, Rapport, Fezzan, 1920.

Guerin, Rapport, 1954.

Lejeune, Carnet monographique du canton du Kawar. 1952.

Le Sourd, Michel, Taghlent 1940; Agadez–Bilma, 1940.

Périé, Monographie du poste de Bilma, 1941.

Prévôt, Rapport, 1909.

Archives du Cercle de Gouré

Grall, Monographie de la région de Gouré, 1939.

Bibliography

Centre Nigérien de Recherches en Sciences Humaines, Niamey
Etude Monographique du territoire de Mirriah, 1947.
Projet de mise en valeur du Dallol Maouri. Etude sociologique, Niamey. FAO Rapport, Programme des Nations Unies pour le développement, 1968, 2 Vols.
Brouin, Un Ilot de vieille civilisation africaine. Le pays de Ouacha (Niger français), 1941.

Archives de la République du Sénégal, Dakar
Lefebvre, Etude sur la question de Bilma, août 1904, 11 G 2 No. 4.
Gadel, H. Rapport sur une tournée en Air ou Azbin, 1905. Territoire militaire du Niger. Rapports, 1904–08. 1 D 200 No. 6.

Nigerian National Archives, Kaduna
Annual Accounts of the Protectorate, 1904–05; SNP 7/6/2945/1905.
Annual Accounts of the Protectorate for 1905–06; SNP 7/7/3517/1906.
Annual Reports, Northern Nigeria, 1900–11.
Annual Report of the Customs Department, 1907; SNP 7/9/330/1908.
Assessment Report, Magumeri District, 1934; MAI PROF 2/2 18A
Blue Book, Protectorate of Northern Nigeria, 1900, 1902, 1905, 1906, 1907, 1914, 1915, 1919.
Bornu Emirate Assessment Report, 1913; SNP 10/286p/1913.
Cargo and Salt Shipped for Lokoja, SNP 7/8/2083/1907.
D. O. Lafia to Resident, Makurdi, 2 December 1942; LAFIA Div 2/1/542.
D. O. Lafia to Resident, Makurdi, 17 December 1942; LAFIA Div 2/1/542.
Estimates, Customs Department, 1903; SNP 18/1 G. 61.
Imperial Institute, Report on Work for year 1908; SNP 7/10/4641/1909.
Imports and Exports, Northern Nigeria, 1907; SNP 7/9/525/1908.
Keana Native Salt, 1948; LAFIA NA 2/1 134.
Maps of Administrative Divisions in Provinces; SNP 7/10 1267/1909.
Mobber District Notebook, Vol. II; MAI PROF 2/4 Acc 33.
Monthly Return of Customs Review, 1906; SNP 7/7/470/1906.
Report on Salt Industry, Awe District, 27 October 1941; LAFIA Div 2/1 542.
Report on Tuareg and Arab Tribes, 1916; Sokprof 3/1 C. 36/1916.
Resident, Nassarawa, Anthropological Notes on Arago, August 1912; SNP 17/8 K 3130.
Sokoto Province, Report for March 1904; Sokprof 2/2/101/1904.
Summary of Caravan Statistics of Nassarawa Province, year ending 31 December 1907.
Backwell, H. F. Re-assessment Report, Illo District, Gando Division, Sokoto Province, 1918; SNP 10/6/511p/1918.
Becklesfall, J. Salt from Bornu Province – Samples of for Transmission to the Imperial Institute for Report, 28 March 1907; SNP 7/8 2281/1907.
Bell, F. W. Assessment Report, Dutsi District, Kano Province, 1911–12; SNP 7/12/2715/1911.
Birtwistle, C. A. Report by the Commercial Intelligence Officer for Southern Nigeria on a Tour made in Northern Nigeria, January to April 1907, SNP 7/8/1765/1907.
  Ilorin Trade, 10 January 1907; SNP 7/8146/1907.
Blakerey, J. E. C. Report for Nassarawa Province, Keffi, 11 January 1909; SNP 7/10/191/1909.
Boyle, French Circle of Ngegmi, 1911; SNP 6/7/87/1911.
Browne, W. Salt from Bornu Province, Report of 19 May 1906; SNP 7/8/2281/1907.
Burdon, J. A. Sokoto Tour, Report No. 8; Sokprof 2/1 129/1903.
Cargill, F. Annual Report on Kano Province for 1907, SNP 7/9/1538/1908.
Cator, D. Nassarawa Province Report for September quarter, 30 September 1909; SNP 7/10/5354/1909.

320

Clarke, J. C. O. Reassessment Report on Keana District, Lafia Emirate, Nassarawa Province, SNP 337/1922.

Dickinson, Salt Rights and Industry, Keana, Lafia Emirate; 8 December 1930; LAFIA Div 2/1 351.

Dunstan, Wyndham R. to Percy Girouard, 5 November 1908; 2427/1907; contained in Mineral Survey, Report on Work, 1908–09, SNP 7/10/3285/1909.

Dwyer, P. M. Annual Report, Ilorin Province, 1906. SNP 7/8/1573/1907.

Ilorin Province, Annual Report, 1906; Ilorprof 120/1906.

Elphinstone, K. V. Nassarawa Province Report No. 31 for quarter ending March 31st 1906; SNP 7/7/165/1906.

Falconer, J. D. Reports to the Geological Survey of Northern Nigeria for 1904; No. 3, Awe, 4 January 1905; No. 5, 22 February 1905; No. 6, Bomanda, 12 March 1905; No. 8, Keana, 15 April 1905; 3513/1904; No. 6, Bomanda, 12 March 1905; No. 8, Keana, 15 April 1905; 3513/1904; contained in Mineral Survey, Report on Work, 1908–09; SNP 7/10/3285/1907.

to His Excellency, 13 March 1908; 1398/1908; contained in Mineral Survey, Report on Work, 1908–09; SNP 7/10/3285/1909.

to Acting Governor, Northern Nigeria, 21 June 1909; Mineral Survey Report on Work, 1908–09, SNP 7/10/3285/1909.

Report on Geological Survey, 1908; SNP 7/10/3285/1909.

Featherstone, E. F. Nguru District Assessment Report, 1930; MAI PROF Acc 42.

Figgis, E. C. Nguru Town: Market; MAI PROF 2/2/1917.

Mongonu District Notebook, 28 February 1936; MAI PROF 2/4 Acc 41.

Foulkes, H. B. Bornu Report, 1902, SNP 15/1 Acc 18.

Assessment Report, Dan Buram District, Kano Province, SNP 7/13/5785/1912.

Frewen, H. M. Assessment Report, Kura District, Kano Province, SNP 7/10/2607/1909.

Assessment Report, Gora District, Kano Province, SNP 7/10/3555/1909.

Girouard, Percy to Elgin, 3 July 1907, 2427/1907; contained in Mineral Survey, Report of Work, 1908–1909; SNP 7/10/3285/1909.

Glenny, H. Q. Assessment Report, Barde's District, Kano Province, SNP 7/10/6166/1909.

Assessment Report, Rano District, Kano Province, SNP 7/10/3272/1909.

Assessment Report, Wombai District, Kano Province, SNP 7/10/5585/1909.

Gowers, W. F. Kano Annual Report, 1913; SNP 10/2/98p/1914.

H., J. D., Kanembu District Notebook, 1926; MAI PROF 2/4 Acc 36.

Hall, J. E. B. Mobber District Notebook, 21 February 1933; MAI PROF 2/4 Acc 40.

Hewby, W. P. Report for Bornu Province, 1905; SNP 7/6/417/1905.

Report on Bornu Province for quarter ending 30 September 1906; SNP 7/7/4634/1906.

Bornu Annual Report, 12 March 1912; SNP 10/182p/1913.

Hoskyns-Abrahall, T. Kano City, Re-assessment, 14 September 1926, SNP 17/8 K 2346.

J. D. H., see under H.

Jones, B. Proposed Well Sites along the Belle–Maiduguri Road, 1932; MAI PROF 3179/1932.

Lawan, Mahomet, Local Salt Production, c. 1941; MAI PROF 2/2 3664.

Lethem, G. J. Assessment Report, Machena District, 1919; SNP 17/12168.

Notes on Monguno District, Bornu Province, SNP 15/317/1921.

Mobber District Notebook; MAI PROF 2/4 Acc 40.

Lugard, F. D. Northern Nigeria Annual Report, 1902, 1903, 1904.

M.-S., P. F. Kanembu District Notebook, 1935, Vol. I; MAI PROF 2/4 Acc 36.

Major, Trade Report, Kano Province, 8 May 1907; SNP 7/8/1867/1907.

Marwick, B. A. Assessment Report, Geidam District, 1938; MAI PROF 2/2 3014.

McIntosh, C. W. Salt Manufacturing Industry, Establishment of; SNP 9/10/1752/1923.

Meek, C. K. Jukon of the Awei District; SNP 17 K 2441.

Milroy, A. L. Gujba District Notebook, January 17, 1927; MAI PROF 2/4 Acc 35.

Bibliography

Morland, T. L. N. Bornu Report, May, 1902, SNP 15/1 Acc 18.
Mundy, G. C. R. Bornu Report No. 4, April 1903; SNP 15/1 Acc 48A.
 Bornu Report No. 5, May 1903; SNP 15/1 Acc 48A.
 Bornu Report No. 8, October 1903; SNP 15/1 Acc 48A.
Niven, C. R. to food controller, Lagos, 16 January 1942; in Local Salt Production, MAI PROF 2/2 3664.
Norton-Traill, H. L. Assessment Report, Keana District, Lafia Division, Nassarawa Province, 27 July 1914; SNP 10/2/120p/1914.
P. F. M.-S., see under M.
Palmer, H. R. History of Katsina, Report No. 2, 1907, SNP 17/8 K. 2076.
 Kano Assessment Report, 1910–11; SNP 7/12/2109/1911.
Patterson, J. R. Assessment Report, Geidam District, 1917; SNP 7/18 609p/1917.
 Special Report on Gumsu District, Dikwa Emirate; SNP 9/2350/1923.
 Mobber District Notebook 1919; MAI PROF 2/4 Acc 40.
Peebles, H. Katsina Emirate, September 1908, SNP 17/8 K 2076.
Reed, L. W. Mobber District Notebook, 5 April 1928; MAI PROF 2/4 Acc 40.
Reynolds, F. G. B. Mobber District Notebook 27 May 1924; MAI PROF 2/4 Acc 40.
Roberts, D. L. Report on Lafia Division, 6 September 1951; LAFIA Div 2/1 351/13.
Rowe, F. Assessment Report, Riverain Jukunawa, Abinsi Administrative District, Munshi Division, Muri Province; 1913; SNP 10/1/2508/1913.
Rowling, C. W. Bosari District Notebook 1928–29; MAI PROF 2/2 Acc 187.
Seccombe, Report in J. Becklesfall, Salt from Bornu Province – Samples of for Transmission to the Imperial Institute for Report, 28 March 1907; SNP 7/8 2281/1907.
Tegetmeier, P. A. Yerwa Assessment Report, 1925; MAI PROF 117/1925 D. 13/Vol. 3.
 Mobber District Notebook, 19 March 1933; MAI PROF 2/4 Acc 40.
Thomson, W. to Resident, Makurdi, 10 March 1949; LAFIA Div 2/1/542.
Tomlinson, G. J. F. Report of 1918; MAI PROF 2/4.
Underwood, R. L. A. Wukari, 14 September 1939; contained in M. H. Varvill, Salt Tax, Awe District, LAFIA Div 2/1 823.
Varvill, M. H. Salt Tax Re-assessment, Awe District, 1937; LAFIA Div 2/1 823.
Vischer, Hans, letter of 13 December 1904, Geidam; in Confidential Papers on the Anglo-French Boundary from Niger to Chad; SNP 15/3 Acc 385 B 1.
Ward, L. S. Assessment Report, Awe, 1920; LAFIA Div 2/1 60; SNP 366p/1920.
Warran, W. S. E. Lafia Emirate, Re-assessment, 1933; SNP 17/3 20197.
Webster, G. Assessment Report, Dan Iya District, Kano Province, SNP 7/13/4055/1912.
Wellman, J. B. Village Life of the Manga of Nguru, 1924; MAI PROF Acc 42.
Wilkinson, Howard, Salt Rights and Industry, Keana, Lafia Emirate, 26 October 1939; LAFIA Div 2/1 351.

Nigerian National Archives, Ibadan
Birtwistle, C. A. Kano, Trade with; CSO 19/1 N 166/1913.
 Hausa trade with Lagos; CSO 19/1/126 N 167/1913.
Fremantle, J. M. letter of 19 May 1913, Zaria; CSO 19/1/126 N 167/1913.
Lagos Blue Books.

Jos Museum
Palmer Papers, Notebook No. 9.

Ghana National Archives, Accra
Salt Trade in Northern Territories via Volta, 5 June 1905; ADM 56/1/39.
Birtwistle, C. A. Ilorin Trade, 10 January 1907; ADM 56/1/57.

322

Rhodes House, Oxford
Gowers, W. F. Notes on Trade in Sokoto Province, February 1911; Mss. Afr. S 662(2).

Public Record Office, London
Daily Return of Persons crossing by the Kraki Ferry and Description of load carried, February 16–May 23, 1897; encl. in William Maxwell to Antrobus, 17 July 1897; CO 96/297.
Altham, E. A. 3 September 1898, enclosed in Director of Military Intelligence to Colonial Office, 2 July 1898. Further Correspondence relating to the Northern Territories, 1898; CO 879/54 No. 564.
Baikie, W. B. to Lord Russell, Bida, 22 March 1862; FO 97/434.
Bida, 22 March 1862; FO 97/434 (letter No. 2).
Dunstan, Wyndham R. First Report of the Results of the Mineral Survey of Northern Nigeria, 1904–5, Colonial Reports, Miscellaneous, No. 32, 1906 [Cd. 2875].
Second Report on the Results of the Mineral Survey, 1904–5, Colonial Reports, Miscellaneous, No. 46, 1908 [Cd. 3914].
Report on the Results of the Mineral Survey, 1906–7, Colonial Reports, Miscellaneous, Northern Nigeria, No. 59, 1909 [Cd. 4719].
Reports of the Results of the Mineral Survey, 1907–8 and 1908–9, Colonial Reports, Miscellaneous No. 79 [Cd. 5899].
Ferguson, George E. Report on Mission to Atabubu, January 1891, CO 96/215.
to W. Bradford Griffith, encl. No. 1 in No. 45, 9 December 1892, encl. in W Bradford Griffith to Marquess of Ripon, 10 January 1893; CO 879/38 No. 448.
Firminger, R. E. to Governor, 20 March 1888, encl. in W. Bradford Griffith to Lord Knutsford, 16 April 1888, CO 96/191.
Goldsmith, in Northern Nigeria, Mineral and Vegetable Products, Colonial Reports, Miscellaneous, No. 26 [Cd. 1939].
Hodgson, F. M. to Chamberlain, 18 July 1899, CO 96/341.
Lang, J. I to Lugard, 3 September 1900, encl. in Lugard to Chamberlain, 24 September 1900; CO 446/11.
Nathan, M. to Chamberlain, 11 September 1903, CO 879/82 No. 736.
Patterson, C. to Comptroller of Customs, 8 February 1899; encl. in No. 103 of 10 March 1899, Low to Chamberlain, CO 96/338.
Rowe to Kimberley, 16 January 1882 in [C 3386].

Archives Nationales – Section Outre-Mer, Paris
Extrait du Rapport, Zinder 13 mai 1904; 11 G 2 (200 Mi 855).
Rapport sur l'exploitation des salines et mares de natron au Territoire Militaire du Niger en 1915, No. 36, Zinder, 7 avril 1916; AOF 11 G 16 (200 Mi 862).
Renseignements sur la vente du sel, 18 oct. 1892; Gabon-Congo XIII (18).
Ayasse, Reconnaissance de N'Guigmi sur Agadem et Bilma, déc. 1904–fév. 1905; 200 D 1, Fond ancien AOF (200 Mi 293).
Destenave, Reconnaissance effectuée dans les îles du Tchad, 10 juin 1902, Fort Lamy; Gabon-Congo IV (15).
Fouchard, 19 fév., 1861; Gabon-Congo XIII (7).
Gadel, Rapport sur une tournée en Air ou Azbin, 27 août au 25 november 1905; 200 D 1 (200 Mi 293).
Lamy, Situation politique du Soudan central à la date du 31 décembre 1899, mission Foureau, Afrique III (42).
Largeau, Rapport sur la situation du pays et protectorats du Tchad, 24 mars 1903; Gabon-Congo II (7).
Lefebvre, Etude sur la question de Bilma, 22 août 1904; 11 G 2 (200 mi 855).

Bibliography

Moll, Situation politique de la région de Zinder–Tchad, 13 mars 1901; Soudan IV (9).
Peroz, Occupation et organisation de la contrée Niger–Tchad en Territoire Militaire IIIe (1900–1901); Tchad I (1).
Plomion, Rapport sur l'escorte de la caravane dans l'Air – 21 sept. 1903 – Notice politique et commerciale sur l'Azbin, 11 G 2 (200 Mi 855).
Reibell, Rapport du 22 octobre 1900, mission Foureau, Afrique III (42).

Institut de France, Paris
Bétrix, Rapport, Fonds Auguste Terrier MS 5935, t. 2.
Colonna di Leca, Extrait de son journal de route, Fonds Auguste Terrier, MS 5935, t. 2.
Cufino, Luigi Djanet et Bilma, Fonds Auguste Terrier MS 5935, t. 2.
Gadel, Rapport sommaire du chef de bataillon Gadel, 1905, Fonds Auguste Terrier MS 5935, t. 2.
Noël, Rapport sur les marches et opérations militaires éffectuees sous la direction du Capitaine Tilho, 30 mai 1904, Fonds Auguste Terrier, MS 5935, t. 1.
Rottier, note sur Djado, Fonds Auguste Terrier MS 5907.
Thérol, Rapport, Fonds Auguste Terrier MS 5935, t. 2

Institut Catholique de Paris
Jean, Rapport sur l'Oasis du Kaouar et note sur le note sur le Tibesti; Documents sur Bilma 1906, Dossier 378 t. I.
Lefebvre au Jean, Zinder, 16 Avril 1906; Documents sur Bilma, Dossier 378 t. I.

II. CORRESPONDENCE

Couty, Phillippe to author, 12 October 1979.
Duffill, M. B. to author, 1 April 1976.
Gac, J. Y. to author, 21 January 1980.
Gavin, R. J. to author, 4 June 1976; 21 September 1977
Gouletquer, P. to author, 3 May 1982
Nicholson, Sharon to author, 16 January 1978.
Sutton, J. E. G. to author, 12 January 1976; 29 October, 1979.

III. FIELD NOTES

Baga, 23 March 1976.
Geidam, 16, 17, and 21 March 1976.
Jajamagi, 20 March 1976.
Maiduguri, 15 March 1976.
Myrria, 21 January 1976.
Nguru, 20 March 1976.
Yusufari, 19 March 1976.

IV. INTERVIEWS

A. Lovejoy Collection (Northern History Research Scheme Library, Ahmadu Bello University, Zaria)
Abbas, Maiunguwar Bakin Zuwo, Kano, 7 July 1973 (b. 1925).
Abdullhamidu Abdulrazaki, Kura, 11 August 1973 (b. c. 1934).
Abubakar Babajo, Zaria, 17 September 1975 (b. c. 1898).
Abubakar, Kudan, 1 December 1975.
Abubakar Muhammadu, Tsaure Fankurun village, Kura District, 4 May 1970, (b. c. 1920).

Abubakar Salga, Bakin Ruwa ward, Kano, 28 December 1969 (b. c. 1887).
Abubakar Usmanu, 'Yan Bundu village, Kano Emirate, 21 March 1970 (b. c. 1898).
Adamu Bagwanje, Kano, 8 November 1969 (b. c. 1885).
Adamu Isma'ila, Garko, Kano Emirate, 23 January 1970 (b. c. 1905).
Ahmadu Ibrahim, Kano, 25 July 1973 (b. c. 1901).
Ahmadu, Minjibir, Kano Emirate, 20 September 1969 (b. c. 1897).
Ahmadu Aci, Gambarawa ward, Katsina, 4 February 1970 (b. c. 1900).
Ahmadu Wanzami, Kano, 28 July 1973.
Alhaji Kuiwar Gabas, Kura District, Kano Emirate, 1 April 1970 (b. c. 1902).
Ali Adamu, Kura, 9 August 1973 (b. c. 1912).
Ali, Shibdawa village, Katsina Emirate, 6 January 1970 (b. c. 1892).
Aliyu and Galadima Salihu, Ribi, 26 April 1976.
Aminu Dahiru, Bakin Zuwo ward, Kano, 8 and 14 July 1973 (b. 1922).
Audu, Makwara Yamma, Kano Emirate, 1 April 1970.
Audu, Unguwar Agalawa, Kura District, Kano Emirate, 1 April 1970 (b. c. 1918).
Audu Ba'are, Mararaba ward, Kano, 1 January 1970 (b. c. 1875).
Audu Isa, Jega, 26 February 1970 (b. c. 1902).
Audu Mohamman, Kano, 14 August 1973 (b. c. 1913).
Audu Zakari, Kura, 11 August 1973 (b. c. 1930).
Baba Dayidu, Kano, 4 September 1969 (b. c. 1899).
Bak'o Madigawa, Kano, 1 December 1969 (b. c. 1889).
Bala Idi, Jani village, Katsina Emirate, 5 February 1970 (b. c. 1892).
Baladari Ali, Damergu village, Kano Emirate, 20 March 1970 (b. c. 1920).
Basharu na Mahu, Gummi, Sokoto Province, 7 March 1970 (b. c. 1883).
Bature, Utai village, Kano Emirate, 23 January 1970 (b. 1891).
Bawa Ibrahim, Jega, 26 February 1970 (b. c. 1910).
Dan Hodio, Tsaure Fankurun village, Kura District, 4 May 1970.
Dan Tsoho Koki, Kano, 5 July 1973 (b. 1929).
Gambo, Katsina, 2 and 3 February 1970.
Gambo Turawa, Katsina, 5 January 1970 (b. c. 1890).
Garba Husaini, Dandi village, Kano Emirate, 11 February 1970 (b. c. 1917).
Garkuwa dan Asiri, Jega, 26 February 1970 (b. c. 1875).
Goje Saba, Kura, 9 August 1973 (b. c. 1923).
Habibu, Kawo village, Kano Emirate, 29 January 1970 (b. c. 1912).
Habu Jibo, 'Yan Bundu village, Kano Emirate, 21 March 1970 (b. c. 1880).
Habu Muhammadu, Katsina, 6 January 1970 (b. c. 1882).
Halidu Adamu, Dandi village, Kano Emirate, 11 February 1970 (b. c. 1907).
Halilu, Kano, 16 August 1973.
Haruna Bakin Zuwo, Kano, 3 and 4 July 1973 (b. 1935).
Hawwa Sule, Dan Mak'eri village, Kano Emirate, 11 February 1970 (b. c. 1910).
Husaini Danjaji, Kano, 26 August 1969 (b. c. 1887).
Ibrahim dan Yaro, Kumurya, Kano Emirate, 27 January 1970 (b. c. 1910).
Ibrahim Isa, Bakin Zuwo ward, Kano, 17 July 1973 (b. 1905).
Ibrahim Muhamma, Dunkura village, Kano Emirate, 27 January 1970 (b. c. 1905).
Idi Abubakar, Garfa, Kano Emirate, 13 February 1970 (b. c. 1908).
Idi Magani, Guzai, Kano Emirate, 13 February 1970 (b. c. 1910).
Ike, Luke, Zaria, 23 January 1976.
Iliyasu, Dunkura village, Kano Emirate, 27 January 1970 (b. c. 1900).
Inusa, Shibdawa village, Katsina Emirate, 6 January 1970 (b. c. 1910).
Isa Madigawa, Kano, 1 January 1970 (b. c. 1915).
Isiaku dan Amadu and Malam Alassan dan Ibrahim, Kano, 16 November 1969.

Isma'ila, Kawo village, Kano Emirate, 29 January 1970.
Kallo Muhammadu, Sumaila, Kano Emirate, 13 February 1970 (b. c. 1888).
Khamed Ibrahim as Khamed el Moumine, Abalak, 28 and 29 January 1976.
Mahamman Alhassan, Kano, 30 August 1973 (b. c. 1878).
Mahamman Bako, Kano, 4 July 1973.
Mahmudu Dayyidu, Bakin Zuwo ward, Kano, 8 July 1973 (b. 1902).
Mahmudu Koki, Kano, 8 and 14 July 1973 (b. 1904).
Makwangiji Jibrin and Malam Bala Ismaila, Awe, 26 April 1976.
Mamman Gabankare, Katsina Emirate, 5 February 1970 (b. c. 1902).
Mato, Gumawa village, Gabasawa District, Kano Emirate, 29 January 1970 (b.c. 1910).
Miko Hamshak'i, Kano, 8 and 10 September 1969, 19 November 1969 (b. 1882).
Muhammad Bello Alkali, Sokoto, 23 February 1970.
Muhammad Lawan Barmo, Katsina, 5 January 1970 (b. c. 1900).
Muhammadu Bayero, Katsina, 3 February 1970 (b. c. 1895).
Muhammadu dan Amarya, Gummi, Sokoto Province, 5 March 1970 (b. c. 1895).
Muhammadu Iya, Awe, 26 April 1976.
Muhammadu Jibirin, Gala village, Sumaila District, Kano Emirate, 13 February 1970 (b. c. 1930).
Muhammadu Kasori, Kano, 24 December 1969 and 1 February 1970 (b. 1902).
Musa Alhasan, Kawo village, Kano Emirate, 29 January 1970 (b. c. 1900).
Musa na Madabo, Kano, 22 December 1969, 1 February 1970 (b. c. 1894).
Musa Urwatu, Katsina, 3 January 1970 (b. c. 1883).
Salihu Kumurya, Kano Emirate, 27 January 1970 (b. c. 1912).
Salisu Yusifu, Kura, 11 August 1973 (b. 1948).
Sa'idu Ladan na Madugu, Gobirawa ward, Sokoto, 23 Feburary 1970 (b. c. 1900).
Suda Sha'aibu, Zangon Beriberi ward, Kano, 22 July 1973 (b. 1914).
Sule Daudu, Dan Mak'eri village, Kano Emirate, 11 February 1970 (b. c. 1900).
Sule na Aba, Jingau ward, Kano City, 30 November 1969.
Sule, Shibdawa village, Katsina Emirate, 6 January 1970 (b. 1899).
Tafida Yakubu Abawa, Kanje, 26 April 1976.
Tsoho Adamu, Kura, 9 August 1973 (b. c. 1933).
Umaru, Garfa, Kano Emirate, 13 February 1970.
Umaru, Tsaure Fankurun village, Kura District, 5 April 1970.
Umaru Mahamma, Tsaure Fankurun village, Kura District, 4 May 1970 (b. c. 1890).
Umaru Musa, Gummi, Sokoto Province, 8 March 1970 (b. c. 1895).
Umaru Sumaila, Kano, 19 August 1973.
Usuman, Kudan, 1 December 1975.
Yahaya Baba Gade-Gade, Kano, 5 and 7 August 1973 (b. 1943).
Yusifu Ibrahim, Kura, 11 August 1973 (b. c. 1905).
Yusufu Hunkuyi, 6 December 1975.

B. M. O. Aliyu Collection (Under supervision of P. E. Lovejoy)
(Northern History Research Scheme Library, ABU Zaria)
Abawa, Ikpeku, Keana, 16 December 1975 (b. c. 1930).
Agbo, Otaki, Keana, 20 December 1975 (b. c. 1925).
Aklo, Osabwa, Keana, 15 December 1975 (b. c. 1915).
Oga, Oyokpa, Keana, 18 December 1975 (b. c. 1925).
Oji, Eladoga, Keana, 21 December 1975 (b. c. 1935).
Onyapa, Ayitogo, Keana, 18 December 1975 (b. 1927).
Onyapa, Odapu, Keana, 17 December 1975 (b. unknown).

Ozegya, Omana, Keana, 18 December 1975 (b. 1945).
Umaru, Keana, 17 December 1957 (b. c. 1915).

C. Augustine Ojobo Collection (Under supervision of P. E. Lovejoy)
(Northern History Research Scheme Library, ABU Zaria)
Oji, Eladoga, Keana, 13 and 19 July 1975 (b. c. 1935).
Onyapa, Ayitogo, Keana, 20 and 22 July 1975 (b. 1927).

D. Innocent E. Agbo Collection (Under supervision of P. E. Lovejoy)
(Northern History Research Scheme Library, ABU Zaria)
Ochagwu, Michael Efiom Edumoga, Edumoga District (Idoma), 16 August 1975.
Ogbona, Ada Obottu, Edumoga District (Idoma), 13 July 1975.
Ogo, Aba Ere Olengbecho, Edumoga District (Idoma), 25 July 1975.

E. Andy Kpurkpur Collection (Under supervision of P. E. Lovejoy)
(Northern History Research Scheme Library, ABU Zaria)
Aba, Adesue Tse Aba (Tiv), 11 July 1975.
Abuur, Malu Lessel, Mbagwa District (Tiv), 6 August 1975.
Aive, Iba Mbabur, Ushongo (Tiv), 29 July 1975.
Ako, Gbise Gbise, Mbayongo District (Tiv), 12 September 1975.
Iarva, T. G. Sai (Tiv), 13 September 1975.
Naiko, Gberindyer Mbaibon, Mbatevem Ukum District (Tiv), 17 September 1975.
Sai, Rev. J. E. I. Harga, Shitire District (Tiv), 10 September 1975.
Shie, Mhambe Mbaakav, Mbatevem District (Tiv), 18 September 1975.
Yade, Ingough Mbadwem (Tiv), 22 September 1975.

F. R. Ade Collection (Under supervision of P. E. Lovejoy)
(Northern History Research Scheme Library, ABU Zaria)
Agbama, Atiri Opiem, Igede Division (Igede), 28 December 1975.
Inakwu, Opiem, Igede Division (Igede), 26 December 1974.

G. Paul Lubeck Collection (Institute of African Studies, University of Ghana, Legon)
Imam al-Juma'a Hajj 'Abdullah b. Hajj al-Hasan, Yendi, 3 August 1968.
Abu Bakr Baba Galadima b. Sarki Muhammad B. Musa B. Mallam Muhammad b. 'Abdullah,
    Yendi, 17 July 1968.
Al-Hajj Idris Kambangna b. Ya Na Imam 'Abdullah b. 'Abd al-Mu'min b. Zakariyya, Yendi, 20
    July 1968.
Muhammad b. Khalid b. Ya'qub b. Muhammad Bawa Mai Kanwa b. Mahmoud, Yendi, 10 July
    1968.

H. K. Yeboa Daaku Collection (Institute of African Studies, University of Ghana, Legon)
Baba, Salaga, summer 1969.
Imam of Daboya, summer 1969.
Kagbanyiche Adzara, Daboya, summer 1969.
Mumuni, Salaga, summer 1969.
Nyaba Abukari, Salaga, summer 1969.
Wasipewura Safo, Daboya, summer 1969.
'X', Kpandai, Gonja, summer 1969.

I. Philip Shea Collection (Appendix to Shea, unpublished, 1975)
Abdu Mai Kano, Kura, Kano Emirate, 23 September 1971.

327

Bibliography

Amadu, Kano City, 29 June 1971.
Badan Ladi, Tofa, Dawakin Tofa District, Kano Emirate, 28 October 1971.
Bawa Halidu, Gwarzo, Gwarzo District, Kano Emirate, 17 December 1970.
Dan Ladi Marini, Rurum, Rano District, Kano Emirate, 21 October 1971.
Garba, Limawa, Kumbotso District, Kano Emirate, 27 October 1971.
Gwadabe, Kano City, 21 June, 10 August 1971.
Inuwa, Kano City, 4 August 1971.
Isiyaku Bunkure, Bunkure, Rano District, Kano Emirate, 30 September 1971.
Na Kurma Sarkin Baba, Dal, Kano Emirate, 7 October 1971.
Sarkin Bugu, Tarai, Rano District, Kano Emirate, 8 October 1971.
Sha'aibu, Kano City, 23 June 1970.
Uban Gila, Rogo, Karaye District, Kano Emirate, November 1971.

J. Bertin Webster Collection (African Studies Centre, Dalhousie University, Halifax)
Acho, Jifi, Kekura, 11 June 1974.
Agwa of Tsohongari, Awe, 14 July 1974.
Kindabi, Kekura, 21 July 1974.
Mohamadu, Kekura, 10 June 1974.
Salihu Usa, Awe, 17 July 1974.
Sarkin Awe and Elders, Awe, 4 June 1974.
Tsumbu, Kekura, 30 June 1974.

V. UNPUBLISHED THESES AND PAPERS

Abdalla, Ismail Hussein, 1981. 'Islamic Medicine and its Influence on Traditional Hausa Practitioners in Northern Nigeria', Ph.D. thesis, University of Wisconsin.
Abubakar, Sa'ad, 1974. 'The Middle Benue Region up to c. 1850', Niger–Benue Valley Seminar, Jos.
Adefuye, Ade, 1974. 'Ozegya Adi Obanseriki of Keana: His Life and Times', Historical Society of Nigeria Conference, Ife.
    1976. 'Keana: The Gift of Salt', Kano Seminar, Kano.
Aku, T. A., 1974. 'The Transformation of Political Authority in Southern Jema'a, c. 1800–1904', BA dissertation, Department of History, Ahmadu Bello University, Zaria.
Aliyu, A. Y., 1973. 'Aspects of Relations between Bornu and Bauchi from Early Times to the First Half of the Nineteenth Century', Borno Seminar, Zaria.
Alkali, Muhammad Bello, 1969. 'A Hausa Community in Crisis. Kebbi in the Nineteenth Century', MA thesis, Ahmadu Bello University, Zaria.
Alkali, Muhammad Nur, 1976. 'Government and Economy in Borno before 1900', Kano Seminar, Kano.
    1978. 'Kanem Borno under the Sayfawa: A Study in the Origin, Growth and Collapse of a Dynasty', Ph.D. Thesis, Ahmadu Bello University, Zaria.
Aude, Lt., 1942. 'Rapport de mission dans la subdivision de Mainé-Soroa', Direction générale santé publique, Dakar.
Baier, Stephen, 1976. 'Local Transport in the Economy of the Central Sudan, 1900–1930', Kano Seminar, Kano.
Beltaro, F., and Bojarski, R., 1971. 'The Possibility of a Salt Industry in Nigeria', Geological Survey of Nigeria, RPT No. 1492, Kaduna.
Bernus, S. and Gouletquer, P., 1973. 'Approche archéologique de la région d'Azelik et de Tegidda-n-tesemt', RCP 322 du CNRS, Niamey.
Bovin, M. S., and Schierup, C., 1975. 'Ethnic and Pan-Ethnic Identities in Borno', seminar paper, Ahmadu Bello University.

Cordell, Dennis, 1972. 'The Awlad Sulayman of Chad and Libya: A Study of Raiding and Power in the Chad Basin in the Nineteenth Century', MA thesis, University of Wisconsin, Madison.
1979. 'The Awlad Sulayman of Libya and Chad: Power and Adaptation along the Southern Stretches of the Tripoli–Borno Route in the Nineteenth Century', Conference on the Trans-Saharan Trade Routes, Tripoli.
Dunbar, Roberta Ann, 1970. 'Damagaram (Zinder, Niger) 1819–1906: The History of a Central Sudanic Kingdom', Ph.D. thesis, UCLA, Los Angeles.
Erim, E. O., n.d. 'The Growth of the Keana Confederacy', seminar paper, Dalhousie University, Halifax.
Faure, H., 1965. 'Inventaire des évaporites du Niger (mission 1963)', Rapport du Bureau de Recherches Géologiques et Minières, Niamey.
Ferguson, Douglas, Edwin, 1973. 'Nineteenth Century Hausaland, being a Description by Imam Imoru of the Land, Economy, and Society of His People', Ph.D. thesis, Los Angeles.
Gavin, R. J., 1973. 'The Borno Economy in the 1920s', Borno Seminar, Zaria.
Gouletquer, P., and Kleinmann, D., 1973. 'Les Salines du Manga, Niger', Niamey, Centre National de la Recherche Scientifique, RCP 322.
Grandin, P., n.d. 'Bilma–Zinder 1946–47. Notes sur l'industrie et le commerce du sel au Kaouar et en Agram', CHEAM, Paris.
Hama, Boubou, 1954. 'Enquête sur le sel. Situation du sel au Niger', Niamey.
Hamani, Djibo, 1975. 'Contribution à l'étude de l'histoire des états hausa. L'Adar précolonial (République du Niger)', Thèse de doctorat de 3ᵉ Cycle, Université de Provence.
Hamman, Mahmoud, 1975. 'The History of Relations between Mambila Borderland and its Eastern Neighbours to 1901', BA dissertation, Ahmadu Bello University, Zaria.
Hautefeuille, C., 'Les Origines de l'Islam au Kawar', CHEAM, Paris.
Keana, Halad Maymako (1983). 'The Historical Evolution and Social Organisation of the Traditional Salt Industry of Nigeria: A Case Study of the Keana Salt Industry in Plateau-State', BA thesis, Department of Sociology, Ahmadu Bello University.
Lange, Dierk, 1977. 'Compte-rendu de la mission au Kawar', CNRS, Niamey.
Lavers, John, 1965. 'The Organisation and Distribution of Trade in the Central Sudan in the Pre-Colonial Period', MA thesis, University of London.
1976. 'Trans-Saharan Trade, c. 1500–1800: A Survey of Sources', Kano Seminar, Kano.
Lovejoy, Paul, E., 1968. 'The Long-Distance Trade of Wadai and Darfur, 1790–1870', seminar paper, University of Wisconsin, Madison.
1976. 'The Salt Industry of the Central Sudan: A Preliminary Survey', Kano Seminar, Kano.
Luxeuil, E., 1959. 'Les Boudoumas. Population lacustre. L'Exploration du lac Tchad', CHEAM, no. 3004, Paris.
Luxeuil, E. and Vial, L., 1938. 'Rapport sur le natron et son exploitation dans la subdivision de Bol et de Rig-Rig'. Gouvernement Générale de l'AEF, Territoire, du Tchad, Département du Kanem.
McDougall, Elizabeth Ann, 1976. 'The Salt Industry in West African History', MA thesis, University of Toronto.
1980. 'The Ijil Salt Industry: Its Role in the Pre-Colonial Economy of the Western Sudan', Ph.D. thesis, University of Birmingham.
Mosrin, 1965. 'Rapport sur la production et la commercialisation du natron', Ministère de l'Économie et Transportation, République du Tchad.
Nasiru, Ibrahim Danyiye, 1973. 'Tuareg and Buzu Immigration into Kano', BA dissertation, Abdullahi Bayero College, Kano.
Nicholson, Sharon, 1976. 'A Climatic Chronology for Africa: Synthesis of Geological, Historical and Meteorological Information and Data', Ph.D. thesis, University of Wisconsin, Madison.
Phoenix, D. A., and Kiser, R. T., 1942. 'Salt Springs, Lafia Division, Benue Province, Northern

Nigeria', Geological Survey of Nigeria, RPT No. 778, Kaduna.

Questiaux, Jean, 1957. 'Quelques aspects de l'économie salinière dans les territoires d' Afrique Nord–occidentale et centrale', thèse de doctorat, Université d'Alger.

Redmond, Patrick M., 1976. 'Some Notes on the Trade in Dried Fish in the Central Savanna. 1800–1930', Kano Seminar, Kano.

Saunders, Margaret O., 1980. 'Hausa Irrigated Agriculture at Mirria, Niger Republic (République du Niger)', African Studies Association Annual Meeting, Philadelphia.

Shea, Philip, 1975. 'The Development of an Export Oriented Dyed Cloth Industry in Kano Emirate in the Nineteenth Century', Ph.D. thesis, University of Wisconsin, Madison.

Simpson, A., 1949. 'Drilling Operations at the Salt Lake near Moi Igbo', Geological Survey of Nigeria, RPT. No. 842A, Kaduna.

Soula, Léon, 1950. 'La Thénardite de Mainé-Soroa (Niger)', thèse, docteur d'état en pharmacie, Université de Marseille.

Sutton, J. E. G., 1975. 'Kebbi Valley. Preliminary Survey, 1975', Zaria Archaeology Paper 5, Ahmadu Bello University, Zaria.

Tambo, David Carl, 1976. 'Pre-Colonial Iron Working on the Jos Plateau', Kano Seminar, Kano.

n.d., 'Trade and Exchange Mechanisms in the Daffo Area of the Jos Plateau'.

Tattam, C. M., 1942. 'Preliminary Report upon the Salt Industries: Eastern Nigeria', Geological Survey of Nigeria, RPT No. 778, Kaduna.

Vikør, Knut S., 1979. 'The Oasis of Salt. The History of Kawar, A Saharan Centre of Salt Production', thesis, University of Bergen.

Webb, James L. A. Jr, 1983. 'Shifting Sands: An Economic History of the Mauritanian Sahara, 1500–1850', Ph.D. thesis, the Johns Hopkins University.

Webster, J. B., n.d. 'Chiefs and Chronology: Jukun Colonies in the Benue Valley', seminar paper, Dalhousie University, Halifax.

VI. PUBLISHED BOOKS AND ARTICLES

(1898). 'Le Commerce des caravannes tripolitaines dans la région du lac Tchad et le Sokoto', *Bulletin du comité de l'Afrique Française, Renseignements Coloniaux*, 8: 208–211.

(1908). 'Native Leather of West Africa', *Bulletin of the Imperial Institute*, 6: 175–181.

(1928). 'The Kano Chronicle', in H. R. Palmer, *Sudanese Memoirs, Being mainly translations of a number of Arabic manuscripts relating to the Central and Western Sudan*, London, III, 92–132.

(1934). 'The Chad Basin Geology and Water Supply', *Bulletin of the Geological Survey of Nigeria*, 15.

(1958). 'Uburu and the Salt Lake', *Nigeria Magazine*, 56: 84–96.

Abadie, Maurice (1927). *La Colonie du Niger*, Paris.

Abir, Mordecai (1965). 'Brokerage and Brokers in Ethiopia in the First Half of the 19th Century', *Journal of Ethiopian Studies*, 3, 1: 1–5.

(1966). 'Salt Trade and Politics in Ethiopia in the "Mamana Masafent" ', *Journal of Ethiopian Studies*, 4, 2: 1–10.

Abubakar, Sa'ad (1977). *The Lamibe of Fombina*, Zaria.

(1979). 'A Survey of the Economy of the Eastern Emirates of the Sokoto Caliphate in the Nineteenth Century', in Yusufu Bala Usman, ed. *Studies in the History of the Sokoto Caliphate. The Sokoto Seminar Papers*, Lagos, 105–124.

(1983). 'Relations Between Borno and Fombina before 1901', in Bala Usman and Nur Alkali, eds. *Studies in the History of Pre-Colonial Borno*, Zaria, 211–236.

Adams, John (1823). *Remarks on the Country Extending from Cape Palmes to the River Congo*, London.

Adamu, Mahdi (1978). *The Hausa Factor in West African History*, Zaria.

(1979). 'Distribution of Trading Centres in the Central Sudan in Eighteenth and Nineteenth Centuries', in Yusufu Bala Usman, ed. *Studies in the History of the Sokoto Caliphate. The Sokoto Seminar Papers*, Lagos, 59–104.

Adamu, Muhammad Uba (1968). 'Some Notes on the Influence of North African Traders in Kano', *Kano Studies*, 4: 43–49.

Adefuye, Ade (1982). 'The Alago Kingdoms: A Political History', in Elizabeth Isichei, ed., *Studies in the History of Plateau State, Nigeria*, London and Basingstoke.

Adeleye, R. A. (1972). 'Hausaland and Borno, 1600–1800', in J. F. A. Ajayi and M. Crowder, eds. *History of West Africa*, New York, I, 497–508.

Afigbo, A. E. (1974). 'The Nineteenth Century Crisis of the Aro Slaving Oligarchy of South-eastern Nigeria', *Nigeria*, 110–112: 66–73.

(1976). 'Pre-Colonial Links between South-eastern Nigeria and the Benue Valley', *Journal of the Historical Society of Nigeria*, 10

Alagoa, E. J. (1970). 'Long-Distance Trade and States in the Niger Delta', *Journal of African History*, Vol. II, 3: 319–329.

Alexander, Boyd (1908). *From the Niger to the Nile*, London, 2 vols.

Alexander, J. A. (1975). 'The Salt Industries of Africa: Their Significance in European Prehistory', in K. W. de Brisay and K. A. Evans, eds. *Salt: The Study of an Ancient Industry*, Colchester, 81–83.

Alhasan, Malam (n.d.). *Tarihin Dagwamba*. (As translated by J. Withers Gill, *A Short History of the Dagomba Tribe*), Accra.

Alkali, Muhammad Nur (1983a). 'The Political System and Administrative Structure of Borno Under the Seifuwa Mais', in Bala Usman and Nur Alkali, eds. *Studies in the History of Pre-Colonial Borno*, Zaria, 101–126.

(1983b). 'Economic Factors in the History of Borno under the Seifuwa', in Bala Usman and Nur Alkali, eds. *Studies in the History of Pre-Colonial Borno*, Zaria, 57–77.

Allen, William and Thomson, T. R. H. (1848). *A Narrative of the Expedition to the River Niger in 1841*, London, 2 Vols.

Al-Tunisi, Muhammed ibn 'Umar (1851). *Voyage au Ouaday* (trans. Perron), Paris.

Ardant du Picq (1931). 'Une Population africaine: les Djerma', *Bulletin du Comité d'études historiques et scientifiques de l'Afrique occidentale Française*, 14, 4.

Arhin, Kwame (1979). *West African Traders in Ghana in the Nineteenth and Twentieth Centuries*, London.

Ayasse, Lt. (1907). 'Première reconnaissance Nguigmi, Agadem, Bilma', *Revue des Troupes Coloniales*, 1: 553–582.

Baier, Stephen (1977). 'Trans-Saharan Trade and the Sahel: Damergu, 1870–1930', *Journal of African History*, 18, 1: 37–60.

(1978). 'A History of the Sahara in the Nineteenth Century', Working paper No. 4, African Studies Center, Boston University, Boston.

(1980a). 'Long-term Structural Change in the Economy of Central Niger', in B. K. Schwartz, and Raymond Dummet, eds., *West African Culture Dynamics: Archaeological and Historical Perspectives*, The Hague, 587–602.

(1980b). *An Economic History of Central Niger*, Oxford.

Baier, Stephen, and King, David J. (1974). 'Drought and the Development of Sahelian Economics, a Case Study of Hausa–Tuareg Interdependence', *Land Tenure Centre Newsletter* (Madison, Wisconsin), 45: 11–21. Madison.

Baier, Stephen, and Lovejoy, Paul E. (1977). 'The Tuareg of the Central Sudan: Gradations in Servility at the Desert Edge (Niger and Nigeria),' in S Miers and I. Kopytoff, eds. *Slavery in Africa: Historical and Anthropological Perspectives*, Madison, 391–411.

Baikie, William Balfour (1856). *Narrative of an Exploring Voyage up the Rivers Kwora and Binue in 1854*, London.

Bargery, G. P. (1934). *A Hausa–English Dictionary and English–Hausa Vocabulary*, London.

Barth, Frederik, ed. (1969). *Ethnic Groups and Boundaries*, Bergen.

Barth, Heinrich (1857). 'Die Imoscharh oder Tuareg, Volk und Land: Eine ethnographische Skizze nach Dr. Barth's Reisewerk', *Petermanns Mitteilungen*, 3: 239–260.

(1857–59). *Travels and Discoveries in North and Central Africa, 1849–1855*, New York, 3 vols.

Bary, Erwin de (1898). *Le dernier Rapport d'un Européen sur Ghât les Touareg de l' Air (journal de voyage d'Erwin de Bary, 1876–1877)*, (Traduit et annoté par Henri Schirmer), Paris.

Beaufoy, Henry (1967). 'Mr. Lucas's Communications', *Proceedings of the Association for Promoting the Discovery of the Interior Parts of Africa*, R. Hallet, ed., I, 47–195, London.

Beauvilain, Alain (1977). *Les Peul du Dallol Bosso*, Niamey.

Belinay, Frédéric de (1938). 'En Kedei sur le Tchad', *Bulletin du Comité de l'Afrique Française, Renseignements Coloniaux*, II: 293–297.

Bell, T. Donald (1960), 'Sodium Chloride in Animal Nutrition', in Dale W. Kaufmann, ed., *Sodium chloride. The Production and Properties of Salt and Brine*, London, 454–469.

Benton, P. A. (1968). *The Languages and Peoples of Bornu*, London, 2 Vols.

Beriel, Marie-Magdeleine (1976). 'Contribution à la connaissance de la région du lac Tchad (Cameroun, Tchad, Nigeria)', *Bulletin de l'IFAN*, sér. B, 38, 2, 411–428.

Bernus, E.; Ahalla, Suleyman; Bernus, S.; Ag Arias, Alatnine (1979). 'Les Jardins d'Azelik', in S. Bernus and Y. Poncet eds. *Programme archéologique d'urgence In Gall–Tegidda-n-tesemt (département d'Agadez). Documents présentation provisioire*, Niamey.

Bernus, E. and Ag Arias, A. (1979). 'Les Kel Fadey, introduction à l'étude des milieux humains actuels', in S. Bernus and Y. Poncet, eds. *Programme archéologique d'urgence In Gall–Tegidda-n-tesemt (département d' Agadez). Documents présentation provisoire*, Niamey, 1–26.

Bernus, E. and Bernus, S. (1972). *Du Sel et des dattes. Introduction à l'étude de la communauté d'In Gall et de Tegidda-n-tesemt*, Niamey.

Bernus, S. and Gouletquer, P. (1976). 'Du Cuivre au sel: Recherches ethno-archéologiques sur la région d'Azelik (campagnes 1973–1975)', *Journal des Africanistes*, 46, 1–2: 7–68.

Bernus, S., Gouletquer, P. and Kleinmann, D. (1976). 'Die salinen von Tegidda-n-tesemt (Niger)', *Ethnographisch–Archaeologische Zeitschrift*, 17: 209–236.

Bernus, S. and Poncet, Y. eds. (1979). *Programme archéologique d'urgence In Gall–Tegidda-n-tesemt (département d' Agadez). Documents présentation provisoire*, Niamey.

Bloch, M. R. (1963). 'The Social Influence of Salt', *Scientific American*, September, 89–98.

Boahen, A. Adu (1962). 'The Caravan Trade in the Nineteenth Century', *Journal of African History*, 3, 2: 349–359.

(1964). *Britain, The Sahara, and the Western Sudan, 1788–1861*, London.

Bouillié, R. (1937). *Les Coutumes familiales au Kanem*, Paris.

Bouquet, Christian (1969). 'La Culture du blé dans les polders du Tchad', *Cahiers d'Outre-Mer*, 22, 86: 203–214.

(1974). *Iles et rives du Sud-Kanem (Tchad)*, Talence, France.

Bovill, E. W. (1922). 'Jega Market', *Journal of the African Society*, 22, 85: 50–60.

ed. (1966). *Missions to the Niger*, London, 4 Vols.

(1968). *The Golden Trade of the Moors*, London, 2nd ed.

Bowdich, Thomas Edward (1819). *Mission from Cape Coast Castle to Ashantee*, London.

Brenner, Louis (1971). 'The North African Trading Community in the Nineteenth-Century Central Sudan', in Daniel F. McCall and Norman R. Bennett, eds. *Aspects of West African Islam*, Boston, 137–150.

(1973). *The Shehus of Kukawa. A History of the Al-Kanemi Dynasty of Bornu*, Oxford.

(1979). 'Muhammad al-Amīn al-Kānimī and Religion and Politics in Bornu', in J. R. Willis, ed., *Studies in West African Islamic History. Vol. 1, The Cultivators of Islam*, London, 160–176.

Bridbury, A. R. (1955). *England and the Salt Trade in the Later Middle Ages*, Oxford.

Brisay, K. W. de, and Evans, K. W., eds. (1975). *Salt. The Study of an Ancient Industry*, Colchester.

Bruel, Georges (1935). *La France equatoriale africaine*, Paris.

Brulard, M. (1958). 'Aperçu sur le commerce caravanier Tripolitaine–Ghat–Niger vers la fin du XIXᵉ siècle', *Bulletin de Liaison Saharienne*, 9: 202–215.

Capot-Rey, R. (1959). 'Le Sel et le commerce du sel au BET (Borkou–Ennedi–Tibesti)', *Travaux de l'Institut de Recherches Sahariennes*, Algiers, 13: 186–193.

Carbou, Henri (1912). *La Région du Tchad et du Ouaddai*, Paris, 2 Vols.

Carl, L. and Petit, J. (1954). *La Ville du sel. (Du Hoggar au Tibesti)*, Paris.

Carter, C. O. (1975). 'Man's Need of Salt', in K. W. de Brisay and K. A. Evans, eds., *Salt. The Study of an Ancient Industry*, Colchester, 13.

Chailley (1954–55). 'La Mission du haut-Soudan et le drame de Zinder', *Bulletin de l'IFAN*, Sér. B, 16: 243–254; 17: 1–58.

Chambert, P. (1908). 'Note sur le cercle de Gouré dans la région de Zinder', *Revue des Troupes Coloniales*, 8: 263–283.

Chapelle, Jean (1980). *Le Peuple tchadien. Ses racines et sa vie quotidienne et ses combats*, Paris.

Chatelain (1917). 'Traditions relatives à l'établissement des Bornouans dans le Dallol Maouri et le pays Djerma', *Bulletin du comité d'études historiques et scientifiques de l'afrique occidentale française*, 358–361.

Chevalier, A. (1903). 'Mission scientifique au Chari et au Tchad', *La Géographie*, 7: 354–360.

(1905). 'Rapport sur une mission scientifique et économique au Chari–lac Tchad', *Nouvelles Archives des Missions Scientifiques et Littéraires*, 13: 7–52.

(1908). *Mission Chari, lac Tchad, 1902–1904, Afrique centrale française*, Paris.

Cheverry, C. (1968). 'Rôle original de la pédogenèse sur la nature et la mode de l'accumulation saline dans certains milieux confinés en région subaride (polders des bordures du lac Tchad)', *Science du Sol*, 2: 33–53.

Chiang, Tao-Chang (1976). 'The Production of Salt in China, 1644–1911', *Annals of the Association of American Geographers*, 66, 4: 516–530.

Chilver, E. M. (1961). 'Nineteenth Century Trade in the Bamenda Grassfields, Southern Cameroons', *Afrika und Ubersee*, Vol. 45, 4: 233–258.

Chudeau, Rene (1906). 'De Zinder au Tchad', *Académie des Sciences, Comptes Rendus Hebdomadaires des séances*, 143: 193–195.

(1907). 'Notes sur les roches alcalines de l'Afrique centrale', *Académie des Sciences, Comptes Rendus Hebdomadaires des Séances*, 145: 82.

(1908). 'Etudes sur le Sahara et le Soudan', *Annales de Géographie*, 17: 34–55.

(1909). *Sahara soudanais*, Paris.

(1925). *Notice sur le Sahara soudanais*, Paris.

Clapperton, H. (1829). *Journal of a Second Expedition into the Interior of Africa*, London.

Clauzel, J. (1960). *Note sur l'exploitation des salines de Taoudeni*, Algiers.

Cline, W. (1950). *The Teda of Tibesti, Borkou and Kawar in the Eastern Sahara*, Menasha, Wisconsin.

Cohen, Abner (1971). 'Cultural Strategies in the Organization of Trading Diasporas', in Claude Meillassoux, ed., *The Development of Indigenous Trade and Markets in West Africa*, London, 266–281.

Cohen, Ronald (1965). 'Some Aspects of Institutionalized Exchange: A Kanuri Example', *Cahiers d'Etudes Africaines*, 5: 353–369.

(1966). 'The Dynamics of Feudalism in Bornu', in Jeffrey Butler, ed., *Boston University Papers on Africa*, Boston, I, 87–105.

(1970). 'Incorporation in Bornu', in Ronald Cohen and John Middleton, eds., *From Tribe to Nation in Africa. Studies in Incorporation Processes*, Scranton, 150–174.

Connah, Graham (1981). *Three Thousand Years in Africa: Man and His Environment in the Lake Chad Region of Nigeria*, Cambridge.

Conte, Edouard (1979). 'Politics and Marriage in South Kanem (Chad): A Statistical Presentation of Endogamy from 1895 to 1975', *Cahiers de l'Office de la Recherche Scientifique et Technique Outre-mer, sér. Sciences Humaines*, 16, 4: 275–295.

(1984). 'Taxation et tribut au Kanem: considerations sur l'accumulation inégale dans une société agropastorale', *Paideuma*, 30: 103–122.

Coppens, Y. (1968). 'L'Epoque haddadienne', in *In Memoriam do Abade Henri Breuil*, Lisbon, I, 207–216.

Cordell, Dennis (1977). 'Eastern Libya, Wadai, and the Sanusiya: A Tariqa and a Trade Route', *Journal of African History*, 18, 1: 37–60.

Cortier, M. (1909). 'Teguidda-n-Tisemt', *La Géographie*, 20, 3: 159–164.

(1912). 'Les Salines du Sahara soudanais', *La Géographie*, 25: 91–98.

(1914). *Mission Cortier, 1908, 1909, 1910*, Paris.

Courtet, H. (1905a). 'Observations géologiques recueillies par la mission Chari–lac Tchad', *Académie des Sciences, Comptes Rendus Hebdomadaires des Séances*, 140: 160–163.

(1905b). 'Les Sels de la région du Tchad', *Académie des Sciences, Comptes Rendus Hebdomadaires des Séances*, 140: 316–318.

Couty, P. (1966). *Sur un secteur intermédiaire dans une économie de savane africaine: le natron*, Fort Lamy.

Crozals, J. de (1886). 'Le Commerce du sel du Sahara au Soudan', *Revue de Géographie Internationale*, Paris, 13: 241–326.

(1896). 'Le Commerce du sel du Sahara au Soudan', *Annales de l'Université de Grenoble*, 8, 1: 33–95.

Curtin, Philip D. (1973). 'The Lure of Bambuk gold', *Journal of African History*, 14, 4: 623–631.

(1975). *Economic Change in Precolonial Africa: Senegambia in the Era of the Slave Trade*, Madison, 2 vols.

(1984). *Cross-Cultural Trade in World History*, Cambridge.

Dainville, Jacques de (1948). 'Habitations et types de peuplement sur la rive occidentale du lac Tchad', *La Revue de Géographie Humaine et d'Ethnologie*, 59–69.

Dalziel, J. M. (1926). 'African Leather Dyes', *Bulletin of Miscellaneous Information, Royal Botanic Gardens, Kew*, 6, 225–238.

(1937). *The Useful Plants of West Tropical Africa*, London.

Daumas, M. J. E., and Chancel, A. de (1856). *Le grand Désert. Itinéraire d'une caravane du Sahara au pays des nègres (Royaume de Haoussa)* Paris.

Dauphinee, James A. (1960). 'Sodium Chloride in Physiology, Nutrition and Medicine', in Dale W. Kaufmann ed., *Sodium Chloride. The Production and Properties of Salt and Brine*, London, 382–453.

Denham, Dixon; Clapperton, Hugh; and Oudney, Walter (1966). *Narrative of Travels and Discoveries in North and Central Africa in the Years 1822, 1823, 1824* (Vols. 2–4 in E. W. Bovill, ed., *Missions to the Niger*, Cambridge).

Dennis, P. (1967). 'Essai sur l'artisanat tchadien', *Africa Turvuren*, Vol. 13, 3/4: 95–100.

Deschamps, G. (1907). 'Le Dagana. Monographie d'un secteur limitrophe du Tchad', *Bulletin de la Société de Géographie d'Alger et l'Afrique du Nord*, 2: 123–143.

(1931). 'Le Lac Tchad, ses bords et son hinterland, il y a trente ans', *Bulletin du Comité de l'Afrique Française, Renseignements Coloniaux*, 4: 173–179.

Destenave, M. (1902–03). 'Rapport sur les îles du Tchad', *Revue Coloniale*, 331–338.

(1903a). 'Exploration des îles du Tchad', *La Géographie*, 7, 421–426; and map 416.

(1903b). 'Deux années de commandement dans la région du Tchad (1900–1902)', *Revue de Géographie*, 53: 4–13.

(1903c). 'Sur les reconnaissances géographiques exécutées dans la région du Tchad, présentée par M. Henri Moissan', *Académie des Sciences, Comptes Rendus Hebdomadaires des Séances*, 136: 575–577.

(1903d). 'Le Lac Tchad. Le lac, ses affluents, les archipels, les habitants, la faune, la flore', *Revue Génerale des Sciences*, 14: 649–662, 717–727.

D'Huart (1904). 'Le Tchad et ses habitants. Notes de géographie physique et humaine', *La Géographie*, 9, 3: 161–176.

Dorward, David (1976). 'Precolonial Tiv Trade and Cloth Currency', *International Journal of African Historical Studies*, 9, 4: 576–591.

Duchemin, Georges (1951). 'La Récolte du sel et les conditions du travail dans les Trarza occidental (Mauritania)', *Bulletin de l'Institut Fondamental de l'Afrique Noir*, sér. B, 13: 853–867.

Duffill, M. B. and Lovejoy, Paul E. (1985). 'Merchants, Porters and Teamsters in the Central Sudan', in Catherine Coquery-Vidrovitch and Paul E. Lovejoy, eds., *The Workers of African Trade*, Beverly Hills, 137–167.

Dupire, M. (1962). *Peuls nomades*, Paris.

Du Puigaudeau, Odette (1940). *Le Sel du désert*, Paris.

Dupuis, Joseph (1824). *Journal of a Residence in Ashantee*, London.

Dyer, Mark (1979). 'Central Saharan Trade in the Early Islamic Centuries (7th–9th Centuries, AD)', African Studies Center, Boston University, Brookline, Mass.

Ekechi, F. K. (1981). 'Aspects of Palm Oil Trade at Oguta (Eastern Nigeria), 1900–1950', *African Economic History*, 10: 35–65.

El-Hachaichi, Mohammed (1912). See Muhammad ibn 'Uthmān al-Hashā'ishi.

Emerit, Marcel (1954). 'Les Liaisons terrestres entre le Soudan et l'Afrique du Nord au XVIIIᵉ et au début du XIXᵉ siècle', *Travaux de l'Institut de Recherches Sahariennes*, 11: 29–47.

Englebert, Victor (1965). 'I Joined a Sahara Salt Caravan', *National Geographic*, 128, 5: 694–711.

Falconer, J. D. (1911). *The Geology and Geography of Northern Nigeria*, London.

Fika, Adamu Mohammed (1978). *The Kano Civil War and British Over-rule, 1882–1940*, Ibadan.

Fisher, H. J. (1975). 'The Central Sahara and Sudan', in Richard Gray, ed., *The Cambridge History of Africa, c. 1600–c. 1790*, Cambridge, 58–141.

Flegel, R. (1880). 'Der Benue von Gande bis Djen', *Petermanns Geographische Mitteilungen*, 220–228.

(1883–1885). 'Der Handel in Nigergebiet und seine voraussichtliche Zukunft', *Mitteilungen der Afrikanischen Gesellschaft in Deutschland*, 4: 134–145.

(1985). *The Biography of Madugu Mohammad Mai Gashin Baki* (trans. and ed. by M. B. Duffill), Los Angeles.

Fonferrier (1923). 'Etudes historiques sur le mouvement caravanier dans le cercle d'Agadez', *Bulletin du Comité d'Etudes Historiques et Scientifiques de l'Afrique Occidentale Française*, 2: 302–314.

Forde, Daryll (1946). 'The Rural Economies', in Margery Perham, ed., *The Native Economies of Nigeria*, London, 29–215.

Fouque, C. (1906). 'La Kanem', *Revue des Troupes Coloniales*, 326–356.

Foureau, Fernand (1894). *Rapport sur ma mission au Sahara 1893–1894*, Paris.

(1895). *Mission chez les Touareg 1894–1895*, Paris.

(1902). *D'Alger au Congo Par le Tchad*, Paris.

(1905). *Documents scientifiques de la mission saharienne (Foureau–Lamy), 1898–1900*, Paris, 3 Vols.

Fourneau, Alfred (1904). 'Deux années dans la région du Tchad', *Bulletin du Comité de l'Afrique Française, Renseignements Coloniaux*, 121–125, 145–152.

335

Bibliography

François, G. (1905). *Notre Colonie du Dahomey. Sa Formation – son dévelopment – son avenir*, Paris.

Fremantle, J. M. (1920). *Gazetteer of Muri Province*, London.

Freydenberg, H. (1907). 'Exploration dans le bassin du Tchad', *La Géographie*, 15: 161–170.

(1908). 'Description géologique de l'itinéraire N'Guigmi–Bilma', *La Géographie*, 17: 111–114.

(1911). *Le Tchad et le bassin du Chari*, Paris.

Fuchs, Peter (1974). 'Sozio-ökonomische Aspekte der Dürrekatastrophe für die Sahara-Bevolkerung von Niger', *Afrika Spectrum*, 74, 3: 308–316.

(1983). *Das Brot der Wüste. Sozio-Ökonomie der Sahara-Kanuri von Fachi*, Wiesbaden.

(1984). 'Die ethnologische Analyse sozio-Okonomischer System: das Beispeil Fachi', *Paideuma*, 30: 123–138.

Gadel, Henri (1907a). 'Notes sur Bilma et les oasis environnantes', *Revue Coloniale*, 51: 361–386.

(1907b). 'Les Oasis de la région de Bilma', *Bulletin de la Société de Géographie de l'AOF*, 2: 85–124.

(1907c). 'Notes sur l'Air', *Bulletin de la Société de Géographie de l'AOF.*, 1: 28–52.

(1907d). 'Notes sur les sections méharistes de la région de Zinder–Tchad', *Revue des Troupes Coloniales*, 2: 288–303; 3: 42–45.

(1908). 'La Pénétration française du Sahara oriental', *Revue des Troupes Coloniales*, 1: 555–581; 2: 101–114.

Gaden, H. (1903). 'Notice sur la résidence de Zinder', *Revue des Troupes Coloniales*, 2: 608–656, 740–794.

(1910). 'Les Salines d'Auolil', *Revue du Monde Musulman*, 12: 436–443.

Gansser, A. (1950). 'Principles of Tanning', *Ciba Review*, 81, 2938–2962.

Garde, G. (1910). *Description géologique des régions situées entre le Niger et le Tchad et à l'est et au nord-est du Tchad*, Paris.

Gardi, René (1952). *Tschad, Erlebnisse in der unberührten Wildnis um den Tschadsee*, Zurich.

(1978). *Tenere, die Wüste, in der man Fische fing*, Bern.

Gast, M. (1965). 'Evolution de la vie économique et structures sociales en Ahaggar', *Travaux de l'Institut des Recherches Sahariennes*, 24: 129–143.

Gaudiche, Cap. (1938). 'La Langue boudouma', *Journal des Africanistes*, 8, 1: 11–32.

Gavin, J. R. (1977). 'The Impact of Colonial Rule on the Ilorin Economy, 1897–1930,' *Centrepoint*, University of Ilorin, 1, 1: 13–52.

Genovese, Eugene D. (1972). *Roll, Jordan, Roll. The World the Slaves Made*, New York.

Gentil, Pierre (1946). *Confins libyens. Lac Tchad Fleuve Niger*, Paris.

Géry, R. (1952). 'Une Industrie autochtone nigérienne: les sauniers du Manga', *Bulletin de l'IFAN*, sér. B, 14: 309–320.

Gilg, Jean-Paul (1963). 'Mobilité pastorale au Tchad occidental', *Cahiers d'Etudes Africaines*, 12: 491–510.

Gilmore, Harlan (1955). 'Cultural Diffusion via Salt', *American Anthropologist*, 57: 1011–1015.

Glanville, R. R. (1930). 'Salt and the Salt Industry of the Northern Province', *Sierra Leone Studies*, 16: 52–56.

Godelier, Maurice (1977). '"Salt Money" and the Circulation of Commodities among the Baruya of New Guinea', in M. Godelier, ed., *Perspectives in Marxist Anthropology*, Cambridge, 127–151.

Good, Charles M. (1972). 'Salt, Trade, and Disease: Aspects of Development in Africa's Northern Great Lakes Region', *International Journal of African Historical Studies*, 5, 4: 543–586.

Gouletquer, P. (1974a). 'The Development of Salt Making in Prehistoric Europe', *Essex Journal*, 8, 1: 2–14.

(1974b). 'Les Bouilleurs de sel', *Sciences et Avenir*, 328: 572–577.

(1974c). 'Niger, Country of Salt', in K. W. de Brisay and K. A. Evans, eds., *Salt: The Study of an Ancient Industry*, Colchester, 47–51.

Gouletquer, P.; Bernus, S., Ahalla, Suleyman; Mahoudan, Hawad; and Fani, Mohammed (1979). 'L'Exploitation du cuivre dans la plaine de l'Eghazer was Agadez,' in S. Bernus, and Y, Poncet, eds., *Programme archéologique d'urgence In Gall–Tegidda-n-tesemt*, Niamey, 80–106.

Gouletquer, P. L. and Kleinmann, D. (1972). 'Les Salines protohistoriques des côtes occidentales de l'Europe', *Actes du 97ᵉ Congrès National des Sociétés Savantes*, Nantes, 17–49.

(1974). 'Les Salines du Manga et leur intérêt dans l'étude des salines protohistoriques en Europe', *Comptes Rendus du 99ᵉ Congrès National des Sociétés Savantes*, Besançon, 21–30.

(1975). 'Structure sociale et commerce du sel dans l'économie touarègue', *Revue de l'Occident Musulman et de la Méditerranée*, Aix-en-Provence, 22: 131–139.

(1978). 'Die Salinen des Mangalandes und ihre Bedeutung fur die Erforschund der prähistorischen Briquetagestatten Europas', *Mitteilungen der Anthropologischen Gesellschaft in Wien*, 108: 41–49.

(1982). 'Les Salines du Manga et les problèmes de l'archéologie ethnographique', *Cahiers du Centre de Recherches Africaines*, 2: 5–19.

Grall, Lt. (1945). 'Le Secteur nord du cercle de Gouré', *Bulletin de l'IFAN*, sér B, 7: 1–46.

Grandin, P. (1951). 'Notes sur l'industrie et le commerce de sel au Kawar et en Agram', *Bulletin de l'IFAN*, sér B, 13: 488–533.

Gray, E. (1945). 'Notes on the Salt-Making Industry of the Nyanja Peoples Near Lake Shirwa', *South Africa Journal of Science*, 41: 465–475.

Greigert, J. and Pougnet, R. (1967). *Essai de description des formations géologiques de la République de Niger*, Paris.

Grove, A. T. (1959). 'A Note on the Former Extent of Lake Chad', *Geographical Journal*, 125: 465–467.

Guinard, A. (1935). 'Les Azalai au Niger', *L'Education Africaine* (Gorée), 89: 27–29.

Gutman, T. E. (1977). 'Review of the Importance of Salt in Historical Literature; with Special Reference to West Mexico', *Katunob*, 9: 88–96.

Hama, Boubou (1967). *Recherches sur l'histoire des Touareg sahariens et soudanais*, Niamey. (1969). *Documents nigériens*, Niamey, 2nd ed.

Harris, Rosemary (1972). 'The History of Trade at Ikom, Eastern Nigeria', *Africa*, 42: 122–139.

Hastings, A. C. D. (1926). *The Voyage of the Day-Spring, Being the Journal of the Late Sir J. H. Glover... Together with Some Account of the Expedition up the Niger R. in 1857*, London.

Hauset, H. (1927). 'Le Sel dans l'histoire', *Revue Economique Internationale*, 3: 270–287.

Hébert, Alexandre (1905). 'Contribution à l'étude chimique des sols, des eaux, et des produits minéraux de la région du Chari et du lac Tchad', *Académie des Sciences, Comptes Rendus Hebdomadaires des Séances*, 140: 163–165.

Hill, Polly (1966). 'Landlords and Brokers: A West African Trading System (with Notes on Kumasi Butchers)', *Cahiers d'Etudes Africaines*, 6: 349–366.

(1972). *Rural Hausa. A Village and a Setting*, London.

(1977). *Population, Prosperity and Poverty: Rural Kano 1900 and 1970*, Cambridge.

Hiskett, M. (1976). 'The Nineteenth-Century Jihads in West Africa', in John E. Flint, ed., *The Cambridge History of Africa, c. 1790–1870*, Cambridge, 125–169.

Hopkins, A. G. (1973). *An Economic History of West Africa*, London.

Hornemann, Friedrich Konrad (1964). *The Journal of Frederick Hornemann's Travels, from Cairo to Mourzouk, the Capital of the Kingdom of Fezzam, in Africa, in the Years 1797–98*, In E. W. Bouvill, ed., *Missions to the Niger*, Cambridge, I, 1–122.

Horowitz, Michael (1972). *The Manga of Niger*, New Haven.

Hunwick, John (1972). 'Songhay, Bornu and Hausaland in the Sixteenth Century', in J. F. A. Ajayi and Michael Crowder, eds., *History of West Africa*, New York, I, 205–212.

Bibliography

Hutchinson, J., Dalziel, J. M., and Hepper, F. N. (1954–72). *Flora of West Tropical Africa*, London, 3 Vols.

Jaffre, Joel; Durou, Jean-Marc; Monod, Théodore (1978). *La Caravane du sel*, Paris.

Jean, Camille-Charles (1909). *Les Touareg du sud-est: leur rôle dans la politique saharienne*, Paris.

Jeannin, P. and Le Goff, J. (1968). 'Questionnaire pour une enquête sur le sel dans l'histoire au moyen âge et aux temps modernes', in Michel Mollat, ed., *Le Rôle du sel dans l'histoire*, Paris, 307–322.

Jeffreys, M. D. W. (1940). 'Some Sources of Salt in Nigeria', *The Nigerian Field*, 9, 1: 37–40.

Joalland, Paul (1901). 'Autour du lac Tchad', *Bulletin de la Société de Géographie Commerciale (Paris)*, 23: 303–319.

(1902). 'Du Niger au Tchad', *Bulletin de la société normande de Géographie*, 5–24.

Johnson, Marion, ed. (n.d.). *Salaga Papers*, Legon, Ghana, 2 Vols.

(1976). 'Calico Caravans: The Tripoli–Kano Trade after 1880', *Journal of African Histroy*, 17, 1: 95–117.

Johnston, H. A. S. and Muffett, D. J. M., eds. (1973). *Denham in Bornu*, Pittsburgh.

Kaufmann, D. W., ed. (1960). *Sodium Chloride*, New York.

Kaunitz, Hans (1956). 'Causes and Consequences of Salt Consumption', *Nature*, November 24: 1141–1144.

Keenan, Jeremy (1972). 'Social Change Among the Tuareg', in E. Gellner and C. Michaud, eds., *Arabs and Berbers*, Lexington, Mass., 345–356.

(1977). *The Tuareg. People of Ahaggar*, New York.

Kleist, Oberleutant von (1907). 'Die Oase Bilma', *Globus*, 91: 65–66.

Klose, H. (1899). *Unter deutschem Flagge: Reisebilder und Betrachtungen*, Berlin.

(1904). 'Produktion und Handel Togos', *Globus*, 86, 5: 69–73; 86, 9: 145–206.

Knops, P. (1970). 'Approvisionnement et emploi du sel au Soudan central et occidental', *Bulletin de la Société Royale Belge d'Anthropologie Préhistorique*, 18: 81–97.

Kondo, Yoshiro (1975). 'The Salt Industry in Ancient Japan', in K. W. de Brisay and K. A. Evans, eds., *Salt. The Study of an Ancient Industry*, Colchester, 61–65.

Krause, G. A. (1888). 'Mit Einer Sklaven Karavane in der Sahara, 5', *Neue Preussische Zeitung*, No. 372, 22 September.

Laborie, Bruneau de (1922). 'Une Semaine de navigation sur le Tchad', *L' Illustration*, 4141: 50–54.

Lacroix, Alfred (1905a). 'Résultats minéralogiques et géographiques de récentes explorations dans l'Afrique occidentale française et dans la région du Tchad', *Revue Coloniale*, 3–31.

(1905b). 'Sur les microgranites alcalins du territoire de Zinder', *Académie des Sciences, Comptes Rendus Hebdomadaires des Séances*, 140: 22–6.

(1905c). 'Les Sels de la région du Tchad. Note de M. H. Courtet', *Académie des Sciences Comptes Rendus Hebdomadaires des Séances*, 140: 316–318.

(1908). 'Sur le chlorure de sodium de l'Oasis de Bilma', *Bulletin de la Société Française de Minéralogie et de Cristallographie*, 40–43.

(1910). 'Sur la thénardite de Bilma', *Bulletin de la Société Française de Minéralogie*, 33: 68.

Lacroix, P.-F. (1975). 'Emghedeshie – "Songhay Language of Agadez" – A travers les documents de Barth', in G. Calame-Griaule, ed., *Origine, convergence et diffusion des langues et civilisations résiduelles de l'Air et de l'Azawaq – documents*, Paris, 1–9.

Lahache, M. and Marre, Francis (1911). 'Le Sel, le natron et les eaux de la région du Tchad', in Jean Tilho, ed., *Documents scientifiques de la mission Tilho, 1906–1909*, Paris, II, 533–588.

Lambert, Robert (1935). 'Les Salines de Teguidda-n'Tessoum', *Bulletin de la Comité d'Etudes Historiques et Scientifiques de l'Afrique Occidentale Française*, 366–371.

(1938). 'Les Salines du Dallol Fogha (Niger)', *Bulletin du Service des Mines de l'AOF*, 1: 49–51.

Lambezat, B. (1962). 'Marchés du Nord-Cameroun', *Cahiers de l'Institut de Science Economique Appliquée*, 5: 85–103.

Lander, Richard (1830). *Records of Captain Clapperton's Last Expedition to Africa ... with the*

Subsequent Adventures of the Author, London, 2 Vols.

Lander, Richard and Lander, John (1858). *Journal of an Expedition to Explore the Course and Termination of the Niger: with a Narrative of a Voyage Down That River to Its Termination*, New York, 2 Vols.

Lange, Dierk (1977). *Le Dīwān des sultans du (Kānem-) Bornū: chronologie et histoire d'un royaume africain*, Wiesbaden.

(1978). 'Progrès de l'Islam et changement politique au Kānem du XIᵉ au XIIIᵉ siècle: Un essai d'interprétation', *Journal of African History*, 19, 4: 495–513.

(1979). 'Un Document de la fin du XVIIᵉ siècle sur le commerce transaharien', *Revue Française d'Histoire d'Outre-Mer*, 47: 211–222.

(1980). 'La Région du Lac Tchad d'après la géographie d'Ibn Saʿīd: Textes et cartes', *Annales Islamologiques*, 16: 149–181.

(1982). 'L'Alun du Kawar: Une exportation africaine vers l'Europe', *Cahiers du Centre de Recherches Africaines*, 2: 21–24.

Lange, Dierk, and Berthoud, Silvio (1977). 'Al-Qasaba et d'autres villes de la route centrale du Sahara', *Paideuma*, 23: 19–40.

Lapie, Pierre Olivier (1943). *My Travels Through Chad*, London.

La Roncière, C. (1919). 'Une Histoire du Bornou au XVIIᵉ siècle par un chirurgien français captif à Tripoli', *Revue de l'Histoire des Colonies Françaises*, 7: 73–88.

Last, D. M. and Al-Hajj, Muhammad (1965). 'Attempts at Defining a Muslim in 19th Century Hausaland and Bornu', *Journal of the Historical Society of Nigeria*, 3, 2: 231–240.

Latham, A. J. H. (1985). 'Palm Oil Exports from Calabar 1812–1887', in Gerhard Liesegang, H. Pasch and A. Jones, eds., *Figuring African Trade*, Berlin.

Lebeuf, Annie M. D. (1959). *Les Populations due Tchad (nord du 10ᵉ parallèle)*, Paris.

Le Coeur, Charles (1943). 'Une Chambre des hôtes dans la ville morte de Djado', *Notes Africaines*, 20: 9–10.

(1969). *Mission au Tibesti – carnets de route, 1933–34*, Paris.

Le Coeur, M. (1947). 'Les Archives de Bilma: enquêtes et enquêteurs', *Notes Africaines*, 33: 24–28.

(1948). 'Les Nomades teda et l'exploitation des palmeraies du Sahara central', *Bulletin de l'Association des Géographes Français*, 194–195: 74–79.

Leo Africanus, Joannes (1956). *Description de l'Afrique*, A. Epaulard, trans., Paris. 2 Vols.

Léotard, J. (1900). 'L'Occupation française du lac Tchad', *Bulletin de la Société Géographique de Marseille*, 24: 452.

Le Rouvreur, A. (1962). *Sahariens et sahéliens du Tchad*, Paris.

Le Sourd, Michel (1946). 'Tarikh el Kawar', *Bulletin de l'IFAN*, sér. B, 8: 1–54.

Lewicki, Tadeusz, ed. (1974). *Arabic External Sources for the History of Africa South of the Sahara*, London.

Lhote, Henri (1933). 'Les Salines du Sahara. La saline de Teguidda N'Tisemt', *La Terre et la Vie*, Paris, 3, 12: 727–735.

(1969). 'Le Cycle caravanier des Touaregs de l'Ahaggar et la saline d'Amadror. Leurs rapports avec les centres commerciaux du Soudan', *Bulletin de' l'IFAN*, sér. B. 31, 4: 1014–1027.

(1972). 'Recherches sur Takedda, ville décrite par le voyageur arabe Ibn Batouta et située en Aïr', *Bulletin de l'IFAN*, sér. B, 34, 3: 429–470.

Lovejoy, Paul E. (1973). 'The Kambarin Beriberi: The Formation of a Specialized Group of Hausa Kola Traders in the Nineteenth Century', *Journal of African History*, 14, 4: 633–657.

(1974). 'Interregional Monetary Flows in the Precolonial Trade of Nigeria', *Journal of African History*, 15, 4: 563–585.

(1978a). 'The Role of the Wangara in the Economic Transformation of the Central Sudan in the Fifteenth and Sixteenth Centuries', *Journal of African History*, 19, 2: 173–193.

(1978b). 'The Borno Salt Industry', *International Journal of African Historical Studies*, 10, 4: 629–668.

339

(1978c). 'Plantations in the Economy of the Sokoto Caliphate', *Journal of African History*, 19, 3: 341–368.

(1980). *Caravans of Kola. The Hausa Kola Trade, 1700–1900*, Zaria.

(1984). 'Commercial Sectors in the Economy of the Nineteenth-Century Central Sudan: The Trans-Saharan Trade and the Desert-side Salt Trade', *African Economic History*, 13: 85–116.

Lovejoy, Paul E., and Baier, Stephen (1975). 'The Desert-Side Economy of the Central Sudan', *International Journal of African Historical Studies*, 7, 4: 551–581.

Low, Victor N. (1972). *Three Nigerian Emirates. A Study in Oral History*, Evanston.

Lukas, J. (1936). 'The Linguistic Situation in the Lake Chad Area in Central Africa', *Africa*, 3: 332–349.

Lyon, G. F. (1821). *A Narrative of Travels in Northern Africa in the Years 1818–1819 and 1820 Accompanied by Geographical Notices of Soudan and of the Course of the Niger*, London.

McCulloch, W. E. (1929). 'An Enquiry into the Dietaries of the Hausa, etc.', *West African Medical Journal*, 3: 8–73.

McDougall, E. A. (1983). 'The Sahara Reconsidered: Pastoralism, Politics and Salt from the Ninth through the Twelfth Centuries', *African Economic History*, 12: 263–286.

(1985a). 'The View from Awdaghust: War, Trade and Social Change in the Southwestern Sahara, Eighth Through Fifteenth Centuries', *Journal of African History*, 26, 1: 1–31.

(1985b). 'The Economics of Islam in the South-Western Sahara, c. 1700–1900, *Journal of Asian and African Studies*.

MacLeod, Olive (1912). *Chiefs and Cities of Central Africa*, London.

Madziga, G. L. (1976). 'Bornu–Mandara Relations to c. 1900', *Nigeria Magazine*, 121: 64–79.

Maglione, G. (1968). 'Présence de gaylussite et de trona dans les natronières du Kanem', *Bulletin de la Sociégé Française de Minéralogie et de Cristallographie*, 91: 388–395.

(1969). 'Premières donnees sur le régime hydro-géochimique des lacs permanents du Kanem (Tchad)', *Cahiers ORSTOM, sér. Hydrobiologie* 3, 1: 121–141.

(1970a). 'La Magadite, silicate sodique de néoformation des faciès évaporitiques du Kanem (littoral nord-est du lac Tchad)', *Bulletin du Service de la Carte Géologique, d'Alsace et de Lorraine*, 23, 3/4: 177–189.

(1970b). 'Le Gisement chloro-sulfaté sodique de Napal (archipel du lac Tchad)', *Cahiers de l'Office de la Recherche Scientifique et Technique Outre-Mer*, sér. géol., 2, 1: 81–94.

(1971). 'Une Example de comportement de la silice en milieu confiné carbonaté sodique: les "natronières" du Tchad', *Bulletin du Service de la Carte Géologique, d'Alsace et de Lorraine*, 24, 4: 255–268.

Maglione, Gilbert, and Tardy, Yves (1971). 'Néoformation pédogénétique d'une zéolite, la mordénite, associée aux carbonates de sodium dans une dépression interdunaire des bords du lac Tchad', *Comptes Rendus, Académie des Sciences*, 272: 772–774.

Malbrant, R.; Receveur, P.; Sabin, R. (1947). 'Le Boeuf du lac Tchad', *Revue d'Elevage et de Médecine Vétérinaire des Pays Tropicaux*, Paris, 1: 37–42.

Maley, J. (1973). 'Mécanisme des changements climatiques aux basses latitudes', *Palaeogeography, Palaeoclimatology, Palaeoecology*, 14: 193–227.

Malval, Jean (1974). *Essai de chronologie tchadienne, 1707–1940*, Paris.

Manning, Patrick (1985). 'Merchants, Porters, and Canoemen in the Bight of Benin: Links in the West African Trade Network', in C. Coquery-Vidrovitch and Paul E. Lovejoy, eds., *The Workers of African Trade*, Beverly Hills, 51–74.

Martel, A. (1961). 'Le Commerce du natron au Fezzan (1895–1899)', *Travaux de l'Institut de Recherches Sahariennes*, 20: 225–236.

Martin, B. G. (1969). 'Kanem, Bornu, and the Fezzan: Notes on the Political History of a Trade Route', *Journal of African History*, 10, 1: 15–27.

Mauny, Raymond (1961). *Tableau géographique de l'ouest africain au moyen âge*, Dakar.

(1962). 'Protohistoire et histoire du Ténéré du Kawar et des régions voisines', in Henri J. Hugot, ed., *Missions Berliet–Ténére–Tchad. Documents scientifiques*, Paris.

Meunier, Dominique (1980). 'Le Commerce du sel de Taoudeni', *Journal Africanistes*, 50, 2: 133–144.

Miege, J.-L. (1975). 'La Libye et le commerce transsaharien au XIXᵉ siècle', *Revue de l'Occident Musulman et de la Méditerranée*, 19: 133–168.

Misrah, Mahomed (1822). 'Narrative of a Journey from Egypt to the Western Coast of Africa', *The Quarterly Journal*, October, 1–16.

Moll, Henry (1901). 'Situation économique de la région de Zinder', *Bulletin du Comité de l'Afrique Française, Renseignements coloniaux*, 9: 197–200.

———— (1910). 'La Mise en valeur du territoire du Tchad: l'élevage, l'exploitation de l'autruche, le miel et la cire', *Bulletin du Comité de l'Afrique Française, Renseignements Coloniaux*, 12: 391–397.

———— (1912). *Une Âme de colonial. Lettres du Lieutenant-Colonel Moll*, Paris.

———— (1913). 'La Mise en valeur du territoire du Tchad: le natron et le sel, le blé', *Bulletin du Comité de l'Afrique Française, Renseignements Coloniaux*, 4: 124–132.

Mollat, Michel, ed. (1968). *Le Rôle du sel dans l'histoire*, Paris.

Monteil, P.-L. (1894). *De Saint-Louis à Tripoli par le Lac Tchad. Voyage au travers du Soudan et du Sahara accompli pendant les années 1890–91–92*, Paris.

Morgan, D. R. (1974). 'Salt Production in Tanzania: Past and Present', *Tanzania Notes and Records*, 74: 31–37.

Moullet, Lt. (1934). 'Le Ténére, Tibesti, Kaouar. Du Tibesti au Hoggar', *Revue des Troupes Coloniales*, 28: 105–125; 269–290.

Mouret (1908a). 'Tournée de reconnaissance dans la région de Bilma', *Bulletin de la Société de Géographie de l'AOF*, 6: 85–101.

———— (1908b). 'Notice succincte sur l'oasis d'Agram', *Bulletin de la Société de Géographic de l'AOF*, 7: 137–187.

Muhammad ibn 'Uthmān al-Hashā'ishī (1912). *Voyage au pays des Senoussia à travers la Tripolitaine et les pays touaregs* (trans. V. Serres), Paris.

Multhauf, Robert P. (1978). *Neptune's Gift. A History of Common Salt*, Baltimore.

Museur, Michel (1977). 'Un Exemple spécifique d'économie caravanière: l'échange sel-mil', *Journal des Africanistes*, 47, 2: 49–80.

Nachtigal, G. (1873). 'Zug mit einer Sklavenkarawane in Baghirmi', *Globus*, 24: 215–218, 231–233.

———— (1874). 'Die tributaren Heidenlander Baghirmi's', *Petermanns Geographische Mitteilungen*, 323–331.

———— (1876). 'Journey to Lake Chad and Neighbouring Regions', *Journal of the Royal Geographical Society*, 46: 396–411.

———— (1876–77). 'Handel im Sudan', *Mitteilungen der Geographischen Gesellschaft in Hamburg*, 2: 305–326.

———— (1877). 'Das Beckan des Tsade und seine Bewohner', *Die Zeitschrift der Gesellschaft fur Erdkunde zu Berlin*, 12: 30–88.

———— (1881). *Sahara et Soudan*, trans. J. Gouidault, Paris.

———— (1980). *Sahara and Sudan. Volume II: Bornu, Kanem, Borku, Ennedi*, trans. from the German, with intro. and notes by A. G. B. Fisher and H. H. Fisher, New York.

Needham, Joseph (1965). *Science and Civilisation in China*, Cambridge, Vol. 4, pt 2.

Nenquin, Jacques (1961). *Salt, a Study in Economic Prehistory*, Bruges.

Newbury, C. W. (1966). 'North African and Western Sudan Trade in the Nineteenth Century: A Re-evaluation', *Journal of African History*, 7, 2: 233–246.

Nicholson, Sharon E. (1978). 'Climatic Variations in the Sahel and Other African Regions During the Past Five Centuries', *Journal of Arid Environments*, 1: 3–24.

———— (1979). 'The Methodology of Historical Climate Reconstruction and its Application to Africa', *Journal of African History*, 20, 1: 31–49.

Bibliography

Nicolaisen, J. (1963). *Ecology and Culture of the Pastoral Tuareg of Ayr and Ahaggar*, Copenhagen.

(1968). 'The Haddad, a Hunting People in Tchad: Preliminary Report of an Ethnographical Reconnaissance', *Folk* (Copenhagen), 10: 91–109.

(1977–78). 'The Pastoral Kreda and the African Cattle Complex; Notes on some Cultural-Historical and Ecological Aspects of Cattle Breeding', *Folk*, Copenhagen, 19–20: 215–307.

Nicolas, Guy (1975). 'Les Catégories d'ethnie et de fraction ethnique au sein du système social hausa', *Cahiers d'Études Africaines*, 15: 399–441.

Niebuhr, Carsten (1790). 'Das Innere von Afrike', *Neues Deutsches Museum, Leipzig*, 3, 10: 963–1004.

Noel, P. (1920). 'Pratiques médicales indigènes au Kaouar (Oasis de Bilma, Sahara oriental)', *L'Anthropologie*, 30: 551–560.

Noma, Alilou (1969). 'Naissance et décadence d'un commerce traditionnel: l'Azalia', in Boubou Hama, ed., *Documents nigériens*, Niamey, 186.

Norris, Edward Graham (1984). 'The Hausa Kola Trade through Togo, 1899–1912: Some Quantifications', *Paideuma*, 30: 161–184.

Northrup, David (1972). 'The Growth of Trade among the Igbo before 1800', *Journal of African History*, 13, 2: 217–236.

Nzekwu, Onuora (1964). 'Keana Salt Camp', *Nigeria Magazine*, 83: 262—278.

Ogunremi, Deji (1975). 'Human Porterage in Nigeria in the Nineteenth Cnentury – A Pillar of the Indigenous Economy', *Journal of the Historical Society of Nigeria*, 8, 1: 37–59.

Overweg (1855). 'Exploration du Tchad', *Revue Coloniale*, 2nd series, 14: 294.

Paden, John N. (1970). 'Urban Pluralism, Integration, and Adaptation of Communal Identity in Kano, Nigeria', in Ronald Cohen and John Middleton, eds., *From Tribe to Nation in Africa. Studies in Incorporation Processes*, Scranton, 242–270.

Pales, Leon (1950). *Les Sels alimentaires, problèmes des sels alimentaires en A.O.F.*, Dakar.

Palmer, H. R. (1928). *Sudanese Memoirs*, Lagos, 3 Vols.

(1929). *Gazetteer of Bornu Province*, Lagos.

(1936). *Bornu, Sahara and Sudan*, London.

Périé and Sellier (1950). 'Histoire des populations du cercle de Dosso', *Bulletin de l'IFAN*, Sér. B, 7, 4: 1015–1074.

Perron, Michel (1924). 'Le Pays Dendi', *Bulletin du Comité d'Études Historiques et Scientifiques de l'Afrique Occidentale Française*, 51–83.

(1926). 'La Rivière de sel du Fogha (colonie du Niger)', *Bulletin de l'Agence Générale des Colonies*, 368–372.

Petermann, Augustus (1851). 'Progress of the African Mission', *Journal of the Royal Geographical Society*, 130–221.

(1985). 'Voyages dans l'Afrique centrale, accomplis dans les années 1850, 1851, 1852, et 1853 par MM. Barth, Overweg, et Vogel', *Revue Coloniale*, 14: 37–114; 279–319, 412–419.

Pias, J. (1962). *Les Sols du moyen et bas Logone du bas Chari*, Paris.

Piault, M. H. (1971). *Histoire Mauri – Introduction à l'étude du processus constitutif d'un état*, Paris.

Pochard, P. (1943). 'Contribution à l'étude des eaux souterraines, des sels et des natrons de la région du Tchad', *Revue des Sciences Médicales, Pharmaceutiques et Vétérinaires de l'Afrique Française Libre, Brazzaville*, 2: 153–183.

Portères, Roland (1950). *Cendres d'origines végétale; sels de cendres comme succédanes du chlorure de sodium alimentaire et catalogue des plantes salifères en Afrique intertropicale et à Madagascar*, Dakar.

Pourriot, R.; Iltis, A.; Leveque-Duwat, S. (1967). 'Le Plancton des mares natronées du Tchad', *International Revue Gesamten Hydrobiologie*, 52, 4: 535–543.

Rabot, Charles (1908). 'De N'Guigmi à Bilma', *La Géographie*, 17: 109–110.

Rattray, R. S. (1913). *Hausa Folk-lore, Customs, Proverbs, etc.*, London, 2 Vols.

Régnier, J. (1961). 'Les Salines de l'Amadror et le trafic caravanier', *Bulletin de Liaison Saharienne*, 43: 234–261.

Reibell, Emile (1931). *Carnet de route de la mission saharienne Foureau–Lamy, 1898–1900*, Paris.

Riad, Mohammed (1960). 'The Jukun: an Example of African Migrations in the Sixteenth Century', *Bulletin de l'IFAN*, sér. B, 22: 476–485.

Richardson, James (1848). *Travels in the Great Desert of Sahara in the Years of 1845 and 1846*, London, 2 Vols.

(1854). *Narrative of a Mission to Central Africa*, London, 2 Vols.

Riou (1920). 'L'Azalay d'Automne 1928', *Bulletin du Comité de l'Afrique Française, Renseignements Coloniaux*, 280–285.

Roberts, A. D., and Sutton, J. E. G. (1968). 'Uvinza and its Salt Industry', *Azania*, 3: 45–86.

Roberts, Richard (1980). 'Long Distance Trade and Production: Sinsani in the Nineteenth Century', *Journal of African History*, 21, 2: 169–188.

Roche, M. A. (1968). 'Première estimation des rapports en sels au Lac Tchad par le Chari', *Cahiers de l'ORSTOM*, sér. *Hydrologie*, 5, I: 55–75.

Rochette, R. (1965a). 'Au Niger: Tibiri, village Maouri', *Revue de Géographie Alpine*, 53: 101–129.

(1965b). 'Au Niger: Kawara Débé, village de mares', *Revue de Géographie Alpine*, 53: 2, 169–203.

Rohlfs, G. (1866). 'Briefe von G. Rohlfs aus Bilma, 1866', *Petermanns Mitteilungen*, 368–370.

(1868). 'Reise durch Nord-Afrika vom Mittelandischem Meere bis Zum Busen von Guinea, 1865 bis 1867, 1. Halfte: Von Tripoli nach Kuka (Fesan, Sahara, Bornu)', *Petermanns Geographischen Mitteilungen Erganzungsheft*, 25.

(1872). 'Reise durch Nord-Afrika ... 2, Halfte: von Kuka nach Lagos (Bornu, Saria, Nupe, Yoruba)', *Petermanns Geographischen Mitteilungen Erganzungsheft*, 34.

Rottier, Cdt. (1924). 'Le Sahara oriental. Kaouar. Djado, Tibesti', *Renseignements Coloniaux de l'Afrique Française (Supplément à l'Afrique Française)*. 1: 1–14; 2: 78–88; 3: 101–108.

Sabatier, F. (1905). 'Les Territoires du lac Tchad', *Bulletin de la Société de Géographie, Marseille*, 24: 295–300.

Salifou, André (1971). *Le Damagaram ou sultanat de Zinder au XIXe siècle*, Niamey.

(1972). 'Malan Yaroh, un grand négociant du soudan centrale à la fin du XIXe siècle', *Journal des Africanistes*, 42: 7–27.

Schultze, A. (1913). *The Sultanate of Bornu* (trans. P. A. Benton), London.

Seetzen, U. J. (1810). "Über das grosse afrikanische Reich Burnu und dessen Nebenländer, und über die Sprache von Affadeh (November 1808)', *Montaliche Correspondenz zur Beförderung der Erd- und Himmels-Kunde*, Hrg. von F. v. Zach, 22: 269–275, 328–341.

(1811). 'Über die Phelláta-Araber südwärts von Fesan, und deren Sprache, nebst einigen Nachrichten von unterschiedlichen umherliegenden afrikanischen Ländern (Oct. 1808)', *Monatliche Correspondenz zur Beförderung der Erd- und Himmels-Kunde*. Hrg. von F. v. Zach, 24: 225–237.

(1812). 'Nouvelles recherches sur l'intérieur de l'Afrique', *Annales des Voyages, de la Géographie et de l'Histoire*, 19: 164–184.

Seidel, H. (1898). 'Salzgewinnung und Salzhandel in Togo'. *Deutsche Kolonialzeitung*, 11: 234–237, 251.

Smith, Abdullahi (1972). 'The Early States of the Central Sudan', in J. F. A Ajayi and Michael Crowder, eds., *History of West Africa*, New York, I, 164–182.

Smith, Mary, ed. (1954) *Baba of Karo. A Woman of the Moslem Hausa*, London.

Smith, M. G. (1959). 'The Hausa System of Social Status', *Africa*, 29, 3: 239–252.

Soula, Léon (1950). *Les Sels alimentaires. Sels du Manga (Niger). La thénardite de Mainé-Soroa*, Dakar.

343

Bibliography

Spittler, Gerd (1984). 'Karawanenhandel und Kamelrazzia bei den Kel Ewey. Die Kontrolle des Salz – und Hirsehandels zwischen Air, Bilma und Kano (1850–1900)', *Paideuma*, 30: 139–160.

Stein, L. (1961). 'Der Handel mit Nahrungsmitteln im Tschad-Seegebiet während des 19. Jahrhunderts', *Veröffentlichungen des Museums für Völkerkunde zu Leipzig*, 2: 639–653.

Stewart, C. C. (1976). 'Southern Saharan Scholarship and the *Bilād al-Sūdān'*, *Journal of African History*, 17, 1: 73–93.

— (1979). 'Diplomatic Relations in Early Nineteenth Century West Africa. Sokoto–Masina–Azaouad Correspondence', in Y. B. Usman, ed., *Studies in the History of the Sokoto Caliphate*, Lagos, 408–429.

Sundström, Lars (1974). *The Exchange Economy of Pre-Colonial Tropical Africa*, London.

Sutton, I. B. (1981). 'The Volta River Salt Trade: The Survival of an Indigenous Industry', *Journal of African History*, 22, 1: 43–61.

Talbot, P. A. (1911a). 'The Buduma of Lake Chad', *Journal of the Royal Anthropological Institute*, 41: 245–259.

— (1911b). 'Lake Tchad', *Geographical Journal*, 38: 269–278.

Tambo, David (1978). 'The "Hill Refugees" of the Jos Plateau: an Historiographical Examination', *History in Africa*, 5: 201–223.

Terrier, A. (1907). 'L'Oasis de Bilma et les oasis environnantes', *Bulletin du Comité de l'Afrique Française, Renseignements Coloniaux*, 17, 8: 287–289.

Tijjani, Kayarj (1979). 'The Force of Religion in the Conduct of Political Affairs and Interpersonal Relations in Borno and Sokoto', in Y. B. Usman, ed., *Studies in the History of the Sokoto Caliphate*, Lagos, 261–277.

— (1983). 'Political and Constitutional Changes in Borno under the Shehu Muhammad al-Amin al-Kanemi. The Case of the Majlis', in Bala Usman and Nur Alkali, eds., *Studies in the History of Pre-Colonial Borno*, Zaria, 127–139.

Tilho, Jean (1906). 'Exploration du lac Tchad (février-mai 1904)', *La Géographie*, 13: 195–214.

— (1910–11). *Documents scientifiques de la mission Tilho, 1906–09*, Paris, 2 Vols.

Truffert, J. (1903). 'Région du Tchad. Le Bahr-el-Ghazal et l'archipel Kouri', *Revue de Géographie*, 52: 481–502; 53: 14–35.

Trystram, J. P. (1958). *Rapport sur le régime foncier des ouaddis du Kanem*, Fort Lamy.

Tubiana, M. J. (1961). 'Le Marché de Hili-ba: moutons, mil, sel et contrebande', *Cahiers d'Études Africaines*, 6: 196–243.

Tubiana, Marie Jose, and Tubiana, Joseph (1977). *The Zaghawa from an Ecological Perspective: Foodgathering, the Pastoral System, Tradition and Development of the Zaghawa of the Sudan and the Chad*, Rotterdam.

Unomah, A. Chukwudi (1982). 'The Lowlands Salt Industry, in Elizabeth Isichei, ed., *Studies in the History of Plateau State, Nigeria*, London and Basingstoke: 151–178.

Urvoy, Y. (1934). 'Chroniques d'Agadès', *Journal des Africanistes*, 4: 145–177.

— (1936). *Histoire des populations du Soudan central (colonie du Niger)*, Paris.

— (1942a). *Petit atlas ethno-démographique du Soudan entre Sénégal et Tchad*, Paris.

— (1942b). *Les Bassins du Niger. Etude de géographie physique et de paléogéographie*, Paris.

— (1949). *Histoire de l'empire du Bornou*, Paris.

Usman, Yusufu Bala, ed. (1979). *Studies in the History of the Sokoto Caliphate. The Sokoto Seminar Papers*, Lagos.

— (1981). *The Transformation of Katsina, 1400–1883*, Zaria.

— (1983). 'A Reconsideration of the History of Relations between Borno and Hausaland before 1804 AD', in Yusufu Bala Usman and Nur Alkali, eds., *Studies in the History of Pre-Colonial Borno*, Zaria, 175–210.

Usman, Yusufu Bala, and Alkali, Nur, eds. (1983). *Studies in the History of Pre-Colonial Borno*, Zaria.

Verger, P. (1964). 'Rôle joué par le tabac de Bahia dans la traite des esclaves au golfe du Benin', *Cahiers d'Études Africaines*, 4: 349–369.

Verlet, M. (1967). 'Le Gouvernement des hommes chez les Yedina du lac Tchad dans le courant du XIXᵉ siècle', *Cahiers d'Études Africaines*, 25: 190–193.

Verlet, Martin, and Hauchecorne, Jean (1974). 'Wheat Cultivation at Lake Chad', in Peter McLaughlin Associates, *Agricultural Development Projects in Francophone Africa*, Commox, B.C.

Vikør, Knut S. (1982). 'The Desert-Side Salt Trade of Kawar', *African Economic History*, 11: 115–144.

Vischer, H. (1909a). 'A Journey from Tripoli Across the Sahara to Lake Chad', *Geographical Journal*, 33: 241–266.

(1909b). 'De Tripoli au lac Tchad', *Géographie*, 20: 349–356.

(1910). *Across the Sahara from Tripoli to Bornu*, London.

Vogel, Eduard (1855). 'Reise nach Central-Afrika: Reise von Tripoli bis zum Tschad See (mars 1852–janv. 1854)', *Petermanns Geographische Mitteilungen*, 237–259.

(1857). 'On the Ivory Trade of Central Africa', *Proceedings of the Royal Geographical Society*, 1: 215–216.

Walckenaer, C. A. (1821). *Recherches géographiques sur l'intérieur de l'Afrique septentrionale*, Paris.

Watts, Michael (1983). *Silent Violence. Food, Famine and Peasantry in Northern Nigeria*, Berkeley and Los Angeles.

Whitting, C. E. J. (1940). *Hausa and Fulani Proverbs*, Lagos.

Wilks, I. (1971). 'Asante Policy Towards the Hausa Trade in the Nineteenth Century', in C. Meillassoux, ed., *The Development of Indigenous Trade and Markets in West Africa*, London 124–141.

Willis, J. S. (1979). 'Introduction: Reflections on the Diffusion of Islam in West Africa', in J. S. Willis, ed., *Studies in West African Islamic History. Vol. 1, The Cultivators of Islam*, London, 1–39.

Works, John A. (1976). *Pilgrims in a Strange Land*, New York.

VII. FILMS

Bernus, Edmond (1972). 'Les Gens du Sel', Comité du film ethnographique, mission ORSTOM-CNRS, 1970.

Fuchs, Peter (1978a). 'Kanuri (Zentralsahara, Oase Fachi) – Salzgewinnung', Film E 2465 des IWF, Gottingen.

(1978b). 'Kanuri (Zentralsahara, Oase Fachi) – Traditioneller Handel', Film E 2466 des IWG, Göttingen.

Index

Abakaliki (town), 50, 51
Abakwariga (ethnic group), 217
abatol (salt basin), 61, 157–158
acha (hungry rice), 86–87, 118
Adamawa (Emirate), 182, 194, 196, 209, 211, 218, 219, 232, 249
Adar (region), 5, 30, 188, 222, 225, 255, 277
Adarawa (ethnic group), 186, 188, 266
Adebour (town), 43, 76, 121, 125, 166, 172, 173, 236
Adefuye, A., 109, 294n1
Adris (town), 165
Afikpo (town), 50–51
Agades (town) 5, 6, 42, 61, 154–155, 158, 171, 177, 182, 183, 188, 207, 222, 225, 228–229, 231, 258, 262
Agalawa (ethnic group), 198, 207, 208, 210, 212, 214, 247, 257, 260, 265, 266–269, 274
agriculture, 91, 114, 116–120, 134–135, 139, 141, 189, 197, 223, 225, 232 235, 259, 263, 277
Ahaggar (region), 183
Aïr Massif (region), 5, 6, 19, 30, 42, 61–62, 141, 155, 185, 187, 189, 222, 225, 228, 230, 255
Akwana (town), 5, 11, 50, 51, 82, 87, 108
Alago (ethnic group), 151, 159, 161–163, 245, 253, 268, 276
Algeria, 7, 10, 106
alifa (title), 223
Alkalawa (town), 201
Alkali, N., 223–224, 225, 237
al-Kanemi, 163, 168–169, 222, 232–233, 238, 255, 256, 258
alum (salt), 27, 59–60, 221
Amadror (region), 10, 19, 39, 45, 79, 94, 106, 179, 218, 261
amersal (salt), 10
Aney (town), 58, 142, 144, 187
Angas (ethnic group), 151
Ankwe (ethnic group), 151, 163
Arabs (*see also* Shuwa, Awlad Sulayman), 147, 183, 188, 190, 239, 266, 272
Ardrash (town), 21, 26, 222
Argungu (town), 246

Ari Kumbomiram (town), 121–122, 172, 173, 273
Aro (ethnic group), 215
Arrigui (Kawar oasis), 34, 58
Arufu (town), 51
Asante, 26–27, 76, 186, 194, 200, 207, 209, 211, 214–215, 218–219, 243, 249
Awlad Sulayman (nomads), 146, 147, 192–193, 238, 241
Awe (town), 5, 11, 19, 33, 35, 50–51, 82–86, 87, 107–109, 149–151, 159–163, 175–176, 216–217, 245, 276
Azara (town), 5, 11, 33, 35, 50–51, 82, 107–108, 150–151, 159–160, 175–176, 216, 245, 276
Azawaq (region), 5, 222, 225, 255
Azelik (town), 30, 31, 88, 119, 139–140, 153–154, 157, 177, 221, 262, 264
baboul, see *kige*

Baga Seyoram (town), 179, 190, 192–196, 232, 233, 242, 270
Bagirmi (state), 71, 129, 182, 191, 240, 241
Bahr el Ghazal (region), 39, 76
Baier, S., 201
Bamenda (region), 30
Bariba states, 179, 219, 249
Barth, Frederick, 252–253, 254
Barth, Heinrich, 45, 61, 73–74, 75, 80–81, 118, 129, 130, 131, 147, 167, 186, 188, 190, 192–196, 199, 203, 217, 220
Bauchi (emirate), 87, 150, 193, 196–197, 211, 215, 216, 222, 245, 246, 268
Bebeji (town), 205, 208
Bedde (ethnic group), 198, 208
Bedo (nomads), 8
Benue Valley, 5, 11, 14, 19, 33, 50–51, 53, 82–86, 88–89, 107–109, 112–113, 119, 149–151, 159–163, 174–176, 179, 192, 196–197, 211, 215, 216–219, 222, 243, 245, 249, 250, 256, 258, 268
Beriberi (ethnic group), 192, 204, 206–207, 209, 260, 266–269
Bernus, S., 140–141, 157–158
beza (salt), 15, 18, 33–34, 56–58, 79, 89, 90, 171, 229